ACT®
Quick Start
Guide

ACT Quick Start Guide

WELCOME TO *ACT PREMIER 2016-2017*

Congratulations on taking the first step to the ACT score you need! Kaplan's *ACT Premier 2016-2017* has a wide range of features you'll use to prepare for Test Day.

In this Quick Start Guide, we'll walk you through everything you'll need to know to take advantage of the book, Practice Tests, DVD, and online resources. We'll help you prep smarter and score higher.

Kaplan's *ACT Premier 2016-2017* gives you everything you need for Test Day. Follow this handy checklist to get your studying on track:

☐ **Register your online companion** for extra practice, Live Online events, video tutorials, Practice Test score reports, and more.

☐ **Set a score goal** based on the schools you're considering applying to. Review admissions information or contact admissions departments for a strong idea of what to aim for.

☐ **Take the online Diagnostic Practice Test: Practice Test 1** to figure out your strong and weak areas.

☐ **Build your study plan** with practice hours, scheduled Practice Tests, and review time leading up to Test Day.

☐ **Review** English, Reading, Math, Science, and Writing concepts.

☐ **Practice, practice, practice** with our quizzes and full-length tests in the book and online.

☐ **Watch the included DVD** containing instruction and tips from elite Kaplan teachers.

YOUR *ACT PREMIER 2016-2017* BOOK

Kaplan's *ACT Premier 2016-2017* is packed with resources to help you get ready for Test Day.

It has:

- A targeted review of key ACT terms and concepts

- Tips and strategies for each exam section and every question type

- Lots of test practice (including three full-length exams in the book and five online)

TAKE ADVANTAGE OF KAPLAN EXCLUSIVES

These powerful tools will help you score higher on Test Day!

SMARTPOINTS™

Throughout the book, you will see Kaplan's SmartPoints. Because the ACT follows established patterns and tests predictable content every year (and because of Kaplan's decades of preparing students for the ACT), Kaplan is able to give you a section-by-section breakdown of which question types will earn you points. This will tell you where you should spend the most time prepping.

SmartPoints rank the skills and topics that are tested most often on the ACT. Build your score to 36 by focusing on the points you need to earn!

USING YOUR ACT ONLINE COMPANION

1. REGISTER YOUR ONLINE COMPANION

The online companion gives you access to even more test prep, including five full-length Practice Tests, video tutorials, registration for Live Online events, quizzes with explanations, and more!

Register your online companion using these simple steps:

1. Go to kaptest.com/booksonline.

2. Follow the on-screen instructions. Please have a copy of your book available.

2. TAKE THE ONLINE DIAGNOSTIC TEST

The Diagnostic Test will help you to do the following:

- **Identify your strengths and weaknesses.** This will help you target your practice time so you can work on the SmartPoints that will get you to your goal.

- **Develop your ACT study plan.** Once you review the results of your Diagnostic Test, you will know where to spend time. Build your study plan based on your needs and schedule.

  – Check your answers carefully, noting how many questions you got right and wrong, how long it took you to answer each question, and how often you skipped questions.

  – Look for patterns. Were you stronger in some areas than others?

- **Know what to expect on Test Day.** The Diagnostic Test provides you with the same timing, sections, and question types as you will see on Test Day, so you'll be ready!

- **Reinforce key skills and earn more points!**

3. GET TO KNOW THE ACT AND CREATE YOUR STUDY PLAN

Remember, your *ACT Premier 2016-2017* program is designed to meet your individual needs.

WHAT DOES THAT MEAN?

- **You're in control.** Study how and when it works best for you.

- **You can customize your study.** We've made your ACT program interactive—you get to mix things up by jumping between the book and the online resources.

Take some time to familiarize yourself with the contents of your *ACT Premier 2016-2017* book. It has all the tools you'll need to conquer the ACT.

4. JOIN A LIVE ONLINE SESSION

Kaplan's ACT Live Online sessions are interactive instructor-led ACT prep lessons that you can participate in from anywhere you can access the Internet.

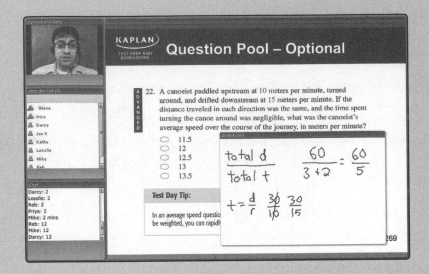

ACT Live Online sessions are held in a state-of-the-art virtual classroom—actual lessons in real time, just like a physical classroom experience. Interact with your teacher and other classmates using audio, instant chat, whiteboard, polling, and screen-sharing functionality. And just like courses at Kaplan centers, ACT Live Online sessions are led by experienced Kaplan instructors.

TO REGISTER FOR AN ACT LIVE ONLINE EVENT:

1. Once you've signed in to your student home page, open your Syllabus.

2. In the Syllabus window, go to the "Live Online Registration" menu option.

3. Click on the link. A separate window will appear with registration instructions.

ACT Live Online events are scheduled to take place throughout the year. Please check your online companion for dates and times!

Please note: Registration begins one month before the session date. Be sure to sign up early, since spaces are reserved on a first come, first served basis.

5. WATCH THE VIDEO TUTORIALS AND TAKE THE ONLINE QUIZZES

In video tutorials, Kaplan's highly rated ACT teachers explain and reinforce the most important concepts from the most important questions. Then, take a quiz on that topic and get automatic feedback.

Video tutorials and quizzes can be accessed only through your online companion.

Here's how:

1. Once you've signed in to your student home page, open your Syllabus.

2. Click on the lesson of your choice.

3. Click on the link for the video you'd like to see or quiz you would like to take. A separate window will appear with your video or quiz.

  Look for the following icons throughout your book. They indicate what is available online for further study.

6. TAKE AN OFFICIAL ACT PRACTICE TEST

Through your online resources, you have access to an official ACT sample test. Take the test for realistic practice, then enter your answers to get your scores and analytics—even for the essay.

Good luck!

TIPS FOR CUSTOMIZING YOUR STUDY PLAN

The most effective study plan will adapt to your individual needs. Here are some helpful tips:

☐ Map the strongest and weakest areas from your Diagnostic Test against the SmartPoints for each area. Make sure the areas you're studying are not only ones where you missed questions, but also where you can substantially raise your score. Some topics matter more than others!

☐ Review the Kaplan content for areas that need the most improvement before starting the quizzes. Kaplan's strategies and tips will help you see the largest increases on your quizzes and Practice Tests.

☐ Make a study calendar for yourself based on your commitments and availability. Don't just figure you'll study "when you have time"—you're too busy for that! Plan your schedule so you know when you *are* studying and when you're *not*.

☐ Use the eight full-length Practice Tests as milestones—don't plan on saving them all for the final weeks. Test yourself periodically and chart your progress.

☐ As time permits, go back to the question types that you aced so you can keep the material sharp.

☐ Take time to practice your essay writing. Understanding the essay requirements and practicing your writing will help you deliver a great essay on Test Day.

☐ Using your Practice Tests and quizzes, reevaluate your strengths and weaknesses regularly. If they change, adjust your plan accordingly.

Related Titles for College-Bound Students

8 ACT Practice Tests

ACT English, Reading, and Writing Prep

ACT Math & Science Prep

ACT for Busy Students

ACT Strategies, Practice & Review

AP Biology

AP Calculus AB & BC

AP Chemistry

AP English Language & Composition

AP English Literature & Composition

AP Environmental Science

AP European History

AP Human Geography

AP Macroeconomics/Microeconomics

AP Physics B & C

AP Psychology

AP Statistics

AP U.S. Government & Politics

AP U.S. History

AP World History

New SAT Premier

New SAT Strategies, Practice & Review

8 Practice Tests for the SAT

Evidence-Based Reading, Writing, and Essay Workbook for the New SAT

Math Workbook for the New SAT

SAT Subject Test: Biology E/M

SAT Subject Test: Chemistry

SAT Subject Test: Literature

SAT Subject Test: Mathematics Level 1

SAT Subject Test: Mathematics Level 2

SAT Subject Test: Physics

SAT Subject Test: Spanish

SAT Subject Test: U.S. History

SAT Subject Test: World History

ACT®
Premier
2016-2017

© 2016 by Kaplan, Inc.

Published by Kaplan Publishing, a division of Kaplan, Inc.
750 Third Avenue, 7th Floor
New York, NY 10017

Printed in the United States of America

10 9 8 7 6 5 4 3

ISBN-13: 978-1-5062-0317-1

Kaplan Publishing books are available at special quantity discounts to use for sales promotions, employee premiums, or educational purposes. For more information or to order books, please call the Simon & Schuster special sales department at 866-506-1949.

Contents

PART TWO: THE ACT TESTS

PART THREE: PRACTICE TESTS AND EXPLANATIONS

Welcome to Kaplan's *ACT Premier 2016-2017*

Are you ready to conquer the ACT?

Kaplan knows a high score on the ACT exam is important to you. A great score can help you stand out from the crowd when applying to colleges and can help you get the scholarships and financial aid to pay for it all.

Kaplan has more than 75 years of experience getting students ready for their exams. We've spent decades building a powerful arsenal of test-taking tools designed with *you* in mind, and the book you have in front of you contains everything you need to score higher on the ACT.

The 2016-2017 edition of Kaplan's *ACT Premier* includes proven ACT strategies, eight realistic ACT Practice Tests (three in the book and five online), a DVD of elite Kaplan teachers providing instruction and tips, and in-depth reviews of every kind of question the ACT will throw at you. Kaplan's ACT tools work. Use them to your advantage, and get ready to score higher on the ACT!

LET'S GET STARTED!

Kaplan's *ACT Premier 2016-2017* has everything you need to get ready for Test Day, but how you use this book is *your* choice. No one knows your test-prep needs and schedule better than you, so we've designed this book to put you in control of the type and amount of study that best suit your needs.

This book is designed to allow you to determine the path your test prep takes. Use it front to back, or jump around and focus on the test sections you need the most help with—it's your call.

In addition to all the great test prep inside the book, we've put a Diagnostic Test online to help you determine your test strengths and weaknesses and focus your study plan. This is a great place to get started.

TAKE THE ONLINE DIAGNOSTIC TEST

Taking the online Diagnostic Test is a great way to figure out where your ACT skills stand and how to structure your study time between now and Test Day. Take the Diagnostic Test and see which sections are your strongest and which will require the most prep.

Here's how to access your ACT Diagnostic Test online:

1. Go to kaptest.com/booksonline.

2. Follow the on-screen instructions. Please have a copy of your book available.

BUILD YOUR ACT STUDY PLAN

Okay, so you've taken the Diagnostic Test. Now what? Well, now that you have a good idea which test sections are your strongest and which need the most attention, you are ready to make the most of this book and build your study plan.

YOUR ACT STUDY PLAN—FIVE STEPS TO SUCCESS

1. Carefully go through the lessons in this book, paying close attention to the areas that focus on the test sections that were weakest on your Diagnostic Test.

2. Do the Warm-Up quizzes after learning how each subject test works, then take the end-of-chapter practice sets to see how well you're progressing. Be sure to read the answers and explanations carefully—they'll help you figure out where you might have gone wrong during your problem-solving and how to get questions like these right on Test Day.

3. Don't hesitate to review challenging concepts more than once. Watch an instructional video or take an extra quiz online. Doing well on the ACT is worth the extra study time!

4. Take time to practice your writing skills for the ACT essay. Use the strategies provided in this book to wow the essay graders on Test Day!

5. As you gain comfort with the various ACT question types and test material, dive into the full-length Practice Tests in the back of the book and online. Don't save all of them for the end—use them to measure your growth and build confidence. Test yourself under realistic Test Day conditions and chart your progress. If your strengths and weaknesses change, adjust your study plan.

Let's get started!

PART ONE

ACT Basics

CHAPTER 1

Introduction to the ACT

Before you plunge into studying for the ACT, let's take a step back and look at the big picture. What's the ACT all about? What does it do for you? How can you prepare for it? What do you need to do to get a high score? This chapter will answer these questions and more.

First, you should think of the ACT as an opportunity, not a barrier. In fact, you should be glad that you're taking it. Really. The purpose of the ACT is to help you get into the college of your choice and get the scholarships you need to pay for it. And it's something you can control: a strong ACT score doesn't depend on how good your high school is, how many college alumni you know, how rich and famous your family is, or whether any of your teachers will swear in a letter of recommendation that you're the greatest scientific mind since Isaac Newton. No, your ACT score only depends on you.

> **✔ EXPERT TUTOR TIP**
>
> If you have two weeks or fewer to prep for the ACT, don't panic. The first thing you should do is become familiar with the test. This chapter is the place to start.

Granted, the ACT is a tough exam, but you should be grateful for that, too. Really. If the ACT were easy, everyone would do well. A good score wouldn't mean much. However, because it is so challenging, the ACT can be your single best opportunity to show what you can do and prove to colleges that you are the candidate of choice—for admission, for advanced placement, and for scholarships.

It's important, though, that you take the test in the right spirit. Don't be timid in the face of the ACT or unfamiliar with what it's going to ask. You can and *must* take control of the test. This book will show you exactly how to do that.

It helps to think of the ACT challenge as a contest—not only between you and the test, but also between you and the other students vying for the same spot at your college of choice. The ACT, after all, provides a way for all college applicants to compete on an even playing field. How do you compete successfully in a fair academic fight? You train—harder and smarter than the next person. First, you learn what challenge is in front of you, then you set a goal and learn all the knowledge and skills you need to succeed. And then, just as importantly, you learn how to show what you know, in ways that the test is designed to reward. You learn how to be a savvy test taker.

FOUR KEYS TO ACT SUCCESS

There are four basic keys to achieving ACT success. Following any of these by itself will improve your score. Following all four together will get you to where you want to be.

1. LEARN THE TEST

The ACT is very predictable. The test makers are excellent at crafting the types of challenges that show what they're trying to see in your score. As a result, the same kinds of questions, testing the same skills and concepts, appear every time the ACT is given. This is to your considerable advantage.

Because the test specifications rarely change, you can learn in advance what to expect on every section. Just a little familiarity can make an enormous difference. Here are a few ways learning the test will boost your score:

- **You'll know the directions.** Why waste valuable time reading directions when you can have them down pat beforehand? You need every second during the test to answer questions and get points.

- **You'll know the difficulty range of questions.** Every question on the ACT is worth the same number of points, and the questions aren't in any order of difficulty. Knowing this, you can plan your approach to recognize the points you can earn quickly and move past the questions that will take too long until you can get back to them. Doing the questions in the order the ACT gives them to you isn't a strategy. Finding every last point you can get *is*.

- **You'll get extra points by guessing.** Unlike other standardized tests, the ACT has no wrong-answer penalty. Knowing how to apply that fact can boost your score significantly. You miss 100 percent of shots you don't take. So if you can't answer a question, guess.

- **You'll know how to write a high-scoring essay.** If you are taking the optional Writing test, learning how it is evaluated will help you get a top score.

We'll help you get a better understanding of the ACT in the next chapter, **The Subject Tests: A Preview.**

2. LEARN THE KAPLAN METHODS AND STRATEGIES

The ACT isn't like the exams you take in school. Most school exams test your memory for what you've just been taught. Instead, the ACT tests your problem-solving skills and how you use them, mostly on unfamiliar content. So instead of worrying about what you do or don't know, focus on learning the Kaplan problem-solving Methods and Strategies to earn you points!

Students miss a lot of ACT questions for no good reason. They see a tough-looking question, say to themselves, "Uh oh, I don't remember how to do that," and start to gnaw on their No. 2 pencils.

However, most ACT questions can be answered without perfect knowledge of the material being tested. Often, all you need to do to succeed on the ACT is to think strategically and creatively. We call this kind of strategic, creative frame of mind the ACT Mind-Set.

How do you put yourself into the ACT Mind-Set? You continually ask yourself questions such as: "What am I being asked? What does this mean? How can I put this into a form I can understand and use? How can I do this faster?" Once you develop some savvy test-taking skills, you'll find yourself capable of working out problems that, at first reading, might have seemed unsolvable. In fact, we'll show you how you can sometimes get right answers when you don't even understand the questions.

There are many, many specific strategies you can use to boost your score. Here are just a few things you'll learn:

- **You'll learn the peculiarities of the ACT format.** Except for the Writing test, the ACT is a multiple-choice test. The correct answer is *always* in front of you—you just have to identify it. We'll show you how to develop specific tactics for each question type to find the correct answer. Wrong answers often take predictable forms as well, so knowing how to recognize them can give you an important edge.

- **You'll learn a plan of attack for each subject test.** We'll show you useful and distinct ways of attacking each subject test. You'll learn the most common questions and content on each section so you know what will get you the most points. You'll learn how to do "question triage"—deciding which questions to do now and which to save for later. You'll learn the Kaplan Method—designed to get you points quickly and systematically—for each ACT subject test. You'll learn gridding techniques to avoid any answer sheet disasters.

- **You'll learn "unofficial" ways of getting right answers fast.** On the ACT, your score is based on whether you get the right answer, not how you decide which choice to select.

That's different from most high school tests, which give credit for showing that you've done questions the "right" way (that is, the way you were taught to do them by your high school teacher). We'll show you how to find creative shortcuts—methods that will save you precious time and net you extra points.

The basic test-smart techniques and strategies for the whole test are covered in the chapter called Taking Control: Your ACT Mind-Set and the Top Ten Strategies. The Kaplan Methods and Strategies for each subject test, plus specific hints, techniques, and strategies for individual question types, are found in the Skill-Building Workouts. These are then summarized in the Strategic Summaries.

3. LEARN THE TESTED MATERIAL

The ACT is designed to test skills and concepts learned in high school and needed for college. But familiarity with the test, coupled with effective test-taking strategies, will take you only so far. For your best score, you need to sharpen the skills and content knowledge that the ACT tests.

The good news is that most of the content on the ACT is covered by sophomore year at most high schools, with the majority of it even earlier than that. So you've probably already learned most of what the ACT expects you to know, but you may need to spend some time remembering or finding better ways to approach the information. That's partly what this book is for—to remind you of the knowledge you already have and to build and refine the specific skills you've developed so far. Here are just a few of the things we'll review:

- How to read graphs and tables efficiently for the Science section.

- The rules for grammar and punctuation (yes, there are consistent and absolute rules, and we'll tell you what they are).

- Math rules for triangles, probabilities, algebraic expressions, and more.

- The difference between generalizations and details, inference and summary, and how to make a passage map that saves you more time than it takes to make it.

- What goes into an excellent persuasive essay, what to leave out, and what to choose if you're running out of time.

4. PRACTICE, PRACTICE, PRACTICE

Practice creates confidence. On Test Day, you need to have the Kaplan Methods and Strategies and the tested concepts ready to go and be relaxed enough to let them all work. So reading and understanding the contents of this book are key, but there's one more step: you need to make the Kaplan Methods part of your everyday routine. The best way to do that is to practice as much as possible.

Test Day will bring its own challenges—you have to be up early to take a long test, in a room full of people you may or may not know, everyone in a state of anticipation and nervousness—and the anxiety is contagious! You'll be the one who doesn't let nerves take over and make you forget what you know about doing well. Your best ally is the confidence practice gives you.

Note: If you don't have time to practice with all of the sections of this book, you can (and should!) practice in the areas you feel weakest.

So here are your four keys to ACT success:

1. Learn the test.

2. Learn the strategies.

3. Learn the material tested.

4. Practice, practice, practice.

Follow these steps, and you'll find yourself just where you want to be: in full command of your ACT test-taking experience, ready to get your highest score. Count on it.

ACT FAQS

Here are some quick answers to the questions students ask most frequently about the ACT.

WHAT IS THE ACT?

As you know, the ACT is a standardized test. That means it tests predefined concepts in predictable ways and is administered to all students the same way. Each time the ACT is administered, it has the same number of questions per section, the same distribution of passages, the same timing, and the same average level of difficulty. You'll learn more about the tested concepts and the predictability of the ACT as you work with this book. For now, you should understand one thing: the more you know about how the test is written and structured, the more in control you'll feel on Test Day. You can only work on the Math section when the proctor announces, "You have the next 60 minutes to work on Section 2," but you don't necessarily need to work on the questions in any particular order. As you learn more about each section, you'll find your own way of approaching the questions with confidence and a plan for earning the most points possible. Your success begins with knowing exactly what to expect on the ACT.

So before anything else, take some time and get to know your test. Let's start with the basics.

The ACT is a three-hour exam (three hours and 40 minutes if you take the optional Writing test) taken mostly by high school juniors and seniors to gain admission to and scholarships for college. It is not an IQ test; it is a test of problem-solving skills—which means you can improve your performance by preparing for common question types.

Because the skills being tested and the format of the test are standardized, the universities get a straightforward and understandable way of comparing students, no matter their academic backgrounds and no matter how grade inflation affects grade point averages. So you can be sure that the admissions offices are going to take a serious look at your test scores.

To evaluate those skills, the ACT utilizes four subject tests: English, Math, Reading, and Science, as well as the optional Writing test. All of the subject tests are primarily designed to test skills rather than knowledge, though some knowledge is required—particularly in English and Math, which test your ability to quickly and accurately apply rules you've learned throughout your school years.

HOW IS THE ACT STRUCTURED?

- The ACT is about three hours long (three hours and 40 minutes with the Writing test). There will be a short break between the Math and Reading subject tests.

- It consists of a total of 215 scored multiple-choice questions and one optional essay.

- It is comprised of four subject tests and an optional Writing test:

    – English (45 minutes, 75 questions)

    – Math (60 minutes, 60 questions)

    – Reading (35 minutes, 40 questions)

    – Science (35 minutes, 40 questions)

    – Writing (40 minutes, 1 essay question)

HOW IS THE ACT SCORED?

The ACT is scored differently from most tests that you take at school. Your ACT score on a test section is not reported as the total number of questions you answered correctly, nor does it directly represent the percentage of questions you answered correctly. Instead, the test makers add up all of your correct answers in a section to get what's called your raw score. They then use a conversion chart, or scale, that matches up a particular raw score with what's called a scaled score. The scaled score is the number that gets reported as your score for that ACT subject test. For each version of the ACT administered, the test maker uses a unique conversion chart that equates a particular raw score with a particular scaled score.

ACT scaled scores range from 1 to 36. Nearly half of all test takers score within a much narrower range: 17–23. Tests and scores on different dates vary slightly, but the data below is based on a recent administration of the test and can be considered typical.

ACT Approximate Percentile Rank*	Scaled (or Composite) Score	Percentage of Questions Correct
99%	33	90%
90%	28	75%
74%	24	63%
49%	20	53%
28%	17	43%

*Percentage of ACT takers scoring at or below given score

Notice that to earn a score of 20 (the national average), you need to answer only about 53 percent of the questions correctly. On most tests, getting only a bit more than half the questions right would not be a passing grade, nor the average. Not so on the ACT. A score of 20 puts you in the middle range of test takers.

The score table includes two very strong scores: 28 and 33. Either score would impress almost any college admissions officer. A 28 would put you in the top 10 percent of the students who take the exam, and a 33 would put you in the top 1 percent. Even a 33 requires getting only about 90 percent of the questions right! So the best-scoring students will probably get at least a dozen questions wrong, but will still get the scores they need to get into college.

> **✔ EXPERT TUTOR TIP**
>
> Just a few questions right or wrong on the ACT can make a big difference. Answering only five extra questions correctly on each subject test can move you from the bottom of the applicant pool into the middle or from the middle up to the top.

If you earn a score of 24, you'll be in about the 74th percentile. That means that you did as well as or better than 74 percent of the test takers—in other words, you're in the top quarter of people who took the ACT. That's a strong score, but notice that to earn this score, you need only about 63 percent of the questions correct. On most tests, a score of 63 percent is probably a D or lower. But on the ACT, it's about a B+.

HOW MANY ACT SCORES WILL YOU GET?

The ACT scaled score we've talked about so far is technically called the Composite score—when people say "I got ___ on the ACT," this is what they're talking about. While the Composite score is really important, you'll see a dozen or more different scores and subscores when you get your ACT results: the Composite score, four (or five) subject scores, and up to eight subscores. Though the subject scores can play a role in decisions or course placement at some schools, the subscores usually aren't as important as the Composite. So feel free to skim over the following chart if you aren't ready to look at subscores.

Here's the full battery of ACT scores (1–36) you'll receive:

English Score (1–36)	Usage/Mechanics subscore (1–18); Rhetorical Skills subscore (1–18)
Mathematics Score (1–36)	Pre-Algebra/Elementary Algebra subscore (1–18); Algebra/Coordinate Geometry subscore (1–18); Plane Geometry/Trigonometry subscore (1–18)
Reading Score (1–36)	Social Studies/Sciences subscore (1–18); Arts/Literature subscore (1–18)
Science Score (1–36)	There are no subscores in Science.
(Optional) Writing Score (1–36)	Ideas and Analysis subscore (1–12); Development and Support subscore (1–12); Organization (1–12); Language Use and Conventions (1–12). This score does not count toward your Composite score, but colleges will see it.
ELA (1–36)	This is the average of your English, Reading, and Writing scores.
STEM (1–36)	This is the average of your Science and Math scores.

HOW DO COLLEGES USE YOUR ACT SCORE?

The most important score is typically the Composite score (which is an unweighted average of the four major subject scores). This is the score used by most colleges and universities in the admissions and scholarship process. The subject scores and subscores may be used for advanced placement or occasionally for scholarships, but they are primarily used by college advisors to help students select majors and first-year courses.

Although many schools deny that they use benchmark scores as cutoffs, students have had mixed experiences, and it's well worth understanding the impact of all of your scores. Highly competitive universities generally decline to accept students with any Composite scores below 22 or 23. For less competitive schools, the benchmark score may be lower than that; for some very selective schools, the cutoff may be higher.

To be clear, no school uses the ACT as an absolute or stand-alone bar to admission; for most applicants, though, a low ACT score can be decisive. As a rule, only students whose backgrounds are extremely unusual or who have overcome enormous disadvantages are accepted if their ACT scores are below the school's benchmark.

SHOULD YOU TAKE THE OPTIONAL WRITING TEST?

The ACT calls the Writing test optional, but you will want to find out whether either your high school (if you're taking the ACT as part of your school's curriculum) or the colleges you're applying to require it. If they do, it's not optional! A list of colleges requiring the test is maintained on the ACT website, www.act.org/aap/writing. If you are unsure about what schools you will apply to, you should plan to take the Writing test. However, testing will be available later if you decide not to take the Writing test and discover later that you need it. This book will give you strong guidance on achieving your best score on the Writing test.

HOW DO SCHOOLS USE THE OPTIONAL WRITING TEST?

The ACT Writing test may be used for either admissions or course placement purposes, and sometimes both. Students who take the Writing test will receive an English score, a Reading score, a Writing score, and a combined ELA score on a 1–36 scale. Copies of the essay (with the graders' comments) will be available online for downloading. Schools that do not require the Writing test will also receive the ELA score for students who have taken the Writing test, unless the school specifically asks *not* to receive those results.

SHOULD YOU GUESS ON THE ACT?

The short answer? Yes! The long answer? Yes, always!

As you've seen, ACT scores are only based on the number of correct answers. But questions you leave blank and questions you answer incorrectly simply don't count for or against your score—unlike some standardized tests, the ACT doesn't have a wrong answer penalty. That's why you should *always* guess on every ACT question you can't answer, even if you don't have time to read it; you have a statistical likelihood of getting each question right just by answering! Though the questions vary enormously in difficulty, harder questions are worth exactly the same as easier ones. So it pays to mark the hardest questions to return to later and to guess on them, and spend your time gaining all the easier points you can find first.

CAN YOU RETAKE THE TEST?

You can take the ACT as many times as you like before it's time for your college applications to be done. If you take it more than once, you can select whichever test score you prefer to be sent to colleges when you apply. However, you can only take advantage of this option if, at the time you register for the test, you do not designate certain colleges to receive your scores automatically. Thus, if you are even possibly interested in taking the test more than once, it is crucial that you not designate any colleges when you register for the test. You can (for a small additional fee) have ACT scores sent to colleges at any time after the scores are reported.

So if you can afford the small extra fee to send the scores again, give yourself the freedom to retake the test (unless you're taking it under the wire and need your scores to reach your target schools ASAP). What this means, of course, is that even if you don't get the score you're looking for the first time, you can give yourself another chance without the schools of your choice seeing every score. The ACT is one of the few areas of your academic life in which you get a second chance. Still, keep in mind that your goal is to get your desired score as soon as possible by using your Kaplan Strategies and Methods. Once you get the score you're looking for, you can breathe a little easier about your college applications!

> ✔ **EXPERT TUTOR TIP**
>
> The ACT is offered many times per year, so plan your prep and testing around the date that will give you the most time to prepare. Consider activities, class tests, and personal plans when setting your prep and test schedule so you can give your preparation the attention it deserves.

ACT REGISTRATION OVERVIEW

- To get a registration packet, see your guidance counselor or contact:

  ACT Student Services
  2727 Scott Boulevard, minizip 46
  P.O. Box 451
  Iowa City, IA 52243-0451
  Phone: (319) 337-1270

- You can also register online at www.actstudent.org.

- Students with disabilities or with other special circumstances can call (319) 337-1332.

- Go online: visit the test maker's website at www.act.org for the latest information on test registration, fees, and content.

- The basic fee at press time for the ACT is $39.50 without the Writing test and $56.50 with the Writing test in the United States. (For students testing outside the United States or Canada, the fee is $79.50 or $96.50 for the ACT with Writing test.) This price includes reports for you, your high school, and up to four college choices. There are additional fees for late registration, standby testing, changing test centers or test dates, and additional services and products.

- In the United States, the ACT is administered in September, October, December, February, April, and June. (The February date is not available in the state of New York.) In selected states, the ACT is also offered in late September. Register early to secure the time you want at the test center of your choice and to avoid late registration fees.

- You may take the ACT as often as you wish. Many students take it twice, once as a junior and again as a senior. There are no limitations on how many times you can take the ACT, but there are some restrictions on how often you can test or how late the schools you're applying to will accept your application.

- Be sure you take your test center admission ticket and acceptable identification with you to the test center. Acceptable forms of identification are a photo ID or a recently published photo with your full name printed. Unacceptable forms of identification are a birth certificate, Social Security card, or any other ID without photo. You will not be admitted without acceptable identification. Check the ACT website at the time of registration and shortly before your test to be sure you have the right documentation.

- Check with ACT, Inc., for all the latest information on the test. Every effort is made to keep the information in this book up-to-date, but changes may occur after the book is published.

- Go online (act.org) to make sure you know ALL the ACT regulations for Test Day. **Note:** Violation of the test rules, such as an alarm going off, a phone ringing in the test room, or use of a unapproved calculator may result in your dismissal from the room and your answer sheet not being scored.

You might be considering whether to take the ACT, the SAT, or both. For more information on the SAT, go to the College Board's website at www.collegeboard.com. While the SAT and ACT have similar purposes, their structure and content are different enough that many people prefer one over the other. Take a sample test of each to find out which will show you at your best for your applications.

CHAPTER 2

The Subject Tests: A Preview

Okay, now you've seen how the ACT is set up. But to really do well, you've got to know something about the ACT subject tests and how each breaks down into points.

Looking at each content area, you want to see a road to 36—a set of questions covering a predictable range of content, with a set number of points that will get you to your goal score on Test Day. The ACT has been very careful and successful in determining which types of questions do the best job of evaluating your overall score. Over the decades that Kaplan has studied this, we've been able to create a road map of your path to 36 points. We call the questions on this road map the *SmartPoints*.

SmartPoints are specific types of questions—like "Detail" in English or "Plane Geometry" in Math—that you can *know* will show up a certain number of times and make up a certain amount of your score on Test Day. What's the benefit of knowing this? You will have no doubt exactly where you *should* and *shouldn't* spend time studying. If you miss half of the questions about circles, it could lower your score up to 3 points. If you miss half of the questions about *sine-cosine-tangent*, it will bring your score down a maximum of 1 point. So which do you want to study?

Want to see how you get to 36 on each section? Here it is:

Point Value	English
7	Connections
6	Verb Tenses
5	Punctuation
5	Word Choice
5	Wordiness
4	Writing Strategy
3	Sentence Sense
1	Organization
36	Total

Point Value	Math
7	Plane Geometry
7	Variable Manipulation
6	Proportions and Probability
6	Coordinate Geometry
3	Operations
3	Patterns, Logic, and Data
2	Number Properties
2	Trigonometry
36	Total

Point Value	Reading
12	Detail
8	Inference
8	Generalization
6	Function
1	Vocab-in-Context
1	Writer's View
36	Total

Point Value	Science
13	Scientific Reasoning
12	Figure Interpretation
11	Patterns
36	Total

You'll be looking in depth at all of the questions as you move through this book, but it will all come back to these points. These are the points you'll be earning to get your score, and you'll be making choices as you go through your preparation about how to invest your time.

In addition to finding the best ways to answer questions, you'll also be studying how to approach each section of the test strategically. Remember: **The questions are not arranged in order of difficulty.** This should change your approach substantially—every question is another chance to raise your score, and you need to find every point you can get, wherever it is.

So here's a preview of the types of questions and strategies you'll see on each of the subject tests. The questions we'll use as examples will be toward the lower end of the difficulty scale here, but later, in the Skill-Building Workouts, we'll challenge you with tougher questions.

After we look at the four required subject tests, we'll give you a preview of the optional Writing test. Let's get started.

ENGLISH

The English test lasts 45 minutes and includes 75 questions. That works out to about 30 seconds per question, but you'll learn in the English chapters to organize your time around whole passages, not individual questions.

You're not tested on spelling or vocabulary on the ACT—there are absolutely no spelling questions of any type, and you won't be asked to define any vocabulary words. Rather, the ACT is designed to test your understanding of the conventions of English—punctuation, grammar, sentence structure—and of rhetorical skills. Rhetorical skills consist of strategies like organizing the text and making sure it's consistently styled and concise. So you'll learn the "things to know" on the English test here, but keep in mind that it is mostly organized around following rules and identifying well-written language.

The average number of questions students get right is higher on the English section than on any other ACT subject area, but that also means there's a harder scoring scale on this section. To earn an average English subscore (a 20, say), you would have to get almost two-thirds of the questions right, while on the rest of the test you would need to get only about half of the questions right.

THE FORMAT

More than half of the English questions follow a standard format. A word, phrase, or sentence in a passage is underlined. You're given four choices: to leave the underlined portion alone (NO CHANGE, which is *always* the first choice) or to replace it with one of three alternatives.

EXAMPLE

…Pike's Peak in Southwest Colorado is named <u>before Zebulon Pike, an early explorer. He</u> traveled through
37
the area, exploring…

37. A. NO CHANGE
    B. before Zebulon Pike became an explorer, and he
    C. after Zebulon Pike, when he
    D. after Zebulon Pike. He

The right answer for number 37 is choice (D). The other choices all have various problems: grammatical, stylistic, and logical. Only choice (D) makes the sentence correct.

Notice that a single question can test several kinds of writing errors. We find that about one-third of the English questions test your ability to write concisely (we call these Wordiness questions), about another third test for logic and sense (Word Choice and Sentence Sense questions), and the remaining one-third test hard-and-fast rules of grammar and punctuation. By recognizing which questions you do best on and which appear most often, you'll know which areas to study.

TO OMIT OR NOT TO OMIT

Some English questions offer, as one of the alternatives, the chance to completely omit, or delete, the underlined portion.

EXAMPLE

Later, Pike fell while valiantly defending America in the War of 1812. <u>It goes without saying that this took place after he discovered Pike's Peak.</u> He actually
40
died near York (now called Toronto)…

40. F. NO CHANGE
    G. Clearly, this must have occurred subsequent to his discovering Pike's Peak.
    H. This was after he found Pike's Peak.
    J. OMIT the underlined portion.

In this case, choice (J) is correct. The idea really does "go without saying." For that reason, it shouldn't be said. On recent ACTs, when OMIT has appeared as a choice, it's been correct more than half of the time. Before choosing OMIT, however, read the passage text *without* the underlined portion to ensure that it is clear and correct that way.

NONSTANDARD-FORMAT QUESTIONS

Some ACT English questions—about 20 per test—don't follow the typical format of presenting you with an underlined portion and three possible revisions; they are referred to as Nonstandard-Format questions. Such questions may ask for the LEAST acceptable alternative to the underlined part, or which of the offered choices best accomplishes a specific goal, or whether to add or delete material, or how to rearrange the passage. For questions like these, it's important to read carefully! Here's an example of how question 40, which you saw earlier, could be presented as a Nonstandard-Format question.

EXAMPLE

…Later, Pike fell while valiantly defending America in the War of 1812. [40] He actually died near York (now called Toronto)…

40. Suppose the author considered adding the following sentence at this point: "It goes without saying that this occurred after he discovered Pike's Peak." Given the overall purpose of the passage, would this sentence be appropriate?

   F. No, because the sentence adds nothing to the meaning of the passage.

   G. No, because the passage is not concerned with Pike's achievements.

   H. Yes, because otherwise the sequence of events would be unclear.

   J. Yes. Though the sentence is not needed, the author recognizes this fact by using the phrase "it goes without saying."

The correct answer for this question is choice (F). Though choice (G) correctly states that the sentence doesn't belong in the passage, it offers a pretty poor reason. The passage *is* concerned with Pike's achievements. Choices (H) and (J) are wrong because they recommend including a sentence that is clearly redundant. Because they often deal with the passage as a whole, many Nonstandard-Format questions occur at the end of a passage.

We think you'll like the English subject test. Picking the best way of saying something, identifying awkward phrases, and playing with the pieces of a passage can be fun. We'll cover strategies for the English question types in the English chapters.

MATH

The Math test is 60 minutes long and includes 60 questions. That works out to one minute per question, but you'll wind up using more time on some questions and less on others.

THE FORMAT

All of the Math questions have the same basic multiple-choice format, with a stand-alone question and five possible answers (unlike questions on the other subject tests, which have only four choices each).

The questions cover a wide range of math topics, from pre-algebra to plane geometry and even a little bit of trigonometry. More emphasis is placed on earlier-level math skills (variable manipulation, order of operations) and less on the higher-level math. This book contains the 100 Key Math Concepts for the ACT to help you review the math content you need.

READING AND DRAWING DIAGRAMS

About one-third of the Math questions either give you a diagram or describe a situation that should be diagrammed. For these questions, the diagrams are crucial—you don't get any points for solving questions in your head, so draw *everything* out.

EXAMPLE

1. The figure below contains five congruent triangles. The longest side of each triangle is 4 meters long. What is the area of the whole figure?

    A. 12.5 square meters

    B. 15 square meters

    C. 20 square meters

    D. 30 square meters

    E. Cannot be determined from the given information.

The key to this question is to let the diagram tell you what you need to know: each triangle represents one-quarter of the area of the square, and the sides of the *square* are 4 meters (you can figure this out because the top side of the square is the hypotenuse of the triangle that makes the "roof"). Since the area of a square can be found by squaring its side, the area of the square is 16 square meters. Thus, each triangle has an area that is one-fourth as much—4 square meters. Since the whole figure consists of *five* triangles, each with area 4, the total area is 5 × 4 = 20. The answer is (C).

> ✔ **EXPERT TUTOR TIP**
>
> In ACT Math questions, the choice "cannot be determined" is rare. When it does appear, it's rarely the right answer, and is almost always wrong in a question that comes with a diagram or for which you can draw one.

HOW TO APPROACH A STORY PROBLEM

About another third of the Math questions are story problems like the following:

EXAMPLE

2. Evan drove halfway home at 20 miles per hour, then sped up and drove the rest of the way at 30 miles per hour. What was his average speed for the entire trip?

    F.   20 miles per hour

    G.   22 miles per hour

    H.   24 miles per hour

    J.   25 miles per hour

    K.   28 miles per hour

A good way to comprehend—and resolve—a story problem like this is to think of a real situation like the one in the story. For example, what if Evan had 60 miles to drive? (You should pick a distance that's easily divisible by both rates.) He would go 30 miles at 30 mph, then 30 miles at 20 mph. How long would it take? Well, 30 miles at 30 mph is one hour; 30 miles at 20 mph is 1.5 hours. That's a total of 60 miles in 2.5 hours; 60 divided by 2.5 gives an average speed of 24 mph. The correct answer is choice (H).

> ✔ **PERFECT SCORE TIP**
>
> Don't let variables or abstract stories confuse you. When you see them, calm down and make them simpler by putting real numbers in for the variables. You'll learn more about this Picking Numbers Strategy in Math Workout 1.

GETTING THE CONCEPT

Finally, about one-third of ACT Math questions directly ask you to demonstrate your knowledge of specific math concepts.

EXAMPLE

3. If angles *A* and *B* are supplementary, and the measure of angle *A* is 57°, what is the measure, in degrees, of angle *B*?

   A. 33

   B. 43

   C. 47

   D. 123

   E. 147

This question requires that you know the concept of supplementary angles: that two angles are *supplementary* when they form a straight line—in other words, when they add up to 180°. Thus, question 3 boils down to this: What number, added to 57, makes 180? The answer is choice (D), 123.

These three types of Math questions, of course, will be discussed more fully in the Math chapters.

READING

The Reading test is 35 minutes long and includes 40 questions. It contains four passages, each followed by 10 questions. You should allow three minutes (or less) to read and mark up the passage. You will then have about 30 seconds per question.

THE FORMAT

There are four categories of reading passages: Prose Fiction, Social Science, Humanities, and Natural Science. You'll always get one passage (or a pair of shorter passages) in each category, always in that order. The passages are about 1,000 words each and are written at about the same difficulty level as college textbooks and readings. After each passage, you'll always find 10 questions.

The Social Science, Humanities, and Natural Science passages are usually formal essays, each with a very specific purpose. Questions expect you to recognize this purpose, comprehend specific facts in the passage, and understand the structure of the essay.

> ✔ **PERFECT SCORE TIP**
>
> You do not have to do the passages in order. For example, if you always have trouble with Prose but are very good at Natural Science, do Natural Science first to make sure you don't run out of time to get those easy points. Develop a personal order that works for you, especially if you have trouble with time.

Prose Fiction passages require you to understand the thoughts, feelings, and motivations of fictional characters, even when these are not explicitly stated in the passage (we'll have a special section on Prose Fiction passages in Reading Workout 3). Note that the *difficulty* of the passages is not objectively different, but you may feel more or less comfortable with some types of writing than others.

Three main Reading SmartPoints—Detail, Inference, and Generalization—account for 28 out of your 36 points. In other words, just getting those three topics right puts you in the 90th percentile! We'll dig into all three in the Reading chapters, but let's take a quick look at each now, since they make up so much of the test.

NAILING DOWN THE DETAILS

Detail questions ask about things stated explicitly in the passage. Your challenge is to find the exact place in the passage where the answer can be found and match the detail from the text in the passage with the correct answer (by locating either similar words or paraphrases). The other choices will try to tempt you by presenting facts from other parts of the passage, bringing in new information, or drawing conclusions that the passage doesn't directly support. But every question has exactly one right answer, and if you can find the specific reference, those points are yours!

The instructions will also encourage you to "refer to the passage." That's a good idea before you look at the answers—find the answer in the passage, predict in your own words what the answer will say, then find it in the answers provided. This will help you to avoid being tempted by wrong answers.

EXAMPLE

When we say "Bach," we almost always refer to Johann Sebastian Bach (1685–1750), but in fact the name "Bach" belongs to a whole family of Baroque German musicians…

(*7 paragraphs and 950 words omitted*)

The works of Johann Christian Bach, J. S. Bach's son, clearly prefigure the rich musical developments that followed the Baroque period. Thus, it is both surprising and unfortunate that the rest of J. S. Bach's family isn't more well-known.

6. According to the author, J. S. Bach is the best-known

   F. German Baroque musician.

   G. member of a musical family.

   H. organist in German history.

   J. composer of Lutheran hymns.

7. Johann Christian Bach was

    A. born earlier than Johann Sebastian Bach.

    B. a composer of the "Romantic" school of music.

    C. a composer whose works are transitional in style.

    D. well-known during his own lifetime.

> ✔ **PERFECT SCORE TIP**
>
> Remember, the scorers do not care about your opinions or ideas about the passage. Base all your answers on what is explicitly written in the passage—not your own knowledge of the material.

You'll see these questions and others from this passage later in the book. For now, notice the phrasing: whether the question says "According to the author" or not, these questions ask for details that are directly stated in the passage. That means no guessing is necessary, no "figuring out," no inferring. Just finding exactly what the author says.

MAKING AN INFERENCE

Most Reading passages also include a large number of Inference questions, which require you to "read between the lines"—to conclude something that *must be true* based on what is in the passage, but is not directly stated.

EXAMPLE

…though schizophrenia and multiple personality disorder (MPD) may be related, and are often confused by laymen, the two terms have radically different meanings…

33. Suppose that a patient has been diagnosed with schizophrenia. Based on the passage, which of the following is LEAST likely?

    A. The patient's doctors immediately assume that the patient also suffers from MPD.

    B. The patient is a layman.

    C. The patient denies that he has MPD.

    D. The patient is related to someone with MPD.

Whereas Detail questions asked specifically about items in the text, look at the language in this Inference question: "Suppose…" Inference questions like this may seem like they're asking you to guess, but that's not how the ACT works! Some of the choices for Inference questions will be definitely false, and some may or may not be true, but the right answer is always something that MUST be true based on what is stated in the passage. We'll see this passage again later.

GETTING THE BIG PICTURE

Along with Detail and Inference questions, the Reading subject test also includes Generalization questions. Some Generalization questions ask about the passage as a whole, requiring you to find the purpose, tone, or structure of the passage. Others ask you to evaluate the writing. Here's a typical Generalization question that might have appeared with the Bach family passage we talked about earlier.

EXAMPLE

9. The author's main point in the passage is to

   A. show that many of the lesser-known members of the Bach family also influenced music history.
   B. argue that J. C. Bach was actually a greater composer than his father, J. S. Bach.
   C. demonstrate that musical talent always runs in families.
   D. dispute the claim that the Bach family was the best-known family of German Baroque musicians.

Language like "the author's main point" or "the passage overall" tells you that you're looking at a Generalization question. To correctly answer these, you need to consider the points that are most important to the passage, and make sure your answer doesn't go far beyond the scope of the passage. Look for verbs like "argue," "show," "prove," or "describe"— passages that do one probably don't do another, so if you're looking at a passage that's just description, "argue" or "prove" might be key words to avoid.

You'll look at the four types of Reading passages and the question types they all have in common in the Reading chapters.

SCIENCE

The Science test is 35 minutes long and includes 40 questions. It has six passages, each with 6 to 7 questions. This breaks down to approximately 5–6 minutes per passage, including questions.

Good news: you don't have to be a scientist to succeed on the ACT Science test. You don't have to know the atomic number of cadmium or the preferred mating habits of the monarch butterfly. All the test requires is common sense and careful reading skills (though a knowledge of standard scientific processes and procedures sure does help). You'll be given passages containing various kinds of scientific information—drawn from the fields of biology, chemistry, physics, geology, astronomy, and meteorology—which you'll have to familiarize yourself with and use as a basis for inferences.

THE FORMAT

On the Science test, the six passages are broken down as follows:

- Two passages with approximately six to seven questions about tables and graphs

- Three passages with approximately six to seven questions about experiments

- One passage with approximately seven questions that presents opposing viewpoints on the same issue

ANALYZING DATA

Up to two-thirds of the questions on the Science test will require you to read data from graphs or tables. On easier questions, you need only identify and report the information on the charts. On harder questions, you will need to draw inferences or note patterns in the data.

EXAMPLE

1. A test taker who scores in approximately the 40th percentile has correctly answered about what fraction of the questions?

   A. $\dfrac{9}{10}$

   B. $\dfrac{2}{3}$

   C. $\dfrac{1}{2}$

   D. $\dfrac{1}{5}$

2. Which of the following best describes the relationship between percentile rank and percent of questions correct?

   F. As percentile rank increases, percent of correct questions also increases.

   G. Percentile rank is inversely proportional to the percent of correct questions.

   H. As percentile rank increases, the percent of correct questions decreases.

   J. As percentile rank decreases, percent of correct questions usually, but not always, also decreases.

The correct answer to question 1 is choice (C). The point for the 40th percentile is slightly above the 50 percent point on the horizontal axis (percent of questions correct), which is the same as $\frac{1}{2}$. Note that this question involves identifying data and then doing a little simple arithmetic (translating a percent into a fraction)—not uncommon for Science questions.

In question 2, the correct answer is choice (F). The points that are higher on the graph (higher percentile) are always farther to the right (higher percentage of correct questions). Note that choices (G) and (H) say essentially the same thing, and thus are wrong for the same reason: they get the relationship backward. Choice (J) is wrong because it says the percent of correct questions does not *always* decrease as percentile rank decreases.

CONDUCTING EXPERIMENTS

Other Science questions require that you understand the way experiments are designed and what they prove. For example, part of a passage might describe an experiment as follows:

EXAMPLE

EXPERIMENT 1

A scientist adds one drop of nitric acid to Beakers A, B, and C. Each beaker contains water from a different stream. The water in Beaker A came from Stream A, that in Beaker B came from Stream B, and that in Beaker C came from Stream C. Precipitates form in Beakers B and C, but not in Beaker A.

12. Which of the following could properly be inferred on the basis of Experiment 1?

   F. Stream A is more polluted than Streams B and C.

   G. Streams B and C are more polluted than A.

   H. Stream A contains material that neutralizes nitric acid.

   J. Streams B and C contain some substance that reacts in the presence of nitric acid.

The correct answer is choice (J). Since a precipitate forms when nitric acid is added to Beakers B and C, which contain water from Streams B and C, something in these streams must be involved. However, we don't know that it is pollution, so choices (F) and (G) are unwarranted. We don't know exactly *why* no precipitate formed in Beaker A, so choice (H) is also an unwarranted conclusion. Scientists *hate* unwarranted conclusions.

> ✔ **PERFECT SCORE TIP**
>
> Remember that like Reading, Science questions will never ask you to make inferences too far beyond what is given. Analyze the data, but DO NOT make unjustified conclusions.

THE PRINCIPLE OF THE THING

The remaining Science questions require you either to logically apply a principle or to identify ways of defending or attacking a principle. In some passages, the question will involve two scientists stating opposing views on the same subject, but this is not *always* the case. A passage might describe a theory that most V-shaped valleys are typically formed by water erosion through soft rock, and be followed by these two Principle questions:

EXAMPLE

16. Which of the following is most likely to be a V-shaped valley?

    F. A valley formed by glaciers
    G. A river valley that is cut into very hard basalt
    H. A valley formed by wind erosion
    J. A river valley in a region of soft shale rocks

17. Which of the following discoveries would most weaken the theory of V-shaped valley formation given in the passage?

    A. Certain parts of many valleys formed by water that are U-shaped
    B. A group of V-shaped valleys almost certainly formed by wind erosion
    C. A group of U-shaped valleys formed by water erosion in hard rock
    D. A group of valleys on Mars that appear to be V-shaped but that are not near any running water

In question 16, the correct answer is choice (J), since this is consistent with the passage as described. The correct answer in question 17 is choice (B). Finding V-shaped valleys *not* formed by water erosion would tend to weaken the theory that they are formed this way. The other answers do not offer evidence about V-shaped valleys on Earth, and thus are irrelevant to a theory about them.

We'll be showing you strategies for each kind of Science question in the three Science chapters.

WRITING

The Writing test is 40 minutes long and is comprised of one essay. The essay prompt will include an issue and three perspectives on the issue. You will be asked to discuss the three perspectives, present your own perspective, and explain the relationship between your perspective and the three perspectives provided by the prompt. You want to support your analysis with specific, relevant support.

You don't have to be a great creative writer to succeed on the ACT Writing test, nor should you be concerned with being "right." Instead, you have to show that you can evaluate an issue, three perspectives, and your own thesis in a coherent, direct way. Furthermore, the essay graders are not primarily concerned with your grammar and punctuation skills, as long as your points are clear. You are being tested on your ability to communicate in writing.

One of the biggest challenges of the Writing test is the time frame. With only 40 minutes to read the prompt, plan your response, draft the essay, and proofread it, you have to work quickly and efficiently. Coming up with a plan and sticking to it are key to succeeding on the Writing test.

THE FORMAT

The Writing test consists of one prompt that lays out the issue, three perspectives, and directions for your response. There are no choices of topic; you have to respond to the topic that is there. Don't worry too much about not knowing anything about the issue you have to write about—test makers craft topics that are broad enough that high school students can be expected to have a point of view regarding the issue presented. And it isn't your point of view, even, that will earn you points, but your ability to clearly state one and explain how it relates to the perspectives provided in the prompt.

WRITING TEST SKILLS

The graders realize that you're writing under time pressure, and they expect you to make some mistakes. **The content of your essay is not relevant; readers are not checking your facts, nor will they judge you on your opinions. They only want to see how well you can evaluate and analyze multiple points of view.**

The ACT identifies the following as the skills tested on the Writing test:

- **Evaluating an issue.** You can demonstrate that you understand the complexity of multiple perspectives by addressing each one individually before providing your own thesis.

- **Stating a clear perspective on an issue.** This means directly providing your own perspective—picking a side.

- **Providing an explanation.** When discussing your own thesis, you are expected to explain the relationship between your ideas and the given perspectives.

- **Providing supporting evidence and logical reasoning.** This means offering relevant support for your opinion and building an argument based on concrete details and examples. Don't just "think" you're right. Be able to prove it.

- **Maintaining focus and organizing ideas logically.** You've got to be organized, avoid digressions, and tie all your ideas together in a sensible way.

- **Writing clearly.** This is the only skill addressing your ability to write directly, and it's limited to clarity.

CHAPTER 3

Taking Control: Your ACT Mind-Set and the Top Ten Strategies

Now that you have a better idea of the kind of questions you'll see on the ACT, it's time to start developing strategies for managing them. In other words, you have to start developing your ACT Mind-Set.

The ACT, as you've seen, isn't a normal test that requires you to rely almost exclusively on your memory of things you've learned. On a normal test, you'd see questions like this:

> The "golden spike," which joined the Union Pacific and Central Pacific Railroads, was driven in Ogden, Utah, in May 1869. Who was president of the United States at the time?

To answer this question, you have to resort to memory dredging. Either you know the answer is Ulysses S. Grant or else you don't. No matter how hard you think, you'll *never* be able to answer this question if you don't remember that fact.

But the ACT doesn't test your memory. The answer to every ACT question can be found on the test—the ACT tests your ability to find the right one. Theoretically, if you read carefully and understand the words and concepts the test uses, you can get any ACT question right.

Notice the difference between the previous regular test question and the following ACT-type question:

EXAMPLE

1. What is the product of n and m^2, where n is an odd number and m is an even number?

   A. An odd number

   B. A multiple of 4

   C. A noninteger

   D. An irrational number

   E. The square of an integer

Aside from the obvious distinction (this question has choices, while the previous one does not), there's another difference: the ACT question tests your ability to understand a situation rather than your ability to remember a fact. Nobody expects you to know off the top of your head what the product of an odd number and the square of an even number is. But the ACT test makers do expect you to be able to roll up your sleeves and figure it out (as we'll do throughout this book).

THE ACT MIND-SET

Most students walk into ACT with the same mind-set they use for normal tests. With their brains on "memory mode," students often panic because they can't seem to "remember" enough to answer the questions. **But you know that's not how to get points. You get points for finding the right answer where it is on the page, not remembering it from before the test started.**

On the ACT, if you understand what a question is really asking, you can almost always answer it. For instance, take the previous math problem. You might have been thrown by the way it was phrased. "How can I solve this problem?" you may have asked yourself. "It doesn't even have numbers in it!"

> ✔ **EXPERT TUTOR TIP**
>
> ACT questions are puzzles to solve. Don't think: "Can I remember?" Think: "Let me figure this thing out!"

But a prepared student isn't surprised by questions like this and knows how to solve them. This Kaplan book will show you a number of ways of solving every question, even if you aren't sure yet how to start. This chapter contains the top ten strategies you'll use to build your ACT Mind-Set!

By the way, the answer to the question is (B). Any odd number (n) times any even number (m or m^2) will be an even number, which eliminates (A), (C), and (D) immediately. But it won't necessarily be a perfect square, which eliminates (E). If you Pick Numbers, you'll see (B) is definitely right. More on that later!

Of course, this doesn't always mean the questions are easy. Many ACT questions are built on basic concepts but are tough to answer nonetheless. The previous problem, for instance, is difficult because it requires some thought to figure out what's being asked and some abstract thinking to deal with variables instead of numbers. This isn't only true in Math—it's the same for every part of the ACT.

The creative, take-control kind of thinking of the ACT Mind-Set is something that will help you on every ACT question you encounter. As you'll see, being in the ACT Mind-Set means reshaping the test-taking experience so that you are in the driver's seat.

It means:

- Answering questions **if** you want to (by guessing on high-difficulty questions rather than spending more time on them than they're worth)

- Answering questions **when** you want to (by skipping tough-but-doable questions and coming back to them after you've gotten all of the easy questions done)

- Answering questions **how** you want to (by using "unofficial" ways of getting correct answers quickly)

That's really what the ACT Mind-Set boils down to: taking control, being creative, and selecting specific questions to answer to get points as quickly and easily as you can.

What follows are the top ten strategies you need to do just that.

> **📶 GO ONLINE**
>
> With three full-length Practice Tests and five more online, you'll get plenty of opportunities to practice the strategies in this chapter.

TOP TEN STRATEGIES FOR MASTERING THE ACT

1. TRIAGE THE QUESTIONS

In a hospital emergency room, the triage nurse is the person who evaluates each patient and decides who gets attention first and who should be treated later. You should do the same thing on the ACT. Every question is worth the same number of points, but they don't all take the same amount of time to solve. Your first job is to find the questions you can get quickly and easily, putting those points in the bank while you go back to work on the ones that will take longer.

Practicing triage is one of the most important ways of controlling your test-taking experience. Follow these steps to approach the test strategically:

- If the question looks comprehensible and reasonably doable, do it right away.

- If the question looks tough and time-consuming, but ultimately doable, skip it for now, circle the question number in your test booklet, and come back to it later. (Make sure to skip that line on your grid, too!)

- If the question looks impossible, forget about it. Guess and move on. *Never* to return unless you have gotten literally every other question right.

> ✔ **EXPERT TUTOR TIP**
>
> The key to question triage is to evaluate questions quickly. If you linger over these decisions, you will lose valuable time on Test Day.

This triage method will ensure that you spend the time needed to do all the quick and easy questions before getting bogged down with tougher ones. Doing the questions in the order they're listed isn't a strategy—it's not a good use of time to spend three minutes struggling on a hard question when you could move on to two or more others that you could answer correctly instead!

Answering easier questions first has another benefit: it gives you confidence to answer harder ones later. Doing problems in the order *you choose* rather than in the order imposed by the test gives you control.

YOUR TRIAGED PLAN OF ATTACK

For the English, Reading, and Science tests, the best plan of attack is to do each passage as a block, because the questions wind up being related to each other. Take a first pass through the questions, doing the easy ones, guessing on the impossible ones, and skipping any that look like they might cause trouble. Then make a second pass (a "cleanup pass"), and do those questions you think you can solve with some elbow grease. Keep an eye on your overall per-passage timing (which you'll learn about in the individual subject test chapters) so you don't spend so long on those elbow grease questions that you take away time from the next passage.

For Math, you use the same two-pass strategy, except you move through the whole subject test twice. Work through the doable questions first, then come back and attack the questions that look possible but tough or time-consuming. The questions are not in order of difficulty, and more importantly *you* will be better at some question types than others, so it's crucial you see every question.

No matter what subject test you're working on, **be extremely careful to grid your answers in the right place.** It's easy to misgrid when you're skipping around, so check your line numbers frequently. And of course, *make sure you have an answer gridded for **every** question by the time the subject test is over!*

2. PUT THE MATERIAL INTO A FORM YOU CAN UNDERSTAND AND USE

ACT questions are rarely presented in the simplest, most helpful way. In fact, your main job for many questions is to figure out what the question means so you can solve it. Since much of the material is presented in a puzzle form, one of your best strategies for taking control is to recast (reword) the material into a form you can handle better. While some methods will only apply to specific question types, many can help you on every section.

MARK UP YOUR TEST BOOKLET

This strategy should be employed on all four subject tests. In Reading and Science, you can reduce the amount of rereading you have to do by circling or underlining main ideas, important transitions, or other items you'll want to return to quickly. Make yourself a road map of the passage, labeling each paragraph so you understand how the ideas all fit together. That way, you'll also know—later, when you're doing the questions—where in the passage to find certain types of information you need.

> ✔ **EXPERT TUTOR TIP**
>
> Write all over your test booklet. Crossing out wrong answers eliminates confusion and helps you to see clearly which answer is correct. Underlining key points when reading passages helps you to determine the main idea.

In Math, you'll have a lot of figuring to do and diagrams to draw. Remember—you don't get extra points for solving the questions in your head, but you do stand to *lose* points if you make a mistake because you didn't write it out. And in English, you'll dramatically improve your chances of finding the right answer if you cross out wrong answers as you identify them.

REWORD THE QUESTIONS

You'll find that you also need to do some recasting of the *questions*. For instance, take this question from a Science passage:

EXAMPLE

Figure 1

15. According to Figure 1, at approximately what latitude would calculations using an estimated value at sea level of $g = 9.80$ m/sec^2 produce the least error?

   A. 0°

   B. 20°

   C. 40°

   D. 80°

Ask yourself: "What does *produce the least error* mean?" We're looking for a solution, like in the Math section—a point on a graph. And we're looking for it in terms of latitude—a degree on the *x*-axis. So the question is really just asking, "At what latitude does 9.80 (*y*-axis) hit the curve?" Now that's a form of the question you can understand, and you can answer it easily: choice (C), which you can get just by reading the chart.

DRAW DIAGRAMS

Often, what the Math section in particular is evaluating is whether you can translate information out of a question and into a diagram, and sometimes it's just easier to solve if you can visualize. For instance, take a look at the following math problem.

EXAMPLE

2. Jason bought a painting with a frame 1 inch wide. If the dimensions of the outside of the frame are 5 inches by 7 inches, which of the following could be the length of one of the sides of the painting inside the frame?

    F. 3 inches

    G. 4 inches

    H. $5\frac{1}{2}$ inches

    J. $6\frac{1}{2}$ inches

    K. 7 inches

Looking at the question the first time, you might be tempted to either just picture it in your head or to subtract 1 from the outside dimensions and assume the inside dimensions are 4 by 6 (and pick choice (G)). Why isn't this the right answer? Take a look at a sketch of it to find out:

Subtracting 1 from 5 by 7 doesn't work because the frame goes all the way around—above and below the painting and to the right and left. So you actually need to subtract 1 from *each side*, much clearer when you look at it—if the outside dimensions are 5 by 7, the inside dimensions must be 3 by 5. Thus, the correct answer is choice (F).

So remember: on the ACT, put everything into a form that you can understand and use.

3. IGNORE IRRELEVANT ISSUES

It's easy to waste time on ACT questions by considering irrelevant issues. Just because an issue looks interesting, or you're worried about something, doesn't make it important.

EXAMPLE

…China was certainly one of the cradles of civilization. It's obvious that, China has a long history. As is the case with other ancient cultures, the early history of China is lost in mythology…

14. F. NO CHANGE

    G. It's obvious that China has a long history.

    H. Obviously; China has a long history.

    J. OMIT the underlined portion.

In this question, there are two big potential distractions. One is figuring out what to do about that comma—you might immediately start looking for a punctuation solution, which you'd find in (G) and might want to select quickly. The other is the subject material—what if you find the history of China interesting? Reading for curiosity means you're not reading to solve questions, so you may have to read again. So we have to focus on the relevant issue: what is the question asking? This question is asking, "Is this sentence right as written? If not, should we fix it or get rid of it?" Looking at it this way, we see that China has an ancient culture and was a cradle of civilization, so it must have a long history. Therefore, the sentence is redundant. Choice (J) is correct.

Remember, you've got limited time, so don't get caught up in issues that won't get you a point.

4. CHECK BACK

Remember, the ACT is not a test of your memory. It's an open-book test. All of the information you need is in the test itself, so don't be afraid to refer to it.

Many questions will contain reference to a specific line, table, graph, or experiment. *Always* refer back to the section referenced—that's what it's there for!

EXAMPLE

1. Isaac Newton was born in 1642 in the hamlet of Woolsthorpe in Lincolnshire, England. But he is more famous as a man of Cambridge, where he studied and taught.

Which of the following does the author imply is a fact about Newton's birth?

    A. It occurred in Lincoln, a small hamlet in England.

    B. It took place in a part of England known for raising sheep.

    C. It did not occur in a large metropolitan setting.

    D. It caused Newton to seek his education at Cambridge.

You might expect the right answer to be that Newton was born in a hamlet, or in Woolsthorpe, or in Lincolnshire. But none of those are offered as choices. Choice (A) is tempting but wrong. Newton was born in Lincolnshire, *not* Lincoln. Choice (B) is actually true, but it's wrong here. As its name suggests, Woolsthorpe was once known for its wool, which comes from sheep, but that's not explained in the passage, so it *cannot* be correct.

The correct answer is choice (C), because a hamlet is a small village. That's not a large metropolitan setting.

Checking back is especially important in Reading and Science because of how many details the passages contain. Often, wrong answers will be misplaced details taken from different parts of the passage or things that don't answer the question properly but that might sound good to you if you aren't careful. By checking back in the passage, you can avoid choosing such tempting wrong choices.

There's another important lesson here: **don't pick a choice just because it contains key words you remember from the passage.** Many wrong choices, like (D) in the previous question, are distortions—they use the right words but say the wrong things. Look for choices that contain the same ideas you find in the passage.

Remember: The best way to avoid choosing misplaced details and distortions is to refer to the passage.

5. ANSWER THE RIGHT QUESTION

This strategy is a natural extension of the last. As we said, **the ACT often includes among the wrong choices for a question the correct answer to a *different* question.** Under time pressure, it's easy to fall for one of these red herrings, thinking you know what's being asked for but finding something else.

EXAMPLE

7. What is the value of $3x$ if $9x = 5y + 2$ and $y + 4 = 2y - 10$?

    A. 5
    B. 8
    C. 14
    D. 24
    E. 72

To solve for x, you need to find y first, because x here is given only in terms of y. To solve for y, you simplify the second equation (the Math section shows you good ways to do this if you need some review) and find that $y = 14$. Great! 14 is (C), so you're done!

Wait a minute. Choice (C), 14, isn't the right answer here, because the question doesn't ask for the value of y—it asks about x. You can use the value of y to find x; however, you do this by plugging the calculated value of y into the first equation.

By plugging 14 in for y, we find $9x = 72$. Great! 72 is (E), so you're done! Wait a minute. (E), 72, isn't the answer either because the question doesn't ask for $9x$. And it doesn't ask for *x* either, so if you picked (B), 8, you'd be wrong as well. The question asks for **3*x***. So you need to solve all the way through for *x*, then multiply by 3 again to get 3*x*: 24, choice (D).

Always check the question again before choosing your answer. In this case, by stopping short of solving all the way through, you might have fallen for three of the other choices. You're doing all the right work—get the right answer too, by answering the right question.

6. LOOK FOR THE HIDDEN ANSWER

On many ACT questions, the right answer is hidden or disguised in one way or another. For example, you might work out a problem and get 1.5 as your answer, but then find that 1.5 isn't among the choices. Then you notice that one choice reads $\frac{3}{2}$. You've found the hidden answer! It pays to think flexibly about numbers.

There's another way the ACT can hide answers. **Many ACT questions have more than one possible right solution, though only one correct choice is given. The ACT will hide that answer by offering one of the less obvious possible answers to a question.**

EXAMPLE

1. If $3x^2 + 5 = 17$, which of the following could be the value of *x*?

    A. −3
    B. −2
    C. 0
    D. 1
    E. 4

You quickly solve this very straightforward problem by simplifying to solve for *x*, which you find to be 2. Having gotten an answer, you confidently look for it among the choices. But 2 isn't a choice. The explanation? This question has two possible solutions, not just one. The square root of 4 can be either 2 *or* −2. So (B) is the answer; it just isn't the one you were looking for.

Keep in mind that though only one right choice for each question will be offered, that right answer may not be the one that occurs to you first. This can lead to second-guessing your work, when you should be looking for the answer you solved for. In this situation, a common mistake is to pick an answer that seems sort of like the answer you're looking for, even when you know it's wrong—it looks "close enough." Don't fall for it—if you know something is wrong, don't select it, and if you don't find your answer, don't assume you're wrong. Try to think of another right way to answer the question.

7. GUESS INTELLIGENTLY

An unanswered question is always wrong, but even a wild guess may be right. The odds are clear: if you have *no idea* and guess, you have a 20 to 25 percent chance (depending on the subject test) of getting the point. If you know at least one wrong answer, your odds go to 25 to 33 percent, and up from there. Your odds if you don't guess? Always 0 percent. *Always* guess on every ACT question you can't answer. Never leave a question blank.

You'll be doing two different kinds of guessing during your two sweeps through any subject test:

1. Blind guessing (which you do mostly on questions you deem too hard or time-consuming to spend time on at all)

2. Strategic guessing (which you do mostly on questions that you do some work on but don't get all the way through)

When you guess blindly, just choose any letter you feel like choosing. Don't fall for any rumors that there is a letter choice that appears most frequently. There's no validity to that—the answers are truly random. So just pick any letter.

When you guess in a strategic way, on the other hand, you've usually done enough work on a question to eliminate at least one or two choices. If you can eliminate any choices, you'll up the odds of guessing correctly.

Here are some fun facts about guessing: If you were to work on only half of the questions on the ACT but get them all right, then guess blindly on the other half of the questions, your composite ACT score would be around 23 (assuming you had a statistically reasonable success rate on your guesses). A 23 would put you in roughly the top quarter of all those who take the ACT. And all you had to do was answer half of the questions correctly.

On the other hand, if you were to hurry and work on all the questions but get only half of them right, you'd earn around a 19, which is below the 50th percentile.

How? Why are you better off answering half and getting them all right than answering all and getting only half right?

Here's the trick: The student who works carefully and answers half of the questions right and skips the others can still take guesses on the unanswered questions—and odds are this student will have enough correct guesses to move up four points, from a 19 to a 23. But the student who works too quickly, answers all the questions, and gets half wrong doesn't have the luxury of taking guesses.

In short, **guess if you can't figure out an answer for any question!**

8. BE CAREFUL WITH THE ANSWER GRID

Your ACT score is based on the answers you select on your answer grid. Even if you work out every question correctly, you won't get the score you earned if you misgrid your answers. So be careful! Don't disdain the process of filling in those little "bubbles" on the grid. Sure, it's mindless, but under time pressure, it's easy to lose control and make mistakes.

It's important to **develop a disciplined strategy for filling in the answer grid.** Many students gain speed by gridding in the answers in groups rather than one question at a time. Give it a try on one of your Kaplan practice tests, if you haven't before. What you should do is this: As you figure out each question in the test booklet, circle your answer. Then, transfer those answers to the answer grid in groups of five or more (until you get close to the end of the section, when you should start gridding answers one by one—you don't want to be caught with ungridded answers when time is called).

Gridding in groups like this cuts down on errors because you can focus on this one task and do it right. It can also save time you'd otherwise spend moving papers around, finding your place, and redirecting your mind. Answering ACT questions takes deep, hard thinking. Filling out answer grids is easy, but you have to be careful, especially if you do a lot of skipping around. Shifting between hard thinking and careful bookkeeping takes time and effort.

During the test, the proctor should warn you when you have about five minutes left on each subject test. But don't depend on proctors! **Rely on your own watch.** When there are five minutes left on a subject test, start gridding your answers one by one. With a minute or two left, start filling in everything you've left blank. Remember: Even one question left blank could cut your score.

9. USE THE LETTERS OF THE CHOICES TO STAY ON TRACK

One oddity about the ACT is that even-numbered questions have F, G, H, J (and, in Math, K) as choices, rather than A, B, C, D (and, again, E in Math). This might be confusing at first, but you can make it work for you. **A common mistake with the answer grid is to accidentally enter an answer one row up or down. On the ACT, that won't happen if you pay attention to the letter in the answer.** If you're looking for an A and you see only F, G, H, J, and K, you'll know you're in the wrong row on the answer grid.

Another advantage of having answers F through K for even-numbered questions is that it makes you less nervous about patterns in the answers. It's common to start worrying if you've picked the same letter a few times in a row. Since the questions have different letters, this can't happen on the ACT. Of course, you could pick the first choice (A or F) for several questions in a row, but this shouldn't worry you. It's common for the answers in the same position to be correct three times in a row, and even four times in a row isn't unheard of. It's all a matter of random order, and sometimes that will look like an intentional pattern. It isn't.

10. KEEP TRACK OF TIME

During each subject test, you have to pace yourself. Trying to answer as many questions as possible until time is called isn't a strategy. On average, English, Reading, and Science questions should take about 30 seconds each, and Math questions should average less than one minute each (full details are available in each individual content area of this book). Remember to take into account the fact that you'll probably be taking two passes through the questions.

A great way to keep track is to set your watch to 12:00 at the beginning of each subject test so it will be easy to check your time. Again, don't rely on proctors, even if they promise that they will dutifully call out the time every 15 minutes. Take control of your own timing.

More basic questions should take less time, and harder ones will probably take more. In Math, for instance, you need to go much faster than one per minute during your first sweep. But at the end, you may spend two or three minutes on each of the harder problems you work out.

TAKE CONTROL

You are the master of the test-taking experience. A common thread in all ten strategies is that you should take control. That's Kaplan's ACT Mind-Set. Do the questions in the order you want and in the way you want. Don't get bogged down or agonize. Remember, you don't earn points for suffering, but you do earn points for moving on to the next question and getting it right.

THE ACT IS NOT SCHOOL

You have spent at least 11 years in school at this point. There, you learned some techniques that will not help you on the ACT. (Want two good examples? "Don't guess on a test" and "If you show your work on math problems, you'll get partial credit.") Many of these school-driven methods will actually work *against* you on the ACT.

Test Day is an exciting and stressful event. Don't approach it with a familiar school mind-set. Instead, practice using the ten strategies in this chapter so that you're rehearsed and confident for Test Day.

Just reading and understanding these strategies once before the test doesn't mean you'll do them effectively on Test Day. The ACT Mind-Set will work only if you use it, so practice!

As you practice, time yourself. Buy or borrow a digital watch, and get used to working

> **⌃ GO ONLINE**
>
> Before going on to the subject-specific workouts, take the online Diagnostic Quiz if you haven't already. You'll learn where to focus your study time.

with it so it doesn't beep at the wrong moment. Your cell phone will be turned off during the test, so you won't be able to use it as a timekeeper.

Practice the various sections of the test at home and take practice tests in single sittings to make sure you're comfortable and ready to get your highest score on Test Day.

BASIC STRATEGY REFERENCE SHEET

THE FOUR KEYS TO ACT SUCCESS

1. LEARN THE TEST

- Learn the directions before Test Day.
- Become familiar with all the subject tests.
- Get a sense of the range of difficulty of the questions.

2. LEARN THE KAPLAN METHODS AND STRATEGIES

- Develop a plan of attack for each subject test.
- Develop a guessing strategy that works for you.
- Find "unofficial" ways of finding answers fast.

3. LEARN THE MATERIAL TESTED

- Bone up on weak areas.
- Find out what is and isn't part of the ACT knowledge base.
- Use the ACT study resources section to review important Math and English concepts.

4. PRACTICE, PRACTICE, PRACTICE

THE TOP TEN STRATEGIES

1. Do question triage.

2. Put the material into a form you can understand and use.

3. Ignore irrelevant issues.

4. Check back.

5. Answer the right question.

6. Look for the hidden answer.

7. Guess intelligently.

8. Be careful with the answer grid.

9. Use the letters of the choices to stay on track.

10. Keep track of time.

PART TWO

The ACT Tests

UNIT 1: ENGLISH

The Basics:

45 Minutes

75 Questions

5 Passages

Pacing:

Pace your time by the passage as opposed to minutes per question.

Spend nine minutes per passage, including questions.

TEST DAY DIRECTIONS AND FORMAT

The directions on the English test illustrate why there's an advantage to knowing them beforehand—they're long, complicated, and if you learn them now, you'll already be racking up points while everyone else is reading the directions on Test Day. The directions on Test Day will look like this:

Directions: In the five passages that follow, certain words and phrases are underlined and numbered. In the right-hand column, you will find alternatives for the underlined parts. In most cases, you are to choose the one that best expresses the idea, makes the statement appropriate for standard written English, or is worded most consistently with the style and tone of the passage as a whole. If you think the original version is best, choose NO CHANGE. In some cases, you will find in the right-hand column a question about the underlined part. You are to choose the best answer to the question.

You will also find questions about a section of the passage or about the passage as a whole. These questions do not refer to an underlined portion of the passage, but rather are identified by a number or numbers in a box.

For each question, choose the alternative you consider best and fill in the corresponding oval on your answer grid. Read each passage through once before you answer the questions that accompany it. For many questions, you must read several sentences beyond the underlined portion to determine the answer. Be sure that you have read enough ahead each time you answer a question.

OUTSIDE KNOWLEDGE

There is some knowledge of grammar rules required. You will learn about all the grammar and punctuation questions the ACT has for you during this test's strategy review. You can find an all-in-one reference in the Grammar and Punctuation Rules to Know section on page 56.

THE INSIDE SCOOP

The ACT is designed to test your understanding of the conventions of written English—punctuation, grammar, sentence structure—and of general rhetorical skills. (Rhetorical skills are more strategic concepts like organizing the text and making sure it's consistently styled and concise.)

The questions *do not* get harder as you proceed through the test.

SMARTPOINTS

Point Value	Topic	Basics Page	Details and Practice
7	**Connections**		
6	**Verb Tenses**		
5	**Punctuation**		
5	**Word Choice**		
5	**Wordiness**		
4	**Writing Strategy**		
3	**Sentence Sense**		
1	**Organization**		

CHAPTER 4

English Part 1: Inside the ACT English Test

As we introduced earlier, Kaplan has a dedicated method for every area of the ACT. Follow these steps to save yourself time, attack the questions strategically, and get your highest score!

THE KAPLAN METHOD FOR ACT ENGLISH

STEP 1: READ UNTIL YOU HAVE ENOUGH INFORMATION TO IDENTIFY THE ISSUE

The instructions on the ACT will tell you to read the whole passage and then answer the questions about it, but remember: You get points for answering questions, not for reading passages. So to balance your time in favor of the questions, read the passage just as far as necessary to answer each question, and then answer them in turn. That being said, don't skip over sentences without questions in them—you'll need to understand the whole passage when you answer summary questions at the end. But for some questions, you'll only need to read a sentence to find the issue being tested. (Keep in mind, issues are not necessarily errors, because some sentences have no errors, and some English questions test your understanding of the passage as a whole.)

STEP 2: ELIMINATE CHOICES THAT DO NOT ADDRESS THE ISSUE

Now that you've identified the issue that the question is testing, read through the answers to see which ones do not address the issue, and cross them out in your book (really do cross them out—this will help you keep track of which answers *can't* be right and will help you guess strategically if needed). Once you've eliminated any choices that don't fix the issue, if you aren't ready to answer, move on to Step 3.

STEP 3: PLUG IN THE REMAINING CHOICES TO SELECT THE MOST CORRECT, CONCISE, AND RELEVANT CHOICE

Finally, try out the remaining choices by plugging them into the sentence or paragraph and seeing how they work. This may mean reading the questions without the underlined phrase to see if OMIT is the best choice. Remember: the best choice will always be *correct* (grammatically), *concise* (short and sweet), and *relevant* (makes sense with the rest of the passage). Make these three words the cornerstone of your decision-making in the English section. When in doubt, just remember *correct, concise, and relevant*.

QUICK TIPS

MIND-SET

- **When in doubt, take it out.** Make sure that everything is written as concisely as possible. If you think something doesn't belong in a sentence, it probably doesn't, so choose an answer that leaves it out. Between two grammatically correct and relevant choices, the shorter one will always be right. Not just better—*right*.

- **Make sure it makes sense.** When switching phrases in and out, it's easy to find grammar but lose logic. Consider sentence formation, making sure that you use complete sentences and not fragments, and that ideas relate logically. For an answer to be correct in ACT English, it must create a sentence that is logically *and* grammatically correct.

- **Trust your eyes and ears.** Mistakes in grammar often look or sound wrong —trust that instinct. Don't choose the answer that "sounds fancy," choose the one that sounds *right*. Review the Grammar and Punctuation Rules to Know on page 56.

SPECIAL STRATEGIES

A few questions will require you to rearrange the words in a sentence, the sentences in a paragraph, or even the paragraphs in a passage. Others may ask questions about the meaning of all or part of the passage, or about its structure. Your approach to these questions should be:

1. **Determine your task.** What are you being asked to do?

2. **Consider the passage as a whole.** Read the sentences around the numbered question to get the big picture—you need to know the points made there. Most passages will have a well-defined theme, laid out in a logical way, so choose the answer that expresses the arrangement of elements that best continues the "flow" of the passage.

3. **Predict your answer.** As you'll see again in the Reading section, making a prediction should give you an idea of what the answer is before looking at the choices.

  Visit your online syllabus—Lesson 5—for more instruction and practice with the Kaplan Method for ACT English.

TIMING: PACING AND APPROACH

Set your watch to 12:00 at the beginning of the subject test. Here's roughly where you should be at the following checkpoints.

12:09 . . . . . One passage finished and answers gridded in

12:18 . . . . . Two passages finished and answers gridded in

12:27 . . . . . Three passages finished and answers gridded in

12:36 . . . . . Four passages finished and answers gridded in

12:45 . . . . . Five passages finished and answers for the entire section gridded in

Note that you should have at least looked at all 75 English questions and made sure you have at least a guess gridded in for every question when time is called.

Organized Approach: Because of the passage-based format, we recommend that you *not* skip around in the English subject test. Move straight from beginning to end, answering all of the questions as you go. Unlike some sections, in English you'll usually have at least a sense of what the right answer should be rather quickly. But remember, even the correct answer will start to sound wrong if you think about it too much!

WHEN YOU'RE RUNNING OUT OF TIME

If you have no time left to even read the last few questions, choose the shortest answer for each one. Remember that OMIT, when it appears, counts as the shortest answer. For questions not based on clarity, pick a letter of the day and just use that. No choice is more likely than any other, so pick one letter and use it for all questions you can't work on.

SCORING

Your performance on the English subject test will be averaged into your ACT Composite Score, weighted equally with your scores on the other three subject tests. You will also receive the following:

- English subject score (1 to 36) for the entire English subject test

- Usage/Mechanics subscore (1 to 18) for questions testing grammar, usage, punctuation, and sentence structure

- Rhetorical Skills subscore (1 to 18) for questions testing strategy, organization, and style

- Writing subscore (2 to 12) for the optional Writing test

- Combined English-Writing score (1 to 36) if you take the optional Writing test

SMARTPOINT BREAKDOWN

Here is a brief overview of what exactly to expect and how much of it you should be expecting.

CONNECTIONS—7 POINTS

Extremely Important

Connection questions test your ability to understand the relationship between ideas. You will have to decide whether the underlined connections words and phrases establish the proper transition. The two most common types of connections tested on the ACT are *cause and effect* (does one idea cause the next?) and *contrast* (are these ideas the same or different?). Other connections tested are *sequence* (did these ideas happen in an order?) and *emphasis* (does one idea exist to emphasize the other?). To find the best connection word or phrase for a question, you must read the non-underlined part of the passage carefully. Sometimes you only need to read the sentence that contains the underlined portion, but other times you need to go back and carefully read the sentence before it as well. Turn to page 96 for more information and practice with this question type, as well as a table of common connection words and phrases.

VERB TENSES—6 POINTS

Very Important

Verb Tense questions test appropriate tense usage in context. Consistency of usage is a priority, and the most commonly tested issue. Unless context makes it clear that more than one time frame is being discussed, verb tense usage should remain consistent in the sentence and with other verbs used in the passage. Turn to page 78 for more information and practice with this question type, as well as a table of commonly tested irregular verbs.

PUNCTUATION—5 POINTS

Important

Punctuation questions test usage of a limited number of punctuation rules. The list is very specific and predictable, so even if you don't think of punctuation as your strongest suit, you can still know which rules will be tested so you can get them right on Test Day! The tested forms of punctuation are: commas, dashes, colons, semicolons, periods, question marks, exclamation points, and apostrophes. Turn to page 74 for a breakdown of each form of punctuation and how it's tested, and refer to the Grammar and Punctuation Rules to Know on page 56 for all tested grammar rules.

WORD CHOICE—5 POINTS

Important

Word Choice questions are the broadest question type on the ACT English test, and they deal primarily with subject-verb agreement and pronoun agreement. They also relate to modifiers and idioms. Each is discussed in more detail on page 81.

WORDINESS—5 POINTS

Important

Wordiness questions test redundancy (saying the same thing twice) and verbosity (using more words than necessary). As you've seen, concise writing is highly valued on the ACT, making it part of the big three in the English Method. Sometimes, an answer on the ACT will be right simply because it's shorter without losing any information. OMIT (removing the underlined portion entirely) is always the shortest answer, and it is often the correct option, as long as it doesn't delete something the sentence needs. Turn to page 93 for a more thorough discussion of wordiness.

WRITING STRATEGY—4 POINTS

Somewhat Important

Writing Strategy questions ask about larger chunks of text, and they always appear with a question stem. These are some of the higher-difficulty questions on the English test and require you to understand the context of the passage. Specifically, these questions deal with tone, consistency, adding or deleting information, and purpose. Follow the Special Strategies listed under Quick Tips. Refer to page 98 for a more thorough discussion of these strategies and Writing Strategy questions in general.

SENTENCE SENSE—3 POINTS

Somewhat Important

Sentence Sense questions test your ability to form proper clauses while fixing run-ons and fragments. Though this skill is not frequently tested directly, understanding independent clauses and dependent clauses is essential to many of the other SmartPoints that test knowledge of grammar, such as Verb Tenses, Punctuation, and Word Choice. Refer to page 70 for a detailed discussion, including everything you need to know for those more frequent question types. As usual, for all things grammar, refer to Grammar and Punctuation Rules to Know on page 56.

ORGANIZATION—1 POINT

Less Important

Organization questions test your understanding of logical sequence. These questions ask you to organize sentences within a paragraph or to organize paragraphs within the passage as a whole. Refer to page 100 for a thorough discussion.

GRAMMAR AND PUNCTUATION RULES TO KNOW

Here they are! Every rule commonly tested on the ACT follows. Go over these now, and refer back to them as often as needed. This is the outside knowledge you're expected to bring with you to Test Day. Get comfortable with each rule.

RULE 1: NUMBER AGREEMENT

The most tested agreement rule on the ACT is this: Singular nouns must match with singular verbs and pronouns, and plural nouns must match with plural verbs and pronouns. A common error in this area involves the use of the word *they*. It's plural, but in everyday speech, we often use it as singular.

WRONG:	"If a student won't study, they won't do well."
PROBLEM:	A *student* (singular) and *they* (plural) don't agree in number.
CORRECTION:	"If students won't study, they won't do well," or "If a student won't study, he or she won't do well."

RULE 2: PRONOUNS IN COMPOUNDS

Another common agreement or matching error concerns compounds, which are phrases that join two words with *and* or *or*.

WRONG:	"The fool gave the wrong tickets to Bob and I."
PROBLEM:	*I* can't be the object of the preposition *to*.
CORRECTION:	"The fool gave the wrong tickets to Bob and me."

Hint: Try dropping the rest of the compound (*Bob and*). "The fool gave the wrong tickets to I" should sound funny to you, which is your first hint it's a problem.

RULE 3: COMMAS OR DASHES AROUND PARENTHETICAL PHRASES

Parenthetical phrases must begin and end with the same punctuation mark. Such phrases can be recognized because, while they add information to a sentence, without them the sentence would still be complete. For instance: "Bob, on his way to the store, saw a large lizard in the street." If you dropped the phrase "on his way to the store," the sentence would still be complete. Thus, this phrase is parenthetical. It could be marked off with commas, parentheses, or dashes, but the same mark is needed at both ends of the phrase.

WRONG:	"Bob—on his way to the store, saw a lizard."
PROBLEM:	The parenthetical phrase starts with a dash but finishes with a comma.
CORRECTION:	"Bob, on his way to the store, saw a lizard."

RULE 4: RUN-ONS AND COMMA SPLICES

You can't combine two complete sentences into one with a comma (though you can with a semicolon or a comma plus a conjunction).

WRONG:	"Ed's a slacker, Sara isn't."
PROBLEM:	Two complete sentences are spliced together with a comma.
CORRECTION:	"Ed's a slacker, but Sara isn't," or "Ed's a slacker; Sara isn't," or "Ed, unlike Sara, is a slacker."

RULE 5: FRAGMENTS

This rule goes hand-in-hand with the previous one. **A sentence must contain at least one complete idea.** A fragment is writing that could be a subordinate part of a sentence but not a whole sentence itself.

WRONG:	"Emily listened to music. While she studied."
PROBLEM:	"She studied" would be a sentence, but *while* makes this a fragment.
CORRECTION:	"Emily listened to music while she studied."

RULE 6: *-ly* ENDINGS (ADVERBS AND ADJECTIVES)

The ACT expects you to understand the difference between adverbs (which often end in *-ly*) and adjectives. The two are similar because they're both modifiers—they modify, refer to, or describe another word or phrase in the sentence. Nouns and pronouns must be modified by adjectives, while verbs, adjectives, and adverbs themselves must be modified by adverbs.

WRONG:	"Anna is an extreme gifted child, and she speaks beautiful too."
PROBLEM:	*Extreme* and *beautiful* are adjectives, but they're supposed to modify an adjective (*gifted*) and a verb (*speaks*) here, so they should be adverbs.
CORRECTION:	"Anna is an extremely gifted child, and she speaks beautifully too."

RULE 7: *-er* AND *-est*, *More* AND *Most* (COMPARATIVES AND SUPERLATIVES)

Whenever you see the endings *-er* or *-est* or the words *more* or *most*, double-check to make sure they're used correctly. Words with *-er* or *more* are only used to compare exactly two things. If there are more than two things involved, use *-est* or *most*.

WRONG:	"Bob is the fastest of the two runners."
PROBLEM:	The comparison is between just two things, so *-est* is inappropriate.
CORRECTION:	"Bob is the faster of the two runners."

RULE 8: COMMONLY INVERTED WORDS

There are several word pairs that we commonly switch around in spoken English, even when it breaks grammatical rules. On the ACT, some of these will be tested, so you will want to know how to use them correctly. Note: Don't get bogged down with these; they will rarely be tested on more than one question total.

GOOD OR *WELL*

Good is an adjective (modifies a noun or pronoun); *well* is an adverb (modifies verbs, adjectives, adverbs).

WRONG:	"Joe did good on the ACT."
PROBLEM:	*Good* is an adjective, but here it's modifying a verb (*did*), so use an adverb.
CORRECTION:	"Joe did well on the ACT."

One exception: *well* can also be an adjective when it means "healthy." So "Joe was well again by the morning of the ACT" is correct.

LIE OR *LAY*

In short, *lie* is something a subject <u>does</u> ("I'm going to lie down for a while"), whereas *lay* is something a subject <u>does to an object</u> ("I'm going to lay the book down for a while.") A reliable way to test this is to replace the word with "put"—if you can ("I'm going to put the book down"), you can use *lay*. If you can't ("I'm going to put down for a while"), you need *lie*.

WHO OR *WHOM*

Your rule to never miss this question again: *who* goes where *he* goes; *whom* goes where *him* goes! If the answer to the question being asked is *he*, the form should be *who*. If the answer is *him*, the form should be *whom*.

WRONG:	"Always remember who you're speaking to."
PROBLEM:	*Who* is wrong. Ask: Speaking to who? Speaking to him, not to he. So it should be *whom*.
CORRECTION:	"Always remember whom you're speaking to."

Some students try to avoid the *who*/*whom* problem by using the word *which* instead. Don't. It's not nice to call people "whiches." Never use the word *which* (or *that*) for a person.

LESS OR *FEWER*

The word *less* is used only for uncountable things. When things can be counted, they are *fewer*.

WRONG:	"I have fewer water than I thought, so I can fill less buckets."
PROBLEM:	You can count buckets; you can't count water.
CORRECTION:	"I have less water than I thought, so I can fill fewer buckets."

BETWEEN OR *AMONG*

The word *between* is used only when there are exactly two things involved. When there are more than two things, or an unknown number of things, use *among*.

WRONG:	"I will walk among the two halves of the class, between the many students in class."
PROBLEM:	Use *between* for two things and *among* for more than two.
CORRECTION:	"I will walk between the two halves of the class, among the many students in class."

RULE 9: *Be* AND *Was* (FORMS OF THE VERB *To Be*)

The ACT tests the use of proper verb forms, especially of the verb *to be*. You must use the following forms. Memorize them if you have to:

Present Tense:	I *am*, we *are*, you *are*, they *are*, he/she/it *is*
Past Tense:	I *was*, we *were*, you *were*, they *were*, he/she/it *was*
Future Tense:	I/we/you/they/he/she/it *will be*
Perfect Tense:	I/we/you *have been*, he/she/it *has been*
Past Perfect:	I/we/you/he/she/it *had been*
Future Perfect:	I/we/you/he/she/it *will have been*

You can decide which form (*am, are, is, were, was, will be, have been, had been, will have been*) is correct by determining what the subject is and what the verb tense is. In many dialects, the words *be* and *was* are used instead of the special forms given. For example, many speakers might say, "They *be* going home" or "They *was* going home." On the ACT, the correct form is "They *are* (or *were*) going home."

RULE 10: PUNCTUATION

The ACT doesn't test uncommon rules of punctuation. However, it does expect you to know what punctuation marks mean and how they are commonly used. Here are some common punctuation marks and their uses:

Use a **comma** (,) or **commas** to do the following:

- Set off items in a list of three or more items

- Combine two independent clauses with a FANBOYS conjunction (For, And, Nor, But, Or, Yet, So)

- Set off an introductory phrase from the rest of the sentence

- Separate nonessential information (something that could be considered a parenthetical phrase) from the rest of the sentence

- **Note:** You may have learned different or even conflicting rules about whether to put a comma before the *and* in a list (known as the serial or Oxford comma), as in this example:

    "At the store, we need bread, juice**, and** eggs."

As opposed to:

    "At the store, we need bread, juice **and** eggs."

Different schools and publications have different rules, but the ACT *does* use the serial/Oxford comma, so you should always be on the lookout for lists!

Use a **semicolon** (;) to do the following:

- Combine two independent clauses when a FANBOYS word is not present.
  "Emily studied for hours; she had a big test the next day."

- Separate items in a series or list if those items already include commas.
  "At the grocery store, George needed milk, eggs, and butter; Alice needed cereal, bread, and juice; and Dan needed apples, water, and ice cream."

Use a **colon** (:) to introduce or emphasize a short phrase, quotation, example, explanation, or list.

    "Peter needed to study three topics before Test Day: punctuation, transitions, and sentence structure."

    "One wild animal causes suburban pet owners more stress than any other: the skunk."

Use a **dash** (—) or **dashes** to set off an explanatory or parenthetical phrase in a sentence.

Use an **apostrophe** (') to do the following:

- Indicate the possessive form of a noun (*not* a pronoun).

- Stand in for a missing letter or letters in a contraction.

SPECIAL RECOGNITION: *Its, It's, or Its'*

Because apostrophes are *not* used to create the possessive form of pronouns (you wouldn't say "it's his' book" or "it's her's car"), the word *its* follows very specific rules:

- *It's* means "It is" or "It has." That's it. There are no other uses for *it's*.

  "It's going to be a little bit before the movie starts."

  "It's been a while since last time we went to the movies."

- *Its* is the possessive form of *it*.

  "The car was safe in its spot when I came outside."

- *Its'* is not a word. Don't use it. Ever. You always mean one of the other forms.

WARM-UP

Now you know what to expect on the English test! You've seen all the pieces of outside knowledge required. You know the Kaplan Method and Strategies. You even know what types of questions you'll see and approximately how many of each. Now you're ready to start making passages correct, concise, and relevant.

Time to put your skills to the test! But take a deep breath. This one is a warm-up. Complete the following passage, and use it to help you determine how to best use the next chapter on English.

The Answers and Explanations follow the passage and reveal which SmartPoint category each question represents. Use your results from this passage and the SmartPoints to prioritize your approach to the next chapter.

Good luck!

FANTASY LITERATURE: IT'S MORE THAN HARRY POTTER

[1]

J. K. Rowling, author of the immensely popular Harry Potter series, has wrought her own special magic in the fantasy genre. Though she may be the best-known fantasy writer to the current <u>generation, she</u> is hardly
₁
the first. A number of others,

<u>many of which</u>, like Rowling, are British, were writing
₂
fantasy novels before J. K. Rowling was born.

[2]

One such writer is George MacDonald, a Scottish minister, best known for his novels *Phantastes* and *Lilith*. MacDonald's work, <u>similar to Rowlings'</u>, showed
₃
that fantasy literature could hold appeal for older children and even adults. In *Phantastes*, a young man named Anodos journeys through a fantasy land where he experiences magical adventures. <u>While</u> *Phantastes*
₄
is a relatively light story, *Lilith*, a much later work by MacDonald, is a

<u>more darker and more provocative</u> tale. In this
₅

<u>novel a character, called</u> Mr. Vane travels through a
₆
fantasy land. There he encounters Lilith, an attractive but troubling fairy princess. In describing Mr. Vane's experiences, MacDonald explores the questions of

1. A. NO CHANGE
   B. generation: she
   C. generation; she
   D. generation. She

2. F. NO CHANGE
   G. of which many
   H. many of whom
   J. many being those

3. A. NO CHANGE
   B. like Rowling's
   C. as with Rowlings'
   D. like with Rowling's

4. F. NO CHANGE
   G. Because
   H. Despite that
   J. Given that

5. A. NO CHANGE
   B. most provocatively dark
   C. darker and most provocative
   D. darker and more provocative

6. F. NO CHANGE
   G. novel, a character called
   H. novel a character called
   J. novel, a character called,

<u>how meaning is found in the condition of being human</u>
                                                    7
and how redemption might be possible.

[3]

       <u>Another British fantasy writer,</u> C. S. Lewis, ac-
                                    8
knowledged

<u>the fact that he felt indebted</u> to George MacDonald. It
                              9
was MacDonald's mythmaking, rather than his writing

style, that Lewis admired. Lewis's *Chronicles of Narnia*,

a tale with mythic power, is a group of seven books tied

together <u>more than</u> the fictional world they describe
          10
than by the narration of a particular character's experi-

ences. Narnia is a magical place where animals can talk

and

<u>time seemed to progress</u> at its own rate. Like Harry Pot-
          11
ter and his mates at Hogwarts, the characters

<u>whom inhabit</u> Narnia struggle with the conflicting
      12
forces of good and evil.

[4]

Yet another fantasy series, occupying fewer printed

7. A. NO CHANGE
    B. human nature and what that means
    C. what it means to be human
    D. how being human has meaning

8. The writer is considering deleting the under-
    lined portion. If this deletion were made, the
    paragraph would primarily lose:

    F. a description of C. S. Lewis's work.
    G. a fact about C. S. Lewis's ethnic origin.
    H. a phrase that relates C. S. Lewis to the
        other novelists discussed.
    J. a description showing contrast between
        C. S. Lewis and George MacDonald.

9. A. NO CHANGE
    B. his feelings of owing a debt
    C. his feeling of indebtedness
    D. that indeed he felt indebted

10. F. NO CHANGE
    G. rather more than
    H. more by
    J. more with

11. A. NO CHANGE
    B. time progresses
    C. time would be progressing
    D. the progress of time is

12. F. NO CHANGE
    G. which inhabits
    H. who inhabits
    J. who inhabit

pages <u>but</u> treating its material in the same broad scope
13
that Rowling does, is J. R. R. Tolkien's *Lord of the Rings*.

Here, the tension

<u>between good and evil are</u> played out in epic scale; the
14
series describes a fellowship of seven characters who

journey together in a quest to dispose properly of the

ring in the title. As Lewis does with Narnia, Tolkien

<u>was inventing</u> a universe, which he calls Middle Earth,
15
and peoples it with a range of characters from mortal

humans to

<u>immortal elves</u> and horrifying creatures called "orcs"
16
and "uruk-hai."

13. A. NO CHANGE
    B. and
    C. however
    D. thus

14. F. NO CHANGE
    G. among good and evil is
    H. between good and evil is
    J. between good or evil are

15. A. NO CHANGE
    B. inventing
    C. invents
    D. invented

16. F. NO CHANGE
    G. elves who are immortal
    H. more immortal elves
    J. elves being immortal

Question 17 asks about the preceding passage
as a whole.

17. Suppose that the writer had been assigned to
    write a brief essay describing the influence
    of earlier fantasy novelists on J. K. Rowling.
    Would this essay successfully fulfill that goal?

    A. Yes, because three fantasy authors are
       discussed along with J. K. Rowling.

    B. Yes, because the issue of an author's
       indebtedness is discussed.

    C. No, because J. K. Rowling is the most
       recent of the writers discussed, and she
       is the only woman.

    D. No, because the essay mentions other
       fantasy novelists but does not discuss
       particular ways that J. K. Rowling was
       influenced by them.

ANSWERS AND EXPLANATIONS

1. A
2. H
3. B
4. F
5. D
6. G
7. C
8. H
9. C

10. H
11. B
12. J
13. A
14. H
15. C
16. F
17. D

1. **The best answer is (A).** The issue is punctuation. Choice (A) correctly uses a comma to set off introductory information from the main part of the sentence. If you don't spot this right away, plug the other choices into the sentence. Choice (B) incorrectly uses a colon to introduce something that is not a list, example, or explanation. Eliminate (C) because it incorrectly uses a semicolon after a dependent clause. Eliminate (D) because it puts a period after a dependent clause. This is incorrect because a dependent clause cannot stand alone as a sentence. Choice (A) is correct.

2. **The best answer is (H).** The issue is pronouns. Whenever you see a pronoun underlined, check to see that it's used correctly. In (F), the pronoun *which* is used incorrectly to refer to people. Recognizing this, you can eliminate (F) and (G). Plug in the other choices to determine the best one. Choice (J) is awkward and certainly wordy compared to (H). Choice (H) is the best answer.

3. **The best answer is (B).** The issue is punctuation, specifically the apostrophe. Eliminate choice (A) because *Rowling,* a singular noun, does not form the possessive by adding *s'*. Knowing this, you can also eliminate (C). Plugging the remaining choices into the sentence, you should be able to tell that (D) is wordy, leaving (B) as the best choice.

4. **The best answer is (F).** The issue is connections. When the underlined portion includes a connections word like *which,* determine the logical relationships that the sentence is expressing. The sentence here conveys the contrast between a *light story* and a *darker and more provocative tale.* Choice (F) is appropriate because *while* expresses this contrast. Eliminate (G) and (J) because they are both cause-and-effect connections. Choice (H) is a contrast connection, but it is not suitable in this particular context. Choice (F) is the best answer.

5. **The best answer is (D).** The issue is word choice. When you see a comparative adjective (one that ends in *-er*) underlined, check to make sure it's used correctly. Here, using the comparative *darker* instead of the superlative *darkest* is correct, because two things are being compared. However, a comparative adjective should never be preceded by the

word *more*. Eliminate (A). This line of thinking should also help you eliminate (B) and (D), which incorrectly use the superlative *most*. Choice (D) is the best answer.

6. **The best answer is (G).** The issue is punctuation. In (F), you should notice that the sentence contains the introductory phrase *in this novel,* which should be set off by a comma. Knowing this, you can eliminate (F) and (H). Plug (G) and (J) into the sentence. Choice (J) is incorrect because it uses a comma after *called,* incorrectly separating a verb from its object. The correct answer is (G).

7. **The best answer is (C).** The issue is wordiness. Choice (A) is wordy. If you don't recognize this immediately, plug in the other choices. Choice (B) is awkward and also a bit wordy. Choice (C) is concise and is the best answer. Choice (D) is wordy and awkward.

8. **The best answer is (H).** The issue is writing strategy. When a question stem asks about what would be lost by deleting a portion, read that portion carefully and consider how it functions in its context. Also, note that the question stem includes the word *primarily.* This means you should determine the most important aspect of the underlined portion. Here, you can eliminate (F) immediately, because the underlined portion says nothing about Lewis's work. Choice (G) is tempting, because the phrase does indicate Lewis's ethnic origin. Choice (H), however, is even better than (G). The phrase in question opens the paragraph, and the word *another* shows continuity between Lewis and the writers discussed in earlier paragraphs. Eliminate (J) because the phrase does not indicate any contrast. Choice (H) is the best answer.

9. **The best answer is (C).** The issue is wordiness. As with many wordiness problems, you may not immediately identify the issue simply by reading (A). Still, read the other choices in the sentence. Choice (C) is slightly shorter and more direct than the others are, so it is the best choice.

10. **The best answer is (H).** The issue is idioms. Choice (F) uses an incorrect idiomatic expression, *tied together…**than.*** Recognizing this, you can eliminate (F) and (G). The correct idiom here is *tied together **by.*** If you know this, you can recognize choice (H) is the best answer. If not, read (H) and (J) in the sentence. Chances are your ear will hear the idiom error in (J). The best answer is (H).

11. **The best answer is (B).** The issue here is sentence sense, particularly as it relates to verb tenses. Whenever you notice an underlined verb, one of the things to check for is whether its tense is consistent with the other tenses in the surrounding context. In (A), the past tense verb *seemed* is inconsistent with the present tense verbs *is* and *describe* used elsewhere in the sentence. Knowing this, you can spot the inconsistency in (C), as well, which uses *would be.* Having eliminated (A) and (C), you should plug the other two into the sentence. Choices (B) and (D) both correctly use the present tense, but (B) is the better choice because (D) is wordy.

12. **The best answer is (J).** The issue is pronouns. When you notice an underlined pronoun, one of the things to check for is that it is the correct form for how it functions in the sentence. Here, *whom* is used incorrectly as the subject of the verb *inhabit*. The pronoun

form *who* is required here. You can eliminate (G) because the pronoun *which* is used only to refer to things, never to people. Read the remaining choices in the sentence to decide which is better. The pronoun *who* can refer to nouns that are either singular or plural. In this case, *who* refers to *characters,* which is plural. The correct verb form, therefore, is *characters who **inhabit.*** Choice (J) is the best answer.

13. **The best answer is (A).** The issue is connections. Whenever you notice a connections word underlined (here, *but*), consider carefully the relationship between the ideas around it. This sentence sets up a contrast: Tolkien's series is shorter, in terms of page count. Still, it treats its material in a broad scope. The word *but* nicely expresses this contrast. Consider the other choices. Choice (B), *and*, is a simple joining word; it doesn't express contrast, so eliminate it. Choice (C) correctly expresses contrast, but it doesn't work in the structure of this particular sentence. Eliminate (D) because *thus* is a cause-and-effect, rather than a contrast, connections word. The best answer is (A).

14. **The best answer is (H).** The issues are word choice and verb usage. When you notice that the word *between* is underlined, pause to ask yourself how many things are being talked about. Here, two things, *good and evil*, are being discussed, so *between* is correct. Notice, also, though, that the underlined portion includes the verb *are*. One thing to check for when you see an underlined verb is subject-verb agreement. Ask yourself what the subject of *are* is. It is *tension,* so the correct verb form here is *is*. Knowing that *between* is correct here and that the correct verb is *is,* you can eliminate (F), (G), and (J).

15. **The best answer is (C).** The issue is sentence sense, especially as it relates to verb tense. When you see an underlined verb, remember to check that its tense is consistent with the tense used in the surrounding context. In the nonunderlined part of this sentence, you find the present tense verbs *does* and *calls*. This is an indication that a present tense verb is needed. Eliminate (A) because it uses a past tense. Eliminate (B) because it uses an *-ing* verb alone as the main verb of a clause. Eliminate (D) because it uses the past tense. The best answer is (C).

16. **The best answer is (F).** The issue is wordiness. You may not be able to identify this issue until you read all of the choices. Choice (F) is clearly the most concise, so it is the best answer.

17. **The best answer is (D).** The issue is writing strategy. The key words to focus on in the question stem are *describing the influence of earlier fantasy novelists on J. K. Rowling.* Ask yourself what the purpose of the essay is. It mentions three fantasy writers who worked before Rowling, but it doesn't specifically describe how they influenced her. Knowing this, you can eliminate (A) and (B). Now consider the reasons provided in (C) and (D). In (C), the fact that Rowling is the most recent of the writers does not mean that the influence of the previous writers must be discussed, and the fact that Rowling is a woman is irrelevant. The reason given in (D) specifically addresses the question posed by the question stem. Choice (D) is the best answer.

SUMMARY

In this chapter, we went over the basic strategy and outside knowledge required to master the ACT English test.

Remember to read through the issue instead of skipping to it. Eliminate when you can, then use your ear and plug in the remaining choice or choices. Listen for what sounds right. Then decide on the answer that is the most *correct, concise, and relevant*.

Make sure the sentence makes sense, and when in doubt, take it out!

To master the ACT English test, combine these strategies with the outside knowledge listed in Grammar and Punctuation Rules to Know. Flag or highlight the rules you still struggle with, then use the following chapter to practice the various question types.

In the next chapter, we'll dive further into each SmartPoint listed. After point-by-point explanations, you'll get to see what each question type looks like on its own and get a chance to practice on those examples. Remember, spend more time mastering question types that are tested more often to maximize your score!

CHAPTER 5

English Part 2: ACT English Strategy in Depth

OVERVIEW

Use this chapter to get familiar with all of the question types on the ACT English test. They are detailed and discussed fully in this chapter, and examples are provided for each type. To get a quick sense of what's to come, refer to the SmartPoint Breakdown in the previous chapter (on page 54). In the last chapter, they were discussed in order of Test Day value, with the more heavily tested SmartPoints listed first. That's generally how you should prioritize your prep time, especially if you are short on time or close to your goal score.

In this chapter, the SmartPoints are discussed in order of building *complexity*, as the knowledge for some question types contributes to other, more frequently tested SmartPoints. So if you have time and want to thoroughly work your English skill set, start at the beginning of the chapter and work your way through.

The chapter ends with Putting It All Together (page 103)—another great resource for those short on time. This section shows how the various question types fit into the passage as a whole.

Enjoy your studies!

The following SmartPoints are shown in order of building complexity, SmartPoint by Smart-Point.

SENTENCE SENSE—3 POINTS

Complexity: Low. Based on grammar and punctuation rules. Relates to: All other grammar-based SmartPoints—Punctuation, Verb Tense, Word Choice, and Connections.

Before we discuss how the ACT tests sentence structure, you need to be comfortable with just a few grammatical terms.

A *sentence* is a group of words that contains these three parts: a subject, a predicate verb, and a complete thought. You will see about 18 questions about sentence structure on the ACT English test.

A sentence is made up of one or more clauses. A *clause* is a group of words that contains a subject and a verb. A clause *may* constitute a complete sentence, but it doesn't necessarily have to. If a clause can stand alone as a sentence, it's called an *independent clause*. If a clause cannot stand alone as a sentence, it's called a *dependent clause*. You will not need to directly identify dependent and independent clauses on Test Day, but you will need to recognize them so you can punctuate them correctly. See if you can label the clauses below as either dependent or independent:

1. _____ because she was my friend

2. _____ she is my friend

3. _____ that I will go to the library

4. _____ I will go to the library

5. _____ although Dana is working tonight

6. _____ Dana is working tonight

7. _____ that all will be well

8. _____ all will be well

9. _____ when I return from vacation next week

10. _____ I return from vacation next week

In this exercise, all of the even-numbered questions are independent clauses. All of the odd-numbered questions are dependent clauses. In each odd-even pair of sentences, the independent clause actually contains fewer words than the dependent clause.

Take a minute to go back to the odd-numbered questions, and circle the first word in each. When you see words such as *because, that, if, whereas,* and *while* in an underlined part of an ACT English passage, sentence structure may be one of the issues tested by that problem.

Remember, just because a group of words in an ACT passage starts with a capital letter and ends with a period, that doesn't necessarily mean it's a proper complete sentence. Be on the lookout for dependent clauses that aren't joined to independent clauses; these would be sentence fragments.

Another kind of sentence structure error is a *run-on sentence*. A run-on sentence contains two or more clauses that are incorrectly strung together. A well-formed sentence can have more than one clause, but the clauses must be joined properly. Before we review the rules for sentence structure, test your present understanding by considering the following incorrect sentence:

> My history teacher requires us to use at least two books in our research, I have to go to the library this weekend.

Can you tell why the sentence structure is wrong? See if you can find one or more ways to correct it.

_____

_____

_____

_____

_____

The sentence is a run-on, because both the part preceding the comma (*My history teacher requires us to use at least two books in our research*) and the part following the comma (*I have to go the library this weekend*) are independent clauses—they could stand on their own as sentences. Joining those two parts with just a comma creates a run-on sentence.

There are several ways to correct a run-on like this one. However, on the ACT, you won't have to choose which way is best; for each multiple-choice question, only one correct choice will be presented.

RULES FOR CORRECTING RUN-ON SENTENCES

The ACT uses three primary fixes for breaking up run-on sentences. Here are the three ways to correctly combine two independent clauses in a single sentence:

1. Use a comma plus a FANBOYS conjunction (*For, And, Nor, But, Or, Yet, So*): *My history teacher requires us to use at least two books in our research**, so** I have to go to the library this weekend.*

2. Use a semicolon between the two clauses. After a semicolon, it is not correct to use a FANBOYS word, but it is acceptable to use a transitional word such as *however, more-over, therefore,* or *nevertheless*:

    *My history teacher requires us to use at least two books in our research**; therefore,**
    I have to go to the library this weekend.*

3. Change one of the independent clauses to a dependent clause by adding a word such as *although, because, despite,* or *since*:

    ***Because** my history teacher requires us to use at least two books in our research, I have
    to go to the library this weekend.*

(You will sometimes have the option to use a period to create multiple sentences, but often the ACT will ask you to properly fit multiple clauses into one sentence.)

      Visit your online syllabus—Lesson 5—for more instruction and
practice with run-on sentences.

VERBS WITH *-ING* RULE

Another common sentence structure rule you should be on the lookout for involves verbs ending with *-ing,* which can easily create sentence fragments. The verb form ending in *-ing* cannot be used without a helping verb, such as *is, was, has, had,* or *have been*, as the main verb in a clause. A helping verb does not show action by itself, but can "help" the main verb show action. Here's an example:

The monkey swinging from tree to tree is incorrect as a complete sentence, because *swinging* is used alone as the main verb. A helping verb is needed. Depending on the context, you might say something like *The monkey is swinging from tree to tree* or *The monkey had been swinging from tree to tree.*

Try these ACT-like questions that test Sentence Sense:

1. Two of our team's best players were injured at the beginning of the <u>season, our</u> team has not been doing well.

    A. NO CHANGE
    B. season, therefore, our
    C. season; so our
    D. season; our

The sentence as it is (choice (A)) is a run-on—the sections before and after the comma are both complete sentences. After identifying this issue, check the choices and eliminate those that don't correct the run-on. Choice (B) is incorrect because a comma cannot join two independent clauses without a FANBOYS conjunction, which *therefore* is not. Choice (C) is wrong because while the semicolon would connect the independent clauses, this answer then adds the word *so*, which makes the second clause dependent. Choice (D) correctly joins two independent clauses with a semicolon and no FANBOYS word.

2. The <u>library, which functioning</u> at times as a social center, is more than just an academic resource.

    F. NO CHANGE

    G. library, which functions

    H. library it functions

    J. library having the function

Notice the *-ing* verb in the underlined section. The sentence as written isn't a run-on, but there is a problem. The phrase *which functioning* probably sounds wrong to your ear, as it uses an *-ing* verb without a helping verb. So choice (F) can definitely be crossed out. Plug in the remaining choices to see which of them fixes the structural problem. Choice (G) doesn't create a problem and is the correct answer. Choice (H) contains the word *it*, which doesn't resolve the issue you've identified. Choice (J) also doesn't resolve the identified issue and sounds just as awkward.

3. My school's French club <u>planning to go</u> to Paris this spring.

    A. NO CHANGE

    B. planning on going

    C. is planning going

    D. is planning to go

Did you notice that an *-ing* verb was used in this question, too? The underlined portion includes *planning,* but a helping verb does not precede this *-ing* verb. Because this is the case, you should have identified sentence structure as the issue and eliminated choice (A). Choice (B) does not address this issue. Both choices (C) and (D) address the issue by adding the helping verb *is*, but (C) introduces a new *-ing* verb (*going*), which makes the sentence wrong again. The correct answer is (D).

PARALLEL STRUCTURE RULE

Items in a series, list, or compound must be parallel in form, meaning all items in a list must have the same "shape"—they must use the same tense, number, helping pronouns, or other structures. Review the examples in this chart:

Check for Parallelism if the Sentence Contains:	Example of Parallel Forms	Parallel Elements in Example
a list	Before you leave, you should **charge** your phone, **clean** your room, and **find** your keys.	Three verb phrases
a compound (words joined by *and* or *or*)	I don't like **swimming** or **hiking**.	Two *-ing* verb forms
an idiomatic phrase like *both...and* and *not only...but also*	It's necessary not only **to prepare thoroughly** but also **to listen carefully**.	Two verb phrases that start with *to*
a comparison	Your **homework** is just as important as your **participation** in class.	Two nouns
related nouns	**Students** who complete all of their homework **assignments** will be rewarded with higher **grades**.	Three plural nouns that are related in the sentence

  Visit your online syllabus—Lesson 5—for more instruction and practice with parallel sentence structure.

PUNCTUATION—5 POINTS

Complexity: Low. Based on grammar and punctuation rules. Relates to: Sentence Sense.

Some of the easiest questions to recognize are Punctuation questions. When you look at the choices, you'll see that they all use the same or nearly the same words, but have different punctuation marks. One great thing about the ACT is that it tests a limited number of punctuation rules.

The questions test commas, dashes, colons, semicolons, periods, question marks, exclamation points, and apostrophes. Review the Grammar and Punctuation Rules to Know section (page 56) for more details.

Comma usage is tested most frequently, followed by semicolon usage.

COMMA RULES

Use commas:

1. To separate introductory words from the main part of the sentence.

   Before you leave the house, you should make sure you've eaten a healthy breakfast.

2. To set off words or phrases that aren't essential to the sentence structure.

   Sonia, who will be playing the role of the lawyer, is a skilled actress.

3. To separate two independent clauses when they're joined by a FANBOYS word (*For, And, Nor, But, Or, Yet, So*).

   Many of my friends drink coffee, but I do not.

4. To separate items in a series.

   Steps involved in a research paper include choosing a topic, conducting the research, writing a first draft, and doing at least one round of revisions.

These four examples are the only uses of the comma that the ACT tests. Learn to recognize when each rule should be applied, and keep in mind the following additional hint: You should avoid unnecessary commas. Sometimes your task on an ACT punctuation question is to remove commas that disturb the flow of a sentence.

SEMICOLON RULES

Use a semicolon to link two independent clauses that are *not* joined by a FANBOYS word.

> I will be missing school to visit colleges; however, my teacher said I will not have to make up the Spanish quiz I will miss.

Certain words are frequently used to connect two independent clauses. These words are acceptable to use after a semicolon:

furthermore	moreover
however	nevertheless
in fact	therefore
indeed	thus

Do *not* use these words after a semicolon:

although	which
despite	where
whereas	that
who	

DASH RULES

Use dashes:

1. To indicate a break in thought.

   You did see the movie—am I right about that?

2. To set off parenthetical information from the main part of a sentence.

Many people find that small necessary items—a wallet, a cell phone, a transit card—are unfortunately very easy to misplace.

APOSTROPHE RULES

Use an apostrophe:

1. To take the place of one or more missing letters in a contraction.

   You can't be late.

2. To show the possessive form of a noun.

   My sister's friends are coming to the party. (This is correct if you're using the singular form, one sister.)

   My sisters' teams both won games this weekend. (This is correct if you're using the plural form, two sisters who play on two separate teams.)

When a question is testing punctuation, think about how the various parts of each sentence relate to one another. Identify the types of clauses, the nonessential information, and the transition words around the underlined punctuation. Recall the rules about commas and semicolons and which words are acceptable with each to join two clauses. Keep these ideas in mind as you try the following questions. To increase your understanding, read each answer explanation before you move on to the next question.

I'm unusual among my friends in that I don't <u>like, to drink coffee</u>. I do enjoy going with them to
1

1. A. NO CHANGE
   B. like to, drink coffee
   C. like to drink coffee
   D. like to drink, coffee

coffee <u>shops because, oddly enough,</u> I appreciate the
2
smell of coffee.

2. F. NO CHANGE
   G. shops, because, oddly enough
   H. shops because oddly, enough,
   J. shops because oddly enough

The convivial atmosphere of our local coffee brewer is also quite appealing to <u>me so,</u> I enjoy spending
3
time there with friends. Fortunately, I

3. A. NO CHANGE
   B. me, so
   C. me; so
   D. me, so,

can get a pretty good cup of tea <u>there, indeed,</u>
                                     4
<u>occasionally</u> I even order hot chocolate. In addition
   4

4. F. NO CHANGE
    G. there indeed, occasionally
    H. there: indeed, occasionally,
    J. there; indeed, occasionally

to the socializing and <u>refreshment, the coffee shop offers</u>
                                        5
me amusement. I have to laugh at the wide array of

available coffee drinks—regular, decaf, espresso,

5. A. NO CHANGE
    B. refreshment, the coffee shop, offers,
    C. refreshment the coffee shop, offers
    D. refreshment; the coffee shop offers

cappuccino, latte, <u>to name just a few,</u> and the amount of
                            6
time it takes my friends to decide what to order.

6. F. NO CHANGE
    G. to name just a few—
    H. to name, just a few,
    J. to name just a few:

I'm baffled by how my very busy friends can give so

much time and attention to something that, no matter

how <u>its' made,</u> still tastes like coffee.
        7

7. A. NO CHANGE
    B. its made,
    C. it's made
    D. it's made,

1. In this sentence, the comma after *like* disturbs the flow of the clause *I don't like to drink coffee.* In this question, remember the hint about avoiding unnecessary commas. The correct answer is (C).

2. Here, the phrase *oddly enough* is nonessential information. If you remove it, the remaining words still make up a correctly formed sentence. Use commas to set off nonessential phrases. The best answer is (F).

3. Think about how this sentence is constructed. It contains two independent clauses, joined by the FANBOYS word *so*. The first clause (*The convivial atmosphere of our local coffee brewer is also quite appealing to me*) can stand alone as a sentence. The second clause (*I enjoy spending time there with friends*) can also stand alone as a sentence. Use a comma after the first independent clause when you're joining two independent clauses with a FANBOYS word. The correct answer is (B).

4. Again, think about sentence structure. You have two independent clauses here. The first is *I can get a pretty good cup of tea there.* The second is *I even order hot chocolate.* The

word between the two clauses, *indeed*, is not a FANBOYS word, so you need a semicolon rather than a comma to join these two independent clauses. The correct answer is (J).

5. This sentence contains only one independent clause. This independent clause, *the coffee shop offers me amusement*, forms the main part of the sentence. The earlier part of the sentence (*In addition to the socializing and refreshment*) is not a clause. It is an introductory phrase. Use a comma to set off an introductory phrase from the main part of the sentence. The correct answer is (A).

6. Be careful here. The incorrect punctuation used in choice (F) can make this sentence confusing to read and understand. Take the sentence apart to determine which words make up the main part of the sentence. The independent clause is *I have to laugh at the wide array of available coffee drinks…and the amount of time it takes my friends to decide what to order*. The words that follow the dash (*regular, decaf, espresso, cappuccino, latte, to name just a few*) constitute parenthetical information that is not part of the sentence's main clause. A dash must be used at the end of the parenthetical expression to properly set it off. The correct answer is (G).

7. This question tests both comma and apostrophe usage. Whenever you see that an underlined portion of an English passage contains an apostrophe, always check that it's used correctly. The spelling *its'* is never correct. If an apostrophe is called for, as it is here, the correct spelling is *it's*. Remember that this spelling is correct whenever it could be replaced by the words *it is*. You have to think about comma rules for this question also. The words *no matter how it's made* are nonessential information. Because you must use commas to set off nonessential information from the rest of the sentence, a comma is required here after *made*. The correct answer is (D).

VERB TENSES—6 POINTS

Complexity: Low-Medium. Based on grammar rules. Relates to: Sentence Sense, Word Choice.

You probably remember that a verb is a word that expresses an action (*draw, eat, walk*) or a word that expresses a state of being (*is, were, was*). Though there are many grammatical rules relating to verbs, there are really only three verb usage rules on the ACT:

1. A verb must agree with its subject.

2. A verb's tense must be logically consistent with time-related phrases in the sentence and other verbs used in the passage.

3. Some verbs can form the past tense in a way other than using *-ed*.

An easy way to know if you have to apply one of these rules is to get used to noticing underlined verbs in the ACT English test. When you notice an underlined verb, ask yourself these questions:

• What is the subject of this verb? Does the underlined verb agree with its grammatical subject?

- Does the tense of the underlined verb make sense in relation to other words in the sentence? Is the underlined verb consistent with other verb tenses used in nearby sentences and the passage as a whole?

- Does this verb form the past tense correctly? Does it sound right?

We'll talk more about subject-verb agreement under the next SmartPoint—Word Choice. For this SmartPoint, we'll focus on the second two questions to make sure we have the verb in the right tense.

> *Does the tense of the underlined verb make sense in relation to other words in the sentence? Is the underlined verb consistent with other verb tenses used in nearby sentences and the passage as a whole?*

To determine if an underlined verb makes sense within its own sentence, watch for time-related phrases and non-underlined verbs. In the following example of illogical verb tense usage, circle the time-related word, and write down the correct verb tense in the space provided:

> Before my parents will let me take the car by myself, I had to [_____] improve my grade-point average considerably.

Here you should have circled the time-related word *before* and the non-underlined verb *will let*. Having noticed these words, you should see that the underlined past-tense verb *had* is not logical in this sentence. Possible corrections include *have to, must,* and *will have to*. On the ACT, only one correct answer will be presented among the choices.

> *Does this verb form the past tense correctly? Does it sound right?*

See if you can make the necessary correction in this sentence:

> Hemingway, along with several other Americans, had went [_____] to Paris to write.

The verb error in this sentence could be corrected in two ways, depending on the context. The key thing to spot here, though, is that *had went* is never correct. It's a good idea to train your ear to listen for past-tense forms that are common errors—the following forms are never correct: *had did, had flied, had wrote, had took*. You don't need to memorize every verb that forms the past tense irregularly (that is, with a spelling other than simply adding *-ed),* but you should be aware that this type of error is sometimes tested on the ACT. Examine the following chart for a list of commonly tested irregular verbs.

Forms of the "Helping Verbs"		
	Present Tense	**Past Tense**
To be	am, are, is	was, were
To have	have, has	had

Examples of Verbs That Use an Irregular Past Tense		
Present	**Past**	**Past Participle (use with *had, has,* or *have*)**
begin	began	begun
come	came	come
do	did	done
drive	drove	driven
know	knew	known
swim	swam	swum
take	took	taken

Try out these ideas on the following passage. Check your work with the Answers and Explanations.

MARY'S ATTIC

I thought the tour of my friend's new house was finished as we came to a stop outside her bedroom on the third floor, but Mary had something else in mind. "Do you want to go up to the attic?" she asked me, her eyes sparkling with mischief. "My dad says no one <u>goes</u> up there for 40 years!"

1. A. NO CHANGE
   B. will have gone
   C. still goes
   D. has gone

I wasn't thrilled about the idea of exploring the dark, musty space overhead. In the past, I <u>would of hesitated</u> whenever Mary suggested risky or dangerous activities, but this time I just nodded, trying to appear nonchalant. Mary yanked on the cord dangling from the wooden door; as if by magic, a staircase unfolded, the bottom step landing directly in front of my feet. I looked up into the looming darkness, imagining cobwebs crawling with eight-legged monsters, and shuddered.

I took a deep breath, hoping Mary wouldn't notice,

2. F. NO CHANGE
   G. hesitated
   H. will hesitate
   J. must hesitate

and gripped the ladder. As I placed my foot on the bot-

tom rung, I wondered how my best friend had failed to

remember I had a terrible fear of spiders. "The sooner

you <u>got</u> this over with, the better," I whispered to my-
     3
self.

3. A. NO CHANGE
    B. had got
    C. get
    D. are getting

All four of the choices for question 1 are grammatically correct, so you can't eliminate anything just based on that. Plugging each into the sentence, however, quickly points out that the issue being tested is the time frame. The speaker is talking about something that has not happened in a long time, so (D), *has gone*, is the answer that fits the context.

The first issue that stands out in question 2 is the idiom use *would of*. That may be how it sounds, but the correct idiom is *would have*. This is not presented as an option, though, so we need to pick the correct time frame. The sentence says *In the past*, so we need a past-tense verb, which only (G) provides.

As written, the phrase *The sooner you got this* in question 3 sounds wrong, which it is; *sooner* refers to something in the future, *got* is in the past. Plugging in choices (C) and (D) makes the choice fairly clear—only (C) is right in context.

WORD CHOICE—5 POINTS

Complexity: Medium. Mostly based on grammar rules. Somewhat based on rhetorical skills. Relates to: Sentence Sense, Verb Tense.

Word Choice questions primarily test:

• Verbs (related to subject-verb agreement)

• Pronouns

They also test:

• Modifiers

• Idioms

We'll look at each one in turn.

VERBS

How to identify and use verbs in the correct tense is discussed in the Verb Tenses section. For Word Choice questions, the tested issue is subject-verb agreement.

Again, when you see a verb underlined, it is testing one of these three usage rules:

1. A verb must agree with its subject.

2. A verb's tense must be logically consistent with time-related phrases in the sentence and other verbs that are used in the passage.

3. Some verbs can form the past tense in a way other than using *-ed*.

Numbers 2 and 3 are discussed under Verb Tenses.

For rule number 1, ask yourself, *What is the subject of this verb? Does the underlined verb agree with its grammatical subject?*

One key thing to remember—and a common trap on the ACT—is that the noun immediately before the verb may not actually be the verb's subject. It may be, but placement is no guarantee.

In this example of incorrect subject-verb agreement, circle the subject and jot down the correction for the underlined verb in the space provided:

> Many of my friends, including everyone in the brass section of the band, is [_____] planning to come to my party.

Recall that the *subject* is who or what is doing the action the verb expresses. In the sentence, you should have circled the word *my friends*, the subject of this sentence. Detecting the incorrect subject-verb agreement here can be tricky because the subject is separated from the verb by several words—a whole dependent clause. As you work through English questions, both in your practice and on Test Day, circle the subject that goes with the underlined verb. Then read the subject and the verb without the words that appear between them. When you do this, you'll hear a mistake more easily. You wouldn't say, *My friends is planning to come*. You would make the correction: *My friends are planning to come*.

Use this chart to study the commonly tested subject-verb agreement rules:

Subject-Verb Agreement		
A verb must agree with its subject noun in person and number.	The noun closest to a verb may not be its subject.	Only the conjunction *and* forms a compound subject that requires a plural verb form.
A stamp sticks to an envelope. Stamps _____ to envelopes.	The chair with the cabriole legs is an antique. MP3 players, small portable devices that play digital audio files, _____ popular with many different demographic groups.	Either Kyle or Trisha is managing the crew. Kyle and Trisha _____ managing the crew. Neither Kyle nor Trisha _____ managing the crew.

The final verb area tested on the ACT is *active voice*. Determining whether or not a sentence is in active voice or *passive voice* requires you to relate subjects to verbs in the context of the sentence as a whole. While both active and passive voice can be grammatically correct, if you have to choose between them to find a right answer on the ACT, you should always select the active voice. You will notice as you practice and take the ACT that the active voice is also usually shorter.

Most sentences in English are worded in what we call the active voice. When a sentence is in the active voice, the subject of the sentence is the person or thing doing whatever action the verb expresses. On the other hand, when a sentence is in the passive voice, the subject of the verb is *receiving* the action instead of *doing* it. In other words, when an active sentence is written in the passive, the subject becomes an object. Some examples will make the difference clear. In the following sentences, the subjects are capitalized and the objects are underlined.

Active Voice: My FAMILY packed the <u>car</u> carefully before we left for vacation.

Passive Voice: The CAR was packed carefully by my <u>family</u> before we left for vacation.

Active Voice: My AUNT gave me a new <u>phone</u>.

Passive Voice: A new PHONE was given to me by my <u>aunt</u>.

The active voice puts the emphasis on the subject. Occasionally, a writer who wants to emphasize the object, rather than the subject, chooses to use the passive voice, but the active voice is desirable most of the time. Once in a while, you may come across an ACT question that tests whether you can recognize the difference. Here's an example:

1. <u>My grandmother's knowledge of knitting having been taught to me by her, I have expanded my skills even further.</u>

   A. NO CHANGE
   B. My grandmother taught me everything she knows about knitting, and I have expanded my skills even further.
   C. Having been taught everything she knows by my grandmother, my knowledge of knitting has been expanded even further.
   D. My grandmother taught me everything she knows about knitting, and my skills have been expanded even further.

The phrasing of this sentence likely sounds very awkward to you, which is your first clue to start looking carefully. In the sentence as written, the preposition *by* alerts you to check for the passive voice. The verb in the first part of the sentence is *taught*, and the grammatical subject is *knowledge*. The person doing the teaching, however, is *my grandmother*. Because the subject is not doing the action (the knowledge is not doing the teaching), this is a passive construction. While this sentence is, technically, grammatically correct, examine the choices to see if an active voice wording is offered. In (B), both the first and second parts of the sentence are written in the active voice, making (B) the best answer. In (C), both the first and second clauses of the sentence are passive. In (D), the first half has been made active, but the second half is still passive.

While the active voice is preferable if all other things are equal, there are some situations in which the passive voice is the only correct choice. The most common instance is in a sentence that begins with a modifying phrase. Consider this example:

2. Tattered and worn after years of use, <u>the old book of poems was still treasured by my grandfather</u>.

    F. NO CHANGE
    G. the poems in the old book were still treasured by my grandfather
    H. my grandfather still treasured the old book of poems
    J. the poems were treasured by my grandfather in the old book

The word *by* in the underlined portion is a clue that the expression is in the passive voice. Remember, though, it's not an absolute rule that the passive voice is always wrong. Sometimes, as in this question, the non-underlined part of the sentence leaves you with no choice but to go with a passive construction. Choice (F) is in the passive form, but look at the other choices to see if any of them are better. The introductory modifying phrase *Tattered and worn after years of use* needs to apply to the noun following it. In choice (G), it is *the poems* that are *tattered and worn*, not the *book*. Similarly, choice (H), although written in the active voice, says it's *my grandfather* who is *tattered and worn*. Choice (J) does the same as (G), making *the poems* the object of the modifying phrase. So, while passive, choice (F) is the correct answer.

PRONOUNS

A *pronoun* is a word that either takes the place of or refers to a noun or another pronoun. Train yourself to spot pronouns in the underlined portion of an ACT English passage. See if you can identify the pronouns in each underlined part of the following paragraph, and write them on the lines provided.

My mother and her work friends, nurses in a large

emergency room, have many interesting stories <u>about</u>
                                                   3
<u>their</u> experiences. Some of these stories are about the
  3
challenges patients face, but some of the funniest stories

are about interactions <u>her and the other nurses have</u>
                              4
with various staff members. Whenever Mom and <u>I have</u>
                                                   5

3. _____

4. _____

5. _____

friends over at the same time, my friends and <u>me always</u>
6

<u>wind up</u> laughing at the things we hear. The story about
6

the doctor who thought <u>their cell phone had been</u> "bor-
7

rowed" by a nurse was hilarious. Mom and her friends

have <u>given we</u> teenagers some good advice: One should
8

not go into the medical field <u>if you don't have</u> a good
9

sense of humor.

6. _____

7. _____

8. _____

9. _____

How did you do at picking out the pronouns? Don't worry if you didn't find them all—we'll discuss the pronouns that you'll see on the ACT. Here are the answers:

3. their

4. her

5. I

6. me

7. their

8. we

9. you

Let's do a quick review of what you need to know about pronouns for the ACT. Any pronoun can be described in terms of two things: case and number. Pronoun *case* refers to how the pronoun is used in a sentence—as a subject or an object. In the sentence *He will call you later,* the pronoun *He* acts as the subject, while the pronoun *you* acts as the object. A pronoun's *number* is either singular or plural. Most personal pronouns take a different form (that is, a different word is used) depending on whether they are used as the subject or object in a sentence and depending on whether they are singular or plural. The following table shows the personal pronouns for which you must consider both case and number.

	Singular	**Plural**
Subject	I, he, she, it,	we, they
Object	me, him, her, it	us, them

Generally, your ear tells you which form of a personal pronoun is correct. The ACT often makes a pronoun question trickier by using a personal pronoun in combination with *and*. You would never say **Him** *went to the store,* but on the ACT, you might see something like

Him and Jesse *went to the store together.* By reading this sentence without the words *and Jesse*, your ear helps you determine that *Him* should be changed to *He* in this sentence.

Examples of correct pronoun usage as subjects and objects:

1. **We** must be respectful in this class, or the teacher will give *us* detention.

2. Kevin and **I** are going skating tonight.

3. The guests said **they** were thankful for the help that *we* volunteers provided.

4. Ginny told **me** there was no need to return the book to *her*.

5. Can you believe my parents said **they** will give *us* the car for the weekend?

Did you notice that the table of personal pronouns above doesn't include the pronoun *you?* The reason for this is that the pronoun *you* takes the same form whether it's used as the subject or object in a sentence. Here's an example:

You must be respectful in the class, or the teacher will give *you* a detention.

However, the ACT does test the pronoun *you* in a different way—by using the word *one* in a sentence that also uses *you*. More about that now!

PRONOUN-SHIFT RULE

A pronoun that can serve a similar purpose as *you* is *one*. But the ACT will test this by making them interchangeable, which they are not. Avoid the *one-you* shift: do not shift between the words *one* and *you* in the same sentence or paragraph.

Here's how the *one-you* shift might look on the ACT:

<u>When one is planning</u> for college, you need to keep many factors in mind.

Here, because the non-underlined part of the sentence uses the word *you*, the underlined part of the sentence should be corrected to *you are*. The sentence could also equalize this by saying *one needs to keep many factors in mind*, but because that section isn't underlined, that isn't an option.

WHICH/WHO/WHOM RULES

In addition to the personal pronouns and the *one-you* shift, another aspect of pronouns frequently tested on the ACT is the use of *who, whom,* and *which*. Fortunately, there are solid rules to learn for this as well!

Who and *whom* intimidate many people, but it's not hard to use them correctly if you think about how each word functions in its sentence or clause. Think about whether it is a subject or an object. Remember this rule: "*Who* goes where *he* goes, and *whom* goes where *him* goes." That is, if you can correctly substitute the pronoun *he* into a sentence, then *who* is correct, but if you can substitute *him* into a sentence, then *whom* is correct.

Which should be used entirely differently—it only applies to nonhuman nouns. So *Which restaurant did you pick?* is correct, while *I invited three friends, one of which has already accepted* is incorrect. Learn to apply these rules:

- Use *which* only to refer to things, never to refer to people.

- Use *who* in a sentence context where *he* or *she* would be correct.

- Use *whom* in a sentence context where *him* or *her* would be correct.

See if you can circle the correct word in the following sentences:

10. My brother, *who/whom* attends the state university, is majoring in history.

11. The baby, *who/which* is only nine months old, has already started walking.

12. A public speaker should keep in mind the audience *who/whom* she is addressing.

13. The company president is the person *which/whom* you need to contact.

14. The principal said that all students *who/whom* skip the pep rally will receive a detention.

15. The head librarian is the one to *which/whom* you must send your résumé.

16. The painting of *which/whom* I write is the work of an unknown genius.

Here are the correct answers, along with explanations to help you apply the rules:

10. *Who* is correct because you'd say **He** *attends the state university.*

11. *Who* is correct, because *the baby* is a person, not a thing.

12. *Whom* is correct because you'd say *She is addressing* **him***.*

13. *Whom* is correct because you're referring to a person and because you'd say *You need to contact* **him***.*

14. *Who* is correct because you'd say **He** *skip[s] the pep rally.*

15. *Whom* is correct because you're referring to a person and because you'd say *You must send your résumé to* **him***.*

16. *Which* is correct because you're referring to the painting—a thing, not a person.

Now let's return to the paragraph you saw at the beginning of this section. This time, it's presented as a test-like passage with multiple-choice answers like on the ACT. Use it to test your understanding of the various pronoun issues.

My mother and her work friends, nurses in a large

emergency room, have many interesting stories <u>about</u>
                                                  17
<u>their</u> experiences. Some of these stories are about the
17
challenges patients face, but some of the funniest stories

are about interactions <u>her and the other nurses have</u>
                              18
with various staff members. Whenever Mom and

<u>I have</u> friends over at the same time, my friends and
19

<u>me always wind up</u> laughing at the things we hear. The
       20
story about the doctor who thought

<u>their cell phone had been</u> "borrowed" by a nurse was
           21
hilarious. Mom and her friends

<u>have given we</u> teenagers some good advice: One should
       22
not go into the medical field

<u>if you don't have</u> a good sense of humor.
       23

17. A. NO CHANGE
    B. about there
    C. on they're
    D. on their

18. F. NO CHANGE
    G. her and the other nurses were having
    H. she and the other nurses having
    J. she and the other nurses have

19. A. NO CHANGE
    B. I would be having
    C. me have
    D. me had

20. F. NO CHANGE
    G. I always wind up
    H. I always winding up
    J. me always winding up

21. A. NO CHANGE
    B. there cell phone had been
    C. they're cell phone had been
    D. her cell phone had been

22. F. NO CHANGE
    G. having gave we
    H. have gave us
    J. have given us

23. A. NO CHANGE
    B. if they don't have
    C. without having
    D. if you aren't having

17. The possessive pronoun *their* is underlined. It is plural, so it correctly refers to *my mother and her friends*. Following step 2 of the Kaplan Method, you can eliminate (B) and (C), which use the incorrect spellings *there* and *they're*. Following step 3 and reading the sentence with (A) and (D), you should be able to eliminate (D). The correct answer is (A).

18. You should notice immediately that the underlined portion uses the pronoun *her*. Ask yourself if it's used correctly. Remember that you should be especially careful whenever you see an underlined pronoun near the word *and*. Think about how the pronoun sounds in context when you momentarily ignore the word that follows *and*. Does it sound correct to say *interactions* her *[has] with other staff members*? No, you would say *interactions* she *has with other staff members*. The issue here is pronoun use. You can eliminate (F) and (G). Following step 3, and reading (H) and (J) into the sentence, you should notice a verb error in (H). The correct answer is (J).

19. Notice the underlined pronoun *I* and determine how it's used in the sentence. Here, *I* is used correctly as the subject of the clause *I have friends over*. Based on pronoun usage, you can eliminate (C) and (D). Then, if you read (B) into the sentence, you can hear that it introduces a verb problem. The correct answer is (A).

20. The underlined portion contains the pronoun *me*, so first you should check to see if it's used correctly. It functions as a subject in the clause *me always wind up laughing*. Pronoun usage is definitely the issue here: the subject pronoun *I* is needed instead. Identifying the issue lets you eliminate (F) and (J). Read the other choices into the sentence, and you'll hear that (H) introduces a verb error. The correct answer is (G).

21. There's an error in this sentence as it's written, but it's not an easy one for your ear to detect. This means that you might have difficulty identifying the issue here. Still, you should notice that the pronoun *their* is underlined. Ask yourself what word in the passage it refers to. *Their* refers to the word *doctor*. The problem is *doctor* is singular, but *their* is plural. Because *doctor* is not underlined, you can't change it, so you have to eliminate the pronoun *their*. Notice that (B) and (C) don't eliminate the pronoun; they simply substitute a different word that sounds the same. Only (D) correctly uses a singular pronoun (*her*) to refer to the singular noun *doctor*. The correct answer is (D).

22. Your ear might help you easily identify the issue here. If not, notice that the underlined portion contains the pronoun *we*, and determine how it's used in the sentence. The fact that the pronoun immediately follows the verb *given* indicates that it's used here as an object; however, *we* is the form to use for a subject, so *we* is incorrect here. Thus, you can eliminate (F) and (G). Read the other two choices. Both correctly use the objective pronoun *us*, but (H) introduces a verb error. The correct answer is (J).

23. The issue in this question is the *one-you* shift. That can be a difficult issue to recognize unless you think to look for it. The fact that the underlined portion includes the pronoun *you* should serve as a red flag. Whenever you notice this word underlined, check the surrounding context for consistency. Because the non-underlined part of the sentence uses the word *one*, it's incorrect to use *you* in the same sentence. Remembering this rule allows you to eliminate (A) and (D). Read the remaining choices into the sentence.

Choice (B) uses the plural pronoun *they* to refer to the singular *one,* so it can't be correct. The correct answer is (C).

      Visit your online syllabus—Lesson 5—for more instruction and practice with pronouns.

Modifiers and idioms are less frequently tested Word Choice issues.

MODIFIERS

A **modifier** is a word or phrase that describes or provides more information about another word. Two different parts of speech—adjectives and adverbs—function as modifiers. Let's look at the two modifier rules that are tested on the ACT.

SINGLE-WORD MODIFIER RULE

Most modifiers are single words that help explain or describe (modify) a simple idea. Commonly, these are adjectives and adverbs. An adjective must be used only to modify a noun or a pronoun. An adverb must be used only to modify a verb, an adjective, or another adverb.

Try the following exercise. Underline the adjective or adverb, and circle the word it logically modifies. Then determine whether the modifier is used correctly. If it isn't, put an X in the space provided. If the modifier is used correctly, put a check in the space provided.

24. _____ Caitlin drove careful on the highway.

25. _____ Carlos worked diligently on the project.

26. _____ I am certainly that the show starts at 8:00.

27. _____ Sarah found it was extreme cold in the tent.

28. _____ Sonnesh is extremely happy.

29. _____ Diligent work leads to success.

You should have identified questions 24, 26, and 27 as being incorrect. Question 24 incorrectly uses the adjective *careful* to modify the verb *drove* (it should be *carefully*). Question 26 incorrectly uses the adverb *certainly* to modify the pronoun *I* (*certain* is correct here). Question 27 incorrectly uses the adjective *extreme* to modify the adjective *cold* (*extremely* is needed here). The other questions are correct. Question 25 uses the adverb *diligently* to modify the verb *worked.* Question 28 uses the adverb *extremely* to modify the adjective *happy.* Question 29 uses the adjective *diligent* to modify the noun *work.*

MODIFYING PHRASE RULE

A **modifying phrase** should be placed as close as possible to the word it modifies. Specifically, when a sentence begins with a modifying phrase, the next noun or pronoun in the sentence *must* be the word that phrase logically modifies. Recall the correct answer to the last question about active voice on page 84.

You can easily spot most introductory modifying phrases because they usually begin with a verb that ends in *-ed* or *-ing*. If you remember this, you'll have no trouble at all with introductory modifiers on the ACT. Let's look at an example:

30. Having just returned from three weeks of primitive camping, <u>sleeping in his own bed was what Matt looked forward to most</u>.

F. NO CHANGE

G. being home in his own bed was what Matt looked forward to most

H. Matt most looked forward to sleeping in his own bed

J. the thing Matt looked forward to most was sleeping in his own bed

If you notice that the sentence starts with a modifying phrase *(Having just returned from three weeks of primitive camping),* you should next ask yourself who or what this phrase logically describes. Once you identify that, you'll find this type of question easy to get right! Logically, the introductory phrase can only be modifying *Matt*—he's the one who went camping. Therefore, *Matt* must immediately follow the phrase, meaning you can eliminate all choices except (H). The key here is paying attention to the non-underlined context of the sentence and using it to determine the right answer.

COMPARATIVE AND SUPERLATIVE RULE

Another modifier issue tests the use of **comparative** and **superlative** adjectives, which are modifiers used to compare items—one thing is *bigger* or *faster* than another, or something is the *most* or *best* of something. These are common parts of speech and important to get right on the ACT. Generally, comparative adjectives end with *-er,* and superlative adjectives end in *-est*. You determine whether the comparative or superlative form of an adjective is correct by asking how many items are being compared.

Use the comparative form of an adjective (for example, *older* or *shorter)* when only two objects are being compared. Use the superlative form of an adjective (for example, *oldest* or *shortest)* when comparing three or more objects.

Because the ACT questions always have exactly one unambiguously correct answer, the context surrounding a comparative or superlative *must* always make it clear how many things are being compared. In the following question, look for a phrase that indicates how many people are involved:

31. Of all my friends, I think Johanna is the <u>most likely to become a doctor</u>.

A. NO CHANGE

B. more likely to become a doctor

C. most likely becoming a doctor

D. most likeliest to become a doctor

If you focused on the word *all,* good for you! The phrase *of **all** my friends* tells you that three or more people are being discussed here—you wouldn't say *all* to refer to two people. This means that the superlative form *most* is correct. Eliminate (B) and plug in the remaining choices. Choice (C) correctly uses the superlative *most likely,* but it creates a sentence sense problem by changing the verb to *becoming,* so eliminate it. You should eliminate (D) as well because the idea of the superlative is already included in the word *most,* so it's incorrect to change *likely* to *likeliest.* Choice (A) is therefore the correct answer.

IDIOMS

The final Word Choice issue tested on the ACT is idiomatic usage. An **idiom** is an expression that is conventionally phrased in a particular way, whether or not there's a firm rule to rely on. These are phrases you've simply heard so often you know how they should be. Idiomatic usage isn't heavily tested on the ACT.

Most often, correct idiomatic usage hinges on prepositions—for example, you would never say, "I'm traveling *at* school." You'd say, "I'm traveling *to* school." In different contexts, though, a different preposition can be correct. For example:

I'm in the math club __ school.

Your ear should tell you that *at* is correct here.

Whenever you notice that the underlined portion of a sentence includes a preposition, think about how it sounds in context to make sure it's idiomatically correct—if your ear tells you something's wrong, it may well be.

Use the following chart to identify Idiom questions and correctly answer them:

Ask	Is a preposition underlined?	Is a verb form that starts with *to* or ends in *-ing* underlined?	Is part of a commonly tested idiomatic expression used somewhere in the sentence?	Does the sentence include the word *barely, hardly,* or *scarcely*?
Check	Determine if the preposition sounds appropriate with other words in the sentence.	Determine if the infinitive, participle, or gerund form is used appropriately.	Check for common idioms such as *either… or* and *neither… nor.*	Watch out for other negative words such as *no, none,* and *not* that would create a double negative.

Here are the most commonly tested prepositions and idioms on the ACT:

Prepositions	Commonly Tested Idiomatic Expressions	Words That Can't Be Paired with Negative Words
at *by* *for* *from* *of* *on* *to* *with*	*as…as* *between…and* *both…and* *either…or* *just as…so* *neither…nor* *not only…but also*	*barely* *hardly* *scarcely*

Sometimes, when you've eliminated two choices and are trying to choose the better one of the remaining two, thinking about correct idiomatic usage will help you select the correct answer.

WORDINESS—5 POINTS

Complexity: Moderate. Based on rhetorical skills. Relates to: None. This is a stand-alone SmartPoint.

Remember the big three words to focus on in the English section. Always use the Kaplan Method, and remember to choose your answer based on the choice that is the most *correct*, *concise*, and *relevant*.

The SmartPoints you've looked at so far all primarily relate to the *correct* part of the big three. They've been based in grammar rules and primarily test mechanics.

Word Choice starts to bridge the gap, as some questions have more to do with rhetorical skill than with making things technically correct, but Wordiness is the first SmartPoint you'll look at that falls entirely outside of grammar rules.

With these next SmartPoints, it's essential to keep the words *concise* and *relevant* in mind, in addition to making sure sentences are correct.

So it's time to get those rhetorical skills rolling. We'll start with the importance of being *concise* to master the Wordiness SmartPoint.

Keep this in mind: sometimes, one choice will be better than another *simply because it's shorter*.

This means that some questions will have more than one choice that is *grammatically correct*, but there is still only one answer the ACT will call *right*. It's easy to lose sight of this when you're working through grammar rules questions and all questions have choices that are cut and dry. Sometimes the grammatically correct answer isn't the only right one.

There are two types of Wordiness errors you can expect to see on the ACT: Redundancy and Verbosity.

REDUNDANCY

Redundancy means saying the same thing twice. This is usually not literally; it may be saying something one way and then repeating the meaning in different words. For example:

> My little brother worked hard on and put a lot of effort into building his sand castle.

What should catch your eye here is that *worked hard on* and *put a lot of effort into* mean pretty much the same thing. Once you've said one, you really don't need the other, so only one phrase should be used, not both.

Fortunately for you, many Redundancy questions come with a built-in clue that Wordiness is the tested issue: the "OMIT the underlined portion" choice. Whenever you see OMIT as a choice, always start by asking yourself: "Is the underlined portion truly necessary, and would anything valuable be lost if the underlined portion were taken out?" If the answers to these questions are "no," then you can confidently select OMIT as the right choice. You should note that when OMIT is offered as a choice, it always appears as the fourth choice. OMIT is the correct answer more than half of the time, so w*hen OMIT is present, always check that choice first!* Try this question:

1. My older sister, who is a sibling of mine, is studying to be a surgeon.

   A. NO CHANGE
   B. , who is of course one of my relatives,
   C. , one of my siblings,
   D. OMIT the underlined portion.

First, notice that OMIT is a choice. Remember, that's your clue to ask yourself whether the underlined portion is necessary. Read around the context to see if the underlined information is already expressed by other, non-underlined words. That *is* the case here, because a sister, by definition, is a sibling. You can eliminate (A) and know that (D) is the correct choice *without even taking the time to read* (B) and (C).

VERBOSITY

Verbosity means simply using more words than are necessary. Verbosity questions don't always include OMIT as a choice, so they are not as easy to spot, but you will often see a difference in the length of the choices. Verbosity results when a long, drawn-out expression is used in place of a shorter one. Read this verbose sentence, and come up with a shorter way of expressing its meaning:

> The student council held a meeting for the purpose of determining what would be the most profitable kind of event for fund-raising.

_____

_____

_____

Here's a more concise way to express the idea:

The student council met to determine the most profitable kind of fund-raising event.

Same idea, far shorter. You may have come up with a different version, which is fine—there are many ways of expressing an idea simply. The key is to notice the wordy phrases that could be replaced with shorter alternatives. Here's how a Verbosity question might look on the ACT:

2. Jonathon wanted to write his history paper in the <u>amount of time that would be the shortest possible</u>.

    F. NO CHANGE
    G. way that would take up the smallest amount of his time possible
    H. least possible time
    J. time that would be the least he could possibly spend on it

As you see again here, the problem with a wordy construction isn't grammatical. Wordiness is a style issue, and that's more subtle. Therefore, you should always work through an English passage remembering that the best ACT style is *concise*. While there's no OMIT choice to serve as a warning here, there is another clue you might notice: Choice (H) is considerably shorter than the other choices. When this is the case, it's often an indication that the issue is wordiness. If you can't determine anything really wrong with one or more choices, always choose the shortest one. In this question, (H) is the correct answer because it's most concise.

Let's look at one more example of an ACT Wordiness question. In this one, the sentence is wordy because it's redundant, but you won't find OMIT as a choice:

3. The intricate figures along the edge of the garden were <u>created and sculpted by</u> the owner of the house.

    A. NO CHANGE
    B. sculpted by
    C. were the creative work of a sculptor who is
    D. the original creation of

Let's look at some ways you can identify that this question tests wordiness, even though OMIT is not the last choice. First, if you're reading carefully, your ear will tell you that *created and sculpted* is redundant, so you can eliminate (A). Here, although *created* doesn't mean exactly the same thing as *sculpted,* the idea of *created* is part of the definition of *sculpted.* Second, you should notice that (B) is shorter than all the others are. Eliminate (C) because it's both redundant (using *creative* and *sculptor*) and verbose. Eliminate (D) because it's not as concise as (B). Choice (B) is the right answer.

CONNECTIONS—7 POINTS

Complexity: Medium-High. Based on rhetorical skills. Relates to: Sentence Sense.

Connections words and phrases are those that express a relationship between ideas. The two most common types of Connections tested on the ACT are Cause-and-Effect and Contrast Connections. Other Connections tested are Sequence and Emphasis. You should thoroughly familiarize yourself with the words and phrases in the following table. Spotting a Connections word on the ACT is a red flag that you need to think about logical relationships—whenever you see a Connections word underlined, you can expect that the other answer choices will also be various Connections words and phrases.

Connections Words and Phrases	
Connections that show addition, continuation, emphasis, or examples	additionally and for example for instance furthermore indeed in addition in fact likewise moreover
Connections that show cause and effect	as a result because consequently leading to since so therefore thus
Connections that show contrast	although but despite even though however nevertheless on the other hand rather though whereas while
Connections that show sequence	finally first if…then last later next second then

Let's look at some examples of how Connections words and phrases are tested on the ACT.

1. Many of my friends enjoy team sports; <u>however</u>, I prefer individual activities such as running and yoga.

    A. NO CHANGE

    B. but

    C. therefore

    D. in addition

Whenever you notice that a Connections word or phrase is underlined, read carefully in the surrounding context to determine how the ideas are related. This sentence has two parts. The first is *many of my friends enjoy team sports*. The second is *I prefer individual activities*. Ask yourself how the two ideas are related. Because *team sports* are different from *individual activities*, the relationship is one of contrast. When you first read the sentence, it should sound logical because *however* is a contrast connection. Indeed, (A) is the best answer here. You can eliminate (C) and (D) because they do not express contrast. Choice (B) does express contrast, but it is not appropriate here because a semicolon is used between the two independent clauses, and a FANBOYS conjunction like *but* is incorrect after a semicolon.

2. <u>Although</u> she has a strong interest in Renaissance art, Elizabeth is eagerly anticipating her trip to Rome.

    F. NO CHANGE

    G. While

    H. Because

    J. Indeed

The presence of an underlined Connections word here should alert you that you need to consider the relationship between ideas in the sentence. There are two ideas here: Elizabeth's interest in Renaissance art and her eager anticipation of her trip to Rome. Ask yourself how these ideas are connected. There is a lot of Renaissance art in Rome, so Elizabeth's interest in it leads her to be excited about her trip. The relationship is one of cause and effect. You can eliminate (F) and (G) because they create contrast. Eliminate (J) because it's an Emphasis Connection and not logical in context. Choice (H) is the correct answer.

3. Restricting sodium in the diet is important to protecting one's health. A main source of dietary sodium is found in canned, microwavable, and other prepared foods. <u>Despite this</u>, another source is the salt people add to their own food at the table.

    A. NO CHANGE

    B. However

    C. In addition

    D. For example

The underlined portion here is a Connections phrase, and it shows contrast. Read the surrounding context carefully to determine if contrast is the appropriate kind of connection here. In this case, you must read not only the sentence that contains the underlined portion, but the sentence before it as well. The previous sentence lists one source of dietary sodium. The sentence containing the underlined segment lists *another source*. Therefore, the appropriate connection here is one that expresses addition or continuation. Choice (C) is the only answer choice that expresses continuation, so it's the correct answer. Eliminate (A) and (B) because they're Contrast Connections. Eliminate (D) because it indicates an example rather than addition or continuation.

4. I would have called you, <u>rather</u> I couldn't because I lost my cell phone.

    F. NO CHANGE

    G. but

    H. moreover

    J. while

Here, ask yourself how losing the cell phone is related to not calling. The writer is saying that *if* she'd had her cell phone, she would have called. Not having the phone prevented the calling; therefore, the appropriate connection here is *contrast*. This question illustrates the importance of reading the answer choices into the sentence. Notice that (F), *rather*, is indeed a Contrast Connection, but it doesn't sound right here. Choice (J), *while*, is also a Contrast Connection that doesn't work in the context. Choice (G) is a Contrast Connection that fits perfectly in the context, and it's the correct answer. Eliminate (H) because it's not a Contrast Connection.

Once you learn to recognize the various Connections words, you should have no trouble with Connections questions on the ACT. Just let the presence of any underlined Connections word remind you to consider the kind of logical relationship expressed in the sentence. Don't worry if a question includes more than one choice in the right category of connections. If that's the case, use your ear to determine which one is appropriate.

WRITING STRATEGY—4 POINTS

Complexity: High. Based on rhetorical skills. Relates to: None. This is a stand-alone SmartPoint.

The last two SmartPoints on the English test are the most complex (Writing Strategy and Organization). Each will always have a question stem (text between the question number and multiple-choice answers stating exactly what is being asked), and you'll need to read further for more information to properly answer these questions. Remember the first step of the Kaplan Method—read until you have enough information to identify the issue. For these two question types, you'll have to consider more of the passage, or the passage as a whole, in order to understand the author's purpose and methods.

But fear not! Though these questions seem intimidating, there are effective strategies to deal with both. The big three for the English test—*correct*, *concise*, and *relevant*—still very much apply.

We'll start with the more common of the two—Writing Strategy.

Writing Strategy questions ask you to choose what kind of phrasing most effectively accomplishes a particular purpose. The most important thing you need to do is to *consider the question stem carefully!* This type of question can ask for a number of different answers, so when you read the question stem, think about what the particular question is asking for. When you focus clearly on what the question is asking, the best answer will usually stand out among the offered choices.

In the following question, underline the key words in the stem *before* looking at the answer choices:

The biologist <u>worked painstakingly for</u>
                                    1
<u>more than a year</u> before her research project
           1
yielded any publishable results.

1. Which of the following choices most effectively conveys that the biologist relied on cooperation with other scientists?

   A. NO CHANGE
   B. needed to discuss methodology with her colleagues
   C. planned many experiments
   D. needed to order several pieces of costly equipment

If you focused on the words *conveys that the biologist relied on cooperation with other scientists,* it's likely that (B) jumped out as the best answer, as the only one that discusses other scientists. Choices (A), (C), and (D) are not incorrect for any grammatical reasons, but they do not fulfill the purpose identified by this question stem. It's helpful to know that, for Writing Strategy questions, the test maker doesn't put ungrammatical or otherwise incorrect language in the answer choices. So if you read through the answer choices looking for what sounds best, you won't get very far. The question stem of a Writing Strategy question is crucial, so read it carefully before you look at the answer choices.

Writing Strategy questions for which you will *not* find a key phrase in the question stem are questions that ask about the effect of adding or deleting a certain phrase or sentence. For questions that ask about deletion, focus on the given phrase, asking yourself what effect it creates for you as a reader. Consider the following example:

The construction site was littered with debris. Scraps of wood, drywall, and various types of nails were scattered on the ground. Even large sheets of roofing materials, some still packaged as they came from the supplier, were lying against the unfinished exterior walls. [2]

2. The author is considering deleting the following sentence:

    Scraps of wood, drywall, and various types of nails were scattered on the ground.

    What would be lost if the author made this deletion?

    F. Information about how long the building site had been unattended
    G. A description of what materials are needed in construction
    H. A suggestion about how to clean the site
    J. Specific details that provide information about what the site looks like

To answer this question, consider the given sentence in the context of the passage. The previous sentence describes the site as *littered with debris*, and the sentence in question lists items that make up that debris. Because it offers specific details describing the debris, (J) is the right answer. If you focus on the given sentence's relation to the sentences around it and how it adds to your understanding of the author's purpose, you shouldn't fall for the wrong answer traps.

Again, for Writing Strategy questions that ask about the effect of deleting information, *consider the context and determine how the information contributes to the writer's purpose.*

ORGANIZATION—1 POINT

Complexity: High. Based on rhetorical skills. Relates to: None. This is a stand-alone SmartPoint.

Organization questions test your understanding of logical sequence in a passage. It's easy to recognize an Organization question because it will involve sentences or paragraphs that are labeled with bracketed numbers in the passage. Some Organization questions ask you to rearrange the order of the sentences within the paragraph or the order of the paragraphs within the whole passage. Other Organization questions present a sentence to be *added* to the passage, and then ask you to determine the best location for the new sentence.

The important thing to keep in mind about Organization questions is that *they are based on logic*. The ACT won't present an Organization question unless there is a clearly discernible logical order to the particular paragraph or passage. Each question on the ACT can have only one possible correct answer, these included. Therefore, the way to succeed with an Organization question is first to recognize that it's testing logical sequence, and then search carefully in the passage for particular words and phrases that provide the key to the correct sequence.

Sometimes a passage is organized according to a rough outline structure. For example, in a passage on nutrition, you might find separate paragraphs that discuss proteins, carbohydrates, fats, and antioxidants. If you were asked where to add a sentence about the antioxidant potential of a particular fruit, you'd put it in the fourth paragraph—the one focusing on antioxidants. Remember to use your reading skills to help you find the best answer to a question like that.

Another organizational format is the chronological sequence. As you read through an English passage that includes an organization question, be alert for specific dates and time references, such as *in 1750* or *before the American Revolution*. Dates and time references can serve as key clues when you need to determine the best location to add new information.

Another format similar to the chronological one is the description of stages in a process. As you read, notice words such as *first, second, then, next, last,* and *finally*. These words serve as clues to help you keep track of sequencing and can be useful if you need to find the best spot in the passage to add information.

As you work on this ACT-like Organization question, underline key words that help you determine the logical sequence:

[1] If you're like most people, you may find that applying to college is a complicated process. [2] This in itself can be time-consuming; you need to search through guidebooks, learn about colleges from their websites, and talk to admissions officers at college fairs. [3] You also need to take standardized tests and continue to maintain your high school grade point average. [4] Then, by the fall of your senior year, you must actually start filling out applications and arranging to have supporting documentation sent to the colleges.

1. Upon reviewing the paragraph and realizing that some information has been left out, the writer composes the following sentence:

   The first challenge is to narrow down a list of places you'd like to study.

   The most logical placement for this sentence would be:

   A. before sentence 1.
   B. after sentence 1.
   C. after sentence 2.
   D. after sentence 3.

Did you find any words to underline in the paragraph? The word *then* in sentence 4 is one indicator of sequence. The sentence to be added, which is stated in the question stem, also contains a sequence clue: *first*. This word indicates that the sentence should most likely be added somewhere near the beginning of the paragraph. To find the right place, plug the new sentence into the passage at the locations described by the answer choices, and think about how it sounds in each context. Notice that sentence 1 introduces the topic of the paragraph. Therefore, it wouldn't make sense to place the additional sentence before that. Read the new sentence *after* sentence 1, and continue reading sentence 2. The additional sentence fits perfectly here because sentence 2 lists several things that must be done in order to *narrow down a list of places*, as the new sentence introduces. You can quickly plug the sentence in at the other locations if you have time, but you should feel pretty confident that you've found the right answer in (B).

The *sentences* in that last passage were numbered. When you notice that a whole passage is presented with numbered paragraphs (the numbers will be in brackets, centered above each paragraph), be aware as you're working through the passage that the paragraphs may not be printed in the most logical order. The other possibility when a passage is printed with numbered paragraphs is that a question will ask where it is most appropriate to add extra information. If a question asks you to add a paragraph, the existing paragraphs will be printed in the most logical order, and you will not see a scrambled paragraphs question for this passage.

For an Organization question that asks you to determine the best ordering of paragraphs, there are several points you should consider. First, glance at each paragraph to determine its topic. You might want to make a brief note in the margin or circle a word or phrase in each paragraph to help you identify the main idea. Second, ask yourself which of the paragraphs sounds like it would make the best introduction to the passage. Third, ask yourself which paragraph sounds most like a concluding paragraph. Usually, simply identifying the most logical introductory and concluding paragraphs is enough to determine the best sequence for all the paragraphs. Sometimes you may have to consider the topics and relationships among the body paragraphs as well.

Consider the following scrambled paragraphs question. Even though we give you only the skeleton of a passage to work with, you should be able to find clues that allow you to determine the best sequence for the paragraphs.

[1]

Carbohydrates in food…

[2]

Protein comes from several sources…

[3]

With each passing decade, scientists learn more about how the components of food affect our health. Nutrition researchers have been aware of the basic building blocks, fats, carbohydrates, and proteins, for years. Fats are…

[4]

While nutritionists have been studying the three building blocks of food for years, they frequently turn their attention to new areas. Cholesterol, for example, came to the attention of nutritionists in the 1970s. It was discovered that heart disease…

[5]

In another development in nutrition, antioxidants began creating a stir in 2000 when…

Question 2 asks about the preceding passage as a whole.

2. For the sake of logic and coherence, paragraph 3 should be placed:

    F. where it is now.

    G. before paragraph 1.

    H. after paragraph 1.

    J. after paragraph 5.

Remember, an Organization question is testing your reading skills. Start by thinking about how paragraph 3 relates to the topics of the other paragraphs. Paragraph 1 discusses carbohydrates, paragraph 2 discusses proteins, paragraph 4 treats cholesterol, and paragraph 5 starts with antioxidants. Now read paragraph 3 carefully. Notice the second sentence: it mentions *carbohydrates* and *proteins,* topics of two of the other paragraphs. Therefore, paragraph 3 would make a good first paragraph because it introduces, at least partially, the rough outline structure of the passage. The right answer is (G).

PUTTING IT ALL TOGETHER

Think of this next section as a quiz we'll work on together.

We've now gone through every SmartPoint you'll ever see on the ACT English Test. But the truth is, on Test Day, they won't be categorized and organized one by one—all SmartPoints will be grouped together within a passage. This next passage will do just that—put everything together, just like on Test Day.

From there, we'll show you how to take the passage apart again, identify the questions you see, and use the strategies from this chapter to deal with them.

Walk through this dress rehearsal with us, and let's see exactly how you can put your newfound skills and strategies into practice in a full passage.

PASSAGE I

ROBINSON CRUSOE: FICTION AND FACT

Most people—even those who've never read Daniel

Defoe's *Robinson Crusoe*—are familiar with the strange

story of the sailor shipwrecked on a far-flung Pacific

island. Relatively few of them, however, know that

Crusoe's <u>story. It was</u> actually based on the real-life
   1

1. A. NO CHANGE

    B. story: was

    C. story, was

    D. story was

adventures of a Scottish seaman, Alexander Selkirk.

Selkirk came to the Pacific as a member of a 1703

privateering expedition led by a captain named William

Dampier. During the voyage, Selkirk became dissatisfied

with conditions aboard the ship.

<u>After a bitter quarrel with his captain, he put Sel-</u>
<u>kirk ashore</u> on tiny Mas a Tierra, one of the islands of
Juan Fernandez, off the coast of Chile.

    Stranded, Selkirk lived there alone—in much the

<u>same manner as</u> Defoe's Crusoe—until 1709, when he
was finally rescued by another English privateer. Upon

his return to England, Selkirk found himself a <u>celebrity,</u>
<u>his</u> strange tale had already become the talk of pubs and
coffeehouses throughout the British Isles. The story even

reached the ears of Richard Steele, who featured it in his

periodical, *The Tatler*. Eventually, <u>he became</u> the subject
of a best-selling book, *A Cruizing Voyage Round the*

World, by Woodes Rogers. <u>While</u> there is some evidence
that Defoe, a journalist, may actually have interviewed

Selkirk personally, most literary historians believe that

it was the reprinting of the Rogers book in 1718 that

served as the real stimulus for Defoe's novel.

2. F. NO CHANGE
   G. Quarreling with his captain, the boat was put ashore
   H. Having quarreled with his captain, Selkirk was put ashore
   J. Having quarreled with his captain, they put Selkirk ashore

3. A. NO CHANGE
   B. same manner that
   C. identical manner that
   D. identical way as

4. F. NO CHANGE
   G. celebrity, but his
   H. celebrity. His
   J. celebrity his

5. A. NO CHANGE
   B. Selkirk became
   C. his became
   D. he becomes

6. F. NO CHANGE
   G. But since
   H. And therefore
   J. OMIT the underlined portion, and start the sentence with *There*.

In *Crusoe*, which <u>has been published</u> in 1719, Defoe
                        7
took substantial liberties with the Selkirk story. For

example, while Selkirk's presence on the island was of

course <u>known for many people</u> (certainly everyone in
            8
the crew that stranded him there), no one in the novel

is aware of Crusoe's survival of the wreck and presence

on the island. Moreover, while Selkirk's exile lasted just

six years, Crusoe's goes on for a much more dramatic,

though less credible, twenty-eight <u>(over four times as</u>
                                          9
<u>long)</u>.
  9
    However, Defoe's most blatant embellishment of the

tale is the invention of the character of Friday, for whom

there was no counterpart whatsoever in the real-life

story.

    <u>Because of</u> its basis in fact, *Robinson Crusoe* is often
       10
regarded as the first major novel in English literature.

<u>Still popular today, contemporary audiences enjoyed</u>
                              11
<u>the book as well.</u>
        11

    In fact, two sequels, in which Crusoe returns to

the island after his rescue, were eventually <u>published.</u>
                                                   12
<u>Though</u> to little acclaim. Meanwhile, Selkirk himself
  12

7. A. NO CHANGE
    B. was published
    C. had been published
    D. will have been published

8. F. NO CHANGE
    G. widely known among people
    H. known about many people
    J. known to many people

9. A. NO CHANGE
    B. (much longer)
    C. (a much longer time, of course)
    D. OMIT the underlined portion.

10. F. NO CHANGE
    G. Despite
    H. Resulting from
    J. As a consequence of

11. A. NO CHANGE
    B. Still read today, Defoe's contemporaries
        also enjoyed it.
    C. Enjoyed by many even then, the book is
        still popular to this day.
    D. Much read in its day, modern audiences
        still find the book compelling.

12. F. NO CHANGE
    G. published, though
    H. published although
    J. published; although

never <u>gave a hoot about returning</u> to the island that had
                    13
made him famous.

Legend has it that he never gave up his eccentric living habits, spending his last years in a cave teaching alley cats to dance in his spare time. One wonders if even Defoe himself could have invented a more fitting end to the bizarre story of his shipwrecked sailor.

13. A. NO CHANGE
    B. evinced himself as desirous of returning
    C. could whip up a head of steam to return
    D. expressed any desire to return

Questions 14–15 ask about the preceding passage as a whole.

14. Considering the tone and subject matter of the preceding paragraphs, is the last sentence an appropriate way to end the essay?

    F. Yes, because it is necessary to shed some doubt on Defoe's creativity.

    G. Yes, because the essay is about the relationship between the real Selkirk and Defoe's fictionalized version of him.

    H. No, because there is nothing "bizarre" about Selkirk's story as it is related in the essay.

    J. No, because the focus of the essay is more on Selkirk himself than on Defoe's fictionalized version of him.

15. This essay would be most appropriate as part of a:

    A. scholarly study of 18th-century maritime history.

    B. study of the geography of the islands off of Chile.

    C. history of privateering in the Pacific.

    D. popular history of English literature.

[1] Only recently has new evidence led many scientists to question the accepted division between birds and dinosaurs. [2] Traditionally, they have been placed in entirely separate classes within the subphylum *Vertebrata*. [3] Birds and dinosaurs don't have many obvious similarities. [4] Birds formed the class *Aves*, while dinosaurs constituted two orders, *Saurischia* and *Ornithischia*, within the class *Reptilia*.

16. To best fulfill the author's purpose, the order of the sentences in the paragraph should be:

    F. 1, 2, 3, 4.

    G. 2, 3, 4, 1.

    H. 3, 2, 4, 1.

    J. 3, 2, 1, 4.

ANSWERS AND EXPLANATIONS

1. **D**	9. **D**
2. **H**	10. **G**
3. **A**	11. **C**
4. **H**	12. **G**
5. **B**	13. **D**
6. **F**	14. **G**
7. **B**	15. **D**
8. **J**	16. **H**

The following explanations are not in numerical order, but grouped by SmartPoints. Again, this is meant to be a walkthrough, and we do this to help you better understand the concepts behind the questions. The more easily you can spot the SmartPoint—the concept the ACT requires you to understand to answer the question correctly—the more confident you'll feel on Test Day.

SMARTPOINT—SENTENCE SENSE (INCLUDING PUNCTUATION)

Questions 1, 12, 4

Question 1

Rule at work: Every sentence must contain a subject and a predicate verb and express a complete thought.

…Relatively few of them, however, know that

Crusoe's <u>story. It was</u> actually based on the real-
        1
life adventures of a Scottish seaman, Alexander

Selkirk.

1. A. NO CHANGE
     B. story: was
     C. story, was
     D. story was

If the underlined section for Question 1 were left as it is, the second sentence of the passage would be incomplete. *Relatively few people know that Crusoe's story* what? To make it make sense, you need to continue the sentence so it can tell us what few people know about Crusoe's story. The three alternatives all do that, but choice (B) introduces an unnecessary colon, while choice (C) adds a comma when there's no pause in the sentence. Choice (D), however, continues the sentence—adding nothing unnecessary but making it complete.

When you are testing a sentence for completeness, don't just look to see if it has a subject and verb—make sure it represents a complete thought.

Question 12

…In fact, two sequels, in which Crusoe returns

to the island after his rescue, were eventually

published. Though to little acclaim.
     12

12.   F.   NO CHANGE
           G.   published, though
           H.   published although
           J.   published; although

Here, the fragment should be more obvious, since the clause that's trying to pass itself off as a sentence—*Though to little acclaim*—contains neither a subject nor a verb. That's the technical reason it's wrong, and if you recognized this immediately, it saved you time.

Clearly, that fragment has to be connected to the sentence before it, so choices (F) and (J) are wrong, since both would leave the fragment isolated. Choice (H) goes too far in the other direction, omitting any punctuation at all between the fragment and the main body of the sentence. The correct choice, (G), does just what we need it to do: it connects the fragment logically to the main sentence and provides a comma to represent the pause between the two clauses.

Question 4

Rule at work: A sentence can have two thoughts, but they must be combined correctly (see below). If none of the answer choices do this, select the choice that creates two separate sentences.

…Upon his return to England, Selkirk found

himself a celebrity, his strange tale had already
             4
become the talk of pubs and coffeehouses

throughout the British Isles.

4.   F.   NO CHANGE
        G.   celebrity, but his
        H.   celebrity. His
        J.   celebrity his

Here we have two complete thoughts: (1) Selkirk found himself a celebrity upon his return, and (2) his tale was popular in pubs and coffeehouses. You can't just run these two complete thoughts together with a comma, as the underlined portion does, and you certainly can't just run them together *without* a comma or anything else, as choice (J) does. You can relate the two thoughts with a comma and a linking word (*and*, for instance), but the word *but* in choice (G) makes no sense. It implies a contrast, while the two complete thoughts are actually very similar. Thus, you should create two sentences, one for each thought, as correct choice (H) does.

Rule at work: There are three ways to connect complete thoughts:

1. Use a semicolon.

2. Use a comma with a FANBOYS (*For, And, Nor, But, Or, Yet, So*) conjunction.

3. Make one of the two thoughts *in*complete (or dependent).

Working with these three possibilities for question 4, you might have seen any of these correct answer choices:

1. Selkirk found himself a celebrity; his strange tale had already…

2. Selkirk found himself a celebrity, *for* his strange tale had already…

3. Selkirk found himself a celebrity *because* his strange tale had already…

SMARTPOINT—VERB TENSE

Question 7

Rules at work: (for all verbs)

1. Use the simplest tense if possible. In most cases, the present, past, and future tenses are all you need.

2. Change tenses only if the sentence doesn't make sense as written.

3. Make sure the verb is singular if it has a singular subject and plural if the subject is plural.

Verbs have an annoying habit of changing form depending on who's doing the action and when that person is doing it. Example: "I *hate* verbs, he *hates* verbs, and we both *have hated* verbs ever since we were kids." You have to be very careful to make sure verbs match their subject and the tense of the surrounding context.

…In *Crusoe*, which <u>has been published</u> in 1719,
                                    7
Defoe took substantial liberties with the Selkirk

story.

7. A. NO CHANGE
   B. was published
   C. had been published
   D. will have been published

The publication of *Robinson Crusoe* took place in 1719—the past, in other words. So the underlined portion, which puts the verb in the present perfect tense, is flawed. Choices (C) and (D), meanwhile, put the verb into tenses normally used to convey a complex time relationship. Choice (C) makes it seem as if publication of the book happened before Defoe took his liberties with the story, but that's nonsensical. Choice (D), meanwhile, does strange things with the time sequence. The book was published in the past; Defoe also took his substantial liberties in the same past. So just use the simple past tense, choice (B).

SMARTPOINT—WORD CHOICE: PRONOUNS

Question 5

Rule at work: A pronoun must agree with the person or thing it is referring to, in person, gender, and number (singular or plural). The reference must be clear; if there is *any* confusion, the sentence must be fixed.

Sometimes the test will throw you a sentence in which the meaning of a pronoun is unclear. You won't be sure to whom or what the pronoun is referring. That's the kind of problem you were given in question 5.

…The story even reached the ears of Richard

Steele, who featured it in his periodical, *The*

Tatler. Eventually, <u>became</u> the subject of a best-
                        5
selling book…

5. A. NO CHANGE
    B. Selkirk became
    C. his became
    D. he becomes

The *intended* meaning of the pronoun *he* here is Selkirk. But what's the closest male name to the pronoun? Richard Steele, publisher of *The Tatler*. Your job is to make it clear whom the pronoun is referring to. Choice (B) takes care of the problem by naming Selkirk explicitly. Choice (C) would create a sense problem—his *what* became the subject of a book? Meanwhile, (D) shifts the verb tense into the present, which makes no sense since this book was written over 250 years ago!

Mistakes of sense often involve pronouns. Make a habit of checking every underlined pronoun as you go along. To what or whom does the pronoun refer? Can you tell? If not, there's an error. Does the reference make sense? If not, there's an error. Make sure it's perfectly clear to what or to whom all pronouns refer.

SMARTPOINT—WORD CHOICE: MODIFIERS

Questions 2, 11

Question 2

Rule at work: A modifier is any word or group of words that describes another. Any and all modifiers must clearly relate to (and be close to) whatever they are describing.

…<u>After a bitter quarrel with his captain, he put</u>
                        2
<u>Selkirk ashore</u> on tiny Mas a Tierra, one of the
        2
islands of Juan Fernandez.

2. F. NO CHANGE
    G. Quarreling with his captain, the boat was put ashore
    H. Having quarreled with his captain, Selkirk was put ashore
    J. Having quarreled with his captain, they put Selkirk ashore

Sentences become confused if a descriptive word, phrase, or clause is separated from the verb, noun, or pronoun that it should be connected to. In the underlined portion of question 2, the phrase *after a bitter quarrel with his captain* should describe the person (or pronoun) that follows next. It doesn't.

The *he* who put Selkirk ashore must be the captain, but it can't be the captain who had *a bitter quarrel with his captain*. That doesn't make sense (unless the captain quarrels with himself). The thing being modified has to be next to the thing modifying it. The person who quarreled with his captain was Selkirk—not the boat and not *they*, whoever *they* are—so choice (H) is correct.

If you recognized the problem with question 2 as a misplaced modifier, that's great and saved you time. However, you didn't have to know the technicalities to get the right answer here. You just had to make the sentence make sense.

Question 11

…<u>Still popular today, contemporary audiences</u>
                                        11
<u>enjoyed the book as well.</u>
              11

11. A. NO CHANGE
    B. Still read today, Defoe's contemporaries also enjoyed it.
    C. Enjoyed by many even then, the book is still popular to this day.
    D. Much read in its day, modern audiences still find the book compelling.

Because of the placement of the noun next to the modifying introduction, the sentence means that contemporary audiences are *still popular today*. That doesn't make sense. The *intended* meaning is that the book is still popular today, as it was then. Choice (C) fixes the sense problem by putting its modifier—*viewed by many even then as a classic*—next to the thing it modifies—*the book*. Notice that the other choices all misplace their modifiers in the same way—they modify *Defoe's contemporaries* in (B) and *modern audiences* in (D).

As a rule of thumb, you should *always* make sure that modifiers are as close as possible to the things they describe.

SMARTPOINT—WORD CHOICE: IDIOMS

Questions 3, 8

Question 3

Rule at work: The correct preposition can vary depending on the sense of the sentence. Many phrases in English are correct because people have agreed to use them in a certain way—no overall rules apply. To master these, listen to what sounds right, or if English is not your native language, study the most common English idioms.

...Stranded, Selkirk lived there alone—in much

the <u>same manner as</u> Defoe's Crusoe—until 1709,
        3
when he was finally rescued by another...

3. A. NO CHANGE
      B. same manner that
      C. identical manner that
      D. identical way as

The sentence as written actually makes sense. Selkirk lived in *much the same manner as* Defoe's Crusoe. The idiom *much the same* calls for *as* to complete the comparison between Selkirk's and Crusoe's ways of life. Note how choices (B) and (C) would create completeness problems—in *much the same* (or *identical*) *manner* that Defoe's Crusoe what? Choice (D), meanwhile, sounds strange. In English, we just don't say *in much the identical way as* because the word *identical* is an absolute. You can't be more or partially identical; you either are or aren't identical to something else. Even if you didn't analyze choice (D) this carefully, it should have just sounded wrong to your ear.

Question 8

...For example, while Selkirk's presence on the

island was of course <u>known for many people</u>
                      8
(certainly everyone in the crew that stranded

him there), no one in the novel is aware of

Crusoe's survival of the wreck and presence on

the island.

8. F. NO CHANGE
      G. widely known among people
      H. known about many people
      J. known to many people

The underlined portion as written is unidiomatic. Selkirk's presence wasn't known *for* many people—it was known *by*, or known *to*, many people. When you're known *for* something, you have a reputation for doing something, which makes no sense in this context. Choice (J) *does* make sense, since it points out that Selkirk's presence on the island was known *to* many people—that is, it was something many people knew about. Choice (G) is unidiomatic; we just wouldn't say *among people* here, since it's not specific enough. That sounds as if we're talking about people as a species. Choice (H) would have been acceptable if it had read *known about* by *many people*, but without the *by*, the correction just wouldn't make sense.

Idioms may be difficult if English is not your first language. You have to think very carefully about the meaning of every word. But if you *are* a native speaker, use your many years of hearing English as a guide. Choose the correction that makes sense.

SMARTPOINT—CONNECTIONS

Questions 10, 6

Question 10

Think about words like *therefore, despite, however,* and *because*. Such words are structural clues—they serve as signposts in the passage to let you know where the author is going and how all of the pieces logically fit together. If the author uses the structural clue *on the other hand*, that means a contrast is coming up; if he or she uses the clue *moreover*, that means that a continuation is coming up—an addition that is more or less in the same vein as what came before.

Remember to refer to the chart on page 96 for a full list of frequently used Connections words listed by category.

…<u>Because of</u> its basis in fact, *Robinson Crusoe* is
     10

often regarded as the first major novel in English

literature.

10. F. NO CHANGE
    G. Despite
    H. Resulting from
    J. As a consequence of

As written, this sentence means that *Crusoe* was regarded as the first major novel because it was based on fact. But that makes no sense. Being based on fact would work against its being regarded as a novel. There's a *contrast* between *basis in fact* (which implies nonfiction) and *first major novel* (which implies fiction). To show that contrast logically, you need a contrast word like *despite*, which only choice (G) provides.

Question 6

….the subject of a best-selling book, *A Cruizing*

Voyage Round the World, by Woodes Rogers.

<u>While</u> there is some evidence that Defoe, a
  6

journalist, may actually have interviewed Selkirk

personally, most literary historians believe that

it was the reprinting of the Rogers book in 1718

that served as the real stimulus for Defoe's novel.

6. F. NO CHANGE
    G. But since
    H. And therefore
    J. OMIT the underlined portion, and start the sentence with *There.*

The structural clue should convey a sense of contrast with the previous sentence. Even though Defoe may have interviewed Selkirk, many believe Defoe's main source was the book by Rogers. *While* provides the needed contrast, making NO CHANGE the correct answer. Choices (G) and (H) have *since* and *therefore,* cause-and-effect words, which make no sense in context. Choice (J) omits a key word and creates a run-on sentence. Remember, don't pick OMIT simply because it's there! It's correct a lot of the time, but not always.

SMARTPOINT—WRITING STRATEGY

Questions 13, 14, 15

Question 13

Rule at work: Every ACT English passage has a voice, or tone. This voice is usually either casual (conversational) or factual (informational). Be sure to make choices that fit the author's voice.

If a passage contains slang, a few exclamation points, and a joke or two, the tone is informal; if it sounds like something from a textbook, the tone is probably formal.

Good style requires that the tone of a piece of writing be the same throughout. Sometimes the underlined portion might not fit the tone of the rest of the passage. If so, it's up to you to correct it.

…Meanwhile, Selkirk himself never <u>gave a hoot about returning</u> to the island that had made him famous.

13. A. NO CHANGE
    B. evinced himself as desirous of returning
    C. could whip up a head of steam to return
    D. expressed any desire to return

Selkirk *never gave a hoot* about going back? No way! There is no other slang in this passage, so it doesn't belong here. Choose (D) because it uses a straightforward, factual tone that fits the passage. Choice (B) is too wordy and formal. Choice (C) is also slang.

Question 14

This question asks about the passage as a whole. Keep in mind the main point of the passage as well as the overall tone and style. For an entire passage to make sense, it has to be consistent throughout, both in content and in tone and style.

14. Considering the tone and subject matter of the preceding paragraphs, is the last sentence an appropriate way to end the essay?

    F. Yes, because it is necessary to shed some doubt on Defoe's creativity.

    G. Yes, because the essay is about the relationship between the real Selkirk and Defoe's fictionalized version of him.

    H. No, because there is nothing bizarre about Selkirk's story as it is related in the essay.

    J. No, because the focus of the essay is more on Selkirk himself than on Defoe's fictionalized version of him.

Think of the passage as a whole. It has been comparing Selkirk's real life with the one that Defoe made up for the character of Robinson Crusoe. Therefore, ending in this way, with an ironic reference wondering whether Defoe could have written a more fitting end to Selkirk's life, is perfectly appropriate. The answer to the question is "yes," which eliminates choices (H) and (J). Choice (G) restates the point of the passage and is the correct answer.

Question 15

If you thought question 15 looked like a Reading question hiding in the English part of the exam, you were right. One reason that you should keep thinking about what the passage means—rather than focusing only on grammar or punctuation rules—is that **the English section includes some questions that test your reading comprehension skills.**

15. This essay would be most appropriate as part of a

    A. scholarly study of 18th-century maritime history.
    B. study of the geography of the islands off of Chile.
    C. history of privateering in the Pacific.
    D. popular history of English literature.

What was this passage principally about? How Defoe's *Robinson Crusoe* was loosely based on the life of a real shipwrecked sailor, Alexander Selkirk. Would that kind of thing belong in a study of geography, (B)? No—the focus is on the fictionalization of a historical person's life, not on the physical features of the islands off Chile. The passage isn't principally about privateering or maritime history either, so choices (C) and (A) are wrong as well. This passage is about the relationship between a true story and a famous fictionalized story. Its tone isn't overly scholarly, so it probably belongs in a popular history of English literature, making choice (D) the right answer.

SMARTPOINT—ORGANIZATION

Question 16

The English section will also have questions that test your grasp of overall structure and purpose in a piece of prose. The test scrambles the order of the sentences in a paragraph (or of the paragraphs in a passage), then asks you to decide on the best order for the scrambled parts. Take a look at this new question:

[1] Only recently has new evidence led many scientists to question the accepted division between birds and dinosaurs. [2] Traditionally, they have been placed in entirely separate classes within the subphylum *Vertebrata*. [3] Birds and dinosaurs don't have many obvious similarities. [4] Birds formed the class *Aves*, while dinosaurs constituted two orders, *Saurischia* and *Ornithischia*, within the class *Reptilia*.

3. To best fulfill the author's purpose, the order of the sentences in the paragraph should be

F. 1, 2, 3, 4.

G. 2, 3, 4, 1.

H. 3, 2, 4, 1.

J. 3, 2, 1, 4.

Here again, the goal is to make it make sense. All of the sentences in this paragraph relate to the differences between birds and dinosaurs. Sentence 3 best introduces this idea, making that the strongest choice for the first sentence. Notice that two of the answer choices begin with sentence 3—(H) and (J). The other two can be eliminated.

Now look again at the logic of the sentences. Because sentence 4 elaborates on the distinction introduced in sentence 2, sentence 4 should immediately follow sentence 2. Only choice (H) has them in that order, so (H) looks like the correct answer.

Just to check, you'll want to read the entire paragraph in the order suggested by choice (H). And if you do, you'll notice that the paragraph makes perfect sense, with sentence 3 introducing the topic, sentences 2 and 4 showing how that topic has been traditionally viewed, and sentence 1 coming in to show how that traditional view is no longer valid.

For questions like this, it's usually a good idea to start by trying to figure out the first (and sometimes the last) sentence, because first and last sentences usually have the most obvious functions in ACT-style paragraphs.

SUMMARY

In this chapter, we went over every SmartPoint and question type you will encounter on the ACT English test. Use this chapter for continued study and reference as you practice English passages and find the skills you need to focus on. Remember: SmartPoints can be organized into grammar-based and rhetorical skills categories.

Grammar-based SmartPoints are:

- Sentence Sense

- Punctuation

- Verb Tense

- Word Choice

Each of these SmartPoints is based on outside knowledge that can be found in the Grammar and Punctuation Rules to Know section on page 56.

The knowledge necessary to master these questions builds from one to the next. If you are struggling with any of these SmartPoints, you should spend more time studying the SmartPoints listed above it as well.

Word Choice has some questions that are based on Rhetorical Skills as well.

The primary *Rhetorical Skills* SmartPoints are:

- Wordiness

- Connections

- Writing Strategy

- Organization

These questions don't require any outside knowledge and don't build off of each other, but they are more complex and often require you to read and understand more of the passage. For these questions, the first step of the Kaplan Method—read until you have enough information—goes beyond the question itself. These Rhetorical Skills questions require you to read through the underlined portion, instead of simply skipping to the sentence with the underlined portion.

When you're ready, move on to the next chapter and try out the English Quiz. Check how you do, SmartPoint by SmartPoint, then come back to this chapter to polish the skills you need.

As always, when deciding on an answer in English, remember the big three: *correct, concise,* and *relevant*!

CHAPTER 6

English Part 3: ACT English Quiz

Showtime!

Treat the following quizzes like the passages you'll encounter on Test Day and see how you do. Make sure to check your answers *after you've completed each passage.* Don't check as you go—you need to start focusing on pacing and timing, and if you review each as you go, you'll either encourage or discourage yourself in a way that won't occur on Test Day.

Keep track of your time, using the guide from the beginning of the English section of this book. Remember to aim for nine minutes on each passage, including all questions. It's okay if you're not there yet; plenty of other English passages are waiting for you in the practice tests later in this book. But make sure you take note so you know what to work on next.

Finally, when checking your answers, take note of the SmartPoints of the questions you miss in particular. Use these quizzes to help you find where to really focus your studying before you move on to those practice tests at the end of the book.

Remember the Kaplan Method—read, eliminate, and find the answer that best fits the big three: *correct*, *concise*, and *relevant*!

ENGLISH QUIZ: PASSAGE 1

Directions: In the following passage, certain words and phrases have been underlined and numbered. You will find alternatives for each underlined portion in the column to the right. Select the one that best expresses the idea, that makes the statement acceptable in standard written English, or that is phrased most consistently with the style and tone of the entire passage. If you feel that the original version is best, select "NO CHANGE." You will also find questions asking about a section of the passage or about the entire passage. For these questions, decide which choice gives the most appropriate response to the given question. For each question in the test, select the best choice, and fill in the corresponding space on the answer folder. You may wish to read each passage through before you begin to answer the questions associated with it. Most answers cannot be determined without reading several sentences around the phrases in question. Make sure to read far enough ahead each time you choose an alternative.

THE WEDDING CAKE HOUSE

Locals in Kennebunk, Maine, have built up a legend around an unusually 19th-century house in that seaside town.

1. A. NO CHANGE
   B. a house unusually of the 19th century
   C. a house unusual of the 19th century
   D. an unusual 19th-century house

In contrast to the frothy white ornamentation that covers much of the house's exterior, it is known as the Wedding Cake House. Building on this name,

2. F. NO CHANGE
   G. Because of
   H. Despite
   J. A consequence of

the wooden carvings were made, the legend suggests, by a newly-wed sea captain, who plied his woodworking talent

3. A. NO CHANGE
   B. a newly-wed sea captain, the legend suggests, made the wooden carvings
   C. the legend suggests that the elaborate wooden carvings were made by a newly-wed sea captain
   D. it has been suggested according to the legend that the wooden carvings were made by a newly-wed sea captain

<u>during lonely hours at sea</u> to surprise his bride upon
        4

his return home.

4. The author is considering deleting the underlined phrase. If this deletion were made, the essay would primarily lose:

   F. a fact that describes the house.

   G. a detail that enhances the romantic nature of the legend.

   H. relevant information about the sea captain's job.

   J. a historical detail.

       The <u>reality is that the</u> truth about the house
               5

departs from the appealing legend about the lovelorn

sailor. The owner of the house, shipbuilder George

Washington

5. A. NO CHANGE

   B. reality of the situation is that

   C. actual honest

   D. OMIT the underlined portion.

<u>Bourne, brought his bride, Jane,</u> to the house in 1825.
           6

The original house was an example of the balance and

6. F. NO CHANGE

   G. Bourne, brought, his bride Jane,

   H. Bourne brought his bride Jane,

   J. Bourne brought his bride, Jane

<u>typifying symmetry on</u> the Federalist architecture of
         7

the time. The two-story house, with a low hipped roof,

multiple large casement windows spanning the front

facade, and <u>the area above the front door taken up by</u>
                  8

<u>a large Palladian window</u>, exemplified geometrical bal-
         8

ance. The elaborate frosting-like designs

7. A. NO CHANGE

   B. symmetry that was typical on

   C. symmetrical type of

   D. symmetry that typified

8. F. NO CHANGE

   G. a large Palladian window occupying the area above the front door

   H. the area above the front door being occupied by a large Palladian window

   J. taking up the area by above the front door, a large Palladian window

being a later addition to this neoclassical house, though
9
they didn't come about in the way the romantic legend

describes.

[1] The transformation of the house from an

example of neoclassic restraint to a building with so

many Gothic overlays that it looked like a wedding cake

resulting from an accident. [2] In 1852,
10

a fire destroyed the barn and shed that were outside the
11
house. [3] The shipbuilder, now retired,

decided on spending his leisure hours carving wooden
12
trim that he could apply to the main house so that its

style, on the surface at least,

would harmonize with the style of his new Gothic barn.
13
[4] Thus, the Wedding Cake House is technically not

an example of the Gothic architecture it appears to

emulate;

 moreover, it remains a neoclassical Federal style house
14
that displays multiple touches of Gothic

9. A. NO CHANGE
   B. were being
   C. were
   D. making up a

10. F. NO CHANGE
    G. was being caused by
    H. had been causing by
    J. was the result of

11. A. NO CHANGE
    B. the barn and shed were destroyed by a
        fire
    C. the barn and shed burning down
    D. a fire destroying the barn and shed

12. F. NO CHANGE
    G. decided to spend
    H. decided that to spend
    J. deciding he would spend

13. A. NO CHANGE
    B. be in harmony to
    C. create the appearance of harmony with
    D. harmonizes with

14. F. NO CHANGE
    G. however
    H. rather
    J. therefore

styling: buttresses arches cornices, and pinnacles [16].
15

15. A. NO CHANGE
    B. styling; buttresses, arches, cornices, and pinnacles
    C. styling, buttresses: arches, cornices, and pinnacles
    D. styling: buttresses, arches, cornices, and pinnacles

16. Upon reviewing this paragraph and finding that some information has been left out, the writer composes the following sentence incorporating that information:

> Bourne, well-traveled and an admirer of the Gothic architecture he had seen in Europe, rebuilt the barn with five tall pinnacles reminiscent of those on the Milan cathedral.

This sentence most logically should be placed after sentence:

    F. 1.
    G. 2.
    H. 3.
    J. 4.

Question 17 asks about the preceding passage as a whole.

17. Suppose the writer's goal had been to write a brief essay describing a house with features of two different architectural styles. Would this essay fulfill that goal?

    A. Yes, because the Wedding Cake House includes elements from both the Federalist and the Gothic styles.
    B. Yes, because the original Federalist style house was associated with a legend.
    C. No, because the Wedding Cake House was originally built in the Federalist style.
    D. No, because the carvings that gave the Wedding Cake House its name are in only the Gothic style.

ANSWERS AND EXPLANATIONS

1. D	**10. J**
2. G	**11. A**
3. C	**12. G**
4. G	**13. A**
5. D	**14. H**
6. F	**15. D**
7. D	**16. G**
8. G	**17. A**
9. C	

1. D

Word Choice

Choice (A) incorrectly uses the adverb *unusually* to modify the adjective *19th-century*. If you recognize this error, your eye will probably be drawn to (D), which corrects the modifier error. Just to make sure, plug in the other two choices. Eliminate (B) because it incorrectly uses the adverb *unusually* to modify the noun *house*. Eliminate (C) because *unusual **of*** is the wrong idiom (*unusual **for*** is correct) and because it's wordy.

2. G

Connections

You should recognize that the underlined segment, *in contrast to,* is a Connections phrase. That's a signal to read the sentence carefully for meaning and look for what the logical connection between ideas is. Here, *the frothy white ornamentation* on *the house's exterior* provides the reason that the house is called the Wedding Cake House. The relationship is one of cause and effect. Having identified this, you can eliminate (F) and (J), both of which are contrast connections. To decide between (G) and (J), plug them into the sentence. Choice (J) is not as concise as (G), so (G) is the best of the four choices.

3. C

Sentence Sense

Pay attention here to the non-underlined context. Ask yourself what the introductory modifier, *building on this name,* is describing. Logically, that word must come next in the sentence. It is *the legend* that builds *on this name.* Only (C) makes *legend* follow the phrase that describes it, so (C) is correct.

4. G

Writing Strategy

Think about the meaning expressed by the phrase under consideration, *during lonely hours at sea.* Read through the answer choices to see which one works. Choice (F) is wrong because the phrase does not describe the house. Choice (G) is correct because it makes the reader think of the sea captain missing his bride. Choice (H) may be tempting, because the sea captain's job does include *lonely hours at sea,* but the paragraph's focus is more on the sea captain and his bride than it is on his job. Choice (J) is wrong because the phrase does not include a historical detail.

5. D

Wordiness

Remember, whenever OMIT is a choice, consider it first (and carefully). This sentence makes sense without the underlined phrase. Indeed, the word *reality* in (A) and (B) repeats the idea of *truth* in the non-underlined portion. Choice (C) is also redundant—there is no need to say *actual honest* before *truth.* Choice (D) is the best answer.

6. F

Punctuation

This sentence contains two nonessential phrases that must be set off by commas. The basic part of the sentence is *The owner of the house…brought his bride…to the house in 1825.* The descriptive phrase *shipbuilder George Washington Bourne* and the name *Jane* are both nonessential information. Choice (F) correctly uses commas to set off this nonessential information. A comma in (G) incorrectly separates the verb *brought* from its object *his bride*. Choice (H) is incorrect because it leaves out the two necessary commas after *Bourne* and *bride*. Choice (J) is incorrect because it omits the necessary comma after *Bourne*. The right answer is (F).

7. **D**
Word Choice

The phrase *symmetry on* is not idiomatically correct here. Identifying that lets you eliminate (A) and (B). Read the other two choices into the sentence. Though the phrase *symmetry of* would be the correct idiom, (C) *symmetrical type of* doesn't make sense. Choice (D) is the correct answer.

8. **G**
Sentence Sense

Check the non-underlined context. This sentence includes a list that starts *a low hipped* **roof,** *multiple large casement* **windows**…Because the list is made up of nouns that describe features of the house, parallelism is best established by putting *a large Palladian* **window** next in the list. If you recognize this, you can eliminate every choice except (G). Choice (H) repeats the parallelism error in (F). Choice (J) is better than (F) and (H), but it still doesn't establish parallelism as clearly as (G), making (G) the right answer.

9. **C**
Sentence Sense

Whenever you notice an -*ing* verb underlined, check to make sure that, if it is used as the main verb in a clause, it has a helping verb with it. Choice (A) is incorrect because *being* is used here without a helping verb as the main verb of the sentence. Eliminate (D) for the same reason. Plug the remaining choices into the sentence. Eliminate (B) because *being* is not necessary with *were*. Choice (C) is the correct answer.

10. **J**
Sentence Sense

Choice (F) uses the -*ing* verb *resulting* as the main verb of the clause without a helping verb, so eliminate it. Read the other choices. Choice (G) is wordy because the word *being* is not necessary here. Choice (H) is wrong because *had been causing* is not the right verb form in context. Choice (J) is the correct answer.

11. **A**
Word Choice

The right answer is (A). Choice (B) is not right because the statement is in the passive voice, which (A) improves. Eliminate (C) because it uses *burning,* an -*ing* verb, as the main verb in a clause without a helping verb. Eliminate (D) because it also uses an -*ing* verb, *destroying,* as the main verb without a helping verb.

12. **G**
Word Choice

You should be able to recognize that (F), *decided* **on spending**, is not the correct idiomatic usage. Choice (G), *decided* **to** *spend,* corrects the idiom error and is the best choice. Read (H) into the sentence. You should hear that it creates sentence structure problems. Eliminate (J) because it uses the -*ing* verb *deciding* as the main verb of a clause. The right choice is (G).

13. **A**
Word Choice

There is no error in (A), so it is the correct answer. Read the other choices into the sentence to confirm this. Choice (B) contains incorrect idiomatic usage, *be in harmony* **to**, and is wordy. Choice (C) is wordy. Choice (D) uses the present tense *harmonizes* and so is inconsistent with the context of the passage, which requires a past tense verb.

14. H
Connections

Whenever you notice a Connections word underlined, such as *moreover* here, remember that you need to read the sentence carefully for meaning to determine the best logical connection. Choice (F), *moreover*, is a transition that expresses emphasis, which is not appropriate here. The first part of the sentence states that the Wedding Cake House is not an example of Gothic architecture. The second part states that the house's style is neoclassical Federal. This calls for a contrast connection. Eliminate (J), *therefore*, because it is a cause-and-effect connection. Choices (G) and (H) are both contrast transitions, but you must read them in the sentence to tell which is best. Choice (H), *rather*, sounds best in the context here.

15. D
Punctuation

Notice that (A) uses a colon to introduce a list. This is correct, but there is another problem here. The word *buttresses*, one of the items in the list, needs to be followed by a comma, so eliminate (A). Having identified that the colon is correct, you should be drawn to (D), which corrects the comma problem in (A). Choice (B) is incorrect because it uses a semicolon when what follows is not an independent clause. Choice (C) is incorrect because it puts the colon in the wrong place.

16. G
Organization

The best way to handle a question like this is to read the sentence to be added into the passage at the locations indicated by the answer choices. Choice (F) seems possible, but it does not resolve the issue as well as (G). The additional sentence introduces Bourne's Gothic-style barn, so it makes sense to add this sentence *before* the existing mention of the *new Gothic barn*. Eliminate (H) because the *new Gothic barn* has already been mentioned in sentence 3. Eliminate (J) because sentence 4 discusses the house, not the barn. Choice (G) is the right answer.

17. A
Writing Strategy

The key words to focus on in the question stem are *describing a house with features of two different architectural styles*. The essay certainly does this, so eliminate (C) and (D). Now look at the reasons given in (A) and (B). The reason provided in (A) relates directly to the question asked in the question stem, so (A) is the correct answer. The reason given in (B) is true according to the essay, but it doesn't address the question in the question stem.

ENGLISH QUIZ: PASSAGE 2

IT'S THE LITTLE THINGS THAT MATTER

[1]

I've <u>lived, in New York City for my entire life,</u> and
                                1
I'm not happy to be leaving it, even

1. A. NO CHANGE
    B. lived in New York City for my entire life
    C. lived in, New York City, for my entire
        life
    D. lived in New York City for my entire
        life,

<u>if the reason is</u> that my mom got a great new job three
        2
states away.

2. F. NO CHANGE
    G. the reason being
    H. being for the reason
    J. because of the reason

<u>Theirs a lot</u> about my life here that I'll miss. It will be
    3
awful having to do senior year in a

3. A. NO CHANGE
    B. Their's a great deal
    C. There's a lot
    D. Theirs a lot

<u>strange place without my friends.</u> That's only part of it,
                    4
though.

4. All of the following choices would appropri-
    ately convey the writer's concerns about a
    new school EXCEPT:
    F. NO CHANGE
    G. different place where I won't know
        anyone
    H. different state
    J. new place with unfamiliar classmates

<u>Being that cell phones and computers are so common,</u>
                        5
it's easier than ever to communicate over a distance, and

I know my buddies and I will stay in touch.

5. A. NO CHANGE
    B. Cell phones and the computer being so
        common,
    C. Among cell phones and the computer,
    D. Between cell phones and the computer,

[2]

Moving means leaving more than my friends. I'll be

leaving and abandoning my childhood home behind. It
     6
may be hard for someone

who's never lived in a city to understand, but my neigh-
     7
borhood is far from impersonal. It really does have the

feel of a village. There are lots of people

who, though not exactly friends are a regular part of my
     8
life. Unlike my friends, these aren't people I know well

enough

staying in contact with after I move. This may sound
     9
odd, but I'll miss them.

[3]

    There's Joe, the old guy who's been the superinten-

dent of my apartment building ever since I can remem-

ber. He's always out sweeping the hallway or cleaning

the laundry room, and he's just a call away to fix a
     10
clogged sink or change a lightbulb in a tall fixture. Joe

has a warm smile and is incredibly nice. I have to admit,

I love that he always keeps a few fun-size chocolate bars

in his toolbox, and he's happy to share his stash with

my sister and I as well. Sure, I can come back and check
     11
on Joe when I visit New York,

and it just won't be the same.
12

[4]

I'll also miss Gen, the quiet woman

6. F. NO CHANGE
   G. saying goodbye to
   H. leaving
   J. parting with and leaving

7. A. NO CHANGE
   B. never having lived
   C. who hadn't ever lived
   D. which hasn't ever lived

8. F. NO CHANGE
   G. who, though not exactly friends, are
   H. who, though not exactly, friends, are
   J. who though not exactly friends, are

9. A. NO CHANGE
   B. to stay in contact
   C. so that staying in contact
   D. for the keeping in touch

10. F. NO CHANGE
   G. room. And
   H. room; and
   J. room,

11. A. NO CHANGE
   B. my sister and me
   C. my sister and I
   D. I and also my sister

12. F. NO CHANGE
   G. so
   H. but
   J. despite that

<u>which runs</u> the green grocer on the corner.
    13

<u>I think most New Yorkers would agree that the corner</u>
                14
<u>grocery is indispensable.</u> Whenever I run in for a drink
    14
or a snack, it seems she's there at the cash register with

her lively kindergarten son, Tang, and now her new

baby. I feel like I've watched Tang grow up.

<u>How old when I come back to visit, who knows, will his</u>
              15
<u>baby sister be?</u> Will the family even still be here? It's so
   15
strange to think that

<u>people who are now seen by me</u> every day may just van-
         16
ish from my life. I'll miss these small connections with

people almost as much as I'll miss my friends.

13. A. NO CHANGE
    B. who runs
    C. who had run
    D. which had been running

14. F. NO CHANGE
    G. For most New Yorkers, they love the corner grocery.
    H. The average New Yorker always needs the corner grocery.
    J. OMIT the underlined portion.

15. A. NO CHANGE
    B. Who knows how old his baby sister will be when I come back to visit?
    C. When his baby sister comes back to visit, who knows how old I will be?
    D. Who knows, when his baby sister comes back to visit, how old I will be?

16. F. NO CHANGE
    G. people I have been now seeing
    H. people I now see
    J. I'm now seeing people

Question 17 asks about the preceding passage as a whole.

17. For the sake of logic and coherence, paragraph 3 should be placed:
    A. where it is now.
    B. before paragraph 1.
    C. after paragraph 1.
    D. after paragraph 4.

ANSWERS AND EXPLANATIONS

1. **D**	10. **F**
2. **F**	11. **B**
3. **C**	12. **H**
4. **H**	13. **B**
5. **D**	14. **J**
6. **H**	15. **B**
7. **A**	16. **H**
8. **G**	17. **A**
9. **B**	

1. D
Punctuation

Choice (A) uses a comma after *lived* that incorrectly breaks up the flow of the sentence. The comma after *life*, however, is used correctly to connect two independent clauses joined by the FANBOYS word *and*. Knowing that this second comma is called for, you can eliminate (B) and (C). Choice (D) is the correct answer.

2. F
Word Choice

The words *even if* in (F) are appropriate because what follows describes a condition. In addition, (G) and (H) incorrectly use the verb form *being*. Choice (J) is redundant: there is no need to say *the reason* with *because*.

3. C
Word Choice

Whenever you see *theirs* underlined, check that it's used correctly. The word *theirs* is a possessive pronoun, which is incorrect in this sentence. The word needed here is *there's* because its meaning is *there is*. Recognizing this, you should eliminate all choices except (C), which is the correct answer.

4. H
Writing Strategy

The key words to focus on in the question stem are *the writer's concerns about a new school*. Choices (F), (G), and (J) all include phrasing that expresses the writer's nervousness about going to school with a different group of students. Choice (H) does not, and because this question asks for the one choice that does not express the writer's concerns, (H) is the right answer.

5. D
Word Choice

Beware whenever you see the phrase *being that* on the ACT. *Being that* is not an acceptable way to say *because*. You can eliminate (A) and plug in the other choices to look for something better. Eliminate (B) because it uses the *-ing* verb *being* without a helping verb as the main verb in a clause. Eliminate (C) because it incorrectly uses *among* when only two things are being discussed. Choice (D), which correctly uses the word *between* when two things are discussed, is the right answer.

6. H
Wordiness

Eliminate (F) because *leaving* and *abandoning* mean the same thing, so the phrase is redundant. Eliminate (J) for the same reason. Plug in the remaining choices. Choice (G) probably sounds all right to your ear, but (H) is more concise, which makes it the right answer.

7. A
Word Choice

Address the pronoun issue first: whenever you see *who's* underlined, make sure that it's in a context in which either *who is* or *who has* makes sense. In this sentence, *who's* correctly stands for *who has*. Now look at verb tense. In this sentence, the past tense verb *has…lived* is correct. Check the other choices just in case. Eliminate (B) because it uses the *-ing* verb *having* without a helping verb as the main verb in the clause. Eliminate (C) because the past tense verb *had…lived* is not the appropriate one here. Eliminate (D) because it incorrectly uses the pronoun *which* to refer to a person. The right answer is indeed (A).

8. G
Punctuation

Think about how the sentence is structured and where the commas are needed. The main part of the sentence is *there are lots of people…who are a regular part of my life*. The phrase *though not exactly friends* is nonessential information and should be set off with commas. Eliminate (F) because it doesn't place a comma after *friends*. Eliminate (H) because, though it correctly sets off the nonessential phrase, it unnecessarily inserts a comma after *exactly*, which breaks up the flow of the sentence. Eliminate (J) because it doesn't use a comma after *who*. The right answer is (G).

9. B
Word Choice

There is an error in (A) because the correct idiomatic usage here is *enough **to stay** in contact*, so eliminate (A). If you identified the idiom issue, (B) should stand out as the correct choice. If not, plug in the remaining choices. Choice (C) introduces a sentence structure problem with *so that*, which doesn't lead to a complete thought. Choice (D) uses the awkward phrasing *for the keeping in touch*. Choice (B) is the right answer.

10. F
Sentence Sense

Choice (F) correctly uses a comma and the FANBOYS word *and* to join two independent clauses. Choice (G) incorrectly begins a sentence with *and*. Choice (H) incorrectly uses a FANBOYS word with a semicolon to join two independent clauses. Choice (J) creates a run-on sentence by using only a comma, without a FANBOYS word, to join two independent clauses. The right answer is (F).

11. B
Word Choice

Whenever you spot an underlined pronoun, check to make sure it's used correctly. In (A), the pronoun *I* is used incorrectly as the object of the preposition *with*. Recognizing this, you should eliminate (A), (C), and (D). Choice (B) correctly uses the object pronoun *me* and so is the correct answer.

12. H
Connections

Choice (F) uses *and*, which is a generic Connections word that doesn't express any particular logical relationship. Read the sentence carefully to see if a more specific Connections word would be appropriate. There are two ideas in this sentence. First is that the writer can come back to visit, and second is that it won't be the same. The second idea expresses some disappointment, so a contrast word is appropriate. Eliminate (G) because *so* expresses cause and effect. Choices (H) and (J) both convey contrast. Read each in the sentence. Choice (H) is correct in context.

13. B
Word Choice

When you notice the word *which* underlined, remember that it should refer only to things, never to people. Here, *which* is used incorrectly to refer to *Gen*. Recognizing this, you can eliminate (A) and (D). Also notice that (C) and (D) use different verb tenses, and plug these choices into the sentence. Pay attention to the broader context of the passage. The predominant tense is the present, so eliminate (C), which uses a past tense. Choice (B) is correct.

14. J
Wordiness

Whenever you notice that an entire sentence is underlined, check to see if OMIT is offered as an answer choice. If it is, that's a clue that you should ask yourself whether the sentence is relevant to the topic of the paragraph. The focus of this paragraph is how much the writer will miss the family at the green grocer. Therefore, a sentence about how most New Yorkers find the green grocer indispensable is not relevant. Choice (J) is the correct answer choice. Having determined this, you don't even need to worry about (G) and (H). If a sentence is irrelevant, don't consider the best way to word it; simply take it out.

15. B
Sentence Sense

If an entire sentence is underlined and OMIT is not offered as an answer choice, that's a clue that you need to find the choice that is most logical and easy to understand. Pay attention to the order of the words and phrases. Choice (A) likely sounds confusing when you read it, which is another good clue that Sentence Sense is the issue. Choice (B) is clear and makes sense, but you should consider the other choices just in case. Choices (C) and (D) are both misleading because it is the writer, not the *baby sister*, who will come *back to visit*. Choice (B) is the right choice.

16. H
Sentence Sense

Choice (F) is probably not going to be the best choice because it uses the passive voice. Read through the answer choices looking for the active voice. Choice (H) is written in the active voice. Choice (G) is wrong because it inappropriately uses a past tense that isn't consistent with the context. Choice (J) is wrong because it uses a present tense (*am seeing*) that isn't consistent with the simple present and future tenses that are used in the passage. Choice (H) is the correct answer.

17. A
Organization

To answer a question that asks you to determine the best ordering of paragraphs, think about which would make the best introduction and which would make the best conclusion. Here, paragraph 1 introduces the topic and serves as the best introduction. Paragraph 4—especially the last two sentences—make it the best conclusion for the essay. Recognizing this lets you eliminate (B) and (D). To decide between (A) and (C), consider the relationship between paragraphs 2 and 3. Paragraph 2 discusses in general the people the writer will miss. Paragraph 3 discusses Joe, a specific one of those people. Therefore, it makes sense to keep paragraph 3 after paragraph 2, making (A) the correct answer.

SUMMARY

Checkup time!

Below, record how many questions you answered correctly.

Next, record how many you answered incorrectly.

Remember, master the Kaplan Method for ACT English and the overall strategies for the English test first. Refer to English Part 1 for these strategies. If you're short on time before Test Day, spend your time with Part 1.

Now, get specific. Look at the Answers and Explanations for each question, and use the chart below to record how many questions you answered correctly and incorrectly in each English SmartPoint.

Point Value	Topic	# Correct	# Incorrect
7	Connections		
6	Verb Tenses		
5	Punctuation		
5	Word Choice		
5	Wordiness		
4	Writing Strategy		
3	Sentence Sense		
1	Organization		

Looking at the Point Value on the left of the chart and how many questions you missed in each category, review the specific areas where you can gain the most points on Test Day. Remember, spend your time on the more heavily tested SmartPoints first!

Keep reviewing using English Part 1 for basics and Part 2 for specific SmartPoints. Then keep practicing using the practice tests later in this book.

With a regular cycle of review and practice, you'll soon be a master of ACT English!

UNIT 2: MATH

The Basics:

60 Minutes

60 Questions

Pacing:

Pace your time per question.

Spend an average of 1 minute per question.

TEST DAY DIRECTIONS AND FORMAT

Here's what the Math directions will look like:

Directions: Solve each problem, choose the correct answer, and then fill in the corresponding oval on your answer document.

Do not linger over problems that take too much time. Solve as many as you can, then return to the others in the time you have left for this test.

You are permitted to use a calculator on this test. You may use your calculator for any problems you choose, but some of the problems may best be done without using a calculator.

Note: Unless otherwise noted, all of the following should be assumed:

1. Illustrative figures are NOT necessarily drawn to scale.

2. Geometric figures lie in a plane.

3. The word *line* indicates a straight line.

4. The word *average* indicates arithmetic mean.

As in the English section, when it comes to directions on the ACT, the golden rule is: Don't read anything on Test Day you already know! Familiarize yourself with everything now, and save yourself time later.

The Math directions don't really tell you much anyway. Of the four special notes at the end of the Math directions, #2, #3, and #4 almost go without saying. Note #1 is pretty important, though—while the rules "bend" a little bit when you have to guess, it's important to know that your eyes *don't* tell you what you need to know about figures; you really do have to do the math. What a figure *looks like* won't reliably get you the right answer.

OUTSIDE KNOWLEDGE

The ACT Math test thoroughly covers rules from a variety of common Math topics, mostly from courses students typically complete by the end of the 11th grade. The outside knowledge required is summed up at the end of this chapter in 100 Key Math Concepts on page 146. The needed math "facts" are also addressed in the strategic discussion throughout this math unit.

THE INSIDE SCOOP

The ACT Math test is designed to measure problem-solving and logical reasoning primarily, but it does test basic computational skills. Covered topics are pre-algebra, algebra, coordinate geometry, plane geometry, and trigonometry.

Questions are not specifically arranged in order of difficulty, but the topics tested *do get more advanced* as you proceed through the test.

SMARTPOINTS

Point Value	Topic	Basics Page	Details and Practice
7	**Plane Geometry**		
7	**Variable Manipulation**		
6	**Proportions and Probability**		
6	**Coordinate Geometry**		
3	**Operations**		
3	**Patterns, Logic, and Data**		
2	**Number Properties**		
2	**Trigonometry**		

CHAPTER 7

Math Part 1: Inside the ACT Math Test

THE KAPLAN METHOD FOR ACT MATH

STEP 1: WHAT IS THE QUESTION?

First, focus on the *question stem* (the part before the answer choices), and make sure you understand the problem. ACT Math questions can have complicated phrasing, and if you don't know *precisely* what you're looking for, you aren't likely to find it. So first, locate the end goal—the objective—and circle it. Do you need to solve for x? Find an odd number? Maybe it's a story problem and you need to find how many adults were admitted to an exhibit, or the number of girls in a classroom. If it is a word problem and you get lost, break the question into pieces and make sure you come away with a clear understanding of what you're looking for. What is the end objective of your work? Again, *circle the question*, or objective as stated in the question stem, when you've found it.

STEP 2: WHAT INFORMATION AM I GIVEN?

Look through the question stem again, and *underline the pieces of information provided.* Ask yourself whether you have everything you'll need to solve the problem, or if there are intermediary steps you'll have to take. By underlining everything, you'll have a place to start, even if you're lost, as the ACT rarely provides information you don't need to solve the problem. Then, examine the format of the answer choices. This can help you determine your strategy. For example, you may think you need to solve for *x* in an equation, but then you see that all of the answers are given *in terms of x*, so you don't actually need to find *x*, just come up with a formula. Additionally, if you are given information in fractions and see answers in decimals, you'll know you need to convert from one to the other at some point.

STEP 3: WHAT CAN I DO WITH THE INFORMATION?

Now that you've gathered the information, time to solve the question. Decide on a plan of attack:

- **Straightforward math.** Do you know how to solve the problem using your math skills? Go for it!

- **Picking numbers.** Are there variables in the answer choices? If so, is there a way to pick some easy-to-use numbers you can plug in for the variable to help you get to the right answer? (This strategy is discussed in depth in the Point Builders section on page 141.)

- **Backsolving.** Are there numbers in the answer choices? What is the question asking for? Is there a way to use the answer choices to get to the right answer? (This strategy is also discussed in the Point Builders section on page 143.)

- **Guess strategically.** If you're really not sure, you can guess—you don't lose points for incorrect answers on the ACT. Try to eliminate as many incorrect choices as you can before guessing, and mark the question in your booklet so you can return to it at the end of the Math test and try again.

STEP 4: AM I FINISHED?

In Step 1, you circled the objective. Check what you circled now. Is that what you found? Have you fully answered the question? Some questions may require several steps, and you may miss the last step if you don't check before you select. The ACT will frequently offer tempting answer choices for students who don't recheck the question. For example, you may need to find the area of a circle and you've only determined the radius—and the radius might be an answer choice! Since you will have identified and marked the question in Step 1, double-checking that you're finished should take only a few seconds, and it can make a real difference on Test Day. If you're stuck, circle the problem in your test book and come back later—always get through the easy questions first.

QUICK TIPS

MIND-SET

- **The end justifies the means.** Your goal is to get as many points as possible, not to demonstrate how great you are at any particular math area, or to show all your work, or get all the "hard" questions—just to get points, plain and simple. That means getting as many correct answers as quickly as possible. If that means doing straightforward questions in a straightforward way, that's fine. But many questions can be solved faster by using Kaplan Methods, such as backsolving and picking numbers, and will make you both faster and more accurate. (Learn these strategies in the Point Builder section on page 140.)

- **Take time to save time.** It sounds paradoxical, but to go your fastest on the Math test, you sometimes have to slow down. Don't just dive in headlong, wildly crunching numbers or manipulating equations without first giving the problem some thought. Remember your priority is the whole section, not just this one question.

- **When in doubt, shake it up.** ACT Math questions are not always what they seem at first glance. Sometimes all you need is a new perspective to break through the disguise. Take a step back and look at the question another way.

SPECIAL STRATEGIES

We offer several recommendations for what to do when you get stuck. If after a few moments of thought you find you still can't come up with a reasonable way of doing the problem, try one of these techniques:

- **Restate.** When you get stuck, try looking at the problem from a different angle. Try rearranging the numbers, changing decimals to fractions, changing fractions to decimals, multiplying out numbers, factoring problems, redrawing a diagram, or doing anything that might help you to look at the problem a bit differently.

- **Remove the disguise.** Find out what the question is really asking—it might not be what the problem appears to ask at first. Find the objective and circle it, especially when you're confused.

- **Try eyeballing.** Even though the directions warn you that diagrams are "not necessarily" drawn to scale, eyeballing is a surprisingly effective guessing strategy. You won't be able to get specifics without doing the math, sometimes, but you will be able to rule some answers out or get a better idea of what you're looking for.

TIMING

You have an average of 1 minute to spend per question. Ideally, you'll be able to spend significantly less time on easy questions so you can buy more time on the hard questions.

Spend about 45 minutes on your first pass through the Math subject test. Do the easier questions, guess on the questions you suspect aren't going to come to you no matter what, and mark the tough ones that you'll want to come back to. Spend the last 15 minutes picking up those questions you skipped on the first pass.

We recommend you grid your answers at the end of every page or two. In the last five minutes or so, start gridding your answers one by one. And make sure that you have an answer (even if it's a blind guess) gridded for every question by the time the test is over.

Don't worry if you have to guess on a lot of the Math questions. You can miss a lot of questions on the Math test and still get a great score. Remember that the average ACT test taker gets fewer than half of the Math questions right!

WHEN YOU'RE RUNNING OUT OF TIME

If at some point you realize you have more questions left than you have time for, be willing to skip around, looking for questions you understand right away. Pick your points, and concentrate on the questions you have the best chance of correctly answering. Just be sure to grid an answer—even if it's just a wild guess—for every question.

SCORING

Your performance on the Math subject test will be averaged into your ACT Composite Score, equally weighted with your scores on the other three major subject tests. You will also receive:

- Math subject score—from 1 to 36—for the entire Math subject test

- Pre-Algebra/Elementary Algebra subscore—from 1 to 18

- Intermediate Algebra/Coordinate Geometry subscore—from 1 to 18

- Plane Geometry/Trigonometry subscore—from 1 to 18

POINT BUILDERS

As we promised, there are many ways to view questions. Here are the top two ways to think outside the box about how to solve any given Math problem.

PICKING NUMBERS

This strategy relates to questions with variables. You can Pick Numbers to make abstract problems—ones that insist on dealing with variables rather than numbers—more concrete. **Use this problem when there are variables in the answer choices.** If there are variables in the answer choices, you won't have to solve for the variables, just determine how they would behave if they were real numbers. Thus, don't assume—pick a real number and see for yourself. Follow these guidelines:

Step 1: Pick a simple number to stand in for the variables, making sure it follows the rules listed in the question stem. Does the number have to be even or odd? Positive or negative? Be careful when using 0 and 1, as they behave differently than most other numbers, but always use easy-to-use numbers.

Step 2: Solve the question using the number you picked.

Step 3: Try out all the answer choices using the number you picked, eliminating those that give you a result you're not looking for.

Step 4: If more than one choice remains, pick a different set of numbers and repeat steps 1–3.

Let's try this strategy on the following problem.

1. Money collected by c charities is to be divided equally. According to donation records, p people gave d dollars each. How much money will each charity receive?

    A. $c/(pd)$
    B. $(pd)/c$
    C. $pd + c$
    D. $(dc)/p$
    E. $(p - c)d$

If the mere thought of this problem gives you a headache, Picking Numbers can provide you with a safe way to quickly get to the answer. The key is to Pick Numbers that make the math easy for you. Since the money will be divided evenly among the charities, Pick Numbers that relate easily to each other to make the math go smoothly. Try 2 for p, 4 for c, and 8 for d. Now the question asks: if 2 people each donated $8 to a trust fund that will distribute the money equally among 4 charities, how much money, in dollars, did each charity receive? So, $16 divided by 4. The answer to this question would be $4, so replace p with 2, d with 8, and c with 4 in each of the answer choices, and see which one comes out to 4.

A. $\dfrac{c}{pd} = \dfrac{4}{2 \times 8} = \dfrac{4}{16} = \dfrac{1}{4}$, which is way too small.

B. $\dfrac{pd}{c} = \dfrac{2 \times 8}{4} = \dfrac{16}{4} = 4$. That's the ticket!

C. $pd + c = 2 \times 8 + 4 = 16 + 4 = 20$. That's too big.

D. $\dfrac{dc}{p} = \dfrac{8 \times 4}{2} = \dfrac{32}{2} = 16$. That's too big.

E. $(p - c)d = (2 - 4) \times 8 = (-2) \times 8 = -16$. That won't work.

Only (B) works, so it must be correct.

Let's try one more common problem type where Picking Numbers can make your life easier.

2. If a is an odd integer and b is an even integer, which of the following must be odd?

F. $2a + b$

G. $a + 2b$

H. ab

J. $a^2 b$

K. ab^2

Rather than try to think this one through abstractly, it's easier to Pick Numbers for a and b. There are rules that predict the evenness or oddness of sums, differences, and products, but there's no need to memorize those rules.

Just say, for the time being, that $a = 3$ (remember, 1 can be used, but is not typically helpful) and $b = 2$. Plug those values into the answer choices, and there's a good chance only one choice will be odd:

F. $2a + b = 2(3) + 2 = 8$

G. $a + 2b = 3 + 2(2) = 9$

H. $ab = (3)(2) = 6$

J. $a^2 b = (3)^2(2) = 18$

K. $ab^2 = (3)(2)^2 = 12$

Choice (G) was the only odd one for $a = 3$ and $b = 2$, so it *must* be the one that's odd no matter *what* odd number a and even number b actually stand for. Even if you're not positive (G) will always be right, you know for a fact that all the others are definitely wrong, which is just as good!

BACKSOLVING

Because you can know for certain that one of the answer choices is right (as opposed to a fill-in-the-blank test), with some ACT Math problems, it may actually be easier to try out each answer choice until you find the one that works, rather than attempt to solve the problem and then look among the choices for the answer. We call this approach Backsolving.

Try it out.

2. All 200 tickets were sold for a particular concert. Some tickets cost $10 apiece, and the others cost $5 apiece. If total ticket sales were $1,750, how many of the more expensive tickets were sold?

    F. 20
    G. 75
    H. 100
    J. 150
    K. 175

There are ways to solve this problem by setting up an equation or two, but if you're not comfortable with the algebraic approach to this one, why not just try out each answer choice? You know one of them will work.

Here's the next part you need to know: when Backsolving, *always start with the middle answer choice*. The numerical answer choices on the ACT are always in ascending order. If you solve for the one in the middle and it comes out too big, you can eliminate it *and the two larger numbers*, and same if it's too small. So trying **one** answer choice can eliminate **three** options.

So start with choice (H). If 100 tickets were sold for $10 each, then the other 100 have to have been sold for $5 each. 100 at $10 is $1,000, and 100 tickets at $5 is $500, for a total of $1,500—too small. There *must* have been more than 100 $10 tickets.

This is great news! If we know it's not (H), and we know (H) is too small, we can eliminate (F) and (G) as well. By solving for one value, we've eliminated three answer choices. Even if you had to stop and guess now, you'd be picking from two answers, not five! So, which answer do we try next? More good news—it doesn't actually matter. If you solve for (J) and it's wrong, the answer must be (K); you don't even have to solve for (K) to know that. So either remaining answer works equally well. That being the case, you should solve for whichever one looks easier, since it's just about doing the math. In this case, 150 looks a little bit easier to solve than 175, so we'll start with (J).

If 150 tickets went for $10, then the other 50 went for $5. So 150 tickets at $10 is $1,500, and 50 tickets at $5 is $250, for a total of $1,750—that's it! The answer is (J), no need to go any further.

Backsolving your way to the answer may not be a method you'd show your algebra teacher, but your algebra teacher won't be watching on Test Day. Remember, all that matters is right answers—it doesn't matter how you get them.

Visit your online syllabus—Lesson 2—for more instruction and practice with Math Point Builders.

SMARTPOINT BREAKDOWN

Here is a brief overview of what exactly to expect and how much of it you should be expecting.

PLANE GEOMETRY—7 POINTS

Extremely Important

Plane Geometry questions test your ability to solve problems related to figures, angles, and lines. Triangles—specifically right triangles—and circles are the two most commonly tested shapes, but you can expect to see questions on a variety of polygons, complex 2-D and simple 3-D shapes. Fortunately, like the rest of the ACT Math test, the number of rules to remember is limited, and they only pertain to simple shapes. Turn to 100 Key Math Concepts on page 146 for a list of these rules. Otherwise, the test will ask you to break down complex figures into recognizable shapes and use problem-solving skills to transfer information throughout a figure. The next chapter has a thorough discussion of each of these concepts and strategies, as well as practice problems, on page 223.

VARIABLE MANIPULATION—7 POINTS

Extremely Important

Variable Manipulation questions extensively test your ability to solve for an unknown quantity given a wide range of information of varying complexity. The simplest questions are pulled from elementary algebra and require you to solve for a single variable. They build up to intermediate algebra, and ask you to solve simultaneous equations, equations involving absolute value, inequalities, or quadratic equations. The tested rules pull extensively from the operations and number properties SmartPoints and can all be found in 100 Key Math Concepts on page 146. However, unlike those SmartPoints—which can be a simpler test of your knowledge of rules—variable manipulation questions involve applying those concepts with adept strategy and problem solving. For a more thorough discussion of these problems, strategies to deal with them, and samples to practice, refer to page 191.

PROPORTIONS AND PROBABILITY—6 POINTS

Very Important

Proportions and Probability questions test a number of key mathematical concepts that involve relating numbers, including percents, ratios, and averages, as well as distance, rate, and time, and of course, probability itself (the likelihood of an event taking place). Refer to 100 Key Math Concepts on page 146 for the three-part formulas essential for this Smart-Point. Memorizing and applying those are key to mastering this section. For more discussion and practice, refer to page 200.

COORDINATE GEOMETRY—6 POINTS

Very Important

Coordinate Geometry questions primarily test knowledge of equations and graphs of lines. This centers around an (x, y) coordinate plane. The Slope-Intercept formula is the most important equation to remember here, as most ACT Coordinate Geometry questions ask about properties of a single, straight line. Slope is paramount, as are the concepts of parallel and perpendicular lines. However, the test will also ask questions that require knowledge of the Midpoint and Distance formulas, quadratics and the associated parabolas, and occasionally the graphs of simple shapes such as triangles and circles. All formulas are listed in 100 Key Math Concepts on page 146 and discussed in detail with strategies on practice on page 217.

OPERATIONS—3 POINTS

Somewhat Important

Like Number Properties, Operations are not directly tested on many questions, but thorough knowledge of them is necessary for many question types, especially Variable Manipulation and Proportions and Probability. Tested operations include all parts of the PEMDAS order of operations (Parenthesis, Exponents, Multiplication, Division, Addition, and Subtraction). Complex Operation questions ask you to perform many of these functions in a single string of numbers. Rarer questions test basic knowledge of imaginary numbers, radicals, and logarithms. All rules for these are listed in 100 Key Math Concepts on page 146. For in-depth discussion and samples of this SmartPoint, refer to page 186.

PATTERNS, LOGIC, AND DATA—3 POINTS

Somewhat Important

Many of these questions don't even look like Math questions at first glance. They often involve pie charts, tables, matrices, and line and bar graphs that would be more at home on the Science subject test. Complex, infrequently tested areas are grouped under this SmartPoint, including Permutations and Combinations, Union and Intersection of Sets, Matrices, and Functions. Fear not, all you need to know is listed, as always, in 100 Key Math Concepts on page 146, and the vast majority of these problems can be solved by calmly identifying what is being asked of you, then using simple, step-by-step logic to get there. Thorough strategy discussion and practice can be found on page 253.

NUMBER PROPERTIES—2 POINTS

Somewhat Important

This is another fundamental SmartPoint, like Operations, that is not often tested directly, but forms a base of knowledge that contributes to a number of other question types, such as Variable Manipulation and Proportions and Probability. Number Properties questions ask you to understand the behavior of numbers, particularly evens and odds and positives and negatives. These questions are ripe for Picking Numbers, discussed earlier in this chapter. It also tests properties of divisibility, such as factors, multiples, and prime numbers. As usual, refer to 100 Key Math Concepts on page 146 for a full list of rules and turn to page 180 for a detailed discussion of strategies for this question type.

TRIGONOMETRY—2 POINTS

Somewhat Important

The fact that the ACT tests Trigonometry scares a lot of test takers. Take a deep breath, because you're about to get good news. Trigonometry is very lightly tested and the questions are extremely predictable. Almost all questions center around sine, cosine, and tangent and some of the most common trigonometric functions. Also good to know: You should expect four trigonometry questions or fewer. Memorize the few rules listed in 100 Key Math Concepts on page 146 and practice them with the more in-depth strategy discussion on page 258, and you can master the Trigonometry portion of the ACT in no time.

100 KEY MATH CONCEPTS

Below is an extensive list of the most frequently tested rules of the ACT Math subject test. Look over this list now and as you review the following chapters, and if you're short on time before Test Day, this is a great place to cram. Otherwise, use this list in conjunction with the SmartPoint-by-SmartPoint discussion in the next chapter, in which the most commonly tested rules are discussed more thoroughly with sample problems similar to the ones you'll see on the ACT.

NUMBER PROPERTIES

1. UNDEFINED

On the ACT, when something is **divided by zero**, it is considered *undefined*. For example, the expression $\dfrac{a}{bc}$ is undefined if either b or c equals 0.

2. REAL/IMAGINARY

A real number is a number that has a **location on the number line**—positive, negative, whole numbers, fractions—all are considered real numbers. Imaginary numbers, on the other hand, are numbers that involve the square root of a negative number.

3. INTEGER/NONINTEGER

Integers are **whole numbers,** which means no fractions, decimals, or mixed numbers; they include both negative and positive numbers, as well as zero.

4. RATIONAL/IRRATIONAL

Any number that can be expressed as a fraction or a repeating decimal is a rational number. This includes numbers like 3, 2/5, −.1666, or .333. **Irrational numbers cannot be expressed precisely as a fraction or decimal.** For the purposes of the ACT, the most important **irrational numbers** are $\sqrt{2}, \sqrt{3},$ and π.

5. ADDING/SUBTRACTING SIGNED NUMBERS

To **add a positive and a negative,** subtract the negative number from the positive number. For instance, −9 + 1 is the same as 1 − 9. Alternately, you can find the difference between the two numbers, and then keep the original sign of the larger number. Again using the example −9 + 1, the difference between 1 and 9 is 8, and since 9 was the larger number, keep the negative sign, so −9 + 1 = −8.

Subtracting a negative number is the same as adding a positive. For example, think of 17 − (−21) as 17 + (+21).

To **add or subtract a string of positives and negatives,** add up all of the positive numbers, and add up all of the negative numbers. Then add those two sums together, keeping the sign of the greater sum. For instance, if you had the string 8 + 3 −12 + 4 − 6 − 5, combine the positives: 8 + 3 + 4 = 15. Combine the negatives: −12 + (− 6) + (−5) = −23. Now combine the two sums: 15 + (−23) = −8.

6. MULTIPLYING/DIVIDING SIGNED NUMBERS

Positives multiplied/divided with other positives are always positive. An even number of negative numbers, when multiplied or divided, will also be positive. However, if there is an odd number of negatives, the multiplication/division will be negative. For instance, (−2) × (−3) = 6, but (−2) × (−3) × (−4) = −24.

7. PEMDAS

When performing multiple operations, remember **PEMDAS,** which means start with anything inside **Parentheses** first, then deal with any **Exponents,** then all of the **Multiplication** and **Division** (left to right), and finally all of the **Addition** and **Subtraction** (left to right).

In the expression $9 − 2 \times (5 − 3)^2 + 6 \div 3$, begin with the parentheses: (5 − 3) = 2. Then do the exponent: $2^2 = 4$, so now the expression is: $9 − 2 \times 4 + 6 \div 3$. Next do the multiplication, 2 × 4 = 8, and division, 6 ÷ 3 = 2, to get 9 − 8 + 2. Finally, subtraction, 9 − 8 = 1, and then the addition, 1 + 2, which equals 3.

8. ABSOLUTE VALUE

The absolute value of something is its distance from zero on the number line, which is why absolute value is always positive. Treat absolute value signs a lot like **parentheses.** Do what's inside them first and then take the absolute value of the result. Don't take the absolute value of each piece between the bars before calculating. In order to calculate $|(-12) + 5 - (-4)| - |5 + (-10)|$, first do what's inside the bars to get: $|-3| - |-5|$, which is $3 - 5$, or -2.

9. COUNTING CONSECUTIVE INTEGERS

To find the number of consecutive integers between two values, **subtract the smallest from the largest and add 1.** So to find the number of consecutive integers from 13 through 31, subtract: $31 - 13 = 18$. Then add 1: $18 + 1 = 19$. There are 19 consecutive integers from 13 through 31.

DIVISIBILITY

10. FACTOR/MULTIPLE

A factor of an integer is any number that divides precisely into that integer (with no remainder). The multiple of an integer is that integer times any number. In other words, factor × factor = multiple. All numbers are both factors and multiples of themselves. Six is a factor of 12, and 24 is a multiple of 12. Twelve is both a factor ($12 \div 12 = 1$) and a multiple ($12 \times 1 = 12$) of itself.

11. PRIME FACTORIZATION

A **prime number** is a positive integer that is divisible without a remainder by only 1 and itself. The number 2 is the smallest prime number and the only even prime number; 1 is not considered prime. To find the prime factorization of an integer, use a factor tree to keep breaking the integer up into factors until **all the factors are prime.** To find the prime factorization of 36, for example, you could begin by breaking it into 4×9:

$$36 = 4 \times 9 = 2 \times 2 \times 3 \times 3$$

12. RELATIVE PRIMES

Two integers are relative primes if they share no prime factors. To determine whether two integers are relative primes, break them both down to their prime factorizations. For example: $35 = 5 \times 7$ and $54 = 2 \times 3 \times 3 \times 3$. They have **no prime factors in common**, so 35 and 54 are relative primes.

13. COMMON MULTIPLE

You can always get a common multiple of two numbers by **multiplying** them, but unless the two numbers are relative primes, the product will not be the least common multiple—the smallest multiple both of those numbers divide into. For example, to find a common multiple for 12 and 15, you could just multiply: $12 \times 15 = 180$.

14. LEAST COMMON MULTIPLE (LCM)

To find the least common multiple, check out the **multiples of the larger number** until you find one that's **also a multiple of the smaller.**

To find the LCM of 12 and 15, begin by taking the multiples of 15: $1 \times 15 = 15$, which is not divisible by 12; $2 \times 15 = 30$, not divisible by 12; nor is 45, which is 3×15. But the next multiple of 15, $4 \times 15 = 60$, is divisible by 12, so it's the LCM.

15. GREATEST COMMON FACTOR (GCF)

The greatest common factor of two numbers is the highest number that divides precisely into each of them without a remainder. To find the greatest common factor, break down both numbers into their prime factorizations, and take **all the prime factors they have in common.** For example, take 36 and 48: $36 = 2 \times 2 \times 3 \times 3$ and $48 = 2 \times 2 \times 2 \times 2 \times 3$. What they have in common is two 2s and one 3, so the GCF is $2 \times 2 \times 3 = 12$.

16. EVEN/ODD

There are rules to predict whether a sum, difference, or product of an expression will be even or odd—"odd times even is even," for example—but there's no need to memorize them. **Pick Numbers like 2 and 3 and see what happens.** Picking Numbers is the easiest and most efficient way to deal with questions dealing with even/odd properties.

17. MULTIPLES OF 2 AND 4

An integer is divisible by 2 if the **last digit is even.** An integer is divisible by 4 if the **last two digits form a multiple of 4.** The last digit of 562 is 2, which is even, so 562 is a multiple of 2. The last two digits make 62, which is not divisible by 4, so 562 is not a multiple of 4. However, 4,928 is divisible by 4 because 28 is divisible by 4.

18. MULTIPLES OF 3 AND 9

An integer is divisible by 3 if the **sum of its digits is divisible by 3.** An integer is divisible by 9 if the **sum of its digits is divisible by 9.** Take the number 957—the sum of the digits is $9 + 5 + 7 = 21$, and 21 is divisible by 3 but 21 is not divisible by 9, so 957 is divisible by 3 but not 9.

19. MULTIPLES OF 5 AND 10

An integer is divisible by 5 if the **last digit is 5 or 0.** An integer is divisible by 10 if the **last digit is 0.** The last digit of 665 is 5, so 665 is a multiple of 5 but not a multiple of 10.

20. REMAINDERS

The remainder is the number left over after division. If you divided 48 by 5, you'd first find the nearest multiple of 5 to 48, which is 45 (9×5). This means 5 goes into 48 nine times, but then there is still 3 left over, which makes the remainder 3.

FRACTIONS AND DECIMALS

21. REDUCING FRACTIONS

To reduce a fraction to lowest terms, **factor out and cancel** all factors the numerator and denominator have in common. For instance, if you had the fraction 28/36, you could reduce this fraction, because both 28 and 36 have a factor of 4 that can be taken out:

$$\frac{28}{36} = \frac{4 \times 7}{4 \times 9} = \frac{7}{9}$$

22. ADDING/SUBTRACTING FRACTIONS

To add or subtract fractions, first find a **common denominator,** and then add or subtract the numerators. Finding a common denominator often involves multiplying one or more of the fractions by a number so that the denominators come out the same:

$$\frac{2}{15} + \frac{3}{10} = \frac{4}{30} + \frac{9}{30} = \frac{4+9}{30} = \frac{13}{30}$$

23. MULTIPLYING FRACTIONS

To multiply fractions, **multiply** straight across—numerator times numerator and denominator times denominator.

$$\frac{5}{7} \times \frac{3}{4} = \frac{5 \times 3}{7 \times 4} = \frac{15}{28}$$

24. DIVIDING FRACTIONS

To divide fractions, **invert** the fraction in the denominator and **multiply.**

$$\frac{1}{2} \div \frac{3}{5} = \frac{1}{2} \times \frac{5}{3} = \frac{1 \times 5}{2 \times 3} = \frac{5}{6}$$

25. CONVERTING A MIXED NUMBER TO AN IMPROPER FRACTION

To convert a mixed number, which is a whole number with a fraction, to an improper fraction, which is a fraction where the numerator is bigger than the denominator, **multiply** the whole number part by the denominator, then **add** the numerator. The result is the new numerator (over the same denominator). To convert $7\frac{1}{3}$ first multiply 7 by 3, then add 1 to get the new numerator of 22. Put that over the same denominator, 3, to get $\frac{22}{3}$.

26. CONVERTING AN IMPROPER FRACTION TO A MIXED NUMBER

To convert an improper fraction to a mixed number, **divide** the denominator into the numerator, and the remainder will be the numerator of the fraction part, with the same

MATH PART 1: INSIDE THE ACT MATH TEST

denominator. For example, to convert $\frac{108}{5}$, first divide 5 into 108, which yields 21 with a remainder of 3. Therefore, $\frac{108}{5} = 21\frac{3}{5}$.

27. RECIPROCAL

The reciprocal of a fraction is the inverse of that fraction. To find the reciprocal of a fraction, switch the numerator and the denominator. The reciprocal of $\frac{3}{7}$ is $\frac{7}{3}$. The reciprocal of 5 (or 5/1, because all whole numbers are over 1) is $\frac{1}{5}$. The product of reciprocals is always 1.

28. COMPARING FRACTIONS

One way to compare fractions is to manipulate them so they have a **common denominator.** For instance, to compare $\frac{3}{4}$ and $\frac{5}{7}$:

$\frac{3}{4} = \frac{21}{28}$ and $\frac{5}{7} = \frac{20}{28}$; $\frac{21}{28}$ is greater than $\frac{20}{28}$, so $\frac{3}{4}$ is greater than $\frac{5}{7}$.

Another way to compare fractions is to convert them both to **decimals.** $\frac{3}{4}$ converts to .75, and $\frac{5}{7}$ converts to approximately .714.

29. CONVERTING FRACTIONS TO DECIMALS

To convert a fraction to a decimal, **divide the numerator by the denominator.** To convert $\frac{5}{8}$, divide 5 by 8, yielding .625. Often, these numbers will start repeating, such as $\frac{1}{6}$. When 1 is divided by 6, the decimal starts repeating almost right away, so it can be written as $1.\overline{66}$ (the line over the 66 means, "repeating").

30. REPEATING DECIMALS

To find a particular digit in a repeating decimal, note the **number of digits in the cluster that repeats.** If there are two digits in that cluster, then every second digit is the same. If there are three digits in that cluster, then every third digit is the same. And so on. For example, the decimal equivalent of $\frac{1}{27}$ is .037037037...which is best written ...$\overline{037}$.

There are three digits in the repeating cluster, so every third digit is the same: 7. To find the 50th digit, look for the multiple of 3 just less than 50—that's 48. The 48th digit is 7, and with the 49th digit the pattern repeats with 0. So, the 50th digit is 3.

31. IDENTIFYING THE PARTS AND THE WHOLE

The key to solving most fraction and percent word problems is to identify the part and the whole. Usually, you'll find the **part** associated with the verb *is/are* and the **whole** associated with the word *of.* In the sentence, "Half of the boys are blonds," the whole is the boys ("*of* the boys"), and the part is the blonds ("*are* blonds"). Sometimes, the problem will give you just the parts: "The ratio of boys to girls is 2 to 3." In this case, we have a part:part relationship. To find the ratio of boys to the total, you would add the parts: 2 + 3 = 5, so the ratio of boys to total (part:whole) is 2 to 5.

PERCENTS

32. PERCENT FORMULA

In percent questions, whether you need to find the part, the whole, or the percent, use the same formula:

Part = Percent × Whole

When you use the formula, be sure to convert the percent into decimal form:

Example: What is 12% of 25?
Setup: Part = .12 × 25

Example: 15 is 3% of what number?
Setup: 15 = .03 × Whole

Example: 45 is what percent of 9?
Setup: 45 = Percent × 9

33. PERCENT INCREASE AND DECREASE

To increase a number by a percent, **add the percent to 100%,** convert to a decimal, and multiply. To increase 40 by 25%, add 25% to 100%, convert 125% to 1.25, and multiply by 40. 1.25 × 40 = 50. To decrease, just subtract the percent from 100%, convert to a decimal, and multiply.

34. FINDING THE ORIGINAL WHOLE

To find the **original whole before a percent increase or decrease,** set up an equation with a variable in place of the original number. Say you have a 15% increase over an unknown original amount, say *x*. You would follow the same steps as always: 100% plus 15% is 115%, which is 1.15 when converted to a decimal. Then multiply to the number, which in this case is *x*, and you get 1.15*x*, then set that equal to the "new" amount.

Example: After a 5% increase, the population was 59,346. What was the population
                before the increase?
Setup: 1.05*x* = 59,346

35. COMBINED PERCENT INCREASE AND DECREASE

When there are multiple percent increases and/or decreases, and the question asks for the combined percent increase or decrease, the easiest and most effective strategy is to pick 100 for the original value and see what happens.

Example: A price went up 10% one year, and the new price went up 20% the next year. What was the combined percent increase?

Setup: First year: 100 + (10% of 100) = 110. Second year: 110 + (20% of 110) = 132. That's a combined 32% increase.

RATIOS, PROPORTIONS, AND RATES

36. SETTING UP A RATIO

To find a ratio, put the number associated with the word **of on top** (as the numerator) and the quantity associated with the word **to on the bottom** (as the denominator), and reduce. The ratio of 20 oranges to 12 apples is $\frac{20}{12}$, which reduces to $\frac{5}{3}$. Be sure to keep the parts in the same order—so if a second ratio of oranges to apples was given, the oranges should be on top and the apples on the bottom.

37. PART-TO-PART AND PART-TO-WHOLE RATIOS

A part-to-part ratio can be turned into two part-to-whole ratios by putting **each number in the original ratio over the sum of the parts.** If the ratio of males to females is 1 to 2, then the males-to-people ratio is $\frac{1}{1+2} = \frac{1}{3}$ and the females-to-people ratio is $\frac{2}{1+2} = \frac{2}{3}$. Or, $\frac{2}{3}$ of all the people are female.

38. SOLVING A PROPORTION

A proportion is two fractions set equal to each other. To solve a proportion, **cross multiply:**

$$\frac{x}{5} = \frac{3}{4}$$
$$4x = 5(3)$$
$$x = \frac{15}{4} = 3.75$$

39. RATE

A rate is any "something per something"—days per week, miles per hour, dollars per gallon, etc. Pay close attention to the units of measurement, since often the rate is given in one measurement in the question and a different measurement in the answer choices. This means you need to convert the rate to the other measurement before you solve the question.

Example: If snow is falling at the rate of one _foot_ every four hours, how many _inches_ of snow will fall in seven hours?

Setup:

$$\frac{1\,\text{foot}}{4\,\text{hours}} = \frac{x\,\text{inches}}{7\,\text{hours}}$$

$$\frac{12\,\text{inches}}{4\,\text{hours}} = \frac{x\,\text{inches}}{7\,\text{hours}}$$

$$4x = 12 \times 7$$

$$x = 21$$

40. AVERAGE RATE

Average rate is _not_ simply the average of the rates. It's the average of the total amounts. The most common rate is speed—distance over time—and the most common question about average rates is average speed—total distance over total time.

$$\text{Average } A \text{ per } B = \frac{\text{Total } A}{\text{Total } B}$$

$$\text{Average speed} = \frac{\text{Total distance}}{\text{Total time}}$$

If the first 120 miles of a journey is at 40 mph and the next 120 miles is at 60 mph, what is the average speed? **Don't just average the two speeds.** Instead, figure out the total distance and the total time. The total distance is 120 + 120 = 240 miles. The times are three hours for the first leg and two hours for the second leg, or five hours total. The average speed, then, is $\frac{240}{5} = 48$ miles per hour.

AVERAGES

41. AVERAGE FORMULA

To find the average of a set of numbers, **add them up and divide by the number of numbers.**

$$\text{Average} = \frac{\text{Sum of the terms}}{\text{Number of the terms}}$$

To find the average of the five numbers 12, 15, 23, 40, and 40, first add them: 12 + 15 + 23 + 40 + 40 = 130. Then divide the sum by 5: 130 ÷ 5 = 26.

42. AVERAGE OF EVENLY SPACED NUMBERS

When you have a set of evenly spaced numbers, such as 10 consecutive numbers, or all the odd numbers between 5 and 35, you can use a shortcut rather than the averages formula. To find the average of evenly spaced numbers, just **average the smallest and the largest.** The average of all the integers from 13 through 77 is the same as the average of 13 and 77: $\frac{13+77}{2} = \frac{90}{2} = 45$.

43. USING THE AVERAGE TO FIND THE SUM

Since the average is just the sum of the numbers divided by the number of numbers, it follows that:

Sum = (Average) × (Number of terms)

If the average of 10 numbers is 50, then they add up to 10 × 50, or 500.

44. FINDING THE MISSING NUMBER

To find a missing number when you're given the average, **use the sum.** If the average of four numbers is 7, then the sum of those four numbers is 4 × 7, or 28. Suppose that three of the numbers are 3, 5, and 8. These numbers add up to 16 of that 28, which leaves 12 for the fourth number.

POSSIBILITIES AND PROBABILITY

45. COUNTING THE POSSIBILITIES

The fundamental counting principle: If there are *m* **ways** one event can happen and *n* **ways** a second event can happen, then there are *m* × *n* **ways** for the two events to happen. For example, with 5 shirts and 7 pairs of pants to choose from, you can put together 5 × 7 = 35 different outfits.

46. PROBABILITY

Probability is always the number of desired outcomes divided by the number of possible outcomes. It can be expressed as a fraction, or sometimes, as a decimal.

$$\text{Probability} = \frac{\text{Favorable outcomes}}{\text{Total possible outcomes}}$$

If you have 12 shirts in a drawer and 9 of them are white, the probability of picking a white shirt at random is $\frac{9}{12} = \frac{3}{4}$. This probability can also be expressed as .75 or 75%.

POWERS AND ROOTS

47. MULTIPLYING AND DIVIDING POWERS

To multiply powers with the same base, **add the exponents:** $x^3 \times x^4 = x^{3+4} = x^7$.

To divide powers with the same base, **subtract the exponents:** $y^{13} \div y^8 = y^{13-8} = y^5$

48. RAISING POWERS TO POWERS

To raise a power to another power, **multiply the exponents:** $(x^3)^4 = x^{3*4} = x^{12}$

49. SIMPLIFYING SQUARE ROOTS

To simplify a square root, **factor out the perfect squares** under the radical, square root them, and put the result in front of the part left under the square root sign (the non-perfect-square factors):

$$\sqrt{12} = \sqrt{4 \times 3} = \sqrt{4} \times \sqrt{3} = 2\sqrt{3}$$

50. ADDING AND SUBTRACTING ROOTS

You can add or subtract radical expressions only if the part under the radicals is the same. In other words, treat it like a variable. Just like 2x + 3x would equal 5x:

$$2\sqrt{3} + 3\sqrt{3} = 5\sqrt{3}$$

In other words, you can only add or subtract the numbers in front of the square root sign—the numbers under the sign stay the same.

51. MULTIPLYING AND DIVIDING ROOTS

You can distribute the square root sign over multiplication and division. The product of square roots is equal to the square root of the product:

$$\sqrt{3} \times \sqrt{5} = \sqrt{3 \times 5} = \sqrt{15}$$

The quotient of square roots is equal to the **square root of the quotient:**

$$\frac{\sqrt{6}}{\sqrt{3}} = \sqrt{\frac{6}{3}} = \sqrt{2}$$

ALGEBRAIC EXPRESSIONS

52. EVALUATING AN EXPRESSION

To evaluate an algebraic expression, **plug in** the given values for the unknowns and calculate according to PEMDAS. To find the value of $x^2 + 5x - 6$ when $x = -2$, plug in -2 for x:

$$(-2)^2 + 5(-2) - 6 = 4 - 10 - 6 = -12$$

53. ADDING AND SUBTRACTING MONOMIALS (COMBINING LIKE TERMS)

To combine like terms, **keep the variable part unchanged while adding or subtracting the coefficients (numbers):**

$$2a + 3a = (2 + 3)a = 5a$$

54. ADDING AND SUBTRACTING POLYNOMIALS

To add or subtract polynomials, **combine like terms:**

$$(3x^2 + 5x - 7) - (x^2 + 12) =$$
$$(3x^2 - x^2) + 5x + (-7 - 12) =$$
$$2x^2 + 5x - 19$$

55. MULTIPLYING MONOMIALS

To multiply monomials, **multiply the numbers and the variables separately:**

$$2a \times 3a = (2 \times 3)(a \times a) = 6a^2$$

56. MULTIPLYING BINOMIALS—FOIL

To multiply binomials, use **FOIL: First, Outer, Inner, Last:**

Example: $(x + 3)(x + 4)$

First multiply the **F**irst terms: $x \times x = x^2$.

Next the **O**uter terms: $x \times 4 = 4x$.

Then the **I**nner terms: $3 \times x = 3x$.

And finally the **L**ast terms: $3 \times 4 = 12$.

Then add and combine like terms: $x^2 + 4x + 3x + 12 = x^2 + 7x + 12$.

57. MULTIPLYING OTHER POLYNOMIALS

FOIL works only when you want to multiply two binomials (an expression with two terms.) If you want to multiply polynomials with more than two terms, make sure you **multiply each term in the first polynomial by each term in the second:**

$$(x^2 + 3x + 4)(x + 5) =$$

$$x^2(x + 5) + 3x(x + 5) + 4(x + 5) =$$

$$x^3 + 5x^2 + 3x^2 + 15x + 4x + 20 =$$

$$x^3 + 8x^2 + 19x + 20$$

FACTORING ALGEBRAIC EXPRESSIONS

58. FACTORING OUT A COMMON DIVISOR

A factor common to all terms of a polynomial can be **factored out.** All three terms in the polynomial $3x^3 + 12x^2 - 6x$ contain a factor of $3x$. Pulling out the common factor yields $3x(x^2 + 4x - 2)$. Remember that if you factor a term out completely, you are still left with 1: in the expression $6x^2 + 9x + 3$, you can factor a 3 out of everything. You're left with $3(2x^2 + 3x + 1)$.

59. FACTORING THE DIFFERENCE OF SQUARES

One of the test maker's favorite classic quadratics is the **difference of squares.**

$a^2 - b^2 = (a - b)(a + b)$

$x^2 - 9$, for example, factors to $(x - 3)(x + 3)$.

60. FACTORING THE SQUARE OF A BINOMIAL

There are two other classic quadratics that occur regularly on the ACT:

$a^2 + 2ab + b^2 = (a + b)^2$

$a^2 - 2ab + b^2 = (a - b)^2$

For example, $4x^2 + 12x + 9$ factors to $(2x + 3)^2$, and $n^2 - 10n + 25$ factors to $(n - 5)^2$. Recognizing a classic quadratic can save a lot of time on Test Day—be on the lookout for these patterns. (HINT: Any time you have a quadratic and one of the numbers is a perfect square, you should check for one of these three patterns.)

61. FACTORING OTHER POLYNOMIALS—FOIL IN REVERSE

To factor a quadratic expression, **think about what binomials you could use FOIL on to get that quadratic expression.** To factor $x^2 - 5x + 6$, think about what **F**irst terms will produce x^2, what **L**ast terms will produce $+ 6$, and what **O**uter and **I**nner terms will produce $-5x$. If there is no number in front of the first term, you are looking for two numbers that add up to the middle term and multiply to the third term. So here, you'd want two numbers that add up to -5 and multiply to 6. (Pay attention to sign—negative vs. positive makes a big difference here!) The correct factors are $(x - 2)(x - 3)$.

62. SIMPLIFYING AN ALGEBRAIC FRACTION

Simplifying an algebraic fraction is a lot like simplifying a numerical fraction. The general idea is to **find factors common to the numerator and denominator and cancel them.** Thus, simplifying an algebraic fraction begins with factoring, which often involves reverse-FOIL.

To simplify $\dfrac{x^2 - x - 12}{x^2 - 9}$, first factor the numerator and denominator:

$$\frac{x^2 - x - 12}{x^2 - 9} = \frac{(x-4)(x+3)}{(x-3)(x+3)}$$

Canceling $x + 3$ from the numerator and denominator leaves you with $\frac{x-4}{x-3}$.

SOLVING EQUATIONS

63. SOLVING A LINEAR EQUATION

To solve an equation, **isolate the variable.** As long as you do the same thing to both sides of the equation, the equation is still balanced. To solve $5x - 12 = -2x + 9$, first get all the x terms on one side by adding $2x$ to both sides: $7x - 12 = 9$.

Then add 12 to both sides: $7x = 21$, then divide both sides by 7 to get: $x = 3$.

64. SOLVING "IN TERMS OF"

To solve an equation for one variable **in terms of** another means to **isolate the one variable that you are solving for on one side of the equation,** leaving an expression containing the other variable on the other side. To solve $3x - 10y = -5x + 6y$ for x in terms of y, isolate x:

$3x - 10y = -5x + 6y$

$3x + 5x = 6y + 10y$

$8x = 16y$

$x = 2y$

65. TRANSLATING FROM ENGLISH INTO ALGEBRA

To translate from English into algebra, look for the key words and work from left to right to turn phrases into algebraic expressions and sentences into equations. Be careful about order, especially when subtraction is called for.

Example: The charge for a phone call is r cents for the first 3 minutes and s cents for each minute thereafter. What is the cost, in cents, of a call lasting exactly t minutes? ($t > 3$)

Setup: The charge begins with r, and then something more is added, depending on the length of the call. The amount added is s times the number of minutes past 3 minutes. If the total number of minutes is t, then the number of minutes past 3 is $t - 3$. So the charge is $r + s(t - 3)$.

INTERMEDIATE ALGEBRA

66. SOLVING A QUADRATIC EQUATION

To solve a quadratic equation, put it in the form of $ax^2 + bx + c = 0$—in other words, set it equal to 0. Then **factor** the left side (if you can), and set each factor equal to 0 separately to get the two solutions. To solve $x^2 + 12 = 7x$, first subtract $7x$ from both sides of the equation, which gives you $x^2 - 7x + 12 = 0$. Then use reverse-FOIL to factor the left side:

$(x - 3)(x - 4) = 0$

$x - 3 = 0$ or $x - 4 = 0$

$x = 3$ or 4

Sometimes the left side might not be obviously factorable. You can always use the **quadratic formula.** Just plug in the coefficients a, b, and c from $ax^2 + bx + c = 0$ into the formula:

$$\frac{-b \pm \sqrt{b^2 - 4ac}}{2a}$$

To solve $x^2 + 4x + 2 = 0$, plug $a = 1$, $b = 4$, and $c = 2$ into the formula:

$$x = \frac{-4 \pm \sqrt{4^2 - 4 \times 1 \times 2}}{2 \times 1}$$

$$= \frac{-4 \pm \sqrt{8}}{2} = -2 \pm \sqrt{2}$$

Whether you use reverse-FOIL or the quadratic equation, you will almost always get two solutions, or roots, to the equation.

67. SOLVING A SYSTEM OF EQUATIONS

You can solve for two variables only if you have two distinct equations. If you have one variable, you only need one equation, but if you have two variables, you need two distinct equations. Two forms of the same equation will not be adequate. If you have three variables, you need three distinct equations, and so on. **Combine the equations in such a way that one of the variables cancels out.** To solve the two equations $4x + 3y = 8$ and $x + y = 3$, multiply both sides of the second equation by -3 to get: $-3x - 3y = -9$. Now add the equations; the $3y$ and the $-3y$ cancel out, leaving $x = -1$:

$$
\begin{aligned}
4x + 3y &= 8 \\
+(-3x - 3y &= -9) \\
\hline
x \quad\quad &= -1
\end{aligned}
$$

Plug that back into either one of the original equations and you'll find that $y = 4$.

68. SOLVING AN EQUATION THAT INCLUDES ABSOLUTE VALUE SIGNS

To solve an equation that includes absolute value signs, **think about the two different cases**—one where what is inside the absolute value sign equals a positive number, and one where it equals a negative number. For example, to solve the equation $|x - 12| = 3$, think of it as two equations:

$x - 12 = 3$ or $x - 12 = -3$

$x = 15$ or 9

Just like with quadratic equations, equations with absolute value signs will have two possible solutions.

69. SOLVING AN INEQUALITY

Solving inequalities works just the same as solving equations—do the same thing to both sides, until the variable you are solving for is isolated—with one exception: When you **multiply or divide both sides by a negative number,** you must **reverse the inequality sign.** To solve $-5x + 7 < -3$, subtract 7 from both sides to get $-5x < -10$. Now divide both sides by -5, remembering to reverse the inequality sign: $x > 2$.

70. GRAPHING INEQUALITIES

To graph a range of values on a number line, use a thick black line over the number line, and at the end(s) of the range, use a **solid circle** if the point *is* **included** or an **open circle** if the point is ***not* included.** The figure here shows the graph of $-3 < x \leq 5$.

COORDINATE GEOMETRY

71. FINDING THE DISTANCE BETWEEN TWO POINTS

To find the distance between points, **use the Pythagorean theorem or special right triangles.** The difference between x_1 and x_2 is one leg and the difference between the y_1 and y_2 is the other leg.

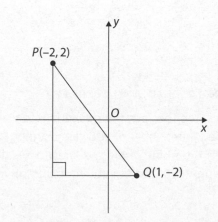

In the figure above, to find the distance between the points P and Q, draw a right triangle where $\overline{PQ}$ is the hypotenuse. This makes a 3-4-5 right triangle, so $\overline{PQ} = 5$.

You can also use the **distance formula:**

$$d = \sqrt{(x_2 - x_1)^2 + (y_2 - y_1)^2}$$

For instance, to find the distance between $R(3, 6)$ and $S(5, -2)$:

$$d = \sqrt{(5 - 3)^2 + (-2 - 6)^2}$$
$$= \sqrt{(2)^2 + (-8)^2}$$
$$= \sqrt{68} = 2\sqrt{17}$$

72. USING TWO POINTS TO FIND THE SLOPE

In mathematics, the slope of a line is often called m.

$$\text{Slope} = m = \frac{\text{Change in } y}{\text{Change in } x} = \frac{\text{Rise}}{\text{Run}} = \frac{y_2 - y_1}{x_2 - x_1}$$

The slope of the line that contains the points $A(2, 3)$ and $B(0, -1)$ is:

$$\frac{y_2 - y_1}{x_2 - x_1} = \frac{-1 - 3}{0 - 2} = \frac{-4}{-2} = 2$$

73. USING AN EQUATION TO FIND THE SLOPE

To find the slope of a line from an equation, put the equation into the **slope-intercept** form:

$$y = mx + b$$

where the slope is m, and b is the y-intercept (the point where the line crosses the y-axis). To find the slope of the equation $3x + 2y = 4$, isolate y, so it's in slope-intercept form:

$$3x + 2y = 4$$

$$2y = -3x + 4$$

$$y = -\frac{3}{2}x + 2$$

The slope is $-\frac{3}{2}$.

74. USING AN EQUATION TO FIND AN INTERCEPT

To find the y-intercept, you can either put the equation into **$y = mx + b$ (slope-intercept)** form—in which case b is the y-intercept—or you can just plug $x = 0$ into the equation and solve for y. The y-intercept is the point where the line crosses the y-axis, which means $x = 0$. To find the x-intercept, plug $y = 0$ into the equation and solve for x.

75. EQUATION FOR A CIRCLE

The equation for a circle of radius r and centered at (h, k) is:

$(x - h)^2 + (y - k)^2 = r^2$

The figure below shows the graph of the equation $(x - 2)^2 + (y + 1)^2 = 25$:

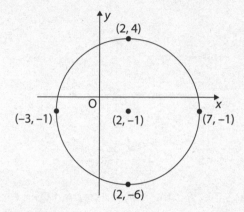

76. EQUATION FOR A PARABOLA

The graph of an equation in the form $y = ax^2 + bx + c$ is a parabola. The figure below shows the graph of seven pairs of numbers that satisfy the equation $y = x^2 - 4x + 3$:

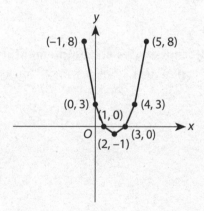

77. EQUATION FOR AN ELLIPSE

The graph of an equation in the form

$$\frac{x^2}{a^2} + \frac{y^2}{b^2} = 1$$

is an ellipse, with $2a$ as the sum of the focal radii (the distance from each foci to the same point on the ellipse), and with foci on the x-axis at $(0, -c)$ and $(0, c)$, where $c = \sqrt{a^2 - b^2}$. The following figure shows the graph of $\dfrac{x^2}{25} + \dfrac{y^2}{16} = 1$:

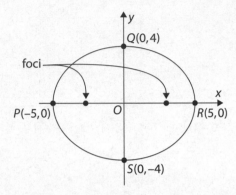

The foci are at $(-3, 0)$ and $(3, 0)$. $\overline{PR}$ is the **major axis,** and $\overline{QS}$ is the **minor axis.** This ellipse is symmetrical about both the x- and y-axes.

LINES AND ANGLES

78. INTERSECTING LINES

When two lines intersect, **adjacent angles are supplementary** (they make a line and add up to 180 degrees), and **vertical angles** (angles across from each other) **are equal.**

In the figure, the angles marked $a°$ and $b°$ are adjacent and supplementary, so $a + b = 180$. Furthermore, the angles marked $a°$ and $60°$ are vertical and equal, so $a = 60$.

79. PARALLEL LINES AND TRANSVERSALS

A line that cuts through two parallel lines is called a transversal. A transversal across parallel lines forms **four equal acute angles and four equal obtuse angles.**

Here, line 1 is parallel to line 2. Angles *a*, *c*, *e*, and *g* are obtuse, so they are all equal. Angles *b*, *d*, *f*, and *h* are acute, so they are all equal.

Furthermore, **any of the acute angles is supplementary to any of the obtuse angles.** Angles *a* and *h* are supplementary, as are *b* and *e*, *c* and *f*, and so on.

TRIANGLES—GENERAL

80. INTERIOR ANGLES OF A TRIANGLE

The three interior angles of any triangle **add up to 180°.**

In the figure above, $x + 50 + 100 = 180$, so $x = 30$.

81. EXTERIOR ANGLES OF A TRIANGLE

An exterior angle of a triangle is equal to the **sum of the remote interior angles**—that is, the two interior angles on the opposite side of the triangle.

In the figure shown here, the exterior angle labeled *x*° is equal to the sum of the remote interior angles 50 and 100: $x = 50 + 100 = 150$.

The three exterior angles of any triangle add up to 360°.

In the figure shown here, $a + b + c = 360$.

82. SIMILAR TRIANGLES

Similar triangles have the same shape: **corresponding angles are equal and corresponding sides are proportional.**

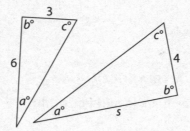

The triangles shown here are similar because they have the same angles. The 3 corresponds to the 4, and the 6 corresponds to the *s*.

83. AREA OF A TRIANGLE

Area of Triangle $= \dfrac{1}{2}$ **(Base)(Height)**

The height must be perpendicular to the base in order to use the area formula. This means if there isn't a right angle, you cannot find the height.

In the right triangle shown here, 4 is the height when the 7 is chosen as the base.

$$\text{Area} = \frac{1}{2}bh = \frac{1}{2}(7)(4) = 14$$

RIGHT TRIANGLES

84. PYTHAGOREAN THEOREM

For all right triangles (triangles with a 90 degree angle), where the hypotenuse is the side opposite the right angle:

$(leg_1)^2 + (leg_2)^2 = (hypotenuse)^2$

If one leg is 2 and the other leg is 3, then:

$$2^2 + 3^3 = c^2$$
$$c^2 = 4 + 9$$
$$c = \sqrt{13}$$

85. SPECIAL RIGHT TRIANGLES

3-4-5

If a right triangle's leg-to-leg ratio is 3:4 or if the leg-to-hypotenuse ratio is 3:5 or 4:5, then it's a 3-4-5 triangle, and you don't need to use the Pythagorean theorem to find the third side. Be on the lookout for multiples of this common pattern—a triangle with side lengths 6-8-10, for instance, is just a 3-4-5 times 2.

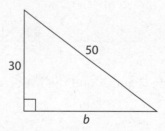

In the right triangle above, one leg is 30 and the hypotenuse is 50. This is 10 times 3-4-5. The other leg is 40.

5-12-13

If a right triangle's leg-to-leg ratio is 5:12 or if the leg-to-hypotenuse ratio is 5:13 or 12:13, then it's a 5-12-13 triangle, and you don't need to use the Pythagorean theorem to find the third side. Just figure out what multiple of 5-12-13 it is (get familiar with the first few multiples of 13, since they appear frequently as the length of the hypotenuse).

Here, one leg is 36 and the hypotenuse is 39. This is 3 times 5-12-13. The other leg is 15.

30°-60°-90°

There are also special right triangles based on angle measurement. The sides of a 30°-60°-90° triangle are in a ratio of $1 : \sqrt{3} : 2$. You don't need to use the Pythagorean theorem.

If the hypotenuse is 6, then the shorter leg is half that, or 3; and then the longer leg is equal to the short leg times $\sqrt{3}$.

45°-45°-90°

The sides of a 45°-45°-90° triangle are in a ratio of $1 : 1 : \sqrt{2}$.

If one leg is 3, then the other leg is also 3, and the hypotenuse is equal to a leg times $\sqrt{2}$, or $3\sqrt{2}$.

OTHER POLYGONS

86. SPECIAL QUADRILATERALS

RECTANGLE

A rectangle is a **four-sided figure with four right angles.** Opposite sides are equal. Diagonals are equal.

Quadrilateral *ABCD* is shown to have three right angles. The fourth angle therefore also measures 90°, and *ABCD* is a rectangle. The perimeter of a rectangle is equal to the sum of the lengths of the four sides, which is equivalent to 2(length + width).

PARALLELOGRAM

A parallelogram has **two pairs of parallel sides.** Opposite sides are equal. Opposite angles are equal. Consecutive angles (angles adjacent to each other) add up to 180°.

In this figure, *s* is the length of the side opposite the 3, so *s* = 3. The perimeter of a parallelogram is the sum of the lengths of all four sides.

SQUARE

A square is a **rectangle with four equal sides and four right angles.**

If *PQRS* is a square, all sides are the same length as *QR*. The perimeter of a square is equal to four times the length of one side.

TRAPEZOID

A **trapezoid** is a quadrilateral (a four-sided figure) with one pair of parallel sides and one pair of nonparallel sides.

In quadrilateral *EFGH*, sides $\overline{EF}$ and $\overline{GH}$ are parallel, while sides $\overline{EH}$ and $\overline{FG}$ are not parallel. *EFGH* is therefore a trapezoid.

87. AREAS OF SPECIAL QUADRILATERALS

Area of Rectangle = Length × Width

The area of a 7-by-3 rectangle is $7 \times 3 = 21$.

Area of Parallelogram = Base × Height

Just like with triangles, the base and the height must be perpendicular to each other, otherwise you cannot calculate the area of the parallelogram. The area of a parallelogram with a height of 4 and a base of 6 is $4 \times 6 = 24$.

Area of Square = (Side)²

The area of a square with sides of length 5 is $5^2 = 25$.

$$\text{Area of Trapezoid} = \left(\frac{base_1 + base_2}{2} \right) \times \text{height}$$

Think of it as the average of the bases (the two parallel sides) times the height (the length perpendicular to the bases—not the side length).

In trapezoid *ABCD*, you can use side *AD* for the height, since it's already perpendicular to the bases. The average of the bases is $\frac{2+14}{2} = 8$, so the area is 5 × 8, or 40.

88. INTERIOR ANGLES OF A POLYGON

The sum of the measures of the interior angles of a polygon is (*n* − 2) × 180, where *n* is the number of sides.

Sum of the Angles = (*n* − 2) × 180 degrees
The eight angles of an octagon, for example, add up to (8 − 2) × 180 = 1,080.

A "regular" shape on the ACT is a shape where all of the angles are the same and all of the side lengths are the same. To find **one angle of a regular polygon,** divide the sum of the angles by the number of angles (which is the same as the number of sides). The formula, therefore, is:

$$\text{Interior Angle} = \frac{(n-2) \times 180}{n}$$

Angle *A*, and all of the other angles, of the regular octagon above measures $\frac{1,080}{8} = 135$ degrees.

CIRCLES

89. CIRCUMFERENCE OF A CIRCLE

Circumference of a Circle = 2π*r*, where *r* is the radius of the circle (the distance from the center of the circle to the edge of the circle).

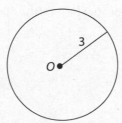

Here, the radius is 3, and so the circumference is 2π(3) = 6π.

90. LENGTH OF AN ARC

An **arc** is a piece of the circumference. Think of it like the crust on a slice of pizza. If n is the measure of the arc's central angle—the angle measure at the center of the circle—then the formula is:

Length of an Arc $= \dfrac{n}{360}(2\pi r)$, or the proportion of the "slice" times the circumference of the circle.

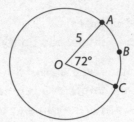

In the figure shown, the radius is 5 and the measure of the central angle is 72°. The arc length is $\dfrac{72}{360}$, or $\dfrac{1}{5}$, of the circumference:

$$\left(\frac{72}{360}\right)2\pi(5) = \left(\frac{1}{5}\right)10\pi = 2\pi$$

91. AREA OF A CIRCLE

Area of a Circle $= \pi r^2$

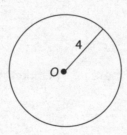

The area of the circle shown is $\pi(4)^2 = 16\pi$.

92. AREA OF A SECTOR

A **sector** is a piece of the area of a circle. Think of it as the whole slice of pizza (crust included!). If n is the measure of the sector's central angle, then the formula is:

Area of a Sector $= \dfrac{n}{360}(\pi r^2)$, or the proportion of the slice times the area of the circle.

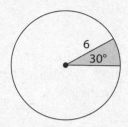

In the figure shown, the radius is 6 and the measure of the sector's central angle is 30°. The sector has $\frac{30}{360}$, or $\frac{1}{12}$, of the area of the circle:

$$\left(\frac{30}{360}\right)(\pi)(6^2) = \left(\frac{1}{12}\right)(36\pi) = 3\pi$$

SOLIDS

93. SURFACE AREA OF A RECTANGULAR SOLID

The surface of a rectangular solid—a box, or a cube, for example—consists of three pairs of identical faces. To find the surface area, find the area of each face and add them up. If the length is l, the width is w, and the height is h, the formula is:

Surface Area = 2lw + 2wh + 2lh

The surface area of the box shown is:

$$2(7 \times 3) + 2(3 \times 4) + 2(7 \times 4) = 42 + 24 + 56 = 122$$

94. VOLUME OF A RECTANGULAR SOLID

Volume of a Rectangular Solid = lwh, in other words, the area of the base times the height.

The volume of a 4-by-5-by-6 box is:

$4 \times 5 \times 6 = 120$

A cube is a rectangular solid with length, width, and height all equal. The volume formula if e is the length of an edge of the cube is:

Volume of a Cube = e^3

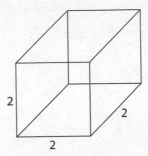

The volume of the cube above is $2^3 = 8$. It's still length times width times height, it's just that in a cube, those are all the same.

95. VOLUME OF OTHER SOLIDS

Volume of a Cylinder = $\pi r^2 h$, which is still just the area of the base times the height.

The volume of a cylinder where $r = 2$ and $h = 5$ is $\pi(2^2)(5) = 20\pi$.

Volume of a Cone $= \frac{1}{3}\pi r^2 h$

The volume of a cone where $r = 3$ and $h = 6$ is:

$$\text{Volume} = \frac{1}{3}\pi(3)^2(6) = 18$$

Volume of a Sphere $= \dfrac{4}{3}\pi r^3$

If the radius of a sphere is 3, then:

$$\text{Volume} = \frac{4}{3}\pi(3)^3 = 36\pi$$

TRIGONOMETRY

96. SINE, COSINE, AND TANGENT OF ACUTE ANGLES

To find the sine, cosine, or tangent of an acute angle (an angle less than 90°), use SOHCAH-TOA, which is an abbreviation for the following definitions:

$$\text{Sine} = \frac{\text{Opposite}}{\text{Hypotenuse}}$$

$$\text{Cosine} = \frac{\text{Adjacent}}{\text{Hypotenuse}}$$

$$\text{Tangent} = \frac{\text{Opposite}}{\text{Adjacent}}$$

In the figure shown:

$$\sin A = \frac{8}{17}$$

$$\cos A = \frac{15}{17}$$

$$\tan A = \frac{8}{15}$$

97. COTANGENT, SECANT, AND COSECANT OF ACUTE ANGLES

Think of the cotangent, secant, and cosecant as the reciprocals of the SOHCAHTOA functions:

$$\text{Cotangent} = \frac{1}{\text{Tangent}} = \frac{\text{Adjacent}}{\text{Opposite}}$$

$$\text{Secant} = \frac{1}{\text{Cosine}} = \frac{\text{Hypotenuse}}{\text{Adjacent}}$$

$$\text{Cosecant} = \frac{1}{\text{Sine}} = \frac{\text{Hypotenuse}}{\text{Opposite}}$$

In the figure shown:

$$\cot D = \frac{2}{3}$$

$$\sec D = \frac{\sqrt{13}}{2}$$

$$\csc D = \frac{\sqrt{13}}{3}$$

98. TRIGONOMETRIC FUNCTIONS OF OTHER ANGLES

To find a trigonometric function of an angle greater than 90°, sketch a circle of radius 1 centered at the origin of the coordinate grid. Start from the point (1, 0) and rotate counter-clockwise until you hit the hypotenuse.

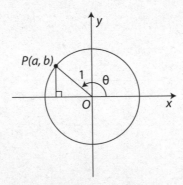

In the "unit circle" setup shown, the basic trigonometric functions are defined in terms of the coordinates a and b:

$$\sin \theta = b$$

$$\cos \theta = a$$

$$\tan \theta = \frac{b}{a}$$

Example: $\sin 210° = ?$

Setup: Sketch a 210° angle in the coordinate plane:

Because the triangle shown in this figure is a 30°-60°-90° right triangle (we know this because the *x*-axis is the first 180 degrees of our angle, which means there are 30 degrees between the *x*-axis and the hypotenuse), we can determine that the coordinates of point *P* are $-\frac{\sqrt{3}}{2}, -\frac{1}{2}$. The sine is therefore $-\frac{1}{2}$.

99. SIMPLIFYING TRIGONOMETRIC EXPRESSIONS

To simplify trigonometric expressions, use the inverse function definitions along with the fundamental trigonometric identity:

$$\sin^2 x + \cos^2 x = 1$$

Example: $\dfrac{\sin^2\theta + \cos^2\theta}{\cos\theta} = ?$

Setup: The numerator equals 1, so:

$$\frac{\sin^2\theta + \cos^2\theta}{\cos\theta} = \frac{1}{\cos\theta} = \sec\theta$$

100. GRAPHING TRIGONOMETRIC FUNCTIONS

To graph trigonometric functions, use the *x*-axis for the angle and the *y*-axis for the value of the trigonometric function. Use special angles—0°, 30°, 45°, 60°, 90°, 120°, 135°, 150°, 180°, etc.—to plot key points.

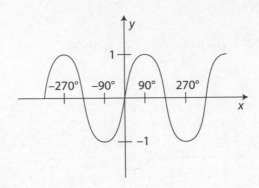

This figure shows a portion of the graph of $y = \sin x$.

SUMMARY

In this chapter, we went over the basics of strategy and the pieces of outside knowledge required to master the ACT Math test.

Remember to circle the real question (what is the objective, the thing you're trying to find?), underline the givens (what info are you going to use to solve the problem?), then examine the format of the answer choices (numbers, decimals, variables, radicals?) before choosing a strategy to solve the problem. Problems often look more complex than they are. Feel free to get to the easy ones first, but don't completely skip a question simply because it looks scary. Do the math if you have it mastered, but remember Point Building strategies such as Picking Numbers and Backsolving. The more tools you have in your repertoire, and the more flexibly you're able to think about a problem, the more prepared you'll be for anything the ACT Math test can throw at you. After you have your answer, remember to check what you circled to be sure you answered the right question.

Think flexibly. You don't have to do problems the "right" way!

To master the ACT Math test, combine these strategies with the outside knowledge listed in 100 Key Math Concepts. Flag or highlight the rules you still struggle with, then use the following chapter to practice the various question types and the strategies you'll need to apply those rules to more complex problems.

Know the outside knowledge, know the test and the question types, and practice the strategies.

CHAPTER 8

Math Part 2: ACT Math Strategy in Depth

OVERVIEW

Use this chapter to become familiar with all of the question types on the ACT Math test. All question types are detailed and discussed fully, and examples are provided for each. To get a quick sense of what's to come, refer to the SmartPoint Breakdown in the previous chapter on page 144. There, they are discussed in order of Test Day weight. The more heavily tested SmartPoints are listed there first. That's also how you should prioritize your time, especially if you are short on it, or close to your goal score. However, the SmartPoints that follow are discussed in order of building complexity, as the knowledge for some areas not commonly tested contributes to other more frequently tested SmartPoints. If you have time, and want to thoroughly work your Math skill set, start at the beginning and work your way through.

The chapter ends with Putting It All Together on page 262. Another great resource for those short on time, you'll get a chance to see how strategies for the Math subject test as a whole can be applied to a variety of question types. With these strategies, even the most complicated questions can be made manageable.

The following SmartPoints are shown in order of building complexity, SmartPoint by SmartPoint.

NUMBER PROPERTIES—2 POINTS

Complexity: Low. Relates to: Operations, Variable Manipulation, Proportions and Probability

Being comfortable with how numbers work can make your life easier on all sorts of math question types on the ACT.

Here are some essential rules and definitions to know:

- ***Integers* include 0 and negative whole numbers.** If a question says "x and y are integers," it's not ruling out numbers like 0 and –1.

- ***Evens and odds* include 0 and negative whole numbers.** Zero and –2 are even numbers; –1 is an odd number.

- ***Prime numbers* do not include 1.** The technical definition of a prime number is a positive integer with exactly two distinct positive integer factors. Two is prime because it has exactly two positive factors: 1 and 2. It is the smallest, and the only even, prime number. Four is not prime because it has three positive factors (1, 2, and 4)—too many! And 1 is not prime because it has only one positive factor (1)—too few!

- ***Remainders* are integers.** If a question asks for the remainder when 15 is divided by 2, don't say "15 divided by 2 is 7.5, so the remainder is .5." What you should say is: "15 divided by 2 is 7 with a remainder of 1."

- ***The $\sqrt{\ }$ symbol represents the positive square root only.*** The equation $x^2 = 9$ has two solutions: 3 and –3. But when you see $\sqrt{9}$, it means positive 3 only.

Remind yourself about evens and odds, and positives and negatives, by filling out these charts (Hint: Pick Numbers if you're stuck):

Know This About Odds and Evens on the ACT

Even × Even = Even Even × Odd = Even Odd × Odd = Odd	Even ± Even = Even Odd ± Odd = Even Even ± Odd = Odd
Even $^{\text{Positive Integer}}$ = Even Odd $^{\text{Positive Integer}}$ = Odd	

Know This About Positives and Negatives on the ACT

Positive × Positive = Positive Negative × Negative = Positive Positive × Negative = Negative	Subtracting a negative number is the same as adding a positive number
Negative $^{\text{Even Exponent}}$ = Positive	Positive Fraction $^{\text{Positive Integer}}$ = Smaller Positive Fraction
Negative $^{\text{Odd Exponent}}$ = Negative	Negative Fraction $^{\text{Positive Integer}}$ = Smaller Negative or Positive Fraction

Let's practice using these rules and the Kaplan Method to work through a tricky Number Properties question.

Know that the Kaplan Method isn't intended to be a rigid procedure, but a set of guidelines that will keep you on track, moving quickly and evading traps.

EXAMPLE

1. If the sum of five consecutive even integers is equal to their product, what is the greatest of the five integers?

    A. 4
    B. 10
    C. 14
    D. 16
    E. 20

STEP 1: WHAT IS THE QUESTION?

Before you can begin to solve this problem, you have to figure out what it's asking. You'll need to know the meanings of *sum, product, consecutive, even*, and *integer*. Put the question stem into words you can understand. What the question stem is really saying here is that when you add up these five consecutive even integers, you get the same thing as when you multiply them.

STEP 2: WHAT INFORMATION AM I GIVEN?

We are not given any numbers in the problem, but we *are* told that we'll be working with consecutive even integers, and we *are* given five answer choices—five numbers that *could* be the final term of the five-even-number sequence. Because the question specifies *even* numbers, the difference between each integer in this series will be 2. And a quick glance at the answer choices tells us they are all positive. Good to know.

STEP 3: WHAT CAN I DO WITH THE INFORMATION?

How are we going to figure out what these five numbers are? We could set up an equation:

$$x + (x - 2) + (x - 4) + (x - 6) + (x - 8) = x(x - 2)(x - 4)(x - 6)(x - 8)$$

That would work. But you may well not have time to create and solve an equation like this! So if that wasn't the first option that came to mind, come up with a better way.

Let's stop and think logically about this one for a moment. When we think about sums and products, it's natural to think mostly of positive integers. With positive integers, we would generally expect the product to be *greater* than the sum. Multiplying makes bigger results than adding.

But what about negative integers? Hmm. Well, the sum of five negatives is negative, and the product of five negatives is also negative. Generally, the product will be "more negative" than the sum, so with negative integers, the product will be *less than* the sum.

So when will the product and sum be the same? How about right at the boundary of positive and negative—that is, around 0? That makes some sense. So try (A)—see if the five consecutive even integers with equal product and sum are: −4, −2, 0, 2, and 4.

$$(-4) \times (-2) \times 0 \times 2 \times 4 = (-4) + (-2) + 0 + 2 + 4$$

The product and sum are both 0. We've done it!

How to Backsolve: The question asks which is the greatest of the integers, so you have to start with the greatest answer choice: (E)—if you start with any other, even if it works you won't know if it's the *largest*. If the largest number is 20, then the other numbers must be 18, 16, 14, 12. Their sum is 20 + 18 + 16 + 14 + 12 = 80. 20 times 18 is already 360, so we know that choice (E) is not correct and is WAY too big! Let's try one a good bit smaller, (C) 14. We want to add: 14 + 12 + 10 + 8 + 6 = 50. Still too big, because 10 times 6 is already 60. So let's try 4, choice (A). 4 + 2 + 0 + (−2) + (−4) = 4 × 2 × 0 x (−2) × (−4) = 0. It works!

The final area of Number Properties you'll need to be aware of is divisibility. Divisibility questions involve factors (including greatest common factor), multiples (including least common multiple), and primes (including prime factorization). All concepts are occasionally tested directly, but more often, a thorough understanding of each will help you navigate through more complex questions from different SmartPoints.

Let's review:

The **factors** of a number divide evenly into that number without a remainder. 2, 4, and 8 are **factors** of 16.

The **multiples** of a number can be divided by that number without a remainder. 4, 8, and 16 are **multiples** of 2.

List all of the factors of 8:

Now, list all of the multiples of 8:

Which task is impossible? Was there any overlap, any numbers that you listed twice?

For the factors of 8, you should have listed 1, 2, 4, 8. That's it. Negative numbers and fractions don't count. Those are all of the factors of 8 that exist.

For the multiples of 8, perhaps you started the task with 8, 16, 24, 32,... Those are all multiples indeed, but there's a problem with listing all of them: The multiples of any number are infinite. They go on forever.

Thus, to keep factors and multiples straight, remember that there are *few factors and many multiples*.

Additionally, notice that 8 was listed twice. Every positive integer is both a factor and a multiple of itself.

To find all factors of a number, you can use a Factor T-Chart.

Try it out with 24.

The rest of the factors were 12 (across from 2), 3 across from 8, and 4 across from 6. To fill out a Factor T-Chart, count up starting from 1 on the left side and see if the number is a factor. If it is, write the factor you need to multiply it by on the right. Continue counting up using the left column until you get to a number that you already have in the right column.

Try it one more time with 45.

Did you find 1 and 45, 3 and 15, 5 and 9?

Great work!

Now ask yourself, is 5 a factor or multiple of 10?

_____.

Is 10 a factor or multiple of 5?

_____.

Your first answer should have been "factor," and your second should be "multiple."

Is every multiple of 8 a multiple of 4?

_____.

Is every multiple of 4 a multiple of 8?

_____.

The first answer here is "yes." The second is "no."

Finally, a **prime number** is an integer that only has itself and 1 as factors.

The first eight prime numbers are 2, 3, 5, 7, 11, 13, 17, and 19. 1 is not prime, and negatives cannot be prime.

The **prime factorization** of an integer is the number broken down into all prime factors. To find prime factorization, pick two factors of the integer (other than itself and 1) and keep finding factors of those integers until all are prime.

For example:

$$84 = 7 \times 12$$

Looking at these factors, we see 7 is prime, but 12 is not. Keep factoring 12.

$$12 = 6 \times 2$$

Of these factors, 2 is prime, but 6 is not.

$$6 = 3 \times 2$$

Both are prime. We're done.

The prime factorization is $7 \times 3 \times 2^2$.

Remember, we pulled the 7 out when it was 84, we pulled two 2's out (which is why we have 2 squared), and we pulled a 3 out.

Try it yourself with 48:

The answer is $2^4 \times 3$.

Here are the definitions of least common multiple and greatest common factor, which you can also find in 100 Key Math Concepts. Review these. Then, let's put it all together and practice a couple of problems.

COMMON MULTIPLE

You can always get a common multiple of two numbers by **multiplying** them, but unless the two numbers are relative primes, the product will not be the least common multiple.

For example, to find a common multiple for 12 and 15, you could just multiply: 12 × 15 = 180. But it's not necessarily the least common multiple (in fact, it's not).

LEAST COMMON MULTIPLE (LCM)

To find the least common multiple, check out the **multiples of the larger number** until you find one that's **also a multiple of the smaller.**

To find the LCM of 12 and 15, begin by taking the multiples of 15. 15 is not divisible by 12; 30 is not; nor is 45. But the next multiple of 15, 60, is divisible by 12, so that's the LCM.

GREATEST COMMON FACTOR (GCF)

To find the greatest common factor, break down both numbers into their prime factorizations, and take **all the prime factors they have in common.** 36 = 2 × 2 × 3 × 3 and 48 = 2 × 2 × 2 × 2 × 3. What they have in common is two 2s and one 3, so the GCF is 2 × 2 × 3 = 12.

PRACTICE

2. How many positive integers less than 50 are multiples of 4 but NOT multiples of 6?

    F. 4

    G. 6

    H. 8

    J. 10

    K. 12

Step 1: The question asks for integers that are multiples of 4 but not multiples of 6.

Step 2: You know the integers are positive and are all less than 50.

Step 3: The multiples of 4 that are less than 50 are 4, 8, 12, 16, 20, 24, 28, 32, 36, 40, 44, and 48. Cross out the multiples of 6: 12, 24, 36, 48.

Step 4: There are eight remaining numbers (4, 8, 16, 20, 28, 32, 40, 44); (H) is correct.

3. If a is the greatest prime factor of 51, and b is the greatest prime factor of 75, what is the value of $a + b$?

    A. 8

    B. 22

    C. 32

    D. 42

    E. 56

Step 1: The question asks for the sum of $a + b$.

Step 2: You know that a equals the greatest prime factor of 51 and b equals the greatest prime factor of 75.

Step 3: Factor out 51 and 75 using factor trees. $51 = 3 \times 17$ and $75 = 5 \times 3 \times 5$.

Step 4: $17 + 5 = 22$; (B) is correct.

> ▶️ 🖥️ Visit your online syllabus—Lesson 4—for more instruction and practice with prime factorization.

OPERATIONS—3 POINTS

Complexity: Low. Relates to: Number Properties, Variable Manipulation, Proportions and Probability

There aren't many questions on the ACT that ask you to simply multiply or divide, but being adept at both is important throughout for answering larger questions.

We'll start by reviewing the order of operations and what it means, then we'll tackle each of the more complex areas of the SmartPoints—Radicals, Imaginary Numbers, and Logarithms.

PEMDAS = Please Excuse My Dear Aunt Sally. This mnemonic will help you remember the order of operations:

P = Parentheses

E = Exponents

M = Multiplication

D = Division

A = Addition

S = Subtraction

Multiplication and division are ordered from left to right.

Addition and subtraction are ordered from left to right.

Example: $30 - 5 \times 4 + (7 - 3)^2 \div 8$

First, perform any operations within parentheses.

$$30 - 5 \times 4 + 4^2 \div 8$$

(If the expression has parentheses within parentheses, work from the innermost out.)

Next, raise to any powers indicated by exponents: $30 - 5 \times 4 + 16 \div 8$.

Then, do all multiplication and division from left to right: $30 - 20 + 2$.

Finally, do all addition and subtraction from left to right: $10 + 2 = 12$.

Try one yourself:

1. $5 - |7 - 9| + 3^2 = ?$

    A. -1

    B. 12

    C. 16

    D. 19

    E. 36

Step 1: $7 - 9 = -2$, so the absolute value portion reduces to 2.

Step 2: $3^2 = 9$

Step 3: (none)

Step 4: $5 - 2 + 9 = 12$. (B) is correct.

WORKING WITH EXPONENTS

The most challenging element of those basic operations is exponents. The ACT tests exponents in a variety of ways. By remembering a few simple rules, you can make your life much easier when dealing with exponents. You'll also be well on your way to understanding more advanced concepts, like radicals and logarithms.

Here are those rules:

In the term $3x^2$, 3 is the coefficient, x is the base, and 2 is the exponent. The exponent refers to the number of times the base is a factor of the expression—the number of times the base is multiplied by itself. For example, 4^3 has 3 factors of 4, or $4^3 = 4 \times 4 \times 4$—it's multiplied by itself 3 times.

An integer times itself is the **square** of that integer ($y \times y$ is the square of y, or y^2).

An integer times itself twice is the **cube** of that integer ($4 \times 4 \times 4$ is the cube of 4, or 4^3).

To multiply two terms with the same base, keep the base and add the exponents.

    $m^4 \times m^7 = m^{4+7} = m^{11}$

EXAMPLE

$$2^2 \times 2^3 = (2 \times 2)(2 \times 2 \times 2) \qquad \text{or} \qquad 2^2 \times 2^3 = 2^{2+3}$$

$$= (2 \times 2 \times 2 \times 2 \times 2) \qquad\qquad\qquad = 2^5$$

$$= 2^5$$

To divide two terms with the same base, keep the base and subtract the exponent of the denominator from the exponent of the numerator.

    $d^{10} \div d^7 = d^{10-7} = d^3$

EXAMPLE

$$4^4 \div 4^2 = \frac{4 \times 4 \times 4 \times 4}{4 \times 4}$$

$$= \frac{4 \times 4}{1} \qquad \text{or} \qquad \begin{aligned} 4^4 \div 4^2 &= 4^{4-2} \\ &= 4^2 \end{aligned}$$

$$= 4^2$$

To raise a power to another power, multiply the exponents.

$$(p^5)^3 = p^{5 \times 3} = p^{15}$$

EXAMPLE

$$(3^2)^4 = (3 \times 3)^4$$

$$= (3 \times 3)(3 \times 3)(3 \times 3)(3 \times 3) \qquad \text{or} \qquad (3^2)^4 = 3^{2 \times 4}$$

$$= 3^8 \qquad\qquad\qquad\qquad\qquad\qquad = 3^8$$

Any nonzero number raised to the zero power is equal to 1. $a^0 = 1$ as long as $a \neq 0$. 0^0 is undefined.

To evaluate a negative exponent, take the reciprocal of the base and change the sign of the exponent.

$$a^{-n} = \frac{1}{a^n} \text{ or } \left(\frac{1}{a}\right)^n$$

EXAMPLE

$$2^{-3} = \left(\frac{1}{2}\right)^3 = \frac{1}{2^3} = \frac{1}{8}$$

A fractional exponent indicates a **root**.

$(a)^{\frac{1}{n}} = \sqrt[n]{a}$ (Read "the nth root of a." If no n is present, the radical sign means a square root.)

EXAMPLE

$$8^{1/3} = \text{the cube root of } 8 = 2$$

WORKING WITH RADICALS

To reverse the process of taking a number to a certain power, via an exponent, you would take the same root of that number, via a radical.

For example, $2^2 = 4$. To reverse this process, we'd take the square root of 4, $\sqrt{4} = 2$.

A radical implies that you're taking the square root of a number, as opposed to the cube root or above. You'll need to be able to work with and simplify radicals on Test Day.

When it comes to the four basic arithmetic operations, we treat radicals in much the same way we would treat variables.

Addition and subtraction: Only like radicals can be added to or subtracted from one another.

EXAMPLE

$$2\sqrt{3} + 4\sqrt{2} - \sqrt{2} - 3\sqrt{3} = \left(4\sqrt{2} - \sqrt{2}\right) + \left(2\sqrt{3} - 3\sqrt{3}\right) \text{ Note: } \sqrt{2} = 1\sqrt{2}$$
$$= 3\sqrt{2} + \left(-\sqrt{3}\right)$$
$$= 3\sqrt{2} - \sqrt{3}$$

Multiplication and division: To multiply or divide one radical by another, multiply or divide the numbers outside the radical signs separately from the numbers inside the radical signs, much like you would with coefficients and variables.

EXAMPLE

$$\left(6\sqrt{3}\right) \times \left(2\sqrt{5}\right) = (6 \times 2)\left(\sqrt{3} \times \sqrt{5}\right) = 12\sqrt{3 \times 5} = 12\sqrt{15}$$

EXAMPLE

$$12\sqrt{15} \div 2\sqrt{5} = (12 \div 2)\left(\sqrt{15} \div \sqrt{5}\right) = 6\left(\frac{\sqrt{15}}{\sqrt{5}}\right) = 6\sqrt{3}$$

EXAMPLE

$$\frac{4\sqrt{18}}{2\sqrt{6}} = \left(\frac{4}{2}\right)\left(\frac{\sqrt{18}}{\sqrt{6}}\right) = 2\left(\sqrt{\frac{18}{6}}\right) = 2\sqrt{3}$$

If the number inside the radical is a multiple of a perfect square, the expression can be simplified by factoring out the perfect square.

EXAMPLE

$$\sqrt{72} = \sqrt{(36 \times 2)} = \sqrt{36} \times \sqrt{2} = 6\sqrt{2}$$

Try putting it all together with this problem.

2. Which of the following is equivalent to $\dfrac{16\sqrt{10} - \sqrt{2}\sqrt{5}}{5}$?

   F. 0

   G. 3

   H. $3\sqrt{2}$

   J. $3\sqrt{10}$

   K. $10\sqrt{10}$

Step 1: $16\sqrt{10} - \sqrt{2}\sqrt{5} = 16\sqrt{10} - \sqrt{10}$

Step 2: $16\sqrt{10} - \sqrt{10} = 15\sqrt{10}$

Step 3: $\dfrac{15\sqrt{10}}{5} = 3\sqrt{10}$. (J) is correct.

The last two concepts to discuss under the Operations SmartPoint also relate to exponents, but are very lightly tested. Logarithms are a shortcut for exponents, similar to the way multiplication is a shortcut for addition. And Imaginary Numbers use exponents to create negative numbers where normally they would not.

Think of logarithms as a way of rearranging a number with a power. $2^3 = 8$ is the same thing as $\log_2 8 = 3$.

The base number, 2, becomes the base of the log and remains the first number listed. The other two switch places.

Try it the other way—remember the base stays the first number listed, and the other two switch places.

$\text{Log}_5 25 = 2$

_____

In standard form, that's $5^2 = 25$.

And that's it. The ACT simply tests your basic knowledge of what logarithms are. Here's a sample problem.

3. If $\log_x(36) = 2$, then $x = ?$

     A. 2
     B. 3
     C. 4
     D. 6
     E. 18

Step 1: $\log_x(36) = 2$ is equivalent to $x^2 = 36$.

Step 2: $x = 6$; (D) is correct.

Though imaginary numbers seem scary, the tested rules on the ACT are just as simple as the ones tested for logarithms.

An **imaginary number** is a number that gives a *negative* result when squared.

So, by definition, $i^2 = -1$.

There are only four values of i you might need to remember:

$$i = \sqrt{(-1)}$$

$$i^2 = -1$$

$$i^3 = -i$$

$$i^4 = 1$$

Because i to the 4th is 1, i^5 cycles back to the beginning and is the same as i to the first. $i^6 = i^2$, $i^7 = i^3$, and $i^8 = i^4 = 1$. We're back to 1 again, thus i^9 starts the process all over, and i cycles through the same four values over and over and over again.

So, then, what is i^{77}?

Should you count every 4, or is there a quicker way?

Try *dividing* by 4.

You'll get 19.25, or 19 with a remainder of 1. Thus, i^{77} is the same as i to the first, just i.

Try this sample problem:

4.   The complex number i is defined as $i^2 = -1$. $(i + 1)^2(i - 1) = ?$

   F. $i - 1$

   G. $i - 2$

   H. $-i + 2$

   J. $-2i + 2$

   K. $-2i - 2$

A complex number can seem scary on the ACT, but this problem defines it for you, so treat it like you would any other variable that you plug numbers into. In this problem, the key is swapping every i^2 with a -1. Begin by simplifying the first term in the expression:

$$(i + 1)^2 = (i + 1)(i + 1) = i^2 + 2i + 1$$
$$= -1 + 2i + 1 = 2i$$

Multiplying this by the second term gets you $2i (i - 1) = 2i^2 - 2i = 2(-1) - 2i = -2 - 2i$

That's the same as (K).

VARIABLE MANIPULATION—7 POINTS

Complexity: Low-Medium. Relates to: Number Properties, Operations

Variable Manipulation questions ask you to put together what you know about number properties and operations to solve for an unknown value, also known as a *variable*.

In the simplest forms of Variable Manipulation questions, keep in mind the order of operations (PEMDAS) and the golden rule of equations:

Whatever you do to one side of the equation, you must do to the other.

To solve for a variable, simply go in the reverse order of PEMDAS, performing the opposite of the operations you see, until the variable is alone on one side of the equation (isolated). The number on the other side will be your answer.

Here's an example. Make sure you have the basics of the process down, then we'll dive into the many wrinkles the ACT will throw at you to see how adept you are at problem solving with variables.

$$2x + 7 = 13$$

Again, we reverse the order of PEMDAS and perform the opposite of the operations we see. The variable has been multiplied by 2 with 7 added to it.

Addition comes first, and the opposite of that function is subtraction.

Subtract 7 from both sides.

Now, our equation is:

$$2x = 6$$

Let's deal with the multiplication. The opposite of that function is division.

Divide both sides by 2, and you have your answer:

$$x = 3$$

Remind yourself how you would use the opposite of the shown functions in the following situations.

    i. $x + 3 = \dfrac{5}{2}$

    ii. $3x = 7$

    iii. $x^2 = 9$

    iv. $\dfrac{x}{7} = 8$

    v. $1\dfrac{1}{5} = x - 2$

Keep in mind that like terms can be combined:

$4x + 2x$ can be simplified to $6x$.

However, terms can only be simplified if they are raised to the same power and use the same variable:

$4x^2 + 2x$ cannot be simplified.

$4x + 2y$ cannot be simplified.

Here's an example of an ACT problem that tests this knowledge.

MATH PART 2: ACT MATH STRATEGY IN DEPTH

1. If $4x + 3 = 9x - 4$, then $x = ?$

   A. $\dfrac{7}{5}$

   B. $\dfrac{5}{7}$

   C. $\dfrac{7}{15}$

   D. $\dfrac{1}{5}$

   E. $-\dfrac{1}{5}$

Step 1: Get the variables on one side of the equation and the constants on the other side by either subtracting $4x$ from both sides of the equation and adding 4 to both sides of the equation, or by subtracting $9x$ from both sides of the equation and subtracting 3 from both sides of the equation. Then divide both sides by the coefficient of x.

Step 2: (A) is correct.

What other method could you have used to solve this problem?

Backsolving, because there are numbers in the answer choices.

Now let's look at some algebraic terminology and build to the first examples of complex variable manipulation: polynomials and quadratic equations.

A *term* is a numerical constant or the product (or quotient) of a numerical constant and one or more variables. Examples of terms are $3x$, $4x2yz$, and $2a/c$.

All of the laws of arithmetic operations, such as the commutative, associative, and distributive laws, are applicable to polynomials as well.

Commutative law: $2x + 5y = 5y + 2x$
$5a \times 3b = 3b \times 5a = 15ab$

Associative law: $(2x + 3x) + 5x = 2x + (3x + 5x) = 10x$
$4s \times (7j \times 2p) = (4s \times 7j) \times 2p = 56sjp$

Distributive law: $3a(2b - 5c) = (3a \times 2b) - (3a \times 5c) = 6ab - 15ac$

Note: The product of two binomials can be calculated by applying the distributive law twice.

EXAMPLE

$(x + 5)(x - 2) = x(x - 2) + 5(x - 2)$
$= x \times x - x \times 2 + 5 \times x - 5 \times 2$
$= x^2 - 2x + 5x - 10$
$= x^2 + 3x - 10$

A simple mnemonic for this is **F**irst **O**uter **I**nner **L**ast, or **FOIL**.

FACTORING ALGEBRAIC EXPRESSIONS

Factoring a polynomial means expressing it as a product of two or more simpler expressions.

Common monomial factor: When there is a monomial factor common to every term in the polynomial, it can be factored out by using the distributive law.

Example: $2a + 6ac = 2a(1 + 3c)$ ($2a$ is the greatest common factor of $2a$ and $6ac$)

Difference of two perfect squares: The difference of two squares can be factored into a product: $a^2 - b^2 = (a - b)(a + b)$.

Example: $9x^2 - 1 = (3x)^2 - (1)^2 = (3x + 1)(3x - 1)$

Polynomials of the form $a^2 + 2ab + b^2$: Any polynomial of this form is equivalent to the square of a binomial. Notice that $(a + b)^2 = a^2 + 2ab + b^2$ (try FOIL).

Factoring such a polynomial is just reversing this procedure.

Example: $x^2 + 6x + 9 = (x)^2 + 2(x)(3) + (3)^2 = (x + 3)^2$

Polynomials of the form $a^2 - 2ab + b^2$: Any polynomial of this form is equivalent to the square of a binomial as well. Here, though, the binomial is the difference of two terms: $(a - b) = a^2 - 2ab + b^2$.

Example: $x^2 - 4x + 4 = (x)^2 - 2(x)(2) + (2)^2 = (x - 2)^2$

Polynomials of the form $ax^2 + bx + c$: Polynomials of this form can nearly always be factored into a product of two binomials. The product of the first term in each binomial must equal the first term of the polynomial. The product of the last terms of the binomials must equal the third term of the polynomial. The sum of the remaining products must equal the second term of the polynomial. Factoring can be thought of as the FOIL method backward.

Example: $x^2 - 3x + 2$

We can factor this into two binomials, each containing an x term. Start by writing down what we know.

$$x^2 - 3x + 2 = (x + ...)(x + ...)$$

We need to fill in the missing term to the right of each binomial. The **product** of the two missing terms will be the last term in the polynomial: 2. The **sum** of the two missing terms will be the coefficient of the second term of the polynomial: -3. Try the possible factors of 2 until we get a pair that adds up to -3. There are two possibilities: 1 and 2, or -1 and -2. Since $(-1) + (-2) = -3$, we can fill -1 and -2 into the empty spaces.

Thus, $x^2 - 3x + 2 = (x - 1)(x - 2)$.

Note: Using FOIL on a factored polynomial is a great way to check your work.

To solve an equation with a polynomial, set it equal to 0, factor it into binomials, then set each of those equal to 0 and solve.

Example: $x^2 - 3x + 2 = 0$

To find the solutions, or roots, start by doing what we did earlier in this chapter—factor it. We can factor $x^2 - 3x + 2$ into $(x - 2)(x - 1)$, making our quadratic equation $(x - 2)(x - 1) = 0$.

We now have an equation where the product of two binomials equals 0. This can only be the case when at least one of the terms is 0. Therefore, to find the roots, we just need to set the two binomials equal to 0 and solve for x. In other words, either $x - 2 = 0$ or $x - 1 = 0$ (or both). Solving for x, we get $x = 2$ or $x = 1$. To check the math, plug 1 and 2 back into the original equation and make sure that both variables satisfy the equation.

$$2^2 - 3(2) + 2 = 0 \qquad\qquad 1^2 - 3(1) + 2 = 0$$
$$4 - 6 + 2 = 0 \qquad\qquad 1 - 3 + 2 = 0$$
$$0 = 0 \qquad\qquad 0 = 0$$

Try out one more.

2. If $x^2 - 4x - 6 = 6$, what are the possible values for x?

    F. 4, 12

    G. −6, 2

    H. −6, −2

    J. 6, 2

    K. 6, −2

Step 1: The question asks for possible values of x.

Step 2: You know that $x^2 - 4x - 6 = 6$.

Step 3: Set the equation equal to zero: $x^2 - 4x - 12 = 0$. FOIL to get $(x - 6)(x + 2) = 0$.

Step 4: x could equal either 6 or −2; (K) is correct.

 Visit your online syllabus—Lesson 4—for more instruction and practice with FOILing.

The other commonly tested area of variable manipulation involves **simultaneous equations.**

Sometimes a problem on the ACT will involve an equation with more than one variable. In general, if you want to find numerical values for all of your variables, you will need as many **distinct** equations as you have variables. Two equations are distinct if neither simplifies into the other.

$x^2 + 2xy + 5y^2 = 5$ and $3x^2 + 6xy + 15y^2 = 15$ are *not* distinct since multiplying the first equation by 3 results in the second.

If we had one equation with two variables, such as $x - y = 7$, there are an infinite number of solution sets because each unique value of x has a different corresponding value for y. If $x = 8$, $y = 1$ (since $8 - 1 = 7$). If $x = 12$, $y = 5$ (since $12 - 5 = 7$). And so forth.

If we are given two distinct equations with two variables, we can combine them to get a unique solution set. This is known as a **system of equations.** There are two ways to do this:

Method I: Combination

Combination involves subtracting a multiple, positive, or negative of one equation from the other. The idea is to choose a multiple such that all but one of the variables is eliminated, solve for that variable, then plug that variable back into the other equation for the *other* variable if necessary.

Example: If $3a + 2b = 12$ and $5a + 4b = 23$, what is the value of a?

Step 1: Start by lining up the equations, one under the other.

$$3a + 2b = 12$$
$$5a + 4b = 23$$

Step 2: Multiply the top equation by 2, to get $4b$ in both.

$$6a + 4b = 24$$
$$5a + 4b = 23$$

Step 3: Subtract to eliminate the b term.

$$
\begin{array}{r}
6a + 4b = 24 \\
-(5a + 4b = 23) \\
\hline
a \quad\ \ = 1
\end{array}
$$

Method II: Substitution

Substitution involves solving for one of the variables in terms of the other in one equation, then substituting that value back into the other equation.

Example: Solve for m and n when $m = 4n + 2$ and $3m + 2n = 16$.

Step 1: We have m in terms of n, so substitute $4n + 2$ for m in the second equation.

$$3(4n + 2) + 2n = 16$$
$$12n + 6 + 2n = 16$$

Step 2: Solve for n.

$$14n = 10$$
$$n = \frac{10}{14} = \frac{5}{7}$$

Step 3: Substitute $\dfrac{5}{7}$ for n in the first equation to solve for m.

$$m = 4n + 2$$
$$m = 4\left(\frac{5}{7}\right) + 2$$
$$= \frac{20}{7} + \frac{14}{7}$$
$$\frac{34}{7}$$

Now that you know both methods, try one more, choosing which one you'd like to use.

3. If $2x + y = -8$ and $-4x + 2y = 16$, what is the value of y?

   A. -4

   B. -2

   C. 0

   D. 2

   E. 4

Step 1: The question asks for the value of y.

Step 2: Because you have two equations with y you're dealing with a system. What strategy can you use to most effectively solve for y?

Step 3: Use combination or substitution. Combination: Multiply the first equation by 2 to get:

$(2)(2x + y) = -8 (2)$
$4x + 2y = -16$
Combine both equations:
$4x + 2y = -16$
$-4x + 2y = 16$
$4y = 0, y = 0$

Substitution: Isolate x in the first equation to get: $2x = -8 - y$.

Divide both sides by 2 to get: $x = \dfrac{(-8 - y)}{2}$.

Substitute that value into that second equation to get:

$\dfrac{-4(-8 - y)}{2} + 2y = 16$; $16 + 2y + 2y = 16$. Simplify to get $4y = 0, y = 0$.

(C) is correct.

The ACT will have many questions involving systems of equations. Some will even be disguised as an entirely different question type. By being adept at Combination or Substitution, you can remove the disguise and efficiently find the answer.

4. What are the (x, y) coordinates of the point of intersection of the line representing the equation $5x + 2y = 4$ and the line representing the equation $x - 2y = 8$?

   F. $(2, 3)$

   G. $(-2, 3)$

   H. $(2, -3)$

   J. $(-3, 2)$

   K. $(3, -2)$

This may look like a coordinate geometry question, but do you really have to graph the lines to find the point of intersection? Remember, the ACT is looking for creative thinkers, not just calculators! Think about it for a moment—what's the special significance of the point of intersection, the one point that the two lines have in common? That's the one point whose coordinates will satisfy *both* equations.

So what we realize now is that this is not a coordinate geometry question at all, but a system-of-equations question. All it's really asking you to do is solve the pair of equations for *x* and *y*. The question has nothing to do with slopes, intercepts, axes, or quadrants. It's a pure algebra question in disguise.

Now that we know we're looking at a system of equations, we can solve the problem using combination and substitution. We'll go through combination, but you can find the same answer using substitution if you prefer.

The first equation has $a + 2y$, and the second equation has $a - 2y$. If we just add the equations, the *y* terms cancel:

$$5x + 2y = 4$$
$$x - 2y = 8$$
$$6x = 12$$

If $6x = 12$, then $x = 2$. Plug that back into either of the original equations, and you'll find that $y = -3$. The point of intersection is $(2, -3)$, and the answer is (H).

  Visit your online syllabus—Lesson 4—for more instruction and practice with systems of equations.

The last (and less common) wrinkles the ACT will test with Variable Manipulation questions are inequalities and absolute values.

INEQUALITIES

Inequality symbols:

> greater than

< less than

≥ greater than or equal to

≤ less than or equal to

Example: $x > 4$ means all numbers greater than 4.

Example: $x < 0$ means all numbers less than zero (the negative numbers).

Example: $x > -2$ means *x* can be -2 or any number greater than -2.

Example: $x \le \frac{1}{2}$ means *x* can be $\frac{1}{2}$ or any number less than $\frac{1}{2}$.

Solving inequalities: Inequalities behave the same way as normal equations with one exception: **Multiplying or dividing by a negative number reverses the inequality's direction.**

Example: $-1(-3x < 2) = 3x > -2$

Example: Solve for x and represent the solution set on a number line: $3 - \dfrac{x}{4} \geq 2$.

1. Multiply both sides by 4.

2. Subtract 12 from both sides.

3. Divide both sides by −1 and change the direction of the sign. $x \leq 4$

Note: The solution set to an inequality is not a single value but a range of possible values. Here, the values include 4 and all numbers below 4.

Try one more.

5. If $8 - 2x > 6$, which of the following describes all of the possible values of x?

    A. $x < -7$

    B. $x > -7$

    C. $x > -2$

    D. $x < 1$

    E. $x > 1$

Step 1: The question asks for the possible values of x.

Step 2: You know that $8 - 2x > 6$.

Step 3: Solve for x—subtract 8 from both sides to get $-2x > -2$. Divide by −2: reverse the directions of the sign.

Step 4: $x < 1$, so (D) is correct.

Now, let's discuss the final concept tested under Variable Manipulation: **absolute value.**

ABSOLUTE VALUE

The absolute value of a number is its distance from 0 on a number line. Thus, because distance cannot be negative, absolute value is always positive or 0.

KNOW THIS ABOUT ABSOLUTE VALUE ON THE ACT

The absolute value of a number is its _____ from zero on the number line.

Because distance cannot be negative, absolute value is always _____.

Number	Absolute Value
7	
−7	
	8
	n

Try out a question. If you don't remember how to work with absolute values in an equation, remember those Point Builders. You don't need to know the "right" way to get to an answer to solve the problem.

For your reference, the "right" way will be discussed after the problem.

6. If $|7 + r| = 3$, what is one possible value of r?

    F.   −10

    G.   −7

    H.   −3

    J.   4

    K.   7

Step 1: The question asks for a possible value of r.

Step 2: You know that the absolute value of $7 + r = 3$.

Step 3: Solve $7 + r = 3$ to get $r = -4$. Now set $7 + r$ to -3. Solve $7 + r = -3$ to get $r = -10$.

Step 4: (F) is correct.

PROPORTIONS AND PROBABILITY—6 POINTS

Complexity: Medium. Relates to: Number Properties, Operations

Proportions and Probability questions involve using what you know about numbers to relate them to each other and find a missing piece.

You'll need to know how to form and calculate percents and ratios (and decimals and fractions along with them). Then, you'll need to apply that knowledge to three-part formulas to find averages, distance/rate/time, and probability.

Let's start by reviewing how to work with fractions and how that translates to finding percents.

FRACTIONS

In the fraction $\dfrac{4}{5}$:

4 ← numerator

— ← fraction bar (means "divided by")

5 ← denominator

Equivalent fractions: The value of a number is unchanged if you multiply the number by 1. In a fraction, multiplying the numerator and denominator by the same nonzero number is the same as multiplying the fraction by 1: The fraction is unchanged. Similarly, dividing the top and bottom by the same nonzero number leaves the fraction unchanged.

EXAMPLE

$$\frac{1}{2} = \frac{1 \times 2}{2 \times 2} = \frac{2}{4}$$

$$\frac{5}{10} = \frac{5 \div 5}{10 \div 5} = \frac{1}{2}$$

Canceling and reducing: Generally speaking, when you work with fractions on the ACT, you'll need to put them in **lowest terms.** This means the numerator and the denominator are not divisible by any common integer greater than 1. The fraction $\frac{1}{2}$ is in lowest terms, but the fraction $\frac{3}{6}$ is not, since 3 and 6 are both divisible by 3. The method we use to take such a fraction and put it in lowest terms is called **reducing.** That simply means to divide out any common multiples from both the numerator and denominator. This process is also commonly called **canceling.**

Example: Reduce $\frac{15}{35}$ to lowest terms.

First, determine the largest common factor of the numerator and denominator. Then, divide the top and bottom by that number to reduce.

$$\frac{15}{35} = \frac{3 \times 5}{7 \times 5} = \frac{3 \times 5 \div 5}{7 \times 5 \div 5} = \frac{3}{7}$$

Addition and subtraction: We can't add or subtract two fractions directly unless they have the same denominator. Therefore, before adding (or subtracting), we must find a common denominator. A common denominator is just a **common multiple** of all the denominators of the fractions. The **least common denominator** is the **least common multiple** (the smallest positive number that is a multiple of all the terms).

EXAMPLE

$\frac{3}{5} + \frac{2}{3} - \frac{1}{2}$. Denominators are 5, 3, 2.

LCM = 5 × 3 × 2 = 30 = LCD

Multiply the numerator and denominator of each fraction by the value that raises its respective denominator to the LCD.

$$\left(\frac{3}{5} \times \frac{6}{6}\right) + \left(\frac{2}{3} \times \frac{10}{10}\right) - \left(\frac{1}{2} \times \frac{15}{15}\right)$$

$$= \frac{18}{30} + \frac{20}{30} - \frac{15}{30}$$

Combine the numerators by adding or subtracting, and keep the LCD as the denominator.

$$= \frac{18 + 20 - 15}{30} = \frac{23}{30}$$

Multiplication: We can easily combine fractions by multiplying straight across the numerators to get a combined numerator, then multiplying across the denominators to get a combined denominator, and finally simplifying as usual. However, we can also make it easier by canceling like terms (with shared factors) diagonally and vertically first.

Example $\frac{10}{9} \times \frac{3}{4} \times \frac{8}{15}$

First, reduce (cancel) diagonally and vertically.

$$\frac{^2\cancel{10}}{_3\cancel{9}} \times \frac{^1\cancel{3}}{_1\cancel{4}} \times \frac{\cancel{8}^2}{\cancel{15}_3}$$

Then, multiply numerators and denominators.

$$\frac{2 \times 1 \times 2}{3 \times 1 \times 3} = \frac{4}{9}$$

Division: Dividing is the same as multiplying by the **reciprocal** of the divisor. To get the reciprocal of a fraction, invert the numerator and the denominator. The reciprocal of the fraction $\frac{3}{7}$ is $\frac{7}{3}$.

Example $\frac{4}{3} \div \frac{4}{9}$

To divide, invert the second term (the divisor), and then multiply as above.

$$\frac{4}{3} \div \frac{4}{9} = \frac{4}{3} \times \frac{9}{4} = \frac{^1\cancel{4}}{_1\cancel{3}} \times \frac{\cancel{9}^3}{\cancel{4}_1} = \frac{1 \times 3}{1 \times 1} = 3$$

PERCENTS

Percents are one of the most commonly used mathematical relationships and are quite popular on the ACT. *Percent* is just another word for *hundredth*. For example, 27% (27 percent) means:

27 hundredths

$\frac{27}{100}$

0.27

27 out of every 100 things

27 parts out of a whole of 100 parts

MAKING AND DROPPING PERCENTS

To make a percent, multiply by 100%. Since 100% means 100 hundredths or 1, multiplying by 100% will not change the value.

Example: $0.17 = 0.17 \times 100\% = 17.0\%$ or 17%

Example: $\dfrac{1}{4} = \dfrac{1}{4} \times 100\% = 25\%$

To drop a percent, divide by 100%. Dividing by 100% will not change the value either.

Example: $32\% = \dfrac{32\%}{100\%} = \dfrac{32}{100} = \dfrac{8}{25}$

Example: $\dfrac{1}{2}\% = \dfrac{\frac{1}{2}\%}{100\%} = \dfrac{1}{200}$

Now, let's look at how **percents** will be tested on the ACT.

In Percent questions, you're usually given two numbers and asked to find a third. The key is to identify what you have and what you're looking for. In other words, identify the part, the percent, and the whole.

Put the numbers and the unknown into the general form:

Part = Percent × Whole

Usually the *part* is associated with the word *is,* and the *whole* is associated with the word *of.*

EXAMPLES

1. In a group of 250 students, 40 are seniors. What percentage of the group are seniors?

    A. 1.6%

    B. 6.25%

    C. 10%

    D. 16%

    E. 40%

The percent is what we're looking for ("What percentage..."); the whole is 250 ("...of the group..."); and the part is 40 ("...are seniors"). Plug these into the general formula:

Part = Percent × Whole

$40 = 250x$

$x = \dfrac{40}{250} = .16 = 16\%$

The answer is (D).

Many ACT percent questions concern percent <u>change</u>. To increase a number by a certain percent, calculate that percent of the original number and add it on. To decrease a number by a certain percent, calculate that percent of the original number and then subtract. For example, to answer the question, "What number is 30 percent greater than 80?" first find 30 percent of 80—that's 24—and add that on to 80: 80 + 24 = 104.

The ACT has ways of complicating percent change problems. Particularly tricky are problems with multiple changes, such as a percent increase followed by another percent increase, or a percent increase followed by a percent decrease, like the following question:

2. If a positive number is increased by 70 percent, and then the result is decreased by 50 percent, which of the following accurately describes the net change?

   F. 20 percent decrease

   G. 15 percent decrease

   H. 12 percent increase

   J. 20 percent increase

   K. 120 percent increase

To get a handle on this one, pick a number. Suppose the original number is 100. After a 70 percent increase, it rises to 170. That number, 170, is decreased by 50 percent, which means it's reduced by half, to 85. The net change from 100 to 85 is a 15 percent decrease—choice (G).

The formula for percent change is:

Percent Change = (Actual Change / Original Amount) × 100%.

Remember, if you're presented with an unknown original value in a percent change problem, that's a perfect time to Pick Numbers! Call the original amount 100, and work through the problem from there.

Try one more percent change question.

3. 750 students attended Lakeland High School in 2009. In 2010, 1,000 students attended Lakeland High School. By what percent did the student body increase in 2010?

   A. 20%

   B. 25%

   C. $33\frac{1}{3}$%

   D. $66\frac{2}{3}$%

   E. 250%

Step 1: The question asks for the percent increase of the student body in 2010.

Step 2: You know the student body populations in 2009 and 2010.

Step 3: Apply the percent change formula:

$$\frac{\text{Actual change}}{\text{Original amount}} \times 100\% = \frac{1,000 - 750}{750} \times 100\% = \frac{250}{750} \times 100\%.$$ This reduces to

$$\frac{1}{3} \times 100\% = 33\frac{1}{3}\%.$$

Step 4: (C) is correct.

The last concept to review before we discuss three-part formulas is **ratios.** Fortunately, the jump from fractions to ratios is a small one, as treating ratios as fractions is often the most efficient way to deal with them mathematically.

RATIOS

A **ratio** is a comparison of two quantities by division.

Ratios may be written with a fraction bar $\left(\dfrac{x}{y} \right)$, with a colon ($x : y$), or in English terms (ratio of x to y). Again, we recommend the first way, since ratios can be treated as fractions for the purposes of computation.

Ratios can (and in most cases, should) be reduced to lowest terms just as fractions are reduced.

Example: Max has 16 books and Marie has 12 books.

The ratio of Max's books to Marie's books is $\dfrac{16}{12}$. (Read "16 to 12.")

$$\frac{16}{12} = \frac{4}{3} \text{ or } 4{:}3$$

In a ratio of two numbers, the *numerator* is often associated with the word *of*, and the *denominator* with the word *to*.

Example: The ratio **of** 3 **to** 4 is $\dfrac{\text{of } 3}{\text{to } 4} = \dfrac{3}{4}$.

We frequently deal with ratios by working with a **proportion.** A proportion is simply an equation in which two ratios are set equal to each other.

PROPORTIONS

Proportions are just two ratios set equal to each other. They are also the most common way ratios are tested on the ACT. You'll need to create two equal ratios, one involving a missing piece. By setting those ratios equal to each other, you form a proportion and can cross-multiply and easily solve for the missing piece.

Make sure only one piece is missing when you set up your proportion. All three of the other pieces need to be in place.

Additionally, make sure your units match before you cross-multiply. When setting up a proportion, ask yourself: are those ratios actually equal to each other?

EXAMPLE

If the ratio of dogs to cats in a pet store is 2:5 and there are 10 dogs, how many cats are in the pet store?

Perhaps you can do this one in your head, but practice setting up a proportion with one missing piece.

The missing piece is the number of cats actually in the pet store. Let's use a variable and say there are x cats in the store.

We know the ratio is 2 dogs to 5 cats, or 2/5.

We can set this equal to our ratio of actual dogs to cats, but make sure you keep in mind which is which when positioning your numbers. In our given ratio, dogs are on top, cats are on the bottom. Our missing piece ratio must be the same for a proper proportion.

$$\frac{2 \text{ dogs}}{5 \text{ cats}} = \frac{10 \text{ dogs}}{x \text{ cats}}$$

Our units match! Now, we can cross-multiply and solve.

$$2x = 50$$

We have 25 cats in the pet store!

The last thing to watch out for with proportions is the type of ratio you're dealing with, whether it's a part-to-part or a part-to-whole ratio.

For instance, let's assume there are only cats and dogs in the pet store. What would be the ratio of dogs to total pets?

Since the two parts of the whole are 2 dogs and 5 cats, we can put those parts together to find that our "whole" is 7 total pets.

Thus, the ratio of dogs to total pets is 2/7. That is a part-to-whole ratio. The ratio of dogs to cats was a part-to-part ratio.

When setting up a proportion, you'll need to match units as you did before, but you'll also need to make sure you're dealing with the same type of ratio on either side of the equal sign.

EXAMPLE

4. The ratio of left-handed people to right-handed people in a class is 1:4. If there are 20 people in the class, how many right-handed people are there?

   F. 1
   G. 4
   H. 5
   J. 16
   K. 20

Step 1:

Left-Handed	+ Right-Handed	= Total
1	4	
		20

Step 2: 1 + 4 = 5

Step 3: The second row is 4 times the first row.

Step 4: Apply the ratio to the second row:

Left-Handed	+ Right-Handed	= Total
1	4	5
4	16	20

(J) is correct. These sorts of questions can also be completed by creating a proportion $\left(\dfrac{4}{5} = \dfrac{x}{20}\right)$, cross-multiplying ($5x = 80$), and solving ($x = 16$).

Finally, to combine ratios, give them a common term.

EXAMPLE

The ratio of a to b is 3 to 4, and the ratio of b to c is 3 to 5. What is the ratio of a to c?

Find a common value for b, since that is our bridge from a to c. In the first ratio, b is 4. In the second, b is 3. In order to cross from a to c, b has to match, which it doesn't now.

To get there, remember to think about ratios as fractions. And remember that we can change fractions as much as we want; we simply need to multiply by another fraction that equals 1.

We want the two to match, so we need a common multiple. The lowest common multiple of 3 and 4 (our two values of b) is 12, so that's what we need.

Thus, let's change our first ratio (a to b is 3/4) so that the denominator equals 12. To get 4 to 12, we need to multiply it by 3. We'll need to do the same thing to our numerator to keep the ratio equal, so we're multiplying the top and bottom by multiplying the whole fraction by 3/3. Our new ratio of a to b is the equivalent ratio 9/12.

Let's do the same thing to our ratio of *b* to *c*, this time making the numerator 12, since that's where we find *b*. *b* is 3 this time, so we'll need to multiply it by 4 and do the same thing to the denominator. Our new ratio of *b* to *c* is 12 to 20.

Now that our *b*'s match, we can cross that bridge from *a* to *c* directly.

Our ratio of *a* to *c* is 9 to 20.

THREE-PART FORMULAS

It's time to jump to three-part formulas! We've laid the groundwork by discussing fractions, percents, ratios, and proportions. Mastering all four will make this next section simple. The ACT will test your knowledge of the above four using the three-part formulas for **average, distance/rate/time,** and **probability.** Let's look at each in turn, along with sample problems.

AVERAGE

The arithmetic **mean,** or **average,** of a group of numbers is defined as the sum of the terms divided by the number of terms.

$$\text{Average} = \frac{\text{Sum of Terms}}{\text{Number of Terms}}$$

Example: Henry buys three items that cost $2.00, $0.75, and $0.25. What is the average price?

$$
\begin{aligned}
\text{Average price} &= \frac{\text{Sum of prices}}{\text{Number of prices}}\\
&= \frac{\$2.00 + \$0.75 + \$0.25}{3}\\
&= \frac{\$3.00}{3}\\
&= \$1.00
\end{aligned}
$$

If we know the average of a group of values and the number of terms in the group, we can find the sum of the terms with the following formula:

$$\text{Sum of Terms} = \text{Average Value} \times \text{Number of Terms}$$

Example: The average daily temperature for the first week in January was 31 degrees. If the average temperature for the first six days was 30 degrees, what was the temperature on the seventh day?

The sum for all seven days is $31 \times 7 = 217$ degrees.

The sum of the first six days is $30 \times 6 = 180$ degrees.

The temperature on the seventh day is $217 - 180 = 37$ degrees.

For evenly spaced numbers, the average is the middle value (or **median,** which we'll discuss shortly). The average of consecutive integers 6, 7, and 8 is 7. The average of 5, 10, 15, and 20 is 12.5 (midway between the middle values, 10 and 15).

It might be useful to try to think of the average as the "balanced" value. In other words, the total deficit of all the values below the average will balance out the total surplus of all the values that exceed the average. The average of 3, 5, and 10 is 6. Three is 3 less than 6 and 5 is 1 less than 6, for a total deficit of $3 + 1 = 4$. This is the same amount by which 10 is greater than 6.

Example: The average of 3, 4, 5, and x is 5. What is the value of x?

Think of each value in terms of its position relative to the average, 5.

3 is 2 less than the average.

4 is 1 less than the average.

5 is at the average.

Together, the three numerical terms have a total deficit of $1 + 2 + 0 = 3$.

Therefore, x must be 3 **more** than the average to restore the balance at 5. So x is $3 + 5 = 8$.

EXAMPLE

5. To earn a B for the semester, Linda needs an average of at least 80 on the five tests. Her average for the first four test scores is 79. What is the minimum score she must get on the fifth test to earn a B for the semester?

    A. 80
    B. 81
    C. 82
    D. 83
    E. 84

The *sum* is the key to a lot of Average questions, as we saw in the previous example. Sums can be combined much more readily than averages. An average of 80 on five tests is more usefully thought of as a combined score of 400 (80×5). To get a B for the semester, Linda's five test scores have to add up to 400 or more. The question stem says her *average* for the first test scores is 79, but we can treat it as though she actually got exactly 79 on all four. So the first four scores add up to $4 \times 79 = 316$. She needs another 84 to get that 316 up to 400. The answer is (E).

One spin the ACT may put on Average questions is to give you an average for part of a group and an average for the rest of the group, and then ask for the combined average.

EXAMPLE

6. In a class of 10 boys and 15 girls, the boys' average score on the final exam was 80 and the girls' average score was 90. What was the average score for the whole class?

F. 83

G. 84

H. 85

J. 86

K. 87

Tempting as it is, don't just average 80 and 90 to get 85. That would work only if the class had exactly the same number of girls as boys, which we know it doesn't, so it can't be a straight average. In this case, there are more girls, so they carry more weight in the overall class average. In other words, the class average should be somewhat closer to 90 (the girls' average) than to 80 (the boys' average). (If you were running short on time and needed to guess, just this information would help you note that the answer *must be* (J) or (K).)

Again, to find the right average, the key is to use the sum. The average score for the whole class is the total of the 25 individual scores divided by 25. We don't have 25 scores to add up, but we can use the boys' average and the girls' average to get two subtotals.

If 10 boys average 80, then their 10 scores add up to 10 × 80, or 800. If 15 girls average 90, then their 15 scores add up to 15 × 90, or 1,350. Add the boys' total to the girls' total: 800 + 1,350 = 2,150. That's the class total, which can be divided by 25 to get the class average: $\frac{2,150}{25} = 86$. The answer is (J).

Median and **Mode** are lightly tested concepts on the ACT that also relate to sets of numbers. Since they are lightly tested, we'll discuss each briefly.

MEDIAN

If a group of numbers is arranged in numerical order, the **median** is the *middle* value if there is an odd number of terms in the set or the *average of the two middle terms* if there is an even number of terms in the set. The median of the numbers 1, 4, 5, 6, and 100 is 5, while the median of the numbers 2, 3, 7, 9, 22, and 34 is $\frac{7+9}{2} = \frac{16}{2} = 8$.

Example: What is the median of the following list of terms: 5, 101, 53, 2, 8, 4, and 11?

Rearranged in numerical order, the list is 2, 4, 5, 8, 11, 53, and 101. The list contains an odd number of terms, so the median is the middle number, or 8.

Remember that in an evenly spaced list of numbers, such as a set of consecutive integers, the median is equal to the mean. However, if the numbers are not spaced evenly, the median will be different from the mean, as you've seen from the examples above.

MODE

The **mode** refers to the term that appears most frequently in a set. If Set A = {1, 5, 7, 1, 3, 4, 1, 3, 0}, the mode would be 1, as it shows up three times—more than any other term.

If more than one term is tied for most frequent, every one of them is a mode.

Example: What is the mode of the following list of terms: 3, 23, 12, 23, 3, 7, 0, 5?

Both 3 and 23 each appear twice, which is more often than any other term, so both 3 and 23 are modes of this list.

If no term shows up more than once, there is no mode.

Finally, be aware of number **sequences.**

An **arithmetic sequence** is formed by adding a common difference to the previous term. If presented with 9, 6, and 3, you may be asked what comes next. You're adding the common difference −3. The next term is 0.

A **geometric or exponential sequence** is formed by multiplying each term by a common number. When given 2, 6, and 18, recognize we are multiplying by 3. We can confirm this by dividing any two consecutive terms. The next term in the sequence is 54.

EXAMPLE

$$\frac{4}{3}, 1, \frac{3}{4}, x, \frac{27}{64}, \ldots$$

7. In the geometric sequence above, what is the value of x?

   A. 0

   B. $\dfrac{1}{2}$

   C. $\dfrac{9}{16}$

   D. $\dfrac{3}{4}$

   E. 2

Step 1: The question asks for the value of x.

Step 2: You're given a pattern of numbers that follow a geometric sequence.

Step 3: Study the pattern to find the common ratio between the numbers. Inspect 1 and

$$\frac{3}{4} \cdot \frac{\frac{3}{4}}{1} = \frac{3}{4}, \text{ the common ratio; multiply } \left(\frac{3}{4}\right)\left(\frac{3}{4}\right) \text{ to get the next term, } \frac{9}{16}.$$

Step 4: Choice (C) is correct. Note that savvy test takers won't have to do any math at all if they think critically about the answer choices: the sequence is centered roughly around $\frac{1}{2}$, so eliminate (A) and (E).

Furthermore, the pattern doesn't repeat, so eliminate (D). Finally, the fractions appear to be getting more complicated, so (C) is much more likely than (B).

DISTANCE/RATE/TIME

A **rate** is a type of ratio that relates two different kinds of quantities. Speed is a common example and relates an amount of distance traveled to the amount of time taken to travel it.

Conversationally, we often interchange the terms *rate* and *speed*. The ACT often does the same, but it's necessary to keep in mind that there could be other rates, such as cost per item or pages per document. Any *x* per *y* is a rate.

Again, the most tested type of rate is speed. Speed can be measured in miles per hour, or kilometers per hour, or meters per second, or really any unit of distance per unit of time.

To find this type of rate, simply divide distance by time.

Rate = Distance/Time.

Shifting the formula, we can also calculate distance given rate and time.

Distance = Rate × Time.

For your reference, to find the time given the other two, we can shift the formula one more time.

Time = Distance/Rate.

EXAMPLE

8. Bob travels 125 miles in $2\frac{1}{2}$ hours. If he travels at the same rate for another 4 hours, how many total miles will he have traveled?

   F. 50
   G. 125
   H. 200
   J. 325
   K. 525

Step 1: $\dfrac{125\,\text{miles}}{2.5\,\text{hours}} = 50\,\text{miles per hour}$

Step 2: $6\frac{1}{2}$ hours

Step 3: D = Rate × Time: 50 miles per hour × $6\frac{1}{2}$ hour = 325 miles; (J) is correct.

Now, try combining your knowledge of proportions with distance, rate, and time to solve the following problem.

Keep careful track of those units of measurement!

Example: A train travels at a speed of 75 miles per hour. How many minutes does it take the train to travel 40 miles?

$$\frac{40\, miles}{75\, miles\, per\, hour} = \frac{40}{75\mathrm{th}}\ of\ an\ hour = \frac{8}{15\mathrm{th}}\ of\ an\ hour = 32\, minutes$$

The final formula to know that deals with distance, rate, and time is for *average speed*. When presented with a multi-part journey at different speeds and tasked with finding the average speed, make sure to follow this formula and *don't just average the speeds!*

Average Speed = Total Distance/Total Time

EXAMPLE

9. A train traveled at a rate of 90 miles per hour for x hours and then at a rate of 60 miles per hour for y hours. Which expression represents the train's average rate in miles per hour for the entire distance traveled?

    A. $\dfrac{540}{xy}$

    B. $\dfrac{90}{x} \times \dfrac{60}{y}$

    C. $\dfrac{90}{x} + \dfrac{60}{y}$

    D. $\dfrac{90x + 60y}{x + y}$

    E. $\dfrac{150}{x + y}$

Step 1: The question asks for the expression that represents the train's average speed for the total distance traveled.

Step 2: You know that the train traveled for 90 miles for x hours and 60 miles for y hours.

Step 3: Use Picking Numbers, and choose easy numbers to plug into the question. If $x = 2$ and $y = 3$, apply the distance formula: $(90)(2) + (60)(3) = 180 + 180 = 360$ miles. Now plug that into the formula for average speed to get $\dfrac{360}{5} = 72$. Plug $x = 2$ and $y = 3$ to find 72:

A. $\dfrac{540}{(3)(2)} = \dfrac{540}{6} = 90$. Eliminate.

B. $\dfrac{90}{2} \times \dfrac{60}{3} = 45 \times 20 = 9$. Eliminate.

C. $\dfrac{90}{2} + \dfrac{60}{3} = 45 + 20 = 65$. Eliminate.

D. $\dfrac{360}{5} = 72$. Keep.

E. $\dfrac{150}{5} = 30$. Eliminate.

Step 4: (D) is correct.

Now, try putting it all together. If you get stuck, remember those Point Builders!

EXAMPLE

10. Jema drives 84 miles in the same time Avery drives 78 miles. Jema drives at a rate 4 miles per hour faster than Avery. How fast did Jema drive?

    F. 42
    G. 46
    H. 48
    J. 52
    K. 56

Step 1: Let *x* equal Avery's speed in miles per hour; *x* + 4 equals Jema's rate.

Step 2:

Drivers	Speed	Distance (miles)
Jema	j	84
Avery	$j - 4$	78

Step 3: If they drove for the same amount of time, solve the distance formula for time $\left(\text{time} = \dfrac{\text{distance}}{\text{rate}} \right)$, and set them equal to each other: $\dfrac{84}{j} = \dfrac{78}{j-4}$. Cross-multiply to get $84j - 336 = 78j$, which equals $6j = 336$; divide both sides by 6 to get $j = 56$. (K) is correct.

Finally, it's time to discuss probability.

PROBABILITY

Don't be intimidated here. **Probability** seems very complex to a lot of students. But it's just a matter of dealing with another three-part formula, and by plugging the values you are given into that formula, you can make probability questions much easier.

Put another way, probability measures the likelihood of an event taking place. It can be expressed as a fraction ("The probability of snow tomorrow is $\frac{1}{2}$"), a decimal ("There is a 0.5 chance of snow tomorrow"), or a percent ("The probability of snow tomorrow is 50%").

When expressed as a fraction, a probability can be read as "x chances in y," where x is the numerator and y is the denominator. So a $\frac{2}{3}$ probability of winning a car could be read as "2 chances in 3 to win a car."

To compute a probability, divide the number of desired outcomes by the number of possible outcomes.

$$\text{Probability} = \frac{\text{Number of Desired Outcomes}}{\text{Number of Possible Outcomes}}$$

Example: If you have 12 shirts in a drawer and 9 of them are white, what is the probability of picking a white shirt at random?

When picking a shirt in this situation, there are 12 possible outcomes, 1 for each shirt. Of these 12, 9 of them are white, so there are 9 desired outcomes.

Therefore, the probability of picking a white shirt at random is $\frac{9}{12} = \frac{3}{4}$. The probability can also be expressed as 0.75 or 75%.

A probability of 0 means that the event has no chance of happening. A probability of 1 means that the event will always happen.

Thus, probability is just another ratio, specifically a part-to-whole ratio. How many parts desired? How many total parts? Finding the probability something *won't* happen is simply a matter of taking the other piece of the pie.

If the probability of picking a white shirt is $\frac{3}{4}$, the probability of not picking a white shirt is $\frac{1}{4}$, or 1 minus the probability that it will happen.

To find the probability that two separate events will both occur, *multiply* the probabilities.

Let's take a look at a couple of examples to see how the ACT can twist probability questions.

EXAMPLE

11. Nancy is picking apples from a display at the grocery store. Of the apples in the display, 24 are red. She randomly picks an apple to purchase. If the probability that she picks a red apple is $\frac{3}{4}$, how many apples are in the display?

    A. 6
    B. 18
    C. 24
    D. 32
    E. 48

Step 1: $\dfrac{\text{Number of Desired Outcomes}}{\text{Total Number of Outcomes}}$

Step 2: You know the number of red apples (24), and you need the total number of apples to solve the problem.

Step 3: Let x equal the total number of apples. Since the probability of picking a red apple is $\dfrac{3}{4}$, $\dfrac{24}{x} = \dfrac{3}{4}$.

Step 4: Cross-multiply to get $3x = 96$, which reduces to $x = 32$. (D) is correct.

EXAMPLE

12. What is the probability of getting exactly one tails from three coin tosses (assume all coins are fair)?

    F. $\dfrac{1}{8}$

    G. $\dfrac{3}{8}$

    H. $\dfrac{1}{2}$

    J. $\dfrac{3}{4}$

    K. $\dfrac{3}{2}$

Step 1: HTH, HHT

Step 2: heads, heads

Step 3: $\left(\dfrac{1}{2}\right)\left(\dfrac{1}{2}\right)\left(\dfrac{1}{2}\right) = \dfrac{1}{8}$

Step 4: There are eight possible permutations of coin tosses, three of which include exactly one tails, so the probability of getting exactly one coin toss to come up tails equals $\dfrac{3}{8}$. (G) is correct.

EXAMPLE

13. A bag contains 3 red marbles, 2 blue marbles, and 7 green marbles. After the first marble is chosen, it is not replaced in the bag. What is the probability of picking two green marbles?

   A. $\dfrac{7}{22}$

   B. $\dfrac{49}{144}$

   C. $\dfrac{6}{11}$

   D. $\dfrac{7}{12}$

   E. $\dfrac{149}{132}$

The question asks for the probability of picking two green marbles. You know the colors and numbers of each type of marble (3 red, 2 blue, and 7 green); you also know that the marbles aren't replaced in the bag. The odds of picking a green marble the first time are

$\dfrac{7}{(2+3+7)} = \dfrac{7}{12}$. Since one green marble is taken out of the bag, the odds of picking a green

marble the second time are $\dfrac{(7-1)}{(12-1)} = \dfrac{6}{11}$. The probability of picking two green marbles is

their product: $\left(\dfrac{7}{12}\right)\left(\dfrac{6}{11}\right) = \dfrac{42}{132} = \dfrac{7}{22}$. (A) is correct.

COORDINATE GEOMETRY—6 POINTS

Complexity: Medium. Relates to: Plane Geometry

Of the highly tested SmartPoint areas, Coordinate Geometry questions have the narrowest scope. Though they can ask about anything and everything related to an (x, y) coordinate plane, they most commonly ask simply about straight lines.

Thus, being very adept at slope and slope-intercept form specifically can allow you to master this SmartPoint quickly and earn the full six points it's worth.

Also note that the ACT does not test parabolas extensively. Most questions involving quadratics are best solved using Variable Manipulation, as opposed to Coordinate Geometry strategies. Similarly, graphs of circles and triangles are best solved using Plane Geometry strategies.

We will discuss the basics of parabolas and how they fit on the coordinate plane at the end of this section, after thoroughly discussing straight lines, slopes, slope-intercept form, and everything you need to know to find the different pieces therein.

The important formulas to remember for lines are the following:

1. Slope-intercept formula: $y = mx + b$, where m is the slope and b is the y-intercept of the line.

2. Midpoint formula: The midpoint of a line segment bounded by the points (x_1, y_1), (x_2, y_2) is $\left(\dfrac{x_1 + x_2}{2}, \dfrac{y_1 + y_2}{2} \right)$.

3. Distance formula: The distance between two points (x_1, y_1), (x_2, y_2) is $D = \sqrt{(x_2 - x_1)^2 + (y_2 - y_1)^2}$.

When dealing with parallel and perpendicular lines, remember that parallel lines have the same slope and perpendicular lines have opposite reciprocal slopes. For example, if the slope of a given line is 5, the slope of a parallel line is also 5. However, the slope of a line perpendicular to these lines is $-\dfrac{1}{5}$. In more general terms, for any line with slope a, the slope of a line perpendicular to it is $-\dfrac{1}{a}$. Also, remember that horizontal lines have a slope of zero, and vertical lines have a slope that is undefined.

EXAMPLE

1. What is the slope of the line perpendicular to the equation $4x + 3y = 9$?

   A. $-\dfrac{4}{3}$

   B. $-\dfrac{3}{4}$

   C. $\dfrac{4}{3}$

   D. $\dfrac{3}{4}$

   E. 3

To find the slope, first you need to put the equation you are given into $y = mx + b$ form. When you do this by solving for y, you can see that the slope of this line is $-\dfrac{4}{3}$ (which you might notice is choice A—a common trap). We are looking for the slope of the line perpendicular to this line. That means that we need the opposite reciprocal slope, which is $\dfrac{3}{4}$, choice (D).

For the Midpoint formula, keep in mind that you're forming two new values, a new value for x and a new value for y. You're trying to find the x value that falls exactly between the two given x's and the y that falls between the given y's. Thus, you're simply finding the average of the given x's and the average of the given y's.

The Distance formula is a derivation of the Pythagorean theorem, which we'll discuss in detail in the Plane Geometry sections. As a quick reminder, the Pythagorean theorem is $a^2 + b^2 = c^2$. For the Distance formula, we are looking for the value of c. To isolate c, we take the square root of the other side of the equation. Think of a as your distance along the x-axis (subtracting your second x from your first). Think of b as your distance along the y-axis (subtracting your second y from your first). If you're looking at a diagonal line, and have found its distance along the x and distance along the y, you've formed a right triangle, with the line you're looking for as the hypotenuse. Simply square a and b, add them together, and take the square root. And there you have the distance formula.

EXAMPLE

2. Point P (−3, 5) and point Q (0, 1) are points on the (x, y) coordinate plane. What is the distance between points P and Q?

    F. 4
    G. 5
    H. 6
    J. 7
    K. 8

There are a couple of ways to solve a distance problem. If you can remember the formula, great! Plug the coordinates into the distance formula:

$$\sqrt{(x_1 - x_2)^2 + (y_2 - y_1)^2}$$

to get:

$$\sqrt{(0 - (-3))^2 + (1 - 5)^2} = \sqrt{(-3)^2 + (4)^2} = \sqrt{9 + 16} = \sqrt{25} = 5$$

If you can't, you can still get this problem correct. Draw a quick graph and plot the two points you are given. Make a triangle once you draw the points, and then determine the lengths of the two legs. You will need to solve for the hypotenuse, but you know how to do this—the Pythagorean theorem! You might also recognize the Pythagorean triplet (3-4-5). Any way you solve it, you will get 5, choice (G).

And that's it! That's all of the outside knowledge you'll need to answer the vast majority of Coordinate Geometry questions. Again, you'll need to know a little bit about parabolas, just in case. And we'll even talk through the formula for a circle on a graph.

But before that, the ACT packs quite a few twists into this test to really make sure you can combine logic with the equations above. This section is primarily about using simple rules for advanced problem solving.

Let's walk through a few examples of how you'll be asked to apply your knowledge of straight lines in a coordinate plane.

When in doubt, draw it out!

And when you're stuck on a straight line coordinate geometry question, see what you can plug into the slope-intercept formula, the most important equation in this section.

EXAMPLE

3. What is the *y*-intercept of the line that passes through the points (1, 21) and (4, 42)?

 A. 0

 B. 7

 C. 9

 D. 14

 E. 19

Step 1: The question asks for the *y*-intercept of a line.

Step 2: You know two points on the line: (1, 21) and (4, 42).

Step 3: What formula can we use to solve this question? Use $y = mx + b$. Find the values of each variable. Identify the slope: $\dfrac{(42 - 21)}{(4 - 1)} = \dfrac{21}{3} = 7$.

Plug in the values of either point; choose (1, 21) and get: $21 = 7(1) + b$.

Step 4: Simplify the equation to get $b = 14$. Choice (D) is correct.

EXAMPLE

4. Which of the following represents the midpoint of $(x + 4, x + 5)$ and $(x + 2, x - 1)$?

 F. $(x - 3, x - 3)$

 G. $(x - 3, x + 3)$

 H. $(x + 3, x - 2)$

 J. $(x + 3, x)$

 K. $(x + 3, x + 2)$

With variables in the answer choices, this question is a great candidate for Picking Numbers. Pick Numbers to check your work.

Step 1: midpoint $= \left(\dfrac{(x_1 + x_2)}{2}, \dfrac{(y_1 + y_2)}{2} \right)$

Step 2: Let $(x_1, y_1) = (x + 4, x + 5)$, and $(x_2, y_2) = (x + 2, x - 1)$.

Step 3: $\dfrac{(x + 4) + (x + 2)}{2} = \dfrac{(2x + 6)}{2} = x + 3$; $\dfrac{(x + 5) + (x - 1)}{2} = \dfrac{(2x + 4)}{2} = x + 2$.

Step 4: (K) is correct.

EXAMPLE

5. Line t in the standard (x, y) coordinate plane has a y-intercept of -3 and is parallel to the line having the equation $3x - 5y = 4$. Which of the following is an equation for line t?

    A. $y = -\dfrac{3}{5}x + 3$

    B. $y = -\dfrac{5}{3}x - 3$

    C. $y = \dfrac{3}{5}x + 3$

    D. $y = \dfrac{5}{3}x + 3$

    E. $y = \dfrac{3}{5}x - 3$

Step 1: $y = mx + b$

Step 2: $3x - 5y = 4$ equals $-5y = -3x + 4$; divide both sides by -5 to get

$y = \dfrac{3}{5}x - \dfrac{4}{5}$.

Step 3: $\dfrac{3}{5}$

Step 4: Choice (E) is the correct answer.

EXAMPLE

6. In the xy-coordinate plane, lines m and n are perpendicular. If line m contains points $(0, 0)$ and $(-3, 1)$, and line n contains points $(-3, 1)$ and $(0, z)$, what is the value of z?

    F. -10

    G. -8

    H. $-\dfrac{1}{3}$

    J. 3

    K. 10

Using the slope formula, you can find that the slope of line m is $\dfrac{(1 - 0)}{(-3 - 0)} = -\dfrac{1}{3}$ and the slope of line n is $\dfrac{(z - 1)}{(0 - (-3))} = \dfrac{z - 1}{3}$. Since the two lines are perpendicular, the slope of line n must be the opposite reciprocal of the slope of m, $-\dfrac{1}{3}$; the slope of n is therefore 3. Set the expression equal to 3 and solve for z:

$\dfrac{z - 1}{3} = 3$

$z - 1 = 9$

$z = 10$. Choice (K) is correct.

Finally, here are the points about more complex graphs you might need to know.

A **parabola** is the graph of a quadratic function, such as $y = x^2$. The graph of a parabola looks like this:

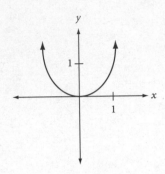

If the coefficient in front of the square is positive, the graph will open upwards. If negative, the graph will open downwards.

Be aware of how the shape and position of parabolas will change with the varying of equations. Often this will be enough to narrow down answer choices, and it may even give you the right one immediately.

EXAMPLE

7. If the parabola $y = (x - 3)^2$ is graphed on the same plane as the parabola $y = x^2$, which of the following will describe the position of $y = (x - 3)^2$ in relation to $y = x^2$?

    A. It will be moved to the left.
    B. It will be moved to the right.
    C. It will be narrower.
    D. It will be moved up.
    E. It will be moved down.

In a question dealing with the movement or change of a parabola, first determine if the transformation is a shift, stretch/compression, or reflection. Addition/subtraction creates a shift. Multiplication by –1 creates a reflection. Multiplication or division by any number other than –1 creates a stretch or a compression.

Next, determine whether the movement is horizontal or vertical. In a horizontal shift, addition means movement left, and subtraction means movement right. In a vertical shift, addition means movement up, and subtraction means movement down.

In this case, 3 is subtracted from x, so it's a shift to the right horizontally (along the x-axis). Choice (B) is correct.

The equation of a circle is $(x - h)^2 + (y - k)^2 = r^2$, where r is the radius of the circle and (h, k) is its center.

The equation of an ellipse is $\dfrac{(x-h)^2}{a^2} + \dfrac{(y-k)^2}{b^2} = 1$, where a represents half of the horizontal axis and b represents half of the vertical axis.

These equations are extremely lightly tested. If you see a question on either, there will only be one.

Finally, you should know how to graph inequalities. A good way to deal with linear inequalities is to simply replace the inequality sign with an equal sign and graph the line. Then depending on what inequality sign the problem uses, shade the appropriate side of the line.

If the inequality sign is:	Line included:	Shaded Area:
<	No	Below line
>	No	Above line
≤	Yes	Below line
≤	Yes	Above line

Commit these relationships to memory, and you will be able to solve inequality graph questions quickly.

PLANE GEOMETRY—7 POINTS

Complexity: Medium. Relates to: Coordinate Geometry

Plane Geometry questions ask primarily about the length of line segments and measure of angles. These lines and angles are placed into shapes and figures of varying complexity. You are tasked with making the figures understandable for yourself so you can find the measures of lines and angles within.

The most commonly tested shapes are triangles (most frequently right triangles) and circles. But you'll also find questions on a variety of other polygons and even unrecognizable two-dimensional figures. Three-dimensional figures are tested as well, but you'll only see regular, uniform three-dimensional shapes on the ACT.

To solve complex Plane Geometry questions, keep these two important steps in mind:

1. Find familiar shapes.

2. Transfer information within those shapes.

We'll work on each of those steps individually, discussing each shape you'll need to know in turn and how to use your knowledge of those shapes to find information and transfer them throughout.

Then, we'll combine those steps to see how these fundamental pieces of knowledge can help you solve even the most complicated Plane Geometry question.

But before we dive into the shapes themselves, let's take a moment to review the basic pieces of Plane Geometry: lines and angles.

LINES AND ANGLES

Lines: A **line** is a one-dimensional geometric abstraction—infinitely long with no width. It is not physically possible to *draw* a line, as any physical line would have a finite length and some width, no matter how long and thin we tried to make it. Two points determine a straight line: given any two points, there is exactly one straight line that passes through them.

Lines: A **line segment** is a section of a straight line, of finite length with two endpoints. A line segment is named for its endpoints, as in segment *AB*. The **midpoint** is the point that divides a line segment into two equal parts.

Example: In the figure shown, *A* and *B* are the endpoints of $\overline{AB}$ and *M* is its midpoint ($\overline{AM}$ = $\overline{MB}$). What is the length of *AB*? $\overline{AM}$ is 6, meaning $\overline{MB}$ is also 6, so $\overline{AB}$ = 6 + 6 = 12.

Two lines are **parallel** if they lie on the same plane and will never intersect each other regardless of how far they are extended. If line ℓ_1 is parallel to line ℓ_2, we write $\ell_1 \| \ell_2$. Parallel lines have the same slope, which is why they never intersect.

Angles: An **angle** is formed whenever two lines or line segments intersect at a point. The point of intersection is called the **vertex** of the angle. Angles are measured in degrees (°).

Angle *x*, ∠*ABC*, and ∠*B* all denote the same angle in the diagram shown here.

An **acute angle** is an angle whose degree measure is between 0° and 90°. A **right angle** is an angle whose degree measure is exactly 90°. An **obtuse angle** is an angle whose degree measure is between 90° and 180°. A **straight angle** is an angle whose degree measure is exactly 180°.

The sum of the measures of the angles on one side of a straight line is 180°.

straight
$(x + y + z = 180)$

The sum of the measures of the angles around a point is 360°.

$a + b + c + d + e = 360$

Two lines are **perpendicular** if they intersect at a 90° angle. The shortest distance from a point to a line is a perpendicular line segment drawn from the point to the line. If line ℓ_1 is perpendicular to line ℓ_2 we write $\ell_1 \perp \ell_2$. If $\ell_1 \perp \ell_2$ and $\ell_2 \perp \ell_3$, then $\ell_1 \parallel \ell_3$:

Two angles are **supplementary** if together they make up a straight angle, i.e., if the sum of their measures is 180°. Two angles are **complementary** if together they make up a right angle, i.e., if the sum of their measures is 90°.

$c + d = 180$ $a + b = 90$

A line or line segment **bisects** an angle if it splits the angle into two equal halves. In the following figure, $\overline{BD}$ bisects $\angle ABC$, meaning $\angle ABD$ has the same measure as $\angle DBC$. The two smaller angles are each half the size of $\angle ABC$.

Vertical angles are a pair of opposite angles formed by two intersecting line segments. At the point of intersection, two pairs of vertical angles are formed. In the following figure, angles a and c are vertical angles, as are b and d.

The two angles in a pair of vertical angles have the same degree measure. In the diagram shown here, $a = c$ and $b = d$. In addition, since ℓ_1 and ℓ_2 are straight lines, $a + b = c + d = a + d = b + c = 180$. In other words, each angle is supplementary to each of its two adjacent angles.

If two parallel lines intersect with a third line (called a *transversal*), each of the parallel lines will intersect the third line at the same angle. In the following figure, $a = e$ (corresponding angles in a transversal), $a = c$ (vertical angles), and $e = g$ (vertical angles). Therefore, $a = c = e = g$ and $b = d = f = h$.

If $\ell_1 \parallel \ell_2$, then $a = c = e = g$ and $b = d = f = h$.

In other words, when two parallel lines intersect with a third line, all acute angles formed are equal, all obtuse angles formed are equal, and any acute angle is supplementary to any obtuse angle.

Now that you know the rules associated with lines and angles, try transferring information to solve the following problems.

EXAMPLE

1. Lines E, F, and G are parallel lines cut by transversal H as shown here. What is the value of $a + b + c + d$?

A. 180°

B. 270°

C. 360°

D. 540°

E. Cannot be determined from the given information

Step 1: The question asks for the value of $a + b + c + d$.

Step 2: You know that line H is a transversal through Lines E, F, and G.

Step 3: Angle a must be supplementary to angle d, and angle b must be supplementary to angle c.

Step 4: The sum of all four angles must be 360°. Choice (C) is correct.

EXAMPLE

2. In the figure shown here, line t crosses parallel lines m and n. What is the degree measure of $\angle x$?

F. 40

G. 50

H. 60

J. 130

K. 140

When a transversal crosses parallel lines, the four acute angles formed are all equal, the four obtuse angles formed are all equal, and any angles that are not equal are supplementary. The angle marked x is obtuse, so it's supplementary to the given 40° angle. $180 - 40 = 140$. The answer is (K).

Next, we'll discuss the most commonly tested shape on the ACT—triangles. We'll review the rules of triangles in general first. Then, we'll move to the most commonly tested type of the most commonly tested shape: right triangles.

GENERAL TRIANGLES

A **triangle** is a closed figure with three angles and three straight sides.

The sum of the measures of the angles in a triangle is 180°.

Each **interior angle** is supplementary to an adjacent **exterior angle.** The degree measure of an exterior angle is equal to the sum of the measures of the other two angles of the triangle (the two not next to the exterior angle), or 180° minus the measure of its adjacent interior angle.

In the figure shown here, a, b, and c are interior angles, so $a + b + c = 180$. d is supplementary to c as well, so $d + c = 180$, $d + c = a + b + c$, and $d = a + b$. Thus, the exterior angle d is equal to the sum of the two remote interior angles—a and b.

The **altitude** (or height) of a triangle is the perpendicular distance from a vertex to the side opposite the vertex. The altitude can fall inside the triangle, outside the triangle, or on one of the sides.

Altitude = $\overline{AD}$

Altitude = $\overline{EH}$

Altitude = $\overline{AC}$

Sides and angles: The length of any side of a triangle is less than the sum of the lengths of the other two sides and greater than their positive difference.

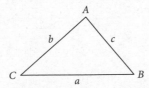

$b + c > a > |b - c|$

$a + b > c > |a - b|$

$a + c > b > |a - c|$

If two sides of a triangle are 8 and 5, the third side has to be greater than the difference, 3, and less than the sum, 13. The third side must fall between those two values in order to form a triangle.

If the lengths of two sides of a triangle are unequal, the **greater angle** lies **opposite the longer side** and vice versa. In the previous figure, if $\angle A > \angle B > \angle C$ then $a > b > c$.

Area of a triangle: The **area** of a triangle refers to the space it takes up.

The area of a triangle is $\frac{1}{2}$ base × height.

Example: The triangle shown here has a base of 4 and an altitude of 3, so we write:

$$A = \frac{1}{2}bh$$
$$= \frac{1}{2} \times 4 \times 3 = 6$$

Remember that the height (or altitude) is perpendicular to the base. Therefore, when two sides of a triangle are perpendicular to each other, the area is easy to find. In a right triangle, we call the two sides that form the 90° angle the **legs.** Then the area is one-half the product of the legs.

Example: In the triangle shown here, we could treat the hypotenuse as the base, since that's how the figure is drawn. If we did this, we would need to know the distance from the hypotenuse to the opposite vertex in order to determine the area of the triangle. A more straightforward method is to notice that this is a **right** triangle with legs of lengths 6 and 8, which allows us to use the alternative formula for the area:

$$A = \frac{1}{2} \times b_1 \times h_1 = \frac{1}{2} \times 6 \times 8 = 24$$

Perimeter of a triangle: The **perimeter** of a triangle is the distance around the triangle. In other words, the perimeter is equal to the sum of the lengths of the sides.

Example: In the triangle shown here, the sides are of lengths 5, 6, and 8. Therefore, the perimeter is 5 + 6 + 8, or 19.

Types of triangles: There are three basic types of triangles: **isosceles, equilateral,** and **scalene.** You will not be tested directly on these types—that is, asked to identify which triangle is which type—but knowing the rules of all three will help you find relevant information quickly. Note that unless you can prove (either because of information provided in the question stem or as you solve for the sides and angles) lengths, angles, or relationships, you cannot tell from the drawing what kind of triangle you are looking at. Figures are not drawn to scale.

Isosceles triangles: An **isosceles triangle** is a triangle that has at least two sides of equal length. The two equal sides are called the **legs,** and the third side is called the **base. Equilateral triangles** are also isosceles, but not all isosceles triangles are equilateral.

Since the two legs have the same length, the two angles opposite the legs must have the same measure. In the figure shown here, $\overline{PQ} = \overline{PR}$ and $\angle R = \angle Q$.

EXAMPLE

3. In isosceles triangle ABC, $\overline{AB}$, and $\overline{BC}$ are congruent. If $\angle CAB = 27°$, what is the measure of $\angle ABC$?

   A. 27°
   B. 54°
   C. 90°
   D. 126°
   E. 153°

Step 1: The question asks for the measure of $\angle ABC$.

Step 2: You know that $\overline{AB}$ and $\overline{BC}$ are congruent lines of $\triangle ABC$ and that $\angle CAB = 27°$.

Step 3: Sketch out $\triangle ABC$. Since $\overline{AB}$ and $\overline{BC}$ are congruent, $\angle BCA$ must also equal 27°. The sum of the interior angles of a triangle equal 180°; therefore, subtract 2(27°) from 180° to get 180° − 54° = 126°.

Step 4: Choice (D) is correct.

Equilateral triangles: An **equilateral triangle** has three sides of equal length and three 60° angles.

$\overline{LM} = \overline{MN} = \overline{LN}$

$\angle L = \angle M = \angle N = 60°$

Scalene triangles: A **scalene triangle** has three sides all of different lengths and three angles all of different measurements. The rules to remember are that the angles will still add up to 180°, the largest angle will be opposite the longest side, and the smallest angle will be opposite the shortest side.

Similar triangles: Triangles are **similar** if they have the same shape (that is, corresponding angles with the same measure). For instance, any two triangles whose angles measure 30°, 60°, and 90° are **similar,** regardless of side length. However, while the lengths will be different, corresponding sides are in the same **ratio** in similar triangles. Triangles are **congruent** if corresponding angles have the same measure and corresponding sides have the same length.

Example: What is the perimeter of $\triangle DEF$?

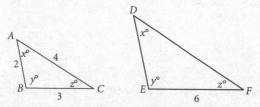

Each triangle has an $x°$ angle, a $y°$ angle, and a $z°$ angle, so they are similar, and corresponding sides are in the same ratio. $\overline{BC}$ and $\overline{EF}$ are corresponding sides—each is opposite the $x°$ angle. Since $\overline{EF}$ is twice the length of $\overline{BC}$, each side of $\triangle DEF$ will be twice the length of its corresponding side in $\triangle ABC$.

Therefore, $\overline{DE} = 2(\overline{AB}) = 4$ and $\overline{DF} = 2(\overline{AC}) = 8$. The perimeter of $\triangle DEF$ is $4 + 6 + 8 = 18$.

The ratio of the **areas** of two similar triangles is the **square** of the ratio of their corresponding lengths. In the previous example, since each side of $\triangle DEF$ is twice the length of its corresponding side in $\triangle ABC$, the area of $\triangle DEF$ must be $2^2 = 4$ times the area of $\triangle ABC$.

$$\frac{\text{Area } \triangle DEF}{\text{Area } \triangle ABC} = \left(\frac{DE}{AB}\right)^2 = \left(\frac{2}{2}\right)^2 = 4$$

Try your hand at these typical ACT problems that test your knowledge of triangle basics, then we'll move on to right triangles.

EXAMPLE

4. In the figure shown here, $\angle B$ is a right angle and the lengths of AB, BC, and CD are given in units. What is the area of $\triangle ACD$, in square units?

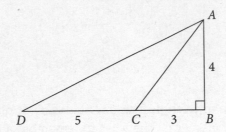

F. 10

G. 12

H. 16

J. 20

K. 32

The formula for the area of a triangle is $A = \dfrac{1}{2}bh$. To apply this formula, you need the base and the height. Here, you can use CD for the base and AB for the height. So:

$$\text{Area} = \frac{1}{2}(CD)(AB) = \frac{1}{2}(5)(4) = 10$$

The answer is (F).

EXAMPLE

5. In the figure shown here, $\triangle ABC$ is similar to $\triangle DEF$. $\angle A$ corresponds to $\angle D$, $\angle B$ corresponds to $\angle E$, and $\angle C$ corresponds to $\angle F$. If the given lengths are of the same unit of measure, what is the value of x?

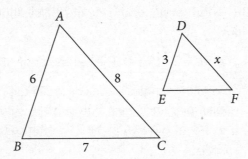

A. 3

B. 3.5

C. 4

D. 5

E. 6

In similar triangles, remember that corresponding sides are proportional. *DE* corresponds to *AB*, and *DF* corresponds to *AC*, so we can set up this proportion:

$$\frac{AB}{DE} = \frac{AC}{DF}$$

$$\frac{6}{3} = \frac{8}{x}$$

$$6x = 3 \times 8$$

$$6x = 24$$

$$x = 4$$

The answer is (C).

Similarly, since the sides are proportional, if you notice that DE (3) is half the length of AB (6), you can immediately know that DF (x) will also be half the length of AC (8).

Right triangles: A right triangle has one interior angle of 90°. The longest side, which lies opposite the right angle, is called the hypotenuse. The other two sides are called the legs. Right triangles have several properties that are frequently tested on the ACT, including the Pythagorean theorem and triplets, which are discussed next. It is important to remember that these rules only apply to right triangles, not other types—you cannot use the Pythagorean theorem on any type of non-right triangle.

PYTHAGOREAN THEOREM

$$(Leg_1)^2 + (Leg_2)^2 = (Hypotenuse)^2$$

or

$$a^2 + b^2 = c^2$$

The **Pythagorean theorem** holds for all right triangles and states that the square of the hypotenuse is equal to the sum of the squares of the legs.

Some sets of integers happen to satisfy the Pythagorean theorem. These sets of integers are commonly referred to as **Pythagorean triplets.** One very common set you might remember is 3, 4, and 5. Since $3^2 + 4^2 = 5^2$, if you have a right triangle with legs of lengths 3 and 4, the length of the hypotenuse would have to be 5. This is the most common kind of right triangle on the ACT, though the sides are generally presented as a multiple of 3, 4, and 5, such as 6, 8, and 10, or 12, 16, and 20. Memorize this ratio and you'll be well on your way to speeding by triangle problems. Another triplet that occasionally appears on the ACT is 5, 12, and 13, or its multiples.

Whenever you're given the lengths of two sides of a right triangle, the Pythagorean theorem allows you to find the third side.

Example: What is the length of the hypotenuse of a right triangle with legs of lengths 9 and 10?

The Pythagorean theorem states that the square of the length of the hypotenuse equals the sum of the squares of the lengths of the legs. Here, the legs are 9 and 10, so we have:

$$\text{Hypotenuse}^2 = 9^2 + 10^2$$
$$= 81 + 100$$
$$= 181$$
$$\text{Hypotenuse} = \sqrt{181}$$

Example: What is the length of the hypotenuse of an isosceles right triangle with legs of length 4?

Since we're told the triangle is isosceles, we know at least two of the sides have the same length. Since we're told the triangle is right, we know the hypotenuse can't be the same length as the legs (the hypotenuse must be longer than the sides on a right triangle—non-right isosceles triangles may also be equilateral). Therefore, the two legs each have length 4, and we can use the Pythagorean theorem to find the hypotenuse.

$$\text{Hypotenuse}^2 = 4^2 + 4^2$$
$$= 16 + 16$$
$$= 32$$
$$\text{Hypotenuse} = \sqrt{32}$$
$$= \sqrt{16} \times \sqrt{2}$$
$$= 4\sqrt{2}$$

You can always use the Pythagorean theorem to find the lengths of the sides in a right triangle. There are, however, two special kinds of right triangles that always have the same ratios.

$1:1:\sqrt{2}$
(for isosceles right triangles—also known as 45-45-90 triangles)

$1:\sqrt{3}:2$
(for 30-60-90 triangles)

These two types of special right triangles are tested often enough that it is to your benefit to memorize them. This will allow you to blow past such problems without having to do any math. If you forget them on Test Day, rest assured that you can still solve the question with the Pythagorean theorem (it will just take longer).

Test your knowledge of right triangles on these typical ACT problems.

EXAMPLE

6. In $\triangle ABC$, $\angle B$ is a right angle. If $\overline{AB}$ is 1 unit long and $\overline{BC}$ is 2 units long, how many units long is $\overline{AC}$?

   F. $\sqrt{3}$

   G. $2\sqrt{3}$

   H. 2

   J. $\sqrt{5}$

   K. 3

The Pythagorean theorem says: $(leg_1)^2 + (leg_2)^2 = (hypotenuse)^2$. Here, the legs have lengths of 1 and 2, so plug them into the formula:

$$(1)^2 + (2)^2 = (hypotenuse)^2$$
$$1 + 4 = x^2$$
$$x^2 = 5$$
$$x = \sqrt{5}$$

The answer is (J).

EXAMPLE

7. A ladder 20 feet long is placed against a wall such that the foot of the ladder is 12 feet from the wall. How many feet above the ground is the top of the ladder?

   A. 8

   B. 12

   C. 15

   D. 16

   E. 18

Step 1: The question asks how far above the ground the top of the ladder is.

Step 2: You know that the ladder is 20 feet long and that the foot of the ladder is 12 feet from the wall.

Step 3: The ladder forms the hypotenuse, the distance from the wall to the ladder is the base, and the wall between the ground and the top of the ladder is the height. There are two ways to solve for this height, the Pythagorean theorem or Pythagorean triplets, and use either to find that the height is 16 (4 × 3:4:5 leaves sides of 12, 16, and 20).

Step 4: Choice (D) is correct.

Now, try a triangle problem that tests your knowledge of multiple aspects of the shape. Remember, when in doubt, draw it out.

EXAMPLE

8. $\triangle ABC$ is isosceles with $\overline{AB} = \overline{CB} = 5$ inches. $\overline{DB}$ is the perpendicular bisector of $\overline{AC}$. The length of $\overline{AC}$ is 4 inches. What is the area of $\triangle ABC$?

F. $\sqrt{21}$

G. $2\sqrt{21}$

H. 10

J. $4\sqrt{21}$

K. 20

Because this question deals with the relationships between multiple pieces on a figure, you'll be most confident answering it if you draw the triangle out. Your figure will be an isosceles triangle with two sides of 5 inches ($\overline{AB}$ and $\overline{CB}$) and a base of 4 inches ($\overline{AC}$). There also needs to be a height drawn from B to $\overline{AC}$, perpendicular at point D.

The area of a triangle is $\frac{1}{2}bh$, and you already have the base: $\overline{AC}$ is 4 inches. To solve for the height ($\overline{DB}$), you need to use the Pythagorean formula. Hypotenuse $\overline{AB}$ is 5, and leg $\overline{DB}$ is 2. $a^2 + (2)^2 = 5^2$, so $a^2 + 4 = 25$, or $a^2 = 21$, or $a = \sqrt{21}$. This is the height of the triangle. Plug this back into the area equation, to get $\frac{1}{2}(4)(\sqrt{21})$, or $2\sqrt{21}$. Choice (G) is correct.

Next, we'll discuss the second most commonly tested shape on the ACT, **circles.** Some challenging circle questions involve ratios and proportions, so if you get stuck, you might want to brush up on your skills in this area by referring to the Proportions and Probability SmartPoint on page 200 if you haven't already.

 Visit your online syllabus—Lesson 4—for more instruction and practice with triangles.

CIRCLES

Circle: The set of all points in a plane at the same distance from a certain point. This point is called the **focus** and lies at the **center** of the circle.

A circle is labeled by its center point: circle O means the circle with center point O. Two circles of different size with the same center are **concentric.**

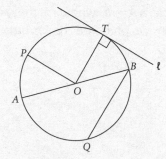

Diameter: A line segment that connects two points on the circle and passes through the center of the circle. In circle O, $\overline{AB}$ is a diameter.

Radius: A line segment from the center of the circle to any point on the circle. The radius of a circle is one-half the length of its diameter. In circle O, $\overline{OA}$, $\overline{OB}$, $\overline{OP}$, and $\overline{OT}$ are all radii.

Chord: A line segment joining two points on the circle. In circle O, $\overline{QB}$ and $\overline{AB}$ are chords. The longest chord in a circle is a diameter.

Central angle: An angle formed by two radii. $\angle AOP$, $\angle POB$, and $\angle BOA$ are three of circle O's central angles.

Tangent: A line outside the circle that touches only one point on the circumference of the circle. A line drawn tangent to a circle is perpendicular to the radius at the point of tangency, meaning it forms a right angle. Line ℓ is tangent to circle O at point T.

Circumference: The distance around a circle is its **circumference.** The number π (pi) is the ratio of a circle's circumference to its diameter. The value of π is usually approximated to 3.14. For the ACT, it is generally sufficient to remember that pi is a little more than 3.

Since π equals the ratio of the circumference to the diameter, a formula for the circumference is $\pi d = 2\pi r$.

Area of a circle: The area of a circle is given by the formula Area = πr^2.

Those are the basics of circles! Know those and you will be ready for ACT circle questions.

Try a couple of sample problems involving these concepts, then we'll look at those central angles and how they can make circle problems more complex with arcs and sectors.

EXAMPLE

9. What is the area, in square inches, of a circle with a diameter of 8 inches?

   A. 4π

   B. 8π

   C. 16π

   D. 32π

   E. 64π

The formula for the area of a circle is $A = \pi r^2$, where r is the radius. If the diameter is 8 inches, then the radius is 4 inches, which we plug into the formula:

$$A = \pi r^2$$

$$= \pi (4)^2$$

$$= 16\pi$$

The answer is (C).

For circle questions, you will almost always want to find the **radius.**

The radius is the most important part of a circle, as the path to everything else (circumference, area, diameter) can start with the radius.

One more…

EXAMPLE

10. What is the area, in square inches, of a circle with a circumference of 2π inches?

    F. $\dfrac{\pi}{2}$

    G. π

    H. 2π

    J. 4π

    K. 8π

As with most circle questions, the first thing you need to do is find the radius. The question tells us that this circle's circumference is 2π. The equation for circumference is $2\pi r$, so if this is equal to 2π, $r = 1$.

Now we can use that to find the area, which is πr^2. If $r = 1$, the area is $\pi (1^2)$, which is just π. The answer is (G).

Before moving on to arcs and sectors, try putting your knowledge of circles and triangles together for our first example of complex shapes. Remember, find familiar shapes and transfer information!

EXAMPLE

11. In the diagram shown here, $\overline{AC}$ is tangent to circle O at point B. $\overline{BD} = \overline{AO} = 6$. What is the length of $\overline{AB}$?

A. 3

B. $3\sqrt{2}$

C. $3\sqrt{3}$

D. 6

E. 12

Step 1: The question asks for the length of $\overline{AB}$.

Step 2: You know that $\overline{AC}$ is tangent to circle O at point B and that $\overline{BD} = \overline{AO} = 6$.

Step 3: Look for hidden triangles within complex figures; we see one in $\triangle ABO$. This is a right triangle, because $\overline{AC}$ is perpendicular to circle O. Its base equals $\frac{1}{2}\overline{BD}$, or 3, and its hypotenuse equals 6. The ratio between sides for a 30-60-90 triangle is $x : x\sqrt{3} : 2x$. If $x = 3$ and $2 - x = 6$, $\overline{AB} = \overline{AB} = x\sqrt{3}$ or $3\sqrt{3}$.

Step 4: Choice (C) is correct.

Arc length and sectors: An **arc** is a portion of the circumference of a circle. In the figure shown here, AB is an arc of the circle, with the same degree measure as central angle AOB. The shorter distance between A and B along the circle is called the **minor arc,** while the longer distance AXB is the **major arc.** An arc that is exactly half the circumference of the circle is called a **semicircle** (meaning half a circle).

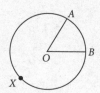

The length of an arc is the same fraction of a circle's circumference as its degree measure is of the degree measure of the circle (360°). For an arc with a central angle measuring *n* degrees, the following applies:

$$\text{Arc length} = \left(\frac{n}{360}\right)(\text{circumference})$$

$$= \frac{n}{360} \times 2\pi r$$

Example: What is the length of arc *ABC* of the circle with center *O* shown here?

The radius is 6, so the circumference is $2\pi r = 2 \times \pi \times 6 = 12\pi$.

Since $\angle AOC$ measures 60°, the arc is $\frac{60}{360} = \frac{1}{6}$ the circumference.

Therefore, the length of the arc is $\frac{12\pi}{6} = 2\pi$.

A **sector** is a portion of a circle bounded by two radii and an arc. In the circle shown here with center *O*, *OAB* is a sector. To determine the area of a sector of a circle, use the same method we used to find the length of an arc. Determine what fraction of 360° is in the degree measure of the central angle of the sector, then multiply that fraction by the area of the circle. In a sector for which the central angle measures *n* degrees, the following applies:

$$\text{Area of sector} = \left(\frac{n}{360}\right) \times (\text{Area of circle})$$

$$= \frac{n}{360} \times \pi r^2$$

Example: What is the area of sector *AOC* in the circle shown here?

A 60° "slice" is $\frac{60}{360} = \frac{1}{6}$ of the circle, so sector *AOC* has an area of

$$\frac{1}{6} \times \pi r^2 = \frac{1}{6} \times \pi \times 6^2 = \frac{1}{6} \times 36\pi = 6\pi.$$

For another way to solve problems involving arc lengths and sectors, recognize that these are all part-to-whole ratios you can set in proportion to each other.

$$\frac{\text{Central angle}}{360\,(\text{the whole angle})} = \frac{\text{Sector area}}{\text{Area of the circle}} = \frac{\text{Arc length}}{\text{Circumference}}.$$

All three ratios are equal to each other. Any two can be used in a proportion to find one missing piece.

Try a sample question.

EXAMPLE

12. In the circle centered at O in the figure shown here, the measure of $\angle AOB$ is 40°. If $\overline{OA}$ is 9 units long, how many units long is minor arc AB?

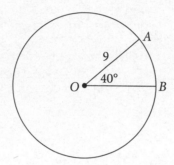

    F. π

    G. 2π

    H. 9

    J. 9π

    K. 40

The central angle of minor arc AB is 40°, which is $\frac{1}{9}$ of the whole circle's 360°. The length of minor arc AB, therefore, is $\frac{1}{9}$ of the whole circle's circumference.

$$C = 2\pi r = 2\pi(9) = 18\pi$$

$$\frac{1}{9}C = \frac{1}{9}(18\pi) = 2\pi$$

The answer is (G).

The only other type of regular polygon you'll see regularly is the **quadrilateral.** We'll discuss those now, before discussing the rest of the regular polygons in general.

QUADRILATERALS

A **quadrilateral** is an enclosed figure with four straight sides and four angles.

The **perimeter** of any quadrilateral is simply the sum of the length of all four sides.

Area for quadrilaterals follows the formula *base × height*, but varies slightly to account for the different types of quadrilaterals.

TYPES OF QUADRILATERALS

A **parallelogram** is a quadrilateral with opposite sides that are *parallel and equal*. The area is calculated simply by multiplying *base × height*, but since parallelograms don't necessarily have sides that form 90° angles, you might have to find an altitude as you would with a triangle.

A **trapezoid** is a quadrilateral with only one set of parallel sides. Those parallel sides form the two bases. To find the area, average those bases and multiply by the height.

EXAMPLE

13. In the figure shown here, $\overline{BE}$ is perpendicular to $\overline{AD}$, and the lengths of $\overline{AB}$, $\overline{BC}$, $\overline{CD}$, and $\overline{BE}$ are given in inches. What is the area, in square inches, of trapezoid *ABCD*?

A. 24

B. 30

C. 32

D. 34

E. 36

The formula for the area of a trapezoid is $A = \left(\dfrac{b_1 + b_2}{2}\right)h$, where b_1 and b_2 are the lengths of the parallel sides. Remember, you could think of it as the height times the average of the bases. You're given the height (3 inches), one base (8 inches), and enough information to figure out the other base. Notice that $\triangle ABE$ is a 3-4-5 triangle, so $AE = 4$ inches. And if you were to drop an altitude down from point *C*, you'd get another 3-4-5 triangle on the right:

Now you can see that the bottom base is 16 inches. Plug these numbers into the formula:

$$A = \left(\frac{b_1 + b_2}{2}\right)h$$

$$= \left(\frac{8 + 16}{2}\right) \times 3$$

$$= 12 \times 3 = 36$$

The answer is (E). If you don't remember the whole equation on Test Day, note that you can also just find the areas of the two side triangles and the rectangle in the middle and add them all up.

Rectangles and **squares** are both types of parallelograms.

A **rectangle** is a parallelogram with four right angles. Thus, because one of the sides of a rectangle always serves as an altitude, we sometimes refer to the formula for area of a rectangle as *length × width* instead of *base × height*. But the principle is the same.

A **square** is a rectangle with four equal sides. We can still multiply the base times the height, but because we have equal sides, it will always be one side times the other without the need to find an altitude. And because those sides are always going to be equal in a square, we can simply say the formula for area of a square is *side²*.

The area of a rectangle is length × width.

The area of a square is side².

EXAMPLE

14. In the parallelogram $WXYZ$ shown here, $\overline{WX}$ is 8 centimeters long. If the parallelogram's perimeter is 30 centimeters, how many centimeters long is $\overline{XY}$?

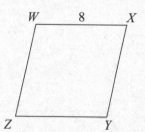

    F. $3\frac{3}{4}$

    G. 7

    H. 8

    J. 11

    K. 14

Step 1: The question asks for the length of $\overline{XY}$.

Step 2: You know that $WXYZ$ is a parallelogram, and $\overline{WX}$ is 8 centimeters long.

Step 3: $\overline{WX} = \overline{ZY} = 8$ and $\overline{WZ} = \overline{XY}$. The perimeter of the parallelogram is $\overline{WX} + \overline{WZ} + \overline{ZY} + \overline{YX}$, or $8 + \overline{WZ} + 8 + \overline{XY} = 30$; $\overline{WZ} + \overline{XY} = 14$. Since opposite sides of a parallelogram are equal, you can divide 14 by 2 to get the length of each $\overline{WZ}$ and $\overline{XY}$, which are each 7.

Step 4: Choice (G) is correct.

Finally, let's discuss **polygons** in general, then we'll dive into more complex shapes and the strategies necessary to deal with them.

POLYGONS

A **polygon** is any closed figure whose sides are straight line segments.

The **perimeter** of a polygon is the sum of the lengths of its sides.

A **vertex** of a polygon is the point where two adjacent sides meet.

A **diagonal** of a polygon is a line segment connecting two nonadjacent vertices.

A **regular polygon** has sides of equal length and interior angles of equal measure.

The number of sides determines the specific name of the polygon. A **triangle** has three sides, a **quadrilateral** has four sides, a **pentagon** has five sides, and a **hexagon** has six sides. Triangles and quadrilaterals are by far the most important polygons on the ACT.

Interior and exterior angles: A polygon can be divided into triangles by drawing diagonals from any given vertex to all other nonadjacent vertices. For instance, the following pentagon can be divided into three triangles. Since the sum of the interior angles of each triangle is 180°, the sum of the interior angles of a pentagon is 3 × 180° = 540°.

Example: What is the measure of an interior angle in the regular hexagon shown here?

Because this is a *regular* hexagon, all angles are equal, so each is equal to one-sixth the sum of the angles. Since we can draw four triangles in a six-sided figure, the sum of the interior angles is 4 × 180° = 720°. Therefore, each interior angle measures $\frac{720}{6} = 120°$.

The formula to represent the total measure of an *n*-sided polygon's interior angles is 180(*n* − 2).

To find the sum of angles of a quadrilateral, you'd take the number of sides (*n* = 4) and plug it into the formula. (4 − 2) × 180. 2 × 180 = 360. The sum of the interior angles of all quadrilaterals is 360.

COMPLEX TWO-DIMENSIONAL SHAPES

Let's walk through samples of how the ACT can ask you to combine your knowledge of shapes and angles to find information within figures that are themselves unrecognizable. These figures can always be broken down into simpler shapes we've already reviewed.

We're getting into Complex Plane Geometry questions now, so remember the two steps discussed earlier:

1. Find familiar shapes.

2. Transfer information.

Those familiar shapes will be triangles, quadrilaterals, and circles. You can use the rules we discussed about each to transfer information from one to the next within a complex figure and find the value you need.

EXAMPLE

15. In the figure shown here, $ABCD$ is a square and $\overline{AB}$ is a diameter of the circle centered at O. If $\overline{AD}$ is 10 units long, what is the area, in square units, of the shaded region?

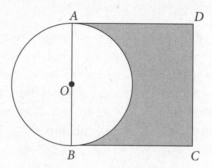

A. $100 - 50\pi$

B. $100 - 25\pi$

C. $100 - \dfrac{25\pi}{2}$

D. $100 - 10\pi$

E. $100 - 5\pi$

This is definitely a question with several steps, but by transferring information from one step to the next, and focusing on what you're being asked for, you can see the way through. As with all ACT Math questions, you should circle what you're being asked for: *the area of the shaded region.* It's not a regular shape, but the shaded region is equal to the area of the whole square minus the area of the semicircle. The area of the square is $10 \times 10 = 100$. The radius of the circle is half of 10, or 5, so the area of the whole circle is $\pi(5)^2 = 25\pi$, and the area of the semicircle is $\dfrac{25\pi}{2}$. The square minus the semicircle, then, is: $100 - \dfrac{25\pi}{2}$. The answer is (C).

EXAMPLE

16. In the figure shown here, $\triangle ABC$ is a right triangle and $\overline{AC}$ is perpendicular to $\overline{BD}$. If $\overline{AB}$ is 6 units long, and $\overline{AC}$ is 10 units long, how many units long is $\overline{AD}$?

F. 3

G. $2\sqrt{3}$

H. 3.6

I. 4

J. $3\sqrt{2}$

At first, this looks like a Pythagorean theorem question. In fact, the two given sides of $\triangle ABC$ identify it as the 6-8-10 version of the 3-4-5 special right triangle. So we know that $\overline{BC} = 8$. So what? How's that going to help us find $\overline{AD}$?

The inspiration here is to realize that this is a "similar triangles" problem. We don't see the word *similar* anywhere in the question stem, but the stem and the figure combined actually tell us that all three triangles in the figure—$\triangle ABC$, $\triangle ADB$, and $\triangle BDC$—are similar. We know the triangles are similar because they all have the same three angles, which we know because they're all right triangles and all share at least one side with another of the triangles. Here are the three triangles separated and oriented to show the correspondences:

In this orientation, it's easy to set up the proportion that will solve the problem:

$$\frac{10}{6} = \frac{6}{x}$$

$$10x = 36$$

$$x = 3.6$$

The answer is (H).

EXAMPLE

17. In the figure shown here, the area of the circle centered at O is 25π, and $\overline{AC}$ is perpendicular to $\overline{OB}$. If $\overline{AC}$ is 8 units long, how many units long is $\overline{BD}$?

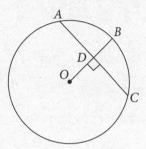

A. 2

B. 2.5

C. 3

D. 3.125

E. 4

This is another complicated one. It's not easy to see how to get BD from the given information. You can use the area—25π—to figure out the radius, and then you'd know the length of OB:

$$\text{Area} = \pi r^2$$
$$25\pi = \pi r^2$$
$$25 = r^2$$
$$r = 5$$

So you know $\overline{OB} = 5$, but what about $\overline{BD}$? If you knew $\overline{OD}$, you could subtract that from $\overline{OB}$ to get what you want. But do you know $\overline{OD}$? This is the place where most people get stuck.

The inspiration that will lead to a solution is that you can take advantage of the right angle at D. Look what happens when you take a pencil and physically add $\overline{OA}$ and $\overline{OC}$ to the figure:

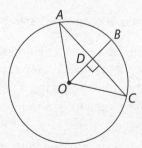

ΔOAD and ΔOCD are right triangles. We found familiar shapes! And when we write in the lengths, we discover some special right triangles:

Now it's apparent that $\overline{OD} = 3$. Since $\overline{OB} = 5$, $\overline{BD}$ is $5 - 3 = 2$. The answer is (A).

Try your hand at finding those familiar shapes one more time.

EXAMPLE

18. What is the area, in square units, of the figure shown here?

   F.   147
   G.   108.5
   H.   91
   J.   60.5
   K. $39 + 7\sqrt{2}$

Step 1: Sketch a line between the intersection of the lines with lengths of 10 and $7\sqrt{2}$, and the right angle beneath it, turning the right half of the shape into a rectangle and a triangle. Sketch a line straight down from the left end of the top side of the figure to divide that trapezoid into a rectangle and a triangle.

Step 2: The figure can be broken into two rectangles and two triangles.

Step 3: The triangle to the left of the figure has a height of 3 and a base of $14 - 10 = 4$. The two rectangles in the middle of the figure can be considered as one 10×3 rectangle. The right triangle to the right of the figure has a base of 7 and a hypotenuse of $7\sqrt{2}$; apply the 45-45-90 triangle formula to determine its height, 7.

Step 4: The area of the triangle on the left equals $\frac{1}{2}(3)(4) = 6$; the area of the rectangle(s) equals $(10)(3) = 30$; the area of the triangle on the right equals $\frac{1}{2}(7)(7) = 24.5$.

Step 5: $6 + 30 + 24.5 = 60.5$. Choice (J) is correct.

Now, try your hand at a question that will ask you to bring all of your knowledge together. This is one of the most complex Plane Geometry questions you'll see on the ACT.

Try it first, then we'll walk through it and go over strategies that can help you master even the most complex of problems.

EXAMPLE

19. In the figure shown here, $\overline{AB}$ is tangent to the circle at A. If the circumference of the circle is 12π units and $\overline{OB}$ is 12 units long, what is the area, in square units, of the shaded region?

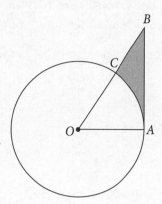

A. $18\sqrt{3} - 6\pi$

B. $24\sqrt{3} - 6\pi$

C. $18\sqrt{3} - 2\pi$

D. $12\pi - 12$

E. $243 - 2\pi$

This is about as hard as they come on the ACT. It is by no means clear how the given information—the circumference of the circle and the length of *OB*—will lead you to the area of the shaded region.

So what do you do? Give up? No. *Don't* just guess immediately unless you're really short on time or you know for sure you can't do the problem.

So then should you just plow ahead blindly and figure out every length, angle, and area you can and see where that leads you? *Well, not exactly.* It would be better to be more systematic.

The key to success with a circuitous problem like this is to focus on your destination— what you're looking for—and think about what you need to get there.

Then go back to the given information and see what you can do to get you going in the right direction. Think about where you're headed before you take even one step; otherwise, you may just have to backtrack.

Your goal is to find the area of the shaded region. That region is a shape that has no name, let alone an area formula. But like most shaded regions on the ACT, this one is the difference between two familiar shapes that *do* have names and area formulas. Think of the shaded region in question 19 as:

(the area of $\triangle AOB$) − (the area of sector $\triangle AOC$)

So now you know what you need: the area of the triangle and the area of the sector.

First, the triangle. You are explicitly given $\overline{OB} = 12$. You are also given that $\overline{AB}$ is tangent to the circle at A, which tells you that $\overline{OA}$ is a radius and that $\angle OAB$ is a right angle. So if you can figure out the radius of the circle, you'll have two sides of a right triangle, which will enable you to figure out the third side and then figure out the area.

You can get the radius from the given circumference. Plug what you know into the formula and solve for r:

$$\text{Circumference} = 2\pi r$$
$$12\pi = 2\pi r$$
$$r = \frac{12\pi}{2\pi} = 6$$
$$\overline{OA} = 6$$

Aha! So it turns out that AOB is no ordinary right triangle. Since one leg—6—is exactly half the hypotenuse—12—you're looking at a 30°-60°-90° triangle. By applying the well-known side ratios $(1 : \sqrt{3} : 2)$ for a 30°-60°-90° triangle, you determine that $AB = 6\sqrt{3}$. Now plug the lengths of the legs in for the base and altitude in the formula for the area of a triangle, and you'll get:

$$\text{Area} = \frac{1}{2}bh$$
$$= \frac{1}{2}\left(6\sqrt{3}\right)(6)$$
$$= 18\sqrt{3}$$

Already it looks like the answer is going to be (A) or (C)—they're the choices that begin with $18\sqrt{3}$. You could just guess choice (A) or (C) and move on, but if you've come this far, you might as well go all the way.

Next, you need to determine the area of the sector. Fortunately, while working on the triangle, you figured out the two things you need to get the area of the sector: the radius of the circle (6) and the measure of the central angle (60°). The radius tells you that the area of the whole circle (πr^2) is 36π. And the central angle tells you that the sector is $\frac{60}{360} = \frac{1}{6}$ of the circle. One-sixth of 36π is 6π. So the area of the shaded region is $18\sqrt{3} - 6\pi$, choice (A).

Finally, let's wrap up plane geometry by looking at **three-dimensional shapes.**

THREE-DIMENSIONAL SHAPES

Fortunately, the ACT only tests regular, uniform three-dimensional figures on the ACT. You won't see any crazy 3-D combinations like you just worked with on a 2-D plane. Questions with 3-D figures can get complex, but still involve finding those familiar 2-D shapes and using them to transfer information.

Those two steps still hold, even for complex questions in 3-D.

The only formulas to remember are **volume** and **surface area.** The only 3-D shapes to be aware of are rectangular solids and right cylinders.

Volume of a rectangular solid = *length × width × height*.

Surface area of a rectangular solid = $2(l \times w) + 2(l \times h) + 2(w \times h)$.

Volume of a right cylinder = $\pi r^2 h$.

EXAMPLE

20. In the figure shown here, a wooden plank is shown with its dimensions in inches. If Marcus wants to spray paint every surface of the plank, how much paint, in square inches, will Marcus need?

    F. 38

    G. 76

    H. 240

    J. 450

    K. 510

Step 1: The question asks how much paint Marcus will need to spray paint a wooden plank; it's asking for surface area.

Step 2: You know the length, width, and height of the plank.

Step 3: Plug in values from the question for surface area formula: $2(30 \times 3) + 2(30 \times 5) + 2(5 \times 3) = 2(90) + 2(150) + 2(15) = 510$.

Step 4: Choice (K) is correct.

Now, try using those two steps for complex plane geometry on one last, very challenging ACT problem, this time involving three dimensions.

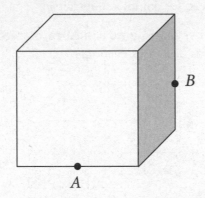

EXAMPLE

21. In the figure shown here, *A* and *B* are midpoints of two edges of the cube. If the cube has edges of length 4, what is the length of line segment $\overline{AB}$ (not shown)?

A. 2

B. $\sqrt{6}$

C. 3

D. $2\sqrt{6}$

E. 6

Step 1: The question asks for the length of $\overline{AB}$, which is not shown.

Step 2: You know the shape is a cube with side lengths of 4.

Step 3: Find or create helpful triangles within the cube. In general, find desired distances by creating a right triangle with the desired distance as the hypotenuse: here the useful triangle has $\overline{AB}$ as its hypotenuse, the length from *B* to the vertex below it as one leg, and a drawn line from that point to *A* as the other leg. While the leg from *B* downward is half the edge length, 2, the length of the other leg is not immediately apparent. That leg is the hypotenuse of another right triangle with one leg from *A* to the vertex to the right, and the other leg from that vertex to the vertex below *B*; the first leg is half the edge length, 2, and the other leg is the whole edge length, 4. Using the Pythagorean theorem, $2^2 + 4^2 = c^2$; $c = \sqrt{20}$, which reduces to $2\sqrt{5}$. This means that the legs of the triangle with *AB* as its hypotenuse are $2\sqrt{5}$ and 2, so apply the Pythagorean theorem again: $(2\sqrt{5})^2 + 2^2 = \overline{AB}^2$; $\overline{AB} = 24$, which reduces to $2\sqrt{6}$.

Step 4: Choice (D) is correct.

PATTERNS, LOGIC, AND DATA—3 POINTS

Complexity: Medium-High. Relates to: Variable Manipulation, Proportions and Probability

Note: Patterns, Logic, and Data questions are lightly tested, and are not knowledge you need to build prowess in other more frequently tested areas (unlike Number Properties, which you need to know for Variable Manipulation).

The concepts tested in both of these SmartPoint areas can be complex, but mostly the rules to remember are simple. And again, they are both tested infrequently.

Thus, before you spend long with either of these two remaining SmartPoints, check your goals and your progress. If you're ready for that last layer to get yourself into the 30s on Math, go ahead and spend time here to drive the lessons home. If you are still building your score and are aiming for something in the 20s, it's likely that your time is better spent in a more highly tested or a more fundamental area.

Remember, prioritize your time based on needs and SmartPoints. These two SmartPoints should be prioritized last.

Still here? Fantastic! Let's get started with Patterns, Logic, and Data.

Patterns, Logic, and Data questions test several more complex concepts of math. However, unlike other ACT SmartPoints, such as Plane Geometry, you don't need to fully understand all iterations of these concepts or to apply them in a multitude of complex ways. The ways they're tested are really pretty direct.

These questions ask you to remember a simple rule or two about each complex topic, just to be sure you're aware of it.

More complex questions in this SmartPoint are actually often better solved using strategies from other SmartPoints. For instance, the most common Patterns, Logic, and Data questions involve functions. Functions are simply dressed-up equations and are best solved using strategies for Variable Manipulations.

However, we'll take a look at the rules you might be asked to know, and we'll walk through a few common sample problems, so you'll be fully prepared. You'll be able to look right past the complex façade and find the clear and often straightforward route to a correct answer.

The tested areas under this SmartPoint are Functions, Permutations and Combinations, Union and Intersection of Sets, and Matrices. We'll tackle each in turn, moving from areas you'll definitely see in at least a question or two to areas you might not see at all.

FUNCTIONS

You'll see at least a question or two on **functions** on the ACT. Think of functions as dressed-up equations.

They are like machines for processing numbers. They take the input—or x values—run them through the equation given with the function, and produce the output, or y values.

EXAMPLE

$f(x) = x^2 + 5x + 9$ is a function.

If given $x = 4$, we have our input.

Simply plug that value in for x in the equation, and solve as you would any number line:

$f(4) = 4^2 + 5(4) + 9 = 16 + 20 + 9 = 45$

$f(4) = 45$

45 is our output, or y value. After we ran the function for the given input, that was the result.

The **domain** of a function is all possible inputs.

The **range** is all possible outputs.

You might see this phrasing on a question:

$f(x) = \dfrac{3}{(x + 2)}$ is defined for all real values except: _____

"Is defined for all real values except" means there is a number that doesn't fit in the domain. If you were to plug one particular number into this equation, the result would be undefined. Can you tell what it is?

The answer is −2. If we plugged in −2, the denominator would be 0 and that would make our output undefined. Thus, −2 is outside of the domain of that function.

One more…

$f(x) = x^2$ has what kinds of numbers in its range? _____

Think about this one, what kind of outputs can we get from this function?

What kind of numbers do you get when you plug in positive values? How about negative ones? See the pattern?

The range for this function is positive numbers and zero. Whenever you square a number, positive or negative, the result is always positive or zero.

Finally, be ready for questions involving **nested functions.** For nested functions, follow the order of operations: start with the innermost parenthesis and work outwards.

EXAMPLE

1. If $f(a) = a^2 + 7$, $g(b) = \sqrt{2b - 7}$, and $h(c) = \sqrt{c^2 + 11}$, what is the value of $h(g(f(3)))$?

    A. 0

    B. 3

    C. 6

    D. 9

    E. 12

Step 1: The question asks for the value of $h(g(f(3)))$.

Step 2: You're given the definition of three functions, and we start with $f(3)$, the innermost function.

Step 3: Solve the value from the inside-out:
$f(3) = (3)^2 + 7 = 9 + 7 = 16$. Substitute 16 into the expression for $f(3)$ to get $h(g(16))$:
$g(16) = \sqrt{2(16) - 7} = \sqrt{(32 - 7)} = \sqrt{25} = 5$
Substitute 5 into the expression for $g(16)$ to get $h(5)$:
$h(5) = \sqrt{5^2 + 11} = \sqrt{25 + 11} = \sqrt{36} = 6$

Step 4: Choice (C) is correct.

Now, put it all together and try one more function question.

EXAMPLE

2. If $f(x) = x^2 + x + 5$, and $g(x) = \sqrt{x}$, then what is the value of $\dfrac{g(4)}{f(1)}$?

    F. $\dfrac{2}{25}$

    G. $\dfrac{2}{7}$

    H. 2

    J. $\dfrac{25}{7}$

    K. 4

Step 1: $g(4) = \sqrt{4}$

Step 2: $\sqrt{4} = 2$

Step 3: $f(1) = (1)^2 + (1) + 5$

Step 4: $(1)^2 + (1) + 5 = 1 + 1 + 5 = 7$

Step 5: $\dfrac{g(4)}{f(1)} = \dfrac{2}{7}$. Choice (G) is correct.

Every other area of this SmartPoint is tested lightly. If you see a question on these areas, you'll see one or two at most.

PERMUTATIONS AND COMBINATIONS

Permutations are sequences in which order matters.

Combinations are groups in which order does not matter.

A locker combination would be an example of a permutation—even if you have the right numbers, it doesn't work if they're out of order. Choosing from a selection of ice cream flavors would be an example of a combination—the order in which you choose doesn't change the end result.

EXAMPLE

3. Jake has 4 types of cheese and 5 types of crackers to make a snack. How many different combinations of one piece of cheese and one cracker are possible for Jake's snack?

    A. 4
    B. 5
    C. 9
    D. 20
    E. 25

Step 1: Combination order doesn't matter.

Step 2: Multiply the number of possibilities for each choice together.

Step 3: $4 \times 5 = 20$; choice (D) is correct.

When dealing with groups of numbers, also keep in mind the **fundamental counting principle:** If an event has a possible outcomes, and another independent event has b possible outcomes, then there are ab ways for the two events to occur together (multiply).

4. How many positive four-digit integers have 3 as their hundreds digit and 5 or 9 as their ones digit?

    F. 180
    G. 190
    H. 200
    J. 210
    K. 220

The question asks for a number of positive four-digit integers. All integers must have 3 as the hundreds digit and either 5 or 9 as the ones digit. If only 3 can go in the hundreds slot, there is only one possibility. There are only two possibilities for the ones slot (5 and 9). There are 10 possibilities for the tens digit (0–9) but only 9 for the thousands slot (1–9). $9 \times 1 \times 10 \times 2 = 180$, or choice (F).

UNION AND INTERSECTION OF SETS

The **union** of sets is what you get when you **combine** the original sets. It includes all elements in either or both.

Example: What is the union of sets {1, 2, 3, 4, 5} and {2, 4, 6, 8, 10}?

To get it, just list everything from both sets once (don't repeat any numbers):

{1, 2, 3, 4, 5, 6, 8, 10}

The **intersection** of sets is what you get when you **overlap** the original sets. It includes only elements *common* to the sets.

Example: What is the intersection of sets {1, 2, 3, 4, 5} and {2, 4, 6, 8, 10}?

To get it, just list the numbers that appear in both:

{2, 4}

MATRICES

Matrices are a set of two or more charts.

To combine matrices, multiply the rows of the first matrix by the columns of the second matrix, and so on. In order to multiply matrices, the number of rows in the first matrix must be the same as the number of columns in the second matrix.

EXAMPLE

5. $\begin{bmatrix} 6 & 1 \\ 6 & 3 \end{bmatrix} \cdot \begin{bmatrix} 2 & 3 \\ 4 & 7 \end{bmatrix} = ?$

A. $\begin{bmatrix} 12 & 3 \\ 20 & 21 \end{bmatrix}$

B. $\begin{bmatrix} 16 & 25 \\ 24 & 39 \end{bmatrix}$

C. $\begin{bmatrix} 12 & 39 \\ 20 & 21 \end{bmatrix}$

D. $\begin{bmatrix} 16 & 22 \\ 25 & 39 \end{bmatrix}$

E. $\begin{bmatrix} 36 & 25 \\ 22 & 16 \end{bmatrix}$

Step 1: The question asks for the product of both matrices.

Step 2: You know the elements of both matrices.

Step 3: Apply the formula: The top left element of the resulting product matrix equals (6 × 2) + (1 × 4) = 12 + 4 = 16; eliminate choices (A), (C), and (E). The bottom left element equals (6 × 2) + (3 × 4) = 12 + 12 = 24; eliminate (D).

Step 4: Choice (B) is correct.

Now let's try a more advanced logic problem. Break this down, step-by-step. What do you know? What rules from earlier sections can help you find what you need to know?

EXAMPLE

6. △*ABC* shown here is an equilateral triangle with an area of 147 square units. What is the area of the shaded region?

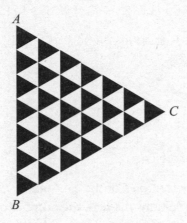

F. 21

G. 28

H. 63

J. 84

K. 98

This question asks for the area of the shaded region. A quick count tells us there are 49 total triangles—28 shaded, and 21 unshaded—meaning the shaded triangles account for $\frac{28}{49}$ of 147 and unshaded account for $\frac{21}{49}$.

Multiply the total area (147) by the fraction of it that is shaded $\left(\frac{28}{49}\right)$ to get the answer: 84, choice (J).

TRIGONOMETRY—2 POINTS

Complexity: High. Relates to: Plane Geometry

Note: As discussed previously, Trigonometry questions are lightly tested and are not required knowledge in order to build prowess in other, more tested areas (unlike Number Properties, which is needed for Variable Manipulation).

MATH PART 2: ACT MATH STRATEGY IN DEPTH

The concepts tested in both of these SmartPoint areas can be complex, but mostly the rules to remember are simple. And again, they are both tested lightly.

Remember, prioritize your time based on needs and SmartPoints. Therefore, prioritize these two SmartPoints last.

Still here? Fantastic! Let's get started with Trigonometry.

We'll discuss the rules to know first, then look at some sample problems to see how the ACT will ask you to apply your knowledge of Trigonometry.

The basic trigonometry functions are the sine, cosine, and tangent functions.

The sine function: $\sin\theta = \dfrac{\text{opposite}}{\text{hypotenuse}}$

The cosine function: $\cos\theta = \dfrac{\text{adjacent}}{\text{hypotenuse}}$

The tangent function: $\text{ten}\,\theta = \dfrac{\text{opposite}}{\text{adjacent}} = \dfrac{\sin\theta}{\cos\theta}$

From those three, we get the mnemonic SOHCAHTOA: Sine = Opposite/Hypotenuse (SOH); Cosine = Adjacent/Hypotenuse (CAH); Tangent = Opposite/Adjacent (TOA).

Values of the previous functions for certain common angles should be committed to memory, as they appear often among ACT Trigonometry questions.

Angle (°)	Sine	Cosine	Tangent
0	0	1	0
30	$\dfrac{1}{2}$	$\dfrac{\sqrt{3}}{2}$	$\dfrac{\sqrt{3}}{3}$
45	$\dfrac{\sqrt{2}}{2}$	$\dfrac{\sqrt{2}}{2}$	1
60	$\dfrac{\sqrt{3}}{2}$	$\dfrac{1}{2}$	$\sqrt{3}$
90	1	0	undefined

In addition to these three basic formulas, there are three inverse formulas: secant, cosecant, and cotangent.

The secant formula: $\csc\theta = \dfrac{1}{\cos\theta} = \dfrac{\text{hypotenuse}}{\text{adjacent}}$

The cosecant formula: $\csc\theta = \dfrac{1}{\sin\theta} = \dfrac{\text{hypotenuse}}{\text{opposite}}$

The cotangent formula: $\cot\theta = \dfrac{1}{\tan\theta} = \dfrac{\cos\theta}{\sin\theta}$

There are also some trigonometric identities that you should be familiar with. The most common are the Pythagorean identities:

$\sin^2\theta + \cos^2\theta = 1$

$1 + \tan^2\theta = \sec^2\theta$

$1 + \cot^2\theta = \csc^2\theta$

Let's try four sample problems so you can get comfortable with how the ACT will test your knowledge of Trigonometry. You can expect to see exactly four Trigonometry problems.

EXAMPLE

1. In the following figure, a surfboard is propped up against a rectangular box. If the board is 7 feet long, which of the following is closest to the height of the box?
    (Note: sin 23° ≈ 0.3907, cos 23° ≈ 0.9205)

    A. 2.7
    B. 3.0
    C. 4.3
    D. 5.6
    E. 6.4

Step 1: Let x equal the height of the triangle.

Step 2: Since the hypotenuse of the triangle is 7 and the height is x, $\sin 23 = \dfrac{x}{7}$.

Step 3: The question tells us that sin 23° ≈ 0.3907, so $\dfrac{x}{7} \approx 0.3907$.

Step 4: Multiply each side by 7 to get $x \approx 2.7349$. Choice (A) is correct.

EXAMPLE

2. The ratio of the lengths of the sides of a right triangle is $2 : \sqrt{5} : 3$. What is the cosine of the smallest angle in the triangle?

F. $\dfrac{2}{3}$

G. $\dfrac{\sqrt{5}}{3}$

H. $\dfrac{2\sqrt{5}}{3}$

J. $\dfrac{9}{10}$

K. 2

The cosine of any angle equals the length of the $\dfrac{\text{hypotenuse}}{\text{adjacent}}$. The smallest angle in a triangle is opposite the smallest side, meaning the side adjacent to the smallest angle is the second biggest side. In this triangle, therefore, the cosine of the smallest angle would be $\dfrac{\sqrt{5}}{3}$. Choice (G) is correct.

EXAMPLE

3. In right triangle ABC, $\sin i = \dfrac{3}{5}$ and $\cos i < 0$. What is the value of $\sec i$?

A. $-\dfrac{3}{5}$

B. $-\dfrac{4}{3}$

C. $-\dfrac{5}{4}$

D. $\dfrac{5}{4}$

E. $\dfrac{5}{3}$

Step 1: Label the opposite side, hypotenuse, and angle in the triangle.

Step 2: Apply the Pythagorean triplet 3-4-5 to the triangle: The missing side length is 4. Secant is $\dfrac{\text{hypotenuse}}{\text{adjacent}}$, or in this case $-\dfrac{5}{4}$.

Choice (C) is correct.

EXAMPLE

4. Line segments $\overline{WX}$, $\overline{XY}$, and $\overline{YZ}$, which represent the three dimensions of the rectangular box shown here, have lengths of 12 centimeters, 5 centimeters, and 13 centimeters, respectively. What is the cosine of $\angle ZWY$?

F. $\dfrac{13\sqrt{2}}{12}$

G. 2

H. $\dfrac{12}{13}$

J. $\dfrac{\sqrt{2}}{2}$

K. $\dfrac{5}{13}$

The cosine of $\angle ZWY$ equals $\dfrac{\text{adjacent}}{\text{hypotenuse}}$. The opposite line, $\overline{YZ}$, equals 13. Determine the length of $\overline{WY}$ by treating the sides of the cube as lengths of a triangle; $\overline{YX} = 5$ and $\overline{WX} = 12$, so use either the Pythagorean theorem or Pythagorean triplets to get the length of $\overline{WY}$, 13. Then solve for $\overline{WZ}$ by using either the theorem or the rules for special triangle 45-45-90 to get the length, $13\sqrt{2}$. $\dfrac{13}{13\sqrt{2}} = \dfrac{1}{\sqrt{2}} = \dfrac{\sqrt{2}}{2}$. Choice (J) is correct.

PUTTING IT ALL TOGETHER

Now, let's dive into some advanced strategies that apply to the ACT Math test as a whole. We've reviewed every SmartPoint and question type you'll see on the ACT Math test. Think of this next section as a dress rehearsal. We'll put your knowledge of those SmartPoints in tandem with the Special Strategies listed in Part 1 on page 139. We'll look at some challenging problems, then we'll show you how to use those strategies to make the problems more manageable on Test Day.

Combine these strategies with the Kaplan Method for the ACT Math test, and continue to work on the specific SmartPoints you need the most. When you're ready, the next chapter is ready and waiting with a quiz.

It's bound to happen at some point on Test Day. You look at a math problem and you don't see what to do. Don't freak out. Think about the problem for a few seconds before you give up—you can still earn those points. **When you don't see the quick and reliable approach right away, shake the problem up a little.** It takes discipline to do this—to force your mind to consider a question a whole new way when your conventional approach stalls. Practice flexible thinking, and try one of these Special Strategies, or "shake-it-up" techniques:

1. **Restate the Question**

2. **Remove the Disguise**

3. **Try Eyeballing**

1. RESTATE THE QUESTION

Often, the way to get over that stymied feeling is to change your perspective. Have you ever watched people playing Scrabble®? In their search to form high-scoring words with the letters on their seven tiles, they frequently move the tiles around in their racks. Sometimes a good word becomes apparent only after rearranging the tiles. One might not see the seven-letter word in this arrangement:

R E B A G L A

But reverse the tiles and a word almost reveals itself:

A L G A B E R

The tiles can spell ALGEBRA.

The same maneuver works on the ACT. **When you get stuck, try looking at the problem from a different angle.** Try rearranging the parts of the equation, changing fractions to decimals, factoring, multiplying out, redrawing the diagram, or just flat-out starting over—anything that might give you the fresh perspective you need to uncover a good solution method.

2. REMOVE THE DISGUISE

Sometimes it's hard to see the quick and reliable method immediately because the true nature of the problem is hidden behind a disguise.

3. TRY EYEBALLING

There is another simple but powerful strategy that should give you at least a 50-50 chance on almost any diagram question: **When in doubt, use your eyes. Trust common sense**

and careful thinking; don't worry if the solid rules or math aren't coming to mind.
For almost half of all diagram questions, you can get a reasonable answer without solving
anything: just eyeball it.

The Math directions say, "Illustrative figures are NOT necessarily drawn to scale," but in fact
they almost **always** are, or at least close enough that you can get close. You're never really
supposed to just eyeball the figure, but it makes a lot more sense than randomly guessing.
Occasionally, eyeballing can at least help you narrow down the choices.

Try these techniques on the following questions:

1. Which of the following is equivalent to $7^{77} - 7^{76}$?

    A. 7
    B. 7^{77-76}
    C. 7^{77+76}
    D. $7(77-76)$
    E. $7^{76}(6)$

2. If $\dfrac{x}{2} - \dfrac{x}{6}$ is an integer, which of the following statements must be true?

    F. x is positive.
    G. x is odd.
    H. x is even.
    J. x is a multiple of 3.
    K. x is a multiple of 6.

3. A geometer uses the following formula to estimate the area A of the shaded portion of a circle, as shown in the following figure, when only the height h and the length of the chord c are known:

$$A = \frac{2ch}{3} + \frac{h^3}{2c}$$

What is the geometer's estimate of the area, in square inches, of the shaded region if the height is 2 inches and the length of the chord is 6 inches?

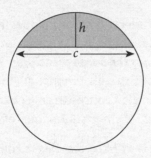

A. 6

B. $6\frac{2}{3}$

C. $7\frac{1}{2}$

D. $8\frac{2}{3}$

E. 12

4. In the following figure, points A, B, and C lie on a circle centered at O. Triangle AOC is equilateral, and the length of OC is 3 inches. What is the length, in inches, of arc ABC?

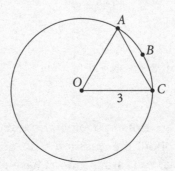

F. 3

G. π

H. 2π

J. 3π

K. 6π

ANSWERS AND EXPLANATIONS

1. **D**
2. **J**
3. **D**
4. **G**

Question 1

Questions like this give a lot of students grief. You know there's a rule, and if you could just remember it you know it would be right, but it's just not coming to mind. **Here's a hint:** ***Think of an easier problem testing the same principles***. The important thing to look for is the basic relationships involved, which will demonstrate the rule—here, we have exponents and subtraction. That subtraction sign causes trouble, because none of the ordinary rules of exponents seem to apply when there is subtraction of unlike terms.

So how would you work with $x^2 - x$? Most test takers could come up with another expression for $x^2 - x$: they'd factor to $x(x - 1)$. Or if the problem asked for $x^{77} - x^{76}$, they'd factor to $x^{76}(x - 1)$. The rule is no different for 7 than for x. Factoring out the x gives you: $7^{76}(7 - 1)$, which is $7^{76}(6)$, or choice (E).

Sometimes an ACT algebra question will include an expression that isn't of much use in its given form. The breakthrough in such a case may be to restate the expression by either simplifying it or factoring it.

Question 2

Re-express: $\dfrac{x}{2} - \dfrac{x}{6} = \dfrac{3x}{6} - \dfrac{x}{6} = \dfrac{2x}{6} = \dfrac{x}{3}$

This form of the expression tells us a lot more. If $\dfrac{x}{3}$ is an integer, then x is equal to three times some integer:

$\dfrac{x}{3} =$ an integer

$x = 3 \times$ an integer

In other words, x is a multiple of 3, choice (J).

Question 3

At first glance, this looks like an esoteric geometry question. Who ever heard of such a formula? But when you think about the question a bit, you realize that you don't really have to understand the formula. You certainly don't have to remember it—it's right there in the question.

In fact, this is not really a geometry question at all. It's just an "evaluate the algebraic expression" question in disguise. All it really asks you to do is plug the given values $h = 2$ and $c = 6$ into the formula:

$$A = \frac{2ch}{3} + \frac{h^3}{2c}$$

$$= \frac{2(6)(2)}{3} + \frac{(2)^3}{2(6)}$$

$$= 8 + \frac{2}{3} = 8\frac{2}{3}$$

Choice (D) is correct.

Question 4

The ACT counts on you taking one glance at this question and giving up. Don't give up on a question too quickly just because it looks like it's testing something you've never seen before. In many such cases, it's really a familiar problem in disguise.

Here's a difficult geometry question that you might just decide to eyeball:

A quick look at this question could easily yield a response such as, "Oh, forget it—that just looks terrible. I'm moving on." But it's a triangle inscribed into a circle. These are simple shapes, and they're right there in front of you. Take another look.

STEP 1: WHAT IS THE QUESTION?

There's an equilateral triangle that connects the center and two points on the circumference of a circle. You're looking for the length of the arc that goes from A to C.

STEP 2: WHAT INFORMATION AM I GIVEN?

You know the length of OC is 3 inches and that AOC is an *equilateral* triangle, that is, a triangle where all sides are equal lengths and all interior angles are 60 degrees. All but one of the answer choices are given in terms of π, so it's likely that a calculation with π would help you find the answer if you were to do a calculation using a formula. But read on, in Step 3 we'll show you that you don't actually need to use a formula to figure this one out!

STEP 3: WHAT CAN I DO WITH THE INFORMATION?

What you're "supposed" to do to answer this question is recall and apply the multi-step formula for the length of an arc. But suppose you don't remember that formula on Test Day. Should you give up and take a wild guess?

No. You can eyeball it. Since you understand that *equilateral* means all sides are equal, you know that side $\overline{AC}$ is 3 inches long. Now look at arc ABC compared to side $\overline{AC}$. Suppose you were an ant, and you had to walk from A to C. If you walked along line segment $\overline{AC}$, it would be a 3-inch trip. About how long a walk would it be along arc *ABC*? Clearly more, but not much more, than 3 inches.

STEP 4: AM I FINISHED?

Now look at the answer choices. Choice (F) is no good—you know the arc is more than 3 inches. All the other choices are in terms of π. Think again of π as "a bit more than 3," and you will quickly see that only one answer choice is in the right ballpark. Choice (G)—π—would be a bit more than 3, which sounds pretty good. Choice (H)—2π—would be something more than 6. Already that's way too big. Choices (D) and (E) are even bigger. It sure looks like the answer has to be (G)—and it is.

Not all ACT students will want to solve this question the textbook way. If you do, great! Go right ahead. If you can't yet, and you'd like to be able to, head to the Plane Geometry section earlier in this chapter. We discuss circles and triangles, and even similar problems involving arc length to a great extent. Solving the problem is **always** more reliable than eyeballing. But when you *don't* know how to solve a diagram problem, or if you think it would take forever to get an answer, eyeballing and eliminating answer choices sure beat wild guessing. Sometimes, as with this question, you might even be able to narrow the choices down to the one that's probably correct.

SUMMARY

In this chapter, we went over every SmartPoint and question type you will encounter on the ACT Math test. Use this chapter for continued study and reference as you practice ACT Math questions and find the skills you need to focus on.

The SmartPoints can be grouped as follows:

The **fundamental** SmartPoints are the two categories of knowledge that form the basis for all other areas of the ACT Math test.

They are:

1. Number Properties

2. Operations

If you find yourself struggling with math conceptually and have trouble grasping the basics of the other SmartPoints, practice here first. This is also a good place to start, just for the sake of establishing a solid foundation.

The **highly tested** SmartPoints are the big four. These SmartPoints are tested inside and out. You'll need to know the basics and be able to apply them with wide variations and tests of many applications.

The big four highly tested ACT SmartPoints are:

1. Variable Manipulation

2. Plane Geometry

3. Proportions and Probability

4. Coordinate Geometry

As you continue to build your score on the ACT Math test, spend the bulk of your time with these four. Test yourself frequently on each, and review them consistently. Mastering these concepts and question types will lead to huge score gains. The bulk of the points on the ACT Math test are contained in this quartet.

The **complex** SmartPoints are the last two. These SmartPoints are not tested extensively and don't form any fundamental knowledge. Prioritize these only when you've mastered the rest and are ready to start aiming for top scores.

They are:

1. Patterns, Logic, and Data

2. Trigonometry

When in doubt, use one of the Special Strategies discussed in Math Part 1 for guidance:

1. Restate the problem.

2. Remove the disguise.

3. Try eyeballing.

When you're ready, move on to the next chapter and try out the Math Quiz. Check how you do, SmartPoint by SmartPoint, then come back to this chapter to polish the skills you need. Good luck!

CHAPTER 9

Math Part 3: ACT Math Quiz

Here we go!

Treat the following quiz questions like those you'll encounter on Test Day, and see how you do. Make sure to check your answers only *after you've completed all 30 questions*! Don't check as you go—you need to start focusing on pacing and timing, and if you review as you go you'll either encourage or discourage yourself in a way that won't occur on Test Day. Keep track of your time. Try to spend one minute per question—aim to spend no more than 30 minutes on the whole quiz. Don't be discouraged if you run over 30 minutes. You'll have plenty more opportunities to practice with the full-length tests at the end of this book. But make note of which questions take you longer than others and how much time it takes you to complete the entire quiz so you know what to work on next.

Finally, when checking your answers, take note in particular of the SmartPoint categories of the questions you miss. Use this quiz to help you find where to spend your study time before you move on to the Practice Tests at the end of the book.

Remember to ask the four questions that comprise the Kaplan Method for ACT Math: What is the question? What information am I given? What can I do with the information? Am I finished? Also, don't forget to use Picking Numbers and Backsolving when applicable.

Directions: Don't linger over questions that are too time-consuming. You may use a calculator (check the ACT website to make sure your calculator is permitted). Some questions, however, may be easier to answer without the use of a calculator.

Note: Unless the question says otherwise, assume all of the following:

1. Illustrative figures are *not* necessarily drawn to scale.

2. All geometric figures lie in a plane.

3. The term *line* indicates a straight line.

4. The term *average* indicates arithmetic mean.

1. If $x^2 + 14 = 63$, $x = $?

   A. 4.5
   B. 7
   C. 11
   D. 14
   E. 24.5

2. The following chart shows the total pizza slice sales for a pizza restaurant over a weekend. If pepperoni slices cost $2.45 and cheese slices cost $1.95, how much did the restaurant earn on Friday from pepperoni and cheese slices?

	Friday	Saturday	Sunday
Cheese	38	46	36
Sausage	43	52	47
Pepperoni	41	49	44

   F. $174.55
   G. $178.00
   H. $179.45
   J. $199.45
   K. $207.80

3. If the average of 292, 305, 415, and x is 343, what is the value of x?

   A. 292
   B. 343
   C. 360
   D. 415
   E. 1,355

4. A jar contains 8 red marbles, 14 blue marbles, 11 yellow marbles, and 6 green marbles. If a marble is selected at random, what is the probability that it will be green?

   F. $\dfrac{2}{39}$

   G. $\dfrac{2}{13}$

   H. $\dfrac{3}{13}$

   J. $\dfrac{8}{39}$

   K. $\dfrac{11}{39}$

5. Each day, Laura bikes to school in the morning and bikes home in the afternoon. If she bikes at a speed of 12 miles per hour and the school is 3 miles from her house, how long does it take her to bike to school and back?

   A. 12 minutes
   B. 15 minutes
   C. 24 minutes
   D. 28 minutes
   E. 30 minutes

6. If $s^2 - 4s - 6 = 6$, what are the possible values of s?

    F. −2, −6

    G. −2, 6

    H. 2, −6

    J. −2, 3

    K. 2, −3

7. The complex number i is defined as $i^2 = -1$. $(i + 1)^2(i - 1) = ?$

    A. $i - 1$

    B. $i - 2$

    C. $- i + 2$

    D. $- 2i + 2$

    E. $- 2i - 2$

8. Each of 50 students had the option of buying either mugs or dinosaurs as museum souvenirs. If 37 bought mugs, 28 bought dinosaurs, and every student bought at least one souvenir, how many students bought both mugs and dinosaurs?

    F. 11

    G. 12

    H. 13

    J. 15

    K. 17

9. Which of the following is a solution to the inequality $-1 \geq -\dfrac{3}{5}x + 2$?

    A. ![number line A]

    B. ![number line B]

    C. ![number line C]

    D. ![number line D]

    E. ![number line E]

10. If $f(x) = 3\sqrt{x^2 + 3x + 4}$, what is the value of $f(4)$?

    F. 4

    G. 12

    H. $3\sqrt{2}$

    J. $4\sqrt{2}$

    K. $12\sqrt{2}$

11. In the following figure, at which point does $\overline{XZ}$ intersect with its perpendicular bisector?

    A. (4, 5)

    B. (2, 4)

    C. (5, 2)

    D. (5, 4)

    E. (3, 2)

12. Which of the following is the equation of the graph shown here?

F. $y = 2x + 1$

G. $y = -2x + 1$

H. $y = -2x - 1$

J. $y = \dfrac{1}{2}x + 1$

K. $y = -\dfrac{1}{2}x + 1$

13. If the first and second terms of a geometric sequence are 3 and 12, what is the expression for the value of the 24th term of the sequence?

A. $a_{24} = 3^4 \times 12$

B. $a_{24} = 3^4 \times 23$

C. $a_{24} = 4^3 \times 12$

D. $a_{24} = 4^{23} \times 3$

E. $a_{24} = 4^{24} \times 3$

14. What is the length of a line segment with endpoints $(3, -6)$ and $(-2, 6)$?

F. 1

G. 5

H. 10

J. 12

K. 13

15. A rectangle has a side length of 8 and a perimeter of 24. What is the area of the rectangle?

A. 16

B. 24

C. 32

D. 64

E. 96

16. A boy who is 4 ft tall stands in front of a tree that is 24 ft tall. If the tree casts a shadow that is 18 ft long on the ground and the two shadows end at the same point, what is the length of the boy's shadow?

F. 3 ft

G. 4 ft

H. 5 ft

J. 6 ft

K. 8 ft

17. An international phone call costs x cents for the first 5 minutes and t cents for each minute after. What is the cost, in cents, of a call lasting exactly v minutes where $v > 5$?

A. $\dfrac{5x + t}{v}$

B. $(5x + 1)\,v$

C. $5x + tv$

D. $x + tv$

E. $x + t(v - 5)$

18. The ramp in the following figure has a 20° angle of elevation and a height of 3 ft. What is the length of the ramp?

F. $\dfrac{3}{\sin 20°}$

G. $\dfrac{3}{\cos 20°}$

H. $\dfrac{\sin 20°}{3}$

J. $\dfrac{\cos 20°}{3}$

K. $3 \cos 20°$

19. In the figure shown here, chord *FG* has a length of 12 and triangle *GOH* has an area of 24. What is the area of the circle centered at *O*?

A. 30π

B. 36π

C. 50π

D. 64π

E. 100π

20. A circle with radius 5 is inscribed in a square. What is the difference between the area of the square and the area of the circle?

F. 25π

G. 50π

H. $50 - 25\pi$

J. $100 - 25\pi$

K. 100

21. If cos *G* = 0.5, which of the following would also equal 0.5?

A. $1 - \sin G$

B. $1 - \tan G$

C. $1 - \dfrac{1}{\sin G}$

D. $1 - \dfrac{1}{\sec G}$

E. $1 - \dfrac{1}{\csc G}$

22. If $0.75x - 13 = 2$, what is the value of *x*?

F. 11.25

G. 14.67

H. 15

J. 16

K. 20

23. The relationship between Fahrenheit and Celsius is $F = \dfrac{9}{5}C + 32$. If the temperature is 68° Fahrenheit, what is the temperature in degrees Celsius?

A. 14°

B. 20°

C. 32°

D. 64.8°

E. 68°

24. A jacket with an original price of $160 is on sale for 15% off. What is the sale price?

    F. $120
    G. $136
    H. $140
    J. $144
    K. $155

25. What is the sum of the prime factors of 60?

    A. 12
    B. 15
    C. 16
    D. 19
    E. 24

26. A local high school is raffling off a college scholarship to the students in its junior class. If a girl has a 0.55 chance of winning the scholarship and 154 of the juniors are girls, how many of the juniors are boys? (Assume that every junior has an equal chance to win.)

    F. 85
    G. 126
    H. 154
    J. 161
    K. 280

27. What is the equation of a line that has a y-intercept of -3 and is parallel to the line $3x = 4 + 5y$?

    A. $y = -\dfrac{3}{5}x + 3$

    B. $y = -\dfrac{5}{3}x + 3$

    C. $y = -\dfrac{5}{3}x - 3$

    D. $y = \dfrac{3}{5}x + 3$

    E. $y = \dfrac{3}{5}x - 3$

28. Circle O has a radius of 5 and $\angle AOB = 45°$. What is the length of arc AB?

    F. 5

    G. $\dfrac{4\pi}{5}$

    H. 3

    J. $\dfrac{5\pi}{4}$

    K. $\dfrac{25\pi}{8}$

29. Square *QRST* is inscribed inside square *ABCD*. If *SR* = 5, what is the area of triangle *QAT*?

   A. 3
   B. 3.125
   C. 4.50
   D. 5
   E. 6.25

30. What is the measure of the angle $\frac{3\pi}{4}$ expressed in degrees?

   F. 45°
   G. 60°
   H. 120°
   J. 135°
   K. 270°

ANSWERS AND EXPLANATIONS

1. **B**	16. **F**
2. **F**	17. **E**
3. **C**	18. **F**
4. **G**	19. **E**
5. **E**	20. **J**
6. **G**	21. **D**
7. **E**	22. **K**
8. **J**	23. **B**
9. **A**	24. **G**
10. **K**	25. **A**
11. **D**	26. **G**
12. **F**	27. **E**
13. **D**	28. **J**
14. **K**	29. **E**
15. **C**	30. **J**

1. **B**

Variable Manipulation

Isolate the variable, then solve for x:

$$x^2 + 14 = 63$$
$$x^2 = 49$$
$$x = \pm 7$$

Choice (B) is 7.

2. **F**

Patterns, Logic, and Data

Take a moment to familiarize yourself with the table before diving into the problem. The question asks for Friday's pepperoni and cheese sales, so be sure that you are reading data from the correct column. On Friday, 41 pepperoni slices were sold at $2.45 per slice, and 38 cheese slices were sold at $1.95 per slice, for sales totaling ($2.45 × 41) + ($1.95 × 38) = $100.45 + $74.10 = $174.55. That's (F).

3. **C**

Operations

If the variable makes the average seem difficult to calculate, consider the sum instead. The average of

four numbers is 343, so their sum must be 343 × 4 = 1,372. Three of the numbers are 292, 305, and 415, so the final number is 1,372 − (292 + 305 + 415) = 1,372 − 1,012 = 360, or (C).

4. **G**

Proportions and Probability

The probability of an event occurring is given by the formula:

$$\text{Probability} = \frac{\text{Number of Desired Outcomes}}{\text{Number of Possible Outcomes}}$$

In this problem, a desired outcome is getting a green marble while a possible outcome is simply getting any marble. There are 8 + 14 + 11 + 6 = 39 total marbles in the jar. Of these, 6 are green, so the probability of getting a green marble is $\frac{6}{39}$, which simplifies to $\frac{2}{13}$. That's choice (G).

5. **E**

Proportions and Probability

Laura lives 3 miles from school, so biking to school and back means a distance of 3 × 2 = 6 miles. Since Laura bikes at a speed of 12 miles per hour and 6 is half of 12, it must take her half an hour, or 30 minutes, to bike both legs of the journey. (E) is correct.

6. **G**

Variable Manipulation

To solve a quadratic equation, first set it equal to 0. Begin by subtracting 6 from both sides of the equation to get $s^2 - 4s - 12 = 0$. To factor this, you will need two factors of −12 that add up to −4. The only pair of factors that meets this criterion is −6 and 2, so the equation factors to $(s + 2)(s - 6) = 0$. For this equation to be true, either $s + 2$ or $s - 6$ (or both) must be 0. Therefore, the two possible solutions of s are −2 and 6. (G) is correct.

7. **E**

Operations

A complex number can seem scary on the ACT, but this problem defines it for you, so treat it like you would any other variable that you plug numbers into. In this problem, the key is swapping every i^2 with a −1. Begin by simplifying the first term in the expression:

$(i + 1)^2 = (i + 1)(i + 1) = i^2 + 2i + 1 = -1 + 2i + 1 = 2i$

Multiplying this by the second term gets you:

$2i(i - 1) = 2i^2 - 2i = 2(-1) - 2i = -2 - 2i$

That's the same as (E).

8. **J**

Patterns, Logic, and Data

In this problem, some of the students bought mugs, some bought dinosaurs, and some bought both. The problem is asking for the number of students who bought both. 37 bought mugs and 28 bought dinosaurs, which accounts for a total of $37 + 28 = 65$ students. Since there are only 50 students in total, $65 - 50 = 15$ students were counted twice. These 15 are the ones who bought both mugs and dinosaurs. That's (J).

9. **A**

Coordinate Geometry

Ignore the number lines for now and focus on the inequality. Inequalities work like normal equations in all aspects except one—when multiplying or dividing by a negative number, remember to flip the inequality sign. To solve the inequality, isolate x:

$$-1 \geq -\frac{3}{5}x + 2$$

$$-3 \geq -\frac{3}{5}x$$

$$-15 \geq -3x$$

$$5 \leq x$$

"Greater than or equal to 5" is represented by a closed circle at 5 with the arrow pointing toward the right. That's (A).

10. **K**

Patterns, Logic, and Data

To find $f(4)$, plug 4 for x into the function $f(x)$ and solve:

$$f(x) = 3\sqrt{x^2 + 3x + 4}$$
$$= 3\sqrt{4^2 + 3(4) + 4}$$
$$= 3\sqrt{16 + 12 + 4}$$
$$= 3\sqrt{32}$$
$$= 3 \times 4\sqrt{2}$$
$$= 12\sqrt{2}$$

So the answer is (K).

11. **D**

Coordinate Geometry

Don't let the triangle fool you—its presence is wholly irrelevant, as you need only $\overline{XZ}$ itself to answer the question. A bisector of a line segment cuts the segment in half, so it must intersect that segment at its midpoint. Therefore, we are actually looking for the midpoint of $\overline{XZ}$. According to the figure, the coordinates of $\overline{XZ}$ are (2, 6) for X and (8, 2) for Z. Plug these points into the Midpoint formula and solve.

$$\text{Midpoint} = \frac{x_1 + x_2}{2}, \frac{y_1 + y_2}{2}$$
$$= \frac{2 + 8}{2}, \frac{6 + 2}{2}$$
$$= \frac{10}{2}, \frac{8}{2}$$
$$= (5, 4)$$

Choice (D) is correct.

12. **F**

Coordinate Geometry

The line crosses the y-axis at (0, 1), so its y-intercept is 1. Eliminate choice (H). A quick look at the four remaining answer choices reveals that each has a different slope, so finding the slope of our line will be enough to answer the question. We already have one point, (0, 1), so pick another point, such as (1, 3), and plug both into the two-point formula for slope:

$$\text{Slope} = \frac{y_2 - y_1}{x_2 - x_1}$$

$$= \frac{3 - 1}{1 - 0}$$

$$= \frac{2}{1}$$

$$= 2$$

The slope is 2 and the y-intercept is 1, so the line is $y = 2x + 1$, which is (F).

13. D

Patterns, Logic, and Data

In a geometric sequence, use the formula $a_n = a_1(r^{n-1})$, where a_n is the nth term in the sequence, a_1 is the first term in the sequence, and r is the amount by which each preceding term is multiplied to get the next term.

The first two terms in this sequence are 3 and 12, so r is $\frac{12}{3} = 4$. Now that we have r, we can plug each known value in the equation and solve for $a_{24} = 3(4^{24-1}) = 3 \times 4^{23}$.

That's (D).

14. K

Coordinate Geometry

To find the distance between two points, plug them into the distance formula and evaluate:

$$\text{Distance} = \sqrt{(x_2 - x_1)^2 + (y_2 - y_1)^2}$$

$$= \sqrt{(-2 - 3)^2 + (6 - (-6))^2}$$

$$= \sqrt{(-5)^2 + 12^2}$$

$$= \sqrt{25 + 144}$$

$$= \sqrt{169}$$

$$= 13$$

(K) is correct.

15. C

Plane Geometry

The perimeter of a rectangle is twice its length plus twice its width, or perimeter = $2l + 2w$. To find the area, you must first determine the value of w, so plug in the values for perimeter and length to solve:

$$\text{Perimeter} = 2l + 2w$$

$$24 = 2(8) + 2w$$

$$24 = 16 + 2w$$

$$8 = 2w$$

$$4 = w$$

So the width is 4. The area of the rectangle is length × width, or $8 \times 4 = 32$. That's (C).

16. F

Plane Geometry

While this problem may look like a geometry problem at first glance, a closer look reveals that each of the three angles of one triangle is congruent to its corresponding angle in the other. The triangles are thus similar and similar triangles have proportional sides, so this is actually a proportion problem. The boy's height is proportional to the tree's height in the same way that the boy's shadow is proportional to that of the tree, so call x the length of the boy's shadow, set up the proportion, and solve for x:

$$\frac{24}{18} = \frac{4}{x}$$

$$24x = 72$$

$$x = 3$$

So the boy's shadow is 3 ft long. That's (F).

17. E

Variable Manipulation

With so many variables in both the question stem and the answer choices, this problem is ripe for Picking Numbers. Pick 10 for x, 3 for t, and 9 for v. Now the problem reads, "An international phone call costs 10 cents for the first 5 minutes and 3 cents for each minute after. What is the cost, in cents, of a call lasting exactly 9 minutes?"

In this case, the first 5 minutes cost 10 cents and there are $9 - 5 = 4$ additional minutes, each of which costs 3 cents, for a total cost of $10 + (4 \times 3) = 10 + 12 = 22$ cents. Plug 10 for x, 3 for t, and 9 for v into each of the choices to see which comes out to 22:

A. $\dfrac{5(10)+3}{9} = \dfrac{53}{9} = 5\dfrac{8}{9}$. Eliminate.

B. $(5(10) + 3)(9) = (50 + 3)(9) = (53)(9) = 477$. Eliminate.

C. $(5 \times 10) + (3 \times 9) = 50 + 27 = 77$. Eliminate.

D. $10 + (3 \times 9) = 10 + 27 = 37$. Eliminate.

E. $10 + 3(9 - 5) = 10 + 3(4) = 10 + 12 = 22$. This works.

Only (E) works, so it must be correct.

18. **F**

Trigonometry

The length of the ramp is the hypotenuse of the right triangle in the figure. Since you have only the side opposite the given angle, use sin 20° to find the hypotenuse:

$$\sin 20° = \frac{\text{opposite}}{\text{hypotenuse}}$$

$$\sin 20° = \frac{3}{\text{hypotenuse}}$$

$$\text{hypotenuse} = \frac{3}{\sin 20°}$$

That's (F).

19. **E**

Plane Geometry

You are given that the area of the triangle inside the circle is 24 and the length of the chord is 12. $\overline{OH}$ comes from the center and is perpendicular to $\overline{FG}$, so the former must be the perpendicular bisector of the latter and $\overline{FH} = \overline{HG} = 6$. Plug this into the area formula to find the length of $\overline{OH}$:

$$\text{Area} = \frac{1}{2}bh$$

$$24 = \frac{1}{2}(6)h$$

$$24 = 3h$$

$$8 = h$$

So $\overline{OH} = 8$, making triangle HOG a 3-4-5 right triangle with legs 6 and 8 and a hypotenuse of 10. The latter also happens to be the radius of the circle, so its area is $\pi r^2 = 10^2\pi = 100\pi$. That's (E).

20. **J**

Plane Geometry

Begin by eliminating (H), as $50 - 25\pi$ is a negative value, and that cannot be correct. Since the problem does not provide you with a figure, draw one to visualize what you are being asked.

Since the circle is inscribed within the square, its radius is half the side of the square. The circle has a radius of 5, so the square has a side of $2 \times 5 = 10$. Therefore, the area of the circle is $5^2\pi = 25\pi$, and the area of the square is $10^2 = 100$. The difference between the area of the square and that of the circle is thus $100 - 25\pi$, which is (J).

21. **D**

Trigonometry

While you may not know the values of most of the choices offhand, you don't need to. Every choice subtracts some value from 1, so the correct answer must subtract an expression that is equal to 0.5. Since secant is the reciprocal of cosine, $\cos G = \dfrac{1}{\sec G} = 0.5$, so (D) is correct.

22. **K**

Variable Manipulation

If the decimal makes this problem seem difficult, convert it into a fraction before solving for x:

$$0.75x - 13 = 2$$

$$\frac{3x}{4} = 15$$

$$3x = 60$$

$$x = 20$$

That's (K).

23. **B**

Variable Manipulation

You are given the equation to convert Fahrenheit to Celsius, so plug 68 in for F and solve for C:

$$F = \frac{9}{5}C + 32$$

$$68 = \frac{9}{5}C + 32$$

$$36 = \frac{9}{5}C$$

$$20 = C$$

That matches (B).

24. **G**

Proportions and Probability

The original price of the jacket is $160, so a 15% sale is a discount of $160 × 0.15 = $24. Therefore, the sale price of the jacket is $160 − $24 = $136. This matches (G).

25. **A**

Number Properties

To find the prime factors of 60, use the prime factorization tree:

So the prime factorization of 60 is 2 × 2 × 3 × 5, and the sum of these factors is 2 + 2 + 3 + 5 = 12. (A) is correct.

26. **G**

Proportions and Probability

There's a lot going on in this problem, so find the most concrete point and begin there. You are told that the chance for a girl to win the scholarship is 0.55. Since this is more than half, there must be more girls than boys in the junior class, so eliminate (H), (J), and (K). The value 0.55 isn't much greater than 0.5, so if you were low on time on Test Day, (G) would be a great guess.

To solve this problem the math way, use the probability formula:

$$\text{Probability} = \frac{\text{number of desired outcomes}}{\text{number of possible outcomes}}$$

Since 0.55 is the probability that a girl would win, the 154 girls are the desired outcomes, and the total number of students (boys and girls) is the number of possible outcomes. Call x this total, and use this formula to solve for x:

$$55 = \frac{154}{x}$$

$$x = \frac{154}{55}$$

$$x = 280$$

With 280 total students and 154 girls, there must be 280 − 154 = 126 boys. That's (G).

27. E
Coordinate Geometry
Begin by converting $3x = 4 + 5y$ into $y = mx + b$ form:

$$3x = 4 + 5y$$

$$3x - 4 = 5y$$

$$\frac{3}{5}x - \frac{4}{5} = y$$

The slope of the line is $\frac{3}{5}$. Parallel lines have the same slope, so the line we are looking for has a slope of $\frac{3}{5}$ and a y-intercept of -3. That's (E).

28. J
Plane Geometry
To find the length of an arc, you will need the measure of the central angle as well as the circumference of the entire circle. In this problem, the central angle is $45°$ and the circumference of the circle is $2\pi(5) = 10\pi$. Plug these values into the proportion and solve:

$$\frac{\text{central angle}}{360°} = \frac{\text{length of arc}}{\text{circumference}}$$

$$\frac{45°}{360°} = \frac{\text{length of arc}}{2\pi r}$$

$$\frac{1}{8} = \frac{\text{length of arc}}{10\pi}$$

$$8 \times (\text{length of arc}) = 10\pi$$

$$\text{length of arc} = \frac{5\pi}{4}$$

That matches (J).

29. E
Plane Geometry
When a square is inscribed within another square like they are in this problem, each of the inner square's vertices bisects one of the outer square's sides, so point Q bisects $\overline{AB}$ and point T bisects $\overline{AD}$. Therefore, $\overline{QA} = \overline{AT}$ and triangle QAT is an isosceles right triangle. Since $QRST$ is a square and $SR = 5$, QR, ST, and TQ also equal 5. Therefore, triangle QAT becomes an isosceles right triangle with a hypotenuse of 5. An isosceles right triangle has sides in the proportion

$x:x:x\sqrt{2}$, so $\overline{QA}$ and $\overline{AT}$ each measure $\frac{5}{\sqrt{2}} = \frac{5\sqrt{2}}{2}$.

Plug these into the area formula and solve:

$$\text{Area} = \frac{1}{2}bh$$

$$= \frac{1}{2} \times \left(\frac{5\sqrt{2}}{2}\right)^2$$

$$= \frac{1}{2} \times \frac{25 \times 2}{4}$$

$$= \frac{1}{2} \times \frac{50}{4}$$

$$= \frac{50}{8}$$

$$= 6.25$$

That's (E).

30. J
Trigonometry
To convert $\frac{3\pi}{4}$ into degrees, substitute 180 for π and solve:

$$\frac{3\pi}{4} = \frac{3 \times 180}{4} = \frac{540}{4} = 135°$$

Choice (J) is correct.

SUMMARY

Time to review!

Use this space to record how many questions you answered correctly.

Now, record how many you answered incorrectly.

Remember to master the Kaplan Method for ACT Math as well as overall strategies for the Math test, like Picking Numbers and Backsolving. Refer to Math Part 1 for those. If you're short on time before Test Day, spend your time with Part 1 to master the essentials.

Now, get specific.

Use the chart below to record how many questions you answered correctly and incorrectly in each Math SmartPoint category.

Point Value	Topic	# Correct	# Incorrect
7	**Plane Geometry**		
7	**Variable Manipulation**		
6	**Proportions and Probability**		
6	**Coordinate Geometry**		
3	**Operations**		
3	**Patterns, Logic, and Data**		
2	**Number Properties**		
2	**Trigonometry**		

Use the chart to review the specific areas in which you can gain the most points on Test Day. Remember to spend more time on the categories with higher SmartPoint values.

Keep reviewing Math Parts 1 and 2 for specific SmartPoints. Then keep practicing using the Practice Tests later in this book.

By regularly reviewing and practicing, you'll become a master of ACT Math!

UNIT 3: READING

The Basics:

35 Minutes

40 Questions

4 Passages or Passage Pairs

Pacing:

Pace your time per passage, or passage pair, as opposed to per question.

Plan to spend a little over eight minutes per passage or passage pair, including reading and answering the questions. The exact pacing is eight minutes and 45 seconds per passage.

TEST DAY DIRECTIONS AND FORMAT

Here's what the Reading directions will say on Test Day:

> **Directions:** There are four passages in this test. Each passage is followed by several questions. After reading a passage, choose the best answer to each question and fill in the corresponding oval on your answer document. You may refer to the passages as often as necessary.

OUTSIDE KNOWLEDGE

No outside knowledge is required. The answers to every question can be found in the passage.

THE INSIDE SCOOP

The ACT Reading test always has the same four passage types in the same order. You can expect to see—in order—Literary Narrative (including prose fiction), Social Science, Humanities, and Natural Science passages. Each passage is about 1,000 words in length (or a pair of two shorter passages that add up to about 1,000 words) and written at the same level of complexity as typical college textbooks and readings.

Paired Passages provide two passages that deal with the same topic or related topics. Some questions ask about only one of the passages, while others ask you to consider both. The passage or passages each question addresses is clearly labeled. When you see Paired Passages, they will replace one of the single passages and will make up about 25% of your Reading score.

The nonfiction passages (Social Science, Humanities, and Natural Science) are written with a clear purpose that you are expected to understand. You'll also need to comprehend specific facts relayed in these essays and the use of structure.

The Prose Fiction passage asks you to focus more on the thoughts, feelings, and motivations of fictional characters, even when these are not explicitly stated in the passage.

The questions *do not* get harder as you proceed through the test.

SMARTPOINTS

Point Value	Topic	Basics Page	Details and Practice
12	**Detail**		
8	**Inference**		
8	**Generalization**		
6	**Function**		
1	**Vocab-in-Context**		
1	**Writer's View**		

CHAPTER 10

Reading Part 1: Inside the ACT Reading Test

THE KAPLAN METHOD FOR ACT READING

STEP 1: ACTIVELY READ THE PASSAGE, TAKING NOTES AS YOU GO

Active reading is the process of asking yourself questions while reading. It's faster than a careful, full read, and slightly slower than a skim. The idea is to quickly get a sense of the big picture of the passage. What's the gist? What's the author's purpose? Remember you're not reading this for fun—you're going to be asked questions about this content, so be ahead of the game by asking yourself what you're reading while you read. Don't get bogged down in the details—you can come back to those if the questions call for it. The passage isn't going anywhere, it's an open-book test. Here are some questions to ask yourself: Why did the author write this paragraph? How does it contribute to the purpose of the passage as a whole?

Next, take brief notes next to each paragraph on what you find from your questioning process. Again, details don't matter at this stage. This isn't meant to be a full outline, but a road map of the passage to guide you once you get to the questions. Find the *purpose* of each paragraph, then jot it in the margins in three to five words to create your passage map. Stick to that word limit, and think of these notes as labels to remind you of what each paragraph contains to help you find information when you get to the questions. Focus on getting the purpose and themes down, as they are much harder to locate on a quick search.

STEP 2: EXAMINE THE QUESTION STEM, LOOKING FOR CLUES

Analyze what the question stem is asking. What type of question is this? Most questions use typical phrasing to let you know if they're asking for details, or a purpose, or an inference. Refer to the particular SmartPoints—breaking down each question type—in Reading Part 2 for examples of these phrases. Now, think about the question stem without looking at the answer choices. Be disciplined; avoid the trap of misleading answers by not looking at any answers until you're fully ready. First, look for line references. If the question stem has one, great! Do your research by looking back at that part of the passage, *even if you feel like you remember it.* Remember to check your map for the big picture of the paragraph and read around the line to collect any details you need. If there is no line reference, that passage map will be invaluable—use it to help you locate what you need. Don't rely on your memory here; you don't get extra points for answering without double-checking. If the question is asking for details, locate those in the passage using the line reference or your map. If the question is asking for bigger-picture information, use the map you've created containing this information.

STEP 3: PREDICT THE ANSWER AND SELECT THE CHOICE THAT BEST MATCHES YOUR PREDICTION

Don't look yet. Now that you've completed your research, you can save yourself time and avoid the temptation of wrong answer choices by forming a prediction of the answer before you peek at the given answer choices. Based on your work in Step 2, state in your own words what you think the answer will be. You'll do so by focusing your attention on the words in the passage. This will help you avoid tempting wrong answers that have less to do with the passage, as well as wrong answers that present details from the passage that are unrelated to the question. Finally, by having a prediction in your head, you'll be able to simply look for an answer choice that matches, instead of having to read and analyze all four choices equally. Evaluating each answer can be a very time-consuming practice on the ACT Reading test, and by predicting, you'll greatly increase your efficiency.

Predict before you peek!

(Note: This method is a huge part of increasing your score on Test Day, but it will take some practice to master it. Thus, we'll discuss it further and give you a chance to practice in the Method Breakdown section on page 293.)

QUICK TIPS

MIND-SET

- **Know where the passage is going.** Read the passages actively, and pay attention to structural clues and key words and sentences to predict and evaluate what the passage is "doing." The easiest way to do this is to create a passage map.

- **Conquer the questions.** Look up the answers directly in the passage; don't be tempted by the choices or your memory.

- **Start with your strengths.** There's no reason to tackle these passages in the order given. Which subject interests you the most? Do you want to do that one first or last? Do you prefer fiction? Science stuff? Passages about people? Get yourself on a roll by starting with the passage that is easiest for you to build confidence and bank your time.

SPECIAL STRATEGIES

PAIRED PASSAGES

If you are tackling a set of paired passages, you want to follow the Kaplan Method for Paired Passages in which you divide and conquer.

THE KAPLAN METHOD FOR PAIRED PASSAGES

Step 1: Read Passage A and answer the questions about it.

Step 2: Read Passage B and answer the questions about it.

Step 3: Answer questions asking about both passages.

The ACT will make clear which questions relate to Passage A, Passage B, and both Passages A and B, which is very helpful. By concentrating on one passage at a time before you tackle questions that discuss both, you can avoid trap answer choices that refer to the wrong passage.

PROSE FICTION PASSAGES

Pay attention to the characters, especially the main character, and who gets the most (or best) lines. Read between the lines to determine unspoken emotions and attitudes. Ask yourself:

- **Who are these people?** What are they like? How do the characters relate to each other?

- **What is their state of mind?** Are they angry, sad, reflective, excited?

- **What's going on?** What's happening on the surface? What's happening beneath the surface?

- **What is the author's attitude toward the characters?** What words indicate a particular tone? Do any phrases suggest the author is either approving of or critical of one of the characters?

NONFICTION PASSAGES

- **Don't be thrown by unfamiliar vocabulary or topics.** The Natural Science passage may take you into strange territory, but remember: this is the Reading test, not the Science test. Everything you need to know will be covered in the passages. If you find a difficult term, odds are the definition will be given to you in context (or else it simply might not matter what the word means). You can get most questions right even if you don't fully understand the passage. Remember, you can find all the answers in the passage.

  Visit your online syllabus—Lesson 2—for more instruction and practice with the Kaplan Method for ACT Reading.

TIMING: PACING AND APPROACH

Take a few seconds at the beginning of the subject test to flip through the four passages, gauging the difficulty of each. Start with the one that best suits your strengths and interests.

Treat each passage and its questions as a block. You have just under nine minutes per block. Spend the first three minutes on your active reading and passage mapping. Use the remaining time researching and answering the questions. Within each block, feel free to skip around and answer the easy questions first. Just make sure to keep track of time so you get to all the questions.

Set your watch to 12:00 at the beginning of the subject test. Although you should go faster if you can, here's roughly where you should be at the following checkpoints:

12:09. . . . . One passage finished and answers gridded in

12:18. . . . . Two passages finished and answers gridded in

12:27. . . . . Three passages finished and answers gridded in

12:35. . . . . Four passages finished and answers for entire section gridded in

Take about 30 seconds (average) per question. Some questions take more time than others (ones with Roman numerals in them and ones that have EXCEPT are examples—these will take longer either to research or to work through and eliminate). So remember, if you feel the need to spend a lot of time to get the right answer, don't. Either guess or skip and come back. (Don't forget to come back, though.)

Don't panic if you can't finish all four passages. Make sure you do a good job on at least three passages—and remember to grid answers (even if they're blind guesses) for all questions by the end. You can get in the mid to high 20s just by doing a great job on three passages. Even if you try all four passages, you probably won't really work on all 40 questions. For many questions, you'll have to guess. Just make sure you guess on the tough ones and actually work on the easy ones!

WHEN YOU'RE RUNNING OUT OF TIME

If you have less than five minutes left for the last passage, do the following:

1. **Look for questions with specific line references and do them.**

2. **Refer to the cited location in the passage and answer the question as best you can, based on what you see there.**

3. **Make sure you have gridded in an answer for every question before time is called.**

SCORING

Your performance on the Reading subject test will be averaged into your ACT Composite Score, weighted equally with your scores on the other three subject tests. You will also receive:

- Reading subject score (1 to 36) for the entire Reading subject test

- Social Science/Sciences subscore (1 to 18) based on your performance on the nonfiction passages drawn from Social Studies and Natural Sciences

- Arts/Literature subscore (1 to 18) based on your performance on the nonfiction passage (drawn from the Humanities) and on the Prose Fiction passage

SMARTPOINT BREAKDOWN

Here is a brief overview of what exactly to expect and how much of it you should be expecting.

DETAIL QUESTIONS—12 POINTS

Extremely Important

Detail questions will ask you about specific points in the passage. These questions are very straightforward; you won't have to draw a conclusion or make an interpretation, just locate the particular detail in the passage and match it to an answer choice. Sometimes the correct answer choice even uses virtually the same wording found in the passage. At other times, the correct answer is a paraphrase of the wording from the passage. For further discussion on Detail questions, and the question stem clues that you will be dealing with, turn to page 328.

INFERENCE QUESTIONS—8 POINTS

Very Important

Inference questions ask you to read between the lines—you'll need to take the next logical step to discover what is implied or suggested by the author. Though you will have to draw a conclusion not directly stated in the passage, be careful not to assume that these questions are a matter of opinion. You will not have to make a wild guess; the correct answer will be logically necessary based on what is stated in the passage, and can best be answered by sticking close to the explicit meaning in the text. Turn to page 333 for discussion and practice with Inference questions, as well as the question stem clues used for this question type.

GENERALIZATION QUESTIONS—8 POINTS

Very Important

Generalization questions ask you to draw conclusions based on larger portions of the passage or the whole passage. You'll need to understand the big picture, as the scope can include whole paragraphs or even the passage in its entirety. Make sure to keep the overall purpose of the passage in mind to answer these questions. Your passage map will be extremely helpful here, showing you how parts of the passage relate to other parts. For further discussion on these questions and the phrases in the question stems that indicate them, turn to page 344.

FUNCTION QUESTIONS—6 POINTS

Important

Function questions ask you to understand the purpose of an essay's structure or order. Specifically, you'll need to interpret why the author used a particular word, phrase, or detail in the passage. Look for the logical flow of a piece to find the correct answer. How does the part referenced fit into that flow? Is it a transition? Does it establish a relationship, such as cause and effect or contrast? You'll need to keep in mind the author's overall purpose to properly answer these questions. Turn to page 336 for more discussion on strategies for this question type and its question stem hints.

VOCAB-IN-CONTEXT QUESTIONS—1 POINT

Less Important

Vocab-in-Context questions ask you to interpret the meaning of a specific word or phrase used in the passage. As implied in the name of the question type, you won't need to bring any outside knowledge of dictionary definitions to answer these questions. In fact, on the ACT they don't often ask about the bigger words you might not recognize. Instead, these questions focus on commonly used words with multiple meanings. You'll have to use the passage to decipher which meaning of the word is most appropriate to the passage. So don't think of these as "Vocab" questions, but as "Context" questions. Page 330 has more strategy discussion for this question type and the typical question stems associated with it

WRITER'S VIEW QUESTIONS—1 POINT

Less Important

Writer's View questions ask you to interpret the intentions or opinions of the author. Because this is often explicit in the nonfiction passages, these questions are mostly found after the Prose Fiction passage. You'll need to take the author's perspective to determine the general attitude felt toward a character or event. Be careful not to confuse what the *characters* think about each other with what the *author* thinks. For strategies and question stem hints associated with Writer's View questions, turn to page 339.

METHOD BREAKDOWN

Active reading and **passage mapping,** the parts that form Step 1 of the Kaplan Method for ACT Reading, are essential techniques to practice to become a master of the Reading test. This method can earn you a great score increase all by itself if you use it effectively.

Thus, without any outside knowledge to review, we'll use this section to really dive into the Kaplan Method.

We'll thoroughly look at active reading and passage mapping. You'll be able to see exactly how to use this first step of the method to full effect. Then, we'll see how it makes the next two steps of the method (answering the questions) that much easier.

Finally, you'll get a chance to practice it all, and then put it all together with the warm-up before we move on to Part 2 and the details on the specific SmartPoints.

Let's get started!

ACTIVE READING

Read *actively* to quickly get a sense of the purpose or main idea of the passage and see how everything fits together to support that main idea. You read *actively* by continually asking yourself questions about what you're reading, trying to get behind the purpose and choices of the author, rather than focusing on details that may or may not be asked about. Look for the general outline of the passage—determine how it's structured. Don't worry about the details. You'll come back for those later. You're not reading slowly and carefully, and you're also not skimming. You're searching for the purpose and the main idea. The process is more like a treasure hunt than a typical read.

Fast, active reading requires more mental energy than slow, passive reading, but it pays off. Those who dwell on details—who passively let the passage reveal itself at its own pace—are sure to run out of time. Don't be that kind of reader! Make the passage reveal itself to you on *your* schedule, by skimming the passage with an eye to structure rather than detail. Look for key words that tell you what the author is doing so you can save yourself time. For instance, read "example" sentences very quickly, just glancing over the words. When an author says "for example," you know that what follows is an example of a general point. Do you need to understand that specific example? Maybe, maybe not. If you do, you can come back and read it when you're attacking the questions. If you *don't* need to know the example for any of the questions, great! You haven't wasted much time on something that won't get you a point.

You actually do this kind of "reading" all the time, and not just when you're reading a book or newspaper. When you watch TV or see a movie, for instance, you can often figure out much of what's going to happen in advance. You see the bad guys run out of a bank with bags of money in their hands, and you can guess that the next thing they'll do is get into a car and drive away in excess of the speed limit. You see a character in an old sitcom bragging to his friends about how great a driver he is, and you know that he's bound to get into a fender bender before the next commercial. **This ability to know where something is going is very valuable. Use it on the ACT.**

To help you know where an author is going, pay careful attention to structural clues. Words like *but, nevertheless*, and *moreover* help you get a sense of where a piece of writing is going. Look for signal phrases (like *clearly, as a result,* or *no one can deny that*) to determine the logic of the passage. These are the same words and phrases described under the Connections SmartPoint in the English test. When you spot these words in a passage, underline them. They provide important clues about the author's purpose and the structure of the passage. Refer to the following table for a list of these words and the type of connections they build.

KEY WORDS THAT INDICATE CAUSE AND EFFECT AND CONTRAST

Cause and Effect	Contrast
as a result	but
as shown by	claims (may suggest that a "claim" isn't)
because	difference
consequently	however
evidence shows	in contrast
for this reason	nevertheless
it follows that	on the other hand
so	some…others
therefore	whereas
thus	while

Of course, the words in the table don't form an exhaustive list, but they do give you an idea of the kinds of words to pay attention to when you need to determine the logical flow and notice what contrasts the writer presents. One thing to notice is that these words are not subject-specific. This is precisely why connections words and phrases are so important. They show up repeatedly in all three nonfiction ACT passages, no matter what topic the passage discusses. You can't predict the exact content of the passages you'll see on Test Day, but you can be certain that cause-and-effect and contrast words and phrases will be present and crucial to your understanding of the passage.

Finding how the pieces fit together is a big step. Use key words to help you spot the structure and the purpose more quickly. Focus on the main idea. How do these puzzle pieces connect? What picture forms when you put them together? The details, remember, you can come back for later when you're doing the questions. **What's important in reading the passage is getting a sense of how those details fit together to express the point or points of the passage.**

PRACTICE KNOWING WHERE YOU'RE GOING

In the following exercise, try to fill in the word or phrase that should come next. For most, there are many possible answers, so don't worry about getting the "right" answer.

1. You'd think that the recipe for a strawberry souffle would be complicated, but my friend's version was_____.

2. I can't believe my good luck! The one time in my life I buy a lottery ticket, I_____.

3. A parked car burns no fuel and causes no pollution. Once the ignition is turned on, however, _____.

4. As their habitat is destroyed, wild animals_____.

5. The new word-processing program was far easier to use than the old one. Moreover, the accompanying instruction booklet explained the commands in a _____way.

6. The new word-processing program was far easier to use than the old one. On the other hand, the accompanying instruction booklet explained the commands in a _____way.

ANSWERS

1. In Sentence 1, the active reader would probably complete the sentence by saying that the friend's version was "actually quite simple" or something similar. How do you know what's coming next here? The structural clue *but* tips you off, telling you a contrast is coming up. You'd think the recipe would be complicated, *but* it's "actually quite simple."

2. In Sentence 2, on the other hand, there's no real structural clue to help you out. However, the *meaning* of the sentence should make clear what's coming up. Because the speaker is marveling at his good luck, he must have won some money. A likely completion would be something like: The one time in my life I buy a lottery ticket, I "win the jackpot."

3. In Sentence 3, we have another contrast, signaled by the clue *however*. A parked car doesn't burn fuel or pollute, so the answer has to be something like "the car starts burning gas and polluting."

4. Sentence 4 demonstrates again that you don't need explicit structural clues to stay ahead. Sometimes all you need is common sense. What do you think would happen to animals whose habitat had been destroyed? Would they thrive? Celebrate? Buy a condo in Florida? No, they'd probably "start dying out." They might even "become extinct."

5. Sentences 5 and 6 show clearly how you can use an author's language to anticipate what point he or she is going to make next. Here, we have identical sentences, except for one small (but very important) difference. One of the sentences in question 5 includes the word *moreover,* indicating continuation or the addition of similar information. The blank should be something close to "in a clear and easy-to-understand" way. It makes sense that "The program was easy to use; moreover, the instructions were easy to understand." The connection in question 6, "on the other hand," indicates contrast. The sentences make sense only if you fill in the blank with "a confusing and unclear" way.

PASSAGE MAPPING

As you actively read, it's important to take notes in the margins. When first trying this, students often figure it will take extra time—obviously reading *and writing things down* takes longer than just reading alone. But having notes saves you far more time when answering questions than it takes during the reading time. Try it out and see! You should organize your notes by paragraph, and write three to five words on the purpose of each. Use the active reading process and those transition words to help you find this purpose quickly.

You may be wondering, wouldn't it be quicker simply to underline a few words in the passage? Underlining is possibly a little quicker, but there's a danger involved—if you read through a paragraph thinking you'll underline what's important, you may find yourself underlining too many details. On the other hand, when you read each paragraph with the goal of determining the author's purpose for that paragraph, there's a certain discipline involved. The mental processing required to decide on a note to jot down in the margin is likely to help you develop a good overall understanding of the passage. Writing a quick note in your own words in the margin is a more active approach than simply underlining words that are already there.

So find the purpose, and write it down. Give yourself a visual guide to the passage while keeping your brain active. You'll understand it better and more quickly this way. You'll also have reference points in the passage when you get to the questions and need to look back to find those details.

Find how the pieces fit, and label those pieces.

Here are some examples of what the purpose of the paragraphs might be:

TYPES OF PURPOSE

State the Thesis

Establish the Tone

Provide a Supporting Argument

Provide Evidence

Give an Opinion

Provide a Counterargument

Give the Backstory or History

That is by no means a comprehensive list, but is a guide to common types of purpose you might find. Note that you should never just write "establish the tone" if you've discovered that to be the purpose of a paragraph. It may well be the purpose, but you should write in your map what that tone actually is—scholarly, personal, humorous, angry, whatever you find it to be. Similarly, what is the opinion or thesis you've spotted? Look for these categories and jot down what it is that fits into them.

TWO PARTS, ONE STEP

Active Reading and passage mapping actually go hand-in-hand, both part of the same process. Here's a step-by-step guide summarizing how to effectively go about Step 1 of the Kaplan Method for ACT Reading:

1. Focus on the big picture. Note the purpose of each paragraph, and don't get bogged down in details.

2. Pay close attention to the first and last paragraphs. They often give great clues for determining the purpose of the passage as a whole.

3. Notice phrasing that indicates an example, such as *an illustration of, for example, for instance, this can be seen when,* or *to illustrate.* Remember that the example is a detail, but the general statement or principle it's illustrating is more general and could be a main idea.

4. Ask yourself questions as you read:

    a. What is the writer's purpose? Is he merely describing and explaining, or does he try to persuade the reader? Notice whether the writer is taking a side on an issue.

    b. What is the tone of the passage? Do you notice any phrasing that is approving, critical, or sarcastic?

    c. What is the internal logic of the passage? Do you notice features of a chronological structure or an outline structure or some of each?

5. Read for contrast, noting when the writer points out differences and contradictions. Pay attention to connection words and phrases that show contrast, such as *although, appears, but, despite, even though, however, in spite of, on the other hand, though,* and *yet.*

6. Notice where and when the writer states an opinion.

7. Notice where and when the writer makes an argument. What point is the evidence supporting? Notice words that direct the flow of an argument such as *as a result, because, consequently, resulting in, therefore,* or *thus.*

TRY IT OUT!

Now that you know how to read actively and create a passage map, put those skills together on an ACT Reading passage. Afterwards, we'll review what your notes could have been. Keep in mind that our suggestions are just a guide. If yours are slightly different, but you still found the purpose, fantastic!

PASSAGE I

By the tenth century most of northern Europe was divided into farming units known as manors…

Line
(5)   Almost always a manor comprised four parts: arable, meadow, waste, and the village area itself. The arable was of course the land which grew the crops on which the inhabitants of the manor subsisted. To maintain fertility and keep down weeds it
(10) was necessary to fallow a part of the cultivated land each year. It was, therefore, usual (though not universal) to divide the arable into three fields. One such field was planted with winter grain, a second with spring
(15) grain, and the third left fallow; the following year, the fallow field would be planted with winter grain, the field in which winter grain had been raised was planted with spring grain, and the third field left fallow.
(20) By following such a rotation, the cycle was completed every three years. Since the fallow field had to be plowed twice in the year in order to keep down the weeds, and the others had to be plowed once, work for the
(25) plow teams extended almost throughout the year. Plowing stopped only at times when all hands were needed to bring in the harvest, or when the soil was too wet

to be plowed, or was frozen. The amount
(30) of land that could be tilled was fixed fairly definitely by the number of plows and plow teams that the manor could muster; and official documents sometimes estimated the wealth and value of a manor in terms of the
(35) number of plows it possessed.

The three great fields lay open, without fences, but were subdivided into numerous small strips (often one acre in size, i.e., the amount of one day's plowing) which
(40) individual peasants "owned." The strips belonging to any one individual were scattered through the three fields in different parts, perhaps in order to assure that each peasant would have strips plowed
(45) early and late, in fertile and infertile parts of the arable land.

Custom severely restricted the individual's rights over his land. The time for plowing and planting was fixed by custom
(50) and each peasant had to conform, since he needed his neighbor's help to plow his strips and they needed his. Uniform cropping was imperative, since on a given day the village animals were turned into the fields to graze
(55) after the harvest had been gathered, and if some individual planted a crop which did not ripen as early as that of his neighbors,

he had no means of defending his field from the hungry animals. If his crop ripened (60) sooner, on the other hand, it could not be garnered without trampling neighboring fields. Moreover, the very idea of innovation was lacking: men did what custom prescribed, cooperated in the plowing and (65) to some extent in the harvesting, and for many generations did not dream of trying to change.

The meadow was almost as important as the arable for the economy of the village. (70) Hay from the meadow supported the indispensable draught animals through the winter. The idea that hay might be sown did not occur to men in medieval times; consequently they were compelled to rely on (75) natural meadows alone. One result was that in many manors, shortage of winter fodder for the plow teams was a constant danger. It was common practice to feed oxen on leaves picked from trees, and on straw from the (80) grain harvest; but despite such supplements the draught animals often nearly starved in winter. In some cases, oxen actually had to be carried out from their winter stalls to spring pastures until some of their strength (85) was recovered and plowing could begin. Thus on many manors, meadow land was

even more valuable than the arable and was divided into much smaller strips (often the width of a scythe stroke).

(90) The waste provided summer pasture for various animals of the manor: pigs, geese, cattle, and sheep. The animals of the whole manor normally grazed together under the watchful eyes of some young children or (95) other attendants who could keep them from wandering too far afield, and bring them back to the village at night. The waste also was the source of wood for fuel and for building purposes, and helped to supplement (100) the food supply with such things as nuts, berries, honey, and rabbits…

The fourth segment of the manor was the village itself, usually located in the center of the arable near a source of (105) drinking water, and perhaps along a road or path or footpath leading to the outside world. The cottages of medieval peasants were extremely humble, usually consisting of a single room, with earthen floor (110) and thatched roof. Around each cottage normally lay a small garden in which various vegetables and sometimes fruit trees were planted. In the village streets, chickens, ducks, and dogs picked up a precarious (115) living.

STEP 1: ACTIVELY READ THE PASSAGE, TAKING NOTES AS YOU GO

Here's a sample passage map. Yours might be similar, but remember, differences are fine as long as you found the purpose for yourself.

Paragraph 1: Intro to manors.

Paragraph 2: Describe arable, part of manor with crops. Seasonal planting cycles.

Paragraph 3: Arable divided into 3 great fields, divided into strips.

Paragraph 4: Custom confined freedoms, limited innovation.

Paragraph 5: Describe meadow. Source of hay for animals, run short in the winter.

Paragraph 6: Describe waste. Summer pasture, source of wood.

Paragraph 7: Describe village. Near water with small cottages.

How close were you? Did you remember to help yourself find the purpose of each paragraph by underlining transition words?

Now, get ready. It's time to use that map on the next steps of the method, to help you start earning those points.

STEP 2: EXAMINE THE QUESTION STEM, LOOKING FOR CLUES

Approaching the Reading questions requires self-discipline. Most test takers have an almost irresistible urge to immediately jump to the answer choices to see what "looks okay." That's not a good idea. Don't peek at the answer choices—there are too many ways to be led astray by tempting "almost" answers.

Read the question stem to identify what the test is asking. Which of the following is it about?

- A detail (what happened)

- The passage as a whole (the big idea)

- An inference (reading between the lines)

- A specific word or phrase used in the passage

Analyzing what the question stem is asking is very important, because the ACT will offer you choices that don't answer the question at hand. It is easy to get the right answer—if you know what you are looking for.

How do you know what you're looking for? There will be clues in the question stem. These clues could be as straightforward as a line reference or as vague as the phrase "as stated in the passage." In both cases, though, you know that you'll be able to find the answer in the passage.

This is where your notes come in handy. On most questions, you won't be able to remember exactly what the passage said about the matter in question. That's okay. In fact, even if you do think you remember, don't trust your memory. Instead refer to the passage and your passage map. Your notes are all waiting to help you find the answers to the 10 questions and to help you find the right spot in the passage.

STEP 3: PREDICT THE ANSWER AND SELECT THE CHOICE THAT BEST MATCHES YOUR PREDICTION

It's extremely important in Reading to **make a habit of answering the question in your own words** (based on your checking of the passage) *before* looking at the answer choices. Predict before you peek. Most students waste enormous amounts of time thinking about answer choices in Reading. If you do that, you'll **never** finish, and you'll get so confused you'll probably get more questions wrong.

Once you have an answer in your head based on what you've read and have rechecked it in the passage, match it to one of the answer choices. Avoid trying to see if they "look right." You wouldn't answer "1.5" on the Math test if you knew the answer was "2." 1.5 isn't "almost" 2. Don't settle for "almost" answers on the Reading test either.

Practice Steps 2 and 3. Use the following question stems to find the information you need and form a prediction. The questions will then be repeated with the answer choices, but get in the habit of researching and predicting before you look.

QUESTIONS

1. The description of the near starvation of the oxen (lines 82–85) serves to:

_____

_____

2. According to the passage, the fact that the peasants' individual strips of land were unfenced subdivisions of larger fields required each peasant to:

_____

_____

3. According to the second paragraph (lines 4–35), the fallow part of the arable had to be plowed a total of how many times in any given calendar year?

_____

_____

4. The passage suggests that the practice of peasants owning strips "scattered through the three fields in different parts" (lines 42–43) was instituted in order to:

_____

_____

5. On the basis of the information in the passage, it may be inferred that people in medieval times did not think of sowing hay because:

_____

_____

6. As it is used in line 61, the word *garnered* means:

_____

_____

7. According to the passage, if one of the arable's three great fields were left fallow one year, it would be:

_____

_____

8. Which of the following conclusions is suggested by the fourth paragraph (lines 47–67)?

_____

_____

9. According to the passage, a manor's value might be judged according to the number of its plows because:

_____

_____

10. According to the passage, summer pasture for a manor's geese would be provided:

_____

_____

1. The description of the near starvation of the oxen (lines 82–85) serves to:

   A. demonstrate how difficult life on the manor was in tenth century northern Europe.

   B. showcase how important work animals were to medieval manors.

   C. emphasize how important natural meadows were to feeding the work animals.

   D. explain why uniform cropping was a critical practice that ensured survival on the medieval manor.

2. According to the passage, the fact that the peasants' individual strips of land were unfenced subdivisions of larger fields required each peasant to:

   F. follow a fixed planting schedule so as to be able to harvest crops at the same time as the other peasants.

   G. harvest crops independently of his neighbors.

   H. limit the size of strips to what could be plowed in a single day.

   J. maintain small garden plots in order to provide his family with enough food.

3. According to the second paragraph (lines 4–35), the fallow part of the arable had to be plowed a total of how many times in any given calendar year?

   A. One

   B. Two

   C. Four

   D. Six

4. The passage suggests that the practice of peasants owning strips "scattered through the three fields in different parts" (lines 42–43) was instituted in order to:

   F. divide resources fairly evenly.

   G. preserve the wealth of elite landowners.

   H. protect the three fields from overuse.

   J. force neighbors to work only their own lands.

5. On the basis of the information in the passage, it may be inferred that people in medieval times did not think of sowing hay because:

   A. hay sowing had not been done in the past.

   B. the need for more hay was not great enough to warrant the extra work.

   C. northern Europeans did not yet have the necessary farming techniques for successful hay cultivation.

   D. the tight schedule of cultivating the arable meant that the peasants had no time to cultivate extra crops.

6. As it is used in line 61, the word *garnered* means:

   F. planted.

   G. watered.

   H. gathered.

   J. plowed.

7. According to the passage, if one of the arable's three great fields were left fallow one year, it would be:

   A. left fallow for two more years in succession.

   B. planted the next year with winter grain only.

   C. planted the next year with spring grain only.

   D. planted with either winter or spring grain the next year.

8. Which of the following conclusions is suggested by the fourth paragraph (lines 47–67)?

    I.   An individual was free to cultivate his own land in any way he wished.

    II. The manor was run according to tradition.

    III. Successful farming required cooperative methods.

    F. I and II only

    G. I and III only

    H. II and III only

    J. I, II, and III

9. According to the passage, a manor's value might be judged according to the number of its plows because:

    A. the more plows a manor had, the less land had to be left fallow.

    B. plows, while not in themselves valuable, symbolized great wealth.

    C. manors with sufficient plows could continue plowing throughout the year.

    D. the number of plows a manor owned determined how much land could be cultivated.

10. According to the passage, summer pasture for a manor's geese would be provided:

    F. next to cottages, within the village.

    G. on the fallow field of the arable.

    H. on the communal ground of the waste.

    J. on the whole of the meadow.

Now, take a look at the answers to see how you did.

KEY TO PASSAGE I

(NONFICTION—SOCIAL STUDIES)

	Answer	Refer to	Type	Comments
1.	C	Lines 68–89	Function	The entire paragraph supports this claim.
2.	F	Lines 52–59	Detail	"Uniform cropping was imperative…"
3.	B	Lines 21–23	Detail	Don't confuse fallow with planted fields.
4.	F	Lines 43–46	Inference	Every peasant got some fertile and some infertile land—inferably, to be fair to each.
5.	A	Lines 62–67, 72–75	Inference	No line reference, so you had to have a sense of the structure to find this.
6.	H	Lines 59–62	Vocab-in-Context	Use context. The crop is ripe, so it must be ready to be gathered.
7.	B	Lines 13–19	Detail	No line reference; otherwise, no problem.
8.	H	Lines 47–67	Inference	I: lines 47–52 say the opposite II: lines 48–52 III: lines 52–62 Statement I is false, so that means (F), (G), and (J) are wrong. That means (H) must be the answer.
9.	D	Lines 33–35	Detail	No line reference; number of plows = amount of land.
10.	H	Lines 90–92	Detail	Whole paragraph devoted to describing waste.

Get comfortable with this method. It might slow you down at first, but with time, it will make you a master of the ACT Reading test. Keep at it!

WARM-UP

Now, you know what to expect on the ACT Reading test. You know what types of questions you'll see and approximately how many of each. You know the Kaplan Method and have had a chance to practice it, step-by-step. It's time to put it together on your own for the first time. Use the following warm-up to practice passage mapping, researching, and predicting.

But take a deep breath. This one is a warm-up. Complete the following passages as well as you can. Make sure to passage map. Get in the habit now to start increasing your efficiency with the process. Check the steps as often as you need to and, again, make sure you research and predict before you peek at the answer choices.

The answers and explanations follow the passage and reveal which SmartPoint category each question was under. Use your results from this passage and the SmartPoints therein to prioritize your approach to the next chapter.

In the next chapter, we'll dive into each SmartPoint listed in this chapter. We'll go over the typical question stems of each, so you can easily recognize them on Test Day. We'll talk through the strategies and give you a chance to practice on samples. Remember, spend more time mastering question types that are tested more often to maximize your score gains!

Good Luck!

PASSAGE I

PROSE FICTION: *The passage is adapted from the novel* The House of Mirth, *written by Edith Wharton and published in 1905. This excerpt concerns Mr. Gryce and Miss Lily Bart and other guests who are visiting at Bellomont, the home of the Trenors.*

The observance of Sunday at Bellomont was chiefly marked by the punctual appearance of the smart omnibus destined to
Line convey the household to the little church
(5) at the gates. Whether any one got into the omnibus or not was a matter of secondary importance, since by standing there it not only bore witness to the orthodox intentions of the family, but made Mrs. Trenor feel,
(10) when she finally heard it drive away, that she had somehow vicariously made use of it.

It was Mrs. Trenor's theory that her daughters actually did go to church every Sunday, but their French governess's convic-
(15) tions calling her to the rival fane, and the fatigues of the week keeping their mother in her room till luncheon, there was seldom any one present to verify the fact. Now and then, in a spasmodic burst of virtue—when
(20) the house had been too uproarious over night—Gus Trenor forced his genial bulk into a tight frock-coat and routed his daughters from their slumber, but habitually, as Lily explained to Mr. Gryce, this parental
(25) duty was forgotten till the church bells were ringing across the park, and the omnibus had driven away empty.

Lily had hinted to Mr. Gryce that this neglect of religious observances was repugnant
(30) to her early traditions, and that during her visits to Bellomont she regularly accompanied Muriel and Hilda to church. This tallied with the assurance, also confidentially imparted, that, never having played bridge
(35) before, she had been "dragged into it" on the night of her arrival and had lost an appalling amount of money in consequence of her ignorance of the game and of the rules of betting. Mr. Gryce was undoubtedly enjoy-
(40) ing Bellomont. He liked the ease and glitter of the life and the luster conferred on him by being a member of this group of rich and conspicuous people. However, he thought it a very materialistic society; there were times
(45) when he was frightened by the talk of the men and the looks of the ladies, and he was glad to find that Miss Bart, for all her ease and self-possession, was not at home in so ambiguous an atmosphere. For this reason,
(50) he had been especially pleased to learn that she would, as usual, attend the young Trenors to church on Sunday morning. As he paced the gravel sweep before the door, his light overcoat on his arm and his prayer-

(55) book in one carefully gloved hand, he reflected agreeably on the strength of character which kept her true to her early training in surrounds so subversive to religious principles.

For a long time, Mr. Gryce and the omni-
(60) bus had the gravel sweep to themselves, but, far from regretting this deplorable indifference on the part of the other guests, he found himself nourishing the hope that Miss Bart might be unaccompanied. The precious minutes were
(65) flying, however. The big chestnuts pawed the ground and flecked their impatient sides with foam. The coachman seemed to be slowly pet-rifying on the box and the groom on the door-step, and still the lady did not come. Suddenly,
(70) however, there was a sound of voices and a rustle of skirts in the doorway, and Mr. Gryce, restoring his watch to his pocket, turned with a nervous start, but it was only to find himself handing Mrs. Wetherall into the carriage.

(75) The Wetheralls always went to church. They belonged to the vast group of human automata who go through life without neglecting to per-form a single one of the gestures executed by the surrounding puppets. It is true that the Bel-
(80) lomont puppets did not go to church, but oth-ers equally important did—and Mr. and Mrs. Wetherall's circle was so large that God was included in their visiting list. After them Hilda and Muriel struggled, yawning and pinning
(85) each other's veils and ribbons as they came. They had promised Lily to go to church with her, they declared, and Lily was such a dear old duck that they didn't mind doing it to please her, though for their own part they would
(90) much rather have played lawn tennis with Jack and Gwen, if she hadn't told them she was coming. The Misses Trenor were followed by Lady Cressida Raith, a weather-beaten person in Liberty silk and ethnological trinkets, who,
(95) on seeing the omnibus, expressed her surprise that they were not to walk across the park. At Mrs. Wetherall's horrified protest that the church was a mile away, her ladyship, after a

glance at the height of the other's heels, acqui-
(100) esced in the necessity of driving, and poor Mr. Gryce found himself rolling off between four ladies for whose spiritual welfare he felt not the least concern.

It might have afforded him some consola-
(105) tion could he have known that Miss Bart had really meant to go to church. She had even risen earlier than usual in execution of her purpose. She had an idea that the sight of her in a grey gown of devotional cut, with her
(110) famous lashes drooped above a prayer-book, would put the finishing touch to Mr. Gryce's subjugation and render inevitable a certain incident which she had resolved should form a part of the walk they were to take together
(115) after luncheon. Her intentions in short had never been more definite, but poor Lily, for all the hard glaze of her exterior, was inwardly as malleable as wax. She was like a water-plant in the flux of the tides, and today the whole
(120) current of her mood was carrying her toward Lawrence Selden.

Why had he come to Bellomont? Was it to see herself?

1. As used in line 49, the word *ambiguous* most nearly means:

   A. misty.

   B. contradictory.

   C. wealthy.

   D. unclear.

2. The phrase *It was Mrs. Trenor's theory* (line 8) is used primarily to indicate that

   F. Mrs. Trenor doesn't care whether or not her daughters attend church.

   G. Mrs. Trenor's understanding and that of the French governess contradict each other.

   H. Mr. and Mrs. Trenor have different beliefs about how best to manage their daughters.

   J. Mrs. Trenor likes to believe that Muriel and Hilda attend church regularly.

3. According to the passage, which of the following statements accurately describes the Wetheralls' attitudes and habits regarding church attendance?

   I. They attend church regularly.

   II. They view Sunday church attendance as a pressing moral obligation.

   III. They feel that church attendance is expected of them.

   IV. They view going to church as something similar to making a social visit.

   A. I, II, III, IV

   B. II, III, IV

   C. III only

   D. I, III, IV

4. It can be inferred from the last paragraph that

   F. Lily never had any intention of meeting Mr. Gryce for church.

   G. Lily is conscious of trying to appear attractive to Mr. Gryce.

   H. Lily's inflexibility can create social problems for her.

   J. Lily's outward appearance of malleability belies her actual resoluteness.

5. The main focus of this passage is

   A. the hypocrisy of the Trenors and their guests.

   B. the uncomfortable interaction between Mrs. Wetherall and Lady Cressida Raith.

   C. Mr. Gryce's interest in Lily Bart.

   D. the manners and morals of the upper classes.

PASSAGE II

SOCIAL SCIENCE: *This passage is adapted from "Assessing the Values of Cultural Heritage," a report published in 2002 by the Advisory Council on Historic Preservation. This selection, written by Marta de la Torre and Randall Mason, examines the challenges involved in determining the cultural significance of historic sites to various groups, including conservation experts and ordinary citizens.*

In recent decades, the concept of what is heritage has evolved and expanded, and new groups have joined specialists in its identifica-
Line tion. These groups of citizens, of profession-
(5) als from other fields, and of representatives of special interests arrive in the heritage field with their own criteria, opinions, and values—which often differ from our own as heritage specialists.

(10) This democratization is a positive development in our field and bears witness to the importance of heritage in today's society. Nonetheless, this aperture has brought new considerations to the discussions and has made
(15) them much more complex. Today the opinions of experts are often a few among many, in an arena where it is recognized that heritage is multivalent and that values are not immutable. In this changed environment, the articulation
(20) and understanding of values have acquired greater importance when heritage decisions are being made about what to conserve, how to conserve it, where to set priorities, and how to handle conflicting interests.

(25) As conservation professionals, we are comfortable with theassessment methods used by traditional heritage experts. However, to identify and measure "social" values, we must venture into new areas. The stakeholders of
(30) social values are usually members of the public who have not traditionally participated in our work or had their opinions taken into consideration. Today, as we recognize the importance of including all stakeholders in the process, we
(35) must turn to other disciplines to bring these new groups into the discussions.

Anthropologist Setha M. Low has introduced ethnographic research as a way of bringing new groups of stakeholders into the
(40) values of identification process. The field of environmental conservation has a relatively long tradition of consultation with broad spectrum of stakeholders. Approaches from the environmental field are often held up as
(45) examples to be emulated in the heritage field. Theresa Satterfield's work in this area has been a model for assessment tools and methods that might be productively applied in our own field. Economists seem to have the most developed
(50) and widely accepted value assessment tools. However, these tools might not be as accurate in measuring cultural values as has been accepted in the past. A number of economists are now searching for ways of honing their tools
(55) to make them more useful in the heritage field. The work of researchers in all three of these areas points us toward collaboration with other disciplines.

A discussion of values, of how social con-
(60) texts shape heritage and conservation, and of the imperative of public participation provides examples of issues that challenge conventional notions of conservation professionals' responsibilities. How to champion conserva-
(65) tion principles (traditional ones, centered on the sanctity and inherent meaningfulness of material heritage) while managing an open democratic process that may conclude by underselling conservation in favor of other social
(70) goals? This issue gets to the essential nature of the field and of conservation as a profession: Are we advocates? Are we neutral professionals and experts?

Conservation professionals are faced
(75) with two particular challenges arising out
of these social and political contexts: power
sharing and collaboration. Broader participation poses a challenge to the roles and
responsibilities of conservation profession-
(80) als: some suggest that bringing conservation
policies and decisions in line with democratic values would undermine the authority
of conservation professionals and would
even amount to an abdication of professional
(85) responsibility. In other words, democratization of conservation decision-making
could contradict the professional devotion
to conservation—what happens when the
democracy of voices decides that a heritage
(90) site can be destroyed? Do we as conservation
professionals have a right, or even a responsibility, to speak against the democratic will?

The probability is not that actual decision-making power will be democratized
(95) but, rather, that the process of value elicita-
tion will be included. Democratization of
the processes of consultation and assessment
of heritage values is not likely to be a threat
to the sovereignty of the field, but it still re-
(100) quires a change of attitude and training. The
inevitability of trade-offs and compromises
and the respectful and meaningful gathering of different modes of valuing have to be
recognized.
(105) Using new methods from different fields
means collaborating with more and different
professionals—anthropologists and economists, for instance. Such collaboration raises
questions about who is in charge of which
(110) part of the process. What are the relative
roles and contributions and responsibilities
of this different cast of characters? Does the
conservation professional's role become that
of an orchestrator of specialists or of one
(115) specialist among others? It seems that the
conservation professional has moved to play
the dual role of specialist and orchestrator.
The tasks associated with the latter function
call for new ways of thinking as well as for
(120) new skills. The challenge ahead is to continue searching for the means to serve the
public good by preserving material remains
of the past.

6. What is the fundamental question addressed by the passage as a whole?

   F. What is the role of the ordinary citizen in determining what conservation professionals should preserve?

   G. What are the best methods to use to ensure reliable conservation of culturally significant sites?

   H. In what ways can anthropologists contribute to the field of conservation?

   J. How is the role of the conservation professional changing in light of social and political concerns about the democratization of conservation activities?

7. A possible drawback of power-sharing and collaboration in the conservation field that the passage refers to is that:

   A. the authority of the specialist would be undermined.

   B. the ordinary citizen lacks knowledge relating to historic sites.

   C. the general public does not express much interest in historic conservation.

   D. most conservation specialists lack the skills needed to lead group collaboration.

8. The phrase "democracy of voices" in line 57 most likely refers to:

   F. the opinion of a large number of ordinary citizens.

   G. a government run by the people.

   H. the viewpoint of a citizen who is politically active.

   J. a traditional influence on decisions about heritage conservation.

9. As used in the passage, the word *orchestrator* (line 114) most nearly means:

   A. manager.

   B. creator.

   C. person with particular expertise.

   D. musical director.

10. The writer's view of the outlook for the conservation field is:

    F. grounded in cynicism.

    G. cautiously optimistic.

    H. tinged with reservations.

    J. fairly pessimistic

PASSAGE III

HUMANITIES: *This passage is taken from a collection of essays about 20th-century British novelists.*

British novelist Barbara Pym has been described as a novelist of manners, a twentieth-
century Jane Austen. Despite this comparison
Line with such a famous literary figure, Pym, for
(5) most of her own life, was relatively unknown.
She came to the attention of the public only
three years before her death when the *Times
Literary Supplement* asked for opinions about
the "most underrated novelist" of the twentieth
(10) century. Barbara Pym was the only novelist
to be named by two of the respondents, the
novelist and poet Philip Larkin and the literary
scholar Lord David Cecil. This recognition
led finally to a surge in her popularity, and
(15) Pym lived to see the publication of most of the
novels she had written previously.

Pym, born in 1913, began writing novels at
the age of 16. Her first effort was titled "Young
Men in Fancy Dress." In 1931, she entered St.
(20) Hilda's College at Oxford, where she read English literature. Following her graduation, she
began working on the novel *Some Tame Gazelle*, centered on the daily lives of two women
in their fifties. Pym based this story on the way
(25) she imagined her life and the lives of her sister
and their friends from Oxford as it might be
thirty years into the future. Pym completed
this novel in 1935 but had no luck in finding
a publisher for it. She kept writing, however,
(30) producing several novels and short stories by
crafting some of her own life experiences into
literary form.

During World War II, Pym worked first at
the Censorship Office in Bristol, England, and
(35) later with the Women's Royal Naval Service in
Naples, Italy. On her return to England, she
worked at the International Africa Institute
in London. Her job as assistant editor for the
journal *Africa* put her in contact with the
(40) world of anthropological scholarship. Her stories include characters who work in academics
and are presented in a mostly appreciative and
humorous way.

Pym's artistic perseverance paid off when
(45) her revision of *Some Tame Gazelle* was finally
accepted by Jonathan Cape, who published
the novel in 1950. Contemporary critics
reviewed this work favorably, so Pym was
finally established as a writer. For the next
(50) decade, Pym enjoyed some success, seeing the
publication of several more novels. *Excellent
Women* was published in 1952, and *Jane and
Prudence* came out the following year. Every
three years until 1961, Pym published a new
(55) novel. Scholars see these first six novels as an
important body of work marking Pym as a
significant author with a unique voice. She
wrote about ordinary people living quiet lives,
often in provincial locations and small towns
(60) in England. The novels include detailed descriptions of characters, clothing, meals, local
gossip, and activities of Anglican clergy and
church members.

Pym's consistent publishing success
(65) throughout the 1950s eventually came to an
end. In 1963, when she presented her next
novel, *An Unsuitable Attachment*, to her
publisher, it was considered out of date and
was rejected. Pym, though disappointed, did
(70) not give up. She submitted the novel to several
other publishers. After receiving several rejections, she revised and resubmitted it. All told,
twenty publishers rejected this novel during
the 1960s. Over the next fifteen years, Pym
(75) fought against losing hope that her writing
would ever again be appreciated. She worked

on yet another book, *The Sweet Dove Died*. This novel, darker than her earlier ones, about an older woman attracted to a much (80) younger man, was again rooted in Pym's personal experience. Like her previous novel, *The Sweet Dove Died* was not accepted by any publishers.

Even though Pym's rejections were com- (85) pounded by health crises, including a cancer diagnosis in 1971 and a stroke in 1974, she continued to write. After retiring from her job at the Africa Institute, she wrote *Quartet in Autumn*, her darkest novel yet, about four (90) office workers facing their own upcoming retirement. When Pym submitted this work to publishers in 1976, it was again rejected by all.

Pym's citation by Philip Larkin in the (95) *Times Literary Supplement* pulled her out of obscurity. Macmillan published *Quartet in Autumn* in 1977 and *The Sweet Dove Died* the following year. *Quartet* was nominated for the Booker Prize, Britain's prestigious (105) literary award. When these last two novels attracted critical attention in England, Macmillan reprinted all of Pym's earlier novels. When American audiences discovered Pym's work, Dutton published all of her novels in (110) the United States. Her work was published in translation, bringing her even wider readership. Despite declining health, Pym worked to finish her last novel, *A Few Green Leaves*, before she died in 1980. Following (115) Pym's death, *An Unsuitable Attachment*, the novel earlier rejected, was published, along with two other novels, *Crampton Hodnet* and *Civil to Strangers*. Pym has continued to generate interest among scholars for her (120) philosophical outlook and distinctive voice.

11. The writer uses the phrase *artistic perseverance* (line 44) to show that:

    A. Pym did not give up when her publishers rejected her work.

    B. Pym worked harder on *Some Tame Gazelle* than she had on "Young Men in Fancy Dress."

    C. rejection at some point is inevitable for all writers.

    D. Pym's subtle artistry was appreciated by contemporary critics.

12. The writer suggests in the first paragraph that:

    F. the article in the *Times Literary Supplement* generated renewed interest in Pym's earlier novels.

    G. the *Times Literary Supplement* rejected several of Pym's short stories.

    H. Pym suffered a stroke in 1974.

    J. Pym enjoyed a long friendship with Philip Larkin and Lord David Cecil.

13. The writer uses the phrase *throughout the 1950s* (line 65) to emphasize that

    A. the 1950s was a stable time for British society.

    B. Pym's success was not consistent throughout her lifetime.

    C. Pym's publishing house saw remarkable success during the 1950s.

    D. *Excellent Women* was one of the novels published during the 1950s.

14. Which of the following novels is *NOT* mentioned in the passage as being related in some way to Pym's personal life?

    F. *Some Tame Gazelle*

    G. *Civil to Strangers*

    H. *The Sweet Dove Died*

    J. *Quartet in Autumn*

15. The writer of this passage adopts a tone that can best be described as:

    A. detached but mildly appreciative.

    B. zealously enthusiastic.

    C. overtly biased.

    D. impatient and critical.

PASSAGE IV

NATURAL SCIENCE: *This passage is adapted from a document describing research done by the United States Geological Survey. The selection below concerns the effects of wind power developments on migrating birds.*

Interest in developing wind power as an alternative renewable energy source has increased in recent years. In the eastern United
Line States, exposed summits or ridge crests in the
(5) Appalachian Mountains have high wind power potential, and numerous wind power projects are being proposed. While generally supportive of energy development from renewable sources, the U.S. Fish & Wildlife Service, state
(10) wildlife agencies, nongovernmental organizations, and the public are concerned about potential impacts of wind power development on wildlife.

During their seasonal migration, large
(15) numbers of birds and bats cross or follow the mountainous landforms used for wind power. Wind power development could potentially impact populations of several species. Baseline information on nocturnally migrating birds
(20) and bats has been collected at some wind power development sites in the Appalachians, generally within a single season. However, a stronger scientific basis is critically needed to assess and mitigate risks at a regional scale.
(25) The United States Geological Survey (USGS) is studying the distribution and flight patterns of birds and bats that migrate at night. Researchers are analyzing weather surveillance radar data (NEXRAD) to allow for a broad
(30) view of spring and fall migration through the Appalachians and to assess the response of migrant birds to mountain ridges and other prominent landforms. Although NEXRAD data provide information on the broad-scale
(35) spatial and temporal patterns of nocturnal migration through the region, the devices generally do not detect bird or bat targets within the altitudinal zone potentially occupied by wind turbines. Therefore, researchers are using

(40) two complementary ground- based techniques—acoustic detection and portable radar sampling—to obtain site-specific information on the abundance and flight characteristics of nocturnal migrants in lower airspace.
(45) USGS is conducting acoustic monitoring at 31 sites scattered throughout the central Appalachians. Researchers are recording the calls made by migrating birds in flight to index the migrants' abundance and species composition
(50) at different locations. Data is being collected in the spring and fall. During the most recent season, there has been minimal disturbance from animals to the recording devices, so data from this season are expected to provide more
(55) complete coverage.

Researchers are working diligently to process and analyze the sound recordings. Because the recording units operate continuously, 24 hours a day, the first step in the
(60) analysis is the identification and separation of the night-time segments from the recordings. These night-time recordings are then scanned for flight calls using sound analysis software called XBAT, developed by Har-
(65) old Figueroa and Matt Robbins. An XBAT extension, developed by Kathy Cortopassi, searches for and flags sounds of a user-specified range of durations with a user-specified range of frequencies. Spectrograms of these
(70) sounds are then reviewed to eliminate sounds that are not bird calls. Sound files can also be scrolled through manually, with flight call spectrograms selected and output. Calls are identified by species, when possible, by
(75) matching them to a reference set. For each hour of sampling at each site, recorded calls are tallied to index migrant abundance within and among nights.

Researchers are continuing to process
(80) these recordings. Preliminary analysis, however, indicates that more flight calls have been recorded at the sites during the fall migrations than during the spring. In addition, during both spring and fall, there is consid-
(85) erable variation among nights, both within and among sites. Researchers have been able to match some of the calls to particular species, but most calls can be placed only in species groups (for example, warblers, spar-
(90) rows, thrushes) because their spectrograms are not clear. Researchers speculate that this lack of clarity occurs because many of the calls are made by birds flying at the outer limits of the recording. The microphones can
(95) record calls up to about 300 meters above ground level.

The acoustic monitoring is supplemented with portable radar sampling at three sites to provide additional data on the passage
(100) of migrants, including their flight altitudes and directions. The data from these radar sampling will be used to model the effects of topography, weather, and other variables on migrant abundance and flight to assess
(105) where and when migrants might be at risk from wind power development.

The data from all these sampling techniques will collectively allow researchers to understand migrant flight dynamics and
(110) behavior and conditions that influence them. Predicted migrant densities and flight characteristics will be mapped region-wide as a function of topographic characteristics, and densities will be summed across dates within
(115) seasons to identify locations over which large numbers of migrants pass, or pass at altitudes within the sweep reach of wind turbine rotors, either consistently or occasionally. This information will be used to
(120) develop a summary map of areas where the risk of migrant interactions with potential wind power projects is expected to be low, moderate, or high.

16. The primary purpose of the passage is to:

    F. discuss ongoing research about the habits of migrating birds and bats to determine how wind power developments will affect them.

    G. persuade the public that the well-being of birds and bats will be threatened by any new wind power developments in the Appalachians.

    H. examine the process of analyzing data collected by acoustic monitoring devices.

    J. argue that XBAT software is essential in investigating the habits of migrating species.

17. According to the passage, the USGS is currently studying the habits of migrating birds:

    A. all across the country.

    B. on a year-round basis.

    C. during the spring and fall.

    D. by using XBAT to analyze NEXRAD data.

18. It can be inferred from lines 51–55, *During the most recent…coverage,* that:

    F. promising results can be obtained only when more complete coverage becomes available.

    G. there have been some disturbances to the recording devices in previous seasons.

    H. researchers are devising data collection techniques that minimize potential interference from wildlife.

    J. further research will be needed to assess and mitigate the risks wind power developments pose for wildlife.

19. The seventh paragraph functions as:

    A. an explanation of how portable radar sampling works.

    B. evidence about the flight altitudes of migrating animals.

    C. a description of how spectrograms are used in acoustic monitoring.

    D. a brief mention of a kind of data collection that is used in conjunction with acoustic monitoring.

20. The goal of the research described in this passage is to:

    F. provide evidence that wind power developments are detrimental to migrating birds and bats.

    G. make use of some sophisticated data collection and analysis techniques, including NEXRAD and XBAT.

    H. determine which areas in the Appalachians could be used as sites for wind power developments while posing minimal threats to migrants.

    J. assess the concerns of various groups, including the U.S. Fish & Wildlife Service, state wildlife agencies, and nongovernmental organizations, regarding wind power projects.

ANSWERS AND EXPLANATIONS

PASSAGE I

SUGGESTED PASSAGE MAP NOTES

Paragraph 1: Omnibus to take people at Bellomont to church

Paragraph 2: Trenors don't often go to church; conversation between Lily and Mr. Gryce

Paragraph 3: Mr. Gryce mostly likes Bellomont; Lily a bit out of place there; Mr. Gryce approving of Lily

Paragraph 4: Mr. Gryce waits for Lily to come out for church

Paragraph 5: Wetheralls and others (the Trenor sisters and Lady Cressida) come for church

Paragraph 6: Lily has sudden change of heart and doesn't follow through on her plan for church; she's curious about Selden

   1. **B**
   2. **J**
   3. **D**
   4. **G**
   5. **C**

1. **The best answer is (B).** For Vocabulary-in-Context questions, start by going back to the sentence where the word is used and make a prediction. If you need to, read a little before and after this sentence. Despite Lily's *self-possession*, she isn't quite comfortable in the _____ atmosphere. Here, *ambiguous* means something that would cause discomfort. For more detail, check the two previous sentences. Mr. Gryce likes the *ease and glitter* of life and Bellomont. The word *however* signals a contrast. Here, the contrast is that Mr. Gryce finds the people at Bellomont to be *materialistic*. Thus, your prediction should relate to contrast. A good prediction would be something like *contrasting* or *contradictory*. Choice (A) is wrong because nothing in the context relates to it. Choice (C) is a misused detail. Choice (D) is a common meaning of *ambiguous*, but not the meaning used here.

2. **The best answer is (J).** For Function questions, look back to the context to make your prediction. Here, *Mrs. Trenor's theory* is something she assumes but can't prove. The governess attends a different church (*a rival fane*), and Mrs. Trenor herself stays in her room until lunch, so neither of them can confirm that the Trenor daughters go to church. Consider also the previous paragraph, which mentions that Mrs. Trenor likes to feel that she's attended church *vicariously* through other members of her household. Put the information from these two paragraphs together and it seems that Mrs. Trenor would like to believe that her daughters go to church, even though she can't prove it. Choices (F) and (G) are contradictions. Choice (H) is out-of-scope—nothing in the passage supports this.

3. **The best answer is (D).** For Roman numeral questions, address each point one-by-one. Remember that you may be able to eliminate certain answer choices even before you have considered all the statements. Statement I is true (line 75); thus, you can eliminate (B) and (C), which exclude it. In considering statement II, pay attention to lines 81–83: *Mr. and Mrs. Wetherall's circle was so large that God was included in their visiting list*. From this sentence, it can be inferred that the Wetheralls view church as more of a social experience than a moral obligation. Statement II is false, which eliminates (A), only leaving (D). You don't need to evaluate statements III or IV, as they appear in both (A) and (D), meaning they must be true no matter what. Once you had it down to (A) or (D), only statement II mattered.

4. **The best answer is (G).** For Generalization questions, consider the specified portion of the passage, and look for particular details that justify your answer. Here, pay careful attention to lines 108–112: *She [Lily] had an idea that the sight of her in a grey gown of devotional cut…would put the finishing touch to Mr. Gryce's subjugation*. The word *subjugation* suggests that Lily wants to use her charms to ensure Mr. Gryce's attraction to her. This prediction best matches (G). Choice (F) is a contradiction. Choice (H) combines the contradiction and out-of-scope traps. Lily is described in this paragraph as being prone to sudden change, the opposite of inflexibility, and the passage doesn't directly refer to any social problems Lily may have. Choice (J) is a distortion of lines 116–118, *Lily, for all the hard glaze of her exterior, was inwardly as malleable as wax*. Choice (J) reverses the details stated here: Lily is actually resolute on the outside but malleable on the inside. Note that *belies* in (J) means *contradicts*.

5. **The best answer is (C).** For this Generalization question, consider the relative emphasis the writer gives to the different characters. In the passage, Lily and Mr. Gryce are discussed more than the Trenors and the Wetheralls, so predict that the answer centers on Lily and Mr. Gryce. Only (C) comes anywhere close. Choice (A) is a misused detail; we can infer that the writer portrays the Trenors and their guests as behaving hypocritically, but this is background, not the main focus. Choice (B) is a misused detail—the interaction between Mrs. Wetherall and Lady Cressida is described, but it is minor. Choice (D) is out-of-scope. It is too general to apply to this passage.

PASSAGE II

SUGGESTED PASSAGE MAP NOTES

Paragraph 1: New groups affecting heritage field

Paragraph 2: Democratization positive but complex

Paragraph 3: Importance of determining social "values"

Paragraph 4: Other fields help bring new groups into values ID process

Paragraph 5: Tension between conservation principles and democratization

Paragraph 6: Resulting challenges

Paragraph 7: Democratization requires changes for professionals

Paragraph 8: Collaboration w/experts outside conservation field

6. **J**
7. **A**
8. **F**
9. **A**
10. **G**

6. **The best answer is (J).** For a broad Generalization question, keep the overall purpose of the passage in mind. Incorrect answer choices may refer to too small a part of the passage. Predict that the purpose of the passage is to address challenges faced by conservation professionals. Choice (J) best captures this purpose. Choice (F) is a distortion. It uses several words from the passage, but it puts the emphasis in the wrong place by focusing on citizens instead of professionals. Choice (G) is out-of-scope. The passage doesn't address particular methods of conservation. Choice (H) is a misused detail. Paragraph 4 discusses contributions from anthropologists, but the focus of the whole passage is much broader.

7. **The best answer is (A).** To predict for a Detail question, refer to your passage map notes to direct you to the right spot in the passage. If the notes don't suggest a particular paragraph to research, skim the passage for the words used in the question stem or words with similar meaning. Here, *power sharing and collaboration* appear in paragraph 6 in the context of *challenges* that are presented by allowing more groups into the discussion. The writer states that *some suggest [that allowing more groups in] would undermine the authority of the conservation professional* (lines 81–84). This prediction leads directly to (A). Choice (B) is out-of-scope. The ordinary citizen's knowledge of historic sites is not mentioned in the passage. Choice (C) is out-of-scope. The passage never states that the general public lacks interest in historic sites. Choice (D) is out-of-scope. The passage doesn't question the leadership skills of *most conservation professionals*.

8. **The best answer is (F).** For an Inference question that asks about the meaning of a phrase, pay close attention to the context of the paragraph. Here, the paragraph refers to *power sharing* (lines 78–79) that might *undermine the authority of conservation professionals* (lines 83–84). There is a tension here between allowing the opinions of new groups into the discussion and maintaining the traditional role of the conservation professionals, because it's possible that the new groups would contradict the professionals. This prediction leads to (F). Choice (G) is out-of-scope. There is nothing in the passage to indicate that *government* works in this context. Choice (H) is out-of-scope. *Politically active* citizens aren't mentioned in the passage. Choice (J) is an opposite. The phrase in question refers to those who might oppose the *traditional influence*.

9. **The best answer is (A).** For Vocab-in-Context questions, read the sentence carefully and, if necessary, the preceding and following sentences to search for clues to predict

the meaning. In this case, the sentence itself presents a contrast. There are two different possibilities for the role of the conservation professional, first, *an orchestrator of specialists* and, second, *one specialist among others.* This contrast suggests that the *orchestrator* is separate from and above the other specialists, so predict that it means something like *leader* or *one who takes priority over.* This prediction fits well with (A). Choice (B) is a distortion that might be tempting if you're thinking of a musical orchestra instead of paying attention to the context. Choice (C) is a distortion that gives too much emphasis to the word *specialist* in the sentence and misses the idea of the orchestrator having a role above and beyond that of *specialist.* Choice (D) is out-of-scope. It draws on a completely different meaning of the word that is not relevant to this passage.

10. **The best answer is (G).** For Writer's View questions, keep in mind the tone of the passage as a whole. For this question, also research in the passage for the area that discusses *the outlook for the conservation field.* To predict, carefully read the last paragraph. It brings up questions about the role of the conservation specialist, but it also poses an answer: *It seems that…orchestrator* (lines 115–117). It mentions changes that will be necessary to meet *the challenge ahead,* but does not suggest that these challenges will be insurmountable. Therefore, predict something like *concerned but hopeful.* This prediction leads directly to (G). Choice (F) is out-of-scope; no cynicism is expressed in this passage. Choice (H) expresses a bleaker view than the passage justifies. The word *tinged* has a negative connotation that makes it sound as though the *reservations* are the primary factor in the writer's outlook. Choice (J) is too negative. The writer mentions the challenges in a hopeful rather than a pessimistic tone.

PASSAGE III

SUGGESTED PASSAGE MAP NOTES

Paragraph 1: Pym's work popular late in her life

Paragraph 2: Early efforts at writing

Paragraph 3: Work history

Paragraph 4: Novels finally published

Paragraph 5: Later novels rejected

Paragraph 6: Continued working

Paragraph 7: Eventual acclaim

11. **A**
12. **F**
13. **B**
14. **G**
15. **A**

11. **The best answer is (A).** For a Function question about a phrase, examine the immediate context to make your prediction. The sentence includes the word *finally* (line 45), which indicates that Pym's success was not immediate. Predict that her a*rtistic perseverance* is used to show that she kept on writing novels even while working at the Africa Institute. This prediction is a good match for (A). Choice (B) is a distortion. The passage doesn't compare how hard Pym worked on stories relative to others. Choice (C) is an extreme. It uses the word *all* and makes a general statement that is much broader than anything expressed in the passage. Choice (D) is a distortion. The context here does mention *contemporary critics* (line 47), but the answer choice inappropriately twists the passage's phrasing *reviewed favorably* (line 48) to appreciating *subtle artistry*.

12. **The best answer is (F).** For a Generalization question about a paragraph, review your notes and the whole paragraph, if necessary. Predict if possible, and if not, work through the answer choices. For the first paragraph, your passage note may refer to Pym's achieving literary success later in life. This is not an exact match but is consistent with (F). Eliminate (G) because it's a distortion; the passage doesn't suggest that it was the *Times Literary Supplement* that rejected Pym's stories. Eliminate (H) because it's a misused detail. This answer choice is indeed true, but it isn't in the first paragraph. Eliminate (J) because it's a distortion. The passage mentions both Philip Larkin and Lord David Cecil, but there is nothing in the passage to suggest that either of them was a friend of Pym. Choice (F) is the only answer remaining, and is correct.

13. **The best answer is (B).** For a Function question asking about a phrase, read the sentence carefully to make your prediction. Here, notice that the sentence describes a contrast: *continued success…came to an end.* Predict that the phrase *throughout the 1950s* is used to develop and emphasize this contrast. This prediction matches well with (B). Choice (A) is out-of-scope. The passage focuses on Pym and makes no general statements about *British society.* Choice (C) is a distortion of the word *success* as it's used in the passage. The *success* mentioned in this sentence is Pym's, not that of her publisher. Choice (D) is a misused detail. It makes a statement that is consistent with the passage, but it doesn't relate to the question posed by the question stem.

14. **The best answer is (G).** For a Detail question phrased with NOT, refer back to the passage to check each answer choice one by one. Eliminate option (F) because lines 24–26 state that *Some Tame Gazelle* is based *on the way she imagined her life…as it might be.* Eliminate (H) because lines 80–81 state that *The Sweet Dove Died* was *again rooted in Pym's personal experience.* Eliminate (J) because *Quartet in Autumn* is described as a novel about retirement that Pym started work on after her own retirement. *Civil to Strangers* is listed as one of the books she wrote, but not discussed in relation to her personal life.

15. **The best answer is (A).** For a Writer's View question, keep the big picture in mind and pay attention to words that indicate the writer's opinion. Here, the overall tone is detached and academic. The writer does appear to admire Pym's persistence, as evidenced by phrases such as *she kept writing, however* (line 29), *Pym's artistic perseverance paid off* (line 44), and *Even though Pym's rejections were compounded…she continued to write* (lines 84–87). Therefore, predict that the tone is primarily detached but colored with

admiration. This prediction matches (A). Choice (B) is out-of-scope. Nothing about the tone of the passage suggests zealousness. Choice (C) is a distortion. The mild admiration implied by the author is not the same as an overt bias. Choice (D) is a contradiction. *Impatient and critical* is the opposite of detached and admiring.

PASSAGE IV

SUGGESTED PASSAGE MAP NOTES

Paragraph 1: Groups concerned about wind power's effects on animals

Paragraph 2: More info needed to determine risks to bats and birds

Paragraph 3: U.S. studying bird and bat migration using radar and other techniques

Paragraph 4: Acoustic monitoring

Paragraph 5: Software used to analyze acoustic data

Paragraph 6: Preliminary results of acoustic monitoring

Paragraph 7: Portable radar technique

Paragraph 8: Data from all techniques to be combined in map

16. F
17. C
18. G
19. D
20. H

16. **The best answer is (F).** For a Generalization question that asks about the purpose of the whole passage, use your passage map and remember not to focus too heavily on particular details. Here, look at the first paragraph to predict that the purpose of the passage is to discuss methods of monitoring the habits of migrating birds and bats in order to determine what threats wind power development may pose to them. Choice (F) is a great match for your prediction. Choice (G) is a contradiction because the passage does not attempt to persuade the reader, only to inform. Choice (H) is a misused detail. It's true that the passage contains information about acoustic monitoring, but that is not the purpose of the passage. Choice (J) is a contradiction based on a misused detail. The passage makes no argument about XBAT being essential and, in any case, XBAT is only a small part of the passage and doesn't address the purpose of the passage as a whole.

17. **The best answer is (C).** For a Detail question, use your passage map or skim the passage for key words in the question stem to help you find the right spot in the passage to read for your prediction. Here, either your notes or skimming should direct you to paragraphs 3 and 4. The question is worded broadly, so your prediction might cover a lot: The USGS is studying the habits of migrating birds in the Appalachians, using

acoustic monitoring, in the spring and fall. The only choice that matches anything in this prediction is (C). Choice (A) is out-of-scope. The passage doesn't mention any studies outside the Appalachian area. Choice (B) is out-of-scope. The passage states that researchers are interested in the habits of migrating bats and birds, and migration doesn't occur all year long. Choice (D) is a distortion. XBAT is described in the passage as a tool for analyzing the acoustic data.

18. **The best answer is (G).** For an Inference question, read the quoted lines carefully and make a prediction that doesn't stray too far from the text. Here, notice that the sentence in question contains an implied contrast: *during the most recent season* is mentioned, suggesting that there's a difference between this season and previous seasons, and the sentence specifies *data from this season are expected to provide more complete coverage*, suggesting that this data is *more* than some other seasons. Predict that the answer has something to do with this contrast, something like *in previous seasons there has been significant interference on the recording devices from animals.* Choice (G) is a great match for this prediction. Choice (F) is an extreme. Nothing in the passage justifies the use of the word *only*. Choice (H) is out-of-scope. This choice goes too far beyond what's stated in the passage. Choice (J) is a contradiction. The meaning of the quoted sentence is that this season's data are expected to be much more useful, not that *further research* is needed.

19.**The best answer is (D).** For a Function question about a paragraph, use your passage map and consider the context of the previous and following paragraphs. Here, paragraph 7 discusses one technique, portable radar, giving this technique much less attention than acoustic monitoring got in paragraphs 4–6. Paragraph 8 discusses all of the research techniques as a whole. Predict that the purpose of paragraph 7 is to briefly introduce a research technique. This prediction matches well with option (D). Choice (A) is a distortion. While the paragraph does discuss portable radar sampling, it doesn't explain how the technique works. Choice (B) is a distortion. Paragraph 7 mentions *flight altitudes* as something portable data sampling is used to investigate, but the paragraph doesn't present any evidence about *flight altitudes*. Choice (C) is a misused detail. Acoustic monitoring and spectrograms are discussed in paragraphs 5 and 6, not paragraph 7.

20. **The best answer is (H).** For a broad Generalization question, keep the purpose of the passage as a whole in mind. Predict that the passage examines research about bird and bat migration in the Appalachians to assess the potential risks of wind power development on these animals. Choice (H) closely matches this prediction. Choice (F) is a distortion. The goal of the research is to determine how detrimental wind power projects could be, not to argue that they *are* detrimental. Choice (G) is a distortion. NEXRAD and XBAT are mentioned in the passage, but the research has a more specific purpose than simply making use of these methods. Choice (J) is a distortion. All of the groups in (J) are mentioned in the passage, but the research discussed is research about bats and birds, not about the concerns of the various people.

  Visit your online syllabus—Lesson 1—for more instruction and practice with passage mapping.

SUMMARY

In this chapter, we talked about the overall strategy necessary to master the ACT Reading test.

You learned how to **actively read** by asking questions as you go and focusing on the big picture. You learned how to **passage map** by finding the purpose and labeling each paragraph with three to five word notations. Remember to use transition words to help you put the pieces together.

After your map is complete, examine the question stem, then find the information you need in the passage. If it's a Detail question, the answer will be waiting for you. Use a line reference or your map to help you locate it. If it's not, use your passage map to help you get the broad sense of purpose necessary to draw whatever conclusion you need. Finally, predict the answer to save time and avoid traps. Only then should you look at the answer choices.

Practice this method. Then, keep practicing it. By learning how to actively read effectively and passage map efficiently, you'll be able to maintain the speed necessary on the ACT Reading passages while still understanding what you need to earn points when you get to the questions.

Keep practicing, and work on the individual question types in the next chapter to help you refine your approach and get the score you covet.

CHAPTER 11

Reading Part 2: ACT Reading Strategy in Depth

OVERVIEW

Use this chapter to get familiar with all of the question types on the ACT Reading test. They are detailed and discussed fully, with examples provided for each. On the Reading test, each question type has certain key phrases repeated in the question stems. We'll review those phrases to help you easily recognize what type of question you're dealing with. Then use the samples to master the specific strategies for each question type. To get a quick sense of what's to come, refer to the SmartPoint Breakdown in the previous chapter on page 291. There, they are discussed in order of Test Day weight. The more heavily tested SmartPoints are listed there first. That's also how you should prioritize your time, especially if you are short on time or close to your goal score. However, the SmartPoints in this chapter are discussed in order of building complexity. We'll discuss the less complex questions first, as they often build the knowledge you'll need to draw for more complex questions. If you have time and want to thoroughly exercise your Reading skill set, start at the beginning and work your way through.

The chapter ends with Putting It All Together on page 347. Another great resource for those short on time, you'll get a chance to see how the various question types fit the various passage types as a whole.

The following SmartPoints are shown in order of building complexity, SmartPoint by SmartPoint.

DETAILS—12 POINTS

Complexity: Low. Can be directly drawn from the passage without the need for interpretation or drawing conclusions.

A *detail* is a specific piece of information.

Detail questions will ask you about individual pieces of the passage. They are designed to test your basic understanding of what you read and ability to find information within the passage. This is far and away the biggest SmartPoint on the ACT Reading test, but remember you don't need to read for or memorize details; they're not going anywhere, as the ACT is an open-book test. Get a basic understanding as you read, to take care of that aspect of the question. As for the primary part of these questions—recalling specific information from the passage—don't rely on your memory! You won't need to map for details or remember them. When you notice a Detail question, just look up the answer in the passage.

But how do you know you're looking at a Detail question? Look for these phrases in the question stem:

Question Stem Indicators

- *As stated in the passage…*
- *According to the author…*
- *According to the passage…*
- *The passage states that…*
- *The writer states that…*
- *All of the following are cited in the passage EXCEPT…*

What all of these phrases have in common is that they refer you back to the passage, and they ask about something that is stated directly, rather than something that is implied.

STRATEGY

Although Detail questions are easy to answer when you know where in the passage to look, it can be challenging to locate the part of the passage that contains the answer. Therefore, it's important to take good notes for your passage map. Again, passage map notes should not include specific details but instead should note the location of details. For example, if a paragraph discusses the career of an artist, don't take notes about specific paintings and critical reactions. Instead, write a short note that describes the general purpose of the paragraph, such as *early career—critics admired*.

Each ACT Reading passage includes many details, but the test presents only 10 questions for each passage. Knowing this means many of the details in each passage will not be relevant to any of the questions. You simply won't need to know them all. So *focus on the big picture* as you read. Do *not* try to guess which details will show up in the questions.

Counterintuitive as it may seem, the best way to score points on Detail questions is by not getting too wrapped up in the details on your first read-through of the passage.

If you're attacking the questions and have difficulty locating a particular detail, don't sweat it. Just circle the question number in your test booklet and make an initial guess. If you have time before the section ends, you can come back to the circled question. Remember you don't have to answer every single question correctly to get a good score. This is especially important to keep in mind for Detail questions. Do your best, but don't obsess. No single question is worth more of your time than any other is.

Two important points to keep in mind:

1. There is one right answer, but there will be other tempting answers. Don't be tempted by "almost" answers. Find the *right* one.

2. "Refer to the passage" in the Reading directions is good advice, since you're not trying to memorize. Predict before you peek! That is, predict in your own words, or by pointing to a specific phrase in the passage, what you think the answer will be before you look at the choices provided.

Then, finish these questions off by matching the detail from the text in the passage with the correct answer. Locate either similar words or paraphrasing.

Note: Many wrong choices will be designed to trip you up by including details from other parts of the passage or by using the same wording as the passage while distorting the meaning. Questions on the ACT Reading test are written to have three wrong answers and *only* one right answer. Some answer choices may appear to be half-right, half-wrong; remember, if an answer choice has *anything* wrong with it, it is not the correct answer! Look for the one choice that is *flawless*.

Typical wrong answer choices on this question type are the following:

Misused details: This is the most common wrong answer on Detail questions. It will tempt you by pulling information directly from the passage. However, that information will not answer this particular question. Use Step 2 before you peek to predict and find the information that *does* answer the question. Your prediction won't match misused details, so you'll be able to avoid this trap.

Distortions: This answer choice uses a detail with a twist. It almost matches what's in the passage, but it changes the details a little bit by combining two of them in an inaccurate way, or by combining a detail in the passage with something else entirely. Thus, the almost-right details become distorted into something entirely wrong. Again, by researching in Step 2 and predicting, you'll have an idea of what is right before you peek at the choices, and you'll be much less likely to fall for the misleading wording of distorted choices.

Don't worry about identifying wrong answer choices. You're not there to decide whether a wrong answer is a distortion or a misused detail. Your job is to find the right answer. It just helps to be aware of how the ACT will attempt to lead you away from that answer.

Now, try out your research and predicting skills on the following Detail questions. Do your best not to peek at the answer choices. Instead, use the question stems to help you seek out the information you need.

EXAMPLES

When we say "Bach," we almost always refer to Johann Sebastian Bach (1685–1750), but in fact the name "Bach" belongs to a whole family of Baroque German musicians…

(7 paragraphs and 950 words omitted)

The works of Johann Christian Bach, J. S. Bach's son, clearly prefigure the rich musical developments that followed the Baroque period. Thus, it is both surprising and unfortunate that the rest of J. S. Bach's family isn't more well known.

1. According to the author, J. S. Bach is the best-known:

    A. German Baroque musician.

    B. member of a musical family.

    C. organist in German history.

    D. composer of Lutheran hymns.

2. Johann Christian Bach was:

    F. born earlier than Johann Sebastian Bach.

    G. a composer of the "Romantic" school of music.

    H. a composer whose works are transitional in style.

    J. well-known during his own lifetime.

The answer for question 1 is (B). Both the first and last sentences in the passage refer to J. S. Bach as the most famous member of a whole family of musicians. You might think J. S. Bach is the best-known German Baroque musician (choice (A)), but that's not what the passage says, so it's wrong.

The answer for question 2 is choice (H). At the end of the passage, the author says that Johann Christian's works "prefigure" the music that followed the Baroque. Thus, it must have had some Baroque characteristics and some new aspects. In other words, it was transitional.

  Visit your online syllabus—Lesson 7—for more instruction and practice with detail questions.

VOCAB-IN-CONTEXT—1 POINT

Complexity: Low. You'll need to make a light interpretation to determine meaning.

As the name implies, Vocab-in-Context questions ask about a word or phrase, but ask about it *as it's used in context*. Your task is to deduce the meaning of that word or phrase as it pertains to the surrounding passage. Thus, to properly answer these questions, you must use the context of the passage.

This question type is infrequent. You'll probably only see between one and three on Test Day. However, they are easy to spot and usually easy to answer quickly once you know the strategies. Because of this, always look for Vocab-in-Context questions and try to answer them. If you have to guess on any question, guess on a harder question that would take you more time to answer. Rack up a few easy points quickly with Vocab-in-Context questions.

So how do you recognize Vocab-in-Context questions? The clues here are simple to spot.

Question Stem Indicators

Phrases indicating meaning or definitions, such as:

- *…most nearly means…*

- *…can most closely be defined as…*

A leading phrase such as:

- *As it is used in the passage…refers to…*

The word or phrase is always printed in italics, and a line reference is always provided.

STRATEGY

1. Look back to the line referenced by the question stem, and pretend the word you're looking to define is actually a blank in the sentence.

2. Read the sentence and look for clues to help you determine what word or phrase would make sense in the blank. Use that word or phrase as your prediction for this question.

3. Look at the answer choices and choose the one closest to your prediction.

Here are some more points to help you with Vocab-in-Context questions:

- Do *not* skip the prediction step! Words used for Vocab-in-Context questions are often chosen because they have more than one meaning. The most common or first meaning that comes to mind is not necessarily the appropriate meaning in the context of the passage. As its name suggests, Vocab-in-Context questions rely on the context of words as used in *this* passage.

- Occasionally, predicting is tough: You may not find any clues within the sentence where the word is used. If that's the case, look at the sentences before and after it. In nearly every case, one of these sentences contains specific clue words to let you predict the meaning of the "blank."

- Connections words and phrases are often the key to making your prediction. Pay particular attention to words such as *yet, but,* and *however.* These contrast clues may tell you that your prediction should be the opposite of another word that's used in the sentence.

Again, the words most frequently tested in this type are common words with multiple meanings, not complex or rare words. Thus, your task is much more about finding context from the passage as opposed to figuring out the definition of a word.

Typical wrong answer choices for this question are other definitions for the tested word.

The most common definition is usually wrong, but it will be among the answer choices. Avoid this trap by using the context of the passage and predicting!

EXAMPLES

One problem is that sunspots themselves are so poorly understood. Observations have revealed that the swirly smudges represent areas of intense *Line* magnetic activity where the sun's radiative energy *(5)* has been blocked, and that they are considerably cooler than bright regions of the sun. Scientists have not been able, however, to determine just how sunspots are created or what effect they have on the solar constant (a misnomer that refers to the sun's *(10)* total radiance at any instant).

The latter question, at least for now, seems to have been resolved by data from the *Solar Maximum Mission* satellite, which has monitored the solar constant since 1980, the peak of the last solar cycle. *(15)* As the number of sunspots decreased through 1986, the satellite recorded a gradual dimming of the sun. Over the past year, as sunspots have proliferated, the sun has brightened. The data suggest that the sun is 0.1 percent more luminous at the peak of the solar *(20)* cycle, when the number of sunspots is greatest, than at its nadir, according to Richard C. Willson of the Jet Propulsion Laboratory and Hugh S. Hudson of the University of California at San Diego.

1. As it is used in the passage, the term *solar constant* (line 9) refers to:

   A. magnetic activity.
   B. the sun's total radiance.
   C. the sun's surface temperature.
   D. wind direction.

2. As it is used in line 17, the word *proliferated* means:

   F. grew in size.
   G. brightened.
   H. decreased in number.
   J. increased in number.

Question 1

Go back to line 9, and predict the meaning of *solar constant* in context. *Sun's radiance at any moment,* which matches (B).

- Choice (A): Misused Detail; this comes from earlier in the passage, but has nothing to do with the solar constant.

- Choice (C): Out-of-Scope; the author does not mention this.

- Choice (D): Misused Detail; while this is in the passage, it has nothing to do with the solar constant.

Question 2

Go back to line 17 and predict a synonym for *proliferated* in context. Predict: *grown in number.* Choice (J) is correct.

- Choice (F): Distortion; growing in physical size is not the same as growing in number.

- Choice (G): Distortion; the *sun* has brightened, not the sunspots.

- Choice (H): Opposite; this is mentioned in the previous sentence, but doesn't apply here.

INFERENCE—8 POINTS

Complexity: Medium. You will need to make conclusions about a small part of the passage.

An *inference* is an unstated conclusion reached by the evidence of stated information. An inference is something that **must** be true, based on what is stated. Not just **can** or **might** be true, but **must**.

Inference questions are the next logical step from Detail questions. Detail questions just ask you to find or know small pieces of information. Inference questions take those same small pieces of the passage, but ask you to know what they logically must mean. The idea is to test your ability to read between the lines.

You'll be able to recognize that you're dealing with Inference questions from the following question stem indicators:

Question Stem Indicators

- *It may be inferred from lines…*

- *The author implies…*

- *The phrase…suggests…*

- *The author suggests…*

- *It is most reasonable to infer…*

- *…most directly supports the conclusion…*

Infer, imply, suggest, and *conclude* are key words to look for.

STRATEGY

You may be tempted to think that such questions are a matter of opinion, that *anything* could be implied, but this is not the case. Although it's true that Inference questions, unlike Detail questions, ask you to draw a conclusion that's not directly stated in the passage, the correct answer to an Inference question will not be a huge logical step away from what is stated in the passage. In other words, to answer an Inference question correctly, do not go too far beyond what's in the passage. The best answer to an Inference question, like the best answer to all ACT Reading questions, is strongly grounded in the words of the passage.

Inference questions refer to a small, localized part of the passage. Read that part of the passage, and come up with a prediction based on what is stated there.

Your passage map will help you determine the overall purpose. Which piece of the purpose is the author putting into place with the line in question?

Remember, the answer is a small step from what is directly stated. It's a conclusion based on the overall themes you've already found. An inference isn't an opinion and it doesn't have to be a guess.

In fact, wrong answer choices are often extreme. They are usually headed in the right direction, but are worded in a way that goes too far. These are the kinds of words and phrases that appear frequently in *extreme* answer traps:

- *absolutely*
- *always*
- *all*
- *best*
- *certainly*
- *ever*
- *in every case*

- *largest*
- *never*
- *no*
- *none*
- *smallest*
- *worst*
- *without a doubt*

An answer choice that contains words or phrases like those listed is not *necessarily* the wrong answer. However, if an answer choice does contain extreme language, you should consider it a trap unless the extreme language is also used in the passage. Ask: "Is this thing really "always" or "never" the case? Literally?" Occasionally it might be, but more often the passage says "This thing sometimes happens," and the extreme answer choice is "This always happens."

The other common wrong answer type on Inference questions is **out-of-scope** answers.

Out-of-Scope traps go beyond what is stated in the passage. The *scope* of a passage refers to what information is covered in the passage. A passage that touches on a large topic has a scope that is broad. A passage that treats a smaller topic in greater depth and detail has a scope that is narrow. Because the correct answer to an ACT Reading question is always based on what is in the passage, you should pay close attention to the scope of the passage when you're considering answer choices and looking for the one that best matches your prediction. If an answer asks you to guess about something the passage doesn't even talk about, that answer is probably out-of-scope.

Again, don't worry about identifying what kind of wrong answers the choices are. Just be aware that both typical wrong answer choices are designed to lure you further away from the written text than you should go. The correct answer will be close to what is stated in the passage.

Practice taking these small steps in the following examples.

EXAMPLES

…though schizophrenia and multiple personality disorder (MPD) may be related, and are often confused by laymen, the two terms have radically different meanings…

1. Which of the following best expresses the relationship between schizophrenia and multiple personality disorder?

    A. They are two terms that describe essentially the same phenomenon.

    B. The two disorders have nothing in common.

    C. Though the two have some similarities, they are fundamentally different.

    D. The two are not exactly alike, but are very close.

2. Suppose that a patient has been diagnosed with schizophrenia. Based on the passage, which of the following is LEAST likely?

    F. The patient's doctors immediately assume that the patient also suffers from MPD.

    G. The patient is a layman.

    H. The patient denies that he has MPD.

    J. The patient is related to someone with MPD.

Note the differences between Detail and Inference questions. Question 1, a Detail question, requires that you understand the explicitly stated idea that schizophrenia and MPD have some connection but are not the same. That's what choice (C) says. Question 2, on the other hand, requires you to apply the idea that the two disorders are different. If they are, it's highly unlikely that doctors would simply assume that a patient suffering from one disorder must suffer from the other; the passage says *laymen* often confuse the two, not that *doctors* do. Therefore, choice (F) is least likely—and therefore correct. The other choices may or may not be true, but nothing in the passage leads us to think one way or the other about them.

The eye of the seal is also uniquely adapted to operate in both air and water. The human eye, adapted to function primarily in air, is equipped with
Line a cornea, which aids in the refraction and focusing of
(5) light onto the retina. As a result, when a human eye is submerged in water, light rays are further refracted and the image is blurry. The seal's cornea, however, refracts light as water does. Therefore, in water, light rays are transmitted by the cornea without distortion,
(10) and are clearly focused on the retina. In air, however,

the cornea is astigmatic, resulting in a distortion
of incoming light rays. The seal compensates for
this by having a stenopaic pupil, which constructs
into a vertical slit. Since the astigmatism is most
(15) pronounced in the horizontal plane of the eye, the
vertical pupil serves to minimize its effect on the
seal's vision.

3. The passage implies that a harbor seal's vision is:

    A. inferior to a human's vision in the water, but superior to it on land.
    B. superior to a human's vision in the water, but inferior to it on land.
    C. inferior to a human's vision both in the water and on land.
    D. equivalent to a human's vision both in the water and on land.

The seal's cornea improves vision in the water (note the comparison to human's underwater vision), but distorts light moving through the air. Another adaptation was then needed to "minimize" distortion, but that doesn't mean distortion is completely eliminated. The correct answer is (B).

FUNCTION—6 POINTS

Complexity: Medium. You will need to make conclusions about a small-to-medium part of the passage.

Function questions task you with understanding the role of certain elements of a passage. They'll ask you why the author used a particular word, sentence, detail, quote, paragraph, or punctuation. These questions test your ability to interpret how the different pieces of a passage fit together. Types of connections, such as cause and effect, sequence, or contrast are important here.

You can recognize these questions from the following clues in the question stems:

Question Stem Indicators

• *The phrase…serves to…*

• *…is meant to…*

• *The author does…in order to…*

Notice that each indicates the idea of finding a purpose.

STRATEGY

To answer these questions, put yourself in the author's place. You make similar decisions when writing your own essays. Why would you use a particular example? Why would you include this paragraph?

Was the piece in question providing evidence or a transition? Was it establishing a relationship?

Refer to your passage map to find the answer. Focus on the big picture for that particular piece, and ask yourself how it fits into the surrounding pieces.

This question is the most like putting together the pieces of a jigsaw puzzle. Again, since you write essays yourself, it will be a puzzle you're familiar with.

Remember those connection words from English and what type of relationship they build. Here they are again for your reference:

	Connections Words and Phrases
Connections that show addition, continuation, emphasis, or examples	additionally and for example for instance furthermore indeed in addition in fact likewise moreover
Connections that show cause and effect	as a result because consequently leading to since so therefore thus

Common wrong answer choices will be **out-of-scope** (page 334) discussed with Inference and Generalization questions, and **distortions** (page 329) discussed with Detail questions.

Now, try recognizing how the pieces fit together with a couple of sample Function questions.

EXAMPLES

Working in a large format (her portrait studies are
usually about 11 inches by 14 inches) and requiring
a long exposure (on the average five minutes), Julia Margaret
Line Cameron produced a large body of work that stands up as
(5) one of the notable artistic achievements of the Victorian
period. The English art critic Roger Fry believed that
her portraits were likely to outlive the works of artists
who were her contemporaries. Her friend Watts, then
a very celebrated portrait painter, inscribed on one of
(10) her photographs, "I wish I could paint such a picture
as this." Her work was widely exhibited, and she
received gold, silver, and bronze medals in England,
the United States, Germany, and Austria. No other
female artist of the nineteenth century achieved such
(15) acclaim, and no other woman photographer has ever
enjoyed such success.

Cameron's work falls into two main categories on
which her contemporaries and people today differ sharply.
Victorian critics were particularly impressed by
(20) her allegorical pictures, many of them based on
the poems of her friend and neighbor Tennyson.
Contemporary taste much prefers her portraits and
finds her narrative scenes sentimental and sometimes
in bad taste, though even the painters of that time
(25) loved to depict subjects such as *Pray God, Bring
Father Safely Home.* Still, today her fame rests upon
her portraits for, as she herself said, she was intent
upon representing not only the outer likeness but
also the inner greatness of the people she portrayed.
(30) Working with the utmost dedication, she produced
photographs of such eminent Victorians as Tennyson,
Browning, Carlyle, Trollope, Longfellow, Watts,
Darwin, Ellen Terry, Sir John Herschel, who was a
close friend of hers, and Mrs. Duckworth, the mother
(35) of Virginia Woolf.

1. The author cites the opinions of an art critic and a "celebrated portrait painter" (lines 6–11) in order to:

    A. illustrate the significance of Cameron's artistic accomplishments.

    B. emphasize Victorian critics' preference for Cameron's allegorical work.

    C. detail the envy Cameron's peers felt toward her.

    D. counter the negative assessments of Cameron's work by more recent critics.

2. The author contrasts assessments of Cameron's work by Victorian era and contemporary critics (lines 19–26) in order to:

   F. argue for the superiority of modern-day assessments of art.

   G. support an earlier claim of how assessments of Cameron's work have changed over time.

   H. argue that Cameron's work has always been held in the highest regard.

   J. dismiss the assessments of modern-day critics.

Question 1

- Choice (A): The author introduces these two assessments directly after lauding Cameron's achievements as "notable." He follows their comments by saying no other woman photographer can match her level of success. The two opinions emphasize how impressive her accomplishments were.

- Choice (B): Misused Detail; this is a Misused Detail from ¶2.

- Choice (C): Out of Scope; don't misconstrue Watts's inscription (lines 8–11); nothing in the paragraph suggests "envy."

- Choice (D): Misused Detail; this is a Misused Detail from ¶2.

Question 2

- Choice (F): Distortion; the author never suggests that one assessment is *superior* to another.

- Choice (G): Correct; in the sentence that precedes the cited lines, the author states, "Her work falls into two main categories on which her contemporaries and people today differ sharply." A strong prediction would be "to describe how critics' opinions of Cameron's work have changed over time."

- Choice (H): Extreme; although critics *usually* praise her work, the author states that "contemporary taste...finds her narrative scenes sentimental and sometimes in bad taste."

- Choice (J): Distortion; the author is not trying to *dismiss* one assessment of Cameron's work.

WRITER'S VIEW—1 POINT

Complexity: Medium-High. You will need to make conclusions about a small-to-large part of the passage.

Writer's View questions ask about something in the passage from the point of view of the writer (or possibly, in the case of a prose fiction passage, the narrator). Writer's View questions refer directly to *the author, the writer, the narrator,* or *the point of view*. The ACT is testing to make sure you can understand tone and intent. Recognize that the author uses a certain order or phrasing for a reason. Function questions ask you what an element does for the passage in relation to the surrounding pieces, whereas Writer's View questions ask you to interpret those pieces to conclude what the author is thinking. What was the intention of writing a particular piece or paragraph? What tone was the author using? All of this leads up to finding the opinion that the author holds.

Look for the following phrasing to indicate a Writer's View question:

Question Stem Indicators

- *The author would most likely agree that*

- *The view of the narrator regarding…appears to be*

- *The author's view of…is*

- *The writer's attitude toward…*

- *From the point of view of…*

- *The author's approach to…*

Notice that each of these indicates the writer and an opinion or point of view.

STRATEGY

Two things you should keep in mind in answering a Writer's View question are:

1. **Keep straight who says what.** If the passage describes multiple viewpoints, make sure you know which viewpoint the author supports or agrees with.

2. **Pay attention to the tone of the passage.** Even a single word such as *fortunately, unfortunately,* or *regrettably* can be a big clue in helping you determine the author's view.

Remember, you should be looking for the "why," or the purpose, in your passage maps. That should lead you to the correct answer.

In prose fiction, when the thesis is obscured, look for opinions expressed both in dialogue and character framing and narration to help you determine which side the author is on.

Here's an opinion not in dialogue:

> Carl had changed, Alexandra felt, much less
> than one might have expected. He had not become
> a self-satisfied city man. There was still something
> homely and wayward and personal about him. Even
> *Line*
> (5) his clothes were unconventional. He seemed to shrink
> into himself as he used to do, as if he were afraid of
> being hurt.

Alexandra is giving her opinion of Carl. It's more likely the author is on her side. Dialogue adds an extra layer, dissociating the author from the opinion, like when Carl gives his counterpoint later:

> Her visitor winced and paused. "You see," he
> said, "measured by your standards here, I'm a
> failure. I couldn't buy even one of your cornfields.
> *Line* I've enjoyed many things in New York, but I've got
> (5) nothing to show for it."

The author distances herself from Carl by letting Carl speak his own mind in dialogue. The author is closer to Alexandra, since they express opinions together without the need for dialogue.

An example of character framing here is the author referring to Carl as "Her visitor." Again, the author is taking Alexandra's perspective by looking at Carl (the visitor) through Alexandra's eyes.

The most common wrong answer choice for Writer's View questions will hold the wrong opinion or intent (perhaps the opinion of a different character or an opposing opinion given to provide the counterargument). This is a **contradiction** trap.

Also, watch out for **extremes** (page 334), as discussed with Inference questions.

Here's an example of how extremes would apply to Writer's View questions:

Suppose a writer says, "Isaac Newton was one of the one most brilliant scientists of his time," and you encounter a question that asks about the writer's opinion of Newton. Consider the following answer choices. Circle any extreme words you notice, and see if you can pick out which one is correct:

    A. Isaac Newton was the most brilliant scientist ever to have lived.

    B. Isaac Newton displayed much brilliance in his scientific work.

    C. Isaac Newton was more brilliant than any of his contemporaries were.

    D. Isaac Newton was the best scientist of his day.

What was the extreme language? You should have spotted the following words:

    A. *most...ever*

    B. no extreme words

    C. *more...than any*

    D. *best*

If you noticed the extreme language, it should be easy to see that option (B) is the correct choice.

In the following examples, practice finding the intent of the author.

EXAMPLES

The distinction between various types of violence is based on the distinction between their respective unconscious motivations. Only the understanding of
Line the unconscious dynamics of behavior permits us to
(5) understand the behavior itself, its roots, its course, and the energy with which it is charged.

Another aspect of reactive violence is the kind of violence that is produced by frustration. We find aggressive behavior in animals, children, and adults
(10) when a wish or a need is frustrated. Such aggressive behavior constitutes an attempt, although often a futile one, to attain the frustrated aim through the use of violence. It is clearly an aggression in the service of life, and not one for the sake of destruction. Since
(15) frustration of needs and desires has been an almost universal occurrence in most societies even to the present day, there is no reason to be surprised that violence and aggression are constantly produced and exhibited.

1. It is most reasonable to infer that the author of the passage believes that:

   A. the frustration of needs and desires is no longer a common aspect of human life.

   B. animals, children, and adults all have similar needs and desires that they attempt to fulfill through violent means.

   C. the examination of the unconscious causes of violence leads to a better understanding of violence itself.

   D. reactive violence is usually sparked by the desire for destruction.

What type of question is this? Generalization, meaning it refers to the author's overall beliefs. Look back at ¶1, which states, *only the understanding of the unconscious dynamics of behavior permits us to understand the behavior itself.* This most closely matches (C).

• Choice (A): Misused Detail; in ¶2, the author refers to this frustration as an *almost universal* occurrence, but nothing indicates that this commonality has ceased.

• Choice (B): Distortion; the author doesn't indicate all of these entities have *similar needs/desires.*

• Choice (D): Opposite; this contradicts the author's statement in lines 7–10.

About 50 miles west of Stonehenge, buried in the peat bogs of the Somerset flatlands in southwestern England, lies the oldest road known to humanity.
Line Dubbed the "Sweet Track" after its discoverer,
(5) Raymond Sweet, this painstakingly constructed

1,800-meter road dates back to the early Neolithic
period, some 6,000 years ago. Thanks primarily to
the overlying layer of acidic peat, which has kept the
wood moist, inhibited the growth of decay bacteria,
(10) and discouraged the curiosity of animal life, the road
is remarkably well-preserved. Examination of its
remains has provided extensive information about the
people who constructed it.

The design of the Sweet Track indicates that
(15) its builders possessed extraordinary engineering
skills. In constructing the road, they first hammered
pegs into the soil in the form of upright Xs. Single
rails were slid beneath the pegs so that the rails
rested firmly on the soft surface of the bog. Then
(20) planks were placed in the V-shaped space formed
by the upper arms of the pegs. This method of
construction—allowing the underlying rail to
distribute the weight of the plank above and thereby
prevent the pegs from sinking into the marsh—is
(25) remarkably sophisticated, testifying to a surprisingly
advanced level of technology.

Undoubtedly, the discovery of the Sweet Track
in 1970 added much to our knowledge of Neolithic
technology. But while study of the remains has
(30) revealed unexpectedly high levels of engineering and
social organization, it must be remembered that the
Sweet Track represents the work of a single isolated
community. One must be careful not to extrapolate
sweeping generalizations from the achievements of
(35) such a small sample of Neolithic humanity.

2. Based on his discussion of the community that built the Sweet Track, which of the fol-
    lowing statements would the author be most likely to make?

    F. The builders' methods were critical to ensuring the preservation of the Sweet
        Track.

    G. Neolithic humanity was much more advanced than scientists had previously
        believed.

    H. The builders of the Sweet Track were more skilled than many archaeologists
        would expect.

    J. No other society has displayed as much skill in woodland management as did
        this group.

It would be hard to predict what the author would say, but you can definitely predict his
overall impression. The author views this community as *surprisingly advanced*, so his statements will be positive, but you also want to be sure not to go too far, as some of the answer
choices do.

Which answer choice matches? Choice (H).

- Choice (F): Misused Detail; in ¶1, the author attributes preservation to peat, not the builders' methods.

- Choice (G): Distortion; in ¶3, the author writes that we *can't* make generalizations about Neolithic humanity.

- Choice (J): Extreme; this community was adept, but it's too strong to say *no other society*.

GENERALIZATIONS—8 POINTS

Complexity: High. You will need to make conclusions about large parts of the passage or the passage as a whole.

Generalization questions ask about large pieces of the passage and task you with putting it all together to draw a supported conclusion. Hopefully, you've actively read and made a map aimed at the big picture—the overall purpose and themes of the passage. This heavily weighted question type will draw upon that global information. These questions are designed to test your grasp of the meaning and tone of the passage as a whole.

They rarely include line references and can ask about a paragraph, a couple of paragraphs, the entirety of the beginning, middle, or end, and even the passage as a whole.

You can know you're dealing with a generalization question from the following question stem clues:

Question Stem Indicators

- *The primary purpose of the passage is to…*

- *The main point of the…paragraph is to…*

The question stems will point to a main idea or purpose and will often end in "to," meaning the first word of the answer choices will be a verb.

STRATEGY

Actively read and take notes in your passage map. That step of the method is extremely important here. Read for the big picture, asking questions about why this passage is being written and how the pieces are fitting together. Practice the method. If you have this down, you'll be well on your way to mastering this complex question type.

Examine the first and last paragraphs. How the passage starts and ends can give you a quick idea of its overall scope and main idea.

If you're stuck, complete other questions with smaller scope first. The Detail questions and Inference questions might help you understand the overall purpose if you missed it on your read-through.

Also, do look at the italicized words preceding the passage. Introductory information can give you vital and quick background information.

Remember that Generalization questions usually end in "to," so the answer choices often begin with a verb. Pay careful attention to this verb and make sure it matches the overall tone of the passage.

Common wrong answer types are **distortions** (discussed under Detail questions on page 329) and **out-of-scope** answers (on page 334).

Be careful not to assume that the main idea of a single paragraph is the main idea of the passage as a whole. This is a common distortion in Generalization questions. Wrong answer choices might also mix in some wrong information with some right information to lead you astray. Predict to avoid this trap.

Here's an example of common out-of-scope answer choices used in Generalization questions. Suppose you see a passage that discusses two medieval philosophers followed by this question:

1. The primary purpose of this passage is to:

    A. give an overview of medieval philosophy.

    B. discuss the merits of a medieval philosopher.

    C. argue that medieval philosophy has been more influential than ancient Greek philosophy.

    D. describe the work of two medieval philosophers.

Did you spot three out-of-scope answer traps here? Choice (A) is out-of-scope because it's too broad. A passage that discusses only two philosophers can't be an overview of all of medieval philosophy. On the other hand, (B) is too narrow. While one or more paragraphs may concern a single medieval philosopher, the passage is about *two* philosophers, and (B) addresses only part of the passage and so is out-of-scope. Choice (C) cannot be correct because Greek philosophy isn't addressed at all in the passage, so it can't be part of the best answer for this question. Choice (D) is the right answer here.

Now, make sure your passage mapping skill is still fresh, and try out the following Generalization questions before we move on to Putting It All Together.

EXAMPLES

With the spread of industry, the exodus of people from the countryside, and the resultant transformation of the urban landscape, city-dwellers of the
Line twentieth century have found themselves living in an
(5) increasingly colorless environment. Veiled in soot, towns and suburbs have lapsed into grimy taciturnity as an all-pervading drabness has overcome our great, sprawling urban complexes.

Improving the quality of life in the city is one
(10) of the primary objectives of street art. Color can

help to save, rehabilitate, or otherwise give new
life to neighborhoods and other urban sites doomed
to demolition, dereliction, or anonymity. The aim
is to provide the city-dweller with the opportunity
(15) to participate in the rebirth of a more human
environment. By its very nature as communal space,
the street lends itself to collective creativity that, in
turn, leads to an enhanced sense of community pride
and well-being.

2. The main idea of the passage is that:

    F. bold colors and street art positively affect urban environments.

    G. modern cities have been ruined by the use of drab colors.

    H. scholars have misunderstood the canons of Greek and Roman architecture.

    J. urban sites should be saved from demolition, dereliction, and anonymity.

• Choice (F): Correct; the main idea relates to the importance of color and public murals to cities.

• Choice (G): Extreme; nothing in the passage supports the idea that modern cities have been *ruined* by drab colors.

• Choice (H): Misused Detail; the author suggests this, but it's too small a point to be the main idea.

• Choice (J): Misused Detail; the author suggests this, but it's too small a point to be the main idea.

However, although the October minimum
remained constant until 1979, the total ozone content
over the Pole was steadily diminishing until, in
Line 1985, public opinion was finally roused by reports
(5) of a "hole" in the ozone layer and observations were
intensified. The culprits responsible for the hole had
already been identified as being supersonic aircraft,
such as the Concorde (although these have now been
exonerated), and the notorious compounds known as
(10) chlorofluorocarbons, or CFCs. Synthesized in 1928
by chemists working at General Motors in the United
States, CFCs are compounds of atoms of carbon,
chlorine, and fluorine. Having the advantage of being
non-flammable, non-toxic, and non-corrosive, they
(15) came into widespread use in the 1950s. They are
widely used in refrigerators, air conditioners, the
"bubbles" in the foam plastic used, for example, in
car seats, and as insulation in buildings.

In 1989, they represented a market valued at over
(20) $1.5 billion and a labor force of 1.6 million. Of the
twenty-five countries producing CFCs, the United
States, France, the United Kingdom, Japan, and
Germany accounted for three-quarters of the total
world production of some 1.2 million tons.

(25)   These figures give some idea of the importance
of the economic interests that are at stake in any
decision to ban the industrial use of CFCs. But, with
CFCs incriminated by scientists, the question arose
as to whether we were prepared to take the risk of
(30) seeing an increase in the number of cases of skin
cancer, eye ailments such as cataracts, or even a
lowering of the human immune defense system, all
effects that would follow further depletion of the
ozone layer.

3.   The main point of the second paragraph (lines 19–24) is to:

    A.   highlight the number of CFCs produced every year.

    B.   criticize the countries responsible for producing CFCs.

    C.   indicate the economic interests at stake in the CFC debate.

    D.   list the most important members of the Montreal Protocol.

At the mention of the second paragraph, you should look back to your passage map, which deals with competition between health and economic interests from CFCs. This matches answer choice (C).

• Choice (A): Misused Detail; this comes from ¶1.

• Choice (B): Distortion; the author offers no such criticism.

• Choice (D): Out-of-Scope; the author doesn't give such a list.

>   Visit your online syllabus—Lesson 7—for more instruction and practice with global questions.

PUTTING IT ALL TOGETHER—NONFICTION

Now that you know what question types to expect, know how to recognize them, and have strategies to deal with each, we'll tackle two full passages together. After all, on the actual ACT, question types won't be isolated. All SmartPoints are grouped together, and you'll have a full passage of information to process in order to find the information you need.

Even the different passage types on Reading bring different challenges. We'll start by looking at those passage types and the challenges they bring. Then, we'll put it all together with full passages and questions. First, we'll fully go through a typical nonfiction passage, then we'll take a look at how the process changes on a Prose Fiction passage.

Think of this section like a quiz that we'll work on together. We'll look at passages as you'd see them on Test Day. Then we'll take the passages apart again, to identify the question types with you, and walk through how to use the strategies from this section to deal with them.

PROSE FICTION—THE FIRST PASSAGE

The Prose Fiction passage is taken from a novel or short story. Because the Prose Fiction passage is centered on characters' thoughts, moods, behaviors, and relationships, it's quite different from the three nonfiction passages.

One aspect of the Prose Fiction passage that can be challenging is that you must infer much of the meaning. Typically, fiction writers don't come right out and make explicit statements. They tend to *show* rather than *tell*. Thus, your ability to understand a prose passage hinges largely on your ability to make appropriate inferences. If you find this challenging, think about watching a movie. The writer and director don't often tell you what to think. Instead, they show you a situation. The music, lighting, and camera angles all affect how you interpret what the characters say and do. Obviously, a piece of literature doesn't use music and cinematography to impart meaning. Nonetheless, a prose passage may be easier for you to understand if you try to visualize it as a movie. Trying to visualize the characters as if they were on film, and not just as words on a page, can help you develop a fuller understanding of the prose passage.

The questions you need to keep in mind on Prose Fiction during your active reading process are different from the questions that help you understand a nonfiction passage. Ask yourself:

- Who are the characters?

- What do details about a character help you understand about that person? The ways the character looks, moves, and speaks can give you important clues.

- What are the characters' emotions, motivations, or opinions? These aspects can help you start to look at the "why" of the characters.

- How are the characters related? You can think of this first in a literal way: Are they friends, relatives, acquaintances, or strangers meeting for the first time? You can also think of this in a more psychological way, asking what connects them: Are they accepting and approving of each other, or are they tied together by negative emotions?

- What is the overall tone of the passage? Is the mood upbeat and joyful or serious and reflective? Do any words create a sense of tension, drama, or excitement?

- What contrasts does the passage present? Is one character portrayed as being different from another in personality, background, or values?

Often, the ACT Prose passage focuses on only a few main characters, but it may include several minor characters as well. As you read through the passage, one of the most important things you must do is develop your understanding of the main characters. If you come across a character that seems more minor, you can underline the name, but don't get distracted by giving equal attention to all the characters. Focus on the most important ones.

SOCIAL STUDIES—THE SECOND PASSAGE

The Social Studies or Social Sciences passage can cover a wide range of topics, including history, anthropology, archaeology, education, psychology, political science, biography, business, geography, sociology, or economics. Because Social Science is a nonfiction passage, remember to apply the usual method of active reading and passage mapping. Look for the connections words that illustrate the logical progression of the passage. Then, find the purpose and focus on the big picture. Topics you might see in a Social Science passage include:

- A reinterpretation of the traditional understanding of an historical event

- A discussion of several scholars who've done work in the field and similarities and differences in their viewpoints

- A presentation of one scholar's view on a topic and why the writer agrees or disagrees with that view

- An explanation of a concept or idea and why it's important in the field of study

- A discussion of the causes of a historical event

- An overview of the work of an important person in the field

This list is merely representative; it certainly doesn't include everything you might find in a Social Science passage. No matter what the topic, your task while actively reading is to grasp the author's purpose for writing.

HUMANITIES—THE THIRD PASSAGE

The Humanities passage broadly relates to human creativity. The visual arts, such as drawing, painting, and sculpture, commonly fall into this category, as do many other areas, such as literature, theatre, music, dance, philosophy, language, communications, film, literary criticism, radio, television, and architecture. As you read the Humanities selection, you should apply all of the active reading questions that you'd use for any nonfiction selection. Some examples of topics that you might be likely to find in a Humanities passage include:

- A discussion of the style of one or more artists and characteristics of the artist's work that make it noteworthy or unique

- A discussion relating to the development of a particular art form, what the origin of the form was, and how it changed over time as different artists used it

- A critical assessment of the work of a particular artist, how the artist's work was received in his own lifetime, and whether scholars in the field have maintained that view or come to a different view

- A chronological tracing of a particular artist's work over time, what the characteristics of the artist's early work were, what periods or stages scholars use to categorize the artist's work, and whether the work of a particular period is valued more highly than work from other periods

Again, this list is not exhaustive. Notice, however, that the outline form and the chronological structure appear in some way in each example. Even though you can't predict the topic you'll see in the Humanities passage, and you may find yourself on Test Day facing a topic you have little familiarity with, you don't need to be intimidated. The practice you've completed with the method will serve you well, and you'll find even an unknown topic will provide the structural clues you need to find the answers.

NATURAL SCIENCE—THE FOURTH PASSAGE

The Natural Science passage could cover any number of technical sciences, including botany, zoology, natural history, biology, chemistry, earth sciences, physics, anatomy, astronomy, ecology, geology, medicine, meteorology, microbiology, physiology, and technology. Don't worry if a Science passage includes technical terms that you aren't familiar with—this is a Reading test, not a Science test. If you need to understand a technical term to answer a question correctly, the term will be explained in the passage. Some examples of the way a topic might be treated in an ACT Natural Science Reading passage include:

- A concept is introduced and several different understandings of it are presented (remember to keep straight who says what).

- A historical view of a scientific concept is contrasted with a contemporary view.

- Several different ways of investigating a particular phenomenon are discussed.

- A first-person narrative discusses personal experience investigating a scientific concern.

- A detached presentation of facts discusses what is known in a particular field.

- A description of the current understanding of a concept is discussed, and suggestions of what researchers might investigate next are presented.

While a Science passage may seem challenging if you don't know much about the particular topic, you should be particularly careful with passages that address topics you *are* familiar with. If you've just studied a particular group of elements in your chemistry class and you find a passage that discusses those elements, your first read-through of the passage will go pretty quickly and comfortably because you've had some previous exposure to the material. When you attack the questions, however, you'll be tempted to rely on your previous knowledge, which is *not* a good approach. The correct answer is always based on something that's stated in the passage—outside knowledge is never tested in this section. So even when you're familiar with a topic (in fact, *especially* when you're familiar with it), it's important to read the question stem carefully and make sure that your prediction is grounded in the passage itself.

If you're unfamiliar with the topic, and it feels like a foreign language, fear not. This isn't the Science test. Everything you need to know is there in front of you. When reading, just avoid getting bogged down by details you don't understand. Find the big picture, and move on. If you get the gist, you can figure out the confusing details later, and only if they ask you to.

PRACTICE—NONFICTION

This passage is taken from the book Invitation to the Theatre, *Third Edition, ©1985 by George Kernodle. Reprinted by permission of Wadsworth, a division of Thomson Learning.*

Tragedy was the invention of the Greeks. In their Golden Age, the fifth century before Christ, they produced the world's greatest
Line dramatists, new forms of tragedy and
(5) comedy that have been models ever since, and a theatre that every age goes back to for rediscovery of some basic principles…

Since it derived from primitive religious rites, with masks and ceremonial costumes,
(10) and made use of music, dance, and poetry, the Greek drama was at the opposite pole from the modern realistic stage. In fact, probably no other theatre in history has made fuller use of the intensities of art. The
(15) masks, made of painted linen, wood, and plaster, brought down from primitive days the atmosphere of gods, heroes, and demons. Our nineteenth- and twentieth-century grandfathers thought masks must have been
(20) very artificial. Today, however, we appreciate their exciting intensity and can see that in a large theatre they were indispensable. If they allowed no fleeting change of expression during a single episode, they could give for
(25) each episode in turn more intense expression than any human face could. When Oedipus comes back with bleeding eyes, the new mask could be more terrible than any facial makeup the audience could endure,
(30) yet in its sculpted intensity more beautiful than a real face.

Most essential of all intensities, and hardest for us to understand, was the chorus. Yet many playwrights today are
(35) trying to find some equivalent to do for a modern play what the chorus did for the Greeks. During the episodes played by the actors, the chorus would only provide a background of group response, enlarging
(40) and reverberating the emotions of the actors, sometimes protesting and opposing but in general serving as ideal spectators to stir and lead the reactions of the audience. But between episodes, with the actors out
(45) of the way, the chorus took over. We have only the words, not the music or dance, and some translations of the odes are in such formal, old-fashioned language that it is hard to guess that they were accompanied
(50) by vigorous, sometimes even wild dances and symbolic actions that filled an orchestra which in some cities was sixty to ninety feet in diameter. Sometimes the chorus expressed simple horror or lament.
(55) Sometimes it chanted and acted out, in unison and in precise formations of rows and lines, the acts of violence the characters were enacting offstage. When Phaedra rushes offstage in *Hippolytus* to hang herself
(60) from the rafters, the members of the chorus, all fifteen of them, perform in mime and chant the act of tying the rope and swinging from the rafters. Sometimes the chorus tells or reenacts an incident of history or legend
(65) that throws light on the situation in the play. Sometimes the chorus puts into specific action what is a general intention in the mind of the main character. When Oedipus

resolves to hunt out the guilty person and
(70) cleanse the city, he is speaking metaphorically,
but the chorus invokes the gods of
vengeance and dances a wild pursuit.

On the printed page, the choral odes
seem static and formal, lyric and philosophical,
(75) emotional letdowns that punctuate the
series of episodes, like intermissions between
two acts of a play. The reader who skips the
odes can get the main points of the play.
A few are worth reading as independent
(80) poems, notably the famous one in *Antigone*
beginning, "Many are the wonders of the
world, but none is more wonderful than
man." Some modern acting versions omit
the chorus or reduce it to a few background
(85) figures. Yet to the Greeks the odes were
certainly more than mere poetic interludes:
the wild Dionysian words and movements
evoked primitive levels of the subconscious
and at the same time served to transform
(90) primitive violence into charm and beauty
and to add philosophical reflections on the

meaning of human destiny.

For production today, we can only
improvise some partial equivalent. In Athens
(95) the entire population was familiar with
choral performances. Every year each of
the tribes entered a dithyramb in a contest,
rehearsing five hundred men and boys
for weeks. Some modern composers have
(100) tried to write dramatic music for choruses:
the most notable examples are the French
composer Darius Milhaud, in the primitive
rhythms, shouts, and chants of his operatic
version of the *Oresteia*; George Gershwin, in
(105) the Negro funeral scenes of *Porgy and Bess*;
and Kurt Weill, in the African choruses for
Lost in the Stars, the musical dramatization
of Alan Paton's novel, *Cry, the Beloved
Country*. For revivals of Greek tragedies we
(110) have not dared use much music beyond a
few phrases half shouted, half sung, and
drumbeats and suggestive melodies in the
background.

A quick preread of the passage should have given you a sense of its general organization:

- *First paragraph:* introduces the topic of Greek tragedy.

- *Second paragraph:* discusses use of masks (artificial but intense).

- *Third and fourth paragraphs:* discuss use of chorus (also artificial but intense).

- *Fifth paragraph:* expands discussion to choral odes.

- *Sixth paragraph:* concludes with discussion of how Greek tragedy is performed today and how it has influenced some modern art.

That's really all the road map you need going into the questions. Aside from that, you should take away the author's main point: Greek tragedy included many artificial devices, but these devices allowed it to rise to a high level of intensity.

1. Combined with the passage's additional information, the fact that some Greek orchestras were 60 to 90 feet across suggests that:

    A. few spectators were able to see the stage.

    B. no one performer could dominate a performance.

    C. choruses and masks helped overcome the distance between actors and audience.

    D. Greek tragedies lacked the emotional force of modern theatrical productions.

2. The phrase "fuller use of the intensities of art" (line 14) most nearly means:

    F. employment of brightly illuminated effects.

    G. good use of powerful, dramatic effects of music, dance, and poetry.

    H. the enjoyment of strong elements of effects on stage.

    J. the utilization of dramatic interactions.

3. The description of the chorus's enactment of Phaedra's offstage suicide (lines 58–63) shows that, in contrast to modern theater, ancient Greek theater was:

    A. more violent.

    B. more concerned with satisfying an audience.

    C. more apt to be historically accurate.

    D. less concerned with a realistic portrayal of events.

4. It can be inferred that one consequence of the Greeks' use of masks was that:

    F. the actors often had to change masks between episodes.

    G. the characters in the play could not convey emotion.

    H. the actors wearing masks played nonspeaking roles.

    J. good acting ability was not important to the Greeks.

5. Which of the following is supported by the information in the second paragraph (lines 8–31)?

    A. Masks in Greek drama combined artistic beauty with emotional intensity.

    B. The use of masks in Greek drama was better appreciated in the 19th century than it is now.

    C. Masks in Greek drama were used to portray gods but never human beings.

    D. Contemporary scholars seriously doubt the importance of masks to Greek theater.

6. The author indicates in lines 68–69 that Oedipus's resolution "to hunt out the guilty person and cleanse the city" was:

    F. at odds with what he actually does later in the performance.

    G. misinterpreted by the chorus.

    H. dramatized by the actions of the chorus.

    J. angrily condemned by the chorus.

7. According to the passage, when actors were present on stage, the chorus would:

    A. look on silently as spectators.

    B. inevitably agree with the actors' actions.

    C. communicate to the audience solely through mime.

    D. react to the performance as an audience might.

8. The main point of the fifth paragraph (lines 72–91) is that choral odes:

   F. should not be performed by modern choruses.

   G. have a meaning and beauty that are lost in modern adaptations.

   H. can be safely ignored by a modern-day reader.

   J. are only worthwhile in *Antigone*.

9. The passage suggests that modern revivals of Greek tragedies "have not dared use much music" (line 109) because:

   A. modern instruments would appear out of place.

   B. to do so would require a greater understanding of how choral odes were performed.

   C. music would distract the audience from listening to the words of choral odes.

   D. such music is considered far too primitive for modern audiences.

10. The author discusses *Porgy and Bess* and *Lost in the Stars* in order to:

    F. show how two modern plays reenact ancient Greek tragedies.

    G. demonstrate the use of music in modern plays.

    H. give examples of two modern-day playwrights who used musical choruses in their dramas.

    J. illustrate how music evokes subconscious emotions in modern-day plays.

  Visit your online syllabus—Lesson 7—for more instruction and practice with the Science passage on the ACT Reading Test.

ANSWERS AND EXPLANATIONS

1. C	6. H
2. G	7. D
3. D	8. G
4. F	9. G
5. A	10. H

The following explanations are not in numerical order, but grouped by SmartPoints. Again, this is meant to be a walkthrough, and we do this to help you better understand the concepts behind the questions. The more easily you can spot the SmartPoint—the concept the ACT requires you to understand to answer the question correctly—the more confident you'll feel on Test Day.

SMARTPOINT—DETAILS

Questions 6 and 7

Question 6

This is a Detail question with a line reference, but to answer the question confidently, you should have also read a few lines *before* and a few lines *after* the cited lines. There, you would have read: "Sometimes the chorus puts into action what is a general intention in the mind of the main character. When Oedipus resolves..." Clearly, the Oedipus example is meant to illustrate the point about the chorus acting out a character's intentions. So choice (H) is correct—they are dramatizing (or acting out) Oedipus's resolution. (By the way, choice (G) might have been tempting, but there's no evidence that the chorus is misinterpreting, just that they're "putting a general intention into specific action.")

Question 7

This is a Detail question without a line reference. Such questions are common on the ACT, and they require that you have a good sense of the structure of the passage as a whole so you can locate the place where the question is answered. Help yourself with this task by passage mapping. If you've done so, the mention of the chorus should lead you to paragraph 3. There, the author claims that the chorus serves to "lead the reactions of the audience"—captured by choice (D).

SMARTPOINT—VOCAB-IN-CONTEXT

Question 2

This stem refers to a word or phrase in the passage and asks you to select the answer that is closest to the meaning in *context*.

Read a little before line 14. Greek drama "made use of music, dance, and poetry" (line 10). This reference matches choice (G), which is the correct answer.

Note: The best answer is not a direct definition of the words. Look instead for the answer that would make the most sense. To check your answer, plug it into the sentence.

SMARTPOINT—INFERENCE

Questions 1, 3, 4, 5, 9

Question 1

Question 1 has no line references to help. Survey the passage. Choice (C) is the only one that is compatible.

Question 3

Research might lead to a prediction of *the chorus emphasizes what's happening on stage*, pointing you to choice (D).

Question 4

Though the stem provides no line reference, the mention of masks should have sent you to the second paragraph of the passage. Lines 23–24 explain that masks "allowed no fleeting change of expression during a single episode." Treat that as your first piece of evidence. Your second comes in lines 24–26: "they [the masks] could give for each episode in turn more intense expression than any human face could." Put those two pieces of evidence together—masks can't change expression *during* a single episode, but they can give expression for each episode *in turn*.

Clearly, the actors must have changed masks between episodes so they could express the different emotions that different episodes required. Choice (F) is correct.

Question 5

Research leads you to the key word *intensity*, which you examined previously in question 2, and which appears in only one answer choice, (A).

Note: The relationship between questions 2 and 5 is a good example of how answering one question can help you answer another. Thus, you may find that if you skip a question the first time, you can answer it during a second pass.

Question 9

Remember, keep your inferences as close to the passage as possible. Don't make wild inferential leaps. An inference should follow naturally and inevitably from the evidence provided in the passage.

Here, by consulting the last paragraph, we find language to lead us to choice (B).

SMARTPOINT—FUNCTIONS

Question 10

Remember that WHY something is discussed is different from WHAT is discussed. Your passage map and the topic sentences in lines 92–109 indicate the main idea for the final paragraph is the modern use of the chorus. Choice (H) is the correct answer.

Note: While choices (G) and (J) may be factually true, they are not the reasons why the author mentions these plays. Choice (F) is false—they are not reenactments of Greek tragedies.

SMARTPOINT—GENERALIZATION

Question 8

Your passage map should indicate the main idea of paragraph 5 relates to choral odes. Skimming that paragraph, you find reference to how the odes seem to people today—"static and formal" (line 73), "like intermissions between two acts of a play" (lines 75–76). Later, the author states, by way of contrast (note the use of the clue word *yet*): "Yet to the Greeks the odes were certainly more than mere poetic interludes." Clearly, the author wants to contrast our modern static view of the odes with the Greeks' view of them as something more. That idea is best captured by choice (G).

PUTTING IT ALL TOGETHER—PROSE FICTION

I recall a mist starting in as I crossed the lawn that afternoon. I was making my way up to the summer house for the purpose of
Line clearing away the remains of his lordship's
(5) taking tea there with some guest a little while earlier. I can recall spotting from some distance…Miss Kenton's figure moving about inside the summer house. When I entered she had seated herself on one of the
(10) wicker chairs scattered around its interior, evidently engaged in some needlework. On closer inspection, I saw she was performing repairs to a cushion. I went about gathering up the various items of crockery from
(15) amidst the plants and the cane furniture, and as I did so, I believe we exchanged a few pleasantries, perhaps discussed one or two professional matters. For the truth was, it was extremely refreshing to be out in the
(20) summer house after many continuous days in the main building and neither of us was inclined to hurry with our tasks…In fact, I was looking out over the lawn to where the mist was thickening down around the poplar
(25) trees planted along the cart-track, when I finally introduced the topic of the previous year's dismissals. Perhaps a little predictably, I did so by saying:

"I was just thinking earlier, Miss Kenton.
(30) It's rather funny to remember now, but you know, only this time a year ago, you were still insisting you were going to resign. It rather amused me to think of it." When I finally turned to look at her, she was gazing
(35) through the glass at the great expanse of fog outside.

"You probably have no idea, Mr. Stevens," she said eventually, "how seriously I really thought of leaving this house. I felt so
(40) strongly about what happened. Had I been anyone worthy of any respect at all, I dare say I would have left Darlington Hall long ago." She paused for a while, and I turned my gaze back out to the poplar trees down
(45) in the distance. Then she continued in a

tired voice: "It was cowardice, Mr. Stevens. Simple cowardice. Where could I have gone? I have no family. Only my aunt. I love her dearly, but I can't live with her for a day
(50) without feeling my whole life is wasting away. I did tell myself, of course, I would soon find some situation.

"But I was so frightened, Mr. Stevens. Whenever I thought of leaving, I just saw
(55) myself going out there and finding nobody who knew or cared about me. There, that's all my high principles amount to. I feel so ashamed of myself. But I just couldn't leave, Mr. Stevens. I just couldn't bring myself to
(60) leave."

Miss Kenton paused again and seemed to be deep in thought. I thus thought it opportune to relate at this point, as precisely as possible, what had taken place earlier
(65) between myself and Lord Darlington. I proceeded to do so and concluded by saying:

"What's done can hardly be undone. But it is at least a great comfort to hear his lordship declare so unequivocally that it
(70) was all a terrible misunderstanding. I just thought you'd like to know, Miss Kenton, since I recall you were as distressed by the episode as I was."

"I'm sorry, Mr. Stevens," Miss Kenton
(75) said behind me in an entirely new voice, as though she had just been jolted from a dream, "I don't understand you."
Then as I turned to her, she went on:
"As I recall, you thought it was only right
(80) and proper that Ruth and Sarah be sent packing. You were positively cheerful about it."

"Now really, Miss Kenton, that is quite incorrect and unfair. The whole matter
(85) caused me great concern, great concern indeed. It is hardly the sort of thing I like to see happen in this house."

"Then why, Mr. Stevens, did you not tell me so at the time?"

(90) I gave a laugh, but for a moment was rather at a loss for an answer. Before I could formulate one, Miss Kenton put down her sewing and said:

"Do you realize, Mr. Stevens, how (95) much it would have meant to me if you had thought to share your feelings last year? You knew how upset I was when my girls were dismissed. Do you realize how much it would have helped me? Why, Mr. (100) Stevens, why, why, why do you always have to pretend?"

I gave another laugh at the ridiculous turn the conversation had suddenly taken. "Really, Miss Kenton," I said, "I'm not sure (105) I know what you mean. Pretend? Why, really…."

"I suffered so much over Ruth and Sarah leaving us. And I suffered all the more because I believed I suffered alone."

1. According to the passage, the author thinks Mr. Stevens is:

   A. worthy of respect.

   B. not considerate of Miss Kenton's feelings.

   C. too formal in his demeanor.

   D. disloyal to his friends.

2. The statement "Had I been anyone worthy of any respect at all, I dare say I would have left Darlington Hall long ago" (lines 40–43) can be interpreted to mean:

   F. no one at Darlington Hall truly respects Miss Kenton.

   G. Miss Kenton has little respect for Mr. Stevens.

   H. Miss Kenton feels she betrayed her principles by staying.

   J. Miss Kenton senses that Mr. Stevens feels superior to her.

3. According to the passage, the intent of Mr. Stevens's recollection of Miss Kenton's desire to resign (lines 29–33) is most likely to:

   A. open up a discussion of an event that had upset Miss Kenton.

   B. turn the conversation to the professional topic of furniture repair.

   C. indulge in nostalgic reminiscences of happier days.

   D. irritate Miss Kenton by mocking the seriousness of that desire.

4. Mr. Stevens gives "a laugh" (line 90) because he is suddenly:

   F. amused.

   G. insecure.

   H. suspicious.

   J. sarcastic.

5. The main point of Miss Kenton's references to her own family (lines 48–52) is that:

   A. she would have nowhere to turn if she left her job.

   B. children often reject those they should love.

   C. she was afraid of discovering that she did not love her aunt.

   D. life becomes very tedious when one visits relatives.

6. What is it that Mr. Stevens describes as "done" (line 67)?

   F. Lord Darlington's earlier conversation with him

   G. Miss Kenton's talk of leaving Darlington Hall

   H. Ruth and Sarah's dismissal

   J. Any talk of Miss Kenton's dismissal

7. As he is revealed in the passage, Mr. Stevens is:

    A. bored with their conversation in the summer house.

    B. increasingly hostile to Miss Kenton's depiction of his actions.

    C. uncomfortable with expressing his deep affection for Miss Kenton.

    D. unaware of how his past behavior had affected Miss Kenton.

8. Which of the following would be out of character for the narrator?

    I.   Pointing out to Miss Kenton why she was unfairly characterizing his actions

    II. Spending time thinking about Miss Kenton's accusations

    III. Ridiculing Miss Kenton for poorly repairing the cushion

    F. I only

    G. II only

    H. I and II only

    J. III only

9. Miss Kenton interacts with Mr. Stevens in a way that can best be described as:

    A. sincere but formal.

    B. indifferent but polite.

    C. timid but angry.

    D. patronizing but kindly.

10. At the end of the passage, Miss Kenton asks, "Why, Mr. Stevens, why, why, why do you always have to pretend?" (lines 99–101) What specific action of Mr. Stevens does she have in mind?

    F. His apparent cheerfulness at Ruth and Sarah's dismissal

    G. His simulation of great affection for her

    H. His phony concern for her own future employment

    J. His empty expressions of sympathy for her own suffering

ANSWERS AND EXPLANATIONS

1. B	6. H
2. H	7. D
3. A	8. J
4. G	9. A
5. A	10. F

Review these Prose-specific questions as you look over your passage map:

1. **Who are these people?** The first paragraphs are peppered with hints about who these people are. Lines 4–5 discuss Mr. Stevens "clearing away the remains of his lordship's taking tea." Lines 12–13 describe Miss Kenton "performing repairs to a cushion." Lines 29–32 discuss her previous plans for resigning. Clearly, Mr. Stevens and Miss Kenton are servants (we later learn—in lines 64–65—that their employer is Lord Darlington).

2. **What is their state of mind?** We read of "the previous year's dismissals" (lines 26–27) and Miss Kenton's intentions to leave the house (lines 37–39) as a result of them. She "felt so strongly about what happened" (lines 39–40), but was afraid to take the step of actually leaving in protest ("It was cowardice," she admits in line 46). It sounds like some other servants were dismissed unfairly last year and that this upset Miss Kenton. Apparently, Mr. Stevens also found the incident distressing (lines 83–87), but Miss Kenton hadn't realized this at the time.

3. **What's going on?** These are obviously very formal people, but there are strong emotions rumbling beneath the surface. It's clear that Miss Kenton is very upset because she didn't realize that Mr. Stevens disapproved of the dismissals, too ("Do you realize, Mr. Stevens, how much it would have meant to me if you had thought to share your feelings last year?"—lines 94–97. And later: "Why, Mr. Stevens, why, why, why do you always have to pretend?"—lines 99–101). We get the impression that Mr. Stevens is not a man who very readily shows his feelings and emotions—as Miss Kenton puts it, he always *pretends*.

4. **What is the author's attitude toward the characters?** Often, there will be a question asking about the author's point of view. Be careful here—don't confuse what the characters think about each other with what the author thinks. The two may not be the same.

Note: The first question here is about Writer's View. Your best bet is to skip the question and leave it for last.

Notice how many Inference questions there are. This is typical of the Prose Fiction passage, where so much information is conveyed implicitly—between the lines. In most cases, you have to read around the specific line references in order to find your answer. If you've done your pre-read properly, however, you should be able to get through most of the questions quickly.

	Answer	Refer to	Type	Comments
1.	B	First two paragraphs	Writer's View	Stevens says he was "amused" and thought it "funny" that she wanted to resign her position. Miss Kenton replies very seriously to his words, saying she doesn't understand him and how he could be so cheerful if he disapproved of the two firings. Miss Kenton has plainly suffered, and Mr. Stevens has not reacted kindly to her pain. The author's sympathy is with Miss Kenton, not Mr. Stevens.
2.	H	Lines 56–57	Inference	"There, that's all my high principles amount to," she says.
3.	A	Lines 29–33, 62–65	Inference	Lines 62–65 show that Mr. Stevens has just been discussing this subject with Lord Darlington and now wants to discuss it with Miss Kenton.
4.	G	Lines 90–91	Inference	He is "at a loss for an answer" and clearly not laughing out of amusement.
5.	A	Lines 47–48	Detail	"Where could I have gone? I have no family."
6.	H	Lines 66–72	Detail	Refers to "the previous year's dismissals," first mentioned in lines 26–27.
7.	D	Throughout	Global	Mr. Stevens's nervous laughs hint that he had no idea how deeply Miss Kenton was affected.
8.	J	Throughout	Inference	I: He does this in lines 83–87. II: He wishes to respond to the accusations in lines 79–82. III: This kind of blatant harshness would be uncharacteristic of so discreet and proper a man.
9.	A	Throughout	Global	Miss Kenton freely expresses her feelings to him throughout, so she is sincere. But she **never** loses her formal language and demeanor.
10.	F	Lines 95–97, 74–82	Inference	She wishes that he "had thought to share [his] feelings"; she was under the impression that he was "positively cheerful about [the dismissals]."

  Visit your online syllabus—Lesson 7—for more instruction and practice with Prose Fiction passages.

SUMMARY

In this chapter, we went over every SmartPoint and question type you will encounter on the ACT Reading test. We then discussed all passage types in their Test Day order. Finally, you had a chance to put your skills to use on a walk-through of a typical nonfiction passage and to see how those strategies changed on a Prose Fiction passage. Use this chapter for continued study and reference as you practice Reading passages and find the skills you need to focus on.

Remember to practice the method first and foremost. If you're comfortable with active reading and can quickly find and map the purpose, you'll be ready for anything the ACT can throw at you. Then, research and predict to avoid traps.

For the questions themselves, remember to stick as closely as possible to what's stated in the passage. Most wrong answer choices will twist things from the passage or provide information outside of the scope of the text. Detail questions will usually have a directly stated answer. Find it and be ready for a paraphrase. But even the other question types, those requiring more inferences and conclusions based on larger pieces of text, will still be rooted in what's written. The answer is in the passage. Find it and state it in your own words.

Don't be afraid to skip around. Start with the easiest passage to conserve time and ease into the section. You can even skip around within the questions for a passage—if you can't find an answer, it's still perfectly okay to guess on this section. No question is worth an abundance of your time.

However, with practice at passage mapping, it won't take long to search the passage for what you need.

When you're ready, move on to the next chapter and try out the Reading Quiz. Check how you do, SmartPoint by SmartPoint, then come back to this chapter to polish the skills you need.

Through it all, keep actively reading and passage mapping to become an ACT Reading master!

CHAPTER 12

Reading Part 3: ACT Reading Quiz

Ready? Great!

Treat the following passages and their questions like those you'll encounter on Test Day to gauge what you need to focus on in your Reading studies. Be sure to check your answers only after you've completed a passage set or after you've completed all four. Do not check as you work—you won't be able to check your answers at all on Test Day, so try to make this practice as realistic as possible.

Keep track of your time. Remember that on Test Day, you'll have approximately 9 minutes per passage and questions, so aim to spend no more than 35 minutes on the whole quiz. Don't be discouraged if you run over 35 minutes, though. You'll have a lot more opportunities to improve your timing with the Practice Tests at the end of this book. Make note of what kinds of passages take you longer to read than others and how much time it takes you to complete the entire quiz.

Finally, when checking your answers, look at the SmartPoint categories of the questions you miss in particular. Use this quiz to help you find where to spend your studying time before you take the Practice Tests at the end of the book.

Remember to make a passage map for each passage and predict answers to the questions before looking at the answer choices.

Directions: This quiz contains four passages, each followed by ten questions. After reading each passage, select the best answer to each question. You may refer to the passages while answering the questions.

PASSAGE I

PROSE FICTION: *This passage is adapted from the novel* The Woman in White *by Wilkie Collins. It was first published in serial form in 1859 and 1860. The narrator, Walter, is a teacher of drawing. His friend, Pesca, is a native of Italy who teaches Italian in England.*

Pesca's face and manner, on the evening when we confronted each other at my mother's gate, were more than sufficient to inform me that something extraordinary had happened.
(5) It was quite useless, however, to ask him for an immediate explanation. I could only conjecture, while he was dragging me in by both hands, that, knowing my habits, he had come to the cottage to make sure of meeting me that
(10) night and that he had some news to tell of an unusually agreeable kind.

We both bounced into the parlor in a highly abrupt and undignified manner. My mother sat by the open window laughing and
(15) fanning herself. Pesca was one of her especial favorites, and his wildest eccentricities were always pardonable in her eyes. From the first moment she found out that the little Professor was deeply and gratefully attached to her
(20) son, she opened her heart to him unreservedly and took all his puzzling foreign peculiarities for granted, without so much as attempting so understand any one of them.

My sister Sarah, with all the advantages of
(25) youth, was, strangely enough, less pliable. She did full justice to Pesca's excellent qualities of heart, but she could not accept him implicitly, as my mother accepted him, for my sake. Her insular notions of propriety rose in perpetual
(30) revolt against Pesca's constitutional contempt for appearances, and she was always more or less undisguisedly astonished at her mother's familiarity with the eccentric little foreigner. I have observed, not only in my sister's case,
(35) but in the instances of others, that we of the young generation are nowhere near as hearty and impulsive as some of our elders. I constantly see old people flushed and excited by the prospect of some anticipated pleasure
(40) which altogether fails to ruffle the tranquility of their serene grandchildren. Are we, I wonder, quite such genuine boys and girls now as our seniors were in their time? Has the great advance in education taken rather
(45) too long a stride, and are we in these modern days just the least trifle in the world too well brought up?

Without attempting to answer those questions decisively, I may at least record that I
(50) never saw my mother and my sister together in Pesca's society without finding my mother much the younger woman of the two. On this occasion, for example, while the old lady was laughing heartily over the boyish manner in
(55) which we tumbled into the parlor, Sarah was perturbedly picking up the broken pieces of a teacup, which the Professor had knocked off the table in his precipitate advance to meet me at the door.

(60) "I don't know what would have happened, Walter," said my mother, "if you had delayed much longer. Pesca has been half mad with impatience, and I have been half mad with curiosity. The Professor has brought some
(65) wonderful news with him, in which he says you are concerned, and he has cruelly refused to give us the smallest hint of it till his friend Walter appeared."

"Very provoking: it spoils the set," mur-
(70) mured Sarah to herself, mournfully absorbed over the ruins of the broken cup. While these words were being spoken, Pesca, happily and fussily unconscious of the irreparable wrong which the crockery had suffered at his hands,
(75) was dragging a large arm-chair to the opposite end of the room, so as to command us all

three, in the character of a public speaker addressing an audience. Having turned the chair
with its back towards us, he jumped into it on
(80) his knees and excitedly addressed his small
congregation of three from an impromptu
pulpit.

"Now, my good dears," began Pesca, "listen
to me. The time has come—I recite my good
(85) news—I speak at last."

"Hear, hear," said my mother, humoring
the joke.

"The next thing he will break, Mamma,"
whispered Sarah, "will be the back of the best
(90) arm-chair."

"Among the fine London Houses where I
teach the language of my native country," said
Pesca, "is one, mighty fine, in the big place
called Portland. The golden Papa there, the
(95) mighty merchant, says, "I have got a letter
from my friend, the Mister, and he wants a
recommend from me, of a drawing-master, to
go down to his house in the country. Perhaps
you know of a drawing master that I can
(100) recommend?"

I address myself to the mighty merchant,
and I say, "Dear sir, I have the man! The first
and foremost drawing-master of the world!"

---

1. It can be inferred from the passage that all
   of the following are true of Professor Pesca
   EXCEPT:

   A. he is familiar with the narrator's daily
      routine.

   B. he is well-trained in public speaking.

   C. the narrator's mother approves of him.

   D. he has not completely mastered the
      subtleties of the English language.

2. A difference between older people and younger people that the narrator finds remarkable is:

   F. younger people are impulsive, while
      older people are more deliberate.

   G. older people tend to be more curious
      than younger people are.

   H. older people fail to display appropriate
      gratitude toward the young.

   J. older people are more likely than
      younger people are to anticipate
      pleasures enthusiastically.

3. According to the passage, the narrator's
   mother has a high opinion of Professor Pesca
   because:

   A. she values intellectual pursuits.

   B. Professor Pesca has been instrumental
      in advancing her son's career.

   C. Professor Pesca feels a grateful attach-
      ment toward her son.

   D. she is the sort of person who can easily
      overlook the fault of others.

4. As used in line 58, the word *precipitate* MOST
   nearly means:

   F. quick.

   G. rude.

   H. faithful.

   J. eccentric.

5. It can be inferred from the first paragraph that:

   A. Pesca frequently visits the narrator's mother.

   B. the narrator does not believe that Pesca shows good judgment.

   C. the narrator fears a hostile confrontation with Pesca.

   D. Pesca visits the cottage fully expecting to meet up with the narrator there.

6. The writer uses the phrase *while he was dragging me in by both hands* (lines 7–8) in order to convey that the narrator:

   F. believes Pesca's actions are characterized by rudeness.

   G. is reluctant to enter his mother's house in the presence of Pesca.

   H. is aware of Pesca's impatience.

   J. is frequently caught off-guard by Pesca's eccentric behaviors.

7. The passage implies that Sarah:

   A. fails to see any good qualities in Professor Pesca.

   B. feels extremely protective toward her brother.

   C. has a strong concern for taking care of material things.

   D. is guilty of neglecting her elderly mother's basic needs.

8. The narrator's questions at the end of the third paragraph suggest that:

   F. the narrator admires the unreserved way that members of the older generation express their feelings.

   G. the narrator believes that Pesca is overly concerned with appearances.

   H. Sarah disapproves of her mother's attitude toward Pesca.

   J. the narrator judges his own generation to be more genuine than his parents' generation.

9. According to the passage, in what order do the following events take place?

   I.   Pesca breaks the teacup.

   II. Pesca arrives at the cottage.

   III. The narrator's mother laughs at the behavior of Pesca and her son.

   IV. The narrator enters the cottage.

   A. II, IV, I, III

   B. II, I, IV, III

   C. IV, II, I, III

   D. IV, III, II, I

10. According to the passage, the narrator wonders:

    F. whether advances in education have gone too far.

    G. if Pesca is entirely trustworthy.

    H. why his mother dislikes Pesca.

    J. why Sarah's attitude is one of perpetual revolt.

PASSAGE II

SOCIAL SCIENCE: *Geographers have suggested different models to describe growth in U.S. cities. These models deal with class structure, which is the basic demographic outcome of an economy. Passage A describes the concentric zone model. Passage B discusses the multiple nuclei model.*

PASSAGE A

The concentric zone model was established by urban geographers Robert Park, Ernest Burgess, and Roderick McKenzie in the early 1920s. The model suggests that the
(5) lower classes live closest to the central business district while the upper classes live farther out because they can afford the commute into the city to work.

The central business district is the com-
(10) mercial center of the city and contains the peak land value intersection, the area with the greatest land value and commercial value. Outside of the central business district is the zone in transition, which usually contains
(15) the slums. Slums are high-density areas of lower-class citizens who live in substandard housing. Many of the people living in this area are new immigrants to the city. Most residences are apartments; these are intermixed
(20) with industrial zones. Because very few people want to live next to industrial zones and their noise and pollution, the value of the housing is usually very low. Many of the apartments in these areas are tenements. Tenements are
(25) rundown apartment buildings that are minimally kept up by landlords because their value is so low. Landlords either barely comply with housing codes or don't comply at all.

Next out from the central business district
(30) is lower-class housing. Typically these are older well-established neighborhoods where working-class families and singles alike tend to purchase homes.

The fourth zone is an area of middle-class
(35) housing where homes get larger as the income of their inhabitants rises. The fifth zone is an upper-class residential area. The houses here are the largest in this area. In some cases, this zone is called a commuter zone because of the
(40) number of people who commute either into the city or to other suburbs for work.

Burgess elaborated on the concentric zone model to include the ideas of "invasion and succession." Invasion and succession refer to
(45) the continued expansion of the central business district and the continual push outwards of the zones. This pushing out process causes the zones to rebuild their infrastructures. Areas that were once low-income residences
(50) and older working-class neighborhoods are converted into apartment buildings. The upper-class continually needs to commute farther and at a greater expense to maintain the lifestyle of the fifth zone.

(55) The concentric zone model was based on Chicago of the early 1900s. The problem with this model is that it reflects a perception about American cities but not the reality. The concentric zone model really does not exist
(60) in the United States today. Many upper- and upper-middle-class residents are moving back into the city, creating wealthy areas relatively close to the urban center. Stretches of upper-class residences usually follow transportation
(65) routes outwards from the central business district rather than occupying zones in concentric circles outward from the city center.

PASSAGE B

The multiple nuclei model was established by Chauncey Harris and Edward Ullman in (70) 1945 and was the first model to suggest that urban growth is independent of the central business district because growth may begin in commercial, industrial, and even residential suburbs outside the central business district. (75) Different industries spring up wherever there are opportunities for growth. According to the multiple nuclei model, growth may occur haphazardly and extend more in one direction than another. The different zones are still based (80) on class, but more emphasis is placed on the extent and type of economic development.

One of the best examples of this model involves airports. Airports are usually located on the outskirts of the city for reasons of space (85) and to limit noise and air pollution. However, around the airport is usually substantial development of hotels, restaurants, and entertainment facilities. This development does not arise from the central business district. (90) Rather, an economic opportunity generated by proximity allows certain companies to prosper around the airport.

Likewise, in this model, industrial development may occur around a port. Ports (95) are located along waterways, and are often a considerable distance from the central business district. However, ports encourage business development that caters to shipping and trade, tourists, and the daily needs of port employees. (100) The multiple nuclei model also takes into account the economic effects of universities.

Around college campuses, there are usually more fast-food restaurants, as well as coffee shops and bookstores. Many universities also (105) construct off-campus housing in surrounding communities for students. Again, development is independent of the central business district.

Although the central business district is still the commercial hub of the city and much (110) development takes place there because of the economic activity, industrial enterprises will usually place a higher priority on being close to an airport or seaport. However, in these areas of growth, one would not likely find (115) high-income housing. That tends to be built in its own area, based on the idea that the wealthy like to live next to the extremely wealthy and so on.

Many American cities follow the multiple (120) nuclei model. Growth occurs where it is needed and where developers can maximize profits, often resulting in edge cities, large commercial centers that offer entertainment and shopping in the suburbs which may approach (125) 100,000 in population. The multiplier effect is the principle that development spurs more develop- ment. When development occurs in a city, more services are needed to meet the needs of the growing population. When more (130) infrastructure is needed, more tradespeople are needed. These people need more grocery stores, gas stations, and so forth, and more services attract more people. The city's tax base increases, supporting even more development (135) through increased amenities such as parks, sports facilities, and better schools.

Questions 11–13 ask about Passage A.

11. According to the passage, where would one expect to find upper-middle-class residents in a modern U.S. city?

    A. Overlapping the boundaries of the fourth and fifth zones

    B. In a wealthy area close to the urban center

    C. Near airports, seaports, or universities

    D. Pushing further outwards due to "invasion and succession"

12. It can be most logically inferred that the main assumption in the concentric zone model is that:

    F. lower classes cannot afford transportation to get to work.

    G. lower classes cannot afford the cost of transportation into the city from outer zones.

    H. lower classes cannot live in the commuter zone because they cannot afford housing there.

    J. lower classes tend to work in the central business district and prefer to live close to work.

13. According to the passage, upper-class and middle-class residents in a modern U.S. city would most likely be located:

    A. in a wealthy area close to the urban center.

    B. in areas that overlap the boundaries of the fourth and fifth zones.

    C. along transportation routes outward from the city.

    D. far away from the city, due to "invasion and succession."

Questions 14–16 ask about Passage B.

14. Based on their locations, airports, ports, and universities can often be categorized as:

    F. central business districts.

    G. nuclei

    H. industrial zones.

    J. commercial hubs.

15. What does the passage cite as the term that accounts for exponential development arising out of development itself?

    A. Exponential growth

    B. Multiplicative effects

    C. Urban sprawl

    D. Multiplier effect

16. According to the passage, how is urban growth related to the central business district?

    F. The central business district is dependent on urban growth for survival.

    G. Urban growth does not necessarily depend on the central business district.

    H. Urban growth thrives within the central business district.

    J. Urban growth is inversely related to the central business district.

Questions 17–20 ask about both passages.

17. The relation between the two passages is such that:

A. Passage A argues one explanation while Passage B argues a competing explanation.

B. Passage A concludes with an observation that Passage B partially supports.

C. Passage A introduces two contradicting models, and Passage B introduces a third model.

D. Passage A concludes by refuting its own presented model and introducing Passage B's model.

18. It can be inferred that the slums and tenements described in Passage A would most likely be found in or around which of the following types of nuclei described in Passage B's model, assuming that each nuclei is geographically separated from the others?

    I. Airports

    II. Seaports

    III. Universities

F. I only

G. III only

H. I and II only

J. I, II, and III

19. If a modern U.S. city has a university, seaport, or airport collocated with the central business district, it can be reasonably inferred that this city would most likely resemble:

A. the concentric zone model of Passage A.

B. none of the models or observations presented.

C. the multiple nuclei model of Passage B.

D. the observations in the final paragraph of Passage A.

20. Given the information provided in the passages, both models suggest that:

F. classes are the only basis for different geographical zones.

G. high-income housing for the upper-class is usually farthest from areas of growth.

H. middle-class and upper-class developments are creating wealthy areas, or "edge cities," close to urban centers.

J. housing zones will not develop systematically or in predictable patterns.

PASSAGE III

HUMANITIES: *This passage focuses on garden design.*

A garden is a living work of art that blends elements of space and mass, light and shade, the natural and the manmade, along with color, scent, texture, and climate. As with any
Line
(5) other art, the evolution of garden design may be seen as reflecting the interests and values of groups of people living in a particular time and place. It is not surprising, then, that the history of the garden illustrates in various ways the
(10) principles of both continuity with and reaction against an existing style in the *jardin anglais*, or the English garden, that became popular in France and other parts of Europe during the mid-18th century.

(15) In the early 18th century, French cultural influence dominated Europe, leading to the popularity of the highly formal garden, sometimes known as the French garden. This garden is characterized by rigidly formulated
(20) geometric patterns in which precision, regularity, and proportion are dominant. The garden at Versailles, one of the largest and best-known formal gardens, is the epitome of the style that was emulated on a smaller scale at other loca-
(25) tions. Typical of the style it represents, the colossal garden at Versailles is based on designs that are strongly geometrical, including areas separated by long straight lines and circular pools dividing symmetrical areas. Canals,
(30) fountains, and statuary are used to emphasize the balanced forms.

Versailles, like many formal gardens, made use of the *bosquet*, a precisely planted grove in which trees are planted so as to be perfectly
(35) aligned according to a pattern. Another feature of the formal garden used extensively at Ver-

sailles is the *parterre*, a sort of garden-within-a-garden. Several types of *parterres* were used, including the *parterre de broderie*, or em-
(40) broidered *parterre*, in which neatly trimmed boxwood shrubs were planted in designs suggestive of botanical shapes. In the embroidered *parterre*, the box plantings were set against turf or colored earth. Other types of *parterres* used
(45) different kinds of flowers and other plants, but the use of a formal pattern was common to all types of *parterres*.

It was in the context of such highly stylized and classical designs that the English
(50) landscape garden came into being. Reaction against formality came in part from the British poet and literary critic Alexander Pope, who in 1713 published an essay on gardening in *The Guardian*. Eschewing the balance, formal-
(55) ity, and rigid symmetry popular in gardens of the time, Pope called instead for the creation of gardens that reflect the "amiable simplicity of unadorned nature." Pope argued that the design of a garden should take its cues from
(60) local topography rather than starting from a preconceived plan that is artificially imposed on the landscape.

In England, two of the most famous designers of landscape style gardens were
(65) William Kent and Lancelot (better known as "Capability") Brown. Kent, a friend of Alexander Pope, drew inspiration from the ideas of the literary critic. Kent, who had studied art in Italy, was highly receptive to Pope's notion
(70) that "all gardening is landscape painting." One of the best examples of Kent's work is found in the garden at Rousham House in Oxford-

shire. This garden, started in 1738, typifies the landscape principle of making the surrounding
(75) countryside an integral part of the experience of the garden. Kent used outlying buildings in a picturesque Gothic style to call attention to the larger surrounding area and the garden's lace within it.

(80)   Following Kent and achieving even greater fame, Capability Brown was the next great English landscape gardener. Fittingly, Brown earned his nickname from his tendency to talk to his clients about the "capabilities" of their
(85) land. Among Brown's most famous works is the landscaping on the grounds of Blenheim Palace in Oxfordshire. Here he created a free-flowing expanse marked by large grassy areas, irregularly shaped bodies of water, and seem-
(90) ingly random plantings of trees, both isolated and in clustered groupings. The naturalistic designs that Brown perfected may be seen as the polar opposite of the highly stylized and artificial designs in the garden at Versailles.
(95) Admirers of the more formal gardens such as the one at Versailles have criticized Brown for destroying some of the best examples of formal gardens in England, while those who appreciate the naturalistic style celebrate Brown's
(100) achievement.

     Capability Brown influenced Humphrey Repton, who continued to create designs that were largely similar to those of his predecessor. In addition, Repton had some literary talent
(105) and in the late 18th and early 19th centuries produced several books documenting the landscape styles that were popular at the time. Though the landscape or "English" style garden eventually saw a decline in popularity in its
(110) country of origin, it enjoyed further longevity in continental Europe, particularly in France.

21. The primary contrast in this passage revolves around:

   A. the relative importance of nature and artificiality in garden design.

   B. the comparative significance of Alexander Pope's and William Kent's garden designs.

   C. two artists working in the same era but producing distinctive though related work.

   D. the dominance of French culture over the English culture during the 18th century.

22. One inference that may be drawn from the fourth paragraph is that:

   F. British poets in the early 18th century rebelled against formality.

   G. a desire to rebel against formality was a crucial element of Alexander Pope's poetry.

   H. creative pursuits in diverse areas did not always exist in isolation from each other.

   J. knowledge of European painting influenced William Kent's garden designs.

23. Based on information in the passage, which statements are true about the garden at Versailles?

    I. It made use of the geometric designs that mimicked botanical forms.

    II. The surrounding landscape was considered a crucial part of the garden's design.

    III. It was featured in a book of garden designs published by Humphrey Repton.

    IV. *Bosquets* and *parterres* were among the pattern designs featured.

    A. I, II, III, IV

    B. II, III, IV

    C. I and IV

    D. IV only

24. As used in line 23, the word *epitome* most nearly means:

    F. best example.

    G. balanced plan.

    H. artistic creation.

    J. inevitable result.

25. According to the passage, the work of Capability Brown:

    A. was strongly influenced by the designs of Humphrey Repton.

    B. was a source of inspiration for Alexander Pope's poetry.

    C. is a subject of some disagreement among critics.

    D. exemplifies the use of geometric forms in garden design.

26. Based on information provided in the passage, which of the following would be *least* likely to be found in a "French garden"?

    F. Two rows of trees planted in precisely parallel lines

    G. Low trimmed bushes planted in circular maze design

    H. Four similar statues each placed in the corners of a square *parterre*

    J. A randomly curved stone path surrounding a large grassy area

27. The writer mentions *Rousham House* (line 72) for the purpose of:

    A. describing gardens that contrast with those found at Blenheim Palace.

    B. providing an example of a famous estate in Oxfordshire.

    C. explaining how the principles of French garden design were adapted to the British landscape.

    D. illustrating an important aspect of William Kent's work.

28. In the passage as a whole, paragraph 2 functions as:

    F. a detailed description of the gardens at Versailles.

    G. an explanation of concepts necessary to differentiate between different gardens.

    H. a criticism of the balanced geometrical designs used in the French style garden.

    J. an argument that statuary and lakes are essential features of a formal garden.

29. The writer mentions *Blenheim Palace* (lines 86–87) in order to:

    A. provide an example of one of Capability Brown's most well-known projects.

    B. suggest that it plays a transitional role in the development of European garden styles.

    C. criticize its designer for destroying a valuable example of the formal French garden.

    D. prove that Oxfordshire was home to more landscape-style gardens than any other county in England.

30. The primary purpose of this passage is to:

    F. present a detailed description of some of the most famous gardens of the 19th century.

    G. argue that a palatial residence cannot be considered complete unless it includes an extensive garden.

    H. support the view that the French and English gardens in the mid-1800s had some significant features in common.

    J. discuss two contrasting styles that are important in the history of garden design.

PASSAGE IV

NATURAL SCIENCE: *This passage is adapted from the paper "Indigenous Uses, Management, and Restoration of Oaks of the Far Western United States." It was issued by the U.S. Department of Agriculture Natural Resources Conservation Service in 2007.*

Today, oaks are plagued with problems. There is lack of regeneration in populations of
Line certain species. Pests such as the acorn weevil and the filbert worm eat away at acorns
(5) and prevent germination. By undermining the root systems of seedlings and saplings, ground-squirrels, gophers, and other small mammals often prevent these young plants from reaching tree size. Severe diseases, such as sudden oak
(10) death, kill many adult oaks. Many mature oaks are having a tough time with fire suppression. In the past, with light surface fires, the oaks had been able to maintain a stronghold where other plants were not able to compete and died
(15) out. Now oaks are being toppled by trees that have a higher tolerance for shade and are not fire-resistant; earlier such trees would have been killed when Native Americans set fires.

Given all of these challenges, the "old-
(20) growth" oaks—the large old valley oaks, Garry oaks, coast live oaks, and canyon live oaks that have huge girth and large canopies—may become a thing of the past. These oaks in particular are important because there are often more
(25) terrestrial vertebrates living in mature oak stands than in seedling and sapling areas. This prevalence of animals occurs because the large crowns of such oaks provide cover and feeding sites for a large variety of wildlife.

(30) The University of California has embarked on an ambitious and necessary research program called the Integrated Hardwood Range-Management Program to explore the significant causes of oak decline and offer varied
(35) solutions. These include investigating the use of grassing regimes that are compatible with

oak seedling establishment, revegetating sites with native grasses to facilitate better germination of oak seedlings, documenting insects
(40) and pathogens that attack oaks, and exploring the ways that native people managed oaks in the past. Scientists at the Pacific Northwest Research Station in Olympia, Washington, and at Redwood National Park in northern
(45) California are reintroducing the burning-practices of Native Americans. When used in Garry oak ecosystems, fires keep Douglas firs from encroaching on the oaks and promote the growth of wildflowers that are important
(50) food plants. Further investigations about these fire practices may be essential in figuring out how to maintain oaks in the western landscape today, given that the fires address many of the factors that are now causing oak decline—from
(55) how to eliminate insect pests of acorns to how to maintain an open structure in oak groves.

Ecological restoration, the traditional approach to woodland maintenance, referred to humans intervening on a very limited time
(60) scale to bring back plants and animals known to have existed in an area historically. However, the decline of oaks, one of the most significant plants to Native Americans, shows us that humans may play an integral part in the
(65) restoration of oak areas. While animals such as jays have been recognized as crucial partners in oak well-being, human actions through the eons may also have been key to the oaks' flourishing.

(70) Sudden oak death, for example, although of exotic origin, may be curtailed locally by thinning around coastal oaks and tan oaks and

setting light surface fires, simulating ancient fire management practices of Native Ameri- (75) cans. Indigenous shrubs and trees that grow in association with oaks are hosts to the sudden oak death pathogen. By limiting the growth of these shrubs, burning that mimics earlier Native American ways may reduce opportunities (80) for disease agents to jump from other plants to oak trees. With a more open environment, it may be harder for sudden oak death to spread.

The oak landscapes that we inherited, which still bear the marks of former Native (85) American interactions, demand a new kind of restoration that complements other forms of ecological restoration. This new kind of restoration could be called *ethnobotanical restoration*, defined as reestablishing the historic plant (90) communities of a given area and restoring

indigenous harvesting, vegetation management, and cultivation practices (seedbearing, burning, pruning, sowing, tilling, and weeding) necessary to maintain these communities (95) in the long term.

Thus, this kind of restoration is not only about restoring plants, but also about restoring the human place within nature. Ethnobotanical restoration is viewed not as a process that (100) can be completed, but rather as a continuous interaction between people and plants as both their fates are intertwined in a region. Using oaks and people once again through harvesting acorns, making products form all parts of the (105) three, knocking the trees, and setting light fires may offer us ways to coexist, receive products from, and benefit the long-term health and well-being of the remarkable oak.

31. All of the following challenges to the health of the oak population are mentioned in the passage EXCEPT:

A. small mammals attacking the root systems of young trees.

B. sudden oak death caused by a pathogen.

C. grazing deer removing bark from the tree trunks.

D. competition from other plants such as shade-tolerant trees.

32. As described in the passage, traditional ecological restoration differs from ethnobotanical restoration in that:

F. ethnobotanical restoration takes place over a longer period of time than ecological restoration.

G. ecological restoration involves introducing particular plants and management practices, whereas ethnobotanical restoration involves only the introduction of plants.

H. only ecological restoration follows historically proven ecological principles.

J. ecological restoration is meant to be used in conjunction with other restorative practices, whereas ethnobotanical restoration is meant to be used in isolation.

33. An important assumption underlying this passage is that:

    A. the decline of the oak population is due primarily to root damage caused by ground squirrels, gophers, and other small mammals.

    B. reinstituting indigenous cultivation practices is likely to be sufficient to restore the health of the oak population.

    C. damage to many species of oak started centuries ago when Native Americans selectively set fires in many areas.

    D. the practices of Native Americans offer lessons to modern researchers about how to promote a healthy oak population.

34. According to the passage, one way to reduce the incidence of sudden oak death is to:

    F. reduce the population of animals that destroy the root systems of the oaks.

    G. control the number of certain shrubs that grow in the vicinity of oak trees.

    H. regulate the importation of the exotic plants that introduced the sudden oak death pathogen to the United States.

    J. plant several varieties of oaks, particularly tan oaks and coastal oaks, to strengthen the oak population in general.

35. The author refers to the *huge girth and large canopies* (line 22) of the old-growth oaks in order to:

    A. provide a description of what the various old-growth oak trees look like.

    B. argue that the old-growth trees are too large to be sustained in a modern ecosystem.

    C. support the explanation of why more vertebrates live in mature oak stands.

    D. indicate that Native Americans valued these trees for their ability to produce shade.

36. The primary purpose of the first paragraph is to:

    F. discuss how oak trees provide a habitat for various animals.

    G. suggest ways in which the declining oak population can be restored.

    H. support the argument that sudden oak death is not as common as rampant forest fires.

    J. describe current challenges to the health of the oak population.

37. Based on the passage as a whole, it is likely that:

    A. human intervention will be crucial in restoring the native oak population.

    B. despite much historical study, it will be impossible to recreate the cultivation practices of early Native Americans.

    C. documentation of the insects and pathogens that attack oak trees is the best way to begin the restoration process.

    D. native shrubs and trees that grow near oaks have served as kindling for many fires that damaged the oak population.

38. The author mentions *trees that have a higher tolerance for shade* (lines 15–16) as an example of:

    F. one type of vegetation that is desirable to plant near oaks.

    G. a currently existing problem that presents a new kind of threat to the oak population.

    H. one of the drawbacks associated with several of the old-growth oak species.

    J. the types of plants Native Americans cultivated.

39. It can be inferred from the third paragraph that:

    A. the oak population in Redwood National Park has faced greater threats than oak populations elsewhere.

    B. native grasses have been shown to deprive oak seedlings of nutrients.

    C. the sudden oak death pathogen has been the primary cause of oak decline.

    D. researchers are interested in finding multiple avenues to restoring the health of the oaks.

40. As stated in the passage, the effect of light surface fires on oaks is to:

    F. promote the health of oaks by limiting vegetation that would compete with them.

    G. reduce the number of oak trees by destroying the acorns before they can seed.

    H. create scars in the bark that allow for the entrance of the sudden oak death pathogen.

    J. harm the oaks by destroying the nests of jays.

ANSWERS AND EXPLANATIONS

PASSAGE I

SUGGESTED PASSAGE MAP

Paragraph 1: Pesca has good news for narrator

Paragraph 2: Narrator's mom likes Pesca

Paragraph 3: Sarah not fond of Pesca; young/old differences

Paragraph 4: Sarah seems older than mom; broken teacup

Paragraph 5: Mom eager for Pesca's good news

Paragraph 6: Sarah's annoyance

Paragraph 7: Pesca sets stage like preacher

Paragraph 8–10: Responses to Pesca

Paragraph 11: Pesca knows rich man who needs drawing teacher

Paragraph 12: Pesca excited to know drawing teacher

ANSWER KEY

1. B	6. H
2. J	7. C
3. C	8. F
4. F	9. B
5. D	10. F

DETAILED EXPLANATIONS

1. B

Inference

For a broad Inference question, quickly review your passage map notes before considering the answer choices. In this case, you must eliminate choices that *are* supported by the passage. Eliminate (A) because line 5 states that Pesca knows the narrator's habits. Choice (B) is not supported by the passage and seems inconsistent with what we've read. Although Pesca consciously uses a dramatic manner to deliver his good news, appearing to act like a preacher addressing his congregation, he does so a bit awkwardly. Nothing in the passage indicates that he is "well-trained" as a public speaker. Eliminate (C) because line 20 states that the narrator's mother "unreservedly" opens her heart to Pesca. Eliminate (D) because Pesca's statements in the passage do not always show strong command of English. For example, in line 96, Pesca says, *he wants a **recommend** from me* instead of *a **recommendation.*** Choice (B) is the correct answer.

2. J

Generalization

For a Generalization question about a contrast, review your passage map notes and skim the passage if necessary to find where in the passage to go for your prediction. In this case, your passage map may direct you to paragraphs 3 and 4. Predict that younger people are not as *impulsive as some of our elders* (lines 36–37) and that *old people [are] excited by the prospect of some anticipated pleasure* (lines 38–39). This prediction fits well with (J). Choice (F) is a distortion; the descriptions of young and old are reversed in this answer choice. Choice (G) is out-of-scope. Nothing in the passage suggests that older people are more curious. Choice (H) is out-of-scope. Older people are not described as ungrateful.

3. C

Detail

For a Detail question, check your passage notes or skim the passage to find the words used in the question stem. Here, your passage map notes should direct you to paragraph 2, where lines 17–20 state that the narrator's mother has favored Pesca since *the first moment she found out that the little Professor was deeply and gratefully attached to her son.* Choice (A) is out-of-scope. The passage says nothing about the narrator's mother valuing intellectual pursuits. Choice (B) is a distortion. While the passage does concern Pesca's recommending the narrator for a job, the narrator's mother doesn't yet know about this when the passage opens. Choice (D) is a distortion. The passage states the narrator's mother overlooks Pesca's faults, but it doesn't suggest that she applies this lenient attitude toward everyone.

4. F
Vocab-in-Context

For a **Vocab-in-Context** question, go back to the sentence and check for context clues that help you predict. The sentence states the Pesca had knocked the teacup off the table while moving to greet the narrator at the door. Paragraph 1 indicates that Pesca is very eager and excited, so predict that he moved *quickly* or *suddenly* toward the door. This prediction matches (F). Choice (G) is a distortion. The passage states that Sarah is *perturbed* by the broken cup, but the narrator doesn't ascribe rudeness to Pesca or his actions. Choice (H) is out-of-scope. Nothing in the sentence or passage indicates that *precipitate* could mean *faithful*. Choice (J) is a distortion. Although Pesca is described as *eccentric* in this passage, his *advance toward the door* is not necessarily described that way.

5. D
Generalization

For a Generalization question about a paragraph, make sure your answer is consistent with everything in the paragraph. It may be tough to predict anything so broad, but you should refer to your passage map note and skim the paragraph before reading the answer choices. Choice (A) is a misused detail from the second paragraph. Choice (B) is out-of-scope. The narrator never questions Pesca's judgment. Choice (C) is out-of-scope. Nothing in the paragraph suggests that a confrontation is likely. Choice (D) is the correct answer. The phrase *knowing my habits* (line 8) suggests that Pesca knows he will find the narrator at his mother's house.

6. H
Function

For a Function question about a phrase, read around the immediate context to make your prediction. Because the narrator suspects that Pesca has come with good news, the narrator probably realizes that Pesca is eager to get him into the house. This prediction fits well with (H). Choice (F) is out-of-scope. There is no evidence suggesting that the narrator finds Pesca to be rude. Choice (G) is out-of-scope. Nothing suggests that the narrator wants to resist Pesca or avoid his company. Choice (J) is a distortion. While the passage does describe Pesca as *an eccentric little foreigner* (line 33), the narrator never says he is caught off-guard by Pesca's eccentricities.

7. C
Generalization

For a Generalization question about a character, start with your passage map notes. In this case, your notes should lead you to paragraphs 3 and 4. Quickly look at these paragraphs to get a feel for how Sarah is portrayed. In addition, skim through the passage for the word *Sarah* to see if any other references will help you with this question. Then read through the answer choices and eliminate. Choice (A) is an extreme. The passage says that Sarah *did full justice to Pesca's excellent qualities of heart, but she could not accept him implicitly* (lines 26–27). This means that Sarah acknowledges that Pesca at least has a good heart, even if she doesn't like everything about him. Choice (B) is out-of-scope because Sarah is not described as being protective of her brother. Choice (C) is justified by lines 70–71 where Sarah is described as *mournfully absorbed over the ruins of the broken cup*. Additional support for this choice is found in lines 89–90, where Sarah is concerned that Pesca will break *the best armchair*. Choice (D) is out-of-scope. The passage says nothing about the basic needs of the narrator's mother not being met.

8. F

Generalization

For a Generalization question about a paragraph, use your passage map notes and quickly review the paragraph to see if you can predict. There's a lot in the third paragraph. Sarah isn't very comfortable with Pesca; the mother seems excited to hear Pesca's good news; the narrator compares old and young, wondering if the young are a little too serious. Don't worry which is most important, but be ready to use the information to judge the answer choices. Choice (F) is the correct answer. It encompasses both the differences between old and young and the narrator's surprise at Sarah's attitude toward Pesca. Choice (G) is a distortion. The passage states that Sarah disapproves of Pesca's *lack* of regard for appearances (lines 30–31). Choice (H) is a distortion. Though lines 27–28 indicates that Sarah doesn't share her mother's opinion of Pesca (*she could not accept him implicitly, as my mother did*), Sarah doesn't express disapproval of her mother's attitude. Choice (J) is a distortion. The narrator asks himself if members of his own generation are *quite such genuine boys and girls now as our seniors were in their time* (lines 41–43), but he doesn't make an explicit statement that his generation is the more *genuine*.

9. B

Detail

For a Roman numeral question about sequence of details, try to determine which event happened first and use that knowledge to eliminate wrong answer choices. In this case, event II must come first. This is justified by lines 8–9:...*knowing my habits, he [Pesca] had come to the cottage to make sure of meeting me.* Thus, eliminate (C) and (D). Now all that remains is to determine whether event IV or I came first, which will determine whether the answer is (A) or (B). Lines 57–59 indicate that Pesca had been inside the cottage and broken the teacup *before* the narrator came inside: *The Professor had knocked [the teacup] off the table in his precipitate advance to meet me at the door.* Therefore (B) is the correct answer.

10. F

Detail

For broadly worded Detail questions, your passage map notes and quick skimming may not direct you to the best part of the passage to refer to. If this is the case, don't spend too much time looking around. Check the answer choices to see if a quick reference to the passage can help you choose the best one. Here, (F) is the right answer, but that may not be immediately apparent. Eliminate (G) because the narrator never questions Pesca's trustworthiness, making this choice out-of-scope. Eliminate option (H) because it's a contradiction. The author states that his mother has a high opinion of Pesca. Choice (J) is a distortion. The phrase *perpetual revolt* describes Sarah's opinion of Pesca's *contempt for appearances* (lines 30–31), but it isn't something the narrator wonders about. Working by elimination is effective for this question. Notice, however, that lines 43–45 (*has the great advance in education taken rather too long a stride?*) directly support (F).

PASSAGE II

SUGGESTED PASSAGE MAP

PASSAGE A

Paragraph 1: Conc. zone—lower classes live closest to central business district (CBD)

Paragraph 2: CBD surrounded by zone in transition w/ slums

Paragraph 3: 3rd zone—lower-class housing

Paragraph 4: 4th zone—middle-class housing; 5th zone—upper-class residential area/commuter zone

Paragraph 5: Invasion & succession—CBD expands and pushes zones out

Paragraph 6: CBD doesn't exist in U.S. today

PASSAGE B

Paragraph 1: Mult. nuclei model—urban growth is ind. of CBD

Paragraph 2: 1st example—airports

Paragraph 3: 2nd example—ports

Paragraph 4: 3rd example—universities

Paragraph 5: Areas of growth don't include high-income housing

Paragraph 6: Mult. nuclei model in U.S. today & has multiplier effect

ANSWER KEY

11. B	**16. G**
12. G	**17. B**
13. A	**18. H**
14. G	**19. D**
15. D	**20. G**

DETAILED EXPLANATIONS

11. B
Detail

For a Detail question, start by using your passage map notes to direct you to the right part of the passage to make your prediction. Here, the final paragraph of Passage A states that the concentric model "does not exist in the United States today" (modern U.S. cities). In addition, this paragraph states, "Many upper- and upper-middle-class residents are moving back into the city, creating wealthy areas relatively close to the urban center." Choices (A) and (D) are both indicative of the concentric model, which the author dismisses as not representative of modern U.S. cities, and (C) refers to details mentioned in Passage B.

12. G
Inference

The concentric zone model is based on the statement that "upper classes live farther out because they can afford the commute into the city to work." The logical assumption that can be inferred is that those other than the upper classes cannot afford the commute from farther out, (G). Choice (F) is too extreme—the argument does not indicate outright that lower classes cannot afford transportation. Choice (H) is out-of-scope as the argument and basis of the model never mentions housing. Choice (J) is also out-of-scope as the passage never addresses where lower classes like to work.

13. A
Detail

The final paragraph of Passage A states that the concentric model "does not exist in the United States today" (modern U.S. cities) and is the only place that "upper-middle-class" residents are cited. The paragraph mentions that they are moving "into the city, creating wealthy areas relatively close to the urban center," (B). Choices (B) and (D) are both indicative of the concentric model, which the author dismisses as not representative of modern U.S. cities, and (C) only applies to upper-class residents as cited in the final paragraph.

14. G
Detail

Airports, ports, and universities are presented as examples of nuclei forming outside the central business district, so (G) is correct. The final paragraph states, "Growth occurs where it is needed and where developers can maximize profits, often resulting in edge cities, large commercial centers that offer entertainment and shopping in the suburbs which may approach 100,000 in population. Choices (H) and (J) are too specific and don't apply to all of the examples in the question.

15. D
Detail

The final paragraph states "the multiplier effect is the principle that development spurs more development." Choice (D) matches exactly.

16. G
Detail

In the first paragraph, the model is described as suggesting that "urban growth is independent of the central business district." Choice (G) matches.

17. B
Inference

Passage A presents an explanation of an urban growth model that the author later describes as obsolete and cites relevant characteristics of modern cities. Passage B presents an explanation of a more recent model and goes as far to say that many American cities follow the it. In the final paragraph of Passage A, elements that the author observes about modern U.S. cities can be traced to similar elements outlined in the final paragraph of Passage B, which yields (B). Choice (A) is incorrect because neither passage argues for a particular model—the explanations are objective. Choice (C) is incorrect because the first passage only introduces one model; the final paragraph is not suggestive of a new model. Choice (D) is incorrect because the conclusion of Passage A never introduces the concept of the nuclei model.

18. H
Inference

According to passage A, the slums and tenements are "intermixed with industrial zones" because "very few people want to live next to industrial zones and their noise and pollution." The second paragraph of Passage B says that if airports were to develop outside the central business district, even though there is noise and pollution, there would still usually be "substantial development of hotels, restaurants, and entertainment facilities." This indicates a commercial district. Additionally, the structure of the passage suggests this is an example of a commercial

suburb, which is not where slums and tenements would be found. In the third paragraph of Passage B, "industrial development may occur around a port," and the structure of the passage indicates this is an example of an industrial suburb, which is where slums and tenements would be found. The fourth paragraph does not describe an area that fits an industrial zone, and the structure of the passage indicates this is an example of a residential suburb, which is not where slums and tenements would be found. Choice (H) is correct.

19. D
Inference

Collocated means "placed side by side," so the question stem is asking about a city in which the central business district is right next to a university, seaport, or airport. The basis of the multiple nuclei model is that areas of development occur in areas outside of the central business district, making (C) incorrect. It would seem most likely then that since these functions would form in the same area, thus growing from the center outward, that the concentric zone model would be the best fit. But the author of Passage A indicates that this model really doesn't exist in practice, thus making choice (A) incorrect. The author of Passage A does give a description of what a modern city would look like in practice if all of these functions were arranged together at the urban center. Choice (D) is correct.

20. G
Inference

Passage A indicates that in the concentric model, the upper-class is the farthest out from where growth occurs at central business districts and "continually needs to commute farther and at a greater expense to maintain the lifestyle of the fifth zone." Additionally, Passage B indicates that in the multiple nuclei model, "one would not likely find high-income housing" in areas of growth. Choice (G) is correct. Choice (F) is true of the concentric model, but not the multiple nuclei model, where "more emphasis is placed on the extent and type of economic development." Choice (H) is true in both passages, but is misused and is not actually true of the concentric model described in Passage A, rather just the observations by the author at the end. Choice (J) is true of the multiple nuclei model as "growth may occur haphazardly and extend more in one direction than another," but not of the concentric model as zones expand in "concentric circles outward from the city center."

PASSAGE III

SUGGESTED PASSAGE MAP

Paragraph 1: Background on garden design; English garden a reaction

Paragraph 2: French garden style; Versailles—geometrical, symmetrical

Paragraph 3: Versailles cont'd—*parterres*

Paragraph 4: Pope started reaction against earlier style, urged focus on nature

Paragraph 5: Kent's work in landscape style

Paragraph 6: Brown; Blenheim Palace—criticized by some

Paragraph 7: Repton; landscape garden style outside of England

ANSWER KEY

21. **A**	26. **J**
22. **H**	27. **D**
23. **C**	28. **G**
24. **F**	29. **A**
25. **C**	30. **J**

DETAILED EXPLANATIONS

21. **A**
Generalization

For a Generalization question, your answer must be based on the passage as a whole. Use your passage notes to help here. Predict that the primary contrast is between the garden at Versailles and the landscape-style garden. The garden at Versailles is described in lines 19–21 as being *characterized by rigidly formulated geometric patterns in which precision, regularity, and proportion are dominant*. Paragraph 4 describes the landscape garden as being a *reaction against formality* (lines 50–51). Predict that the answer has something to do with the difference between a highly formal style and a more natural style. This prediction matches best with (A). Choice (B) is a distortion. Although Kent is mentioned in the passage as a designer of gardens, Pope is not. Choice (C) is a distortion. Although three garden designers are mentioned (Kent, Brown, and Repton), their work is described as largely continuous, not *distinctive*. Choice (D) is a misused detail. The dominance of French culture is cited, but in passing, not as a major element of the passage.

22. **H**
Generalization

For a Generalization question about a paragraph, use your passage notes. Paragraph 4 discusses a poet's influence on the field of garden design. The best answer will be consistent with this idea, and option (H) matches well. Choice (F) combines the out-of-scope and distortion answer traps. It's out-of-scope because the passage focuses on landscape design, not poetry. The phrase *rebel against formality* in option (F) is a distortion of the phrase *reaction against formality* (lines 50–51), which is used in the passage in relation to garden design, not poetry. Choice (G) is out-of-scope. Alexander Pope's interests were only discussed in relation to gardens, not his own poetry. Choice (J) is a misused detail. The reference to Kent's study of art in Italy comes in paragraph 5, but this question stem asks about an inference based on paragraph 4.

23. C
Detail

For a Roman numeral Detail question, consider each statement separately, and eliminate answer choices when you find a statement isn't true. Based on lines 40–42, statement I is true. Knowing this, we can eliminate (B) and (D). We still have to consider statements II and III (we don't need to verify IV, as it appears in both of our remaining options). Statement II is not true of the garden at Versailles. The surrounding landscape is mentioned in the passage as being important in Kent's landscape style garden (lines 73–76). Statement III is not true. Though that passage states that Repton *produced several books documenting the landscape styles that were popular at the time* (lines 106–107), Versailles is not described as having a landscape-style garden. Knowing that either or both statements II and III aren't true, you can eliminate (A), only leaving (C).

24. F
Vocab-in-Context

For Vocab-in-Context questions, pay attention to clues in the sentence that tell you what the word means. In this case, reading the previous sentence is also helpful. The previous sentence describes the style of garden known as the "French" garden, suggesting that the garden at Versailles is presented as an *example* of this style. This leads to a prediction of *example,* which option (F) matches nicely. Choice (G) is a misused detail. While the garden at Versailles exhibits a *balanced plan,* that is not presented as representative of all. Choice (H) is a misused detail. Though *artistic style* is relevant to the passage, it doesn't fit in this context. Choice (J) is out-of-scope. There's no cause-and-effect relationship indicated here, so *result* doesn't work in this context.

25. C
Detail

For a Detail question, your passage map notes can help you know where to look to make your prediction. For this question, look back to paragraph 6. The question is broadly worded, so it's hard to make a precise prediction. Skim the paragraph so you're familiar with what it says: The grounds at Blenheim Palace are a famous example of Brown's work, and they reflect the naturalistic style; Brown has been criticized for destroying great examples of formal gardens. Read through the answer choices and eliminate as you go. Choice (A) is a contradiction. Repton followed Brown, so Brown could not have been influenced by him. Choice (B) combines the distortion and out-of-scope answer traps. Although Pope is mentioned in the passage, Brown is not discussed as a source of inspiration for Pope's poetry. Choice (C) fits with your general prediction, particularly taking into account lines 95–100, *Admirers of the more formal gardens…Brown's achievement.* Choice (D) is a contradiction. The passage states that Brown, instead of using geometrical forms, created *a free-flowing expanse, marked by…irregularly shaped bodies of water and seemingly random plantings* (lines 87–90).

26. J
Generalization

For a Generalization question such as this one, determine what information you need to take from the passage. Your prediction should involve referring to the passage to make sure you're clear about how a *French garden* is described. Your passage map notes direct you to paragraph 2, where the French garden is described as featuring *precision, regularity, and proportion* (lines 20–21). With this in mind, consider each answer choice and eliminate choices that don't match. Choice (F) is a contradiction because *precisely planted parallel lines* might easily have appeared in a French garden. Choice (G) is also a contradiction. *A circular maze design* features the geometry that is characteristic of a French garden. Choice (H) is a contradiction because the statues placed in the four corners of a square exemplify the geometrical form and symmetry found in a French garden. Choice (J) is the correct answer. The *random curve* and *large grassy area* do not fit in the highly stylized plan of a French garden as it's described in the passage.

27. D
Function

For Function questions, pay attention to context and think about the writer's purpose. Your passage map notes should tell you that the purpose of paragraph 5 is to discuss William Kent's work. The immediate context states that Rousham House is *one of the best examples of Kent's work* (line 71). This makes a great prediction and nicely fits with (D). Choice (A) is a misused detail. Blenheim Palace is not discussed in connection with Kent's work. Choice (B) is a distortion. While Rousham House is indeed described as an example of something, it is not presented as *an example of a famous estate*. Choice (C) is both a misused detail and a contradiction. French design principles have nothing to do with Rousham House, and the passage never says that French design principles were adapted to the English landscape.

28. G
Generalization

For a Generalization question that asks how a paragraph functions, use your passage map notes, and consider the passage as a whole. Predict that paragraph 2 discusses the French garden, with the garden at Versailles as an illustration, and that it's used to show the contrasts between the French style and the landscape style used in England. This prediction lines up nicely with (G). Choice (F) is a distortion. While paragraph 2 does describe the garden at Versailles, the description is brief, and this option says nothing about how the paragraph fits into the passage as a whole. Choice (H) is a contradiction. Nothing in paragraph 2 indicates criticism of the French garden style. Choice (J) is a distortion. It's true that *statuary* is mentioned in paragraph 2, but the author never argues that statues are essential to the style.

29. A
Function

For a Function question that asks about a detail, consider the context of the sentences surrounding it. The context states that Blenheim Palace is *among Brown's most famous work* (line 85). Predict that Blenheim Palace is used to illustrate Brown's work. This prediction matches (A). Choice (B) is a distortion. The passage does treat the development of garden styles, but the focus is on the French style that came *before* the landscape style Brown worked in. If the writer were suggesting that Brown's style is *transitional,* he would have to state what style followed it, and the passage doesn't do this. Choice (C) is a misused detail. It's true that the paragraph indicates some have criticized Brown for destroying examples of formal gardens, but the writer doesn't say that Brown destroyed a formal garden in carrying out his work at Blenheim, nor necessarily join those criticizing. Choice (D) combines the out-of-scope and extreme traps. The writer never even states, much less attempts to prove, that Oxfordshire has more landscape gardens than anyplace else. The phrasing *more… than any other* in this answer choice should alert you that it may be an extreme trap.

30. J
Generalization

For a Generalization question about the purpose of the whole passage, use your passage map notes to predict, and avoid tempting wrong answers that address only part of the passage. Here, your prediction should include something about the difference between the two styles of garden design discussed in the passage. Choice (J) is a great match. Choice (F) is out-of-scope. Its description *some of the most famous gardens of the 19th century* is too broad. Choice (G) is out-of-scope. *Palatial residences* are not mentioned as such and are not the focus of the passage. Choice (H) is a distortion. Though both garden types are discussed, the author focuses on their differences, not their similarities.

PASSAGE IV

SUGGESTED PASSAGE MAP

Paragraph 1: Problems facing oak populations

Paragraph 2: Importance of "old-growth" oaks

Paragraph 3: Research being done to learn about problems and solutions

Paragraph 4: Ecological restoration

Paragraph 5: Sudden oak death

Paragraph 6: Def. of ethnobotanical restoration

Paragraph 7: Importance of people in ethnobotanical restoration

ANSWER KEY

31. C	36. J
32. F	37. A
33. D	38. G
34. G	39. D
35. C	40. F

DETAILED EXPLANATIONS

31. C
Detail

For a Detail question that uses EXCEPT, go straight to the answer choices and check the passage for each one. Eliminate (A) because it's cited in lines 5–9. Eliminate (B) because *sudden oak death* is mentioned in line 6, and the *pathogen* that causes it is mentioned in lines 10–11. Eliminate (D) because it's mentioned in lines 15–17. Choice (C) is the correct answer because the passage says nothing about grazing deer.

32. F
Detail

When a Detail question asks you to describe a contrast, make sure you read enough to determine what

the passage says about both things contrasted. Here, review paragraph 6 to predict that ethnobotanical restoration is a new approach that involves introducing plants and practices that were used in the past and working on long-term maintenance (lines 98–102). Research in paragraph 4 to predict that ecological restoration is used in a limited time frame and refers only to introducing plants and animals that were historically present (lines 57–61). Choice (F) matches perfectly with the time frame the prediction points to. Choice (G) is a distortion because ecological restoration isn't described as involving *management practices*. Choice (H) is a contradiction because both types of restoration are described as being historically based. Choice (J) is a distortion. The descriptions of the two kinds of restoration are reversed in the wording of this answer choice.

33. D
Generalization

A Generalization question about an underlying assumption may be tough to make a prediction for. Still, try making a quick prediction that addresses the purpose of the passage, then check through the answer choices. In this case, your prediction might be something along the lines of *restoring the health of the oak populations is an important endeavor*. None of the answer choices matches this prediction exactly, but (D) comes close, and it is true that the writer values the practices of Native Americans. But be sure the other answers don't provide something closer to your prediction. Choice (A) is a misused detail. Damage done to oaks by small mammals is mentioned, but it is not described as being the primary cause of the oaks' decline. Choice (B) is a distortion; you should pay special attention to the word *sufficient* in this choice. While ethnobotanical restoration does include bringing in Native American practices, the passage describes ethnobotanical restoration as something that *complements other forms of ecological restoration* (lines 86–87). Choice (C) is a contradiction. Line 12 refers to fires set by Native Americans as protection for oaks by limiting the growth of other trees that competed with oaks. Choice (D) matches your prediction best, and is the right answer.

34. **G**
Detail

For a Detail question, use passage map notes to guide you to the right part of the passage. Paragraph 5 discusses sudden oak death. It states that a way to reduce the spread of sudden oak death is to limit the growth of shrubs that harbor the sudden oak death pathogen. Choice (G) matches this prediction. Choice (F) is a misused detail. Animals that destroy the root systems of oaks are described as a problem, but not as a cause of sudden oak death. Choice (H) combines the misused detail and out-of-scope traps. Sudden oak death is described as having an *exotic origin* (line 71), but there is nothing in the passage about regulating imports. Choice (J) combines the misused detail and out-of-scope traps. There is nothing in the passage suggesting that planting tan oaks and coastal oaks will strengthen the oak population in general.

35. **C**
Function

When a Function question asks about a phrase, consider the sentence it appears in and the sentences before or after, if necessary. Here, predict that the phrase *huge girth and large canopies* describes trees in *mature oak stands* (lines 25–26), which the passage states are home to more small animals (the *terrestrial vertebrates* in line 25) than younger trees are. This prediction fits with (C). Choice (A) is a misused detail. It's true that the phrase describes the appearance of the trees, but that doesn't address the author's purpose for describing this appearance. Choice (B) is out-of-scope. The passage never says that the trees are too large for a modern ecosystem. Choice (D) is a misused detail. Both *Native Americans* and *shade* are mentioned in the passage, but not in the context of the oaks' *huge girth and large canopies.*

36. **J**
Function

When a Function question asks about the purpose of a paragraph, keep in mind how its topic relates to the passage as a whole. Here, predict that paragraph 1 introduces the topic by discussing problems facing oak trees. Choice (J) is a great match for this prediction. Choice (F) is a misused detail. The animals that live in oaks are mentioned in paragraph 2, not paragraph 1. Choice (G) is a misused detail. This statement is true of the passage as a whole but doesn't relate to the first paragraph. Choice (H) is a distortion. The passage mentions both fires and sudden oak death but doesn't compare their effects.

37. **A**
Generalization

For a broad Generalization question, keep the entire passage in mind. Predict that the passage concerns problems facing oaks and proposed solutions. Choice (A) goes a little beyond this prediction but is consistent with the passage because solutions to the problems involve human intervention. Choice (B) is a contradiction. Lines 90–92 discuss *restoring indigenous…cultivation practices* as though it's reasonable to expect that such things can be accomplished. Choice (C) is an extreme. Though the passage mentions the pathogen and *pests* (line 55), it doesn't say that dealing with them is the *best* way to start the restoration process. Choice (D) is a distortion. The fires that are mentioned in the passage (e.g., line 12) are described as protecting the oak population, not damaging it. Choice (A) is the correct answer.

38. **G**
Function

For a Function question about a particular detail, focus on the immediate context to make your prediction. Here, pay attention to the first part of the sentence: now *oaks are being toppled by trees that have a higher tolerance for shade* (lines 15–16). Predict that the shade-tolerant trees are overpowering the oaks. This prediction works well with (G). Choice (F) is an opposite: because shade-tolerant trees are *toppling* the oaks, it would not be good to plant them near the oaks. Choice (H) is a distortion. The passage mentions *old-growth oaks* but doesn't describe them as being at all shade-tolerant. Choice (J) is a distortion. The passage mentions *Native Americans* but doesn't say that they planted the highly shade-tolerant trees.

39. D

Generalization

For a Generalization question about a paragraph, use your passage map notes to keep the purpose of the paragraph in mind. Here, predict that the best answer will have something to do with finding ways to improve the declining strength of the oak population. Choice (D) fits perfectly with this prediction. Choice (A) is a misused detail. Redwood National Park is mentioned in the paragraph, but nothing in the paragraph suggests that oaks there are in worse shape than they are elsewhere. Choice (B) is a contradiction. The paragraph states that native grasses can *facilitate better germination of oak seedlings.* Choice (C) is a misused detail.

Although sudden oak death is mentioned in the passage, nothing is said about it in paragraph 3. (This answer choice also uses the extreme language *primary cause,* which should put you on alert.)

40. F

Detail

If your passage map notes do not direct you to a particular place in the passage to answer a Detail question, skim the passage quickly for a phrase from the question stem or another phrase that means something similar. Here, the exact phrase *light surface fires* appears in line 12. Read the sentence and predict that *they,* here referring to the oaks, *were able to maintain a stronghold* (line 13) because the fires kept in check plants that competed with the oaks, which matches (F) perfectly. Choice (G) is a distortion. The passage does mention acorns, but not in connection with fires. Choice (H) is out-of-scope. The passage does not say anything about scars forming on the bark of oak trees. Choice (J) is a distortion. *Jays* are mentioned in the passage, but not in relation to fires.

SUMMARY

Time to review!

Use this space to record how many questions you answered correctly.

Now, record how many you answered incorrectly.

Remember: Master the Kaplan Method for ACT Reading as well as overall strategies for the Reading Test like passage mapping and predicting. Refer to Reading Part 1 for more tips on those. If you're short on time before Test Day, spend your time with Part 1.

Now, get specific.

Use the chart below to record how many questions you answered correctly and incorrectly in each Reading SmartPoint category.

Point Value	Topic	# Correct	# Incorrect
12	Detail Questions		
8	Inference Questions		
1	Writer's View Questions		
8	Generalization Questions		
6	Function Questions		
1	Vocab-in-Context Questions		

Use the chart to review the specific areas in which you can gain the most points on Test Day. Remember to spend more time on the categories with higher SmartPoint values.

Keep reviewing Reading Parts 1 and 2 for specific SmartPoints. Then, keep practicing using the Practice Tests toward the end of this book.

By regularly reviewing and practicing, you'll become an ACT Reading all-star!

UNIT 4: SCIENCE

The Basics:

35 Minutes

40 Questions

6 Passages

Pacing:

Pace your time per passage as opposed to per question.

Spend roughly five to six minutes on each passage, going through the text, charts, and graphs and answering the questions.

TEST DAY DIRECTIONS AND FORMAT

Here's what the Science directions will say on Test Day:

> **Directions:** There are six passages in this test. Each passage is followed by several questions. After reading a passage, choose the best answer to each question and fill in the corresponding oval on your answer document. You may refer to the passages as often as necessary. You are NOT permitted to use a calculator on this test.

OUTSIDE KNOWLEDGE

You don't need to be a scientist to ace this section of the ACT, which primarily tests your ability to read and understand, not call on background knowledge. It helps to have a basic understanding of scientific terms and concepts, but you won't have to rely on any outside knowledge to answer the questions. Just like Reading, the answers are always in the passage.

THE INSIDE SCOOP

The purpose of the Science test is to test your scientific reasoning skills, as opposed to your ability to remember information from your high school science classes.

The six passages are drawn from four basic areas of science—biology, chemistry, earth and space sciences, and physics. Expect one to two passages on each subject, but again, you're not expected to bring outside knowledge of these areas of science to the test.

You'll see three types of passages:

1. *Data representations* will simply show you data, occasionally with a brief passage beforehand to introduce the charts and graphs. No experiments or theories are involved. Expect two passages with six to seven questions each.

2. *Research summary* passages will describe experiments and show you charts and graphs of the results. You'll need to interpret the data and understand the scientific method employed. Expect three passages with six to seven questions each.

3. *Conflicting viewpoints* will describe a phenomenon, then two or more scientists will offer opinions on the cause of that phenomenon. You'll need to understand the conflicting opinions and the evidence associated with each. Expect one passage with seven questions.

The questions *do not* get harder as you proceed through the Science test.

SMARTPOINTS

Point Value	Topic	Basics Page	Details and Practice
13	**Scientific Reasoning**		
12	**Figure Interpretation**		
11	**Patterns**		

CHAPTER 13

Science Part 1: Inside the ACT Science Test

THE KAPLAN METHOD FOR ACT SCIENCE

On the Science test, the Kaplan Method varies depending on the passage type. Below is the basic method for all sections, but refer to the Method Breakdown on page 400 later in this chapter for an in-depth discussion of how to apply and alter these strategies to the various passage types.

STEP 1: MAP THE PASSAGE, IDENTIFYING AND MARKING THE PURPOSE, METHOD, AND RESULTS OF THE EXPERIMENT

Get an overview of the text, searching for the Purpose, Method, and Results. Don't get bogged down in the details; you can give everything else a quick read and come back later if the question requires it. Simply find the Purpose and Method within the text, take a moment to understand each, then get an overview of the Results.

Underline the Purpose. The Purpose is the "why" of the experiment. What were the researchers trying to learn, to do, to prove? Look for the infinitive form of the verb in the first paragraph to help you find this quickly. Examples: The Scientists are trying…"to determine," "to calculate," "to discover"…etc.

Bracket the Method. This is the "how" of the experiment. What did the researchers actually *do*? This is separate from the Purpose—for example, they didn't "try to learn ___," they "heated the mixture," etc. It usually involves changing one variable while keeping the others constant and describes how they are setting up their processes to answer the question outlined in the Purpose. For the first experiment, look for what you could see them doing. The Method won't be thinking or calculating; it will involve physically putting things in place. For any experiments past the first, focus on what is changing. What's different each time?

Star the Results. These are usually listed in charts and graphs, but may be in paragraph form. A high percentage of the questions on the ACT Science test will come from analyzing the data. Thus, move quickly through the text, understanding the Purpose and Method, so you can spend a little time analyzing the Results in Step 2.

STEP 2: SCAN FIGURES, IDENTIFYING VARIABLES AND PATTERNS

Here's where you can analyze the data. This shouldn't be a long process, but by giving each chart and graph an overview as you go, focusing on a few key things, you'll be better prepared to find answers quickly once you get to the questions.

Scan figures: This is the overview step. Get a sense of what is being represented by looking at the labels of charts, the axes of graphs, and the variables and how they change.

Identify variables: Now, dive into the variables. How do they relate to the experiment? Look specifically for independent variables and dependent variables. Which are the scientists changing themselves (independent), and how does that affect the one(s) they are observing (dependent)? If scientists wanted to see whether temperature affected how fast a student could read, the temperature would be the independent variable, and the speed of the student would be the dependent. Note: On a coordinate graph, the independent variable will often appear on the *x*-axis; the dependent will appear on the *y*.

Patterns: Finally, get a sense for how the different parts of the graph vary in relation to each other. Specifically, look at the independent and dependent variables (or other important variables) and determine if they vary directly or inversely. (Direct variation is where they both increase or decrease together. Inverse variation is where as one increases, the other decreases.)

STEP 3: FIND SUPPORT FOR THE ANSWER IN THE PASSAGE

Always refer back to the passage before looking at the choices and selecting one. Make sure you read charts and graphs accurately and that you do not confuse different kinds of units. It helps to answer the question in your own words. Form a prediction of what you think the answer will be. Don't rely too much on your knowledge of science. Match your answer with one of the choices.

QUICK TIPS

MIND-SET

- **Look for patterns.** Usually, the exact data contained in Science passages is not as important as the *changes* in the data are. Look for extremes (maximums and minimums), critical points (points of change), and variation (direct and inverse).

- **Know your direction.** There are two kinds of scientific reasoning—general-to-specific and specific-to-general. *Always* be aware of when scientists are inferring a specific case from a general rule and when they are using specific data to form a (general) hypothesis.

- **Refer, don't remember.** Don't even think of trying to remember data. As with the Reading test, there is always more data than could possibly be asked about. The data is **always** there, right on the page, for you to refer to when needed.

SPECIAL STRATEGIES

READING TABLES AND GRAPHS

When reading tables and graphs, you should ask yourself:

- What does the figure show?

- What are the units of measurement?

- What is the pattern in the data?

EXPERIMENTS

Remember how experiments work. There is typically (though not always) a control group (a group in which the results are known and not changing) plus an experimental group or groups. In a well-designed experiment, the only difference between the groups will be a variation in the factor that's being tested. Ask yourself:

- What's the factor that's being varied intentionally (the independent variable)?

- What's the factor that changes as a result (the dependent variable)?

- What's the control group, if any?

- What do the results show? What differences exist between the results for one group and those for another?

CONFLICTING VIEWPOINTS PASSAGE

Spend a little more time than usual on the pre-reading step of the Conflicting Viewpoints passage. Focus on the two points of view—what are the scientists arguing about? What do they agree on, if anything? What do they differ on? Identify the following for each scientist:

- **Basic theory statement** (usually the first sentence of Scientist 1, and in the middle for Scientist 2)

- **Major pieces of data behind the theory** (keeping in mind whether each supports the scientist's own theory or weakens the opposing scientist's theory)

  Visit your online syllabus—Lesson 8—for more instruction and practice with the Kaplan Method for ACT Science.

TIMING: PACING AND APPROACH

Some Science passages are a lot harder than others, and they're not arranged in order of difficulty, so you might want to **take a few seconds at the beginning of the subject test to page through the passages, gauging the difficulty of each one.** You may wish to skip an entire passage if it seems very difficult (but remember that a very difficult passage may have very easy questions).

As in Reading, treat each passage and its questions as a block. Get the easy questions on the first pass through and save the tougher ones for the second pass. For any questions that look like they will take far too long to answer, take an educated guess.

Set your watch to 12:00 at the beginning of the subject test. Although you should go faster if you can, here's where you should be at the following checkpoints:

12:05 . . . . . One passage finished and answers gridded in

12:10 . . . . . Two passages finished and answers gridded in

12:15 . . . . . Three passages finished and answers gridded in

12:20 . . . . . Four passages finished and answers gridded in

12:25 . . . . . Five passages finished and answers gridded in

12:30 . . . . . Six passages finished and answers gridded in

Don't spend time agonizing over specific questions. Avoid thinking long and hard about the answer choices. If you've spent a minute or so on a question and don't seem to be making any headway, make your best guess and move on.

Don't panic if you can't finish all six passages, but try to do a good job on at least five of them. Make sure you remember to grid answers (even if they're blind guesses) for all questions by the end of the test.

WHEN YOU'RE RUNNING OUT OF TIME

If you have less than three minutes left for the last passage, do the following:

4. **Look for questions that refer to specific experiments or to specific graphs or tables.**

5. **Refer to the cited location in the passage and answer the question as best you can, based on what you see there.**

6. **Make sure you have gridded in an answer for every question before time is called.**

SCORING

Your performance on the Science subject test will be averaged into your ACT Composite score, weighted equally with your scores on the other three major subject tests. You will also receive:

- A Science subject score—from 1 to 36—for the entire Science subject test

Unlike the other three subject scores, the Science score is not divided into subscores.

SMARTPOINT BREAKDOWN

Here is a brief overview of what exactly to expect and how much of it you should be expecting.

SCIENTIFIC REASONING—13 POINTS

Extremely Important

Scientific Reasoning questions ask you to think like a scientist. These are the conclusion- and inference-based questions on the ACT Science test. This SmartPoint is the reason you need to gather information from the passages and can't just skip to the charts and graphs. This is also the primary question type of the Conflicting Viewpoints passage. These questions task you with understanding the way experiments are designed and what they prove. You might even have to take the next step and figure out what the scientists should do next. They might also ask you to either logically apply a principle or identify ways of defending or attacking a principle. For a discussion of the different questions that fit into this category, and strategies for dealing with each, turn to page 438.

FIGURE INTERPRETATION—12 POINTS

Extremely Important

Figure Interpretation questions task you with locating data. These are data-based questions on which you don't need to draw a conclusion. Simply examine the charts and graphs carefully, and you'll find the answer you need. On the more difficult Figure Interpretation questions, the data necessary to answer the question can be hidden within complex charts and graphs. Still, with a diligent search, you'll be able to find the answer. For a strategy discussion of this question type, and how to efficiently search for your answer in both simple and complex figures, turn to page 418.

PATTERNS—11 POINTS

Extremely Important

Patterns questions ask you to interpret trends in data. These are data-based questions on which you'll need to draw conclusions or make inferences. Most commonly, you'll need to describe the relationships between variables. Do they vary directly or inversely? You may need to find this pattern within a chart or graph containing a multitude of data. More difficult questions will ask you to describe what would happen to new data points, or determine how a new variable would behave. Just like in Reading, the answer to any questions that involve an inference will be a small step from the data you can see and will follow the pattern established. Always assume the patterns you can see won't change drastically. Refer to page 427 for strategies to isolate variables and find patterns even amidst complex data, and how to use existing data to find what would happen next.

METHOD BREAKDOWN

Because the passage types on Science are so different from each other, both in terms of how they are structured and what information you'll need to know to answer the questions, the method for Science is the most fluid of all Kaplan Methods.

With every other Kaplan Method, you should use one set of practices to efficiently work through the entire section. With the Kaplan Method for ACT Science, you'll gain efficiency by varying your approach to each passage type.

We'll use this section to take a closer look at the different passages and how you can approach each to effectively answer their typical questions.

RESEARCH SUMMARY

Three passages. Six to seven questions each.

Use the standard method, discussed earlier in this chapter (page 395).

This is the only passage type on which both the information in the text and the information in the data are likely to be equally important. All three of the SmartPoints can be tested here.

Step 1: The passage starts with text giving explanatory background and describing the overall process. The **Purpose** can usually be found at the end of this first paragraph. Underline it when you find it. Remember to look for the infinitive form of the verb to find it quickly (to determine, to calculate, to discover, to study).

Then, you'll usually have a paragraph dedicated to each of the different experiments the scientists perform to achieve their purpose. In the first such paragraph, look for the **Method** and bracket it. Here, focus on the steps of the process you could see the scientists do. In the paragraphs describing each subsequent method or experiment, focus on what's changing. What are they doing differently this time?

With Research Summaries, perform a quick read of the text. You don't need to be thorough. Find the Purpose and Method, take an extra moment to be sure you understand those two aspects of the process, and move on. Refer to the surrounding text as you need to in order to help you understand the Purpose and Method, and you'll be ready for any Scientific Reasoning questions with this passage.

Step 2: After the text, the passage will usually contain charts and graphs relaying the results. Go through the usual process of Step 2 of the Kaplan Method with these charts and graphs to prepare yourself for any Figure Interpretation or Pattern questions.

Scan the figures to give yourself a sense of the results. Were the scientists aiming for something in particular in their purpose? Did they achieve it?

Identify the independent and dependent variables. What variable were they changing themselves? What variable changed as a result? When in doubt, the independent variable will be on the *x*-axis and the dependent variable will be on the *y*-axis.

Finally, look for patterns, especially between the independent and dependent variables, but if there are other variables present, get a quick sense for how those vary as well.

Step 3: Support your answer. Predict for any questions that involve conclusions. Don't rely on your memory! You can expect all three question types here, so be ready to find data, interpret patterns, and draw conclusions based on the process of the scientists.

DATA REPRESENTATION

Two passages. Six to seven questions each.

Skip straight to Step 2 of the Kaplan Method discussed earlier in this chapter on page 396.

Only the information in the data is important in these passages. If there is text, it will simply be a description of the data on display in the charts and graphs.

The two tested SmartPoints are Figure Interpretation and Patterns. Scientific Reasoning does not appear in this passage type.

Skim the text, if there is any, to simply get a sense of the data to come. Remember, if it does throw in a question regarding a detail from the text, you can always go back and look.

But your time is better spent looking over the data on this particular passage type.

Suppose you saw the following graph in a Science passage:

Scan the figure and ask, "What does this figure show? What are the units of measurement?" Well, the graph shows air temperature at various altitudes at Test Site #3—the title tells us that. The temperature is measured in °C (degrees Celsius) on the *y*-axis. We can assume the km above sea level is the independent variable, and the air temperature is dependent; when we look for patterns, we notice they vary inversely. As km above sea level increases, air temperature decreases.

Then you'll just move on! You don't need to focus on what the specifics are until a *question* asks you. Until it's going to earn you points, it just doesn't matter!

However, there are going to be questions like "What is the temperature at 2 km above sea level?" To answer, find 2 km on the *x*-axis. Draw a line straight up until you intersect the line. Then draw a straight line from this point to the *y*-axis. Use your pencil—the graphs are often pretty small, and eyeballing won't always give you an accurate enough estimate. Here, you can see that the temperature at 2 km is about 5°.

Data will also appear in the form of tables. Suppose you come across this in a passage:

Concentration of *E. Coli* in Cooling Pool B	
DISTANCE FROM EFFLUENT PIPE 3	**1,000S OF E. COLI PER CENTILITER**
0 m	0.4
5 m	5.6
10 m	27.6
15 m	14.0
20 m	7.5

Again, you'll scan to identify what the figure shows and the units of measurement (percent doesn't have units, time is in seconds). This time, don't linger on independent and dependent variables. It's not as important when there isn't an experiment. Do a quick check for patterns. You'll notice the distance increases constantly, but concentration goes up, and then down; there isn't a regular pattern. And that's okay! Sometimes, the variables won't have a clear relationship. Get a sense for how each one changes throughout, and move on. More specific analysis can wait until it'll earn you points.

For your reference, the fact that distance is listed on the left, and has consistent intervals of 5, means it is likely the independent variable, and concentration would be the dependent. Just consider how an experiment would be done—you're much more able to take concentration measurements every 5 meters than to measure distances according to *E. coli* concentration.

The questions on this table might ask "Five meters from Effluent Pipe 3, how many thousands of *E. coli* are found per centiliter of water?" To answer, find 5 in the "Distance" column (the row of boxes on the far left, running down). Follow the 5 m row over to the "1,000s of *E. Coli*" column. The value in that box is 5.6. There are 5.6 thousands per centiliter.

You might also be asked to identify trends in the data in a table. You'll be ready, since you've already noticed how the *E. coli* values change as you go down the distance column. They go up from 0.4 to 27.6, and then they start to go down.

These skills form the basics of graph and table reading. More complex questions will build from these fundamental skills, and we'll discuss them in detail under the corresponding SmartPoints in the next chapter.

CONFLICTING VIEWPOINTS

One passage. Seven questions each.

Employ a different method for this unique Science passage:

The Kaplan Method for Conflicting Viewpoints Passages

1. **Read the introductory text and the first author's viewpoint,** then answer the questions that ask *only about the first author's viewpoint.*

2. **Read the second author's viewpoint,** then answer questions that ask *only about the second author's viewpoint.*

3. **Answer the questions that refer to both authors' viewpoints.**[*]

Focus on the opinions of each scientist as you read, and <u>underline the opinions</u> when you find them. The opinion of the first scientist will often be in the first or second sentence. The opinion of the second scientist will often be in the middle of the paragraph. The second scientist will often start by refuting the first, then transition to his or her unique opinion. With more than two scientists, look in the first or second sentence for each.

This passage has a heavy focus on Scientific Reasoning questions. It's the only passage you'll want to take the time to read carefully.

Notice, though, that you'll take the unique approach of only reading one scientist at a time, then answering the questions that relate to him or her, as opposed to just reading straight through as you're used to. This approach keeps each scientist's points fresh in your mind and keeps you from confusing their viewpoints. Practice this intermittent approach plenty, so it becomes a habit for this passage type by Test Day.

Structure: Each Conflicting Viewpoints passage is structured in generally the same way. There is an opening paragraph (or two) that explains some background information about a particular phenomenon. Generally, the opening paragraph is a statement of fact. It often supplies you with a few definitions of key terms.

Next, a scientist will offer one opinion on or possible explanation for the phenomenon. A second scientist will then offer a different opinion on or explanation for the phenomenon. Sometimes, a third or fourth scientist weighs in.

Each scientist will offer different evidence to support his or her viewpoint. Usually, these viewpoints will contradict each other. That's okay. Your job isn't to decide who is right and who is wrong, but to recognize each viewpoint and understand how each scientist uses evidence to support a viewpoint.

Questions: The questions following a Conflicting Viewpoints passage test your ability to follow a scientist's line of reasoning. They might ask you why a scientist included a particular detail in his or her argument or to apply a line of reasoning to a different situation. They might ask you to predict, based on what's written, what a scientist might think about a related topic.

Questions might also introduce new information and ask whether the new information weakens or strengthens one or both of the arguments. They might ask you to identify points of agreement between the two scientists (Hint: Look for answer choices drawn from the opening text). Conversely, a question might ask you to identify a point of disagreement.

Finally, some questions will test your reading comprehension, with phrasing like, "According to the passage, polypeptide molecules are…" or "The passage indicates that…" These questions are similar to those on the Reading test, and you'll handle them just as you would a Reading question: by going back to the passage to find your answer.

The most important thing to remember as you're taking the ACT Science test is that *answering questions*, not reading the passage, earns you points. Even though you should carefully read the Conflicting Viewpoints passage, it's still important to avoid getting caught up in the complex details.

Always spend your time on the questions on every type of Science passage. That's where the payoff is.

WARM-UP

Now you know what to expect on the ACT Science test. You know the three passage types you'll see and what those passages will look like. You also know the Kaplan Method and how it changes for each passage type. You know the three big categories of question types and how they fit into the passage types, so you can be ready to view the different ways the ACT Science test will throw information at you. Then you can process that information quickly, know what to look for, and get to the questions to start earning points. You know the basics. Now it's time to work on one of each passage type and practice applying those strategies.

But take a deep breath. This one is a warm-up. Complete the following passages as well as you can. Refer back to the Method Breakdown as often as you need to in order to make your process efficient from the get-go. Make sure you're approaching each passage with the unique mind-set detailed in that section. Get the information you need, specific to that passage type, and get to the questions.

The answers and explanations follow the passages and reveal which SmartPoint category each question was under. Use your results from this Warm-Up and the SmartPoints to prioritize your approach to the next chapter.

In the next chapter, we'll dive into each SmartPoint. We'll talk through the strategies for simple and complex versions of each question type and give you a chance to practice on samples. Know what to expect, and take away the intimidation factor of the Science test.

Good luck!

PASSAGE I

Data Representation

As the prevalence of wild wetland decreases with human population growth and urban sprawl, efforts have begun to create new wildlife habitats. In particular, scientists have studied the feasibility of conserving amphibian species by creating artificial ponds. Several studies have documented the natural process of *colonization* of artificial ponds with microorganisms (spirogyra and protozoans), aquatic plant life (*Nymphaea odorata* and *Eleocharis acisularis*), and both amphibian larvae and grown amphibians (*Hyla regilla*, *Rama sylvatica*, and *Ambystoma macrodactylum*) over time (see Figure 1).

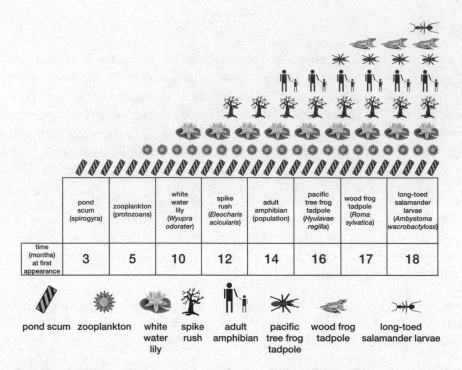

	pond scum (spirogyra)	zooplankton (protozoans)	white water lily (*Wyupra odorater*)	spike rush (*Eleocharis acicularis*)	adult amphibian (population)	pacific tree frog tadpole (*Hyulavae regilla*)	wood frog tadpole (*Roma sylvatica*)	long-toed salamander larvae (*Ambystoma wacrobactyloss*)
time (months) at first appearance	3	5	10	12	14	16	17	18

pond scum   zooplankton   white water lily   spike rush   adult amphibian   pacific tree frog tadpole   wood frog tadpole   long-toed salamander larvae

Figure 1 (Note: Species are organized according to their appearance over time.)

As colonization progresses, amphibian larvae gradually displace vegetative cover. The larvae populations were estimated by trapping and counting the number of larvae in 1 m^3 of pond water at the edge of the pond and multiplying this number by the circumference of the pond in meters. Percent vegetative cover was estimated using aerial photography to determine the fraction of pond surface area obscured by aquatic plant life. Figure 2 shows the change over time of percent vegetative cover with the presence of tadpoles and larvae in one pond.

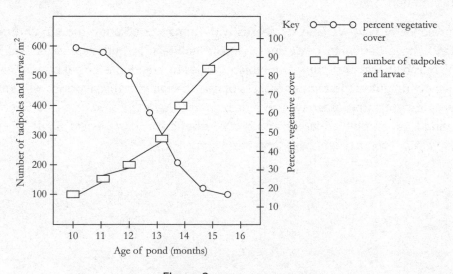

Figure 2

Scientists also wished to determine how the final abundance of adult amphibian species correlated with several key physical characteristics of the artificial ponds. Their findings are summarized in Figure 3.

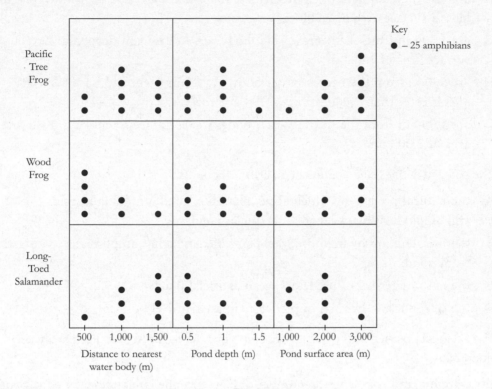

Figure 3

1. According to Figure 1, how would the colonization of an artificial pond best be characterized at 14 months?

   A. The pond would contain a mixture of algae, aquatic plants, and amphibian larvae.

   B. The pond would contain a mixture of aquatic plants and adult amphibians.

   C. The pond would contain a mixture of algae, aquatic plants, and adult amphibians.

   D. The pond would contain a mixture of algae, amphibian larvae, and adult amphibians.

2. Given the information in Figure 3, long-toed salamanders can be found in the greatest numbers in artificial ponds that:

   F. are less than 1,000 m from the nearest water body, are at least 1 m deep, and have a surface area of 2,000 m² or greater.

   G. are 1,500 m from the nearest water body, are at least 1 m deep, and have a surface area of 1,000 m².

   H. are 500 m from the nearest water body, are 1.5 m deep, and have a surface area greater than 2,000 m².

   J. are 1,500 m from the nearest water body, are 0.5 m deep, and have a surface area of 2,000 m².

3. The passage defines *colonization* of an artificial pond as:

   A. the natural process by which algae, plant life, adult amphibians, and amphibian larvae appear in an artificial pond.

   B. the introduction by man of algae, plant life, and adult amphibians to an artificial pond.

   C. the natural arrival of predators to an artificial pond.

   D. the introduction by man of predators to an artificial pond.

4. The scientists estimated the number of amphibian larvae present in each artificial pond by:

   F. trapping and counting the number of larvae in one cubic meter of edge pond water, then multiplying by the surface area of the pond in meters squared.

   G. trapping and counting the number of larvae in one cubic meter of edge pond water, then multiplying by the circumference of the pond in meters.

   H. trapping and counting the number of larvae in one cubic meter of central pond water, then multiplying by the circumference of the pond in meters.

   J. trapping and counting the number of larvae in one cubic meter of central pond water, then multiplying by the surface area of the pond in meters squared.

PASSAGE II

Research Summary

Friction is the force acting between two surfaces in contact with each other. Students wished to determine the amount of force required to overcome the force of friction between two unmoving objects. To conduct their experiment, they rested a block of wood on top of a larger wooden plane. Next, they set a weight atop the wooden block. Then, a tangential force was applied to the wooden block and measured with a spring scale, as diagrammed in Figure 1. The tangential force required to cause the wooden block to begin sliding across the plane was recorded.

Figure 1 (Note: Assume the mass of the spring scale is insignificant.)

EXPERIMENT 1

Students placed a wooden block with a surface area of 100 cm² in the apparatus depicted in Figure 1. A tangential force was applied, and the force at which the block began to slip was recorded in newtons (N). The experiment was repeated using weights of differing masses atop the wooden block. The forces required to cause the wooden block to slip were recorded in Table 1.

Table 1

Mass of Weight (kg)	Tangential Force (N)
0.5	6.1
1.0	12.3
1.5	18.8
2.0	24.5
2.5	30.6

EXPERIMENT 2

Experiment 1 was repeated using a wooden block of the same mass as in Experiment 1, but a surface area of 200 cm². The mass of the weight atop the block was varied as in Experiment 1, and the tangential forces required to cause the block to slip were recorded in Table 2.

Table 2

Mass of Weight (kg)	Tangential Force (N)
0.5	6.1
1.0	12.3
1.5	18.8
2.0	24.5
2.5	30.6

EXPERIMENT 3

In this experiment, the coefficient of friction between the wooden block and the plane was lowered by the application of grease to the plane. The procedures from Experiment 1 were repeated using the wooden block and weights from Experiment 1.

Table 3

Mass of Weight (kg)	Tangential Force (N)
0.5	3.6
1.0	6.2
1.5	9.4
2.0	12.3
2.5	15.3

5. Which of the following statements best explains why the students varied the mass of the weight atop the wooden block in Experiment 1? The students wanted to:

   A. measure the amount of downward force between the wooden block and the plane.

   B. vary the amount of tangential force on the wooden block.

   C. study how different materials affect friction.

   D. vary downward force between the wooden block and the plane.

6. Which of the following factors was NOT directly controlled by the students in Experiment 3?

   F. The tangential force required to move the wooden block

   G. The mass of the weight atop the wooden block

   H. The coefficient of friction between the wooden block and the plane

   J. The surface area of the side of the wooden block in contact with the plane

7. Several students were asked to push a box to the other end of their classroom. Based on the results of the experiments, how could the students minimize the amount of force necessary to push the box? The students could:

   A. rotate the box so that the side with the smallest area is in contact with the ground.

   B. decrease the coefficient of friction between the box and the floor by painting the bottom of the box with grease.

   C. pull the box instead of pushing the box.

   D. increase the mass of the box by adding weights.

8. If Experiment 2 is continued using a 3 kg mass atop the wooden block, the tangential force required for the block to slip will be approximately:

F. 18.5 N.

G. 24.5 N.

H. 30.6 N.

J. 36.8 N.

PASSAGE III

Conflicting Viewpoints

Acids are chemical compounds that are today most fundamentally defined as having a pH less than 7.0—that is, a hydrogen ion activity greater than pure water—when dissolved in water and which are capable of donating a proton. Bases are chemical compounds with a pH higher than 7.0 and are commonly understood as compounds that can accept protons. Before chemists developed the modern model of acid and base behavior, there were many attempts to explain their observable qualities; especially the observable qualities of acids (sour taste, an ability to turn blue vegetable dye red, an ability to conduct an electric current, and, most notably, an ability to react with certain compounds and give off hydrogen or carbon dioxide gas). Two historical definitions of acids follow.

LAVOISIER DEFINITION

Lavoisier believed that all acids showed the same observable properties because they contained one common substance. Because he primarily knew of strong acids such as HNO_3 and H_2SO_4, he believed that this common substance was oxygen (O). He believed that a metal, reacting with an acid, would combine with the oxygen in the acid to produce a *calx* (a metal oxide). The calx would then further react with the acid to form a salt. Hydrogen, the other component of water, was released as a gas. The reaction could also run in reverse. Water, combined with a salt and calx, would produce an acid. Oxygen, according to Lavoisier, was the driving force behind the reaction. In fact, Lavoisier himself actually recognized and named the element oxygen, deriving the word from the Greek for "acid-producer."

Lavoisier further believed that the other portions of the acidic compound were responsible for the acid's specific individual properties and called this other portion the "acidifiable base." He had no further understanding of bases.

LIEBIG DEFINITION

Liebig primarily studied organic acids such as CH_3CO_2H (acetic acid) and $C_3H_6O_3$ (lactic acid). According to the Liebig definition, it was not oxygen but rather hydrogen (H) that was responsible for the common properties of an acid. However, not all compounds containing hydrogen could be considered acidic; Liebig defined an acid as a hydrogen-containing compound in which the hydrogen could be replaced by a metal. The hydrogen would then be released as a gas. Liebig recognized a base as a substance capable of *neutralizing* an acid (neutralization is the process by which an acid is transformed into a salt and water and no longer displays the common characteristics of an acid), but had no theoretical understanding of how and why bases worked.

9. Which of the following assumptions was made by Lavoisier?

   A. All acids combine with oxygen as they react.

   B. Acids cannot be broken down into other compounds.

   C. All acids contain oxygen.

   D. Any compound that contains oxygen is an acid.

10. Suppose an acid is allowed to react completely with a metal. Which of the following statements about acids is most consistent with the information presented in the passage?

   F. If the Lavoisier definition is correct, the oxygen in the acid will have donated a proton in the reaction.

   G. If the Lavoisier definition is correct, the hydrogen in the acid will have accepted a proton in the reaction.

   H. If the Liebig definition is correct, the oxygen in the acid will have donated a proton in the reaction.

   J. If the Liebig definition is correct, the hydrogen in the acid will have accepted a proton in the reaction.

11. The Liebig definition states that the hydrogen in an acid is capable of being replaced by metal. Which of the following findings, if true, could be used to *counter* this definition?

   A. Acids, when reacted, release pure hydrogen gas.

   B. Acids, when neutralized, form solutions with a pH equal to that of pure water.

   C. In the reaction of sulfuric acid (H_2SO_4) with sodium hydroxide (NaOH), sodium sulfate (Na_2SO_4) and water are formed.

   D. Some acids, when completely reacted, form pure minerals in water.

12. Adherents of which definition, if either, would predict that hydrochloric acid (HCl) has a pH of less than 7?

   F. The Lavoisier definition only

   G. The Liebig definition only

   H. Both the Lavoisier definition and the Liebig definition

   J. Neither the Lavoisier definition nor the Liebig definition

ANSWERS AND EXPLANATIONS

PASSAGE I

1. **C**

2. **J**

3. **A**

4. **G**

1. C

Here's one example of a question asking us to find one or more pieces of data in a simple data presentation. Fortunately, the question stem makes our job easy and tells us right where we need to go to find our answer: Figure 1. When we look back at Figure 1, we can see that algae (pond scum and zooplankton) appear between 3 and 5 months, aquatic plants (white water lily and spike rush) show up after 10 to 12 months, and an adult amphibian population is present at 14 months. That fits (C).

We can see that (A) and (D) are incorrect because they state that amphibian larvae are present in the pond at 14 months. Figure 1 shows that the first amphibian larvae (Pacific tree frog tadpoles) don't appear until 16 months. Choice (B) doesn't include algae, so it is likewise incorrect.

2. J

This question asks us to put together two or more pieces of data from a simple data presentation. We're directed to Figure 3 and asked to figure out which artificial ponds have the most long-toed salamanders. The key beside Figure 3 explains that each dot represents 25 amphibians.

Long-toed salamanders are represented by the bottom row in Figure 3. There are 25 in ponds that are 500 m from the nearest water body, 75 in ponds 1,000 m from the nearest water body, and 100 in ponds that are 1,500 m from the nearest water body. Similarly, the maximum number of long-toed

salamanders is found in ponds that are 0.5 m deep and have a surface area of 2,000 m². This fits (J).

3. A

This question is testing our ability to find the definition of a term used in the written part of the passage. The term *colonization* first appears in the first paragraph. It says, "Several studies have documented the natural process of *colonization* of artificial ponds with microorganisms (spirogyra and protozoans), aquatic plant life (*Nymphaea odorata* and *Eleocharis acisularis*), and both amphibian larvae and grown amphibians (*Hyla regilla*, *Rama sylvatica*, and *Ambystoma macrodactylum*) over time…" We can infer from this sentence that the process of colonization refers to the natural process by which plants and animals come to inhabit a pond. This best matches (A).

We could also approach this question by examining the answer choices. Choice (B) is incorrect because it states that colonization is the "introduction by man" of plants and animals into the pond, which contradicts the information in paragraph 1. Choice (C) mentions predators, which aren't mentioned anywhere in the passage, and (D) mentions both introduction by man and predators, neither of which is supported by the passage. That leaves us with just (A).

4. G

This question is testing our ability to understand the scientists' methods. Numbers of amphibian larvae are shown on the left-hand axis of Figure 2, so we should start by reading the paragraph just before Figure 2. It states, "The larvae populations were estimated by trapping and counting the larvae in 1 m³ of pond water at the edge of the pond and multiplying this number by the circumference of the pond in meters." This is correctly restated in (G).

Notice that only subtle changes make the other choices incorrect. Choice (F) substitutes surface area for circumference, (H) substitutes central pond water for edge water, and (J) makes both substitutions.

PASSAGE II

5. **D**

6. **F**

7. **B**

8. **J**

5. **D**

This question tests our understanding of the experimental design. What was the point of putting weights on top of the wooden block? The students wanted to be able to increase the downward force of the wooden block without changing the wooden block itself. By placing different masses on top of the same wooden block, they could increase or decrease the downward force between the wooden block and the plane. Choice (D) is correct. Choice (A) is tempting because it uses much of the same language, but they're not trying to *measure* the amount of downward force—they know what that is (the mass of the weight)—they're trying to *vary* it. Choice (B) is a distortion. They're not trying to *vary* the amount of tangential force, they're trying to *measure* it. Choice (C) is incorrect; they're not using different materials.

6. **F**

The key to answering this question correctly is the phrase "directly controlled" in the question stem. While all of the answer choices represent variables that changed over the course of Experiment 3, only one was NOT "directly" controlled by the students: the tangential force required to move the wooden block, (F).

This question tests your knowledge of *dependent* and *independent* variables. Choice (G) was an *independent* variable—it varied, but the researchers controlled it. Same for option (H): the researchers directly affected this by applying grease. Choice (J) isn't a variable at all; the surface area of the blocks remains the same in all cases.

7. **B**

To answer this question, we'll have to draw from the passage as a whole, so it's best to save this one for last, when our understanding of the passage will be most complete.

According to the passage, which factors lead to a decrease in the amount of tangential force required to move a block (or, in this case, a box)? Experiment 1 shows us that decreasing the downward force on the box will make it easier to push, but this doesn't match any of the answer choices. In fact, (D) states the exact opposite of this idea, so we can eliminate it.

Experiment 2 shows us that, contrary to what our intuition might tell us, increasing the surface area does not increase the amount of tangential force required to move the box. Rotating the box so that the side with the smallest area is in contact with the ground, then, won't make it any easier to push, and we can eliminate (A).

Experiment 3 shows us that decreasing the coefficient of friction between two surfaces by spreading one with grease decreases the tangential force needed to push a block. Spreading one side of the box with grease, however messy, would then make the box easier to push, so (B) is correct.

Note that the passage never mentioned the difference between a push and a pull, so (C) must be incorrect as well, as it is out-of-scope.

8. **J**

Research Summaries passages will have a few of the same question types that we see in Data Representation passages. Here, we're asked to extrapolate a pattern from Table 2. Answer this question after reading Experiment 2, but before looking at Experiment 3. The mass of the weight in Table 2 varies from 0.5 to 2.5 kg, and the tangential force increases steadily as the mass increases. Because the tangential force required to move a block with a 2.5 kg mass atop it is 30.6 N, and each 0.5 kg increase results in an approximately 6 N increase in tangential force, we need an answer choice close to 36 N. Only (J) fits the bill.

PASSAGE III

9. C

10. F

11. D

12. G

9. **C**

The passage states that "Lavoisier believed that all acids showed the same observable properties because they contained one common substance." In the next sentence, the passage goes on to state that "he believed that this common substance was oxygen (O)." So according to Lavoisier, all acids contain one common substance, and that substance is oxygen. Choice (C) is correct.

Choice (A) is a misused detail. Acids don't *combine* with oxygen, they *contain* oxygen. If we were to rush through this question because it looks pretty easy, we might fall into this wrong answer trap.

Choice (B) is incorrect. The Lavoisier definition never states that acids cannot be broken down into other compounds. Quite the opposite—the definition states that acids can react with metals to produce hydrogen gas and a salt.

Choice (D) is also a misused detail. The Lavoisier definition states that all acids contain oxygen, but we cannot conclude from this statement that all compounds containing oxygen are acids.

10. **F**

This question requires us to combine information in the passage with information in the question stem to support one of the viewpoints. As is typical with "which of the following" type questions, it's easiest to begin this one by moving straight to the answer choices.

To know which choice is correct, we need to know what the passage says about protons. That information appears in the opening paragraph. The

first sentence says that "[a]cids are chemical compounds...capable of donating a proton." So if acids donate protons, and a hypothetical acid has reacted with a metal, it is consistent with the Lavoisier definition to state that the oxygen in the acid donated a proton, eliminating (G) and (J).

This is only discussed in the Lavoisier passage, meaning (H) is also out-of-scope, leaving (F) as correct.

11. **D**

In a "which of the following" question, we should go straight to evaluating the answer choices against the passage—in this case, the Liebig definition.

Choice (A) strengthens the idea that hydrogen in an acid is capable of being replaced by a metal, because it supports the idea that the hydrogen in an acid is released (though it doesn't speak to what that hydrogen might be replaced by). Eliminate this one.

Choice (B) doesn't tell us whether the hydrogen has been replaced by a metal. Eliminate it.

Choice (C) supports the Liebig definition, as the hydrogen in the acid has been replaced in the final product by a metal (Na), so it is certainly not correct.

Choice (D) would counter the Liebig definition, as the hydrogen in an acid can't be replaced by a metal if pure metals in water are formed. It is correct.

12. **G**

The opening paragraph states, "Acids are chemical compounds that are today most fundamentally defined as having a pH less than 7.0." So this question stem is really asking us to decide who would predict that HCl is an acid.

According to the Lavoisier definition, all acids contain oxygen (O). According to the Liebig definition, all acids contain hydrogen (H). Hydrochloric acid, which contains hydrogen and not oxygen, would only be expected to be an acid according to the Liebig definition. Choice (G) is correct.

SUMMARY

In this chapter, we talked about all of the strategy basics you need to master the ACT Science test.

Remember to vary your approach to tackle each passage type as efficiently as possible.

For Research Summaries, quickly read the text, looking for the Purpose and Method. Analyze the charts and graphs to find the independent and dependent variables and the patterns relating the two.

For Data Representation, skim the text and skip Step 1 of the Kaplan Method. Spend longer diving into the charts and graphs. Identify the variables when you can, and look for patterns.

For Conflicting Viewpoints, change it up entirely. Read the text carefully, underlining the opinions of the scientists when you find them. Read the introduction and Scientist 1, then answer the questions about Scientist 1 only. Then, read each subsequent scientist and do the same. Finally, answer the questions about more than one scientist last.

For all passage types, support your answers by looking back at the text, charts, and graphs. Don't rely on your memory, and don't get bogged down in the details.

Learn to recognize each passage type quickly. Keep practicing the various methods so you can handle each in stride on Test Day with maximum efficiency.

As always, the points come from the questions. Refer to the next chapter for a detailed discussion of each question type.

The Science test can be very intimidating, but its complexity only disguises a Reading test with scientific words. Know what to expect, know what information to look for to help yourself get to the questions quickly, and you can master the ACT Science test.

CHAPTER 14

Science Part 2: ACT Science Strategy in Depth

OVERVIEW

Use this chapter to get familiar with all of the question types on the ACT Science test. They are detailed and discussed fully, and examples are provided for each. To get a quick sense of what's to come, refer to the SmartPoint Breakdown in the previous chapter (page 399). In that chapter, they are discussed in order of Test Day weight. The more heavily tested SmartPoints are listed there first. That's also how you should prioritize your time, especially if you are short on it, or close to your goal score. However, the SmartPoints in this chapter are discussed in order of building complexity. The knowledge necessary for simpler questions often builds to the conclusions you'll need to draw for the complex ones. Each individual Science SmartPoint can also vary in complexity, and we'll work from simple to complex within all three SmartPoint categories, as we do the same from SmartPoint to SmartPoint. If you have time, and want to thoroughly work your Science skill set, start at the beginning and work your way all the way through.

The chapter ends with Putting It All Together on page 458. This is another great resource for those short on time; you'll get a chance to see how all three question types fit into the three passage types.

The following SmartPoints are shown in order of building complexity, SmartPoint by SmartPoint.

FIGURE INTERPRETATION—12 POINTS

Complexity: Low-Medium. The information needed can be found explicitly in the charts and graphs.

Figures on the ACT Science test are charts or graphs designed to present data. Figure Interpretation questions task you with studying these diagrams to locate a particular piece of information. And that's it. These questions simply test your ability to carefully read and locate data on a figure. No interpretation or conclusions are necessary. They can be complex, by nature of intricate charts and graphs that are more difficult to read, but by cutting through the distracting information, the correct answer to every Figure Interpretation question will still be right there waiting for you. The most advanced thinking you'll need to do with this question type is comparing a few numbers from least to greatest or combining a few to find sums or differences. Basically, you'll need to locate more than one piece of data and perform simple numerical evaluations.

That said, the ACT will throw complex charts and graphs at you. Thus, a few strategies for finding data efficiently will help.

Let's start by reviewing a few basic science terms. Again, the ACT Science test doesn't task you with remembering everything from your high school science classes. The answers can always be found in the passage. But by remembering a few basic terms and science processes, you can be more familiar with what you're seeing, and navigate the charts and graphs more easily.

BASIC SCIENCE TERMINOLOGY

The ACT most often uses the International System of Units (SI), which includes meters (m), kilograms (kg), seconds (s), ampere (A), Kelvin (K), mole (mol), as well as liters (L). However, it's not impossible that you'll see feet (ft), pounds (lb), degrees Celsius (°C), or even Fahrenheit (°F). You should be comfortable using derivatives of these units as well—milliliters (mL) and grams (g), for example. In most cases, all you'll need is to understand that these are units of measurements, but in some cases you might need to know which is larger than which.

You should know what it means to create a *solution* (a mixture in which a *solute* is dissolved into a *solvent*) and to *dilute* (thin or weaken). You should understand terms such as *density* (mass per unit volume) and *force* (that which causes a mass to accelerate).

This is by no means an exhaustive list of terms you may encounter, but it represents the general level of terminology you should be comfortable with. More specific terms and pieces of equipment (such as a *bomb calorimeter*) will generally be explained within the text.

SIMPLE QUESTION STRATEGIES

FINDING BASIC INFORMATION IN THE PASSAGE

This is the basic skill tested in Figure Interpretation questions. Your pencil is the key. If a question asks you to find a point on a graph, for example, draw a line up from the *x*-axis and over to the *y*-axis. You can even use a second pencil to keep your lines straight. Often, the graphs are printed pretty small, and eyeballing just isn't accurate enough.

When you find the right piece of data in a table, circle it as a visual aid. The wrong answer choices usually include the values just above or below the correct one, and it's very easy for your eyes to accidentally skip up or down a row in a table.

COMPARING AND COMBINING DATA

You might be asked to combine or compare data from two or more simple presentations. These questions will involve finding more than one data point and using your basic math skills to combine or compare.

To compare data, circle all of the relevant points in the graph or table. This will help you to focus on only what's asked and exclude any possible distractions. Most often, questions of this type will ask you to order from least to greatest (or vice versa). For example, you may be shown a table that lists the viscosity of several liquids and asked to order them from most to least viscous.

Other questions will ask you to combine data. Usually, this just means adding or subtracting the numbers. These questions will often ask you to find the difference between two data points.

Remember that on a first read, some questions (like some figures) will appear pretty complicated. Remind yourself that complicated questions are really just questions that ask you to put together a few simple steps. Take the question one step at a time, and you'll find that getting the answer is much easier than it first appeared.

Now, try out some simple Figure Interpretation questions. Then, we'll increase the complexity.

EXAMPLES

Many proteins undergo denaturation upon heating. A denatured protein is unfolded and can no longer perform its normal biological functions. Denaturation usually occurs over a temperature range. Some proteins can fold back (renature) into their original conformation when the temperature is decreased. A series of experiments was performed to determine the denaturation and renaturation behavior of three different proteins.

EXPERIMENT 1

Fifteen separate 15-mL samples of each of the proteins ribonuclease (Rase), carboxypep-tidase (Case), and hexokinase (Hase) were heated slowly from 20°C to 160°C and cooled slowly back to 20°C. After every 5°C increase in temperature, 0.002 mL of each sample was removed and chemically analyzed to determine the temperature at which denaturation occurred. After every 5°C decrease in temperature, 0.002 mL of each sample was removed and analyzed to determine the temperature at which renaturation occurred. The results of the experiment are shown in Table 1.

Table 1			
Protein	**Molecular weight (amu)**	**Denaturation temperature range (°C)**	**Renaturation temperature range (°C)**
Rase	856	135–145	110–135
Case	672	150–155	60–140
Hase	759	85–95	—

EXPERIMENT 2

Solubility is also a measure of protein denaturation. A protein can be considered fully denatured when its solubility drops to zero. Each 0.002-mL sample of ribonuclease, car-boxypeptidase, and hexokinase was dissolved in 10 mL of ethyl alcohol, and its solubility was measured. The solubility measurements were taken in 5°C increments as the samples were heated from 20°C to 160°C and again as they were cooled from 160°C to 20°C. The results are shown in Figure 1 and Figure 2.

Figure 1

Figure 2

1. A fourth protein, ovalbumin, denatures between 115°C and 130°C and renatures between 70°C and 100°C. According to Figure 1, its solubility curve would:

    A. peak at 85°C.

    B. peak at 95°C.

    C. peak at 105°C.

    D. peak at 115°C.

2. According to Figures 1 and 2, what would most likely be the solubility of Case in 10 mL of ethyl alcohol at 0°C?

    F. 0.055 g/mL

    G. 0.045 g/mL

    H. 0.015 g/mL

    J. 0.0 g/mL

Question 1

• Where in the passage should we look for information about denaturation ranges and solubility? *Table 1, Figure 1, and Figure 2*

• What patterns do we notice in the figures? *The beginning of the denaturation range is the peak of the solubility curve.*

• So where does ovalbumin peak? *At 115°C*

• Which answer choice matches? Choice (D).

Question 2

• Where in the passage should we look for an answer? *Figure 1 or Figure 2* (either one, but Figure 1 would be easier)

- How must we use the figure to locate Case's solubility at 0°C? *Carefully draw a line extending the graph until it crosses 0°C.*

- What is the approximate solubility at 0°C? *just under 0.05 g/mL*

- Which answer choice matches? Choice (G).

Table 1		
Date	**Nitrate concentration (mg/L)**	**Phosphate concentration (mg/L)**
Dormitory 1		
June 1	19.1	8.3
June 2	17.7	6.6
June 3	18.5	9.2
June 4	19.1	9.0
June 5	22.5	7.9
Dormitory 2		
June 1	23.9	9.8
June 2	26.4	10.1
June 3	23.1	10.8
June 4	22.7	9.5
June 5	19.5	8.6

Table 2			
Date	**Suspended sediment concentration (mg/L)**	**Nitrate concentration (mg/L)**	**Phosphate concentration (mg/L)**
Stream 1			
June 1	33.5	35.5	7.1
June 2	42.0	33.4	9.3
June 3	512.9	36.8	52.6
June 4	1,668.2	62.4	102.9
June 5	687.5	57.0	55.7
Stream 2			
June 1	12.3	11.3	6.7
June 2	18.4	26.5	12.9
June 3	24.1	29.7	26.8
June 4	19.2	21.3	16.4
June 5	12.3	12.5	9.2

3. According to the data in Table 1, on which date was the nitrate concentration from Dormitory 2 the highest?

    A. June 1
    B. June 2
    C. June 3
    D. June 4

4. According to the data in Table 2, on which date were nitrate concentrations from Stream 2 the highest?

    F. June 1
    G. June 2
    H. June 3
    J. June 4

Question 3

- Read Step 3 on page 174. Then read the question stem on page 175.

- Where in the passage should you look for an answer? *Table 1*

- Where in Table 1 should we look? *Dormitory 2, nitrate concentration column*

- On which date was the nitrate concentration highest? *on June 2*

- Which answer choice matches? Choice (B).

Question 4

- Where in the passage should you look for an answer? *Table 2*

- Where in Table 2 should you look? *Stream 2, nitrate concentration column*

- On which date was the nitrate concentration highest? *on June 3*

- Which answer choice matches? Choice (H)

LOCATING DATA WITHIN COMPLEX PRESENTATIONS

Nothing is more intimidating than a science chart with lots of lines heading in all different directions, except for maybe a chart with lots of lines and a few random Greek letters. But keep your cool! The ACT doesn't expect that you have your PhD. The complex charts and graphs might look scary, but remind yourself that they're designed to be comprehensible to high school students just like you. In other words, they *look* complicated, but in fact are just going to ask you to find a few points on them.

As you read the passage containing the complex figure for the first time, skim the paragraph preceding the figure for an explanation of what it shows. Read the axis labels and any legend or key accompanying the figure so you know what you're looking at, but then stop there.

When a question asks you specifically about the complex figure, the key is to focus only on the relevant information and block out everything else that's going on. Often, complex figures are only complex because they show how more than one variable behaves at a time. Use your pencil to trace only the curve that applies to the question at hand, and you'll find that the figure often isn't really as complex as it first appeared.

COMPARING AND COMBINING DATA FROM COMPLEX PRESENTATIONS

Comparing and combining data from complex presentations isn't any more difficult than comparing and combining data from simple presentations. What's harder is *finding* the appropriate data in the midst of a complex presentation.

A complex presentation or figure usually involves the presence of lots of variables in one giant table, a bizarre-looking graph with three or more lines, at least one of which is zigzag-ging, and some kind of strange units, especially angstroms (Å) (that's 0.1 nanometer, usually used for wavelength). But finding data on a line about angstroms is no harder than finding data on a line about Fahrenheit. It's just a different word.

To find the right data in a complex presentation, use the same skills you would on any other Figure Interpretation question: Look to the axes to find units (which can point you to the correct variable), and use your pencil to highlight only the appropriate data. Then focus on the precise calculation the question stem is asking for. Sometimes you'll need to figure out which piece of data is bigger or rank the data from least to greatest. Sometimes you'll have to add or subtract values. The actual calculations you make will be very simple. Calculators aren't allowed on the Science test, and you'll never need one.

The skills for all Figure Interpretation questions are the same, and they're fundamental. Keep calm when looking at complex figures, and use your pencil so that you don't get lost. Make sure to find exactly what the question stem is asking for, and you'll master this SmartPoint.

Try using your pencil to navigate these more complex charts and graphs.

Examples

Directions: First, read and map the passage, identifying and marking the Purpose, Method, and Results of the experiment.

The survival of plant life depends heavily on the availability of nitrogen in the environment. Although about 72% of Earth's atmosphere consists of N^2 gas, this form of nitrogen is inaccessible to plants, since a plant cell is incapable of breaking the triple bond between the two nitrogen atoms. Certain bacteria in soil, however, are capable of processing N^2 into ammonia (NH^4), a form of nitrogen that plants can utilize. This process is called *nitrogen fixation*. Plant roots extract nitrogen in the form of ammonia from the soil and release back into the soil various forms of nitrogen as metabolic byproducts. After a plant dies, it also releases various forms of nitrogen as it decays. Figure 1 shows how the concentration of ammonia in the soil affects the growth rate of a certain bean plant.

Figure 1

5. According to Figure 1, the minimum ammonia concentration that allows for a maximum bean plant growth rate is approximately:

A. 2 ppm.

B. 3 ppm.

C. 5 ppm.

D. 7 ppm.

Question 5

Step 1: Scan the figure, identifying variables and patterns. *Step 2:* The figure compares the growth of the bean plant and the ammonia concentration. The question asks at what concentration of ammonia does the maximum bean plant growth occur? *Step 3:* Locate the maximum plant growth, which is at 10 cm. This growth occurs when the ammonia concentration is 5 ppm. Choice (C) is the correct answer.

Directions: First, actively read the passage, then answer the questions. Remember to underline the Purpose, bracket the Method, and star the Results.

The extent to which a solute will dissolve in a given solvent is dependent on several factors, including conditions of temperature and pressure, and the electrochemical natures of the solute and solvent. A high school chemistry teacher assigned 24 students the project of measuring the solubilities in distilled water of several pairs of common sodium (Na) and potassium (K) salts at various temperatures. The pairs were NaCl and KCl, $NaNO_3$ and KNO_3, and $NaClO_3$ and $KClO_3$. All measurements were conducted under normal atmospheric pressure. After pooling and averaging all the data, the students plotted solubility curves to produce the following graph.

6. Based on the data in the passage, which solute exhibits the greatest variation of solubility with temperatures between 0°C and 60°C?

   F. NaCl

   G. KCl

   H. KNO_3

   J. $KClO_3$

7. For which of the following salts would it be possible to dissolve more than 0.65 g/mL at 65°C?

   A. Any of the Na salts

   B. Any of the K salts

   C. Either of the NO_3 salts

   D. Either of the ClO_3 salts

Question 6

The question asks which substance changes most in its solubility curve between 0 and 60 degrees Celsius. Look at the graph and determine which curve displays the most change. The correct answer is KNO_3, or (H).

Question 7

The question asks which of the salts can be dissolved more than 0.65g/mL at 65 degrees Celsius. Refer to the graph. Look for salts whose solubility curves exceed 0.65g/mL at 65 degrees Celsius. Choice (C) is correct.

  Visit your online syllabus—Lesson 8—for more instruction and practice with interpreting figures.

PATTERNS—11 POINTS

Complexity: Low-Medium to High-Medium. The information needed can be interpreted and inferred from the charts and graphs.

Patterns questions ask you to bring your analytical skills to charts and graphs. Figure Interpretation questions simply require you to find information. Patterns questions will ask you to find data and then relate it to other information or take a new piece of information and insert it where it belongs. To answer them correctly, you'll need to find trends in the data. First, you need to be aware of the increases and decreases of any single variable, and then you'll have to decipher whether other variables increase or decrease in the same way, the opposite way, or in an unrelated way. By finding these trends, you can draw conclusions as to what the experiment found, and you'll be able to insert new data just by discovering how it fits with the trend.

Let's review the basic skills of Patterns questions.

DETERMINING THE RELATIONSHIP BETWEEN TWO VARIABLES

Determining the relationship between two variables means observing how one variable changes in response to another. A scientist studying the relationship between the number of cars on the highway and the number of accidents, for example, will record the number of cars she counts in one hour along with the number of accidents. Then she'll list her results in a table, with the number of cars in one column and the number of accidents in another. Or perhaps she'll graph them, with the number of cars on the *x*-axis and the number of accidents on the *y*-axis. Suppose these are her results:

Your job is to understand by looking at the graph how the number of accidents changes with the number of cars. In this example, you can see that as the number of cars increases, the number of accidents increases. That's it! You might notice slight variations—the curve dips slightly from 100 to 200 and seems to increase more quickly at the end (curve instead of straight line), but these are minor variations that certainly don't change the overall trend. You now have the basic process of comparing variables and finding patterns!

You'll also need to keep an eye out for critical points.

CRITICAL POINTS

To find out how critical points can help you evaluate data, take a look at the graph representing the concentration of *E. coli* (a common type of bacterium) in Cooling Pool B.

Concentration of *E. coli* in Cooling Pool B

Notice how the concentration is low very near Effluent Pipe 3. From there, it rises until about 10 meters away from the pipe, then it falls again, tapering off as you get farther from the pipe. There's a critical point, then, right around 10 meters from Effluent Pipe 3. Somehow, that vicinity is most conducive to the growth of *E. coli*. As you move closer to or farther away from that point, the concentration falls off. So, in looking to explain the data, you'd want to focus on that location—10 meters from the pipe. What is it about that location that's so special? What makes it the hot new place for *E. coli* to see and be seen?

Now, see if you can find the relationships in this figure:

Hours of Sunlight	Air Temperature (Fahrenheit)		
	Chamber 1	Chamber 2	Chamber 3
2	73.23	75.67	78.87
4	71.23	75.79	79.78
6	69.23	74.76	81.34
8	67.23	79.87	82.12
10	65.23	80.65	83.06

What happens in Chamber 1? What do you think the temperature is going to be after 12 hours of sunlight? Do you notice the pattern? The temperature goes down by 2 degrees for every 2 hours of sunlight. The temperature is going to be 63.23 degrees.

As the number of hours of sunlight increases, what happens to the temperature in Chamber 2? When you look at the data, there doesn't appear to be a relationship. This is a valid answer.

Based on the data, what do you think the temperature will be after one hour of sunlight in Chamber 3? Well, as the number of hours of sunlight increase, the temperature in the chamber increases. So if you had to predict what would happen after only one hour of sunlight, then according to the table, it is going to be less than 78.87 degrees.

Now, let's make things slightly more complex, then we'll dive into some examples.

UNDERSTANDING THE RELATIONSHIP BETWEEN VARIABLES IN A COMPLEX DATA PRESENTATION

Understanding the relationship between variables will remain a primary skill in passages with complex data presentations. The basic methods are the same as those discussed with simpler question strategies, but you'll have to focus harder to zero in on the variables you need and ignore the ones you don't.

Work methodically. Locate one variable at a time (check the axes of a graph or the left-most column and top row of a table for your variables). If you can't find them, look for the appropriate units: If a question asks for temperature, look for °C or °F.

When you find your variables, ask yourself how one changes as the other increases or decreases. Then match your answer to the choices. Again, these complex questions often reduce to a series of a few simple steps. Take them one step at a time, and you'll find getting the answer is far easier than it looks!

INTERPOLATING POINTS

Interpolation simply means "reading between." So interpolating points just means "figuring out what happens *between* data points"—some questions will ask you to approximate values in between those actually shown in the passage. Again, this is a lot easier than it sounds.

Suppose, for example, a passage contains a table—say, one that lists distance in multiples of 10 cm in one column and corresponding intensity in the other—and you're asked to find the intensity at 15 cm. Your job would be to look for the values of intensity at 10 cm and 20 cm, and make a guess halfway in between those. Easy!

If you're looking at a graph, the task is similar. Look for the values just below and above the point in question, and make a guess somewhere in the middle. Then simply match your guess to the answer choices.

TRANSLATING INFORMATION INTO A TABLE, GRAPH, OR DIAGRAM

Occasionally, a question will ask you to generate your own graph, table, or diagram. This sounds difficult, but these are usually easy if you know how to find patterns. That's because a) the graphs are usually very straightforward, and b) you don't actually have to generate them. You just have to pick the correct plot out of four choices.

To identify the correct plot, first check the general trend of the data by looking at the slope of the curve or the values in the table. Is the data you're looking for increasing, decreasing, or staying the same? Match the shape you're looking for to the answer choices.

If more than one choice remains after you check the trends, check individual values. If the information in the passage indicates that the data should have a specific value at a given point, look for the choice that contains that point. It shouldn't take more than a few seconds to backtrack your way to the correct answer.

Now, put your skills at finding patterns to the test on the following passage.

EXAMPLES

Although the effective acceleration due to gravity at the Earth's surface is often treated as a constant ($g = 9.80$ m /sec^2), its actual value varies from place to place because of several factors.

First, a body on the surface of any rotating spheroid experiences an effective force perpendicular to the rotational axis and proportional to the speed of rotation. This centrifugal force, which counteracts gravity, varies with latitude, increasing from zero at the poles to a maximum at the equator. In addition, because the Earth "bulges" at the equator, a body at equatorial sea level is farther from the center of the Earth than is a body at polar sea level. Figure 1 shows the variation of mean values of g at sea level resulting from both effects; the contribution from "bulging" is about half that from rotation.

Figure 1

Measurements of g also vary depending on local rock density and altitude. Table 1 shows the effect of altitude on g at various points above sea level.

Table 1	
Altitude above Sea Level (km)	**Variation in g(m/sec^2)**
1	−0.0031
5	−0.0154
10	−0.0309
25	−0.0772
30	−0.1543

1. Given the information in the passage, which of the following most closely approximates the value of g at a point 10 km high along the equator?

   A. 9.75 m/sec^2

   B. 9.80 m/sec^2

   C. 9.81 m/sec^2

   D. 9.87 m/sec^2

2. Suppose that the Earth stopped rotating but still "bulged." Based on information from the passage, the value of g at sea level at the equator would be:

   F. exactly 9.80 m/sec^2.

   G. greater than 9.78 m/sec^2.

   H. exactly 9.78 m/sec^2.

   J. less than 9.78 m/sec^2.

3. According to the information in Figure 1, the value of *g*:

    A. changes by a greater average amount per degree latitude between 30° and 60° than it does near the equator or poles.

    B. changes by a greater average amount per degree latitude near the equator or poles than it does between 30° and 60°.

    C. increases by an average of 5.8 m/sec^2 per degree latitude from the equator to the poles.

    D. decreases by an average of 3.1×10^{-3} m/sec^2 per degree latitude from the equator to the poles.

Question 1 requires that you read both Figure 1 and Table 1 properly. It asks for the value of *g* at the equator (that information comes from Figure 1), but at an altitude of 10 km above sea level (that information comes from Table 1). Figure 1 tells you that the value of *g* at the equator at sea level would be 9.78 m/sec^2. But at 10 km above sea level, according to Table 1, *g* would be slightly lower, 0.0309 m/sec^2 lower, to be precise. So 9.78 minus 0.0309 would be about 9.75 m/sec^2. That's (A).

Question 2 asks you to suppose that rotation effects (one of the two factors affected by latitude) ceased, but that the Earth still bulged at the equator. What would be the value of *g*? Well, again, rotation tends to "counteract" gravity, so without rotation, then *g* would be "less counteracted"—it would go up, in other words. That means (reading from Figure 1 again) that *g* at 0° latitude (the equator) would, in the absence of rotation, go up from its current value of 9.78. That's why (G) is correct.

Question 3 can also be answered just by reading Figure 1. It asks you to describe what the graph tells you about the value of *g*. As we saw, the value rises slowly as you head away from 0° latitude (the equator), rises more rapidly in the middle latitudes, and slows down again near 90° latitude (the poles). That's best described by (A). (Choice (B) gets it backward—remember to read the choices carefully!) Choices (C) and (D) would involve you in some extensive calculations, at the end of which you'd realize that they were not true. But there's no reason to get that far. If you find yourself doing extensive calculation, you should know that you're on the wrong track. ACT Science will involve simple calculation only.

IDENTIFYING AND USING COMPLEX RELATIONSHIPS BETWEEN VARIABLES

Even extremely complex questions regarding intricate charts and graphs will often come down to the same basic skill of relating variables that you've developed throughout this SmartPoint. Remember, these relationships are often pretty straightforward, and that will be true even in the most difficult of passages. As one variable increases by a constant amount, the other increases or decreases by a constant amount. Occasionally, the relationship will be more complex; as one variable doubles, for example, the other will quadruple. This is known as an **exponential** relationship and is the most common sort of complex relationship on the ACT Science test.

If you suspect a complex relationship between variables, be sure to look at more than one data point. For example, if doubling the quantity of a solution quadruples the reaction time, check to see what tripling the quantity does (it should multiply the reaction time by nine). Take those extra few seconds to make sure you're seeing what you think you're seeing, but only get into this level of detailed analysis if the question asks you to. The basic relationship might be enough.

Mostly, you'll be tasked with using this complex relationship, as opposed to identifying exactly what it is. Nail down the relationship between the two variables, and use that to predict what will happen next.

EXTRAPOLATING FROM DATA

Extrapolating from data means predicting the value of a data point that falls beyond the range given. The rule here is to assume the data trends continue as indicated by the table or graph. If you see a line graphed as straight from 1 to 100 on the x-axis, assume it continues to be straight. If it's a curve that's beginning to level off at the top, assume that leveling trend continues. If a table shows a variable steadily increasing, you can safely assume that subsequent values not shown on the table continue to increase.

NEW RESULTS

Other questions will ask you to predict the results of a hypothetical new trial or experiment. The key in these is to identify *which* patterns and trends apply to the question at hand. The question stem will give you clues to figure out where you need to look.

You might see a question that asks you to do the reverse; that is, instead of asking what results come from new conditions, it'll ask which conditions would yield new results. The method for answering is the same: identify the relevant experiment that manipulates the variable in question, find the trend in the data, and use that trend to identify the conditions that will give you the desired result.

The bottom line with additional trials and experiments questions is that the answer is in the passage. Additional trials and experiments must conform to the data you've already been given. Be wary of answer choices that stray too far from the passage.

Now, try putting your skills at understanding variables and relationships together on these more complex Patterns questions.

EXAMPLES

A high school physics class wished to determine the best way of calculating D, a snowmobile's total braking distance. They defined D as the total distance a snowmobile requires to stop from the moment the driver first sees a "stop" signal until the snowmobile comes to a complete stop.

The class used two methods. In Method 1, *S* is the distance traveled before the driver could begin the braking process when a driver reaction time of 0.8 sec was assumed, and *T* is the average distance traveled after the brakes were applied. Method 2 assumes that *D* is simply the initial speed in ft/sec times 2 sec. Table 1 shows the results of both methods with various initial speeds.

Table 1					
Initial speed (mi/hr)	**Initial speed (ft/sec)**	**Method 1**			**Method 2**
		S (ft)	**T (ft)**	**D (ft)**	**D (ft)**
25	37	30	28	58	74
35	51	41	75	116	102
45	66	53	144	197	132
55	81	65	245	310	162

The class then plotted the *D* they calculated through Method 1 and the *D* they calculated through Method 2. The results are shown in Figure 1.

Figure 1

4. According to Figure 1, if a snowmobile is traveling at an initial speed of 75 mi/hr, what will its *D* be according to Method 2?

F. Less than 100 ft

G. Between 105 and 200 ft

H. Between 205 and 300 ft

J. Greater than 300 ft

Question 4

Apply Step 2 of the Kaplan Method and take a few seconds to examine the figure. *Step 2:* Table 1 shows the snowmobile's initial speed. The columns under Method 1 show the distance traveled by the snowmobile driver from when he saw the stop signal to when he actually reacted and began stopping; the distance required to actually stop; and the total required braking distance from the start of the signal. The column under Method 2 shows a total stopping distance, assuming stopping distance is simply twice the initial speed in ft/sec. Initial speed is given in units of both mi/hr and ft/sec. Every other measurement is given in ft.

Figure 1 shows a plot of initial speed versus stopping distance for Method 1 and Method 2. The units of the x-axis are mi/hr, and the y-axis is in feet.

Continue the straight line that represents Method 2 to 75 mi/hr or use Table 1 to estimate D. The straight line from Figure 1, if extended, gives D of about 225 feet, or (H). Looking at Table 1, each 10 mi/hr increase in initial speed increases D by about 30 ft. So an initial speed of 75 mi/hr would have a D that's about 60 feet greater than the D at 55 mi/hr, or about 222 feet, also (H).

Directions: Read the following passage and answer the questions.

A conductor's resistance (R) is defined as the extent to which it opposes *conductivity* (the flow of electricity). Resistance depends not only on the conductor's resistivity ($Ů$), but also on the conductor's length (L) and cross-sectional area (A). The resistivity of a conductor is a physical property of the material and varies with temperature. A research team designing a new appliance was researching the best type of wire to use in a particular circuit. The most important consideration was the wire's resistance. The team studied the resistance of wires made from four metals—gold (Au), aluminum (Al), tungsten (W), and iron (Fe). Two lengths and two *gauges* (diameters) of each type of wire were tested at 20°C. The results are recorded in Table 1.

Note: Area of circle = πr^2

Table 1				
Material	**Resistivity (μΩ/cm)**	**Length (cm)**	**Cross-sectional area (mm²)**	**Resistance (μΩ)**
Au	2.44	1.0	5.26	46.4
Au	2.44	1.0	1.31	186.0
Au	2.44	2.0	5.26	92.8
Au	2.44	2.0	1.31	372.0
Al	2.83	1.0	5.26	53.8
Al	2.83	1.0	1.31	216.0
Al	2.83	2.0	5.26	107.6
Al	2.83	2.0	1.31	432.0
W	5.51	1.0	5.26	105.0
W	5.51	1.0	1.31	421.0
W	5.51	2.0	5.26	210.0
W	5.51	2.0	1.31	842.0
Fe	10.00	1.0	5.26	190.0
Fe	10.00	1.0	1.31	764.0
Fe	10.00	2.0	5.26	380.0
Fe	10.00	2.0	1.31	1,528.0

5. Of the wires tested, resistance increases for any given material as which parameter decreases?

   A. Length
   B. Cross-sectional area
   C. Resistivity
   D. Gauge

6. Given the data in Table 1, which of the following best expresses resistance in terms of resistivity (ρ), cross-sectional area (A), and length (L)?

   F. $\dfrac{\rho A}{L} \times 100$

   G. $\dfrac{\rho L}{A} \times 100$

   H. $\rho A L \times 100$

   J. $\dfrac{A L}{\rho} \times 100$

7. Which of the following wires would have the highest resistance?

    A. A 1-cm aluminum wire with a cross-sectional area of 3.31 mm^2

    B. A 2-cm aluminum wire with a cross-sectional area of 3.31 mm^2

    C. A 1-cm tungsten wire with a cross-sectional area of 0.66 mm^2

    D. A 2-cm tungsten wire with a cross-sectional area of 0.66 mm^2

8. According to the information given, which of the following statements is (are) correct?

    I. 10-gauge wire has a larger diameter than 16-gauge wire.

    II. Gold has a higher resistivity than tungsten.

    III. Aluminum conducts electricity better than iron.

    F. I only

    G. II only

    H. III only

    J. I and III only

9. Which of the following graphs best represents the relationship between the resistivity of a tungsten wire and its length?

A.

C.

B.

D.

Question 5

According to Table 1, decreasing the cross-sectional area of a given wire always increases resistance, so (B) is correct.

• Choice (A) is incorrect; Table 1 shows that resistance goes up with length, which is the opposite of the relationship you're looking for.

• Choice (C) is incorrect; resistivity is constant for each material and can't be increased or decreased.

- Choice (D) is tricky; gauge varies *inversely* with cross-sectional area, so it varies *directly* with resistance.

Question 6

Since you just determined in the previous question that resistance goes up as area (*A*) goes down, cross off any answer choices that don't have *A* in the denominator. That's everything but (G), which is the correct answer.

Question 7

Compare choices two at a time. The wires in (A) and (B) are both made of aluminum and have the same cross-sectional area; only their lengths are different. Doubling the length doubles the resistance, so (B) will have higher resistance than (A). Cross off (A). Similarly, (D) will have higher resistance than (C), so eliminate (C). Choices (B) and (D) differ in both cross-sectional area and material. You can approximate from Table 1 that (B) will have a resistance of about 230 (about halfway between the resistance for a 2-cm aluminum wire with a cross-sectional area of 5.26 and the same wire with a cross-sectional areas of 1.31). Choice (D) will have a resistance of about double that of the 2-cm tungsten wire with a cross-sectional area of 1.31, or about 1,700. That's higher than 230, the resistance of (B), so (D) is correct.

Question 8

Check the diagram above Table 1 to see whether a 10-gauge wire has a larger diameter than a 16-gauge wire. It does, so eliminate (G) and (H), because they don't contain statement I. You don't have to check statement II, because it's not in any of the remaining choices. To deduce if statement III is true, you'll have to check Table 1. It shows that the resistance of an iron (Fe) wire is much higher than that of an aluminum (Al) wire with the same length and cross-sectional area. How does that relate to conductivity? The first sentence of the passage defines the resistance of a conductor as "the extent to which it opposes *conductivity* (the flow of electricity)." Since iron has a higher resistance than aluminum, iron must not conduct electricity as well. Therefore, statement III is true, and (J) is correct.

Question 9

Table 1 shows that the resistivity of a material doesn't change when wire length changes. Therefore, the graph of resistivity versus length for a tungsten wire (or any other wire) is a horizontal line, and (D) is correct.

    Visit your online syllabus—Lesson 8—for more instruction and practice with patterns.

SCIENTIFIC REASONING—13 POINTS

Complexity: Medium to High. The information needed can be inferred and concluded from the text of the passages.

Scientific Reasoning questions are the only ones that really require you to use the text. You'll almost never see these questions in Data Representation passages. They form about a third of Research Summary questions, and they are the most common questions on Conflicting Viewpoints passages.

In Research Summary questions, you'll be asked to understand the hypothesis being tested, how it's being tested, and whether or not the scientists reached the goals they were seeking. In other words, you need a good grasp of the Purpose and Method, and how they affect the Results. You might also be asked to conclude what the scientists should do next.

In Conflicting Viewpoints passages, you'll be asked to understand all viewpoints, how they could be strengthened or weakened, and their similarities and difference. You might also be asked how the viewpoints can be strengthened or weakened by new evidence.

UNDERSTANDING HYPOTHESES

While you'll likely never be asked to directly identify the hypothesis for an experiment, the ACT does test your understanding of hypotheses in general. So what is a hypothesis? It's the scientists' guess at the answer to the question they're asking (which is the Purpose you've already identified). Understand that a hypothesis is not a *statement of fact,* but rather one possible explanation for a phenomenon. "The sky is blue" is not a hypothesis. Scientist 1 saying "The sky is blue because of the salinity of evaporation off the oceans" and Scientist 2 saying "The sky appears blue not because of the salinity of the oceans, but because of the speed of Earth's rotation" are conflicting hypotheses.

Usually, the ACT makes it pretty clear when they're giving you a hypothesis, so you don't have to worry about ever coming up with one on your own. You'll see dead giveaways when you're dealing with a hypothesis question, like "If Scientist 1's hypothesis is correct..." You do need to understand how to support or weaken that hypothesis or how to further test it.

Supporting a hypothesis means backing it up with more information that fits the hypothesis. Weakening it means finding information that contradicts the hypothesis. To further test a hypothesis, you'll need to ask yourself what else you need to know to confirm or disprove this guess.

SELECTING HYPOTHESES, CONCLUSIONS, OR PREDICTIONS FROM THE DATA

Occasionally, you'll be asked to identify valid hypotheses or conclusions based on what is written in the passage. Your job is never more complicated than distinguishing the correct choice from among three choices that *must* be wrong.

To answer these questions, first go back to the passage. Find where it discusses the information in the question stem, and see if you can predict the answer. If you can, great. If you can't, then see if you can identify the fatal flaw in each of the incorrect answer choices. Often, these flaws will be pretty obvious: some choices might reference information that has absolutely nothing to do with the passage, some might reference an unrelated detail from another part of the passage, and still others might reverse the correct relationship.

UNDERSTANDING THE TOOLS IN A SIMPLE EXPERIMENT

The opening paragraph or experiment descriptions of Research Summary passages might contain a complex-looking diagram, like this one:

In other words, some of the Experimental Setup diagrams will look pretty unfamiliar and complicated. Don't let that worry you! Treat a figure like this as you would any other figure on the ACT: Summarize the gist of it, and then move on. You can look at it in more detail when you come to a question that relates to it.

Other tools involved in a simple experiment are the same tools you've used in your high school science labs. Remember, the ACT assumes you've taken at least two years of science, and that usually includes a certain amount of lab work. You should be familiar with what it means to measure temperature, measure quantities of liquids, record masses, record physical observations, and carry out many of the other routine tasks required by a high school science lab.

UNDERSTANDING A SIMPLE EXPERIMENTAL DESIGN

Remember to look for the Method on Research Summary passages. Ask yourself, "How did they set up their experiment? Which were the variables that the researchers changed? Which variables changed in response? What did the researchers record in their results?"

Remember that experiments on the ACT, while they may look complicated at first glance, are usually very straightforward. Some basic equipment will be set up and a few trials will be run. Only a handful of variables will be manipulated. The passages usually look much harder at first glance than they really are.

IDENTIFYING A CONTROL IN AN EXPERIMENT

Remember to find the independent and dependent variables as you proceed through Step 2 of the Kaplan Method. Sometimes, which variable is which will be made clear by the Purpose in Step 1. These will provide valuable hints to how and why the researchers did what they did. As a quick reminder: **Independent variables** are the variables deliberately manipulated by researchers; the ones researchers control. **Dependent variables** are those that are observed to change in response to the independent variables.

When researchers are trying to figure out the effects of the independent variables they're studying, they'll want to weed out effects caused by other variables they're not thinking of or measuring—the humidity of the room for a chemistry experiment, the amount of rainfall this year for an outdoor biology experiment, or any other factor that's not in their control or on their radar.

To do this, they'll usually run what's called a *control*. Think of this as a "blank" experiment of sorts; the experiment run without any of the independent variables in it at all. For example, if researchers are measuring how three patches of sunflowers grow when they're fed three different kinds of nutrient solutions, they may plant a fourth patch of sunflowers fed only water. The water-fed patch would be the experiment's control.

IDENTIFYING SIMILARITIES AND DIFFERENCES BETWEEN EXPERIMENTS

Questions asking you to identify the similarities and differences between experiments are a guarantee on the ACT, but luckily, finding the answer is straightforward. You may have already located this information using the Method. Usually, it's printed in the paragraph below the *Experiment 1, 2,* or *3* headings. Often, you'll see an explanation of Experiment 2 along the lines of "Scientists repeated Experiment 1, but brought the temperature of the solution to 25°C." Then, looking at the description of Experiment 1, you'll find that the scientists ran that experiment at 15°C.

You should also look quickly at the results the scientists achieved with each experiment. These are almost always printed in tables in Research Summaries passages, and the tables are usually pretty small (the biggest tables are found in Data Representation passages). Column 1 usually contains the independent variables and column 2 the dependent variables. If the first columns of the two tables match, you'll know that the researchers ran basically the same experiment again, with one minor difference. If the first columns are different, you'll know that the researchers varied more than just the temperature at which the experiment was run.

Now, try out these strategies, with the Kaplan Method for Research Summary passages to answer the Scientific Reasoning questions on the sample passage that follows.

EXAMPLES

The Brazilian tree frog (*Hyla faber*) exchanges gases through both its skin and lungs. The exchange rate depends on the temperature of the frog's environment. A pair of experiments was performed to investigate this dependence.

EXPERIMENT 1

Fifty frogs were placed in a controlled atmosphere that, with the exception of temperature, was designed to simulate their native habitat. The temperature was varied from 5°C to 25°C, and equilibrium was attained before each successive temperature change. The amount of oxygen absorbed by the frogs' lungs and skin per hour was measured, and the results for all the frogs were averaged. The results are shown in Table 1.

Table 1		
	Moles O_2 absorbed/hr	
Temperature (°C)	Skin	Lungs
5	15.4	8.3
10	22.7	35.1
15	43.6	64.9
20	42.1	73.5
25	40.4	78.7

Table 2		
	Moles CO_2 eliminated/hr	
Temperature (°C)	Skin	Lungs
5	18.9	2.1
10	43.8	12.7
15	79.2	21.3
20	91.6	21.9
25	96.5	21.4

1. Which of the following factors did researchers intentionally vary?

    A. The number of frogs studied

    B. The humidity of the frogs' simulated habitats

    C. The temperature of the frogs' simulated habitats

    D. The amount of oxygen in the frogs' simulated habitats

2. Which of the following best explains why the researchers allowed the temperature in the simulated habitats to achieve equilibrium before each temperature change? The researchers wanted to allow:

   F. time for additional oxygen to be removed from the habitats.

   G. time for the frogs to adjust their oxygen absorption to the new temperature.

   H. time for the researchers to increase or decrease carbon dioxide levels in the habitats.

   J. time for the habitats' humidity level to adjust to the new temperature.

3. Which of the following best explains why the frogs were placed in a controlled atmosphere designed to simulate their native habitats?

   A. The researchers wanted to manipulate some variables but leave other elements as they naturally are.

   B. The researchers wanted to exclude natural predators from the frogs' environment.

   C. The researchers wanted to be able to control the frogs' food supply.

   D. The researchers wanted to be able to control the frogs' oxygen intake.

Question 1

Step 1: Cover the answer choices for question 1 and read the question stem. *Step 2:* Think about what you already figured out. What did the researchers do? What did they intentionally vary? *Temperature*; (C) is correct.

• Choice (A): Did researchers vary the number of frogs? *No, this is explained in the passage.*

• Choice (B): Humidity? *No, humidity is not mentioned in tables.*

• Choice (D): Amount of oxygen? *No, tempting, but this is what was measured, not what was varied.*

Question 2

Step 1: Again, cover the answer choices, then read the question stem. Without going back to the passage, why would the scientists want to achieve equilibrium? *They want to let things settle out before taking a measurement. Step 2:* Which answer choice matches your prediction? Choice (G) is correct.

• Choice (F): Did researchers remove oxygen from the habitat? *No, they measured oxygen.*

• Choice (H): Did researchers add or remove carbon dioxide? *No, they measured that, too.*

• Choice (J): Did the humidity level change during these experiments? *Humidity is not mentioned in the experiment.*

Question 3

Choice (A) is correct; the purpose of this experiment is to investigate how temperature affects the rate of exchange of gas.

ADDITIONAL TRIALS AND EXPERIMENTS

The Research Summaries passages on the ACT might contain questions asking you to take the experiments one step further, by identifying trials or experiments that would give researchers more information. To answer these questions correctly, you'll have to build on the skills listed earlier: You must understand how experiments are set up and recognize the independent and dependent variables.

The secret to answering questions about new trials or experiments is to determine, from the question stem, exactly what the researchers need to know that they don't already. Then all you have to do is identify which answer choice addresses just this variable, while keeping the others constant. Watch out for answer choices that identify variables already explored in previous trials or experiments—they're there to confuse you by looking familiar. Also, avoid answer choices that stray too far from the topic; don't be drawn to answer choices that look confusing and complicated.

NEW INFORMATION

Sometimes, the questions following a Research Summaries passage will introduce new information. That information might come in the form of text in the question stem or a new table or graph. Your job with these questions is to figure out how this new information relates to what's already stated in the passage and find an answer choice that works with both the passage and the new information.

Questions with new information can be confusing on first read. One strategy is to save these questions for last. That gives you a chance to become more familiar with the information in the passage before you try to integrate additional data.

Now, put your skills and strategies together and try your hand at complex Scientific Reasoning questions.

EXAMPLES

Directions: Read the passage and answer the corresponding questions.

A solution is defined as a mixture of two or more substances. The *solvent* is the liquid into which the *solute*, usually a solid or gas, is dissolved. Solutions that can conduct an electrical current are called *electrolytes*. The current is conducted through an electrolyte by the solute. Solutions that cannot conduct an electric current are called *nonelectrolytes*. The voltage of a current traveling through a solution can be measured by a device called a voltmeter. A simple circuit, consisting of a battery, solution, electrodes, light emitting diode (LED), and voltmeter, is diagrammed in Figure 1.

Figure 1

Researchers conducted the following experiments to determine whether increasing the solute in a solution or increasing the temperature of the solution would increase the solution's conductivity.

EXPERIMENT 1

Researchers mixed five solutions, each containing 10.0 grams (g) of solute dissolved in 100 milliliters (mL) of water at 35°C. Water was also tested for conductivity without the addition of solute. The results of Experiment 1 are shown in Table 1.

Table 1	
Solute	**Voltmeter reading (volts)**
Water (H_2O)	0.0
Sodium chloride (NaCl)	5.4
Glucose ($C_{12}H_{22}O_{11}$)	0.0
Potassium fluoride (KF)	5.1
Magnesium chloride ($MgCl_2$)	1.6
Acetic acid ($HC_2H_3O_2$)	1.9

EXPERIMENT 2

The researchers repeated Experiment 1, this time tripling the amount of solute in each solution to 30.0 g. The solute was again dissolved in 100 mL of water at 35°C. The results of Experiment 2 are shown in Table 2.

Table 2	
Solute	**Voltmeter reading (volts)**
Water (H_2O)	0.0
Sodium chloride (NaCl)	10.6
Glucose ($C_{12}H_{22}O_{11}$)	0.0
Potassium fluoride (KF)	9.7
Magnesium chloride ($MgCl_2$)	2.6
Acetic acid ($HC_2H_3O_2$)	3.0

EXPERIMENT 3

Experiment 2 was repeated with 30.0 g of solute dissolved in 100 mL of water. This time, however, researchers heated the water to 70°C. The results of Experiment 3 are shown in Table 3.

Table 3	
Solute	**Voltmeter reading (volts)**
Water (H_2O)	0.0
Sodium chloride (NaCl)	1.3
Glucose ($C_{12}H_{22}O_{11}$)	0.0
Potassium fluoride (KF)	13.1
Magnesium chloride ($MgCl_2$)	4.0
Acetic acid ($HC_2H_3O_2$)	4.9

4. According to the results of all three experiments, which effects would be most appropriate to test next to learn more about conductivity in a solution?

   F. How temperature influences conductivity

   G. How solute color influences conductivity

   H. How water influences conductivity

   J. How different solvents influence conductivity

5. Which of the following objectives best explains why H_2O alone was tested in all three experiments?

    A. To test whether H_2O was the solute or the solvent

    B. To determine the amount of conductivity that could be attributed to H_2O

    C. To test whether H_2O would dissolve all of the salts equally

    D. To prove that H_2O conducts electricity well

Question 4

What do the results of the experiments suggest? *Certain solutes increase conductivity, higher concentration increases conductivity, heat usually increases conductivity, sometimes decreases.*

Which answer choice would be reasonable to test next? Choice (J).

- Choice (F): Temperature has already been tested.

- Choice (G): There is no information that suggests solute color influences conductivity, so that would not the best variable to test next.

- Choice (H): Water has already been tested.

Question 5

When is water tested in each experiment? *first*

What is changed in the water? *temperature, in Experiment 3*

Why was water tested each time? *as a control, to see what reaction is attributable to water as the solvent instead of to each solute*

Which answer choice matches this prediction? Choice (B).

- Choice (A): Water, as a liquid, is always the solvent.

- Choice (B): This describes water as the control for the experiment.

- Choice (C): How thoroughly each salt was dissolved was not tested.

- Choice (D): This was not being tested.

UNDERSTANDING THE VIEWPOINTS

Some of the questions that accompany a Conflicting Viewpoints passage will simply test your ability to identify key issues or assumptions in each individual viewpoint. They're typically rather straightforward and reliably contain wrong answer choices that draw from other authors' viewpoints to trick you. That's why it's important to follow the Kaplan Method for Conflicting Viewpoints passages.

Remember, this Kaplan Method is completely different from the other two. Here it is again as a reminder:

THE KAPLAN METHOD FOR CONFLICTING VIEWPOINTS PASSAGES

1. Read the introductory text and the first author's viewpoint, then answer the questions that ask only about the first author's viewpoint.

2. Read the second author's viewpoint, then answer the questions that ask only about the second author's viewpoint.

3. Answer the questions that refer to both authors' viewpoints.

This Kaplan Method will require that you skip around in the questions. That's fine. There's no rule saying you have to answer the questions in the order in which they appear. And you'll find that it's much, much easier to deal with Conflicting Viewpoints passages when you minimize your opportunities to confuse the two (or three, or four) viewpoints.

IDENTIFYING SIMILARITIES AND DIFFERENCES BETWEEN VIEWPOINTS

You might see questions that ask you to identify a point on which the authors agree or a point on which they disagree. Remember to underline each author's main point as you're reading. Then when it's time to identify similarities and differences, you'll have the essence of their viewpoints highlighted.

Answer these questions immediately after you answer all the questions that deal with just one viewpoint at a time. Questions that ask you to identify similarities or differences are typically among the easier questions in the passage, so they're great for giving you a chance to make sure you have the subtleties of each viewpoint nailed down.

SUPPORTING AND WEAKENING VIEWPOINTS

It's common to see at least one question asking you to identify whether information supports or weakens the view of one or both authors. Typically, these questions will introduce new information or data, and your job will be to determine whether the data supports or weakens a viewpoint.

Information supports a viewpoint if it offers data that makes the viewpoint even more likely to be true. Conversely, information weakens a viewpoint if it contradicts some part of it. The information doesn't have to prove a viewpoint to be true in order to support it, and it doesn't have to prove it false to weaken it. You're simply supposed to judge whether the information adds to or detracts from any part of the viewpoint.

Try your hand at these strategies on the following samples.

EXAMPLES

While the *focus* (point of origin) of most earthquakes lies less than 20 km below Earth's surface, certain unusual seismographic readings indicate that some activity originates at considerably greater depths. Below, two scientists discuss the possible causes of deep-focus earthquakes.

SCIENTIST 1

Surface earthquakes occur when rock in Earth's crust fractures to relieve stress. However, below 50 km, rock is under too much pressure to fracture normally. Deep-focus earthquakes are caused by the pressure of fluids trapped in Earth's tectonic plates. As a plate is forced down into the mantle by convection, increases in temperature and pressure cause changes in the crystalline structure of minerals such as serpentine. In adopting a denser configuration, the crystals dehydrate, releasing water. Other sources of fluid include water trapped in pockets of deep-sea trenches and carried down with the plates. Laboratory work has shown that fluids trapped in rock pores can cause rock to fail at lower shear stresses. In fact, at the Rocky Mountain Arsenal, the injection of fluid wastes into the ground accidentally induced a series of shallow-focus earthquakes.

SCIENTIST 2

Deep-focus earthquakes cannot result from normal fractures because rock becomes ductile at the temperatures and pressures that exist at depths greater than 50 km. Furthermore, mantle rock below 300 km is probably totally dehydrated because of the extreme pressure. Therefore, trapped fluids could not cause quakes below that depth. A better explanation is that deep-focus quakes result from the slippage that occurs when rock in a descending tectonic plate undergoes a phase change in its crystalline structure along a thin plane parallel to a stress. Just such a phase change and resultant slippage can be produced in the laboratory by compressing a slab of calcium magnesium silicate. The pattern of deep-quake activity supports this theory. In most seismic zones, the recorded incidence of deep-focus earthquakes corresponds to the depths at which phase changes are predicted to occur in mantle rock. For example, little or no phase change is thought to occur at 400 km, and indeed, earthquake activity at this level is negligible. Between 400 and 680 km, activity once again increases. Although seismologists initially believed that earthquakes could be generated at depths as low as 1,080 or 1,200 km, no foci have been confirmed below 700 km. No phase changes are predicted for mantle rock below 680 km.

6. Scientists 1 and 2 agree on which point?

    F. Deep-earthquake activity does not occur below 400 km.

    G. Fluid allows tectonic plates to slip past one another.

    H. Water can penetrate mantle rock.

    J. Rock below 50 km will not fracture normally.

7. Which of the following is evidence that would support the hypothesis of Scientist 1?

   A. The discovery that water can be extracted from mantle-like rock at temperatures and pressures similar to those found below 300 km

   B. Seismographic indications that earthquakes occur 300 km below the surface of Earth

   C. The discovery that phase changes occur in the mantle rock at depths of 1,080 km

   D. An earthquake underneath Los Angeles that was shown to have been caused by water trapped in sewer lines

8. Both scientists assume that:

   F. deep-focus earthquakes are more common than surface earthquakes.

   G. trapped fluids cause surface earthquakes.

   H. Earth's crust is composed of mobile tectonic plates.

   J. deep-focus earthquakes cannot be felt on Earth's crust without special recording devices.

9. To best refute Scientist 2's hypothesis, Scientist 1 might:

   A. find evidence of other sources of underground water.

   B. record a deep-focus earthquake below 680 km.

   C. find a substance that doesn't undergo phase changes even at depths equivalent to 680 km.

   D. show that rock becomes ductile at depths of less than 50 km.

10. According to Scientist 1, the earthquake at Rocky Mountain Arsenal occurred because:

    F. serpentine or other minerals dehydrated and released water.

    G. fluid wastes injected into the ground compressed a thin slab of calcium magnesium silicate.

    H. fluid wastes injected into the ground flooded pockets of deep-sea trench.

    J. fluid wastes injected into the ground lowered the shear stress failure point of the rock.

11. Scientist 2's hypothesis would be strengthened by evidence showing that:

    A. water evaporates at high temperatures and pressures.

    B. deep-focus earthquakes can occur at 680 km.

    C. stress has the same effect on mantle rock that it has on calcium magnesium silicate.

    D. water pockets exist at depths below 300 km.

12. The information in the passage indicates that:

  F. most earthquakes originate near Earth's surface.

  G. most earthquakes originate hundreds of kilometers below Earth's surface.

  H. deep-sea earthquakes often are caused by volcanic activity.

  J. earthquakes are Earth's most destructive natural phenomenon.

Question 6

On what do the scientists agree?

- Choice (F): Not discussed by Scientist 1

- Choice (G): Scientist 1 disagrees

- Choice (H): Not discussed by Scientist 2

- Choice (J): Agreed upon by both scientists; *correct*

Question 7

What is Scientist 1's hypothesis? *Deep-focus earthquakes are caused by fluid pressure.*

What information would support this? *evidence of fluid pressure, evidence demonstrating difference in earthquake activity between areas that do and do not have fluid pressure*

- Choice (A): This agrees with Scientist 1's conclusion that fluid pressure can be found at deep-focus levels. *Correct*

- Choice (B): Irrelevant—we know this already from Scientist 2.

- Choice (C): This is Scientist 2's argument.

- Choice (D): This demonstrates that fluid causes earthquakes, but they are shallow-level, not deep-focus.

Question 8

What viewpoint does this question ask about? *both*

What do the scientists agree on? *that deep-focus earthquakes are different, that types of earthquakes have shared causes*

- Choice (F): Do the scientists say deep-focus earthquakes are more common than surface earthquakes? *No—rejected in first sentence*

- Choice (G): Rejected by Scientist 1 in first sentence

- Choice (H): Do scientists agree that Earth's crust is made of mobile tectonic plates? *Yes—otherwise main earthquake theories wouldn't make any sense. Correct.*

- Choice (J): Neither scientist describes whether earthquakes can be felt.

Question 9

What is Scientist 2's hypothesis? *Deep-focus earthquakes are caused by rock undergoing "phase change in crystalline structure."*

How could Scientist 1 refute this hypothesis? *prove that something else causes deep-focus earthquakes, prove that phase changes do not cause earthquakes, prove that phase changes do not occur, disprove any part of Scientist 2's argument*

Which answer choice does this?

- Choice (A): Scientist 2's argument does not hinge on *other sources* of water.

- Choice (B): Scientist 2 argues that deep-focus earthquakes are a result of phase changes and that no phase changes exist below 680 km. If deep-focus earthquakes do exist below 680 km, Scientist 2 is wrong about either the existence of phase changes, the cause of earthquakes, or both. *Correct*

- Choice (C): Finding *a substance* that does not undergo phase change would not disprove earthquake theory.

- Choice (D): Showing ductility of rocks at shallow levels would not disprove Scientist 2's theory that rocks are ductile at deeper levels.

Question 10

Where will you find the answer to this question? *Scientist 1*

What does Scientist 1 say caused this earthquake? *the injection of fluid wastes into the ground*

Which answer does this reflect? Choice (G), (H), and (J) *all say "fluid wastes injected into the ground…"*

Read further. What else does Scientist 1 say causes earthquakes in general? *"Fluids trapped in rock pores can cause rock to fail at lower shear stresses."*

Which answer reflects this? *Only (J) supports this.*

Question 11

What is Scientist 2's hypothesis? *Deep-focus earthquakes are caused by rock undergoing "phase change in its crystalline structure."*

What evidence would support this? *evidence that fluid pressure exists at levels as described in argument, evidence that rock ductility occurs as described, evidence that earthquakes occur only at levels described in argument*

Which answer choice does this?

- Choice (A): This is irrelevent.

- Choice (B): This has not been disputed.

- Choice (C): Calcium magnesium silicate has been shown in a laboratory to undergo the phase shift Scientist 2 describes. If mantle rock responds the same way, that would support Scientist 2's conclusion. *Correct*

- Choice (D): Opposite: Scientist 2 argues that rock at that level is dehydrated.

Question 12

Whose viewpoint does this question ask about? *neither scientist's*

When should you answer this question? *first*

Which answer choice is supported by the entire passage?

- Choice (F): Sentence one confirms. *Correct*

- Choice (G): Sentence 1 refutes.

- Choice (H): Volcanic activity is not mentioned.

- Choice (J): The *most destructive natural phenomenon* is not discussed.

MORE ON STRENGTHENING AND WEAKENING VIEWPOINTS

Some complex questions might introduce new information, then ask you *why* the new information supports or weakens a viewpoint.

Questions that introduce new information sometimes look really confusing. The information might look overly complex or appear at first to have nothing to do with the rest of the passage. Remember that the questions don't rely on any outside knowledge, so you *do* have the information you need to answer them. Break these questions down into a series of simple steps, and always start by making sure you understand each viewpoint. Remember that information supports a viewpoint if it makes it more likely to be true and weakens it if it makes the viewpoint less likely to be true.

MAKING PREDICTIONS BASED ON VIEWPOINTS

Questions that ask you to make predictions based on the viewpoints are particularly common with the more technical passages. These questions often require you to apply a viewpoint to a specific process, or a hypothetical situation, and make a prediction about the outcome. For example, one recent ACT Conflicting Viewpoints passage presented four viewpoints about gene replication in bacteria. The questions accompanying this passage were focused almost exclusively on predicting the order in which the genes would be copied according to each viewpoint.

Confusion is the biggest source of error in these situations. Make sure you minimize potential confusion by reading one viewpoint at a time, and then answering the questions that apply to just that viewpoint.

HYPOTHESES, CONCLUSIONS, AND PREDICTIONS SUPPORTED BY TWO VIEWPOINTS

Another complicated question type will ask you to find hypotheses, conclusions, and predictions that are supported by two or more viewpoints or pieces of information. Again, your job is to find an answer choice that is compatible with both viewpoints or with one viewpoint and some additional information. Make sure you understand exactly what each viewpoint states, or how the viewpoint in question relates to the additional information in the question stem, before you answer the question. A big source of error on the ACT Science test is moving to the answer choices before you know what you're looking for. Make sure you have a guess in mind before reading the answer choices. For questions that ask "which of the following," it's generally quicker to evaluate the answer choices without making a guess, but you need to be certain that you know how to tell whether each choice is correct before you start.

GENERAL COMPLEX QUESTIONS

Sometimes, the ACT makes a question complex by veering far from what is directly stated in the passage. They might do this by introducing seemingly unrelated concepts, asking you to make a prediction or draw a conclusion that feels abstract, or asking you to apply a scientist's reasoning to an entirely new situation.

Complex questions ARE answerable. Start by making sure you understand exactly what the author is saying. Reread the relevant parts of the passage and summarize the main idea in your own words. Then go straight to the answer choices. Three will contain fatal flaws—look for these. The most common kind of wrong answer choice uses ideas drawn from the wrong parts of the passage (for example, ideas in the opening information or another author's viewpoint). Also, look out for answer choices that use just the right words but actually state the exact opposite of what is true, answer choices that use key words from the passage but aren't relevant to the question at hand (these are always tempting because they *look* so good), and answer choices that are outside of the scope of the passage. An answer choice doesn't have to be one you'd come up with on your own to be correct—it just has to be true according to the passage.

Finally, remember that you do have a time limit. Don't spend too much time on any one question. Guess, circle it in your test booklet, and come back for another look if you have time when you finish the section.

Let's wrap up this Scientific Reasoning section by looking at a complex Conflicting Viewpoints passage.

EXAMPLES

An increasing number of individuals over 50 develop type II diabetes, which occurs when the body does not produce enough insulin or when the cells ignore the insulin and as a result, the body's blood sugar level rises dangerously. Although type II diabetes occurs in people of all ages and races, it is more common in adults. Several hypotheses have been proposed to explain the cause of type II diabetes.

DIETARY HYPOTHESIS

Most Americans consume too much sugar. Sugar from food is absorbed into the bloodstream, and insulin is required for the body to be able to use that sugar. In a study of individuals 18–25 years old who consumed more than the recommended amount of sugar daily, and were thus considered at risk for developing type II diabetes, it was shown that the majority had significantly elevated levels of sugar in their blood but normal levels of insulin. When these individuals received small injections of insulin once a day, their blood sugar levels decreased to more normal levels. If abundant levels of sugar are supplied by the diet, sugar dissolving insulin injections should be given to avoid type II diabetes.

GENETIC HYPOTHESIS

Genes, which primarily come from parents and grandparents, contribute to many medical problems that individuals will experience through life. Type II diabetes mainly depends on one's genes, but also on one's lifestyle. Diabetes occurs when the pancreas produces little or no insulin or when the insulin it produces does not work properly. As individuals grow older, the processes of their bodies do not run as efficiently as they did when the individuals were younger. Therefore, the same behaviors may be more detrimental to a person when he or she is older than when he or she was younger, especially for those over the age of 50. This is the main reason that type II diabetes is more common in adults.

Scientists compared the genetics and lifestyles of four groups of individuals over 50. The results are shown in the following table.

Group	Attributes	% with type II diabetes
A	One parent with type II	55%
B	Healthy lifestyle, no parents with type II	20%
C	One parent with type II and healthy lifestyle	40%
D	Two parents with type II	70%

EXERCISE HYPOTHESIS

A lack of exercise results in high body fat content, and a high body fat content does not allow the body to work efficiently. Conversely, regular weight-bearing exercise can boost the body's efficiency. One study showed that 10 weeks of weight training lowered blood sugar in adults over 50. A second study on another group of adults over 50 showed that walking two miles a day for 12 weeks also lowered blood sugar levels.

13. The Genetic Hypothesis best explains why type II diabetes is more common in which of the following groups?

   A. Individuals under the age of 25 as opposed to individuals over the age of 25
   B. Individuals over the age of 25 as opposed to individuals under the age of 25
   C. Individuals over the age of 50 as opposed to individuals under the age of 50
   D. Individuals under the age of 50 as opposed to individuals over the age of 50

14. According to the Genetic Hypothesis, adults who have had their pancreas removed should exhibit:

   F. increased blood insulin levels.
   G. decreased blood sugar levels.
   H. increased blood sugar levels.
   J. decreased body fat content.

15. Supporters of the Dietary Hypothesis might criticize the experimental results in the Exercise Hypothesis for which of the following reasons?

   A. Not enough sugar was included in the diets of the test subjects in both groups.
   B. The sugar intake of the individuals in the two groups was not monitored.
   C. The genetics of each individual in both groups should have been determined.
   D. Type II diabetes is more common in children than adults.

16. Assume that individuals with elevated blood sugar levels have a greater chance of developing type II diabetes. How would supporters of the Genetic Hypothesis explain the experimental results presented in the Dietary Hypothesis?

   F. The test subjects probably had high levels of sugar in their diets.
   G. The test subjects did not perform any weight-bearing exercise.
   H. The test subjects probably had no occurrence of type II diabetes in their genetic backgrounds.
   J. The test subjects were given too little insulin.

17. How might proponents of the Dietary Hypothesis explain the results of Group D in the Genetic Hypothesis experiment?

    A. Insulin supplements should not have been taken by this group.

    B. These individuals and both parents had an unhealthy diet that was high in sugar.

    C. More genetic background should be researched for all the groups.

    D. Not enough insulin was given to this group to affect the onset of type II diabetes.

18. The experiments cited in the Genetic Hypothesis and in the Exercise Hypothesis are similar in that each test subject:

    F. has at least one parent with type II diabetes.

    G. was given a shot of insulin.

    H. had their pancreas previously removed.

    J. was an adult over 50 years old.

Question 13

What is the Genetic Hypothesis? *Type II diabetes is mainly caused by genetic predisposition, but all people become less able to produce insulin as they age.*

What age group does this suggest is most likely to develop type II diabetes? *older individuals*

What answer choices can we eliminate? *Choice (A) and (D)*

Does the passage suggest type II diabetes would be more common in people over 25 or people over 50? *over 50*

Which answer choice does this correspond to? *Choice (C)*

Question 14

What does the Genetic Hypothesis paragraph say about the pancreas? *It produces insulin.*

What would happen without a pancreas? *The body would produce little or no insulin.*

What would occur in a body with little or no insulin? *Blood sugar would increase.*

Which answer choice does that match? *Choice (H)*

Question 15

What is the Dietary Hypothesis? *Adults have too much sugar, so are at high risk unless they take insulin.*

How is this different from the Exercise Hypothesis? *The Exercise Hypothesis attributes the elevated blood sugar level to increased body fat, whereas the Dietary Hypothesis attributes elevated blood sugar to increased sugar intake.*

Which answer choice illustrates the difference between these two hypotheses? *Choice (B)*

Question 16

What is the difference between the Genetic Hypothesis and the Dietary Hypothesis? *The Dietary Hypothesis attributes type II diabetes to sugar intake in adults; the Genetic Hypothesis attributes it to a combination of genetics and decreased ability to produce insulin.*

What do the experimental results in the Dietary Hypothesis show? *Adults who consume more than the recommended amount of sugar have elevated blood sugar levels, which decrease when insulin is introduced.*

What would proponents of the Genetic Hypothesis look for in these results? *Genetic history of type II diabetes in test subjects*

Which answer choice does this match? *Choice (H)*

Question 17

What are the results of Group D in the Genetics Hypothesis experiment? *70% of individuals with two parents with type II diabetes have type II diabetes as well.*

What do proponents of the Dietary Hypothesis attribute type II diabetes to? *High sugar intake without insulin*

To what would Dietary Hypothesis supporters attribute the high incidence of type II diabetes in Group D? *High sugar intake in subjects*

Which answer matches that prediction? *Choice (B)*

Question 18

Who were the individuals in the Genetic Hypothesis experiment? *various individuals over age 50*

Who were the individuals in the Exercise Hypothesis experiment? *various individuals over age 50*

Which answer choice matches? Choice *(J)*

PUTTING IT ALL TOGETHER—CONFLICTING VIEWPOINTS

Now, you know what question types to expect and have strategies to deal with each. On the ACT, the questions won't be grouped by type. They will be mixed together within a passage.

As you know, not all passage types contain an equal balance of the three question types. The passage types themselves have different strategies accordingly. You'll still need to be ready to use the skills for different question types in the context of the various passages.

Thus, we'll work through one more of each passage type together. Think of this section as your dress rehearsal. Be ready to use the different methods for each passage type, and employ the strategies from this chapter when we get to the questions.

PRACTICE—CONFLICTING VIEWPOINTS

Tektites are natural, glassy objects that range in size from the diameter of a grain of sand to that of a human fist. They are found in only a few well-defined areas, called strewn fields. Two theories about the origin of tektites are presented here.

SCIENTIST 1

Tektites almost certainly are extraterrestrial, probably lunar, in origin. Their forms show the characteristics of air-friction melting. In one study, flanged "flying saucer" shapes similar to those of australites (a common tektite form) were produced by ablating lenses of tektite glass in a heated airstream that simulated atmospheric entry.

Atmospheric forces also make terrestrial origin extremely improbable. Aerodynamic studies have shown that because of atmospheric density, tektite-like material ejected from the Earth's surface would never attain a velocity much higher than that of the surrounding air, and therefore would not be shaped by atmospheric friction. Most likely, tektites were formed either from meteorites or from lunar material ejected in volcanic eruptions.

Analysis of specimen #14425 from the *Apollo 12* lunar mission shows that the sample strongly resembles some of the tektites from the Australasian strewn field. Also, tektites contain only a small fraction of the water that is locked into the structure of terrestrial volcanic glass. And tektites never contain unmelted crystalline material; the otherwise similar terrestrial glass produced by some meteorite impacts **always** does.

SCIENTIST 2

Nonlocal origin is extremely unlikely, given the narrow distribution of tektite strewn fields. Even if a tightly focused jet of lunar matter were to strike the Earth, whatever was deflected by the atmosphere would remain in a solar orbit. The next time its orbit coincided with that of the Earth, some of the matter would be captured by Earth's gravity and fall over a wide area.

There are striking similarities not only between the composition of the Earth's crust and that of most tektites but also between the proportions of various gases found in the Earth's atmosphere and also the vesicles of certain tektites.

Tektites were probably formed by meteorite impacts. The shock wave produced by a major collision could temporarily displace the atmosphere above. Terrestrial material might then splatter to suborbital heights and undergo air-friction melting upon reentry. And tektite fields in the Ivory Coast and Ghana can be correlated with known impact craters.

1. The discovery that many tektites contain unmelted crystalline material would:

   A. tend to weaken Scientist 1's argument.

   B. tend to weaken Scientist 2's argument.

   C. be incompatible with both scientists' views.

   D. be irrelevant to the controversy.

2. Which of the following is a reason given by Scientist 2 for believing that tektites originate on the Earth?

   F. The density of the Earth's atmosphere would prevent any similar lunar or extraterrestrial material from reaching the Earth's surface.

   G. Tektites have a composition totally unlike that of any material ever brought back from the moon.

   H. Extraterrestrial material could not have been as widely dispersed as tektites are.

   J. Material ejected from the moon or beyond would eventually have been much more widely distributed on Earth.

3. Scientist 1 could best answer the point that some tektites have vesicles filled with gases in the same proportion as the Earth's atmosphere by:

   A. countering that not all tektites have such gas-filled vesicles.

   B. demonstrating that molten material would be likely to trap some gases while falling through the terrestrial atmosphere.

   C. suggesting that those gases might occur in the same proportions in the moon's atmosphere.

   D. showing that similar vesicles, filled with these gases in the same proportions, are also found in some terrestrial volcanic glass.

4. How did Scientist 2 answer the argument that tektite-like material ejected from the Earth could not reach a high enough velocity relative to the atmosphere to undergo air-friction melting?

   F. By asserting that a shock wave might cause a momentary change in atmosphere density, permitting subsequent aerodynamic heating

   G. By pointing out that periodic meteorite impacts have caused gradual changes in atmospheric density over the eons

   H. By attacking the validity of the aerodynamic studies cited by Scientist 1

   J. By referring to the correlation between tektite fields and known impact craters in the Ivory Coast and Ghana

5. The point of subjecting lenses of tektite glass to a heated airstream was to:

   A. determine their water content.

   B. see if gases became trapped in their vesicles.

   C. reproduce the effects of atmospheric entry.

   D. simulate the mechanism of meteorite formation.

6. Researchers could best counter the objections of Scientist 2 to Scientist 1's argument by:

   F. discovering some phenomenon that would quickly remove tektite-sized objects from orbit.

   G. proving that most common tektite shapes can be produced by aerodynamic heating.

   H. confirming that active volcanoes once existed on the moon.

   J. mapping the locations of all known tektite fields and impact craters.

7. Which of the following characteristics of tektites is LEAST consistent with the theory that tektites are of extraterrestrial origin?

   A. Low water content

   B. "Flying saucer" shapes

   C. Narrow distribution

   D. Absence of unmelted material

ANSWERS AND EXPLANATIONS

1. A
2. J
3. B
4. F
5. C
6. F
7. C

Use the introduction to reveal the issue at hand—namely, tektites, which are small glassy objects found in certain areas known as strewn fields. The conflict is about the *origin* of these objects: in other words, where did they come from?

Scientist 1's theory is expressed in his first sentence: "Tektites almost certainly are extra-terrestrial, probably lunar, in origin." Put that into a form you can understand: Scientist 1 believes that tektites come from space, probably the moon. On the other hand, Scientist 2 has an opposing theory, also expressed in her first sentence: "Nonlocal origin is extremely unlikely." In other words, it's unlikely that tektites come from a nonlocal source; they probably come from a *local* source, i.e., right here on Earth. The conflict is clear. One says that tektites come from space; the other says they come from Earth. You might have even labeled the two positions "space origin" and "Earth origin."

Scientist 1 presents three points of data:

1. Tektite shapes show characteristics of "air-friction melting" (supporting the theory of space origin).

2. "Atmospheric forces" wouldn't be great enough to shape tektite-like material ejected from Earth's surface (weakening the theory of Earth origin).

3. Tektites resemble moon rocks gathered by *Apollo 12* but not Earth rocks (strengthening the theory of space origin).

Complete question 3 at this point, before you move on to Scientist 2.

Question 1

Question 1 asks how it would affect the scientists' arguments if it were discovered that many tektites contain unmelted crystalline material. Well, Scientist 1 says that tektites never contain unmelted crystalline material and that the terrestrial glass produced by some meteorite impacts always does. Therefore, by showing a resemblance between tektites and Earth materials, this discovery would weaken Scientist 1's argument for extraterrestrial origin. Thus, (A) is the correct answer.

Question 2

For question 2, you had to identify which answer choice was used by Scientist 2 to support the argument that tektites are terrestrial in origin. You should have been immediately drawn to (J), which expresses what we've identified above as Scientist 2's first data point. Choice (F) is not discussed by Scientist 2. As for (G), Scientist 2 says that tektites do resemble Earth materials, but never says that they don't resemble lunar materials. And (H) gets it backwards; Scientist 2 says that extraterrestrial material would be widely dispersed and that the tektites are not widely dispersed, therefore they cannot be extraterrestrial.

Question 3

For question 3, you need to find the best way for Scientist 1 to counter the point that some tektites have vesicles filled with gases in the same proportion as the Earth's atmosphere. First, make sure you understand the meaning of that point. If the tektites contain gases from Earth's atmosphere, how could they have been formed in space? Scientist 1 could say that not all tektites have such gas-filled vesicles—choice (A)—but that's not a great argument. If any reasonable number of them do, Scientist 1 would have to come up with an alternative explanation. But if, as (B) suggests, Scientist 1 could demonstrate that tektites are molten as they fall through Earth's atmosphere, and would be likely to trap some terrestrial gases while falling, this would explain how tektites might have come from beyond Earth and still contain Earth-like gases. Choice (C) is easy to eliminate if you know that the moon's atmosphere is extremely thin and totally different in composition from Earth's atmosphere, but if you don't know that, it's still inconsistent with the passage—we know that the tektites are altered as they go through Earth's atmosphere, so this doesn't explain how the trapped gas made it to Earth. Finally, (D) would weaken Scientist 1's hypothesis by equating tektites with terrestrial volcanic glass.

Now, read the information for Scientist 2. Scientist 2 also presents three points of data:

1. Any matter coming from space would "fall over a wide area" instead of being concentrated in strewn fields (weakening the theory of space origin).

2. There are "striking similarities" between tektites and the composition of the Earth's crust (strengthening the theory of Earth origin).

3. Meteorite impacts could create shock waves, explaining how terrestrial material could undergo air-friction melting (strengthening the theory of Earth origin and counteracting Scientist 1's first point).

Obviously, you won't have time to write out the supporting data for each theory the way we've done above. **What's important is that you have an idea of what data supports which theory.** The questions, once you get to them, will then force you to focus.

Question 4

In question 4, you're asked how Scientist 2 answered the argument that tektite-like material ejected from the Earth could not reach a high enough velocity to undergo air-friction melting. Well, that was Scientist 2's third data point. The shock wave produced by a major meteorite collision could momentarily displace the atmosphere right above the impact site (meaning the air moved out of the way for a brief time). So when the splattered material reentered the atmosphere, it would undergo air-friction melting. That's basically what (F) says, making it the correct answer. Choice (J) is tempting because it is mentioned in the same paragraph, but the impact craters in the Ivory Coast and Ghana are mentioned as supporting correlations between tektites and meteorites, not explanations. Note: All questions for this passage are Scientific Reasoning, as is typical of a Conflicting Viewpoints passage.

Question 5

In question 5, the concept of subjecting lenses of tektite glass to a heated airstream was mentioned toward the beginning of Scientist 1's argument. The point was to simulate the entry of extraterrestrial tektite material through Earth's atmosphere, which matches choice (C).

Question 6

Question 6 shows again why it pays to keep each scientist's viewpoint straight. You can't counter the objections of Scientist 2 to Scientist 1's argument unless you know what Scientist 2 was objecting to. Scientist 2's first data point is the only one designed to shoot holes in the opposing viewpoint. There, Scientist 2 takes issue with the idea that lunar material could strike the Earth without being dispersed over a far wider area than the known strewn fields. But, as correct choice (F) says, if researchers found some force capable of pulling tektite-sized objects from orbit *quickly*, it would remove the objection that Scientist 2 raises in her first paragraph. The tektite material would strike the Earth or be pulled away quickly, instead of remaining in a solar orbit long enough to be captured by the Earth's gravity and subsequently be distributed over a wide area of the Earth.

Question 7

Question 7 wasn't too tough if you read the question stem carefully. You want to find the tektite characteristic that is LEAST consistent with the theory that tektites came from the moon or beyond. This is Scientist 1's theory, so you want to pick the answer choice that doesn't go with his argument. Scientist 1's evidence *does* include tektites' low water content, "flying saucer" shapes, and absence of unmelted material. The only answer choice that he didn't mention was the narrow distribution of the strewn fields. And with good reason: That's part of Scientist 2's argument *against* an extraterrestrial origin. So the correct answer is (C).

PUTTING IT ALL TOGETHER—RESEARCH SUMMARY

The following flowchart shows the steps used by a chemist in testing sample solutions for positive ions of silver (Ag), lead (Pb), and mercury (Hg).

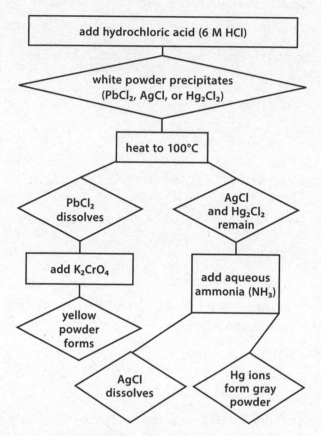

The following experiments were performed by the chemist:

EXPERIMENT 1

Hydrochloric acid (6 M HCl) was added to samples of four unknown solutions labeled 1, 2, 3, and 4. A white powder precipitated out of solutions 1, 2, and 3; no precipitate formed in solution 4.

EXPERIMENT 2

Each of the sample solutions from Experiment 1 was placed in a 100°C water bath for 15 minutes. The precipitate in solution 1 redissolved completely; solutions 2 and 3 still contained a white powder; solution 4 was unchanged. Solutions 2 and 3 were centrifuged to remove the precipitates, which were retained for further testing. Potassium chromate (K_2CrO_4) was then added to each sample. A bright yellow precipitate formed in solutions 1 and 2; none formed in solutions 3 or 4.

EXPERIMENT 3

The white powder centrifuged from solutions 2 and 3 in Experiment 2 was treated with aqueous ammonia (NH_3). The precipitate from solution 2 returned into solution, while that from solution 3 produced a gray powder.

1. Which conclusion is best supported by the results of Experiment 1 alone?

    A. Silver ions are present only in solution 3.

    B. No ions are present in solution 4.

    C. Lead ions are present in solutions 1, 2, and 3.

    D. No positive ions of silver, mercury, or lead are present in solution 4.

2. Based on the experimental results, which ions did solution 2 contain?

    F. Lead ions only

    G. Lead and silver ions only

    H. Silver and mercury ions only

    J. Silver ions only

3. The yellow precipitate that formed in Experiment 2 was most likely:

    A. $AgCl$.

    B. Hg_2Cl_2.

    C. $PbCrO_4$.

    D. Ag_2CrO_4.

4. The experimental results suggest that if lead chloride ($PbCl_2$) were treated with aqueous ammonia (NH_3), the results would be:

    F. a bright yellow precipitate.

    G. a light gray precipitate.

    H. a powdery white precipitate.

    J. impossible to determine from the information given.

5. A student proposed that the analysis could be carried out more efficiently by heating the samples to 100°C before adding the 6 M HCl. This suggestion is:

    A. a bad idea; since $PbCl_2$ will not precipitate out of solution at this temperature, lead ions would be undetectable.

    B. a bad idea; the hot solutions could not be safely centrifuged.

    C. a good idea; the number of steps would be reduced from 3 to 2, saving much time and effort.

    D. a good idea; the chloride-forming reaction would proceed faster, eliminating the necessity for a 15-minute water bath.

ANSWERS AND EXPLANATIONS

1. D
2. G
3. C
4. J
5. A

Let's review the basics of General to Specific and Specific to General Scientific thinking as you look over the passage and think like a scientist.

GENERAL TO SPECIFIC

In some cases, scientists have already discovered a law of nature and wish to apply their knowledge to a specific case. For example, a scientist may wish to know how fast a pebble (call it Pebble A) will be falling when it hits the ground three seconds after being dropped. The scientist could use the known general principle of gravity to calculate the specific information she needs. You could think of this kind of logic as *general-to-specific*. The scientist uses a *general* principle (the acceleration of any object falling on Earth) to find a *specific* fact (the speed of Pebble A).

SPECIFIC TO GENERAL

Scientists use a different kind of thinking to discover a new law of nature. In this case, they examine many specific facts and then draw a general conclusion about what they've seen. For example, a scientist might watch hundreds of different kinds of frogs live and die and might notice that all of them developed from tadpoles. She might then announce a conclusion: all frogs develop from tadpoles. You could think of this kind of logic as *specific to general*. The scientist looks at many *specific* frogs to find a *general* rule about all frogs. Because not every case can be tested, this conclusion is a *hypothesis*, not a *fact*, but it may be so well-documented that it becomes the equivalent of a law.

In your science classes in school, you mostly learn about general-to-specific thinking. Your teachers explain general rules of science to you and then expect you to apply these rules to answer questions and solve problems. Some ACT Science questions are like that as well. But the majority are not. **Most ACT Science questions test specific-to-general thinking.** The questions test your ability to see the kinds of patterns in specific data that, as a scientist, you would use to formulate your own general hypotheses.

In this series of experiments, the general principle is known—silver, lead, and mercury will precipitate or dissolve when certain things are done to them—and the scientists are using this principle to test certain substances in order to identify them. In fact, this is more like a procedure than an experiment, since there's no control group. But the same kind of experimental thinking—using the results of varying procedures to make reasonable inferences about what's happening—will get you your answers.

This passage also introduces the idea of a flowchart. Basically, the flowchart indicates an order of procedures. You follow the flowchart from top to bottom. The things in squares indicate what's done to a specimen; the things in diamonds indicate possible results.

SMARTPOINT—FIGURE INTERPRETATION

Question 4

The passage does not provide any evidence for what would happen. The lead chloride is treated on one side of the flowchart, and the aqueous ammonia treatment is only on the other side of the flowchart. We cannot draw any conclusions at all, so the answer is (J).

SMARTPOINT—PATTERNS

Question 5

Heating all of the samples first would substantially change the results. We know, for example, that the $PbCl_2$ dissolves back into the solution at 100°C, meaning we would never see it in the first place if the heating were to be the first step. This matches answer (A). Choice (B) also says this is a bad idea, but safety is not addressed in this passage.

SMARTPOINT—SCIENTIFIC REASONING

Question 1

If any Ag, Pb, or Hg ions were present, they would have precipitated out as powder. Choice (B) may at first be tempting, but is too extreme—we're only testing for three specific ions, not all ions, so we cannot argue that no ions at all are present. Choice (A) is not supported because the same thing happened in three solutions, and we don't know enough about the precipitate yet to say it is lead, so (C) is not correct.

Question 2

This question combines a number of pieces of information, but can be walked through methodically. We know from the flowchart that heating causes lead (Pb) to dissolve. Since solution 2 still has precipitate after heating (in Experiment 2), it must have something other than lead in it—either or both silver or mercury. This eliminates (F). However, we also know that when potassium chromate is added to lead (again on the left side of the flowchart), a yellow powder forms. This also happens in solution 2 in Experiment 2, so there must be lead in it. This eliminates (H) and (J), only leaving (G), which matches all the information provided.

Question 3

This question requires careful examination of the order of events in the experiment. The yellow precipitate formed in Experiment 2 when potassium chromate was added. This was done after the white precipitate was removed from solutions 2 and 3. We know from the right side of the flowchart that the white precipitate was silver- and mercury-based. So when those solutions were centrifuged, the silver and mercury were removed, only leaving the dissolved lead. The yellow precipitate that formed in Experiment 2 when potassium chromate was added, therefore, must be lead-based, which only matches (C).

PUTTING IT ALL TOGETHER—FIGURE INTERPRETATION

This is the last passage we'll work on before the quiz, and we'll throw you into the deep end now so you can see what a complex and intimidating ACT Science passage looks like. Fear not, we'll use this passage to show you how you can earn points on even the most difficult of ACT Science passages, without needing to know exactly what's going on.

Neutrinos (n) are subatomic particles that travel at approximately the speed of light. They can penetrate most matter, because they are electrically neutral and effectively massless.

Generally accepted theory holds that the nuclear reactions that power the sun create vast quantities of neutrinos as byproducts. Three proposed stages (PPI, PPII, and PPIII) of the most important solar reaction are shown in Figure 1, along with their neutrino-producing subpaths. Equations for the subpaths are shown in Table 1, as are the predicted neutrino energies and fluxes.

Figure 1

Table 1

Subpath name	Subpath equation	Neutrino energy (MeV)	Expected flux on Earth ($10^{10} cirr^2 sec^{-1}$)
p-p	$_1H^1 + {_1}H^1 \rightarrow {_1}H^2 + \beta^+ + n$	0.42	6.06781
p-e-p	$_1H^1 + \beta^- + {_1}H^1 \rightarrow {_1}H^2 + n$	1.44	0.01524
$Be^7\dagger$	$_4Be^7 + \beta^- \rightarrow {_3}Li^7 + n$	0.87	0.43924
$Be^7\dagger\dagger$	$_4Be^7 + \beta^- \rightarrow {_3}Li^7 + n$	0.38	0.04880
B^8	$_5B^8 \rightarrow {_4}Be^8 + \beta^+ + n$ 54	14.05	0.00054

Be^7† signifies subpath 1   Be^7†† signifies subpath 2

1. According to the information presented in the passage, which of the following stages or subpaths should contribute the smallest portion of the total solar neutrino flux on Earth?

    A. p-p
    B. PPI
    C. PPII
    D. PIII

2. Of the neutrinos that are produced in the subpaths described in the passage, which type can have the greatest energy?

    F. n_1
    G. n_2
    H. n_3
    J. n_4

3. Based on the information presented in the passage, the percentage of solar neutrinos produced by Be^7 subpath 2 is approximately:

    A. 1.2%.
    B. 10%.
    C. 12%.
    D. 90%.

4. Solar neutrinos are detected through a reaction with 37Q for which the minimum neutrino energy is approximately 0.8 MeV. Of the neutrinos discussed in the passage, this method would detect:

    F. all of the neutrinos produced in PPI and PPII.
    G. some of the neutrinos produced in PPI, PPII, and PPIII.
    H. only neutrinos produced in Be^7 subpath 1 of PPII.
    J. only neutrinos produced in PPIII.

5. The symbol β represents a beta particle, a particle emitted during nuclear decay. Beta particles may be positively or negatively charged. During which of the following subpaths are beta particles emitted?

    I. p-p
    II. p-e-p
    III. B^8

    A. II only
    B. I and III only
    C. II and III only
    D. I, II, and III

ANSWERS AND EXPLANATIONS

1. **D**
2. **J**
3. **A**
4. **G**
5. **B**

Confused? If so, don't sweat it. **Some ACT questions are so hard that even your teachers would have a hard time getting them correct just based on the science.**

The good news is that you don't have to understand a passage to get at least some of the questions right. You're demonstrating your Reading skills foremost, not your understanding of neutrinos. Here's how you might have approached the passage:

GETTING POINTS EVEN IF YOU DON'T GET THE POINT

Your pre-read of the introduction should have told you that the passage is about neutrinos coming from the sun. But that may be all you were able to get from this, so start there: This is about neutrinos, which come from the sun. Figure 1 and Table 1 may not have added much, but if you didn't panic, you might have noticed a few things: Figure 1 has some really odd-looking equations, it has three areas (PPI, PPII, and PPIII), and it has some really big parts and some really small parts. If you look at the *x*-axis of the chart, you'll see what those big parts and small parts mean: Whatever PPI, PPII, and PPIII are, the first is 88 percent, the second is only 12 percent, and the third is only 0.01 percent. Table 1 then relates subpaths to energy to flux. What *are* those? These are less clear, but Table 1 shows how they relate.

SMARTPOINT—FIGURE INTERPRETATION

Question 1

Here we go. Question 1 asks which stage or subpath contributes the smallest portion of neutrino flux. That sounds familiar. We saw both subpaths and fluxes in Table 1, and those PPI-III in the answer choices are definitely from Figure 1. A look back at Table 1 doesn't contribute much, but a look at Figure 1 reminds us of two things: 1) "p-p" isn't a stage like PPI-III, and 2) whatever PPI-III are, PPIII is only 0.001 of the total. That makes (D) a very tempting option, and indeed, (D) is correct for question 1.

Question 2

This one's not much friendlier. But it asks which of these n_1–n_4 neutrinos has the greatest energy, so that at least tells us what we're looking for: something with n_1–n_4 and energy. The third column in Table 1 is clearly about neutrino energy, and the last line of it is way bigger than any of the others. What that last line is or means is hard to say, but it's the most energy. It doesn't relate directly to n_1–n_4, though—those are all in Figure 1—but it does relate to subpath name B[8] in the first column, and *that* only appears in one other place: next to an arrow pointing to n_4 in Figure 1. So take a gamble; choose n_4—which is (J)—for this question. If you did that, you'd still have gotten another point, still without really understanding much more than before.

Question 4

Things get a little harder with question 4, but you still might have gotten the answer if you were methodical. Here we get some mumbo jumbo about 37Q, but that doesn't match *anything* in the tables, so we can and should ignore it. The part of the question that should have caught your eye was the bit about a minimum neutrino energy of 0.8 MeV. Neutrino energy was represented in the third column of Table 1. According to that table, only three subpaths have an energy greater than 0.8—p-e-p (with 1.44), Be^7† (with 0.87), and B^8 (the champion, with 14.06); in other words, the second, third, and fifth rows. Those three appear to be "fine"—they would be detected, because they're above 0.8 MeV.

The first and fourth rows don't look as good—they aren't going to be detected, because they're under 0.8. But what are those? The first is p-p. That's part (but not all) of the PPI portion of Figure 1. The rest of PPI is p-e-p, which is fine. So *some but not all* of PPI is safe. This actually tells us the answer right away, because it eliminates (F), (H), and (J), but let's push all the way through. The fourth row—Be^7††—also isn't safe, at only 0.38, so what is that? That appears on Figure 1 to be a small part of PPII, the rest of which is Be^7†, which is also fine at 0.87. So again, *some* of PPII is fine, some is not. This answer—that some of PPI and some of PPII will be detected—is enough to tell us that (G) is correct, and it is.

SMARTPOINT—PATTERNS

Question 3

Question 3 refers to Be^7 subpath 2. You may have noticed in the note under Table 1 that the Be^7†† signifies subpath 2. So in the question, where it says "Be^7 subpath 2," we can substitute "Be^7††." So far, so good. Notice that the choices are all percentages. Where are percentages mentioned? In Figure 1. So find Be^7†† in Figure 1. You find it in the area of PPII, which is 12 percent of the *x*-axis in that chart. But notice that Be^7†† represents only *part* of that part of the figure—10 percent, to be exact. So 10 percent of 12 percent would be 1.2 percent. That's (A). It's also the correct answer.

SMARTPOINT—SCIENTIFIC REASONING

Question 5

Finally, question 5 talks about beta particles. Well, looking at both tables, that little beta symbol (β) appears only in the "subpath equation" column of Table 1. There, we find beta symbols in the equations for *all* of the subpaths in the table. That may lead you to believe that all three Roman numerals should be included, and no one would blame you for choosing

(D) (I, II, and III). You would have been wrong, but you can't win them all when you're winging questions you don't really understand.

Going back to the question, you notice it's asking in which subpaths beta particles are *emitted*, and if you reason that in the subpath equations everything *before* the arrow is what you start with and everything *after* the arrow is what you finish with, you might be able to make a better guess. You would realize that those equations with a beta symbol *after* the arrow were ones in which a beta particle was *emitted*. In that case, then, you would have seen that the equations for p-p and B^8 do have beta particles emitted, while the rest do not. That would have led you to (B)—I and III only—which is the correct answer.

The moral of the story, of course, is **don't give up on a passage just because you don't understand it.** You may not be able to get *every* point associated with the passage, but you may be able to get at least one or two (or three or four). Remember: The test is designed in such a way that you can *figure out* many of the questions, even if you don't know the subject area.

SUMMARY

In this chapter, we went over every SmartPoint on the ACT Science test, and the strategies to use for each at their various complexities.

We also saw how the SmartPoints fit into the three different passage types; you had a chance to use the distinct methods for each passage type discussed in the previous chapter and the strategies for each question type within those passages.

Use this chapter for continued study and reference as you practice Science passages and find the skills you need to focus on.

Remember, don't get bogged down in the details and don't let complexity scare you. All of the information you need to answer the questions can be found in the passage. You can even answer most of the questions without a clear understanding of meaning. Carefully search the data for Figure Interpretation questions, relate variables for Pattern questions, and think like a scientist for the sake of Scientific Reasoning.

Continue to rehearse the Kaplan Methods. Being able to quickly recognize what passage type you're dealing with, then diving in with the appropriate strategy to find the information you need are important skills. Use the quiz in the next chapter, when you're ready, to practice each Kaplan Method again. Refer back to this chapter and the previous chapter as often as necessary. Build these habits now to increase your efficiency on Test Day.

Use the strategies to find the info you need and nothing more. Get to the questions. Research your answer and earn points to master the ACT Science test!

CHAPTER 15

Science Part 3: ACT Science Quiz

All set? Let's go!

Treat the following passages and their questions like those you'll encounter on Test Day to gauge what ACT Science test skills you need to hone. Make sure to check your answers only after you've completed a passage and its questions or after you've completed all three. Do not check as you work—you won't be able to check your answers at all on Test Day, so try to make this practice as realistic as possible.

Keep track of your time. Remember that on Test Day, you will have 35 minutes to read 7 passages and answer 40 questions. The passages will draw from biology, chemistry, earth and space science, and physics. Passages will be Data Representation, Research Summaries, or Conflicting Viewpoints. Make sure you take note of which kinds of passages and questions present a greater challenge for you so you can review the Kaplan Methods for those and practice more.

Finally, when you are reviewing your answers, make sure you make special note of the SmartPoint categories of the questions you missed. Use this quiz to help you figure out where to spend your studying time before tackling the Practice Tests at the end of the book.

Remember: Read the passage, taking notes as you go, skim the figures, and attack the questions. Keep in mind the specific methods for each type of passage.

Directions: This quiz contains three passages, each followed by a series of questions. After reading each passage, select the best answer to each question. You may refer to the passages while you answer the questions.

PASSAGE I

Table 1 below shows the percent composition of Earth's atmosphere by volume[*], temperature, and pressure according to elevation above a specific location. An elevation of 0 kilometers represents sea level, the surface of Earth. Temperature is given in degrees Celsius and pressure in mmHg.

Table 1

Atmospheric layer	Elevation (km)	Pressure (mmHg)	Temperature (°C)	Concentration (% by volume)				
				N_2	O_2	He	H_2	H_2O
Troposphere	0	1000	25	78.08	20.94	0.0005	0.00005	2
	15	100	−45	78.08	20.94	0.0005	0.00005	1
Stratosphere	50	10	−5	78.08	20.94	0.0005	0.00005	0.25
Mesosphere	90	3	−90	78.08	20.94	0.0005	0.00005	0
Thermosphere	200	1	900	0	99.78	0.0005	0.00005	0
	500	0.001	1,500	0	0	99.6	0.4	0
Exosphere	1000	0.0001	0	0	0	0.05	99.05	0

*Percent composition by volume is equivalent to the mole-fraction of the gas—i.e., the number of molecules of the gas over the total number of molecules in any given volume.

The temperature in Earth's atmosphere does not vary continuously with elevation. Figure 1, which follows, shows the complex relationship between elevation and temperature in Earth's atmosphere.

Figure 1

Image and associated databases are available from the National Oceanic and Atmospheric Administration, U.S. Department of Commerce, www.srh.noaa.gov/srh/jetstream/atmos/atmprofile.

1. According to the data presented in Table 1, what is the percent concentration of O_2 at 50 km?

    A. 99.78

    B. 78.08

    C. 20.94

    D. 0.005

2. The percent concentrations of which of the following gases are constant below an elevation of 90 km?

    F. N_2, O_2, and H_2O only

    G. H_2O only

    H. N_2, O_2, and H_2 only

    J. N_2, O_2, He, and H_2 only

3. Which of the following graphs represents the relationship between O_2 concentration and elevation?

    A.

    B.

    C.

    D.

4. According to Table 1, the concentration of H_2O at 10 km is approximately:

    F. 1%.

    G. 1.5%.

    H. 2%.

    J. 10%.

5. A group of researchers sent up a weather balloon from their lab. The balloon sent back a temperature reading of –20°C. Given the information in Figure 1, which of the following elevations could possibly be the elevation of the balloon?

    A. 7 km

    B. 23 km, 59 km, or 116 km

    C. 3 km, 23 km, 35 km, or 72 km

    D. 7 km, 37 km, 59 km, or 116 km

6. Suppose a rocket malfunctions on its way into outer space. The last readings the rocket sent to Earth before the malfunction were an atmospheric O_2 concentration of 33.75%, an H_2O concentration of 0%, and a temperature of 285°C. At what elevation did the rocket likely malfunction?

    F. 10 km

    G. 50 km

    H. 100 km

    J. 500 km

7. According to the information in Figure 1, between 50 and 85 km, as elevation increases:

    A. temperature increases.

    B. temperature decreases.

    C. temperature decreases, then increases.

    D. temperature increases, then decreases.

PASSAGE II

Before it can be considered safe to drink, water pumped from the ground or piped from an above-ground reservoir must be treated to remove contaminants. Suspended particles of organic and inorganic matter, parasites such as *Giardia,* bacteria, and toxic metal ions, especially lead (Pb), arsenic (As), and copper (Cu), must be removed for the water to be considered safe for consumption. Several methods of water filtration were investigated by scientists.

METHOD 1

Water was filtered through a rapid sand filter. The funnel-shaped filter is constructed from an upper layer of activated carbon and a thicker layer of sand below that, as shown in Diagram 1. Particles too large to pass through the spaces between grains of sand are trapped in the upper layers of sand, and smaller particles are trapped in pore spaces or adhere to the sand. Rapid sand filters do not remove a significant number of dissolved metal ions. The efficiency of particle removal was tested using filters of different depth. Data are shown in Table 1.

Diagram 1

Table 1

Filter Depth (m)	Particles Removed (%)	Time for Filter Efficiency to Drop to 50% (hours)
0.6	95	2
0.8	98	3
1.0	99	4
1.2	99	5

METHOD 2

After filtering through the rapid sand filter, the water was pumped into storage tanks and treated with various concentrations of chlorine to destroy parasites and bacteria. Data are shown in Table 2.

Table 2

Chlorine Concentration (parts per million)	Parasites and Bacteria Killed (%)
0.10	75
0.15	98
0.20	99.9
0.25	99.99
0.30	99.99

METHOD 3

The final step of water purification involves the removal of dangerous dissolved metal ions. To reduce these concentrations, a reverse osmosis filter was used (Diagram 2). The size of the pores in the filter was varied, and the percentage of metal ions removed was calculated for each pore size. Data are shown in Table 3.

Diagram 2

Table 3

Pore Size (angstroms)	As Removed (%)	Cu Removed (%)	Pb Removed (%)
2	62	78	85
3	59	77	98
4	51	68	92
5	47	62	84
6	30	56	70

8. How would the results of chlorinating water be affected, if at all, if excess chlorine-free water was accidentally added to the water in the chlorination tanks?

   F. The percentage of bacteria and parasites killed would decrease.

   G. The percentage of bacteria and parasites killed would increase.

   H. The percentage of bacteria and parasites would not change.

   J. The percentage of bacteria killed would increase while the percentage of parasites killed would decrease.

9. Which of the following statements about pore size is consistent with the results of Method 3?

   A. Increasing pore size results in an increased amount of Cu removed.

   B. Increasing pore size results in an increased amount of bacteria and parasites killed.

   C. Decreasing pore size results in an increased amount of As removed.

   D. Decreasing pore size requires more time to filter heavy metal ions.

10. Which of the following procedures would yield more information about the effects of chlorine concentration on parasites and bacteria in water?

    F. Determining what percentage of parasites and bacteria are killed by ultraviolet light exposure

    G. Determining what percentage of parasites and bacteria are killed during the process of rapid sand filtering

    H. Determining how the nutrient content of the water changes with chlorine concentration

    J. Determining what percentages of individual types of parasites and bacteria are killed at different chlorine concentrations

11. Scientists were concerned that sediment particles contained within the rapid sand filters were contributing to the amount of particulate matter in the water exiting the filter. Which of the following procedures would best allow the scientists to investigate this issue?

    A. Filtering pure water through the filter and measuring the amount of particulate matter in the water exiting the filter

    B. Testing the amount of dissolved metal ion in the water before and after filtering

    C. Adding additional sediment particles to the water before filtering

    D. Measuring the amount of sediment in the water before and after filtering

12. Over-chlorinating water can result in the production of potentially harmful chemical byproducts called trihalomethanes (THMs). If chlorine concentrations above 0.25 parts per million (ppm) can result in dangerous levels of THMs in the water supply, which of the following chlorine concentrations should scientists recommend to best purify drinking water of parasites and bacteria?

    F. 0.15 ppm

    G. 0.20 ppm

    H. 0.25 ppm

    J. 0.30 ppm

13. Molecules of zinc (Zn) are very close in size to molecules of Cu. If the percentage of Zn ions in water was also measured before and after reverse osmosis filtration, what relationship, if any, would scientists expect to see between pore size and percent Zn removal?

    A. As pore size increased, the percentage of Zn removed would increase.

    B. As pore size increased, the percentage of Zn removed would decrease.

    C. As pore size increased, the percentage of Zn removed would first increase, then decrease.

    D. As pore size increased, the percentage of Zn removed would first decrease, then increase.

14. If a city's water contained equal amounts of As, Cu, and Pb, a reverse osmosis filter with which pore size would remove the most heavy metals?

    F. 2 angstroms

    G. 3 angstroms

    H. 4 angstroms

    J. 5 angstroms

PASSAGE III

The *molecular geometry* of a molecule is the three-dimensional appearance of that molecule. Molecular geometry determines many of the properties of a substance, most notably its phase of matter, reactivity, polarity, and magnetism. While molecular geometries can be determined absolutely through X-ray crystallography or quantum mechanical modeling, they can also be predicted with the *valence shell electron-pair repulsion* (VSEPR) theory.

The VSEPR theory uses Lewis structures (diagrams that show the bonding between atoms and lone electron pairs in a molecule) to predict the molecular geometry of covalently bonded molecules. VSEPR theory states that the shape of a molecule is determined by the repulsions between the bonded and nonbonded pairs of electrons in the outer shell of the molecule's central atom. These electron pairs arrange themselves as far apart as possible to minimize repulsion. There are five basic molecular geometries:

1. *Linear.* In a linear molecule, two electron pairs are arranged in a line around a central atom. The bond angle between the electron pairs is 180°.

2. *Trigonal planar.* A molecule with trigonal planar geometry has three electron pairs arranged around a central atom, with a bond angle of 120° between electron pairs.

3. *Tetrahedral.* In a molecule with tetrahedral geometry, the central atom is surrounded by four electron pairs, each with bond angles of 109.5°.

4. *Trigonal bipyramidal.* Molecules with this geometry contain five electron pairs. The bond angles are 90°, 120°, and 180°.

5. *Octahedral.* Molecules with octahedral geometry contain six electron pairs around one central atom. Bond angles are 90° and 180°.

Two students discuss the molecular geometry of water (H_2O).

STUDENT 1

Predicting the shape of a molecule is relatively straightforward. A molecule's shape will always be determined by the number of electron pairs around the central atom. The number of electron pairs corresponds to the number of atoms that are bound to the central atom of the molecule. For example, water contains two hydrogen atoms bound to one atom of oxygen, giving the molecule a linear geometry.

STUDENT 2

The geometry of a molecule is dependent on the number of atoms bound to the central atom of that molecule. However, the geometry of a molecule is also dependent on the presence of electron pairs around the central atom that are not bonded to any atoms. These nonbonded electron pairs also have a negative charge and therefore repel the electrons that are bound to atoms, influencing the shape of a molecule. Because one molecule of water contains two nonbonded electron pairs around a central oxygen atom and two electron pairs bonded to hydrogen atoms, it has a tetrahedral geometry.

15. According to the passage, electron pairs tend to:

    A. attract each other.

    B. prefer a linear geometry.

    C. arrange themselves close to each other.

    D. arrange themselves as far apart as possible.

16. Based on Student 2's explanation, the south (negatively charged) end of a magnet will repel the south end of another magnet because:

    F. positive charges always attract each other.

    G. negative charges always repel each other.

    H. a positive and negative charge always attract each other.

    J. a positive and a negative charge always repel each other.

17. Suppose a molecule of sulfur dioxide (SO_2) was found to have a bond angle of 120° and contain one nonbonded electron pair. If true, this finding would most likely support the viewpoint(s) of:

    A. Student 1 only.

    B. Student 2 only.

    C. both Student 1 and Student 2.

    D. neither Student 1 nor Student 2.

18. Quantum mechanical models suggest that a molecule of sulfur hexafluoride (SF_6) contains no nonbonded electron pairs. Both students would predict that a molecule of SF_6 would have:

    F. an octahedral geometry.

    G. a trigonal bipyramidal geometry.

    H. bond angles of 90°, 120°, and 180°.

    J. a bond angle of 109.5°.

19. Suppose that the model presented by Student 1 is correct. Based on the information provided, what would be the bond angle in a molecule of perchlorate ion (ClO_4^-)?

    A. 180°

    B. 120°

    C. 109.5°

    D. 90°

20. Based on the model presented by Student 1, a molecule of ammonia (NH_3) would have a:

    F. trigonal planar geometry, because three atoms of H are bound to one central atom of N.

    G. trigonal planar geometry, because three atoms of H and one unbound electron pair are bound to one central atom of N.

    H. tetrahedral geometry, because three atoms of H are bound to one central atom of N.

    J. tetrahedral geometry, because three atoms of H and one unbound electron pair are bound to one central atom of N.

21. Which of the following diagrams showing the relationship between an electron pair's bonded status and the relative strength of the repulsive force is consistent with Student 2's assertions about the shape of a water molecule, but is NOT consistent with Student 1's assertions about the shape of a water molecule?

A.

C.

B.

D.

22. Measurements made through X-ray crystallography show that the repulsive force of nonbonded electron pairs is greater than the repulsive force of bound electron pairs. Based on the information provided, this finding would most likely weaken the viewpoint(s) of:

F. Student 1 only.

G. Student 2 only.

H. both Student 1 and Student 2.

J. neither Student 1 nor Student 2.

ANSWERS AND EXPLANATIONS

PASSAGE I

1. C
2. J
3. A
4. G
5. D
6. H
7. B

1. C

Figure Interpretation

This is a classic example of a question asking us to locate data from within a complex data presentation. Table 1 has nine rows and nine columns, and contains an awful lot of information. To zero in on the data we need to answer this question, we should start by looking for the column labeled "O_2." (Hint: it's the sixth column.) Then use a pencil to follow that column down until we reach the 50 km row. Underline the 50 km row, and see where it meets the line down the O_2 row. It's easy for your eyes to accidentally skip up, down, or over a row in such a big table, so marking the row and column you need will help avoid unnecessary errors. The correct answer is (C), 20.94%.

2. J

Figure Interpretation

Here's a great example of a comparing data question. The question asks us to list the gases with constant concentrations below an elevation of 90 km. To answer, we need to underline the 90 km row in Table 1 (again, this makes it easier to keep track of). Which gases have concentrations that don't change

above this line? N_2, O_2, He, and H_2. The correct answer is (J).

Choice (G) is a trap. Notice that the question stem asks for concentrations "below an elevation of 90 km." Below 90 km means less than 90 km, which on the table means the rows *above* 90 km. If we had read that "below" literally and read down on the table, we might have picked (G).

3. A

Figure Interpretation

This question asks us to translate information from a table into a graph. Looking at the answer choices, we can see that the graph we are asked to generate doesn't contain specific points (in fact, there are no numbers at all on any of the graphs in the answer choices), merely an approximation of the general shape of the curve we would expect to see.

To find the correct graph, look at the column for O_2 concentration in Table 1 (that's the sixth column from the left). From 0 to 90 km, concentration remains constant at 20.94%. Then, at 200 km, it spikes to 99.8%. Above 500 km, it's 0%. So we're looking for a chart that stays flat, then peaks, then drops to 0.

Choice (A) best represents this trend. Notice that (D) shows the steep rise, but not the drop back down to zero, and (C) shows the drop down to zero, but not the steep rise to 99.8%.

4. G

Patterns

This question tests our ability to interpolate between two data points. Table 1 doesn't directly give us a value for percent H_2O concentration at 10 km, but it does give us the percent concentrations at 0 and 15 km (which are 2% and 1%, respectively). Our job is to read in between the lines. Since 10 km is between 0 and 15 km, we need to find the answer choice between 2% and 1%. The only one given is (G), 1.5%. Could 1.5 be slightly off? Sure, but it has to be the right answer.

5. D
Figure Interpretation
Here's another question testing our ability to combine data from a complex presentation. The curve in Figure 1 zigzags a few times and crosses over –20°C more than once. To identify the elevations that could measure –20°C, we should draw a line up from –20°C on the x-axis. We can see that the line intersects the curve four times. Tracing left to the y-axis from those four points of intersection, we can see that possible elevations at –20°C are approximately 7 km, 37 km, 59 km, and 116 km. That matches (D).

Choice (A) is a trap testing whether you just stop at the first point of intersection (about 7 km), or keep following the line up. Choice (C) is a trap designed to catch you if you weren't paying attention to units and the presence of a double y-axis. The left y-axis is in km and the right one is in miles. Choice (C) provides the correct values for this question in miles, but labels the answer in km, so it appears consistent with all the other choices.

6. H
Figure Interpretation
This question requires us to combine information from two complex sources: Table 1 and Figure 1. Our first clue is that the O_2 concentration at the elevation of malfunction is 33.75%. The O_2 concentration is given in Table 1, so we should start by checking there; it shows that the O_2 concentration rises from 20.94% above 90 km. Without going any farther, we know we can eliminate (F) and (G). Our rocket is definitely above these elevations.

Our next clues are an H_2O concentration of 0% and a temperature of 285°C. The H_2O concentration is

0% for any elevation above 90 km, so that doesn't give us any additional information. Temperature, however, is an important clue. According to Figure 1, a temperature of 285°C only occurs above 90 km once, at about 100 km. Choice (H), then, is the correct answer.

7. B
Figure Interpretation
Here's a question asking us to understand the relationship between variables in a complex data presentation. Fortunately, this question makes our job a bit easier by restricting elevation to between 50 and 85 km. We should start by drawing a horizontal line through 50 km and a second horizontal line through 85 km. Now we can focus on only the relevant section of the curve. We can see clearly that between our two lines, as elevation increases, temperature decreases. This is stated in (B).

PASSAGE II

8. **F**

9. **C**

10. **J**

11. **A**

12. **H**

13. **B**

14. **G**

8. F
Patterns
You're asked to predict how the accidental addition of chlorine-free water would affect the results obtained in Method 2. To answer, consider the relationship between the chlorine concentration and the percentage of bacteria and parasites killed. A quick glance back at Table 2 clearly shows that as

chlorine concentration increases, the percentage of bacteria and parasites killed also increases.

What, then, will happen to the concentration of chlorine in the water if chlorine-free water is introduced? Chlorine-free water would dilute the concentration of chlorine. This decrease in concentration would decrease the percentage of bacteria and parasites killed, so (F) is correct.

9. C

Scientific Reasoning

Remember that some Research Summaries questions will ask you to evaluate the experimental results, just like Data Representation questions. Here, we're asked to examine the relationship between pore size and heavy metal removal.

Begin by looking back over Table 3. For both As and Cu, an increase in pore size results in a decrease in the percentage of heavy metal removed. For Pb, percentage removed increases when pore size is increased from 2 to 3 angstroms, and then decreases as pore size increases further.

Only (C) gets the relationship right (though the wording is a bit confusing—"decreasing" pore size means you have to read the table from bottom to top, which isn't how one usually approaches a table). Note that choices (B) and (D) don't relate to Method 3 at all and that (A) gets the relationship backward.

10. J

Scientific Reasoning

The effect of chlorine concentration on parasites and bacteria was examined in Method 2. Further investigations about chlorine concentration should test something not already studied in Method 2, but relevant to the experiment at hand. Only (J) identifies an experiment that would give us additional information about the effects of chlorine concentration on parasites and bacteria; it suggests finding out how specific kinds of parasites and bacteria each respond to chlorine concentration.

Choices (F) and (G) are incorrect because they do not offer any additional information about how *chlorine concentration* affects parasites and bacteria. Choice (H) is incorrect because we're asked to find out more about the effects of chlorine concentration on parasites and bacteria, not nutrient content.

11. A

Scientific Reasoning

The question stem tells us that the scientists are concerned that sediment contained within the rapid sand filter itself is contributing to the amount of particulate matter in the water exiting the filter. To test whether this is an issue, it would make sense for the scientists to run pure, particle-free water through the filter and see if any sediment particles are contained in the water exiting the filter, as in (A). If sediment particles are found in the water exiting the filter, their suspicion is verified.

Choice (B) is irrelevant to the issue of particles within the filter. Heavy metal ions are discussed in Method 3, but have no bearing on the particle-removing rapid sand filters discussed in Method 1.

Choice (C) is also incorrect. Adding additional sediment to the water before filtering won't tell scientists anything about whether the filter itself is adding particles to the water. Choice (D) is likewise incorrect. The amount of sediment in the water is already being measured before and after filtering, to determine the percentage of sediment removed by each filter. It offers us no additional information.

12. H

Scientific Reasoning

Many questions on the ACT Science test will introduce some additional information, either in the form of information within the question stem, as is the case here, or in the form of additional tables or graphs. Our task in this situation is to integrate this new information with the information already in the passage.

To answer this question, we must look back at Table 2. It shows that chlorine concentrations of 0.10 ppm kill 75% of parasites and bacteria, concentrations of 0.15 ppm kill 98% of parasites and bacteria, concentrations of 0.20 ppm kill 99.9% of parasites and bacteria, and concentrations of 0.25 ppm and higher kill 99.99% of parasites and bacteria. The question stem, however, tells us that concentrations *over* 0.25 ppm result in dangerously high THM levels. Scientists should, then, recommend that water be treated with the lowest chlorine concentration that still kills the highest percentage of parasites and bacteria. That would be 0.25 ppm, as in (H).

13. **B**

Patterns

Here, we are asked to predict the results of an additional measurement in an experiment. Scientists didn't measure the percentage of zinc removed by reverse osmosis filtration. However, we're told in the question stem that zinc molecules are about the same size as copper molecules. Table 3 shows us that pore size is directly related to the percentage of each metal that is removed. We can infer, then, that if zinc is about the same size as copper, it will be removed by the reverse osmosis filter similarly to copper.

How is the percentage of copper removed related to pore size? We should resist the temptation to speed through this question by answering from memory. It only takes a few more seconds to double-check the table!

A quick scan down the Cu column shows us that as pore size increases, the percentage of copper removed decreases. This matches (B).

14. **G**

Scientific Reasoning

This question asks us to determine which set of experimental conditions gives us a specified result. In this case, the specified result is the greatest amount of heavy metals removed.

To investigate, we should look back to Table 3. It shows that as pore size increases, the percent of As and Cu removed decreases. However, notice that Pb doesn't exactly follow this trend. At 2 angstroms, 85% of Pb is removed. But at 3 angstroms, 98% of Pb is removed. That's a different trend and underscores the importance of evaluating *all* of the data before answering a question. Once pore size is increased over 3 angstroms, the percentage of Pb removed sharply plummets. Even knowing this much, though, allows us to eliminate (H) and (J).

To determine whether 2 angstroms or 3 angstroms is the best answer, we must evaluate, approximately, which size results in more total metal removed. We're told in the question stem that the city's water contains equal amounts of As, Cu, and Pb. The decrease in the percent of As and Cu removed when pore size is increased from 2 to 3 angstroms is tiny (3% and 1% respectively), but the increase in Pb removed is significant (13%). We don't need a calculator (and aren't allowed one anyway!) to realize that more metal is removed at 3 angstroms than at 2 angstroms. Choice (G) is correct.

PASSAGE III

15. D

16. G

17. B

18. F

19. C

20. F

21. D

22. H

15. D
Scientific Reasoning

Remember that Conflicting Viewpoints passages can look a lot like Reading passages. Here's a question that exemplifies that point; it tests our ability to locate and comprehend information from within the passage (information that just happens to be scientific, of course!). This is also a great question to answer first, because it doesn't require you to read either viewpoint yet.

To answer, we need to scan back through the opening information in the passage to find where it discusses electron pairs. That's in the second half of the second paragraph, which reads, "VSEPR theory states that the shape of a molecule is determined by the repulsions between the bonded and nonbonded pairs of electrons in the outer shell of the molecule's central atom. These electron pairs arrange themselves as far apart as possible to minimize repulsion."

The last sentence perfectly matches (D), which is correct.

Notice that (A) and (C) get it exactly backward. This is a common wrong answer format. Choice (B) brings up a detail from later in the passage and uses it inappropriately, another common wrong answer format.

16. G
Patterns

To answer this question, we must apply what we know about charge from Student 2's explanation to a new situation (namely, magnets). What does Student 2 believe about negative charges? We should go back to the passage to find out.

Student 2 states that "nonbonded electron pairs also have a negative charge and therefore repel the electrons that are bound to atoms." This means that both bound and nonbound electron pairs have a negative charge and that the two repel. We can conclude that negative charges repel each other.

Based on this theory, the south (negatively charged) end of a magnet will repel the negatively charged end of another magnet because negative charges always repel each other. This matches (G).

17. B
Patterns

This is a great example of the kind of question that can seem pretty complicated at first glance. It introduces a new type of molecule, gives us a bond angle, and asks us to figure out whose viewpoint is supported. But like most other Science questions, it breaks down to a series of relatively simple steps when we approach it methodically.

The chemical formula of sulfur dioxide is given to us in the question stem (SO_2). This is important because Student 1 states that you can determine the shape of a molecule from the chemical formula alone. All you have to do is count the "number of atoms that are bound to the central atom of a molecule." So we know that Student 1 would predict that a molecule of SO_2 would look just like a molecule of H_2O, and according to him, a molecule of H_2O has a linear geometry. Unfortunately, the question stem doesn't give us the geometry of sulfur dioxide, just the bond angle, so we have a little more work to do.

To find the bond angle in a molecule with linear geometry, we need to consult the opening information again. That defines a linear molecule as having a bond angle of 180°. So to put it all together, we know that Student 1 would believe that sulfur dioxide has a linear geometry and a bond angle of 180°. If it actually has a bond angle of 120°, that does not support Student 1's viewpoint. So we know the answer isn't (A) or (C).

Now we need to determine whether the fact that sulfur dioxide has a bond angle of 120° supports the viewpoint of Student 2. He states that "the geometry of a molecule is also dependent on the presence of electron pairs around the central atom that are not bonded to any atoms" and that because water contains two nonbonded pairs of electrons and two atoms bonded to the central atom, it has a tetrahedral geometry.

If a molecule of sulfur dioxide contains one non-bonded electron pair and two bound electron pairs, Student 2 would predict that it would have a trigonal planar geometry. According to the passage, this geometry has a bond angle of 120°. This is consistent with Student 2's viewpoint, so (B) is correct.

18. F
Scientific Reasoning

This question is asking us to make another prediction about molecular shape. This time, however, we're dealing with a situation in which Student 1 and Student 2 are in agreement. That's because according to the question stem, sulfur hexafluoride (SF_6) doesn't contain any nonbonded electron pairs, and these nonbonded electron pairs are the source of the two students' disagreement.

The question, then, is pretty straightforward. We have a central atom (S) with six atoms (F) bound to it. According to the information in the passage, molecules that contain six electron pairs around a central atom will have an octahedral geometry. Choice (F) is correct.

19. C
Scientific Reasoning

It would be wise to answer this question before reading Student 2's viewpoint to minimize confusion.

Student 1 believes that "a molecule's shape will always be determined by the number of electron pairs around the central atom" and that "the number of electron pairs corresponds to the number of atoms that are bound to the central atom of the molecule." Because a molecule of perchlorate ion (ClO_4^-) contains four O atoms around one central Cl atom, it should have a tetrahedral geometry.

The names of the possible shapes aren't given in the answer choices, just bond angles. According to the information in the passage, molecules with a tetrahedral geometry have bond angles of 109.5°, so (C) is correct.

20. F
Scientific Reasoning

Here's another question we should answer before going on to read Student 2's viewpoint. Student 1 believes that the number of atoms bound to the central atom of a molecule determines the number of electron pairs around the central atom, and thus the shape of the molecule. If ammonia (NH_3) contains three H molecules around one N molecule, it should have a trigonal planar geometry. Choice (F) is correct.

If we look at (G) and (J), we can see that the wrong choices are drawn from either Student 2's viewpoint alone or a combination of Student 1's and Student 2's viewpoints. Choice (H) incorrectly applies Student 1's viewpoint to predicting the geometry of NH_3. Answering this question before we go on to read Student 2's viewpoint will help us avoid a lot of potential confusion.

21. D
Scientific Reasoning

The first step in answering this question is to make sure we know exactly what Student 1 and Student 2 assert about the strength of the repulsive force of bonded and nonbonded electron pairs.

Student 1 claims that nonbonded electron pairs don't factor into the shape of a molecule at all. That's why water has a linear geometry, he says. Student 2 claims that nonbonded electron pairs exert a repulsive force equal in magnitude to the repulsive force exerted by bonded electron pairs. That's why he believes a molecule of water, which contains two bonded and two nonbonded electron pairs, should have a tetrahedral geometry.

So we're looking for a diagram that shows the relative strength of the repulsive force to be equal for bonded and nonbonded electron pairs. This is consistent with (D), which shows the two bars to be of equal length. Choice (D), then, is correct.

Note that the question stem asks us to determine which answer choice is consistent with Student 2's viewpoint and not Student 1's. It doesn't matter what we might know about the repulsive force of bonded and nonbonded electrons or which student is actually right in this case (if either). Our job is simply to identify the diagram that is consistent with the viewpoints in the passage.

22. **H**

Scientific Reasoning

According to the passage, Student 1 believes that nonbonded electron pairs don't factor into the shape of a molecule. Measurements that prove nonbonded electron pairs *do* show a repulsive force would weaken his viewpoint, because this would allow them to influence the shape of the molecule. We can eliminate (G) and (J).

We're not done, though. We still need to determine whether this information weakens the viewpoint of Student 2. He believes that nonbonded electron pairs behave just like bonded electron pairs in determining the shape of a molecule. If measurements were to show that nonbonded electron pairs exerted a repulsive force *greater* than that of bound electron pairs, his viewpoint would also be weakened—nonbonded electron pairs could not be counted on to behave just like bound electron pairs and would have an even greater influence on the shape of a molecule than he believes. His viewpoint would also be weakened, so (H) is correct.

SUMMARY

Time to review!

Use this space to record how many questions you answered correctly.

Now, record how many you answered incorrectly.

Remember to review and master the Kaplan Method for ACT Science, as well as the strategies for specific passage and question types. Refer to Science Part 1 for those. If you're short on time before Test Day, spend your time with Part 1.

Now, get specific.

Use the chart below to record how many questions you answered correctly and incorrectly in each Science SmartPoint category.

Point Value	Topic	# Correct	# Incorrect
13	**Scientific Reasoning**		
12	**Figure Interpretation**		
11	**Patterns**		

Use the chart to review the specific areas in which you can gain the most points on Test Day. Remember to spend more time on the categories with higher SmartPoint values.

Keep reviewing Science Parts 1 and 2 for specific SmartPoints. Then, keep practicing using the Practice Tests toward the end of this book.

By regularly reviewing and practicing, you'll become an ace at ACT Science!

UNIT 5: WRITING

The Basics:

40 Minutes

1 Prompt

Pacing:

Take up to 8 minutes to read the prompt and create a plan. Spend 30 minutes producing the essay. Save 2 to 3 minutes at the end for proofreading.

TEST DAY DIRECTIONS AND FORMAT

This is a test of your writing skills. You will have forty (40) minutes to write an essay in English. Before you begin planning and writing your essay, read the writing prompt carefully to understand exactly what you are being asked to do. Your essay will be evaluated on the evidence it provides of your ability to do the following:

- Express judgments by evaluating the three perspectives given in the prompt, taking a position on an issue, and explaining the relationship among all four ideas
- Develop a position by using logical reasoning and by supporting your ideas
- Maintain a focus on the topic throughout the essay
- Organize ideas in a logical way
- Use language clearly and effectively according to the conventions of standard written English

You may use the unlined pages in this test booklet to plan your essay. **You must write your essay in pencil on the lined pages in the answer folder.** Your writing on those lined pages will be scored. You may not need all the lined pages, but to ensure you have enough room to finish, do NOT skip lines. You may write corrections or additions neatly between the lines of your essay, but do NOT write in the margins of the lined pages. **Illegible essays cannot be scored, so you must write (or print) clearly.**

If you finish before time is called, you may review your work. Lay your pencil down immediately when time is called.

OUTSIDE KNOWLEDGE

No outside knowledge is required.

THE INSIDE SCOOP

This is an optional part of the ACT, as far as your registration for Test Day is concerned. Whether or not it is truly optional depends on whether your high school or the colleges you're applying to require it. If they do, it isn't optional! If you're not sure what schools you're applying to, or whether they require it, consider it mandatory—far better to have it and not need it than need it and not have it. Either way, it's an area on which, with some advance practice and planning, you can get a high score, so you should be prepared to take it with confidence.

The ACT Writing test is designed to gauge your ability to compose a clear and logical argument and effectively present that argument in written form.

The essay prompt will present a specific issue and three perspectives. You are asked to analyze multiple perspectives on a complex issue and to arrive at a point of view on that issue. Then you must state your point of view clearly and support it with clear and relevant examples.

The essay is *argument based*, not *fact based*. That is, you're being tested on what you can effectively argue, not what you know about the topic. Does this mean facts aren't relevant? Yes and no—you will not be scored based on whether your facts are *true* or not, but you will be scored based on whether you use facts effectively. In an essay about being active in your community, for example, if you attribute the quote "Ask not what your country can do for you; ask what you can do for your country" to Ronald Reagan, you will be factually wrong, but you will be using an effective piece of evidence anyway. So you will get credit for effective use of information, even though that was said by John F. Kennedy.

SMARTPOINTS

As there is only one prompt for the Writing Test, there are no SmartPoints. All strategies apply to the whole section.

CHAPTER 16

Writing Part 1: Inside the ACT Writing Test

THE KAPLAN METHOD FOR ACT WRITING

STEP 1: PROMPT

Read about the issue and be sure you understand clearly what the core arguments are. You cannot get a high score without clearly responding to each perspective individually. Once you've determined what each perspective is arguing, pick a position on the issue. There is no right or wrong answer, and you can partially or fully agree or disagree with the perspectives provided. You should plan a thesis that you can *best defend*, whether that's what you personally believe or not. Be aware that **multiple** sides can be effectively defended; there's no "easy" or "right" side.

STEP 2: PLAN

Take up to 8 minutes to complete Steps 1 and 2. You want to be sure to strategically plan your essay before you write. Most students skip this step on Test Day! Take this time to plan so you know what you're trying to accomplish and can put forth your best first draft. Begin by stating your thesis. Since you already decided upon a stance during Step 1, now compose a sentence that states your position clearly. Then, focus on what kinds of reasoning and examples you can use to discuss not only your position but also the three perspectives provided in the prompt. Choose the best specific, relevant examples you can brainstorm.

You'll use one in each body paragraph, and the strongest body paragraphs discuss real-world evidence rather than hypothetical positions.

STEP 3: PRODUCE

Write your draft, sticking closely to your plan. In about 30 minutes, you should aim to produce five well-developed paragraphs with topic sentences and supporting details. You're not scored on how many words or paragraphs you write but on the strength of what you put down. Be very sure to include an introductory paragraph stating your position and a concluding sentence, because without those two framing statements, you're missing fundamental ingredients your essay needs. As you produce your essay, write as neatly as possible—words that cannot be read cannot be scored.

STEP 4: PROOFREAD

Always leave yourself the last couple of minutes to review your work—this time spent proof-reading is definitely to your benefit. Very few of us can avoid the occasional confused sentence or omitted word when we write under pressure, and a missed word can affect the meaning of a sentence. Again, graders can only score what they read, not what you might mean. Therefore, always quickly review your essay to be sure your ideas are clearly stated. Also, by leaving yourself this 2-minute buffer at the end, you'll avoid having to rush your conclusion. Remember, that's the last thing your essay grader will read, and you want to go out strong.

QUICK TIPS

MIND-SET

- **Don't wait until Test Day to practice.** Regardless of what issue is raised in the prompt, the directions and objectives will be the same. Practicing this type of essay beforehand will save you time since you will know what to expect. As other students are looking at the directions for the first time, you will already be reading through the issue and perspectives, ready to start planning the points you will discuss.

- **Refresh your memory about school subjects, current events, personal experiences, and activities—anything.** By doing so, you strengthen mental connections to those ideas and details, making it easier to use them as specific, relevant support for your thesis on Test Day. Again, the important thing to remember is that real-world evidence is far more powerful than hypothetical stances. Saying "This is right because I believe it" will never be as strong as saying "This is right—look at all this evidence."

SPECIAL STRATEGIES

You must be very focused in order to write a complete, coherent essay in 40 minutes. You can use Kaplan's Essay Template to guide your overall organization.

KAPLAN'S ESSAY TEMPLATE

¶1:   **Introductory paragraph**

- Introductory statement
- Thesis

¶2:   **1st body paragraph**

- Describe Perspective One
  - Strengths/Weaknesses
  - Insights it offers/Insights it fails to consider
  - Persuasive/Fails to persuade
- Specifically state whether you agree, disagree, or partially agree/disagree with this perspective

¶3:   **2nd body paragraph**

- Describe Perspective Two
  - Strengths/Weaknesses
  - Insights it offers/Insights it fails to consider
  - Persuasive/Fails to persuade
- Specifically state whether you agree, disagree, or partially agree/disagree with this perspective

¶4:   **3rd body paragraph**

- Describe Perspective Three
  - Strengths/Weaknesses
  - Insights it offers/Insights it fails to consider
  - Persuasive/Fails to persuade
- Specifically state whether you agree, disagree, or partially agree/disagree with this perspective

¶5:   **4th body paragraph**

- Describe your thesis
  - Provide specific, relevant support
  - Discuss the strengths/weaknesses of your thesis
  - Explain how your thesis compares and contrasts with Perspectives One, Two, and Three
- Include a single concluding sentence at the end of your fourth body paragraph to wrap up your essay

Stick to the template as you write the essay. Don't change your essay halfway through, even if another idea suddenly comes to you—it might derail the essay! Keep your focus on the issue and don't digress.

TIMING

With only 40 minutes, efficient use of time is critical. Divide your time as follows:

Approximately 8 minutes—Read the prompt and plan your essay.

Approximately 30 minutes—Draft your essay, sticking to the plan.

Approximately 2 minutes—Proofread and correct any errors.

WHEN YOU'RE RUNNING OUT OF TIME

On the Writing test, you won't be able to guess on the last few questions when you're running out of time, as you can on the other tests. Thus, practice the timing carefully to avoid losing coherence toward the end. If you do start running out of time, shorten one of your first three body paragraphs and go straight to the last body paragraph so that you have time to discuss your thesis. Be sure to end your essay with a single concluding statement. The conclusion is a necessary component of your essay, and its exclusion will cost you more than a strong body paragraph will gain you. Even when you're rushed, try to allow 1 to 2 minutes to proofread for errors that affect clarity.

SCORING

Two trained readers score your essay on a scale of 1–6 along the 4 Writing Test domains; those scores are added to arrive at your Writing subscores (each from 2 to 12). Essays can get a zero if they are left blank, entirely off-topic, illegible, or written in a language other than English. If there's a difference of more than 1 point between the two readers' scores (for example, one reader gives you a 3 and the other a 5), your essay will be read by a third reader. Readers evaluate the essays *holistically*, judging the overall quality of each, and do not assign separate scores for specific elements such as grammar or organization.

A Writing score will also be recorded. Your Writing score is calculated from your domain scores and is reported on a scale of 1–36.

Statistically speaking, there will be few essays that score 12 out of 12 for all four Writing Test domains. If each grader gives your essay a 4 or 5 for each of the four domains (making your subscores 8–10), that will place you within the upper range of those taking the exam.

METHOD BREAKDOWN

STEP 1: PROMPT

The ACT Writing prompt usually relates to a topic that is broad enough for high school students to be able to relate to it. In most cases, the subject will be something fairly innocuous, like the possible advantages of including mandatory career-readiness programs in high schools. If by chance the prompt describes a situation you feel strongly about, be sure to still present your argument in a careful, thoughtful manner. Do NOT write an overly emotional response. You are being gauged on the strength of your argument, not the strength of your feelings.

Here's an example of a typical ACT Writing prompt:

BILINGUAL ACCREDITATION

While the United States has just one official national language, English is certainly not the only language in which Americans communicate. In fact, bilingual fluency is highly desirable in many professions, including business, education, and medicine. In an effort to ready students for success in their future careers, some high schools may consider instituting programs that would offer bilingual accreditation to students who successfully complete a significant portion of their schooling in a language other than English. Since bilingual certification is not a necessary component of traditional education, should schools be expected to explore this option for interested students? As American high schools aim to remain competitive as measured by increasingly rigorous international education standards, innovative programs such as bilingual certification may prove to be essential.

Read and carefully consider these perspectives. Each discusses relevant aspects of offering bilingual accreditation.

Perspective One	Perspective Two	Perspective Three
Schools should encourage bilingual fluency but should not be expected to offer special classes or programs. School administrators need to work on strengthening the existing curriculum rather than overcomplicating instruction by attempting to incorporate additional programs that do not reinforce traditional education.	Offering bilingual accreditation weakens the core of high school curriculum. A large enough portion of the student population already struggles to maintain passing grades when taught in English, and adding other languages would likely add to that number.	Bilingual accreditation should be offered, but it needs to be thoughtfully implemented. Courses taught in languages other than English need to be carefully selected to ensure that this program does not affect the integrity of the high school diploma.

ESSAY TASK

Write a unified, coherent essay in which you evaluate multiple perspectives regarding bilingual accreditation. In your essay, be sure to:

- Analyze and evaluate the perspectives given
- State and develop your own perspective on the issue
- Explain the relationship between your perspective and those given

Your perspective may be in full agreement with any of the others, in partial agreement, or wholly different. Whatever the case, support your ideas with logical reasoning and detailed, persuasive examples.

PLANNING YOUR ESSAY

You may wish to consider the following as you think critically about the task:

Strengths and weaknesses of the three given perspectives
- What insights do they offer, and what do they fail to consider?
- Why might they be persuasive to others, or why might they fail to persuade?

Your own knowledge, experience, and values
- What is your perspective on this issue, and what are its strengths and weaknesses?
- How will you support your perspective in your essay?

As you read, be sure you understand the argument clearly. In this case, the argument is "Should schools be expected to explore bilingual accreditation for interested students, even though it is not a necessary component of traditional education?" You know you have the right question in this case because it is stated clearly in the prompt, but it may not always be. If the question is not stated this clearly, make sure you think through the issue thoroughly enough that you can take one clear position, being careful to not overcomplicate your thesis. Based on the structure of the prompt, you can use the three perspectives to help you determine your position. In this case, you can say, "High schools should promote bilingualism but shouldn't be required to offer bilingual classes," "High schools should avoid bilingual options," or "High schools should offer bilingual accreditation if it is carefully implemented." For this prompt, you do not want to try to argue all three positions since these perspectives feature diverse arguments.

STEP 2: PLAN

Take up to 8 minutes to analyze the prompt (Step 1) and build a plan before you write. This step is critical—a successful plan leads directly to a high-scoring essay. Focus on what kinds of reasoning and examples you can use to support your position.

Note: If you find you have better supporting evidence for a position different from the one you originally thought you would take, *change your position*.

Kaplan's Essay Template is an excellent way to organize your essay before you begin to write. This can easily be done in the 4 to 6 minutes you will invest in planning, and doing so will make the actual production *much* faster and smoother. Take a few minutes to write down notes about the prompt in Step 1. Then organize your notes using Kaplan's Essay Template. Your outline may look similar to the following:

¶1:   **Introductory paragraph**

- Introductory statement
- Thesis—***Schools should offer bilingual accreditation as long as courses offered in languages other than English are carefully selected.***

¶2:   **1st body paragraph**

- Describe Perspective One—***Students should be encouraged to become bilingual, but schools do not have the time or resources to add a bilingual certification program.***

    - Strengths/Weaknesses—***focuses on real-life concerns about curriculum***
    - Insights it offers/Insights it fails to consider—***fails to consider that bilingual accreditation could enhance curriculum***
    - Persuasive/Fails to persuade—***fails to persuade by ignoring possible benefits***

- Specifically state whether you agree, disagree, or partially agree/disagree with this perspective—***disagree***

¶3:   **2nd body paragraph**

- Describe Perspective Two—***Bilingual accreditation should not be included in any capacity because it will make school even harder than it is now.***

    - Strengths/Weaknesses—***considers how students may feel about the program***
    - Insights it offers/Insights it fails to consider—***does not consider the fact that some students struggle in school because English is not their primary language***
    - Persuasive/Fails to persuade—***fails to persuade because it dismisses the program without considering how it could help students***

- Specifically state whether you agree, disagree, or partially agree/disagree with this perspective—***disagree***

¶4:   **3rd body paragraph**

- Describe Perspective Three—***Bilingual accreditation should be offered, but it needs to be carefully organized so that all students receive education of the same quality.***

    - Strengths/Weaknesses—***considers the benefits to students***
    - Insights it offers/Insights it fails to consider—***does not consider that all courses taught in high schools are carefully selected***
    - Persuasive/Fails to persuade—***persuades because it recognizes that offering additional opportunity without sacrificing overall integrity benefits students***

- Specifically state whether you agree, disagree, or partially agree/disagree with this perspective—***agree***

¶5:   4th body paragraph

- Describe your thesis—***All students should have the opportunity to pursue bilingual accreditation as long as this opportunity is in addition to traditional course offerings; schools should accommodate students who wish to take classes in multiple languages as well as students who want to study only in English.***

  - Provide specific, relevant support—***traditional foreign language courses provide a foundation for this program***
  - Discuss the strengths/weaknesses of your thesis—***program is available to all students, which is good in terms of opportunity, but could be difficult to implement***
  - Explain how your thesis fits in among Perspectives One, Two, and Three—***agrees with Perspective Three***

- Include a single concluding sentence at the end of your fourth body paragraph to wrap up your essay.

Information banks: Don't wait until Test Day to think of examples you can use to support your ideas. Regardless of what question is raised in the prompt, you will draw your support from the things you know best and are most comfortable writing about—things you know a fair amount of concrete detail about.

Refresh your memory about your favorite or most memorable books, school subjects, historical events, personal experiences, activities—anything. By doing so, you strengthen mental connections to those ideas and details, making it easier to connect to the right examples on Test Day.

With that in mind:

- Use an effective *hook* to bring the reader in.
- Use *transitions* regularly—these are the "glue" that holds your ideas together.
- End with a *bang* to make your essay memorable.

Using a "hook" means avoiding an essay that opens (as thousands of other essays will): "In my opinion, … because …" Your opinion is not compelling to a reader who has graded hundreds of essays on the same subject. Make it something more exciting than that!

In today's global economy, students are looking for ways to ready themselves for an increasingly international future.

A "bang" means a closing that ties the essay together. A good choice can be a clear, succinct statement of your thesis in the essay or a vivid example that's right on point.

Enhancing instruction is always better than restricting learning, especially when the result is effective communication, desirable skills, and valuable experiences.

In summary, a good plan:

- Responds to the prompt
- Has an introduction
- Has strong examples, usually one per paragraph
- Has a strong conclusion

STEP 3: PRODUCE

You are not graded directly on word count, but graders know that filling out a thorough argument takes time and space—it will be hard to present all the elements of a strong argument in few words or only a couple of paragraphs. Nonetheless, don't think about your *number of words*; instead, think about the *strength of your arguments.*

Organization counts. Graders are far more able to follow—and be compelled by—your argument if they can see its distinct ingredients.

Write neatly. Graders may give you a zero if your essay is impossible to read. If your handwriting is a problem, print.

Stick with the plan. Resist any urge to introduce new ideas—no matter how good you think they are—or to digress from the central focus or organization of each paragraph.

Use topic sentences. Each paragraph should be organized around a topic sentence that you should finish in your mind before you start to write. These may begin as follows:

- *One example …*
- *Another example …*
- *Therefore, we can conclude …*

You don't have to write it this way in the essay, but completing these sentences in your mind ensures that you focus on the idea that organizes each paragraph.

Choose words carefully. Use vocabulary you know well. New or fancy words that you have learned recently often stick out in a negative way. Using unfamiliar words in an essay often produces awkward, confusing thoughts—the opposite of what you want. Instead of impressing the graders, you would obscure your ideas. Two more points to keep in mind:

1. **Avoid using *I* excessively.** You are absolutely allowed to use personal examples ("At my school, we had this issue just last year, and I was very involved in the discussion …"), but avoid using your opinions or beliefs *as evidence* ("I really think …" "I believe …" "In my opinion …"). You base your argument on weak ground when it is founded on your thoughts, not what you can prove.

2. **Avoid slang.** Your tone should be personal and natural but academic. This is a school paper. Abbreviations such as those you might use in text messaging, online, or in personal emails are not appropriate here; at best, they're unprofessional, and at worst, the grader won't know what you're talking about.

Use transitions. Think about the relationship between ideas as you write and spell out your concepts clearly. Doing so allows the readers to follow your reasoning easily, and they'll appreciate it. **Use key words from the prompt as well as the kinds of words you've learned about in Reading that indicate contrast, opinion, relative importance, and support.**

Don't sweat the small stuff. Do not obsess over every little thing. If you cannot remember how to spell a word, do your best and just **keep going.** Even the top-scoring essays can have minor errors. The essay readers understand that you are writing first drafts and have no time for research or revision.

STEP 4: PROOFREAD

Always leave yourself 2 or 3 minutes to review your work—the time spent will definitely pay off. Very few of us can avoid the occasional confused sentence or omitted word when we write under pressure. Quickly review your essay to be sure your ideas are clearly stated.

Don't hesitate to make corrections to your essay—this is a timed first draft, not a term paper. But keep your writing clearly readable: use a single line through deletions and an asterisk to mark where text should be inserted.

> ✔ **EXPERT TUTOR TIP**
>
> Use a caret ^ or an asterisk * to insert a word or words. Write a backward *P* to create a new paragraph. Cross words out with one line. Don't make a mess!

During proofreading, remind yourself that **you don't have time to revise substantially.** This isn't the time for inserting new paragraphs, radically changing your tone, or (worst yet) changing your mind. Use your practice essays to learn the types of mistakes you tend to make and look for them.

COMMON ERRORS

- Omitted words
- Sentence fragments
- Misplaced modifiers
- Misused words—especially homonyms like *their* for *there* or *they're*
- Spelling errors

COMMON STYLE PROBLEMS

- Choppy sentences (combine some)
- Too many long, complex sentences (break some up)
- Too many stuffy-sounding words (replace with simple words)
- Too many simple words (add a few college-level words)

SUMMARY

In this chapter, we went over the method you can use to write a high-scoring essay on the ACT Writing test.

Remember, the idea is to write a comprehensive analysis of three perspectives in addition to presenting your own thesis. When explaining your thesis, take a distinct stance and support your argument with clear, logical evidence.

Make sure to plan! You can get a good score on the ACT Writing test just by presenting clear points and using proper structure. Know what points you are going to make beforehand to avoid writing an essay that sounds like a stream of consciousness.

The ideal structure: Put your thesis and a hook into your first paragraph. Have four body paragraphs, each with a distinct supporting point and evidence. Make sure you don't bring up any new points in your concluding sentence. Just wrap things up neatly.

Leave yourself a couple of minutes to proofread. Doing so will also give you a time buffer—in case your writing runs long, you won't have to cut your essay short.

In the next chapter, you'll go over each piece of the essay in detail, learning how to craft each piece to maximize your score.

Work on the sections you most need, whether it's crafting a compelling hook for your introduction and a clear thesis or using well-developed evidence to drive a body paragraph home with the reader.

Put the pieces together at the end of these Writing chapters by completing a sample Writing test and reviewing your strengths and weaknesses.

Keep an eye on where you're going. Take a clear side on the issue, create a plan for your essay, and follow through. When you do these things, you're well on your way to mastering the ACT Writing test.

CHAPTER 17

Writing Part 2: ACT Writing Strategy in Depth

OVERVIEW

Use this chapter to get familiar with how to properly form the pieces of an essay for the ACT Writing test.

We'll go over each in turn, paragraph by paragraph.

For the introductory paragraph, we'll discuss how to create a thesis (the most important sentence of your essay) and how to draw the reader in with a hook.

For the body paragraphs, we'll discuss further how to include coherent analysis and specific evidence. We'll also look at the proper way to discuss your own perspective.

For the concluding sentence, we'll discuss how to properly bring the essay to a close.

Finally, you'll get a chance to put it all together in response to a prompt, and we'll discuss how your essay will be graded. Essays are scored holistically, meaning that the graders form a general impression rather than checking whether an essay contains specific pieces. We'll discuss how the pieces should fit together and flow from one to the next so you can maximize your score potential.

PARAGRAPH BY PARAGRAPH

THE INTRODUCTION

You've likely been writing essays for as long as you've been in school, and you may have had multiple teachers tell you at various points the "one right way" to write an essay. If you've come to suspect there may not really be "one right way," you're in good company. What good essays do have in common, however, is a set of ingredients. Some of these ingredients are optional and vary based on individual taste, but some are necessary to successfully produce an academic essay.

Think about a sandwich. You can have any kind of bread and any kind of fillings you like, but if you don't have a piece of bread on each side and something in the middle, you don't have a sandwich. In a formal essay like this, the introduction and conclusion are your bread, and your body paragraphs are your filling. Exactly what you will put in, what will it look like, and what it will do—all these things are yours to decide. But without the key ingredients of introduction, conclusion, and body paragraphs, you don't have a sandwich.

Your introductory paragraph needs to fulfill certain roles. It must do the following:

- Introduce the argument. By the end of the first paragraph, a person who has just picked up your essay should know what is being discussed and what the main arguments are.

- Acknowledge the three perspectives provided in the prompt.

- Establish your side of the argument. We'll talk more about your **thesis statement** soon, but do know this is where it goes. You may have heard before that your thesis should be the first sentence of the first paragraph or the last sentence of the first paragraph, or any other sentence, but rest assured that it should just be *somewhere* in the first paragraph. Readers should go into the second paragraph (the first body paragraph) knowing which side you're on.

- Set the tone for the essay. While your essay should be academic in style, that still leaves some wiggle room. Will your essay be fierce and uncompromising? Gentle but persuasive? Personal and humorous? Use whatever tone comes most naturally to you; just make sure to keep it consistent throughout the essay. Sudden changes of voice will distract readers.

If you've included the items listed above, you have an introduction! The thesis is the most important component of this paragraph because it tells readers what to expect from the rest of your essay, so let's dig into it further.

THE THESIS STATEMENT

Before you can create a thesis, you need to understand the issue. Start with Step 1 and read the prompt. To help you focus on the topic, underline key words in the prompt as you read. Key words are the nouns and verbs that form the backbone of the prompt. You'll also use these words in your essay to keep your writing on topic.

After reading the prompt, move to Step 2, making your plan. You should write a brief plan before you start producing your essay, but you don't need to do this immediately after reading the prompt. Take a minute to think about the three perspectives posed in the prompt. Do you have an immediate and strong reaction to them? Sometimes, you'll know right away how you feel about the issue, and ideas and examples will pop into your head even as you're reading the prompt. At other times, you might be a little less certain. Perhaps all three perspectives seem equally valid, and you can think of reasons to support all of them. In this case, don't spend too long deliberating. Remember, the issues posed in ACT prompts are chosen precisely because three reasonable people might have legitimate reasons for supporting those views. Your essay score is not affected by which viewpoint you choose to defend.

Again, don't spend too much time deciding which perspective to support. Choose one viewpoint and jot down a list of evidence you can use to support that viewpoint. Once you've chosen a perspective, you need to formulate a good thesis statement. A thesis statement is a clear, simple sentence that describes the position you will support in your essay. A strong thesis statement:

- Answers the question in the prompt
- Leaves no doubt about where you stand on the issue
- Doesn't necessarily contain reasons for your position but does set the stage for your presentation of evidence that will follow

WRITING EXERCISE 1

Using the "Bilingual Accreditation" prompt from the previous chapter, consider each of the following sentences and put an asterisk next to the ones you think would make a good thesis sentence:

1. _____ I've always enjoyed learning languages other than English.

2. _____ Learning foreign languages serves several educational purposes.

3. _____ Bilingual certification is an innovative program that should be offered to high school students.

4. _____ Learning languages other than English actually distracts students from learning well.

5. _____ Bilingual accreditation would unfairly reward students who already know other languages.

6. _____Schools should focus on improving the existing curriculum instead of adding new programs like bilingual certification.

7. _____ While students should have the opportunity to learn other languages, bilingual certification should not be offered since teaching classes in languages other than English will make it harder to ensure that every student is receiving the same type and quality of education.

8. _____ Teachers tend to give better grades to students they know speak more than one language.

Sentences 3, 6, and 7 are the most appropriate thesis sentences. Sentences 2, 4, and 5 all discuss bilingual programs, but they don't state a position on the question in the prompt. These sentences might be appropriate as part of your argument in the essay, but they can't act as a thesis statement. Sentences 1 and 8 do not relate to the issue in the prompt and should not be featured in your essay.

1. Although this sentence discusses learning languages other than English, it does not state a position relating to the question in the prompt.

2. Although this sentence discusses foreign languages, it does not state a position relating to the question in the prompt. This sentence might be appropriate as part of your argument in the essay, but it can't act as a thesis statement.

3. This is an appropriate thesis sentence.

4. Although this sentence discusses the issue presented in the prompt, it does not state a clear position in regard to the three perspectives. This sentence might be appropriate as part of your argument in the essay, but it can't act as a thesis statement.

5. Although this sentence discusses bilingual accreditation, it does not state a position relating to the question in the prompt. This sentence might be appropriate as part of your argument in the essay, but it can't act as a thesis statement.

6. This is an appropriate thesis sentence.

7. This is an appropriate thesis sentence.

8. Although this sentence discusses bilingual certification, it does not state a position relating to the question in the prompt.

DEMONSTRATING UNDERSTANDING OF COMPLEXITY

One thing an ACT essay grader expects to find in a top-scoring essay is an indication that the writer understands the complexity of the question in the prompt. The strongest ACT essays not only effectively discuss all three perspectives but also illustrate an understanding of the ramifications of each position.

BODY PARAGRAPHS

Each body paragraph must push the argument along. Since the perspectives follow a clear sequence ("First this perspective, then this perspective, then this perspective, and finally my own perspective"), your body paragraphs should follow that sequence as well.

EVIDENCE

Now that you know what an appropriate thesis statement is, let's consider what your evidence should look like. The use of **evidence** (real-world examples) is highly effective, as it takes the argument off the page and grounds it in real issues.

The most important thing to remember when selecting evidence is that it should be specific and relevant to your topic. During Step 2: Plan, identify your examples and reasons in brief notes, but in Step 3: Produce, you'll actually flesh out your evidence. Now it's important to develop your evidence with specifics. A problem many unprepared students have with the ACT essay is talking in generalities instead of presenting specific evidence that supports their thesis. This happens because they are writing under time pressure without planning sufficiently. With practice, however, you will avoid this common pitfall.

Prepare solid examples by reading newspapers, staying informed about current events (local, national, and world), and reading opinion articles and blogs. Doing so in the weeks leading up to Test Day will both provide you with a wealth of real-world examples and expose you to strong writing examples.

INFORMATION BANKS

Don't wait until Test Day to think about what subjects you can draw on for your examples to create animated and engaging essays. Examples can be drawn from anywhere: your life experience, a story you saw on the news, etc. So prepare yourself by refreshing your memory about your favorite subjects—collect examples that can be used for a variety of topics.

Don't hesitate to use your examples broadly. If the topic is about school, that doesn't mean you have to use school-based examples. It's better to write about things that you are comfortable with and know a lot about. Just be sure to make clear how they are relevant to the essay's topic.

And there you have the pieces of an excellent body paragraph! Before you move on, though, make sure to wrap up.

You'll want to produce an evidence sandwich. In other words, you don't want to just jump into or out of your specific example. You take care of the entry to your evidence with your topic sentence. This gives the reader an idea of the main point that evidence is supporting. Then end your paragraph by reminding the reader what your evidence proved. In other words, put a second piece of bread on that sandwich before moving on.

CONCLUSION

In the last chapter, we discussed the importance of leaving time to write a strong conclusion, even if you need to cut a body paragraph a little short. Remember: Without a conclusion, you don't have a full formal essay, and your score will reflect that. Your conclusion serves several purposes:

- It ties all of your body paragraphs together. ("Considering all of these arguments together…")
- It reminds the reader of the centrality of your argument. ("Ultimately, we must remember the most important point…")
- It provides a chance to leave a lasting impression on the reader. ("We cannot overlook the importance of this issue…")

Make sure your conclusion does all of the following:

- Restates your thesis, not by repeating it word for word but by paraphrasing it to remind the reader of your main idea.
- Summarizes your points. Again, don't repeat them all, but reference them briefly to reinforce their strength and relationship to your thesis.
- Wraps up the argument. By this point in the essay, you should be writing with the assumption that your reader agrees with you. Close with clear language about the rightness and importance of your argument.

PUTTING IT ALL TOGETHER

LANGUAGE

In your practice for the ACT English test, you're learning rules and principles to help you make the best choices about wording in the English passages. It's important that you keep these rules and principles in mind for the ACT Writing test as well. Remember that the last step of the Kaplan Method for ACT Writing is to proofread. If you spend an adequate amount of time on the prompt, plan, and produce steps, you'll have only a few minutes to proofread. Let's give some attention to the best ways to use this time effectively.

BE CAREFUL WITH PRONOUNS!

When you're writing under pressure, as you are on the ACT, it's easy to make some grammatical mistakes that affect the logic of your essay. The use of pronouns is an area that many students have trouble with. If you train yourself to pay attention to pronouns and think about what's involved in using them correctly, it will be easier to catch pronoun problems and correct them even when you're proofreading quickly. Everything you know about pronouns that you apply to the English test also holds true for the Writing test. Refresh yourself on the guidelines described here.

PRONOUN REFERENCE RULE

A pronoun refers to a noun or another pronoun. Do not use a pronoun if the sentence it's in or the sentence before it doesn't contain a word for the pronoun to refer to logically.

PRONOUN NUMBER RULE

A pronoun must agree in number with the noun or pronoun it refers to. Do not use a plural pronoun to refer to a singular noun.

PRONOUN SHIFT RULE

Do not switch between the words *one* and *you* in a given context.

For most people, it's easier to spot mistakes in something written by someone else. It can be tough to identify errors in your own writing, but pronouns are an area you can easily work on. Try the following pronoun exercise.

WRITING EXERCISE 2

In the following essay excerpts, watch for errors in the use of pronouns. Circle the mistakes and write down the corrections.

1. When one works hard on academics all semester, you expect to get some kind of recognition.

   _____

2. School authorities shouldn't try to control the lives of students completely. If a student doesn't want to perform community service, they shouldn't have to.

   _____

3. The school administration has given a lot of thought to the value of the honor roll. They feel that by doing away with the honor roll, students will lose motivation to work hard.

   _____

4. Our school administration is debating whether or not to allow the use of films in the classroom. They say that movies are effective at capturing the interest of students.

   _____

5. A girl who has attended a single-sex school is likely to report that they feel teachers take their opinions seriously.

   _____

6. The student council exists to serve the student body. Therefore, they should have the responsibility of electing the representatives.

   _____

7. A bilingual classroom doesn't help a non-native English speaker learn English quickly. They should get tutoring and extra help, but they should attend classes in English.

_____

8. I've read the newspaper every day for the past five months, and they say that education is one of the most pressing issues in the upcoming election.

_____

9. Every student deserves the right to wear what they want to, within reasonable boundaries of course.

_____

10. Educators, because they have more experience, know what's best for students. They should be the ones who determine new course offerings.

_____

This exercise should have increased your awareness of incorrect pronoun usage. Question 1 is incorrect because it shifts between *one* and *you*. Many of the others are incorrect because the pronoun *they*, which is plural, appears without a plural noun to which it could logically refer. Here are some corrections you could have made. Note that you might have come up with different revisions that effectively correct the pronoun errors.

1. When one works hard on academics all semester, **one expects** [*not* you expect] to get some kind of recognition.

2. School authorities shouldn't try to control the lives of students completely. If a student doesn't want to perform community service, **he or she** [*not* they] shouldn't have to.

3. The school administration has given a lot of thought to the value of the honor roll. **Administrators** [*not* They] feel that by doing away with the honor roll, students will lose motivation to work hard.

4. Our school **administrators are** [*not* administration is] debating whether or not to allow the use of films in the classroom. They say that movies are effective at capturing the interest of students.

5. A girl who has attended a single-sex school is likely to report that **she feels** [*not* they feel] teachers take **her** [*not* their] opinions seriously.

6. The student council exists to serve the student body. Therefore, **students** [*not* they] should have the responsibility of electing the representatives.

7. A bilingual classroom doesn't help **non-native English speakers** [*not* a non-native English speaker] learn English quickly. They should get tutoring and extra help, but they should attend classes in English.

8. I've read the newspaper every day for the past five months, and **many reporters and columnists** [*not* they] say that education is one of the most pressing issues in the upcoming election.

9. **All students deserve** [*not* Every student deserves] the right to wear what they want to, within reasonable boundaries of course.

10. **Educators, because they have more experience, know what's best for students and should be the ones who determine new course offerings.** [The problem is that "they" in the original sentence could logically refer to either "students" or "educators." You could also correct the problem by simply changing "they" to "educators" instead of rewriting the whole sentence.]

AVOID SLANG AND CLICHÉS

Although some slang words and expressions are acceptable in ordinary conversation, you should avoid slang in your ACT essay. The purpose of the essay is to present a logical argument based on reasoning and evidence, and the language you choose should reflect the serious-ness of the task. As you practice, become sensitive to the tone of various expressions. If you think something is slang or too informal, ask yourself if there's a more appropriate phrasing.

Like slang, clichéd language is best avoided in your ACT essay. A cliché is a worn-out, over-used expression. Your essay should show that you're taking a fresh and thoughtful approach to the question posed, and the overuse of clichés undercuts the serious and thoughtful attention you bring to your argument.

WRITING EXERCISE 3

In the following sentences, circle slang and clichéd expressions. Write an alternative in the space provided.

1. Most kids don't have time to hold jobs during the school year.

_____

2. The idea of making math teachers give writing assignments to students is just crazy.

_____

3. Politicians say they have everyone's best interests in mind, but those guys don't really see the big picture.

_____

4. It's true that some kids do act like jerks, but the entire student body shouldn't have to pay for the misbehavior of a few bad apples.

_____

5. If this change is implemented, all students will have the chance to get the best ever education.

_____

6. It's been shown over and over again that everyone needs encouragement.

_____

Phrases like "kids" and "crazy" and "best ever" detract from your argument by sounding far too casual. You're trying to gain points for seriousness and care, so your language should reflect maturity of writing. Here are some corrections you could have made. Note that you might have come up with different revisions that also avoid slang or clichés.

1. Most students don't have time to work during the school year.

2. Math class is not the best environment for the assignment and grading of writing projects.

3. While politicians claim to have the public's best interests in mind, they are often too far removed from everyday life to really understand it.

4. While some misbehavior is unavoidable at any school, most students conduct themselves appropriately, and they should not be punished for the actions of few.

5. If this change is implemented, a better education will be available to all students.

6. It has been repeatedly demonstrated that encouragement is good for everyone.

USE CORRECT AND VARIED SENTENCE STRUCTURE

Sentence structure is tested directly on the ACT English test, but it's also very important for the essay you produce on the Writing test. To apply the principles of correct sentence structure in your essay, think about how you combine groups of words into sentences. You can avoid sentence fragments by making sure that each sentence includes a subject and a verb and expresses a complete thought. You can avoid run-ons by making sure that ideas are joined with proper punctuation and connections (transitions) words. The following exercise is designed to help you review what you learned about sentence structure in the English section of this book.

WRITING EXERCISE 4

Following is a run-on sentence. Write out three acceptable ways to correct it.

Teenagers value driving as a privilege, most work hard to be safe drivers.

1. _____

2. _____

3. _____

Here are our answers, each followed by a general guideline.

1. Because teenagers value driving as a privilege, most work hard to be safe drivers. [Use a connections word to introduce the first clause.]

2. Teenagers value driving as a privilege, so most work hard to be safe drivers. [Use a comma followed by a FANBOYS word to combine the two clauses.]

3. Teenagers value driving as a privilege; therefore, most work hard to be safe drivers. [Use a semicolon and a non-FANBOYS connections word to combine the two clauses.]

Varied sentence structure means sentences of different lengths. Your essay shouldn't use all short, choppy sentences, but you should use some shorter sentences to provide variety among longer, complicated sentences. During Step 4: Proofread, you're likely to find spots in your essay where you can make a few quick adjustments—say, inserting a word or changing the punctuation—to help you improve your sentence structure. If you follow the guidelines for properly combining clauses into sentences, your essay's sentence structure should be in good shape.

AVOID UNNECESSARY REPETITION

When you're writing an essay under very tight time constraints, as you must on the ACT, it's easy to find yourself using the same words and phrases frequently. Such repetition can detract from the effectiveness of your essay. It's true that you need to stay focused on the topic. However, if you use the same words and phrases repeatedly, it's a sign that you may not be developing your ideas thoroughly. Thus, the first remedy for needless repetition comes in the planning stage: Make sure you've reflected carefully on your viewpoint. To earn a high score, you must go beyond the ideas offered in the prompt by expanding upon your own position with reasoning and evidence. Thinking through your plan and writing brief notes in the test booklet help to ensure that you'll develop your ideas adequately during the production step. It can also help if you think of some synonyms for key words and phrases that are important to the topic.

WRITING EXERCISE 5

Imagine that the topic of your essay question somehow relates to academic success. Take a few minutes to write down some words and phrases that might be relevant.

_____

_____

_____

_____

There are no right or wrong answers here, and, of course, the words and phrases you choose to use in your essay will depend upon the focus of the particular question and the angle from which you approach it. Some phrases that relate to academic success are *academic achievement, excellence, scholarship, academic arena, intellectual development, effective learning strategies, motivation, diligence.*

Although thinking carefully during the planning step can help you minimize repetition in your essay, when you are proofreading, watch for any repetition that may have crept in. Making a slight change in a word or phrase takes only a few seconds and can introduce greater variety and effectiveness to your choice of vocabulary.

WRITING EXERCISE 6

The following examples include unnecessary repetition and could be made more concise. In each example, underline the repeated words and phrases, and then rewrite the example to be less wordy and more varied in word choice.

1. Funding arts programs is important to student achievement. Studies show that musical training leads to increased student achievement.

   _____

   _____

2. Bilingual education is an important topic in education today. Bilingual education is necessary for students whose first language is not English.

   _____

   _____

3. My school allocates too much money to sports programs. I know many students who don't participate in sports. Money allocated to sports programs doesn't benefit them. The school could achieve a better balance by allocating more money to programs that promote social activities and creative pursuits.

   _____

   _____

   _____

4. School newspapers serve several important functions. One of them is to let students decide what is worthy of publication and what is not. This function of a school newspaper would be completely taken away if a panel of teachers were to take over the decisions about what is worthy of publication.

_____

_____

_____

For many students, proofreading is the most difficult part of writing. Remember, the ACT essay readers don't expect your essay to be flawless. However, you can improve your writing by making just a few small corrections during the proofreading step. Don't worry if you didn't make the same corrections that we did. However, do work on identifying repetition and wordiness in your own writing. Here are some possible ways of correcting the examples. We've reprinted them and highlighted repetition and wordiness in boldface type.

1. Funding arts programs is important to **student achievement.** Studies show that musical training leads to increased **student achievement.**

   Funding arts programs is important because studies show that musical training leads to increased student achievement [or "academic performance"].

2. **Bilingual education** is an important topic in **education** today. **Bilingual education** is necessary for students whose first language is not English.

   Bilingual education is an important topic today because public schools serve many students whose first language is not English.

3. My school **allocates** too much **money** to **sports programs.** I know many students who don't participate in **sports. Money** allocated to **sports programs** doesn't benefit them. The school could achieve a better balance by **allocating** more **money** to **programs** that promote social activities and creative pursuits.

   My school allocates too much money to sports programs. This funding doesn't benefit the many students I know who are not athletically inclined. The school could achieve a better balance by directing more resources to social activities and creative pursuits.

4. **School newspapers** serve several important **functions.** One of them is to let students decide what is **worthy of publication and what is not.** This **function** of a **school newspaper** would be completely taken away if a panel of teachers were to take over the decisions about **what is worthy of publication.**

   School newspapers serve several important functions, one of which is giving students the opportunity to decide what is appropriate for publication. This function would be removed if the determination about what is worthy of publication were made by a panel of teachers instead of by students.

SCORING

Step	A High-Scoring Essay	A Low-Scoring Essay
Step 1: Prompt	Clearly develops a position on the prompt	Does not clearly state a position
Step 2: Plan	Supports with concrete, relevant examples	Is general, repetitious, or overly simplistic
Step 3: Produce	Maintains clear focus and organization	Digresses or has weak organization
Step 4: Proofread	Shows competent use of language	Contains errors that reduce clarity

Kaplan has found this approach useful in our many years of experience with hundreds of sample essay statements on a wide range of tests. Let's look at what the test makers tell you about how the essays are scored.

To score a 4, you must:

- Answer the question
- Support ideas with examples
- Show logical thought and organization
- Avoid major or frequent errors that make your writing unclear

Organization and clarity are key to an above-average essay. If the reader can't follow your train of thought—if ideas aren't clearly organized or if grammatical errors, misspellings, and incorrect word choices make your writing unclear—you can't do well.

To score a 5, all you have to add to a 4 is:

- Address the topic in depth

In other words, offer more examples and details. The test graders love specific examples, and the more concrete your examples are, the more they clarify your thinking and keep you and your essay focused.

To score a 6, all you have to add to a 5 is:

- Make transitions smoother and show variety in syntax and vocabulary

Use words from the prompt to tie paragraphs together rather than rely exclusively on connectors like *however* and *therefore*. Vary your sentence structure, sometimes using simple sentences and other times using compound and complex ones. Adding a few college-level vocabulary words will also boost your score.

Scoring the essay	In your essay, you must...	Your essay will not be affected by...
• The essay is scored by two readers, who assess your essay on 4 domains. Each scorer assigns a score from 1–6 for each domain. • The domain scores are combined to generate 4 essay subscores between 2–12. • Your subscores are used to calculate a final Writing score from 1–36. • The essay is scored holistically. • Your ACT essay score is *not* included in your ACT Composite score. When you take this optional Writing test, you receive an additional score called ELA score, which is an average of your subscore in English, Reading, and Writing. The ELA score is between 1–36.	• answer the assignment question! • show an understanding of the issue • show an understanding of the complexity of the issue • have a distinct introduction and conclusion • use effective organization • have effective development of ideas • maintain sustained focus • demonstrate effective language use • use effective transitions • not have errors that detract from clarity and readability	• which point of view you choose to defend • factual errors • a few minor spelling or grammatical errors

What does it mean for an essay to be scored holistically?

Your essay is scored *holistically*. That means it is based on the reader's overall impression of your writing skill, not a tally of points you got "right" or "wrong."

VIEW FROM THE OTHER SIDE: GETTING YOUR SCORE AND GRADING ESSAYS

GETTING YOUR SCORE

We've referenced the idea a few times that your essay score is *holistic*—that is, it reflects the grader's overall impression of your writing skill, rather than a strict equation of "right" and "wrong" answers. There is not, for example, an automatic point deduction for a misspelled word or a misused punctuation mark. However, an essay riddled with poor punctuation and spelling will be harder for a grader to give a high score. Still, there are elements essay graders consistently look for as hallmarks of strong writing. The grading criteria include:

• Does the author discuss all three perspectives provided in the prompt?

• Is the author's own perspective clearly stated?

• Does the body of the essay assess and analyze each perspective?

• Is the relevance of each paragraph clear?

- Does the author start a new paragraph for each new idea?
- Is each sentence in a paragraph relevant to the point made in that paragraph?
- Are transitions clear?
- Is the essay easy to read? Is it engaging?
- Are sentences varied?
- Is vocabulary used effectively? Is college-level vocabulary used?

While a perfect essay will address all of these points, a strong essay that gets a 4 or 5 from each grader will have to do fairly well on most of the points. An essay that misses any of them completely or does many of them at a very low level will have a hard time getting a high score, and the more basic the requirement, the more it affects your score. For example, while an otherwise-strong essay that has only basic transitions can still do well, an essay that doesn't directly answer the question cannot score higher than a 2 from each grader.

GRADING ESSAYS

Let's look at some sample essays based on the "Bilingual Accreditation" prompt we've seen. Evaluate each essay against the points we've discussed, and give it a score.

SAMPLE ESSAY 1

Some people think schools should encourage bilingualism but should not be expected to offer special classes or programs. Other people think offering bilingual accreditation weakens high school classes. Others say bilingual accreditation should be offered but it needs to be thoughtfully implemented. In my opinion, schools should definitely give the option of bilingualism.

Firstly, schools should always encourage bilingualism. Students better in life with more than one language. Second, weakening high school doesn't make sense. More languages mean more learning.

Finally and most importantly, there should be bilingual accreditation. Students won't be able to cognizant and value diverse languages if not given the opportunity. Extra certification on diplomas is good for getting kids into college. So high schools should have bilingual accreditation.

Score: _____ /6

It should have been fairly easy to see that this isn't a strong essay. This essay would get a score of 2 or 3 out of 6. The author does state a clear opinion, but half of the essay is a direct copy of the prompt—the graders will notice this and those sentences won't help the score. The time and space spent just quoting the prompt was completely wasted—it earned the writer zero points.

The rest of the essay is organized and uses transition words (*firstly* and *finally*). The author states her thesis, acknowledges the three perspectives provided in the prompt, and then offers a conclusion. However, none of this is discussed fully enough—no concrete details or examples are given. In the second paragraph, for instance, the author should have added examples that demonstrate how encouraging bilingual education is both beneficial to students and not a threat to the quality of high school curriculum.

The language is understandable, but there are significant errors affecting clarity. For instance, the second sentence of paragraph 2 is a fragment—there is no verb. Some vocabulary words are used without a clear understanding of their meaning: In paragraph 3, "won't be able to cognizant" is incorrect; perhaps the student meant "won't be able to understand."

It is possible that the writer couldn't think of good ideas to support each point, waited too long to start writing, and had to write in a hurry.

Let's look at another essay. Read it quickly and decide how you would score it.

SAMPLE ESSAY 2

Some people think that schools should provide enough education in a different language for students to be certified as bilingual. Others think this will weaken the curriculum. Still others think the accreditation should be offered but carefully administered so that graduation from that school would indicate the completed high school curriculum, and this is the option I agree with.

The first option is to encourage bilingual fluency but not add any bilingual classes. Instead, the school administrators should make the existing curriculum better so that traditional education is really good. Certainly a high school curriculum should be as good as it can be and we should always be looking for ways to make it better. That often means adding new courses.

The second alternative is to not provide any bilingual education because there are enough students struggling with the curriculum in English. But this is a very weak argument because no one is suggesting that all students need to take bilingual classes, so just having those classes would not necessarily affect struggling students' grades.

Finally, people argue that students should be given the opportunity to learn in other languages and be accredited as bilingual, but that the courses given need to be carefully selected. In reality, all classes need to be carefully selected so this not a problem for bilingual classes. And if the classes selected were all optional, not required, it would not affect students who still want to learn everything in English. Since core classes might be given in two languages, and students select which one they want, all students still study the core curriculum and preserve the integrity of the diploma.

Being bilingual in a world with international interaction can't help but be useful. Expanding courses offered in a curriculum is always better than restricting them, especially when they serve such an important need as the ability to communicate with others in their own language. I fully support option three.

Score: _____ /6

This essay is pretty good—it would earn a 4. The position is clearly stated, and some supporting reasoning is given.

However, the reasoning is too general and the writing is too ordinary to earn the top score. Let's see how it could be improved.

TURNING A 4 INTO A 6

The essay plunges right into the first point of view offered in the prompt. It could be improved by introducing the issue with a general statement, like:

> In today's world where international education standards are very high and the U.S. needs to remain competitive, educators are looking for ways to enhance high school curriculum. One way is offering classes in languages other than English.

In the last sentence of the first paragraph, the writer indicates that she agrees with Perspective Three. It is good to include your thesis in the introductory paragraph, but it would be better to make it clear where the position from the prompt ends and the author's position begins, perhaps like this:

> Still others think the accreditation should be offered but carefully administered so that graduation from that school would indicate the completed high school curriculum, and this is the option I agree with. <u>I would further argue that carefully implemented bilingual programs suit students who want to become fluent in two languages, but do not prevent others from pursuing their entire education in English.</u>

The second paragraph is relevant and organized—it covers one of the three positions offered in the prompt. But it would be better if the writer discussed this perspective using real-life information, such as:

> For instance, computer courses didn't exist a few years ago, but they are in the schools now because it's important for people to be able to use computers. It's the same thing with bilingual courses. Most of the world uses English as a second language and many people speak at least two languages. So it's only right that to stay competitive, U.S. students should be fluent in two languages too; this is particularly important in careers that require international work. Also, the argument simply says that these classes would only be for interested students, so it doesn't affect everyone. And finally, how can the schools encourage bilingual fluency if they don't provide a place for students to practice another language?

The third paragraph addresses Perspective Two. Discussing concrete ideas would bolster the essay. Plus, graders look to see if writers are able to provide analysis regarding how the perspectives relate to each other. For example:

> Students who struggle with the existing curriculum may find classes in another language, which may even be their home language. It may be more interesting, and they will do better overall. As I wrote before, adding important classes, such as computers, does not diminish the curriculum but strengthens it because it makes it more relevant to people today. Since bilingual classes are not required and therefore would not affect a student struggling to learn in English (and may even help if the student can take a class in his native language), this is an imprudent option and should not be implemented.

Paragraph four is pretty good, but expanding the discussion helps to increase your score. For instance:

> Schools have always taught languages in high school, so a French or Spanish course taught as a bilingual class makes perfect sense. Bilingual classes are also appropriate for students who do well and want to challenge themselves. So a French literature class can be taught in French while students read in French also.

The fifth paragraph reiterates the writer's thesis, but it could benefit from reorganization and additional development, like:

> Being bilingual in a world with international interaction can't help but be useful. I fully support option three <u>because it opens up possibilities for all students without denying anyone a full high school curriculum leading to a meaningful diploma. Recognizing the benefits of being bilingual, and making bilingual courses available but optional, is the best of both worlds.</u> Expanding courses offered in a curriculum is always better than impeding them, especially when they serve such an important need as the ability to communicate with others in their own language.

Here's how this essay would look with the improvements we've suggested:

> In today's world where international education standards are very high and the U.S. needs to remain competitive, educators are looking for ways to enhance high school curriculum. One way is offering classes in languages other than English. Some people think that schools should provide enough education in a different language for students to be certified as bilingual. Others think this will weaken the curriculum. Still others think the accreditation should be offered but carefully administered so that graduation from that school would indicate the completed high school curriculum, and this is the option I agree with. I would further argue that carefully implemented bilingual programs suit students who want to become fluent in two languages, but do not prevent others from pursuing their entire education in English.

The first option is to encourage bilingual fluency but not add any bilingual classes. Instead, the school administrators should make the existing curriculum better so that traditional education is really good. Certainly a high school curriculum should be as good as it can be and we should always be looking for ways to make it better. That often means adding new courses. For instance, computer courses didn't exist a few years ago, but they are in the schools now because it's important for people to be able to use computers. It's the same thing with bilingual courses. Most of the world uses English as a second language, and many people speak at least two languages. So it's only right that to stay competitive, U.S. students should be fluent in two languages too; this is particularly important in careers that require international work. Also, the argument simply says that these classes would only be for interested students, so it doesn't affect everyone. And finally, how can the schools encourage bilingual fluency if they don't provide a place for students to practice another language?

The second alternative is to not provide any bilingual education because there are enough students struggling with the curriculum in English. But this is a very weak argument because no one is suggesting that all students need to take bilingual classes, so just having those classes would not necessarily affect struggling students' grades. Students who struggle with the existing curriculum may find classes in another language, which may even be their home language. It may be more interesting, and they will *do* better overall. As I wrote before, adding important classes, such as computers, does not diminish the curriculum but strengthens it because it makes it more relevant to people today. Since bilingual classes are not required and therefore would not affect a student struggling to learn in English (and may even help if the student can take a class in his native language), this is an imprudent option and should not be implemented.

Finally, people argue that students should be given the opportunity to learn in other languages and be accredited as bilingual, but that the courses given need to be carefully selected. In reality, all classes need to be carefully selected so this not a problem for bilingual classes. And if the classes selected were all optional, not required, it would not affect students who still want to learn everything in English. Since core classes might be given in two languages, and students select which one they want, all students still study the core curriculum and preserve the integrity of the diploma. Schools have always taught languages in high school so a French or Spanish course taught as a bilingual class makes perfect sense. Bilingual classes are also advantageous for students who do well and want to challenge themselves. So a French literature class can be taught in French while students read in French also.

Being bilingual in a world with international interaction can't help but be useful. I fully support option three because it opens up possibilities for all students without denying anyone a full high school curriculum leading to a meaningful diploma. Recognizing the benefits of *being bilingual, and making bilingual courses available but optional, is the best of both worlds. Expanding courses offered in a curriculum is always better than restricting them, especially when they serve such an important need as the ability to communicate with others in their own language.*

This is now a 6 essay. It addresses the task fully and concretely. It addresses all three perspectives, refutes two opposing arguments, and then moves to the bulk of the author's own reasoning. The first paragraph introduces all the lines of reasoning that will be used, demonstrating that the writer knew right from the start where this essay was headed. The development of ideas is clear and logical, and the paragraphs reflect this organization.

The author shows a high level of skill with language. The transitions between paragraphs are clear and guide the reader through the reasoning. The sentence structure varies throughout the passage and is at times complex.

So what did we do to our 4 to make it a 6?

- We added examples and detail.
- We varied sentence structure and added stronger vocabulary (*diminish*, *imprudent*, *advantageous*).
- While length alone doesn't make a 6, we added detail to our original essay.
- The conclusion, rather than being lost in the fifth paragraph, is now a strong, independent statement that concisely sums up the writer's point of view.

SUMMARY

In this chapter, we went over all of the necessary pieces of a great essay for the ACT Writing test. Use this chapter to work on the individual pieces.

Then, we saw how those pieces are put together into an overall essay, and you had a chance to work on some general skills.

Finally, you learned the details of how an essay is scored and had a chance to put that into practice and score some essays yourself.

Use this knowledge as you practice your essay with prompts in the next chapter. Time yourself accurately, and score your essays honestly. That will help you find which aspects are your areas of opportunity.

Remember to keep practicing. Use Kaplan's Essay Template each time you work on an essay so that you will be able to easily organize your ideas on Test Day. If you're unable to fairly assess yourself, get a second opinion. Have someone else help you by reading your essay and assessing how clear it is.

Refine the pieces and practice the flow. Soon enough, you'll be able to master the ACT Writing test.

CHAPTER 18

Writing Part 3: ACT Writing Quiz

Here we go!

Treat the following essay like the one you'll encounter on Test Day and see how you do.

Starting the moment you read the prompt, keep track of your time. Allot 40 total minutes, divided up according to the Kaplan Method. Remember to take a good 3 minutes to read and fully understand the prompt so you can respond to it effectively, another 5 minutes to plan your essay so you know you have all the pieces, about 30 minutes producing, and the last 2 minutes proofreading and making *minor* edits.

Finally, take the time to read and evaluate your essay, asking yourself the same questions the graders will on Test Day, and give yourself a grade. If you'd like a second opinion on your score, get one! An English teacher or friend or family member with strong writing skills can help you fine-tune your skills. Use this practice essay to know where to focus your energy for the Practice Tests at the end of the book.

Remember the Kaplan Method—Understand the Prompt, Make a Plan, Produce Your Essay, and Proofread!

Directions: This is a test of your writing skills. You will have forty (40) minutes to write an essay in English. Before you begin planning and writing your essay, read the writing prompt carefully to understand exactly what you are being asked to do. Your essay will be evaluated on the evidence it provides of your ability to do the following:

- Express judgments by evaluating the three perspectives given in the prompt, taking a position on an issue, and explaining the relationship among all four ideas

- Develop a position by using logical reasoning and by supporting your ideas

- Maintain a focus on the topic throughout the essay

- Organize ideas in a logical way

- Use language clearly and effectively according to the conventions of standard written English

ENDANGERED SPECIES

Conservation status systems help governments and policy organizations prioritize and allocate resources to support the survival of imperiled species. In the United States, laws such as the Endangered Species Act provide a policy framework for implementing efforts to protect at-risk wildlife and ecosystems. These laws are often directly focused on mitigating the negative man-made effects of commercial expansion and land use. However, some activist groups support the broader goal of preventing the extinction of any species, regardless of whether or not humans are the cause of endangerment. Should regulatory efforts to protect endangered species be limited to offsetting the role of humans in placing wildlife at risk? Considering the global scope of conservation issues, the careful consideration and coordination of advocacy priorities could lead to improved policy outcomes.

Read and carefully consider these perspectives. Each suggests a particular way of thinking about the protection of endangered species.

Perspective One	Perspective Two	Perspective Three
Humans have the unique ability, through technological capability and scientific progress, to benefit the environment through the protection of wildlife and ecosystems. Conservation efforts should be open to any at-risk species, regardless of the known causes of endangerment.	Conservation policies are regularly met with the challenge of an ever-increasing number of species to save. With limited conservation resources available, funding priorities are too often biased in favor of publicly well-known animals and plants. Conservation decisions should instead be driven by scientific models that pinpoint sources of risk and identify high-value targets for species protection.	To shape effective policy, a distinction should be drawn between species at risk due to human and nonhuman factors. Well-intentioned conservation programs often carry unintended consequences that can create new environmental hazards despite successful species protection. Conservation policy should therefore be focused in a narrow way to repair the known negative effects of human activities on an ecosystem.

Essay Task

Write a unified, coherent essay in which you evaluate multiple perspectives on policies designed to protect endangered species. In your essay, be sure to:

- Analyze and evaluate the perspectives given
- State and develop your own perspective on the issue
- Explain the relationship between your perspective and those given

Your perspective may be in full agreement with any of the others, in partial agreement, or wholly different. Whatever the case, support your ideas with logical reasoning and detailed, persuasive examples.

Planning Your Essay

Use a blank sheet of paper to generate ideas and plan your essay. You may wish to consider the following as you think critically about the task.

Strengths and weaknesses of the three given perspectives:

- What insights do they offer, and what do they fail to consider?
- Why might they be persuasive to others, or why might they fail to persuade?

Your own knowledge, experience, and values:

- What is your perspective on this issue, and what are its strengths and weaknesses?
- How will you support your perspective in your essay?

MODEL ESSAY

Here's one possible way to approach this essay prompt. Remember that the opinion you express is less important than the way you present it. Notice that this response includes a logically arranged argument with specific examples.

Most people have heard politicians argue about global warming and environmentalists ask for donations to help save the rain forest. Some people believe that humans should be responsible for assisting any and all plants and animals that are at risk of extinction. Since it is impossible to save every species, however, it makes more sense to use scientific reasoning to determine which plants and animals should be saved. While it is interesting to know which species are affected by purely human factors and which are affected by non-human influences, such a determination should not affect environmental policy.

The idea of saving the rain forest is a noble one, and there are plenty of plants and animals close by that could also use our help, but trying to help every at-risk species is costly and time-consuming and would ultimately prove unsuccessful. Some organisms are more important to the overall ecosystem than others, and that should be taken into account. If polluted water is affecting animals at the top of a food chain, like alligators, it makes sense to work to protect the alligators rather than a species at the very bottom of the food chain, like earthworms. If the alligators die out, the entire food chain will deteriorate quickly. If earthworms become extinct, it will certainly create problems, but it is more likely that other animals can adapt to take the place of earthworms than to replace alligators.

Just as we can use zoological observations that demonstrate alligators are at the top of the food chain, we can use other scientific evidence to guide our choices. Currently, scientists are studying the naked mole rat because it is said to be immune to cancer. Since the naked mole rat may provide information that can lead to medical breakthroughs, we should protect that particular species. Protecting the earth is a great responsibility, and we should do so wisely.

As we act responsibly to repair some of the damage we may have done to the environment, we should focus on efforts that will provide the most benefit to both humans and the overall ecosystem. Whether an issue arises from man-made or natural causes, we should work to save species that we can confidently say are highly important to maintaining a global balance between human progress and natural wildlife. For example, if the bee population suddenly declined due to an unexpected gene mutation, we shouldn't refrain from saving the species just because humans didn't cause the mutation. Bees are responsible for extremely important pollination efforts, and their demise should not be dismissed lightly.

Humans should embrace the fact they can change the environment around them for the better. No matter what the reason—human or natural—if scientists determine that a species should be saved, money and time should be spent to make that happen. We can't wait until after alligators, naked mole rats, or bees are gone to try to do something. We need to plan ahead, use scientific reasoning, and allocate resources so that the world that sustains us continues to do just that.

SUMMARY

Checkup time!

Record what score you believe your essay would earn.

Now, identify three items that you believe went very well.

Next, identify three items you could improve to raise your score on Test Day.

Did your essay have a strong introduction and conclusion, with five paragraphs total? Did you use real-world examples? Did you discuss all three perspectives? Go back over chapters 16 and 17 for a review of the basics and supporting ideas so you can continue improving. Then, keep practicing using the Practice Tests later in this book.

With a regular cycle of review and practice, you'll soon be a master of the ACT Writing test!

CHAPTER 19

Last-Minute Tips

Is it starting to feel like your whole life is a buildup to the ACT? You've known about it for years, you've worried about it for months, and now you've spent at least a few hours in solid preparation for it. As Test Day gets closer, you may find your anxiety is on the rise. Don't worry. After the preparation you've received from this book, you're in good shape for Test Day.

> ✔ **EXPERT TUTOR TIP**
>
> If it is close to the ACT and you know there is one specific subject test you are not prepared for, do as many practice questions from that test as possible. Practice really does bring you closer to perfection.

To calm any pretest jitters you may have (and assuming you've left yourself at least some breathing time before your ACT), let's go over some last-minute strategies for the few days before and after Test Day.

THREE DAYS BEFORE THE TEST

- If you haven't already done so, take one of the full-length Practice Tests in this book under timed conditions. This book comes with eight Practice Tests—three in the back of the book, five online. Even better, visit your online syllabus for an official ACT practice test. Take the test and enter you answers online to receive a score report that highlights your strengths and opportunities. You can even submit your official ACT essay to be graded by an expert Kaplan instructor. You can also find practice questions on the official ACT website at www.actstudent.org.
- Try to use all of the techniques and tips you've learned in this book. Take control. Approach the test strategically and confidently.

WARNING: Don't take any more practice ACTs within 48 hours before the test! Doing so will probably exhaust you, hurting your scoring potential on the actual test. You wouldn't run a marathon the day before the real thing, would you?

TWO DAYS BEFORE THE TEST

- **Go over the results of your Practice Test.** Don't worry too much about your score or whether you got a specific question right or wrong. Remember—the Practice Test doesn't count. But do examine your performance on specific questions with an eye to how you might get through each one more quickly and with greater accuracy on the actual test to come.

- **After reviewing your test, identify which topics have the most points left for you to earn.** Review the pages that deal most with those topics and do more practice questions.

- **This is the last study day—review a couple of the more difficult principles we've covered, do a few more practice problems, and call it quits.** It doesn't pay to make yourself crazy right before the test. You've prepared. You'll do well.

THE DAY BEFORE THE TEST

- **Don't study.**

- **Do find something stimulating to do.** Do a puzzle, read a good book, exercise, go for a walk. Don't just sit around or do something brainless (TV marathon, etc.); do things that will make you feel good and energized. Of course, don't work so hard that you can't get up the next day!

- **Get together an "ACT survival kit" containing the following items:**

  - Watch (preferably digital)

  - At least three sharpened No. 2 pencils and pencil sharpener

  - Two erasers

  - Photo ID card (if you're not taking the test at your high school, make sure your ID is official)

  - An approved calculator

  - Your admission ticket

  - Snack and a bottle of water—there's a break, and you'll probably get hungry

  - Confidence!

- **Know exactly where you're going and how you're getting there.** It's a good idea to visit your test center sometime before Test Day so you know what to expect on the big day.

- **Get a good night's sleep.** Go to bed early and allow for some extra time to get ready

> ✔ **EXPERT TUTOR TIP**
>
> Make sure you prepare the things you will need the day before. It is not worth getting stressed the morning of because you cannot find your calculator or pencils.

in the morning. Make sure your rest schedule is roughly in line with your usual sleep pattern. If you normally go to bed at 10, don't go to bed at 7 the night before Test Day. That will just confuse your body and disrupt your rest.

THE MORNING OF THE TEST

- **Eat breakfast.** Protein is brain food, but don't eat anything too heavy or greasy. Don't drink a lot of coffee if you're not used to it; bathroom breaks cut into your time, and too much caffeine—or any other kind of stimulant—is a bad idea for your blood sugar and sustained energy (the test is four hours long, including breaks and hearing the proctoring instructions). Like sleep, get what your body needs, but don't deviate too far from your usual. If you normally have a small breakfast, add some protein and enough to keep yourself full, but don't turn it into a lumberjack breakfast that will make you ill.

- **Dress in layers** so that you can adjust to the temperature of the test room.

- **Read something.** Warm up your brain with a newspaper or a magazine. Don't let the ACT be the first thing you read that day.

- **Be sure to get there early.** Allow yourself extra time for traffic, mass-transit delays, and any other possible problems.

- **If you can, go to the test with a friend** (even if he or she isn't taking the test). It's nice to have somebody supporting you right up to the last minute.

DURING THE TEST

- **Don't get rattled.** If you find your confidence slipping, remind yourself how well you've prepared. You've followed the keys to ACT success, and you have practiced. You know the test; you know the strategies; you know the material tested. You're in great shape, as long as you relax! Take a step back and re-approach the question.

- **Even if something goes really wrong, don't panic.** If the test booklet is defective— two pages are stuck together or the ink has run—try to stay calm. Raise your hand, and tell the proctor you need a new book. If you accidentally mis-grid your answer page or put the answers in the wrong section, again, don't panic. Raise your hand, and tell the proctor. He or she might be able to arrange for you to re-grid your test after it's over, when it won't cost you any time.

Good luck! With all of your practice and Kaplan's strategies under your belt, we know you'll do great on the ACT.

AFTER THE TEST

Once the test is over, put it out of your mind. If you don't plan to take the ACT again, shelve this book and start thinking about more interesting things.

You might walk out of the ACT thinking that you could have done better. This is a normal reaction. Lots of people—even the highest scorers—feel that way. You tend to remember the questions that stumped you, not the many that you knew. If you're really concerned, call Kaplan for advice. Also, call us if you had any problems with your test experience—a proctor who called time early, a testing room whose temperature hovered just below freezing. We'll do everything we can to make sure that your rights as a test taker are preserved!

However, we're positive you performed well and scored your best on the exam because you followed our ACT Personalized Strategies and practiced with your eight Practice Tests. Be confident that you were prepared, and celebrate in the fact that the ACT is a distant memory.

If you want more help or just want to know more about the ACT, college admissions, or Kaplan prep courses for the ACT, give us a call at 1-800-KAP-TEST or visit us at www.kaptest.com. We're here to answer your questions and to help you in any way we can. Also, be sure to return one last time to your online syllabus and complete our survey. We're only as good as our successful students!

Congratulations on all you've accomplished. You're ready for your highest score and to show colleges you're the student they should accept for admission. We're excited for you, so get excited for your new opportunities as well, and let us know how you do!

PART THREE

Practice Tests and Explanations

Practice Test One

HOW TO TAKE THESE PRACTICE TESTS

These three Practice Tests are Kaplan-created tests, similar to the actual ACT. Before taking a Practice Test, find a quiet room where you can work uninterrupted for three and a half hours. Make sure you have a comfortable desk, your calculator, and several No. 2 pencils. Use the answer sheet to record your answers. Once you start a Practice Test, don't stop until you've finished. Remember: You can review any questions within a subject test, but you may not jump from one subject test to another.

You'll find the answers and explanations to the test questions immediately following each test.

ACT Practice Test One
ANSWER SHEET

ENGLISH TEST

1. Ⓐ Ⓑ Ⓒ Ⓓ 11. Ⓐ Ⓑ Ⓒ Ⓓ 21. Ⓐ Ⓑ Ⓒ Ⓓ 31. Ⓐ Ⓑ Ⓒ Ⓓ 41. Ⓐ Ⓑ Ⓒ Ⓓ 51. Ⓐ Ⓑ Ⓒ Ⓓ 61. Ⓐ Ⓑ Ⓒ Ⓓ 71. Ⓐ Ⓑ Ⓒ Ⓓ
2. Ⓕ Ⓖ Ⓗ Ⓙ 12. Ⓕ Ⓖ Ⓗ Ⓙ 22. Ⓕ Ⓖ Ⓗ Ⓙ 32. Ⓕ Ⓖ Ⓗ Ⓙ 42. Ⓕ Ⓖ Ⓗ Ⓙ 52. Ⓕ Ⓖ Ⓗ Ⓙ 62. Ⓕ Ⓖ Ⓗ Ⓙ 72. Ⓕ Ⓖ Ⓗ Ⓙ
3. Ⓐ Ⓑ Ⓒ Ⓓ 13. Ⓐ Ⓑ Ⓒ Ⓓ 23. Ⓐ Ⓑ Ⓒ Ⓓ 33. Ⓐ Ⓑ Ⓒ Ⓓ 43. Ⓐ Ⓑ Ⓒ Ⓓ 53. Ⓐ Ⓑ Ⓒ Ⓓ 63. Ⓐ Ⓑ Ⓒ Ⓓ 73. Ⓐ Ⓑ Ⓒ Ⓓ
4. Ⓕ Ⓖ Ⓗ Ⓙ 14. Ⓕ Ⓖ Ⓗ Ⓙ 24. Ⓕ Ⓖ Ⓗ Ⓙ 34. Ⓕ Ⓖ Ⓗ Ⓙ 44. Ⓕ Ⓖ Ⓗ Ⓙ 54. Ⓕ Ⓖ Ⓗ Ⓙ 64. Ⓕ Ⓖ Ⓗ Ⓙ 74. Ⓕ Ⓖ Ⓗ Ⓙ
5. Ⓐ Ⓑ Ⓒ Ⓓ 15. Ⓐ Ⓑ Ⓒ Ⓓ 25. Ⓐ Ⓑ Ⓒ Ⓓ 35. Ⓐ Ⓑ Ⓒ Ⓓ 45. Ⓐ Ⓑ Ⓒ Ⓓ 55. Ⓐ Ⓑ Ⓒ Ⓓ 65. Ⓐ Ⓑ Ⓒ Ⓓ 75. Ⓐ Ⓑ Ⓒ Ⓓ
6. Ⓕ Ⓖ Ⓗ Ⓙ 16. Ⓕ Ⓖ Ⓗ Ⓙ 26. Ⓕ Ⓖ Ⓗ Ⓙ 36. Ⓕ Ⓖ Ⓗ Ⓙ 46. Ⓕ Ⓖ Ⓗ Ⓙ 56. Ⓕ Ⓖ Ⓗ Ⓙ 66. Ⓕ Ⓖ Ⓗ Ⓙ
7. Ⓐ Ⓑ Ⓒ Ⓓ 17. Ⓐ Ⓑ Ⓒ Ⓓ 27. Ⓐ Ⓑ Ⓒ Ⓓ 37. Ⓐ Ⓑ Ⓒ Ⓓ 47. Ⓐ Ⓑ Ⓒ Ⓓ 57. Ⓐ Ⓑ Ⓒ Ⓓ 67. Ⓐ Ⓑ Ⓒ Ⓓ
8. Ⓕ Ⓖ Ⓗ Ⓙ 18. Ⓕ Ⓖ Ⓗ Ⓙ 28. Ⓕ Ⓖ Ⓗ Ⓙ 38. Ⓕ Ⓖ Ⓗ Ⓙ 48. Ⓕ Ⓖ Ⓗ Ⓙ 58. Ⓕ Ⓖ Ⓗ Ⓙ 68. Ⓕ Ⓖ Ⓗ Ⓙ
9. Ⓐ Ⓑ Ⓒ Ⓓ 19. Ⓐ Ⓑ Ⓒ Ⓓ 29. Ⓐ Ⓑ Ⓒ Ⓓ 39. Ⓐ Ⓑ Ⓒ Ⓓ 49. Ⓐ Ⓑ Ⓒ Ⓓ 59. Ⓐ Ⓑ Ⓒ Ⓓ 69. Ⓐ Ⓑ Ⓒ Ⓓ
10. Ⓕ Ⓖ Ⓗ Ⓙ 20. Ⓕ Ⓖ Ⓗ Ⓙ 30. Ⓕ Ⓖ Ⓗ Ⓙ 40. Ⓕ Ⓖ Ⓗ Ⓙ 50. Ⓕ Ⓖ Ⓗ Ⓙ 60. Ⓕ Ⓖ Ⓗ Ⓙ 70. Ⓕ Ⓖ Ⓗ Ⓙ

MATHEMATICS TEST

1. Ⓐ Ⓑ Ⓒ Ⓓ Ⓔ 11. Ⓐ Ⓑ Ⓒ Ⓓ Ⓔ 21. Ⓐ Ⓑ Ⓒ Ⓓ Ⓔ 31. Ⓐ Ⓑ Ⓒ Ⓓ Ⓔ 41. Ⓐ Ⓑ Ⓒ Ⓓ Ⓔ 51. Ⓐ Ⓑ Ⓒ Ⓓ Ⓔ
2. Ⓕ Ⓖ Ⓗ Ⓙ Ⓚ 12. Ⓕ Ⓖ Ⓗ Ⓙ Ⓚ 22. Ⓕ Ⓖ Ⓗ Ⓙ Ⓚ 32. Ⓕ Ⓖ Ⓗ Ⓙ Ⓚ 42. Ⓕ Ⓖ Ⓗ Ⓙ Ⓚ 52. Ⓕ Ⓖ Ⓗ Ⓙ Ⓚ
3. Ⓐ Ⓑ Ⓒ Ⓓ Ⓔ 13. Ⓐ Ⓑ Ⓒ Ⓓ Ⓔ 23. Ⓐ Ⓑ Ⓒ Ⓓ Ⓔ 33. Ⓐ Ⓑ Ⓒ Ⓓ Ⓔ 43. Ⓐ Ⓑ Ⓒ Ⓓ Ⓔ 53. Ⓐ Ⓑ Ⓒ Ⓓ Ⓔ
4. Ⓕ Ⓖ Ⓗ Ⓙ Ⓚ 14. Ⓕ Ⓖ Ⓗ Ⓙ Ⓚ 24. Ⓕ Ⓖ Ⓗ Ⓙ Ⓚ 34. Ⓕ Ⓖ Ⓗ Ⓙ Ⓚ 44. Ⓕ Ⓖ Ⓗ Ⓙ Ⓚ 54. Ⓕ Ⓖ Ⓗ Ⓙ Ⓚ
5. Ⓐ Ⓑ Ⓒ Ⓓ Ⓔ 15. Ⓐ Ⓑ Ⓒ Ⓓ Ⓔ 25. Ⓐ Ⓑ Ⓒ Ⓓ Ⓔ 35. Ⓐ Ⓑ Ⓒ Ⓓ Ⓔ 45. Ⓐ Ⓑ Ⓒ Ⓓ Ⓔ 55. Ⓐ Ⓑ Ⓒ Ⓓ Ⓔ
6. Ⓕ Ⓖ Ⓗ Ⓙ Ⓚ 16. Ⓕ Ⓖ Ⓗ Ⓙ Ⓚ 26. Ⓕ Ⓖ Ⓗ Ⓙ Ⓚ 36. Ⓕ Ⓖ Ⓗ Ⓙ Ⓚ 46. Ⓕ Ⓖ Ⓗ Ⓙ Ⓚ 56. Ⓕ Ⓖ Ⓗ Ⓙ Ⓚ
7. Ⓐ Ⓑ Ⓒ Ⓓ Ⓔ 17. Ⓐ Ⓑ Ⓒ Ⓓ Ⓔ 27. Ⓐ Ⓑ Ⓒ Ⓓ Ⓔ 37. Ⓐ Ⓑ Ⓒ Ⓓ Ⓔ 47. Ⓐ Ⓑ Ⓒ Ⓓ Ⓔ 57. Ⓐ Ⓑ Ⓒ Ⓓ Ⓔ
8. Ⓕ Ⓖ Ⓗ Ⓙ Ⓚ 18. Ⓕ Ⓖ Ⓗ Ⓙ Ⓚ 28. Ⓕ Ⓖ Ⓗ Ⓙ Ⓚ 38. Ⓕ Ⓖ Ⓗ Ⓙ Ⓚ 48. Ⓕ Ⓖ Ⓗ Ⓙ Ⓚ 58. Ⓕ Ⓖ Ⓗ Ⓙ Ⓚ
9. Ⓐ Ⓑ Ⓒ Ⓓ Ⓔ 19. Ⓐ Ⓑ Ⓒ Ⓓ Ⓔ 29. Ⓐ Ⓑ Ⓒ Ⓓ Ⓔ 39. Ⓐ Ⓑ Ⓒ Ⓓ Ⓔ 49. Ⓐ Ⓑ Ⓒ Ⓓ Ⓔ 59. Ⓐ Ⓑ Ⓒ Ⓓ Ⓔ
10. Ⓕ Ⓖ Ⓗ Ⓙ Ⓚ 20. Ⓕ Ⓖ Ⓗ Ⓙ Ⓚ 30. Ⓕ Ⓖ Ⓗ Ⓙ Ⓚ 40. Ⓕ Ⓖ Ⓗ Ⓙ Ⓚ 50. Ⓕ Ⓖ Ⓗ Ⓙ Ⓚ 60. Ⓕ Ⓖ Ⓗ Ⓙ Ⓚ

READING TEST

1. Ⓐ Ⓑ Ⓒ Ⓓ 6. Ⓕ Ⓖ Ⓗ Ⓙ 11. Ⓐ Ⓑ Ⓒ Ⓓ 16. Ⓕ Ⓖ Ⓗ Ⓙ 21. Ⓐ Ⓑ Ⓒ Ⓓ 26. Ⓕ Ⓖ Ⓗ Ⓙ 31. Ⓐ Ⓑ Ⓒ Ⓓ 36. Ⓕ Ⓖ Ⓗ Ⓙ
2. Ⓕ Ⓖ Ⓗ Ⓙ 7. Ⓐ Ⓑ Ⓒ Ⓓ 12. Ⓕ Ⓖ Ⓗ Ⓙ 17. Ⓐ Ⓑ Ⓒ Ⓓ 22. Ⓕ Ⓖ Ⓗ Ⓙ 27. Ⓐ Ⓑ Ⓒ Ⓓ 32. Ⓕ Ⓖ Ⓗ Ⓙ 37. Ⓐ Ⓑ Ⓒ Ⓓ
3. Ⓐ Ⓑ Ⓒ Ⓓ 8. Ⓕ Ⓖ Ⓗ Ⓙ 13. Ⓐ Ⓑ Ⓒ Ⓓ 18. Ⓕ Ⓖ Ⓗ Ⓙ 23. Ⓐ Ⓑ Ⓒ Ⓓ 28. Ⓕ Ⓖ Ⓗ Ⓙ 33. Ⓐ Ⓑ Ⓒ Ⓓ 38. Ⓕ Ⓖ Ⓗ Ⓙ
4. Ⓕ Ⓖ Ⓗ Ⓙ 9. Ⓐ Ⓑ Ⓒ Ⓓ 14. Ⓕ Ⓖ Ⓗ Ⓙ 19. Ⓐ Ⓑ Ⓒ Ⓓ 24. Ⓕ Ⓖ Ⓗ Ⓙ 29. Ⓐ Ⓑ Ⓒ Ⓓ 34. Ⓕ Ⓖ Ⓗ Ⓙ 39. Ⓐ Ⓑ Ⓒ Ⓓ
5. Ⓐ Ⓑ Ⓒ Ⓓ 10. Ⓕ Ⓖ Ⓗ Ⓙ 15. Ⓐ Ⓑ Ⓒ Ⓓ 20. Ⓕ Ⓖ Ⓗ Ⓙ 25. Ⓐ Ⓑ Ⓒ Ⓓ 30. Ⓕ Ⓖ Ⓗ Ⓙ 35. Ⓐ Ⓑ Ⓒ Ⓓ 40. Ⓕ Ⓖ Ⓗ Ⓙ

SCIENCE TEST

1. Ⓐ Ⓑ Ⓒ Ⓓ 6. Ⓕ Ⓖ Ⓗ Ⓙ 11. Ⓐ Ⓑ Ⓒ Ⓓ 16. Ⓕ Ⓖ Ⓗ Ⓙ 21. Ⓐ Ⓑ Ⓒ Ⓓ 26. Ⓕ Ⓖ Ⓗ Ⓙ 31. Ⓐ Ⓑ Ⓒ Ⓓ 36. Ⓕ Ⓖ Ⓗ Ⓙ
2. Ⓕ Ⓖ Ⓗ Ⓙ 7. Ⓐ Ⓑ Ⓒ Ⓓ 12. Ⓕ Ⓖ Ⓗ Ⓙ 17. Ⓐ Ⓑ Ⓒ Ⓓ 22. Ⓕ Ⓖ Ⓗ Ⓙ 27. Ⓐ Ⓑ Ⓒ Ⓓ 32. Ⓕ Ⓖ Ⓗ Ⓙ 37. Ⓐ Ⓑ Ⓒ Ⓓ
3. Ⓐ Ⓑ Ⓒ Ⓓ 8. Ⓕ Ⓖ Ⓗ Ⓙ 13. Ⓐ Ⓑ Ⓒ Ⓓ 18. Ⓕ Ⓖ Ⓗ Ⓙ 23. Ⓐ Ⓑ Ⓒ Ⓓ 28. Ⓕ Ⓖ Ⓗ Ⓙ 33. Ⓐ Ⓑ Ⓒ Ⓓ 38. Ⓕ Ⓖ Ⓗ Ⓙ
4. Ⓕ Ⓖ Ⓗ Ⓙ 9. Ⓐ Ⓑ Ⓒ Ⓓ 14. Ⓕ Ⓖ Ⓗ Ⓙ 19. Ⓐ Ⓑ Ⓒ Ⓓ 24. Ⓕ Ⓖ Ⓗ Ⓙ 29. Ⓐ Ⓑ Ⓒ Ⓓ 34. Ⓕ Ⓖ Ⓗ Ⓙ 39. Ⓐ Ⓑ Ⓒ Ⓓ
5. Ⓐ Ⓑ Ⓒ Ⓓ 10. Ⓕ Ⓖ Ⓗ Ⓙ 15. Ⓐ Ⓑ Ⓒ Ⓓ 20. Ⓕ Ⓖ Ⓗ Ⓙ 25. Ⓐ Ⓑ Ⓒ Ⓓ 30. Ⓕ Ⓖ Ⓗ Ⓙ 35. Ⓐ Ⓑ Ⓒ Ⓓ 40. Ⓕ Ⓖ Ⓗ Ⓙ

ENGLISH TEST

45 Minutes—75 Questions

Directions: In the following five passages, certain words and phrases are underlined and numbered. In the right-hand column are alternatives for each underlined portion. Select the one that best conveys the idea, creates the most grammatically correct sentence, or is the most consistent with the style and tone of the passage. If you decide that the original version is best, select NO CHANGE. You may also find questions that ask about the entire passage or a section of the passage. These questions will correspond to small numbered boxes in the text. For these questions, decide which choice best accomplishes the purpose set out in the question stem. After you've selected the best choice, fill in the corresponding oval in your Answer Grid. For some questions, you'll need to read the context in order to answer correctly. Be sure to read until you have enough information to determine the correct answer choice.

PASSAGE I

ORIGINS OF URBAN LEGENDS

[1]

Since primitive times, societies have <u>created, and told</u> legends. Even before the development of written language, cultures would orally pass down these popular stories.

[2]

2 These stories served the dual purpose of entertaining audiences and of transmitting values and beliefs from generation to generation.

1. **A.** NO CHANGE
   B. created then subsequently told
   C. created and told
   D. created, and told original

2. Suppose that the author wants to insert a sentence here to describe the different kinds of oral stories told by these societies. Which of the following sentences would best serve that purpose?

   F. These myths and tales varied in substance, from the humorous to the heroic.
   G. These myths and tales were often recited by paid storytellers.
   H. Unfortunately, no recording of the original myths and tales exists.
   J. Sometimes it took several evenings for the full story to be recited.

GO ON TO THE NEXT PAGE ⟶

<u>Indeed</u> today we have many more permanent ways
   3
of handing down our beliefs to future generations, we

continue to create and tell legends. In our technological

society, a new form of folktale has emerged:

<u>the</u> urban legend.
 4

3. **A.** NO CHANGE
   B. However,
   C. Indeed,
   D. Although

4. **F.** NO CHANGE
   G. it is called the
   H. it being the
   J. known as the

[3]

Urban legends are stories we all have heard; they

are supposed to have really happened, but are never

<u>verifiable however.</u> It seems that the people involved can
         5
never be found. Researchers of the urban legend call the

elusive participant in such supposed "real-life" events a

FOAF—a Friend of a Friend.

5. **A.** NO CHANGE
   B. verifiable, however.
   C. verifiable, furthermore.
   D. verifiable.

[4]

Urban legends have some characteristic features.

They are often humorous in nature with a surprise

<u>ending and a conclusion.</u> One such legend is the tale of
              6
the hunter who was returning home from an unsuccess-

ful hunting trip. On his way home, he accidentally hit

and killed a deer on a deserted highway. Even though he

knew it was illegal, he decided to keep the deer, and he

<u>loads it in</u> the back of his station wagon. As the hunter
      7
continued driving, the deer,

6. **F.** NO CHANGE
   G. ending.
   H. ending, which is a conclusion.
   J. ending or conclusion.

7. **A.** NO CHANGE
   B. loaded it in
   C. is loading it in
   D. had loaded it in

<u>he was</u> only temporarily knocked unconscious by the
   8
car, woke up and began thrashing around. The hunter

panicked, stopped the car, ran to hide in the roadside

ditch, and watched the enraged deer destroy his car.

8. **F.** NO CHANGE
   G. which being
   H. that is
   J. which was

GO ON TO THE NEXT PAGE →

[5]

One legend involves alligators in the sewer systems of major metropolitan areas. According to the story, before alligators were a protected species, people vacationing in Florida purchased baby alligators to take home as souvenirs.

Between 1930 and 1940, nearly a million alligators in Florida were killed for the value of their skin, used to make expensive leather products such as boots and wallets.
     After the novelty of having a pet alligator wore off, many people flushed their baby souvenirs down toilets. Legend has it that the baby alligators found a perfect growing and breeding environment in city sewer systems, where they thrive to this day on the ample supply of rats.

[6]

In addition to urban legends that are told from friend to friend, a growing number of urban legends are passed along through the Internet and email. One of the more popular stories are about a woman who was unwittingly charged $100 for a cookie recipe she requested at an upscale restaurant. To get her money's worth, this woman supposed copied the recipe for the delicious cookies and forwarded it via email to everyone she knew.

9. A. NO CHANGE
    B. species; people
    C. species. People
    D. species people

10. F. NO CHANGE
     G. Because their skin is used to make expensive leather products such as boots and wallets, nearly a million alligators in Florida were killed between 1930 and 1940.
     H. Killed between 1930 and 1940, the skin of nearly a million alligators from Florida was used to make expensive leather products such as boots and wallets.
     J. OMIT the underlined portion.

11. A. NO CHANGE
     B. would be about
     C. is about
     D. is dealing with

12. F. NO CHANGE
     G. woman supposedly
     H. women supposedly
     J. women supposed to

GO ON TO THE NEXT PAGE

[7]

Although today's technology enhances our ability to tell and retell urban legends, the Internet can also serve as a monitor of urban legends. <u>Dedicated to commonly told urban legends, research is done by many websites.</u> According to those websites, most legends, including the ones told here, have no basis in reality.

13. **A.** NO CHANGE

      B. Many websites are dedicated to researching the validity of commonly told urban legends.

      C. Researching the validity of commonly told urban legends, many websites are dedicated.

      D. OMIT the underlined portion.

Questions 14–15 ask about the preceding passage as a whole.

---

14. The author wants to insert the following sentence:

    > Other urban legends seem to be designed to instill fear.

    What would be the most logical placement for this sentence?

    F. After the last sentence of paragraph 3
    G. After the second sentence of paragraph 4
    H. Before the first sentence of paragraph 5
    J. After the last sentence of paragraph 6

15. Suppose that the author had been assigned to write an essay comparing the purposes and topics of myths and legends in primitive societies and in our modern society. Would this essay fulfill that assignment?

    A. Yes, because the essay describes myths and legends from primitive societies and modern society.
    B. Yes, because the essay provides explanations of possible purposes and topics of myths and legends from primitive societies and modern society.
    C. No, because the essay does not provide enough information about the topics of the myths and legends of primitive societies to make a valid comparison.
    D. No, because the essay does not provide any information on the myths and legends of primitive societies.

PASSAGE II

HENRY DAVID THOREAU: A SUCCESSFUL LIFE

What does it mean to be successful? <u>Do one</u> measure success by money? If I told you about a
¹⁶

<u>man: working</u> as a teacher, a land surveyor, and a
¹⁷
factory worker (never holding any of these jobs for more than a few years), would that man sound like a success to you? If I told you that he spent

16. F. NO CHANGE
    G. Does we
    H. Does one
    J. Did you

17. A. NO CHANGE
    B. man who worked
    C. man and worked
    D. man, which working

<u>two solitary years living alone</u> in a small cabin that he
₁₈
built for himself and that he spent those years looking at

plants and writing in a diary—would you think of him

as a celebrity or an important figure? What if I told you

that <u>he rarely ventured</u> far from the town where he was
₁₉
born, that he was thrown in jail for refusing to pay his

taxes, and that he died at the age of forty-five? Do any of

these facts seem to point to a man whose life should be

studied and emulated?

You may already know about this man. You may

even have read some of his writings. His name <u>was:</u>
₂₀
<u>Henry David Thoreau, and he</u> was, in addition to the
₂₀
jobs listed above, a poet, an essayist, a naturalist, and

a social critic. Although the facts listed about him

may not seem to add up to much, he <u>was, in fact a</u>
₂₁
tremendously influential person. Along with writers

such as Ralph Waldo Emerson, Mark Twain, and Walt

Whitman, Thoreau helped to create the first literature

and philosophy that most people identify as <u>unique</u>
₂₂
American.

In 1845, Thoreau built a <u>cabin. Near</u> Walden Pond
₂₃
and remained there for more than two years, living

alone, fending for himself, and observing the nature

around him. He kept scrupulous notes in his diary,

notes that he later distilled into his most famous work

titled *Walden*.

18. **F.** NO CHANGE
    G. two years living alone
    H. two solitary years all by himself
    J. a couple of lonely years living in solitude

19. **A.** NO CHANGE
    B. he is rarely venturing
    C. he has rare ventures
    D. this person was to venture rarely

20. **F.** NO CHANGE
    G. was Henry David Thoreau and he
    H. was: Henry David Thoreau; and he
    J. was Henry David Thoreau, and he

21. **A.** NO CHANGE
    B. was, in fact, a
    C. was in fact a
    D. was in fact, a

22. **F.** NO CHANGE
    G. uniquely
    H. uniqueness
    J. the most unique

23. **A.** NO CHANGE
    B. cabin. On
    C. cabin, by
    D. cabin near

GO ON TO THE NEXT PAGE ⇒

<u>*Walden* is read by many literature students today.</u>
24

[1] To protest slavery, Thoreau refused to pay his taxes in 1846. [2] Thoreau was a firm believer in the abolition of slavery, and he objected to the practice's extension into the new territories of the West. [3] For this act of rebellion, he was thrown in the Concord jail. 25

Thoreau used his writing to spread his message of resistance and <u>activism; he published</u> an essay entitled
26
Civil Disobedience (also known as *Resistance to Civil Government*). In it, Thoreau laid out his argument for refusing to obey unjust laws.

Although Thoreau's life was very brief, <u>his</u> works
27
and his ideas continue to touch and influence people. Students all over the country—all over the world—continue to read his essays and hear his unique voice, urging them to lead lives of principle, individuality, and freedom. 28 To be able to live out the ideas that

burn in <u>the heart of a person</u>—surely that is the mean-
29
ing of success.

24. F. NO CHANGE
G. This book is read by many literature students today.
H. Today, many literature students read *Walden*.
J. OMIT the underlined portion.

25. What is the most logical order of sentences in this paragraph?
A. NO CHANGE
B. 3, 2, 1
C. 2, 1, 3
D. 3, 1, 2

26. F. NO CHANGE
G. activism, he published:
H. activism, he published
J. activism, he published,

27. A. NO CHANGE
B. he's
C. their
D. those

28. The purpose of this paragraph is to:
F. explain why Thoreau was put in jail.
G. prove a point about people's conception of success.
H. suggest that Thoreau may be misunderstood.
J. discuss Thoreau's importance in today's world.

29. A. NO CHANGE
B. one's heart
C. the heart and soul of a person
D. through the heart of a person

GO ON TO THE NEXT PAGE

> Question 30 asks about the preceding passage as a whole.

30. By including questions throughout the entire first paragraph, the author encourages the reader to:

    F. answer each question as the passage proceeds.

    G. think about the meaning of success.

    H. assess the quality of Thoreau's work.

    J. form an opinion about greed in modern society.

PASSAGE III

THE SLOTH: SLOW BUT NOT SLOTHFUL

[1]

More than half of the world's <u>currently living plant</u> and
                                          31
animal species live in tropical rain forests. Four square miles of a Central American rain forest can be home to up to 1,500 different species of flowering plants, 700 species of trees, 400 species of birds, and 125 species of mammals. Of these mammals, the sloth is one of the most unusual.

[2]

Unlike most mammals, the sloth is usually upside down. A sloth does just about everything upside down, including sleeping, eating, mating, and giving birth. <u>Its' unique</u> anatomy allows the sloth to spend most of
    32
the time hanging from one tree branch or another, high in the canopy of a rain forest tree. About the size of a large domestic <u>cat, the</u> sloth hangs from its unusually
                          33
long limbs and long, hooklike claws.

31. A. NO CHANGE
    B. currently existing plant
    C. living plant
    D. plant

32. F. NO CHANGE
    G. It's unique
    H. Its unique
    J. Its uniquely

33. A. NO CHANGE
    B. cat; the
    C. cat. The
    D. cat, but the

GO ON TO THE NEXT PAGE →

Specially designed for limbs, the sloth's muscles seem to
                                          34
cling to things.
    34

[3]

In fact, a sloth's limbs are <u>so specific</u> adapted to
                              35
upside-down life that a sloth is essentially incapable

of walking on the ground. <u>Instead, they</u> must crawl or
                              36
drag itself with its massive claws. This makes it easy to

see why the sloth rarely leaves its home in the trees.

<u>Because</u> it can not move swiftly on the ground, the sloth
   37
is an excellent swimmer.

[4]

[38] A sloth can hang upside down and, without

34. F. NO CHANGE

G. The sloth's muscles seem to cling to things for specially designed limbs.

H. The muscles in a sloth's limbs seem to be specially designed for clinging to things.

J. OMIT the underlined portion.

35. A. NO CHANGE

B. so specific and

C. so specified

D. so specifically

36. F. NO CHANGE

G. Instead, it

H. However, they

J. In addition, it

37. A. NO CHANGE

B. Despite

C. Similarly,

D. Though

38. The author wants to insert a sentence here to help connect paragraph 3 and paragraph 4. Which of the following sentences would best serve that purpose?

F. Of course, many other animals are also excellent swimmers.

G. Another unique characteristic of the sloth is its flexibility.

H. In addition to swimming, the sloth is an incredible climber.

J. Flexibility is a trait that helps the sloth survive.

GO ON TO THE NEXT PAGE ▷

moving the rest of its <u>body turn</u> its face 180 degrees so
                              39

that it <u>was looking</u> at the ground. A sloth can rotate
              40
its forelimbs in all directions, so it can easily reach the

leaves that make up its diet. The sloth can also roll itself

up into a ball in order to <u>protect and defend itself from</u>
                                     41

predators. <u>The howler monkey, another inhabitant of</u>
                                        42
<u>the rain forest, is not as flexible as the sloth.</u>
                         42

[5]

The best defense a sloth has from predators such as

jaguars and large snakes, though, is its camouflage. Dur-

ing the rainy season, a sloth's thick brown or gray fur is

usually covered with a coat of blue-green <u>algae. Which</u>
                                                   43
helps it blend in with its forest surroundings. Another

type of camouflage is the sloth's incredibly slow move-

ment: it often moves less than 100 feet during a 24-hour

period.

[6]

It is this slow movement that earned the sloth its

name. *Sloth* is also a word for laziness or an aversion to

work. But even though it sleeps an average of 15 hours a

day, the sloth isn't necessarily lazy. It just moves, upside

39. A. NO CHANGE
   B. body turns
   C. body, it has the capability of turning
   D. body, turn

40. F. NO CHANGE
   G. had been looking
   H. will have the ability to be looking
   J. can look

41. A. NO CHANGE
   B. protect itself and defend itself from
   C. protect itself so it won't be harmed by
   D. protect itself from

42. F. NO CHANGE
   G. Another inhabitant of the rain forest, the howler monkey, is not as flexible as the sloth.
   H. Not as flexible as the sloth is the howler monkey, another inhabitant of the rain forest.
   J. OMIT the underlined portion.

43. A. NO CHANGE
   B. algae, which
   C. algae, being that it
   D. algae

GO ON TO THE NEXT PAGE ⟶

down, at its own slow pace through its world of rain

forest trees. 44

44. The author is considering deleting the last sentence of paragraph 6. This change would:

F. diminish the amount of information provided about the habits of the sloth.

G. make the ending of the passage more abrupt.

H. emphasize the slothful nature of the sloth.

J. make the tone of the essay more consistent.

Question 45 asks about the preceding passage as a whole.

---

45. The author wants to insert the following description:

An observer could easily be tricked into thinking that a sloth was just a pile of decaying leaves.

What would be the most appropriate placement for this sentence?

A. After the last sentence of paragraph 1

B. After the third sentence of paragraph 2

C. Before the last sentence of paragraph 5

D. Before the first sentence of paragraph 6

GO ON TO THE NEXT PAGE

PASSAGE IV

FIRES IN YELLOWSTONE

During the summer of 1988, I watched Yellowstone National Park go up in flames. In June, <u>fires ignited by lightning</u> had been allowed to burn unsuppressed
₄₆
because park officials expected that the usual summer rains would douse the flames. However, the rains never <u>will have come</u>. A plentiful fuel supply of fallen logs and
₄₇
pine needles was available, and winds of up to 100 miles per hour whipped the spreading fires along and carried red-hot embers to other areas, creating new fires. By the time park officials succumbed to the pressure of public opinion and <u>decide</u> to try to extinguish the
₄₈

<u>flames. It's</u> too late. The situation remained out of con-
₄₉
trol in spite of the efforts of 9,000 firefighters who were using state-of-the-art equipment. By September, more than 720,000 acres of Yellowstone had been affected by fire. <u>Nature was only able to curb the destruction</u>; the
₅₀
smoke did not begin to clear until the first snow arrived on September 11.

<u>Being that I was</u> an ecologist who has studied
₅₁
forests for 20 years, I know that this was not nearly the tragedy it seemed to be. Large fires are, after

46. **F.** NO CHANGE
    G. fires having been ignited by lightning
    H. fires, the kind ignited by lightning,
    J. fires ignited and started by lightning

47. **A.** NO CHANGE
    B. came
    C. were coming
    D. have come

48. **F.** NO CHANGE
    G. are deciding
    H. decided
    J. OMIT the underlined portion.

49. **A.** NO CHANGE
    B. flames, it's
    C. flames, it was
    D. flames; it was

50. **F.** NO CHANGE
    G. Only curbing the destruction by able nature
    H. Only nature was able to curb the destruction
    J. Nature was able to curb only the destruction

51. **A.** NO CHANGE
    B. Being that I am
    C. I'm
    D. As

GO ON TO THE NEXT PAGE ⟩

all, necessary <u>in order that the continued health in</u>
                                            52
<u>the forest ecosystem be maintained.</u> Fires thin out
                        52
overcrowded areas and allow the sun to reach species of

plants stunted by shade. Ash fertilizes the soil, and fire

smoke kills forest bacteria. In the case of the lodgepole

pine, fire is essential to reproduction: the <u>pines' cone</u>
                                                  53
open only when exposed to temperatures greater than

112 degrees.

    The fires in Yellowstone did result in some loss of

wildlife, but overall, the region's animals proved to be

fire-tolerant and fire-adaptive. <u>However,</u> large ani-
                                        54
mals

such as bison were often seen <u>grazing, and</u> bedding
                                      55
down in meadows near burning forests. Also, the fire

posed little threat to the members of any endangered

animal species in the park.

    My confidence in the natural resilience of the forest

has been borne out in the years since the fires ravaged

Yellowstone. <u>Judged from recent pictures of the park</u>
                                56

the forest was not destroyed; <u>it</u> was rejuvenated.
                                  57

---

52. **F.** NO CHANGE

    G. for the continued health of the forest ecosystem to be maintained.

    H. in order to continue the maintenance of the health of the forest ecosystem.

    J. for the continued health of the forest ecosystem.

53. **A.** NO CHANGE

    B. pines cones'

    C. pine's cones

    D. pine's cone

54. **F.** NO CHANGE

    G. Clearly,

    H. In fact,

    J. Instead,

55. **A.** NO CHANGE

    B. grazing; and bedding

    C. grazing: and bedding

    D. grazing and bedding

56. **F.** NO CHANGE

    G. Recent pictures of the park show that

    H. Judging by the recent pictures of the park,

    J. As judged according to pictures taken of the park recently,

57. **A.** NO CHANGE

    B. they

    C. the fires

    D. I

GO ON TO THE NEXT PAGE →

> Questions 58–59 ask about the preceding passage as a whole.

58. The writer is considering inserting the following true statement after the first sentence of the second paragraph:

> Many more acres of forest burned in Alaska in 1988 than in Yellowstone Park.

Would this addition be appropriate for the essay?

F. Yes, the statement would add important information about the effects of large-scale forest fires.

G. Yes, the statement would provide an informative contrast to the Yellowstone fire.

H. No, the statement would not provide any additional information about the effect of the 1988 fire in Yellowstone.

J. No, the statement would undermine the author's position as an authority on the subject of forest fires.

59. Suppose that the writer wishes to provide additional support for the claim that the fire posed little threat to the members of any endangered animal species in the park. Which of the following additions would be most effective?

A. A list of the endangered animals known to inhabit the park

B. A discussion of the particular vulnerability of endangered species of birds to forest fires

C. An explanation of the relative infrequency of such an extensive series of forest fires

D. A summary of reports of biologists who monitored the activity of endangered species in the park during the fire

PASSAGE V

MY FIRST WHITE-WATER RAFTING TRIP

[1]

White-water rafting <u>being</u> a favorite pastime of
　　　　　　　　　　 60
mine for several years. I have drifted down many challenging North American rivers, including the Snake, the

Green,

and the <u>Salmon, and there are many other rivers in</u>
　　　　　　　 61
<u>America as well.</u> I have spent some of my best moments
　　　 61
in dangerous rapids, yet nothing has matched the thrill

60. F. NO CHANGE

G. have been

H. has been

J. was

61. A. NO CHANGE

B. Salmon, just three of many rivers existing in North America.

C. Salmon; many other rivers exist in North America.

D. Salmon.

GO ON TO THE NEXT PAGE ⟹

I experienced facing my <u>first, rapids, on the Deschutes</u>
                                          62
<u>River.</u>
62

[2]

My father and I spent the morning floating down
a calm and peaceful stretch of the Deschutes in his
wooden MacKenzie river boat. This trip <u>it being</u> the
                                                    63
wooden boat's first time down rapids, as well as mine.

<u>Rapids are rated according to a uniform scale of relative</u>
                                          64
<u>difficulty.</u>
64

[3]

<u>Roaring, I was in the boat approaching Whitehorse</u>
                                          65
<u>Rapids.</u> I felt much like a novice skier peering down her
65
first steep slope: I was scared, but even more excited.

The water <u>churned and covering me</u> with a refreshing
                        66
spray. My father, toward the stern, controlled the oars.

The carefree expression he usually wore on the river had

been replaced<u>, and instead he adopted</u> a look of intense
                            67
concentration as he maneuvered around boulders

dotting our path. To release tension, we began to holler

62. **F.** NO CHANGE
   G. first: rapids on the Deschutes River.
   H. first rapids; on the Deschutes River.
   J. first rapids on the Deschutes River.

63. **A.** NO CHANGE
   B. it happened that it was
   C. was
   D. being

64. **F.** NO CHANGE
   G. Rated according to a uniform scale, rapids are relatively difficult.
   H. (Rapids are rated according to a uniform scale of relative difficulty.)
   J. OMIT the underlined portion.

65. **A.** NO CHANGE
   B. It roared, and the boat and I approached Whitehorse Rapids.
   C. While the roaring boat was approaching Whitehorse Rapids, I could hear the water.
   D. I could hear the water roar as we approached Whitehorse Rapids.

66. **F.** NO CHANGE
   G. churned, and covering me
   H. churning and covering me
   J. churned, covering me

67. **A.** NO CHANGE
   B. with
   C. by another countenance altogether:
   D. instead with another expression;

GO ON TO THE NEXT PAGE ➡

like kids on a roller-coaster, our voices echoing <u>across</u>
68
the water as we lurched violently about.

[4]

Suddenly we came to a jarring halt <u>and we stopped;</u>
69
the left side of the bow was wedged on a large rock. A

whirlpool swirled around us; if we capsized, we would

be sucked into the undertow. Instinctively, I threw all

of my weight toward the right side of the tilting boat.

Luckily, <u>it was</u> just enough force to dislodge us, and
70
we continued on downstream to enjoy about 10 more

minutes of spectacular rapids.

[5]

Later that day, we went through Buckskin Mary

Rapids and Boxcar Rapids. When we pulled up on the

bank that evening, we saw that the boat had received its

first scar: <u>that scar was a</u> small hole on the upper bow
71
from the boulder we had wrestled with. In the years to

come, we went down many rapids and the boat

<u>receiving many</u> bruises, but Whitehorse remains the
72
most

68. **F.** NO CHANGE
  G. throughout
  H. around
  J. from

69. **A.** NO CHANGE
  B. which stopped us
  C. and stopped
  D. OMIT the underlined portion.

70. **F.** NO CHANGE
  G. it's
  H. it is
  J. its

71. **A.** NO CHANGE
  B. that was a
  C. which was a
  D. a

72. **F.** NO CHANGE
  G. received many
  H. received much
  J. receives many

GO ON TO THE NEXT PAGE

memorable rapids of all. [73]

73. Which of the following concluding sentences would most effectively emphasize the final point made in this paragraph while retaining the style and tone of the narrative as a whole?

   A. The brutal calamities that it presented the unwary rafter were more than offset by its beguiling excitement.

   B. Perhaps it is true that your first close encounter with white water is your most intense.

   C. Or, if not the most memorable, then at least a very memorable one!

   D. Call me crazy or weird if you want, but white-water rafting is the sport for me.

Questions 74–75 ask about the preceding passage as a whole.

---

74. The writer has been assigned to write an essay that focuses on the techniques of white-water rafting. Would this essay meet the requirements of that assignment?

   F. No, because the essay's main focus is on a particular experience, not on techniques.

   G. No, because the essay mostly deals with the relationship between father and daughter.

   H. Yes, because specific rafting techniques are the essay's main focus.

   J. Yes, because it presents a dramatic story of a day of white-water rafting.

75. Suppose that the writer wants to add the following sentence to the essay:

> It was such a mild summer day that it was hard to believe dangerous rapids awaited us downstream.

What would be the most logical placement of this sentence?

   A. After the last sentence of paragraph 1

   B. After the last sentence of paragraph 2

   C. Before the first sentence of paragraph 4

   D. After the last sentence of paragraph 4

IF YOU FINISH BEFORE TIME IS CALLED, YOU MAY CHECK YOUR WORK ON THIS SECTION ONLY. DO NOT TURN TO ANY OTHER SECTION IN THE TEST.   **STOP**

MATHEMATICS TEST

60 Minutes—60 Questions

Directions: Solve each of the following problems, select the correct answer, and then fill in the corresponding space on your answer sheet.

Don't linger over problems that are too time-consuming. Do as many as you can, then come back to the others in the time you have remaining.

The use of a calculator is permitted on this test. Though you are allowed to use your calculator to solve any questions you choose, some of the questions may be most easily answered without the use of a calculator.

Note: Unless otherwise noted, all of the following should be assumed.

1. Illustrative figures are *not* necessarily drawn to scale.
2. All geometric figures lie in a plane.
3. The term *line* indicates a straight line.
4. The term *average* indicates arithmetic mean.

1. In a recent survey, 14 people found their mayor to be "very competent." This number is exactly 20% of the people surveyed. How many people were surveyed?

   A. 28
   B. 35
   C. 56
   D. 70
   E. 84

2. A train traveled at a rate of 90 miles per hour for x hours, and then at a rate of 60 miles per hour for y hours. Which expression represents the train's average rate in miles per hour for the entire distance traveled?

   F. $\dfrac{540}{xy}$

   G. $\dfrac{90}{x} \times \dfrac{60}{y}$

   H. $\dfrac{90}{x} + \dfrac{60}{y}$

   J. $\dfrac{90x + 60y}{x + y}$

   K. $\dfrac{150}{x + y}$

3. In a certain string ensemble, the ratio of men to women is 5:3. If there are a total of 24 people in the ensemble, how many women are there?

   A. 8
   B. 9
   C. 10
   D. 11
   E. 12

4. If $x \neq 0$, and $x^2 - 3x = 6x$, then $x = ?$

   F. −9
   G. −3
   H. $\sqrt{3}$
   J. 3
   K. 9

GO ON TO THE NEXT PAGE

5. Two overlapping circles below form three regions, as shown:

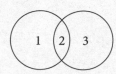

What is the maximum number of regions that can be formed by three overlapping circles?

A. 5

B. 6

C. 7

D. 8

E. 9

6. If $x^2 + 6x + 8 = 4 + 10x$, then x equals which of the following?

F. −2

G. −1

H. 0

J. 1

K. 2

7. Nine less than the number c is the same as the number d, and d less than twice c is 20. Which two equations could be used to determine the value of c and d ?

A. $d - 9 = c$
   $d - 2c = 20$

B. $c - 9 = d$
   $2c - d = 20$

C. $c - 9 = d$
   $d - 2c = 20$

D. $9 - c = d$
   $2c - d = 20$

E. $9 - c = d$
   $2cd = 20$

8. An ice cream parlor offers five flavors of ice cream and four different toppings (sprinkles, hot fudge, whipped cream, and butterscotch). There is a special offer that includes one flavor of ice cream and one topping, served in a cup, sugar cone, or waffle cone. How many ways are there to order ice cream with the special offer?

F. 4

G. 5

H. 12

J. 23

K. 60

9. At a recent audition for a school play, 1 out of 3 students who auditioned were asked to come to a second audition. After the second audition, 75% of those asked to the second audition were offered parts. If 18 students were offered parts, how many students went to the first audition?

A. 18

B. 24

C. 48

D. 56

E. 72

10. One number is 5 times another number, and their sum is −60. What is the lesser of the two numbers?

F. −5

G. −10

H. −12

J. −48

K. −50

GO ON TO THE NEXT PAGE

11. In the following figure, which is composed of equilateral triangles, what is the greatest number of parallelograms that can be found?

A. 6

B. 9

C. 12

D. 15

E. 18

12. The circle in the following figure is inscribed in a square with a perimeter of 16 inches. What is the area of the shaded region?

F. 4π

G. $16 - 2\pi$

H. $16 - 4\pi$

J. $8 - 2\pi$

K. $8 - 4\pi$

13. How many positive integers less than 50 are multiples of 4 but *not* multiples of 6 ?

A. 4

B. 6

C. 8

D. 10

E. 12

14. Given that $f(x) = (8 - 3x)(x^2 - 2x - 15)$, what is the value of $f(3)$?

F. -30

G. -18

H. 12

J. 24

K. 30

15. A class contains five juniors and five seniors. If one member of the class is assigned at random to present a paper on a certain subject, and another member of the class is randomly assigned to assist him, what is the probability that both will be juniors?

A. $\dfrac{1}{10}$

B. $\dfrac{1}{5}$

C. $\dfrac{2}{9}$

D. $\dfrac{2}{5}$

E. $\dfrac{1}{2}$

16. In triangle XYZ shown, $\overline{XS}$ and $\overline{SZ}$ are 3 and 12 units, respectively. If the area of triangle XYZ is 45 square units, how many units long is altitude $\overline{YS}$?

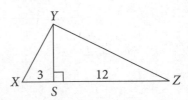

F. 3

G. 6

H. 9

J. 12

K. 15

GO ON TO THE NEXT PAGE ⟹

17. At which y-coordinate does the line described by the equation $6y - 3x = 18$ intersect the y-axis?

    A. 2
    B. 3
    C. 6
    D. 9
    E. 18

18. If $x^2 - y^2 = 12$ and $x - y = 4$, what is the value of $x^2 + 2xy + y^2$?

    F. 3
    G. 8
    H. 9
    J. 12
    K. 16

19. What is the area in square units of the following figure?

    A. $39 + 7\sqrt{2}$
    B. 60.5
    C. 91
    D. 108.5
    E. 147

20. A carpenter is cutting wood to make a new bookcase with a board that is 12 feet long. If the carpenter cuts off three pieces, each of which is 17 inches long, how many inches long is the remaining fourth and final board? (A foot contains 12 inches.)

    F. 36
    G. 51
    H. 93
    J. 108
    K. 144

21. If $x^2 - 4x - 6 = 6$, what are the possible values for x ?

    A. 4, 12
    B. −6, 2
    C. −6, −2
    D. 6, 2
    E. 6, −2

22. If −3 is a solution for the equation $x^2 + kx - 15 = 0$, what is the value of k ?

    F. 5
    G. 2
    H. −2
    J. −5
    K. Cannot be determined from the information given.

23. If the lengths of all three sides of a triangle are integers, and one side is 7 inches long, what is the smallest possible perimeter of the triangle, in inches?

    A. 9
    B. 10
    C. 12
    D. 15
    E. 18

GO ON TO THE NEXT PAGE

24. If $0° < \theta < 90°$ and $\sin \theta = \dfrac{\sqrt{11}}{2\sqrt{3}}$, then $\cos \theta = ?$

   F. $\dfrac{1}{2\sqrt{3}}$

   G. $\dfrac{1}{\sqrt{11}}$

   H. $\dfrac{2}{\sqrt{3}}$

   J. $\dfrac{2\sqrt{3}}{\sqrt{11}}$

   K. $\dfrac{11}{2\sqrt{3}}$

25. Which of the following expressions is equivalent to $\dfrac{\sqrt{3+x}}{\sqrt{3-x}}$ for all x such that $-3 < x < 3$?

   A. $\dfrac{3-x}{3+x}$

   B. $\dfrac{3+x}{3-x}$

   C. $\dfrac{-3\sqrt{3+x}}{\sqrt{3-x}}$

   D. $\dfrac{\sqrt{9-x^2}}{3-x}$

   E. $\dfrac{x^2-9}{3+x}$

26. In a certain cookie jar containing only macaroons and gingersnaps, the ratio of macaroons to gingersnaps is 2 to 5. Which of the following could be the total number of cookies in the cookie jar?

   F. 24

   G. 35

   H. 39

   J. 48

   K. 52

27. What is the sum of $\dfrac{3}{16}$ and 0.175?

   A. 0.3165

   B. 0.3500

   C. 0.3625

   D. 0.3750

   E. 0.3875

28. What is the maximum possible area, in square inches, of a rectangle with a perimeter of 20 inches?

   F. 15

   G. 20

   H. 25

   J. 30

   K. 40

29. $\dfrac{\dfrac{3}{2}+\dfrac{7}{4}}{\left(\dfrac{15}{8}-\dfrac{3}{4}\right)-\left(\dfrac{4+3}{-4+3}\right)} = ?$

   A. $\dfrac{3}{8}$

   B. $\dfrac{2}{5}$

   C. $\dfrac{9}{13}$

   D. $\dfrac{5}{2}$

   E. $\dfrac{8}{3}$

30. If $x - 15 = 7 - 5(x - 4)$, then $x = ?$

   F. 0

   G. 2

   H. 4

   J. 5

   K. 7

GO ON TO THE NEXT PAGE

31. The following sketch shows the dimensions of a flower garden. What is the area of this garden in square meters?

9 meters

9 meters

13 meters

 A. 31
 B. 85
 C. 99
 D. 101
 E. 117

32. What is the slope of the line described by the equation $6y - 3x = 18$?

 F. -2
 G. $-\dfrac{1}{2}$
 H. $\dfrac{1}{2}$
 J. 2
 K. 3

33. Line m passes through the point $(4,3)$ in the standard (x,y) coordinate plane and is perpendicular to the line described by the equation $y = -\dfrac{4}{5}x + 6$. Which of the following equations describes line m ?

 A. $y = \dfrac{5}{4}x - 2$
 B. $y = -\dfrac{5}{4}x + 6$
 C. $y = -\dfrac{4}{5}x - 2$
 D. $y = -\dfrac{4}{5}x + 2$
 E. $y = -\dfrac{5}{4}x - 2$

34. Line t in the standard (x,y) coordinate plane has a y-intercept of -3 and is parallel to the line having the equation $3x - 5y = 4$. Which of the following is an equation for line t ?

 F. $y = -\dfrac{3}{5}x + 3$
 G. $y = -\dfrac{5}{3}x - 3$
 H. $y = \dfrac{3}{5}x + 3$
 J. $y = \dfrac{5}{3}x + 3$
 K. $y = \dfrac{3}{5}x - 3$

35. If $y = mx + b$, which of the following equations expresses x in terms of y, m, and b ?

 A. $x = \dfrac{y - b}{m}$
 B. $x = \dfrac{b - y}{m}$
 C. $x = \dfrac{y + b}{m}$
 D. $x = \dfrac{y}{m} - bx$
 E. $x = \dfrac{y}{m} + b$

GO ON TO THE NEXT PAGE

36. In the following figure, $\overline{AB} = 20$, $\overline{BC} = 15$, and $\angle ADB$ and $\angle ABC$ are right angles. What is the length of $\overline{AD}$?

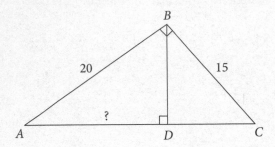

   F. 9
   G. 12
   H. 15
   J. 16
   K. 25

37. In the standard (x,y) coordinate plane shown in the figure, points A and B lie on line m, and point C lies below it. The coordinates of points A, B, and C are $(0,5)$, $(5,5)$, and $(3,3)$, respectively. What is the shortest possible distance from point C to a point on line m?

   A. 2
   B. $2\sqrt{2}$
   C. 3
   D. $\sqrt{13}$
   E. 5

38. For all $x \neq 8$, $\dfrac{x^2 - 11x + 24}{8 - x} = ?$

   F. $8 - x$
   G. $3 - x$
   H. $x - 3$
   J. $x - 8$
   K. $x - 11$

39. Points A and B lie in the standard (x,y) coordinate plane. The (x,y) coordinates of A are $(2,1)$, and the (x,y) coordinates of B are $(-2,-2)$. What is the distance from A to B?

   A. $3\sqrt{2}$
   B. $3\sqrt{3}$
   C. 5
   D. 6
   E. 7

40. In the following figure, $\overline{AB}$ and $\overline{CD}$ are both tangent to the circle as shown, and $ABCD$ is a rectangle with side lengths $2x$ and $5x$ as shown. What is the area of the shaded region?

   F. $10\pi x^2$
   G. $10x^2 - \pi x^2$
   H. $10x^2 - 2\pi x$
   J. $9\pi x^2$
   K. $6\pi x^2$

GO ON TO THE NEXT PAGE

41. If $0° < \theta < 90°$ and $\cos \theta = \dfrac{5\sqrt{2}}{8}$, then $\tan \theta = ?$

   A. $\dfrac{5}{\sqrt{7}}$

   B. $\dfrac{\sqrt{7}}{5}$

   C. $\dfrac{\sqrt{14}}{8}$

   D. $\dfrac{8}{\sqrt{14}}$

   E. $\dfrac{8}{5\sqrt{2}}$

42. Consider fractions of the form $\dfrac{7}{n}$, where n is an integer. How many integer values of n make this fraction greater than 0.5 and less than 0.8 ?

   F. 3

   G. 4

   H. 5

   J. 6

   K. 7

43. The figure below shows two tangent circles. The circumference of circle X is 12π, and the circumference of circle Y is 8π. What is the greatest possible distance between two points, one of which lies on the circumference of circle X and one of which lies on the circumference of circle Y ?

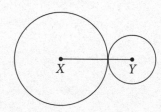

   A. 6

   B. 10

   C. 20

   D. 10π

   E. 20π

44. $\sqrt{(x^2 + 4)^2} - (x + 2)(x - 2) = ?$

   F. $2x^2$

   G. $x^2 - 8$

   H. $2(x - 2)$

   J. 0

   K. 8

45. If $s = -3$, then $s^3 + 2s^2 + 2s = ?$

   A. -15

   B. -10

   C. -5

   D. 5

   E. 33

46. How many different numbers are solutions for the equation $2x + 6 = (x + 5)(x + 3)$?

   F. 0

   G. 1

   H. 2

   J. 3

   K. Infinitely many

47. In square $ABCD$ shown, $\overline{AC} = 8$. What is the perimeter of $ABCD$?

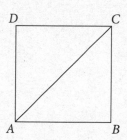

   A. $4\sqrt{2}$

   B. 8

   C. $8\sqrt{2}$

   D. 16

   E. $16\sqrt{2}$

GO ON TO THE NEXT PAGE ⟩

48. The front surface of a fence panel is shown here with the lengths labeled representing inches. The panel is symmetrical along its center vertical axis. What is the surface area of the front surface of the panel in square inches?

- 30
- 36
- 4

- **F.** 144
- **G.** 132
- **H.** 120
- **J.** 80
- **K.** $64 + 6\sqrt{5}$

49. In the following figure, O is the center of the circle, and C, D, and E are points on the circumference of the circle. If $\angle OCD$ measures 70° and $\angle OED$ measures 45°, what is the measure of $\angle CDE$?

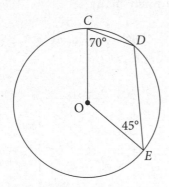

- **A.** 25°
- **B.** 45°
- **C.** 70°
- **D.** 90°
- **E.** 115°

50. Which of the following systems of equations does NOT have a solution?

- **F.** $x + 3y = 19$
  $3x + y = 6$
- **G.** $x + 3y = 19$
  $x - 3y = 13$
- **H.** $x - 3y = 19$
  $3x - y = 7$
- **J.** $x - 3y = 19$
  $3x + y = 6$
- **K.** $x + 3y = 6$
  $3x + 9y = 7$

51. What is the 46th digit to the right of the decimal point in the decimal equivalent of $\frac{1}{7}$?

- **A.** 1
- **B.** 2
- **C.** 4
- **D.** 7
- **E.** 8

52. Which of the following inequalities is equivalent to $-2 - 4x \leq -6x$?

- **F.** $x \geq -2$
- **G.** $x \geq 1$
- **H.** $x \geq 2$
- **J.** $x \leq -1$
- **K.** $x \leq 1$

GO ON TO THE NEXT PAGE

53. If $x > 0$ and $y > 0$, $\dfrac{\sqrt{x}}{x} + \dfrac{\sqrt{y}}{y}$ is equivalent to which of the following?

   A. $\dfrac{2}{xy}$

   B. $\dfrac{\sqrt{x} + \sqrt{y}}{\sqrt{xy}}$

   C. $\dfrac{x + y}{xy}$

   D. $\dfrac{\sqrt{x} + \sqrt{y}}{\sqrt{x + y}}$

   E. $\dfrac{x + y}{\sqrt{xy}}$

54. In the following diagram, $\overline{CD}$, $\overline{BE}$, and $\overline{AF}$ are all parallel and are intersected by two transversals as shown. What is the length of $\overline{EF}$?

   F. 2

   G. 3

   H. 4

   J. 6

   K. 9

55. What is the area, in square units, of the square whose vertices are located at the (x,y) coordinate points indicated in the following figure?

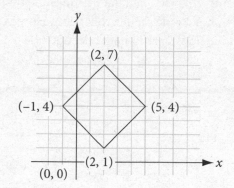

   A. 9

   B. 12

   C. 16

   D. 18

   E. 24

56. Compared to the graph of $y = \cos \theta$, the graph of $y = 2 \cos \theta$ has:

   F. twice the period and the same amplitude.

   G. half the period and the same amplitude.

   H. twice the period and half the amplitude.

   J. half the amplitude and the same period.

   K. twice the amplitude and the same period.

GO ON TO THE NEXT PAGE

57. Brandy has a collection of comic books. If she adds 15 to the number of comic books in her collection and multiplies the sum by 3, the result will be 65 less than 4 times the number of comic books in her collection. How many comic books are in her collection?

    A.   50

    B.   85

    C. 110

    D. 145

    E. 175

58. One empty cylinder has three times the height and twice the diameter of another empty cylinder. How many fillings of the smaller cylinder would be equivalent to one filling of the larger cylinder?

(Note: The volume of a cylinder of radius r and height h is $\pi r^2 h$.)

    F.   6

    G. $6\sqrt{2}$

    H. 12

    J. 18

    K. 24

59. What is the perimeter of a 30°-60°-90° triangle with a long leg of 12 inches?

    A. $5\sqrt{3} + 12$

    B. $4\sqrt{3} + 18$

    C. $8\sqrt{3} + 18$

    D. $12\sqrt{3} + 12$

    E. $12\sqrt{3} + 18$

60. A baseball team scores an average of x points in its first n games and then scores y points in its next and final game of the season. Which of the following represents the team's average score for the entire season?

    F. $x + \dfrac{y}{n}$

    G. $x + \dfrac{y}{n+1}$

    H. $\dfrac{x + ny}{n+1}$

    J. $\dfrac{nx + y}{n+1}$

    K. $\dfrac{n(x + y)}{n+1}$

READING TEST

35 Minutes—40 Questions

Directions: There are four passages in this test. Each passage is followed by several questions. After reading a passage, choose the best answer to each question and fill in the corresponding oval on your Answer Grid. You may refer to the passages as often as necessary.

PASSAGE I

PROSE FICTION

This passage is adapted from the novel Emma *by Jane Austen. It was originally published in 1815.*

Emma Woodhouse, handsome, clever, and rich, with a comfortable home and happy disposition, seemed to unite some of the best blessings of existence. She had lived
Line
(5) nearly twenty-one years in the world with very little to distress or vex her. She was the youngest of the two daughters of a most affectionate, indulgent father, and had, in consequence of her sister's marriage, been
(10) mistress of his house from a very early period. Her mother had died too long ago for her to have more than an indistinct remembrance of her caresses, and her place had been taken by an excellent governess
(15) who had fallen little short of a mother in affection.

Sixteen years had Miss Taylor been in Mr. Woodhouse's family, less as a governess than a friend, very fond of both daughters,
(20) but particularly of Emma. Between them it was more the intimacy of sisters. Even before Miss Taylor had ceased to hold the nominal office of governess, the mildness of her temper had hardly allowed her
(25) to impose any restraint. The shadow of authority being now long passed away, they had been living together as friend and friend very mutually attached, and Emma doing just what she liked, highly esteeming Miss
(30) Taylor's judgment, but directed chiefly by her own. The real evils, indeed, of Emma's situation were the power of having rather

too much her own way, and a disposition to think a little too well of herself; these were
(35) the disadvantages which threatened alloy to her many enjoyments. The danger, however, was at present so unperceived, that they did not by any means rank as misfortunes with her.

(40) Sorrow came—a gentle sorrow—but not at all in the shape of any disagreeable consciousness. Miss Taylor married. It was Miss Taylor's loss which first brought grief. It was on the wedding-day of this beloved
(45) friend that Emma first sat in mournful thought of any continuance. The wedding over, and the bride-people gone, she and her father were left to dine together, with no prospect of a third to cheer a long evening.
(50) Her father composed himself to sleep after dinner, as usual, and she had then only to sit and think of what she had lost.

The marriage had every promise of happiness for her friend. Mr. Weston was
(55) a man of unexceptionable character, easy fortune, suitable age, and pleasant manners. There was some satisfaction in considering with what self-denying, generous friendship she had always wished and promoted the
(60) match, but it was a black morning's work for her. The want of Miss Taylor would be felt every hour of every day. She recalled her past kindness—the kindness, the affection of sixteen years—how she had taught her
(65) and how she had played with her from five years old—how she had devoted all her

GO ON TO THE NEXT PAGE ▷

powers to attach and amuse her in health—
and how she had nursed her through the
various illnesses of childhood. A large
(70) debt of gratitude was owing here, but the
intercourse of he last seven years, the equal
footing and perfect unreserve which had
soon followed Isabella's marriage, on their
being left to each other, was yet a dearer,
(75) tenderer recollection. She had been a friend
and companion such as few possessed:
intelligent, well-informed, useful, gentle,
knowing all the ways of the family, interested
in all its concerns, and peculiarly
(80) interested in her, in every pleasure, every
scheme of hers—one to whom she could
speak every thought as it arose, and who
had such an affection for her as could never
find fault.
(85)   How was she to bear the change? It was
true that her friend was going only half a
mile from them, but Emma was aware that
great must be the difference between a Mrs.
Weston, only half a mile from them, and
(90) a Miss Taylor in the house. With all her
advantages, natural and domestic, she was
now in great danger of suffering from intellectual
solitude.

1. According to the passage, what are the great-
    est disadvantages facing Emma?

    A. Her father is not a stimulating conversa-
       tionalist, and she is bored.

    B. She is lonely and afraid that Mrs.
       Weston will not have a happy marriage.

    C. She is used to having her way too much,
       and she thinks too highly of herself.

    D. She misses the companionship of her
       mother, her sister, and Miss Taylor.

2. The name of Emma's sister is:

    F. Mrs. Weston.

    G. Isabella.

    H. Miss Taylor.

    J. Mrs. Woodhouse.

3. As described in the passage, Emma's relation-
    ship with Miss Taylor can be characterized as:

    A. similar to a mother-daughter relation-
       ship.

    B. similar to the relationship of sisters or
       best friends.

    C. weaker than Emma's relationship with
       her sister.

    D. stronger than Miss Taylor's relationship
       with her new husband.

4. As used in line 33, *disposition* can most closely
    be defined as:

    F. a tendency.

    G. control.

    H. placement.

    J. transfer.

5. Which of the following are included in
    Emma's memories of her relationship with
    Miss Taylor?

    I.   Miss Taylor taking care of Emma
         during childhood illnesses

    II. Miss Taylor entertaining Emma

    III. Miss Taylor teaching her mathemat-
         ics

    IV. Miss Taylor scolding her for being
         selfish

    A. I, III, and IV only

    B. I and III only

    C. II, III, and IV only

    D. I and II only

GO ON TO THE NEXT PAGE

6. It is most reasonable to infer from Emma's realization that "great must be the difference between a Mrs. Weston, only half a mile from them, and a Miss Taylor in the house" (lines 88–90) that:

    F. Miss Taylor will no longer be a part of Emma's life.

    G. Emma is happy about the marriage because now she will have more freedom.

    H. Emma regrets that her relationship with Miss Taylor will change.

    J. Emma believes that her relationship with Miss Taylor will become stronger.

7. Based on the passage, Emma could best be described as:

    A. sweet and naïve.

    B. self-centered and naïve.

    C. self-centered and headstrong.

    D. unappreciative and bitter.

8. The passage suggests that the quality Emma values most in a friend is:

    F. charisma.

    G. devotion.

    H. honesty.

    J. intelligence.

9. How does Emma view Mr. Weston?

    A. She thinks that he is an excellent match, and it required considerable self-sacrifice not to pursue him herself.

    B. She considers him to be a respectable if somewhat average match for her friend.

    C. She sees him as an intruder who has carried away her best friend in "a black morning's work" (line 60).

    D. She believes he is an indulgent, easily swayed man, reminiscent of her father.

10. From the passage, it can be inferred that Emma is accustomed to:

    F. behaving according to the wishes of her affectionate father.

    G. taking the advice of Miss Taylor when faced with deciding upon a course of action.

    H. doing as she pleases without permission from her father or governess.

    J. abiding by strict rules governing her behavior.

PASSAGE II

SOCIAL SCIENCE

The period of active experimentation to develop the airplane began in the 1890s. Many scientists and engineers attempted to solve the problem in the decade following, but with limited progress until Orville and Wilbur Wright made the first successful powered, heavier-than-air flight in 1903. Both of the passages below discuss aspects of the Wright brothers' invention.

PASSAGE A

What about the method used by the Wright brothers allowed them to succeed where so many scientists, engineers, and crackpots had failed to make progress for a dozen years? In
Line
(5) the decade leading up to their success, there had been so many unsuccessful attempts that newspaper reporters became jaded, tired of investigating each yokel who claimed to have made an airplane. In fact, the reporter present
(10) at that historical first flight didn't even bother to take his camera out of its bag, deciding that two unassuming brothers from Ohio without college educations would be two more in a long line. Instead, the Wrights, quite systematically
(15) and without much fuss or outside assistance, changed the world dramatically in 1903. What made Orville and Wilbur so different from the rest of the pack?

GO ON TO THE NEXT PAGE ⇒

Most inventors of the time were working
(20) on their planes with a fairly simple and logical
approach: They would design an airplane, build
it, test it in the field, and then use the results of
that test to tinker with their designs in an attempt to improve the next model. The problem
(25) with this method, though, was that the field
test of a new airplane only provided information about whether it flew or not, for how
long, and how high. There was no way of knowing whether the wings were good but the
(30) engine was bad, or the shape was right but
the materials were too heavy. With no way of
discerning which parts worked and which
parts didn't, inventors' second attempts often
flew worse than their initial ones, because
(35) their creators had inadvertently removed
design features that were effective and exag-
gerated features that were not.

The Wright brothers proved to be adept
scientists. With their keen analytical insight
(40) and love of engineering and all things mechanical, they were able to escape that endless loop
of misguided "improvements." They worked
on their machine one aspect at a time. After
familiarizing themselves with all the published
(45) literature on flight, they began working on a
method of control. They theorized that twisting the wings one way or another would steer
a craft. Instead of building an entire airplane
to test their theory, they built a five-foot bi-
(50) plane kite. Sure enough, twisting the wings
controlled the craft laterally. Having settled
that aspect of the craft's design, they turned
to wing shape.

After building two failed gliders based
(55) on their original design, the brothers realized
that it was too expensive and time consuming
to continue designing and making whole
machines. As an alternative, they invented
the first wind tunnel with instruments capable
(60) of quantifying the lift and drag of wing segments. In this wind tunnel, they could test
wings alone for their efficiency and aerody-
namics. In the process of testing 80 to 200
wing shapes in this way, they disproved a com-

(65) monly accepted theory of lift (called "Smeaton's
coefficient") and settled on a new and highly
efficient wing shape for their craft.

The Wrights returned to the wind tunnel
to perfect designs for their propeller and
(70) then designed an effective four-cylinder
engine to power the craft. When the time
came to marry all of these carefully designed
components into a complete craft, there was
no guesswork involved. The Wright brothers
(75) knew they had built an airplane, and they
knew that each piece was beautifully designed and perfectly functioning. That first historic flight was merely proof of their scientific
genius.

PASSAGE B

(80)   Few people recognize that the Wright
brothers are tragic figures in American
history. Today, they are hailed as great inventors, but during their lives they were scorned
and discredited publicly, even though the
(85) entire world copied their successful designs.
The prevailing opinion among those who
made airplanes was that two rustic, uneducated fellows from Ohio could never have
accomplished such a historic feat, let alone
(90) deliberately marry the disparate components
of air travel that are required for successful
flight. They hadn't paid their dues to the
scientific community. The French aviation
community especially mocked the brothers,
(95) and the secrecy of Orville and Wilbur during
the years in which they prepared their patents
only fueled derision of and doubts about
their accomplishments.

The Wright brothers finally received a
(100) U.S. patent for their system of lateral control,
perhaps their most important contribution to
aviation, in May of 1906. Manufacturers
unwilling to pay the modest fee the brothers
asked for use of their system launched a vast
(105) and sadly successful smear campaign against
the brothers, impugning the importance of
their contribution to flight. Some European
countries simply refused to issue the brothers

GO ON TO THE NEXT PAGE →

a patent, and as a result airplane manufacturers (110) in those countries could legally copy the Wrights' technology unchecked.

In the midst of the legal battle over rights and license fees against several airplane manufacturers, Wilbur sadly succumbed to typhoid (115) fever. He was thus deprived of seeing his claims vindicated in court, and, though Orville was accorded a tidy sum, this small victory was hardly commensurate with the enormous contribution the two brothers had made. The (120) court case also did nothing to compensate the brothers for the taxing and unfair period of ridicule and doubt and the obstinate refusal by much of the world to acknowledge their achievements. Perhaps most tellingly, the Smithsonian Museum (125) didn't display the brothers' historic craft until 1948, when it finally bestowed on them the title of the first men to fly in a heavier-than-air craft. Sadly, this was too little, too late, as the brothers had both passed away.

Questions 11–13 ask about Passage A.

---

11. The main purpose of Passage A is to:

A. describe how the Wright brothers were regarded.

B. emphasize the process of designing the airplane.

C. criticize the attitude of other inventors.

D. explore the practical application of science.

12. What does Passage A suggest about the method used by most inventors at the time of the Wright brothers?

F. They did not take Smeaton's coefficient into account.

G. They scorned the methods used by the Wright brothers.

H. They weren't able to learn effectively from previous failures.

J. They didn't believe it was possible to build an airplane.

13. Passage A suggests that the wind tunnel played what role in the Wright brothers' research?

A. It provided more reliable data than their experiments with kites.

B. It allowed them to isolate single aspects of design from other considerations.

C. It helped them develop a method of twisting the wings to control the plane laterally.

D. It confirmed the accuracy of Smeaton's coefficient.

Questions 14–16 ask about Passage B.

---

14. In Passage B, the author mentions a "legal battle" (line 112) in order to:

F. emphasize the poor way in which the Wright brothers were treated.

G. illustrate the dangers of publicizing new knowledge.

H. help explain why the Wright brothers' discovery was of little importance.

J. suggest a reason for Wilbur's fatal illness.

15. What does Passage B suggest about the Smithsonian Museum's choice to display the brothers' historic craft in 1948?

A. It was a small victory for Orville, who lost his brother Wilbur to typhoid fever.

B. It was a direct result of the obstinate refusal by much of the world to acknowledge their achievements.

C. While it was a great honor, it did not fully atone for the poor treatment of the brothers.

D. The historic craft would have been displayed sooner if European countries had issued the brothers a patent.

GO ON TO THE NEXT PAGE

16. In Passage B, the statement "They hadn't paid their dues to the scientific community" (lines 92–93) is presented as the opinion of:

    F. the French aviation community.

    G. the Wright brothers.

    H. the author.

    J. those who made airplanes.

Questions 17–20 ask about both passages.

17. The author of Passage B would likely agree that the "inventors of the time" (line 19) mentioned in Passage A:

    A. thought that the Wright brothers didn't actually make the first airplane.

    B. didn't believe that the Wright brothers deserved credit for the magnitude of their achievement.

    C. were grateful for the breakthrough that the Wrights had engineered.

    D. felt the Wright brothers had likely copied the design from a more accomplished inventor.

18. In lines 72 and 90, "marry" most nearly means:

    F. prove.

    G. test rigorously.

    H. bring together.

    J. satisfy.

19. According to Passage A, while the brothers "hadn't paid their dues to the scientific community" (lines 92–93), as mentioned in Passage B, they were indeed skilled inventors because:

    A. they designed an airplane, built it, tested it in the field, and then used the results of that test to adjust their designs.

    B. they used analytical insight to work on machines one aspect at a time to perfect their design.

    C. they invented the first wind tunnel, which was a greater accomplishment than inventing the first successful aircraft.

    D. their claims were eventually vindicated in court, and Orville received monetary reimbursement.

20. Both passages provide support for the idea that the Wright brothers:

    F. used a method of scientific inquiry that was different from everyone else's.

    G. were poorly treated following their discovery.

    H. were exceptional scientists.

    J. should have protected the rights to their discovery more carefully.

PASSAGE III

HUMANITIES

This passage is excerpted from A History of Women Artists, *© 1975 by Hugo Munsterberg; Clarkson N. Potter (a division of Random House, Inc.), publisher. Reprinted by permission of the author's family.*

There can be little doubt that women artists have been most prominent in photography and that they have made their greatest
Line contribution in this field. One reason for
(5) this is not difficult to ascertain. As several

GO ON TO THE NEXT PAGE ➡

historians of photography have pointed out, photography, being a new medium outside the traditional academic framework, was wide open to women and offered them
(10) opportunities that the older fields did not....

All these observations apply to the first woman to have achieved eminence in photography, and that is Julia Margaret Cameron....Born in 1815 in Calcutta into an
(15) upper-middle-class family and married to Charles Hay Cameron, a distinguished jurist and member of the Supreme Court of India, Julia Cameron was well-known as a brilliant conversationalist and a woman of personality
(20) and intellect who was unconventional to the point of eccentricity. Although the mother of six children, she adopted several more and still found time to be active in social causes and literary activities. After
(25) the Camerons settled in England in 1848 at Freshwater Bay on the Isle of Wight, she became the center of an artistic and literary circle that included such notable figures as the poet Alfred Lord Tennyson and the
(30) painter George Frederick Watts. Pursuing numerous activities and taking care of her large family, Mrs. Cameron might have been remembered as still another rather remarkable and colorful Victorian lady had it not
(35) been for the fact that, in 1863, her daughter presented her with photographic equipment, thinking her mother might enjoy taking pictures of her family and friends. Although forty-eight years old, Mrs. Cameron took
(40) up this new hobby with enormous enthusiasm and dedication. She was a complete beginner, but within a very few years she developed into one of the greatest photographers of her period and a giant in the
(45) history of photography. She worked ceaselessly as long as daylight lasted and mastered the technical processes of photography, at that time far more cumbersome than today, turning her coal house into a darkroom
(50) and her chicken house into a studio. To her, photography was a "divine art," and in it she found her vocation. In 1864, she wrote

triumphantly under one of her photographs, "My First Success," and from then until her
(55) death in Ceylon in 1874, she devoted herself wholly to this art.

Working in a large format (her portrait studies are usually about 11 inches by 14 inches) and requiring a long exposure
(60) (on the average five minutes), she produced a large body of work that stands up as one of the notable artistic achievements of the Victorian period. The English art critic Roger Fry believed that her portraits were
(65) likely to outlive the works of artists who were her contemporaries. Her friend Watts, then a very celebrated portrait painter, inscribed on one of her photographs, "I wish I could paint such a picture as this."...Her
(70) work was widely exhibited, and she received gold, silver, and bronze medals in England, America, Germany, and Austria. No other female artist of the nineteenth century achieved such acclaim, and no other woman
(75) photographer has ever enjoyed such success.

Her work falls into two main categories on which her contemporaries and people today differ sharply. Victorian critics were particularly impressed by her allegorical
(80) pictures, many of them based on the poems of her friend and neighbor Tennyson.... Contemporary taste much prefers her portraits and finds her narrative scenes sentimental and sometimes in bad taste. Yet,
(85) not only Julia Cameron, but also the painters of that time loved to depict subjects such as *The Five Foolish Virgins* or *Pray God, Bring Father Safely Home*. Still, today her fame rests upon her portraits for, as she herself
(90) said, she was intent upon representing not only the outer likeness but also the inner greatness of the people she portrayed. Working with the utmost dedication, she produced photographs of such eminent
(95) Victorians as Tennyson, Browning, Carlyle, Trollope, Longfellow, Watts, Darwin, Ellen Terry, Sir John Herschel, who was a close friend of hers, and Mrs. Duckworth, the mother of Virginia Woolf.

GO ON TO THE NEXT PAGE

21. Which of the following conclusions can be reasonably drawn from the passage's discussion of Julia Margaret Cameron?

    A. She was a traditional homemaker until she discovered photography.

    B. Her work holds a significant place in the history of photography.

    C. She was unable to achieve in her lifetime the artistic recognition she deserved.

    D. Her eccentricity has kept her from being taken seriously by modern critics of photography.

22. According to the passage, Cameron is most respected by modern critics for her:

    F. portraits.

    G. allegorical pictures.

    H. use of a large format.

    J. service in recording the faces of so many twentieth century figures.

23. The author uses which of the following methods to develop the second paragraph (lines 11–56)?

    A. A series of anecdotes depicting Cameron's energy and unconventionality

    B. A presentation of factual data demonstrating Cameron's importance in the history of photography

    C. A description of the author's personal acquaintance with Cameron

    D. A chronological account of Cameron's background and artistic growth

24. As it is used in the passage, *cumbersome* (line 48) most closely means:

    F. difficult to manage.

    G. expensive.

    H. intense.

    J. enjoyable.

25. When the author says that Cameron had found "her vocation" (line 52), his main point is that photography:

    A. offered Cameron an escape from the confines of conventional social life.

    B. became the main interest of her life.

    C. became her primary source of income.

    D. provided her with a way to express her religious beliefs.

26. The main point of the third paragraph is that Cameron:

    F. achieved great artistic success during her lifetime.

    G. is the greatest photographer who ever lived.

    H. was considered a more important artist during her lifetime than she is now.

    J. revolutionized photographic methods in the Victorian era.

27. According to the passage, the art of photography offered women artists more opportunities than did other art forms because it:

    A. did not require expensive materials.

    B. allowed the artist to use family and friends for subject matter.

    C. was nontraditional.

    D. required little artistic skill.

28. *The Five Foolish Virgins* and *Pray God, Bring Father Safely Home* are examples of:

    F. portraits of celebrated Victorians.

    G. allegorical subjects of the sort that were popular during the Victorian era.

    H. photographs in which Cameron sought to show a subject's outer likeness and inner greatness.

    J. photographs by Cameron that were scoffed at by her contemporaries.

GO ON TO THE NEXT PAGE →

29. According to the passage, which of the following opinions of Cameron's work was held by Victorian critics but is NOT held by modern critics?

   A. Photographs should be based on poems.

   B. Her portraits are too sentimental.

   C. Narrative scenes are often in bad taste.

   D. Her allegorical pictures are her best work.

30. The author's treatment of Cameron's development as a photographer can best be described as:

   F. admiring.

   G. condescending.

   H. neutral.

   J. defensive.

PASSAGE IV

NATURAL SCIENCE

This passage discusses aspects of the harbor seal's sensory systems.

The harbor seal, *Phoca vitulina*, lives amphibiously along the northern Atlantic and Pacific coasts. This extraordinary
Line mammal, which does most of its fishing at
(5) night when visibility is low and in places where noise levels are high, has developed several unique adaptations that have sharpened its acoustic and visual acuity. The need for such adaptations has been
(10) compounded by the varying behavior of sound and light in each of the two habitats of the harbor seal—land and water.

While the seal is on land, its ear operates much like the human ear, with sound waves
(15) traveling through air and entering the inner ear through the auditory canal. The directions from which sounds originate are distinguishable because the sound waves arrive at each inner ear at different times.
(20) In water, however, where sound waves travel faster than they do in air, the ability of the brain to differentiate arrival times between each ear is severely reduced. Yet it is crucial for the seal to be able to pinpoint the exact
(25) origins of sound in order to locate both its offspring and its prey. Therefore, the seal has developed an extremely sensitive quadraphonic hearing system, composed of a specialized band of tissue that extends
(30) down from the ear to the inner ear. In water, sound is conducted to the seal's inner ear by this special band of tissue, making it possible for the seal to identify the exact origins of sounds.

(35) The eye of the seal is also uniquely adapted to operate in both air and water. The human eye, adapted to function primarily in air, is equipped with a cornea, which aids in the refraction and focusing
(40) of light onto the retina. As a result, when a human eye is submerged in water, light rays are further refracted and the image is blurry. The seal's cornea, however, refracts light as water does. Therefore, in water, light
(45) rays are transmitted by the cornea without distortion and are clearly focused on the retina. In air, however, the cornea is astigmatic, resulting in a distortion of incoming light rays. The seal compensates for this by
(50) having a stenopaic pupil, which constricts into a vertical slit. Since the astigmatism is most pronounced in the horizontal plane of the eye, the vertical pupil serves to minimize its effect on the seal's vision.

(55) Since the harbor seal hunts for food under conditions of low visibility, some scientists believe it has echolocation systems akin to those of bats, porpoises, and dolphins. This kind of natural radar involves
(60) the emission of high-frequency sound pulses that reflect off obstacles such as predators, prey, or natural barriers. The reflections are received as sensory signals by the brain, which processes them into an image. The

GO ON TO THE NEXT PAGE ▷

(65) animal, blinded by unfavorable lighting conditions, is thus able to perceive its surroundings. Such echolocation by harbor seals is suggested by the fact that they emit "clicks," high-frequency sounds produced in (70) short, fast bursts that occur mostly at night, when visibility is low.

Finally, there is speculation that the seal's whiskers, or vibrissae, which are unusually well developed and highly (75) sensitive to vibrations, act as additional sensory receptors. Scientists speculate that the vibrissae may sense wave disturbances produced by nearby moving fish, allowing the seal to home in on and capture prey.

31. The harbor seal's eye compensates for the distortion of light rays on land by means of its:

   A. vibrissae.

   B. cornea.

   C. stenopaic pupil.

   D. echolocation.

32. The passage implies that a harbor seal's vision is:

   F. inferior to a human's vision in the water, but superior to it on land.

   G. superior to a human's vision in the water, but inferior to it on land.

   H. inferior to a human's vision both in the water and on land.

   J. equivalent to a human's vision both in the water and on land.

33. According to the passage, scientists think vibrissae help harbor seals to catch prey by:

   A. improving underwater vision.

   B. sensing vibrations in the air.

   C. camouflaging predator seals.

   D. detecting underwater movement.

34. According to the passage, the speed of sound in water is:

   F. faster than the speed of sound in air.

   G. slower than the speed of sound in air.

   H. the same as the speed of sound in air.

   J. unable to be determined exactly.

35. According to the passage, which of the following have contributed to the harbor seal's need to adapt its visual and acoustic senses?

   I. Night hunting

   II. The need to operate in two habitats

   III. A noisy environment

   A. I and II only

   B. II and III only

   C. I and III only

   D. I, II, and III

36. Which of the following claims expresses the writer's opinion and not a fact?

   F. The human eye is adapted to function primarily in air.

   G. When the seal is on land, its ear operates like a human ear.

   H. The "clicks" emitted by the harbor seal mean it uses echolocation.

   J. The need for adaptation is increased if an animal lives in two habitats.

37. The passage suggests that the harbor seal lives in:

   A. cold ocean waters with accessible coasts.

   B. all areas with abundant fish populations.

   C. most island and coastal regions.

   D. warm coastlines with exceptionally clear waters.

GO ON TO THE NEXT PAGE

38. According to the passage, a special band of tissue extending from the ear to the inner ear enables the harbor seal to:

    F. make its distinctive "clicking" sounds.

    G. find prey by echolocation.

    H. breathe underwater.

    J. determine where a sound originated.

39. The author compares harbor seal sensory organs to human sensory organs primarily in order to:

    A. point out similarities among mammals.

    B. explain how the seal's sensory organs function.

    C. prove that seals are more adaptively successful than humans.

    D. prove that humans are better adapted to their environment than seals.

40. According to the passage, one way in which seals differ from humans is:

    F. that sound waves enter a seal's inner ear through the auditory canal.

    G. the degree to which their corneas refract light.

    H. that seal's eyes focus light rays on the retina.

    J. that seals have adapted to live in a certain environment.

IF YOU FINISH BEFORE TIME IS CALLED, YOU MAY CHECK YOUR WORK ON THIS SECTION ONLY. DO NOT TURN TO ANY OTHER SECTION IN THE TEST.   **STOP**

SCIENCE TEST

45 Minutes—40 Questions

Directions: There are several passages in this test. Each passage is followed by several questions. After reading a passage, choose the best answer to each question and fill in the corresponding oval on your Answer Grid. You may refer to the passages as often as necessary. You are NOT permitted to use a calculator on this test.

PASSAGE I

The following table contains some physical properties of common optical materials. The refractive index of a material is a measure of the amount by which light is bent upon entering the material. The transmittance range is the range of wavelengths over which the material is transparent.

Table 1

Physical Properties of Optical Materials				
Material	Refractive index for light of 0.589 µm	Transmittance range (µm)	Useful range for prisms (µm)	Chemical resistance
Lithium fluoride	1.39	0.12–6	2.7–5.5	Poor
Calcium fluoride	1.43	0.12–12	5–9.4	Good
Sodium chloride	1.54	0.3–17	8–16	Poor
Quartz	1.54	0.20–3.3	0.20–2.7	Excellent
Potassium bromide	1.56	0.3–29	15–28	Poor
Flint glass*	1.66	0.35–2.2	0.35–2	Excellent
Cesium iodide	1.79	0.3–70	15–55	Poor

*Flint glass is lead oxide–doped quartz.

1. According to the table, which material(s) will transmit light at 25 µm?

   A. Potassium bromide only
   B. Potassium bromide and cesium iodide
   C. Lithium fluoride and cesium iodide
   D. Lithium fluoride and flint glass

2. A scientist hypothesizes that any material with poor chemical resistance would have a transmittance range wider than 10 µm. The properties of which of the following materials contradicts this hypothesis?

   F. Lithium fluoride
   G. Flint glass
   H. Cesium iodide
   J. Quartz

GO ON TO THE NEXT PAGE ⟶

3. When light travels from one medium to another, total internal reflection can occur if the first medium has a higher refractive index than the second. Total internal reflection could occur if light were traveling from:

   A. lithium fluoride to flint glass.

   B. potassium bromide to cesium iodide.

   C. quartz to potassium bromide.

   D. flint glass to calcium fluoride.

4. Based on the information in the table, how is the transmittance range related to the useful prism range?

   F. The transmittance range is always narrower than the useful prism range.

   G. The transmittance range is narrower than or equal to the useful prism range.

   H. The transmittance range increases as the useful prism range decreases.

   J. The transmittance range is wider than and includes within it the useful prism range.

5. The addition of lead oxide to pure quartz has the effect of:

   A. decreasing the transmittance range and the refractive index.

   B. decreasing the transmittance range and increasing the refractive index.

   C. increasing the transmittance range and the useful prism range.

   D. increasing the transmittance range and decreasing the useful prism range.

6. Which of the following materials would provide the greatest range of transmittance as well as the greatest useful range for prisms?

   F. Lithium fluoride

   G. Sodium chloride

   H. Quartz

   J. Flint glass

PASSAGE II

Osmosis is the diffusion of a solvent (often water) across a semipermeable membrane from the side of the membrane with a lower concentration of dissolved material to the side with a higher concentration of dissolved material. The result of osmosis is an equilibrium—an even distribution—on both sides of the membrane. In order to prevent osmosis, external pressure must be applied to the side with the higher concentration of dissolved material. *Osmotic pressure* is the external pressure required to prevent osmosis. The apparatus shown was used to measure osmotic pressure in the following experiments.

EXPERIMENT 1

Aqueous (water-based) solutions containing different concentrations of sucrose were placed in the closed side of the apparatus. The open side was filled with water. The sucrose solutions also contained a blue dye that binds to sucrose. The osmotic pressure created by the piston was measured for each solution at various temperatures. The results are given in Table 1.

GO ON TO THE NEXT PAGE ⟩

Table 1

Concentration of sucrose solution (mol/L)	Temperature (K)	Osmotic pressure (atm)
1.00	298.0	24.47
0.50	298.0	12.23
0.10	298.0	2.45
0.05	298.0	1.22
1.00	348.0	28.57
0.50	348.0	14.29
0.10	348.0	2.86
0.05	348.0	1.43

EXPERIMENT 2

Sucrose solutions of four different organic solvents were investigated in the same manner as in Experiment 1 with all trials at 298 K. The results are shown in Table 2.

Table 2

Solvent	Concentration of sucrose solution (mol/L)	Osmotic pressure (atm)
Ethanol	0.50	12.23
Ethanol	0.10	2.45
Acetone	0.50	12.23
Acetone	0.10	2.45
Diethyl ether	0.50	12.23
Diethyl ether	0.10	2.45
Methanol	0.50	12.23
Methanol	0.10	2.45

7. Osmotic pressure can be calculated using the formula $\Pi = MRT$, where Π represents the calculated osmotic pressure, M = mol/L, R is a constant equal to 0.0821 and T is temperature in Kelvins. Which of the following can be inferred from the data in Table 1?

  I. In order to maintain osmotic pressure, temperature must stay constant.

  II. Temperature and volume must have an inverse relationship in order to maintain a constant osmotic pressure.

  III. Osmotic pressure will increase as volume and temperature increase.

  A. I only

  B. II only

  C. III only

  D. II and III only

8. According to the experimental results, osmotic pressure is dependent upon the:

  F. solvent and temperature only.

  G. solvent and concentration only.

  H. temperature and concentration only.

  J. solvent, temperature, and concentration.

9. According to Experiment 2, if methanol was used as a solvent, what pressure must be applied to a 0.5 mol/L solution of sucrose at 298 K to prevent osmosis?

  A. 1.23 atm

  B. 2.45 atm

  C. 12.23 atm

  D. 24.46 atm

10. A 0.10 mol/L aqueous sucrose solution is separated from an equal volume of pure water by a semipermeable membrane. If the solution is at a pressure of 1 atm and a temperature of 298 K:

    F. water will diffuse across the semipermeable membrane from the sucrose solution side to the pure water side.

    G. water will diffuse across the semipermeable membrane from the pure water side to the sucrose solution side.

    H. water will not diffuse across the semipermeable membrane.

    J. water will diffuse across the semipermeable membrane, but the direction of diffusion cannot be determined.

11. In Experiment 1, the scientists investigated the effect of:

    A. solvent and concentration on osmotic pressure.

    B. volume and temperature on osmotic pressure.

    C. concentration and temperature on osmotic pressure.

    D. temperature on atmospheric pressure.

12. Which of the following conclusions can be drawn from the experimental results?

    I. Osmotic pressure is independent of the solvent used.

    II. Osmotic pressure is only dependent upon the temperature of the system.

    III. Osmosis occurs only when the osmotic pressure is exceeded.

    F. I only

    G. III only

    H. I and II only

    J. I and III only

13. What was the most likely purpose of the dye placed in the sucrose solutions in Experiments 1 and 2?

    A. The dye showed when osmosis was completed.

    B. The dye showed the presence of ions in the solutions.

    C. The dye was used to make the experiment more colorful.

    D. The dye was used to make the onset of osmosis visible.

GO ON TO THE NEXT PAGE

PASSAGE III

A series of experiments was performed to study the environmental factors affecting the size and number of leaves on the *Cycas* plant.

EXPERIMENT 1

Five groups of 25 *Cycas* seedlings, all 2–3 cm tall, were allowed to grow for 3 months, each group at a different humidity level. All of the groups were kept at 75°F and received 9 hours of sunlight a day. The average leaf lengths, widths, and densities are given in Table 1.

Table 1

% Humidity	Average length (cm)	Average width (cm)	Average density* (leaves/cm)
15	5.6	1.6	0.13
35	7.1	1.8	0.25
55	9.8	2.0	0.56
75	14.6	2.6	0.61
95	7.5	1.7	0.52

*Number of leaves per 1 cm of plant stalk

EXPERIMENT 2

Five new groups of 25 seedlings, all 2–3 cm tall, were allowed to grow for three months, each group receiving different amounts of sunlight at a constant humidity of 55%. All other conditions were the same as in Experiment 1. The results are listed in Table 2.

Table 2

Sunlight (hrs/day)	Average length (cm)	Average width (cm)	Average density* (leaves/cm)
0	5.3	1.5	0.32
3	12.4	2.4	0.59
6	11.2	2.0	0.56
9	8.4	1.8	0.26
12	7.7	1.7	0.19

*Number of leaves per 1 cm of plant stalk

EXPERIMENT 3

Five new groups of 25 seedlings, all 2–3 cm tall, were allowed to grow at a constant humidity of 55% for three months at different daytime and night-time temperatures. All other conditions were the same as in Experiment 1. The results are shown in Table 3.

Table 3

Day/night temperature (°F)	Average length (cm)	Average width (cm)	Average density* (leaves/ cm)
85/85	6.8	1.5	0.28
85/65	12.3	2.1	0.53
65/85	8.1	1.7	0.33
75/75	7.1	1.9	0.45
65/65	8.3	1.7	0.39

*Number of leaves per 1 cm of plant stalk

14. Based on the data in Experiment 3, which day/night temperatures produced the smallest leaves?

    F. 85/85

    G. 85/65

    H. 75/75

    J. 65/85

15. Which of the following conclusions can be made based on the results of Experiment 2 alone?

    A. The seedlings do not require long daily periods of sunlight to grow.

    B. The average leaf density is independent of the humidity the seedlings receive.

    C. The seedlings need more water at night than during the day.

    D. The average length of the leaves increases as the amount of sunlight increases.

16. Seedlings grown at a 40% humidity level under the same conditions as in Experiment 1 would have average leaf widths closest to:

    F. 1.6 cm.
    G. 1.9 cm.
    H. 2.2 cm.
    J. 2.5 cm.

17. According to the experimental results, under which set of conditions would a *Cycas* seedling be most likely to produce the largest leaves?

    A. 95% humidity and 3 hours of sunlight
    B. 75% humidity and 3 hours of sunlight
    C. 95% humidity and 6 hours of sunlight
    D. 75% humidity and 6 hours of sunlight

18. Which variable remained constant throughout all of the experiments?

    F. The number of seedling groups
    G. The percent of humidity
    H. The daytime temperature
    J. The nighttime temperature

19. It was assumed in the design of the three experiments that all of the *Cycas* seedlings were:

    A. more than 5 cm tall.
    B. equally capable of germinating.
    C. equally capable of producing flowers.
    D. equally capable of further growth.

20. As a continuation of the three experiments listed, it would be most appropriate to next investigate:

    F. how many leaves over 6.0 cm long there are on each plant.
    G. which animals consume *Cycas* seedlings.
    H. how the mineral content of the soil affects the leaf size and density.
    J. what time of year the seedlings have the darkest coloring.

PASSAGE IV

The resistance (R) of a conductor is the extent to which it opposes the flow of electricity. Resistance depends not only on the conductor's resistivity (ρ) but also on the conductor's length (L) and cross-sectional area (A). The resistivity of a conductor is a physical property of the material that varies with temperature.

A research team designing a new appliance was researching the best type of wire to use in a particular circuit. The most important consideration was the wire's resistance. The team studied the resistance of wires made from four metals—gold (Au), aluminum (Al), tungsten (W), and iron (Fe). Two lengths and two gauges (diameters) of each type of wire were tested at 20°C. The results are recorded in the following table.

10-gauge wire
$A = 5.26$ mm²

16-gauge wire
$A = 1.31$ mm²

2.59 mm

1.29 mm

Note: area of circle = πr^2

GO ON TO THE NEXT PAGE ▷

Table 1

Material	Resistivity (mV–cm)	Length (cm)	Cross-sectional area (mm²)	Resistance (mV)
Au	2.44	1.0	5.26	46.4
Au	2.44	1.0	1.31	186.0
Au	2.44	2.0	5.26	92.8
Au	2.44	2.0	1.31	372.0
Al	2.83	1.0	5.26	53.8
Al	2.83	1.0	1.31	216.0
Al	2.83	2.0	5.26	107.6
Al	2.83	2.0	1.31	432.0
W	5.51	1.0	5.26	105.0
W	5.51	1.0	1.31	421.0
W	5.51	2.0	5.26	210.0
W	5.51	2.0	1.31	842.0
Fe	10.00	1.0	5.26	190.0
Fe	10.00	1.0	1.31	764.0
Fe	10.00	2.0	5.26	380.0
Fe	10.00	2.0	1.31	1,528.0

21. Of the wires tested, resistance increases for any given material as which parameter is decreased?

A. Length

B. Cross-sectional area

C. Resistivity

D. Gauge

22. Given the data in the table, which of the following best expresses resistance in terms of resistivity (ρ), cross-sectional area (A), and length (L)?

F. $\dfrac{\rho^A}{L}$

G. $\dfrac{\rho^L}{A}$

H. ρAL

J. $\dfrac{AL}{\rho}$

23. Which of the following wires would have the highest resistance?

A. A 1-cm aluminum wire with a cross-sectional area of 0.33 mm²

B. A 2-cm aluminum wire with a cross-sectional area of 0.33 mm²

C. A 1-cm tungsten wire with a cross-sectional area of 0.33 mm²

D. A 2-cm tungsten wire with a cross-sectional area of 0.33 mm²

24. According to the information given, which of the following statements is (are) correct?

   I. 10-gauge wire has a larger diameter than 16-gauge wire.

   II. Gold has a higher resistivity than tungsten.

   III. Aluminum conducts electricity better than iron.

F. I only

G. II only

H. III only

J. I and III only

GO ON TO THE NEXT PAGE ⟩

25. Which of the following graphs best represents the relationship between the resistivity of a tungsten wire and its length?

A.

B.

C.

D.

26. If the length of the wires were increased to 4 cm, what could be expected in terms of resistance?

F. Resistance would increase, but only with a 10 gauge wire.

G. Resistance would decrease, but only with a 16 gauge wire.

H. Resistance would not change because 2 cm is the maximum length that affects resistance.

J. Resistance would increase on both the 10 and 16 gauge wires.

PASSAGE V

How does evolution occur? Two views are presented here.

SCIENTIST 1

Evolution occurs by natural selection. Random mutations are continually occurring in a species as it propagates. A number of these mutations result in traits that help the species adapt to environmental changes. Because these mutant traits are advantageous, the members of the species who possess them tend to survive and pass on their genes more often than those who do not have these traits. Therefore, the percentage of the population with an advantageous trait increases over time. Long necks evolved in giraffes by natural selection. The ancestors of giraffes had necks of various sizes; however, their average neck length was much shorter than the average neck length of modern-day giraffes. Since the food supply was limited, the individuals with necks on the long range of the spectrum had access to more food (the leaves of trees) and therefore were more likely to survive and pass on their traits than individuals with shorter necks. Therefore, the proportion of the individuals with long necks was slightly greater in each subsequent generation.

SCIENTIST 2

Evolution occurs by the inheritance of acquired characteristics. Characteristics that are acquired by an individual member of a species during its lifetime are passed on to its offspring. Therefore, each generation's traits are partially accounted for by all the changes that occurred in the individuals of the previous generation. This includes changes that occurred as a result of accidents, changes in the environment, overuse of muscles, etc. The evolution of long necks of giraffes is an example. Ancestors of giraffes had short necks and consequently had to stretch their necks to reach the leaves of trees that were their main source of food. This repeated stretching of their necks caused them to elongate

GO ON TO THE NEXT PAGE ⟹

slightly. This trait was passed on, so that the individuals of the next generation had slightly longer necks. Each subsequent generation also stretched their necks to feed; therefore, each generation had slightly longer necks than the previous generation.

27. Both scientists agree that:

   A. the environment affects evolution.

   B. the individuals of a generation have identical traits.

   C. acquired characteristics are inherited.

   D. random mutations occur.

28. How would the two hypotheses be affected if it were found that all of the offspring of an individual with a missing leg due to an accident were born with a missing leg?

   F. It would support Scientist 1's hypothesis, because it is an example of random mutations occurring within a species.

   G. It would refute Scientist 1's hypothesis, because it is an example of random mutations occurring within a species.

   H. It would support Scientist 2's hypothesis, because it is an example of an acquired characteristic being passed on to the next generation.

   J. It would support Scientist 2's hypothesis, because it is an example of random mutations occurring within a species.

29. Which of the following characteristics can be inherited according to Scientist 2?

   I. Fur color

   II. Bodily scars resulting from a fight with another animal

   III. Poor vision

   A. I only

   B. II only

   C. I and III only

   D. I, II, and III

30. Scientist 1 believes that the evolution of the long neck of the giraffe:

   F. is an advantageous trait that resulted from overuse of neck muscles over many generations.

   G. is an advantageous trait that resulted from a random mutation.

   H. is an advantageous trait that resulted from a mutation that occurred in response to a change in the environment.

   J. is a disadvantageous trait that resulted from a random mutation.

31. The fundamental point of disagreement between the two scientists is whether:

   A. giraffes' ancestors had short necks.

   B. evolved traits come from random mutations or from the previous generation.

   C. the environment affects the evolution of a species.

   D. the extinction of a species could be the result of random mutations.

GO ON TO THE NEXT PAGE ⟹

32. Suppose evidence was found that suggested that before the discovery of fire, human skin lacked the nerve endings necessary to detect extreme heat. Which of the following pieces of information, if true, would most seriously weaken the hypothesis of Scientist 2?

    F. Human skin is capable of generating nerve endings with new functions during life.

    G. The total number of nerve endings in the skin of a human is determined at birth and remains constant until death.

    H. An excess of nerve endings that are sensitive to extreme heat is a relatively common human mutation.

    J. No evidence exists to suggest that an excess of nerve endings that are sensitive to heat could be acquired through mutation.

33. The average height of a full-grown person today is significantly greater than was the average height of a full-grown person 1,000 years ago. If it was proven that the increase in average height was due only to evolutionary changes, how would Scientist 1 most likely explain this increase?

    A. People genetically prone to growing taller have been more likely to produce offspring over the last 1,000 years.

    B. Over the last 1,000 years, improvements in nutrition and medicine have led to greater average growth over a person's lifetime, and this growth has been passed from one generation to the next.

    C. Increased height is not a trait that can be acquired through mutation.

    D. Measurements of average height were less accurate 1,000 years ago than they are today.

PASSAGE VI

Bovine spongiform encephalopathy (BSE) is caused by the spread of a misfolded protein that eventually kills infected cattle. BSE is diagnosed postmortem from the diseased cavities that appear in brain tissue and is associated with the use in cattle feed of ground-up meat from scrapie-infected sheep. A series of experiments was performed to determine the mode of transmission of BSE. The results of both experiments are provided in Table 1.

EXPERIMENT 1

Sixty healthy cows were divided into two equal groups. Group A's feed included meat from scrapie-free sheep; and Group B's feed included meat from scrapie-infected sheep. Eighteen months later, the two groups were slaughtered and their brains examined for BSE cavities.

EXPERIMENT 2

Researchers injected ground-up sheep brains directly into the brains of two groups of 30 healthy cows. The cows in Group C received brains from scrapie-free sheep. The cows in Group D received brains from scrapie-infected sheep. Eighteen months later, both groups were slaughtered and their brains examined for diseased cavities.

Table 1

Group	Mode of transmission	Scrapie present	Number of cows infected with BSE*
A	feed	no	1
B	feed	yes	12
C	injection	no	0
D	injection	yes	3

*As determined visually by presence/absence of spongiform encephalopathy

GO ON TO THE NEXT PAGE ⟶

34. Based on the information provided in Table 1, a cow is at greatest risk for contracting BSE if the cow:

    F. consumes meat from scrapie-free sheep.

    G. consumes meat from scrapie-infected sheep.

    H. is injected with ground-up sheep brains from scrapie-free sheep.

    J. is injected with ground-up sheep brains from scrapie-infected sheep.

35. Which of the following hypotheses was investigated in Experiment 1?

    A. The injection of scrapie-infected sheep brains into cows' brains causes BSE.

    B. The ingestion of wild grasses causes BSE.

    C. The ingestion of scrapie-infected sheep meat causes scrapie.

    D. The ingestion of scrapie-infected sheep meat causes BSE.

36. What is the purpose of Experiment 2?

    F. To determine whether BSE can be transmitted by injection

    G. To determine whether BSE can be transmitted by ingestion

    H. To determine whether ingestion or injection is the primary mode of BSE transmission

    J. To determine the healthiest diet for cows

37. Which of the following assumptions is made by the researchers in Experiments 1 and 2?

    A. Cows do not suffer from scrapie.

    B. A year and a half is a sufficient amount of time for BSE to develop in a cow.

    C. Cows and sheep suffer from the same diseases.

    D. Cows that eat scrapie-free sheep meat will not develop BSE.

38. A researcher wishes to determine whether BSE can be transmitted through scrapie-infected goats. Which of the following experiments would best test this?

    F. Repeating Experiment 1, using a mixture of sheep and goat meat in Group C's feed

    G. Repeating Experiments 1 and 2, replacing sheep with healthy goats

    H. Repeating Experiments 1 and 2, replacing healthy sheep with healthy goats and scrapie-infected sheep with scrapie-infected goats

    J. Repeating Experiment 2, replacing healthy cows with healthy goats

39. What is the control group in Experiment 1?

    A. Group A

    B. Group B

    C. Group C

    D. Group D

GO ON TO THE NEXT PAGE

40. Which of the following conclusions can be drawn based on the results of the experiments?

> I. Cows that are exposed to scrapie-infected sheep are more likely to develop BSE than cows that are not.
>
> II. BSE is only transmitted by eating scrapie-infected sheep meat.
>
> III. A cow that eats scrapie-infected sheep meat is more likely to develop BSE than a cow that is injected with scrapie-infected sheep brains.

F. II only

G. III only

H. I and III only

J. II and III only

WRITING TEST

40 Minutes—1 Question

Directions: This is a test of your writing skills. You will have forty (40) minutes to write an essay in English. Before you begin planning and writing your essay, read the writing prompt carefully to understand exactly what you are being asked to do. Your essay will be evaluated on the evidence it provides of your ability to do the following:

- Express judgments by evaluating the three perspectives given in the prompt, taking a position on an issue, and explaining the relationship among all four ideas
- Develop a position by using logical reasoning and by supporting your ideas
- Maintain a focus on the topic throughout the essay
- Organize ideas in a logical way
- Use language clearly and effectively according to the conventions of standard written English

You may use a separate piece of paper to plan your essay. *You must write your essay in pencil on the lined pages provided after the prompt.* Your writing on those lined pages will be scored. You may not need all the lined pages, but to ensure you have enough room to finish, do NOT skip lines. You may write corrections or additions neatly between the lines of your essay, but do NOT write in the margins of the lined pages. *Illegible essays cannot be scored, so you must write (or print) clearly.*

DO NOT OPEN THIS BOOKLET UNTIL TOLD TO DO SO.

GO ON TO THE NEXT PAGE ▷

CAREER READINESS PROGRAMS

High school curricula are designed to ready students for future career paths, many of which include higher education. Whether or not students choose to attend college, a comprehensive high school education provides an essential foundation. Some educators argue that high schools have an obligation to provide career readiness training for students who do not intend to pursue a college degree. Should high schools invest time and money to develop programs for students who do not wish to continue their education beyond 12th grade? Given the many factors that students weigh when considering if, where, and when to attend college, it is prudent for educators to explore programs that contribute to a better-skilled workforce.

Read and carefully consider these perspectives. Each offers suggestions regarding high school–based career readiness programs.

Perspective One	Perspective Two	Perspective Three
Rather than concentrating solely on students who may not pursue higher education, high schools should help all students develop valuable skills for the workforce. Requiring students to complete classes that focus on key cognitive strategies, content knowledge, and relevant skills and techniques will help them enter the workforce, either immediately after high school or later in their lives.	Career-readiness training should be provided for students who do not wish to pursue college, and it should be particularly targeted at students who are at risk for dropping out. When their high school experience is reframed as training for successful careers rather than government-mandated learning, students can succeed where they may previously have failed.	Students who do not want to pursue higher education should not be given additional accommodations in high school, because they should not be provided any incentives to not attend college. College is the best way to learn how to be productive in the workforce, and students should be encouraged to attend since it is in their best interest.

ESSAY TASK

Write a unified, coherent essay in which you evaluate multiple perspectives on high school–based career readiness programs. In your essay, be sure to:

- analyze and evaluate the perspectives given
- state and develop your own perspective on the issue
- explain the relationship between your perspective and those given

Your perspective may be in full agreement with any of the others, in partial agreement, or wholly different. Whatever the case, support your ideas with logical reasoning and detailed, persuasive examples.

GO ON TO THE NEXT PAGE ⟩

PLANNING YOUR ESSAY

You may wish to consider the following as you think critically about the task:

Strengths and weaknesses of the three given perspectives

- What insights do they offer, and what do they fail to consider?
- Why might they be persuasive to others, or why might they fail to persuade?

Your own knowledge, experience, and values

- What is your perspective on this issue, and what are its strengths and weaknesses?
- How will you support your perspective in your essay?

_____

_____

_____

_____

_____

_____

_____

_____

_____

_____

_____

_____

_____

_____

_____

_____

_____

GO ON TO THE NEXT PAGE ⟶

Practice Test One
ANSWER KEY

ENGLISH TEST

1. C	11. C	21. B	31. D	41. D	51. D	61. D	71. D
2. F	12. G	22. G	32. H	42. J	52. J	62. J	72. G
3. D	13. B	23. D	33. A	43. B	53. C	63. C	73. B
4. F	14. H	24. J	34. H	44. G	54. H	64. J	74. F
5. D	15. C	25. C	35. D	45. C	55. D	65. D	75. B
6. G	16. H	26. F	36. G	46. F	56. G	66. J	
7. B	17. B	27. A	37. D	47. B	57. A	67. B	
8. J	18. G	28. J	38. G	48. H	58. H	68. F	
9. A	19. A	29. B	39. D	49. C	59. D	69. D	
10. J	20. J	30. G	40. J	50. H	60. H	70. F	

MATHEMATICS TEST

1. D	9. E	17. B	25. D	33. A	41. B	49. E	57. C
2. J	10. K	18. H	26. G	34. K	42. H	50. K	58. H
3. B	11. D	19. B	27. C	35. A	43. C	51. E	59. D
4. K	12. H	20. H	28. H	36. J	44. K	52. K	60. J
5. C	13. C	21. E	29. B	37. A	45. A	53. B	
6. K	14. H	22. H	30. K	38. G	46. G	54. G	
7. B	15. C	23. D	31. C	39. C	47. E	55. D	
8. K	16. G	24. F	32. H	40. G	48. G	56. K	

READING TEST

1. C	6. H	11. B	16. J	21. B	26. F	31. C	36. H
2. G	7. C	12. H	17. B	22. F	27. C	32. G	37. A
3. B	8. G	13. B	18. H	23. D	28. G	33. D	38. J
4. F	9. B	14. F	19. B	24. F	29. D	34. F	39. B
5. D	10. H	15. C	20. H	25. B	30. F	35. D	40. G

SCIENCE TEST

1. B	6. G	11. C	16. G	21. B	26. J	31. B	36. F
2. F	7. D	12. F	17. B	22. G	27. A	32. G	37. B
3. D	8. H	13. D	18. F	23. D	28. H	33. A	38. H
4. J	9. C	14. F	19. D	24. J	29. D	34. G	39. A
5. B	10. G	15. A	20. H	25. D	30. G	35. D	40. G

ANSWERS AND EXPLANATIONS

ENGLISH TEST

PASSAGE I

1. C
Category: Punctuation
Difficulty: Medium
Getting to the Answer: Choice (C) is the correct and most concise answer choice. Choice A uses an unnecessary comma. Choice B is unnecessarily wordy. Choice D is redundant—if the societies created the legends, there is no need to describe the legends as "original."

2. F
Category: Writing Strategy
Difficulty: High
Getting to the Answer: The question stem gives an important clue to the best answer: The purpose of the inserted sentence is "to describe the different kinds" of stories. Choice (F) is the only choice that does this. Choice G explains how the stories were told. Choice H explains why more is not known about the stories. Choice J describes the length of some stories.

3. D
Category: Connections
Difficulty: Medium
Getting to the Answer: Choices A, B, and C create run-on sentences. Choice (D) describes a relationship that makes sense between our "many more permanent ways of handing down our beliefs" and the fact that "we continue to create and tell legends." It also creates a complete sentence.

4. F
Category: Verb Tenses
Difficulty: Low
Getting to the Answer: Choices H and J are ungrammatical after a colon. Choice G is unnecessarily wordy.

5. D
Category: Wordiness
Difficulty: Medium
Getting to the Answer: Choices A, B, and C are redundant or unnecessarily wordy. Because the contrasting word *but* is already used, *however* is repetitive and should be eliminated.

6. G
Category: Wordiness
Difficulty: Low
Getting to the Answer: Choices F, H, and J are all redundant. The word *conclusion* is unnecessary because the word *ending* has already been used.

7. B
Category: Verb Tenses
Difficulty: Medium
Getting to the Answer: Choice (B) is the only choice that is consistent with the verb tense established by *knew* and *decided*.

8. J
Category: Verb Tenses
Difficulty: Medium
Getting to the Answer: Choice F creates a run-on sentence and also makes it seem that the hunter, not the deer, "was only temporarily knocked unconscious by the car." Choices G and H use incorrect verb tenses.

9. A
Category: Punctuation
Difficulty: High
Getting to the Answer: Choice B is incorrect because the words preceding the semicolon could not be a complete sentence on their own. Choice C would create a sentence fragment. Choice D would create a run-on sentence.

10. J
Category: Wordiness
Difficulty: Medium
Getting to the Answer: Regardless of the sequence of the words, the information provided in F, G, and H is irrelevant to the passage's topic of urban legends.

11. C
Category: Verb Tenses
Difficulty: Medium
Getting to the Answer: The subject of the sentence is *One*, so the verb must be singular. Choices B and D use incorrect verb tenses.

12. G
Category: Word Choice
Difficulty: Low
Getting to the Answer: Choice F creates a sentence that does not make sense. Choices H and J use the plural *women* instead of the singular *woman*.

13. B
Category: Sentence Sense
Difficulty: Medium
Getting to the Answer: Choice (B) most clearly expresses the idea that several websites research "the validity of commonly told urban legends." Because this information is relevant to the topic of urban legends, "OMIT the underlined portion" is not the best answer.

14. H
Category: Writing Strategy
Difficulty: High
Getting to the Answer: Paragraph 4 describes an urban legend that is "humorous in nature." Paragraph 5 describes a rather frightening legend: alligators living underneath the city in the sewer system. The sentence "Other urban legends seem to be designed to instill fear" is an appropriate topic sentence for paragraph 5, and it also serves as a needed transition between paragraph 4 and paragraph 5.

15. C
Category: Writing Strategy
Difficulty: Medium
Getting to the Answer: Although paragraph 1 provides *some* general information about the purpose and topics of the myths and legends of primitive societies, no specifics are given. This makes (C) the best answer.

PASSAGE II

16. H
Category: Verb Tenses
Difficulty: Medium
Getting to the Answer: Correct choices here could be *do you* or *does one*. The latter appears in (H).

17. B
Category: Punctuation
Difficulty: Medium
Getting to the Answer: Choice A incorrectly uses a colon. Choices C and D are grammatically incorrect.

18. G
Category: Wordiness
Difficulty: Medium
Getting to the Answer: *Solitary* and *alone* are redundant in the same sentence. Choices H and J also have redundancy.

19. A
Category: Word Choice
Difficulty: Low
Getting to the Answer: The underlined portion is clearest the way it is written.

20. J
Category: Punctuation
Difficulty: Medium
Getting to the Answer: The colon is incorrect, so eliminate F and H. Because this sentence is a compound sentence, a comma is needed before *and*.

21. B
Category: Sentence Sense
Difficulty: Medium
Getting to the Answer: *In fact* is nonessential—it should be set off by commas.

22. G
Category: Word Choice
Difficulty: Medium
Getting to the Answer: *American* (an adjective) is the word being modified. Therefore, the adverb form of *unique—uniquely—* is needed.

23. D
Category: Sentence Sense
Difficulty: Low
Getting to the Answer: "Near Walden Pond…" is a long sentence fragment. The best way to fix the error is to simply combine the sentences by eliminating the period.

24. J
Category: Sentence Sense
Difficulty: Medium
Getting to the Answer: This paragraph and the ones that immediately follow outline Thoreau's life. His influence on the people of today is not discussed until the end of the essay. Therefore, the underlined sentence does not belong here.

25. C
Category: Organization
Difficulty: High
Getting to the Answer: Sentence 3 logically follows sentence 1. Choice (C) is the only choice that lists this correct order.

26. F
Category: Punctuation
Difficulty: Medium
Getting to the Answer: There is one independent clause on each side of the semicolon, so the sentence is punctuated correctly. Choice G would need *and* after the comma to be correct. Choices H and J create run-on sentences.

27. A
Category: Word Choice
Difficulty: Low
Getting to the Answer: A possessive pronoun is needed because the works belong to Thoreau. Eliminate B and D. Choice C relates to more than one person, so it is incorrect as well.

28. J
Category: Writing Strategy
Difficulty: Medium
Getting to the Answer: This paragraph discusses Thoreau's impact on modern society; only (J) expresses the correct topic.

29. B
Category: Wordiness
Difficulty: Medium
Getting to the Answer: Choices A, C, and D are excessively wordy.

30. G
Category: Writing Strategy
Difficulty: High
Getting to the Answer: The use of questions prompts a reader to think about the answers to those questions. Choice F is too literal, and J is too broad for the topic of the essay. Choice H is incorrect because the author establishes the quality of Thoreau's work.

PASSAGE III

31. D
Category: Wordiness
Difficulty: Medium
Getting to the Answer: Because the word *live* is used later in the sentence, A, B, and C contain redundant information.

32. H
Category: Word Choice
Difficulty: Low
Getting to the Answer: In this sentence, the *its* must be possessive because the "unique anatomy" belongs to the sloth. The word describing *anatomy* must be an adjective, not an adverb.

33. A
Category: Punctuation
Difficulty: Medium
Getting to the Answer: The comma is correctly used in (A) to separate the nonessential descriptive phrase "about the size of a large domestic cat" from the rest of the sentence.

34. H
Category: Sentence Sense
Difficulty: Medium
Getting to the Answer: The information about the sloth's limbs is relevant to the topic, so it should not be omitted. Choice (H) clearly and directly expresses how the sloth's muscles are designed to allow this animal to cling to things.

35. D
Category: Word Choice
Difficulty: Medium
Getting to the Answer: *Adapted* needs to be modified by an adverb, so (D) is the best choice.

36. G
Category: Connections
Difficulty: Medium
Getting to the Answer: *Instead* describes the right relationship between the two sentences. The

pronouns must be consistent, and because *its* is already used in the sentence, (G) is the best choice.

37. D
Category: Connections
Difficulty: Low
Getting to the Answer: Choice (D) is the only choice that correctly establishes the relationship between the sloth's inability to "move swiftly on the ground" and its ability to swim.

38. G
Category: Writing Strategy
Difficulty: High
Getting to the Answer: Choice (G) connects the sloth's unique characteristics discussed in paragraph 3 with the description of its flexibility in paragraph 4.

39. D
Category: Punctuation
Difficulty: Medium
Getting to the Answer: Choice (D) correctly uses the second comma necessary to separate the phrase "without moving the rest of its body" from the rest of the sentence. Choice C can be eliminated because it is unnecessarily wordy.

40. J
Category: Verb Tenses
Difficulty: Medium
Getting to the Answer: Choice (J) is the only choice that contains a verb tense consistent with the sentence.

41. D
Category: Wordiness
Difficulty: Low
Getting to the Answer: Choices A, B, and C contain redundant information.

42. J
Category: Wordiness
Difficulty: Medium
Getting to the Answer: This information about the howler monkey is irrelevant to the topic of the passage.

PRACTICE TEST ONE ANSWERS AND EXPLANATIONS

43. B

Category: Sentence Sense

Difficulty: Medium

Getting to the Answer: Choice A creates a sentence fragment. Choice C is unnecessarily wordy and awkward. Choice D creates a run-on sentence.

44. G

Category: Writing Strategy

Difficulty: Medium

Getting to the Answer: The last sentence aptly concludes the entire passage, and removing it would make the ending more abrupt.

45. C

Category: Organization

Difficulty: High

Getting to the Answer: The description of the sloth's "camouflage" is in paragraph 5.

PASSAGE IV

46. F

Category: Verb Tenses

Difficulty: Medium

Getting to the Answer: The underlined portion is best left as is. The other answer choices make the sentence unnecessarily wordy.

47. B

Category: Verb Tenses

Difficulty: Low

Getting to the Answer: The verb tense must agree with the tense that has been established up to this point. The passage is in the past tense, so (B) is correct.

48. H

Category: Verb Tenses

Difficulty: Medium

Getting to the Answer: As with the answer to the previous question, the simple past tense is correct.

49. C

Difficulty: Medium

Category: Verb Tenses

Getting to the Answer: Choice A creates a sentence fragment and uses an incorrect verb tense. Choice B also uses the wrong verb tense. Choice D incorrectly uses a semicolon, as the words preceding the semicolon do not constitute an independent clause.

50. H

Category: Sentence Sense

Difficulty: High

Getting to the Answer: In the context of the rest of the passage, only (H) makes sense. The firefighters' attempts to extinguish the flames failed; *only* nature could stop the fire with the first snowfall.

51. D

Category: Wordiness

Difficulty: Medium

Getting to the Answer: Choices A and B are unnecessarily wordy and awkward. Choice C creates a run-on sentence.

52. J

Category: Wordiness

Difficulty: Medium

Getting to the Answer: All of the other answer choices are unnecessarily wordy and/or repetitive.

53. C

Category: Verb Tenses

Difficulty: High

Getting to the Answer: From the plural verb *open*, you can determine that the best answer will contain *cones*. This makes (C) the only possible answer, as the apostrophe is incorrectly used in B.

54. H

Category: Connections

Difficulty: Medium

Getting to the Answer: This is the only choice that makes sense in the context of the passage. The sighting of the large animals near burning forests is used as evidence that the animals of the region were "fire-tolerant and fire-adaptive."

55. D
Category: Punctuation

Difficulty: Medium

Getting to the Answer: The comma in A is unnecessary because the sentence has a list of only two examples, not three. The semicolon in B is incorrectly used because "and bedding down" does not begin an independent clause. The colon in C is incorrectly used because it is not being used to introduce or emphasize information.

56. G
Category: Sentence Sense

Difficulty: High

Getting to the Answer: The problem with "judging from recent pictures of the park" is that the phrase is modifying *forest*, and a forest obviously can't judge anything. The phrase would have been correct if the sentence had read "judging from the recent pictures of the park, I think that the forest was not destroyed." In this case, the phrase would modify *I*, the author, who is capable of judging. Choice (G) takes care of the problem by rewriting the sentence to eliminate the modifying phrase.

57. A
Category: Word Choice

Difficulty: Low

Getting to the Answer: The pronoun refers to *forest*.

58. H
Category: Writing Strategy

Difficulty: Medium

Getting to the Answer: The introduction of information about fires in Alaska is unwarranted, so F and G can be eliminated. Choice J is incorrect because the additional information would actually uphold the author's position as an authority.

59. D
Category: Writing Strategy

Difficulty: High

Getting to the Answer: The reports mentioned in (D) directly substantiate the author's claims much more than do any of the other answer choices.

PASSAGE V

60. H
Category: Verb Tenses

Difficulty: Medium

Getting to the Answer: Choice F creates a sentence fragment, and G incorrectly uses a plural verb with a singular subject. The verb tense of the paragraph makes (H) a better choice than J.

61. D
Category: Wordiness

Difficulty: Medium

Getting to the Answer: The final part of the sentence "…and there are many other rivers in America as well" is completely irrelevant to the rest of the sentence and the paragraph, in which the author discusses white-water rafting and the rivers she's rafted.

62. J
Category: Punctuation

Difficulty: Medium

Getting to the Answer: Choice F is wrong because *rapids* is essential information and should not be set off by commas. Choice G is wrong because what follows the colon is not an explanation. Choice H is incorrect because what follows the semicolon cannot stand alone as a sentence.

63. C
Category: Wordiness

Difficulty: Low

Getting to the Answer: Choices A and D create sentence fragments, and B is extremely awkward.

64. J
Category: Wordiness
Difficulty: Medium
Getting to the Answer: This sentence is irrelevant to the topic of the passage.

65. D
Category: Word Choice
Difficulty: Medium
Getting to the Answer: This sentence makes it sound as though the author were roaring, not the rapids; *roaring* is a misplaced modifier. Choice B doesn't fix the problem because the reader has no idea what *it* refers to. Choice C has *the boat* roaring. Choice (D) is the clearest choice.

66. J
Category: Sentence Sense
Difficulty: Medium
Getting to the Answer: Either the word *cover* must be in past tense, or the structure of the sentence must change. Choice (J) does the latter.

67. B
Category: Wordiness
Difficulty: Medium
Getting to the Answer: Choice (B) is the simplest, most concise way of expressing the idea. Replacing "and instead he adopted" with "with" and removing the comma make the sentence much less awkward.

68. F
Category: Word Choice
Difficulty: Low
Getting to the Answer: Choices G and J make it sound as though the author were in the water. Choice (F) expresses the idea more accurately than H does.

69. D
Category: Wordiness
Difficulty: High
Getting to the Answer: The phrase "and we stopped" is redundant because "we came to a jarring halt" says the same thing much more expressively. Omit the underlined portion.

70. F
Category: Word Choice
Difficulty: Low
Getting to the Answer: "It was" is fine here because the author is telling her story in the past tense. Choices G and H are in the present tense, and J incorrectly introduces the possessive form.

71. D
Category: Wordiness
Difficulty: Medium
Getting to the Answer: The other answer choices are unnecessarily wordy; the simplest choice, (D), is the best.

72. G
Category: Verb Tenses
Difficulty: Medium
Getting to the Answer: The participle *receiving* has to be changed into a verb in the past tense, *received*, in order to be consistent with *went*. Choice (G) is correct as opposed to H, because the number of bruises something has can be counted, necessitating *many* bruises, not *much* bruises.

73. B
Category: Writing Strategy
Difficulty: Medium
Getting to the Answer: Choice A wouldn't work as a concluding sentence because its style and tone are off; nowhere in the passage does the writer use language such as "brutal calamities" and "beguiling excitement." Also, the writer and her father were not "unwary rafters." Choice C contradicts the writer's main theme that nothing was as memorable as her first ride through the rapids. This is also a sentence fragment. The tone in D, "call me crazy or weird…," is much different from the writer's. Choice (B) closely matches the author's style and tone while restating the main theme of the passage.

74. F

Category: Writing Strategy

Difficulty: Medium

Getting to the Answer: This essay relates a personal experience of the writer: her first time rafting down a rapids. There is very little mention of the techniques of white-water rafting, so the essay would not meet the requirements of the assignment. Choice G is incorrect because the essay does not focus on the relationship between father and daughter but on their first rafting experience together.

75. B

Category: Organization

Difficulty: High

Getting to the Answer: The sentence foreshadows things to come, so it must appear toward the beginning of the essay. That eliminates C and D. The second paragraph is about the peaceful setting, so (B) is the most sensible answer.

MATHEMATICS TEST

1. D

Category: Proportions and Probability

Difficulty: Medium

Getting to the Answer: You know that 14 people are 20% of the total, and you need to find 100% of the total. You could set up an equation, or you could multiply 14 by 5, because 100% is 5 times as much as 20%. The number of people surveyed is 14×5, or 70.

2. J

Category: Proportions and Probability

Difficulty: Medium

Getting to the Answer: One safe way to answer this question is by Picking Numbers. For instance, if you let $x = 2$ and $y = 3$, the train would have traveled $90 \times 2 + 60 \times 3 = 360$ miles in 5 hours, or $\frac{360}{5} = 72$ miles per hour. If you then plug $x = 2$ and

$y = 3$ into the answer choices, it's clear that the correct answer is (J). No other answer choice equals 72 when $x = 2$ and $y = 3$.

3. B

Category: Proportions and Probability

Difficulty: High

Getting to the Answer: If the ratio of men to women is 5:3, then the ratio of women to the total is $3:(3 + 5) = 3:8$. Because you know the total number of string players is 24, you can set up the equation $\frac{3}{8} = \frac{x}{24}$ to find that $x = 9$. Also, without setting up the proportion, you could note that the total number of players is 3 times the ratio total, so the number of women will be 3 times the part of the ratio that represents women.

4. K

Category: Variable Manipulation

Difficulty: Medium

Getting to the Answer: In a pinch, you could Backsolve on this question, but this one is fairly easy to solve algebraically:

$$x^2 - 3x = 6x$$

$$x^2 = 9x$$

Now you can divide both sides by x because $x \neq 0$:

$$\frac{x^2}{x} = \frac{9x}{x}$$

$$x = 9$$

5. C

Category: Patterns, Logic, and Data

Difficulty: Medium

Getting to the Answer: With visual perception problems such as this one, the key is to play around with possibilities as you try to draw a solution. Eventually, you should be able to come up with a picture like this:

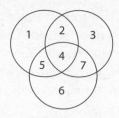

6. K

Category: Variable Manipulation

Difficulty: High

Getting to the Answer: This problem could be solved algebraically, but look at the answer choices. They are all simple numbers, making this a great opportunity for Backsolving. Begin with H.

Plugging in 0, you get:

$$(0)^2 + 6(0) + 8 = 4 + 10(0)$$

$$8 = 4$$

Because 8 does not equal 4, you know this isn't the correct answer. But it is difficult to know which answer to try next. Should you aim higher or lower? If you're unsure of which direction to go, just try whatever looks easiest. Choice J, 1, looks like a good candidate:

$$(1)^2 + 6(1) + 8 = 4 + 10(1)$$

$$1 + 6 + 8 = 4 + 10$$

$$15 = 14$$

So J doesn't work either, but it looks like the numbers are getting closer, so you're going in the right direction. Try (K) just to be sure.

$$(2)^2 + 6(2) + 8 = 4 + 10(2)$$

$$4 + 12 + 8 = 4 + 20$$

$$24 = 24$$

Choice (K) is the correct answer.

7. B

Category: Variable Manipulation

Difficulty: Medium

Getting to the Answer: Translate piece by piece:

"Nine less than c" indicates subtraction: $c - 9$.

"Nine less than c is the same as the number d": $c - 9 = d$. There's one equation. The answer is either (B) or C.

"d less than" also indicates subtraction: $- d$.

"d less than twice c is 20": $2c - d = 20$. There's the second equation.

Choice (B) matches what you found.

8. K

Category: Proportions and Probability

Difficulty: Medium

Getting to the Answer: To determine the total number of possible arrangements on a question like this one, simply determine the number of possibilities for each component and then multiply them together. There are three ways of serving the ice cream, five flavors, and four toppings. Therefore, there are $3 \times 5 \times 4 = 60$ ways to order ice cream, and (K) is correct.

9. E

Category: Proportions and Probability

Difficulty: High

Getting to the Answer: Backsolving is a great technique to use for this problem. Start with C. The director asked 1 out of 3 students to come to the second audition and $\frac{1}{3}$ of 48 is 16, so 16 students were invited to a second audition. Then 75% of 16, which is $\frac{3}{4}(16) = 12$ students, were offered parts. The question states that 18 students were offered parts, so you already know that C is too small.

(You can also, thus, eliminate A and B.) Because

the director invited $\frac{1}{3}$ of the students to a second audition, the number of students at the first audition must be divisible by 3. (You can't have a fraction of a student.) That eliminates D, leaving only (E).

10. K
Category: Variable Manipulation
Difficulty: Medium
Getting to the Answer: Begin by translating the English into math: $x + 5x = -60$, $6x = -60$, so $x = -10$, and the two numbers are -10 and -50. Thus, the lesser number is -50.

By the way, this is where most people mess up. They forget that the lesser of two negative numbers is the negative number with the larger absolute value (because *less* means *to the left of* on the number line):

11. D
Category: Patterns, Logic, and Data
Difficulty: High
Getting to the Answer: You're looking for the total number of parallelograms that can be found among the triangles, and parallelograms could be formed two ways from these triangles, either from two adjacent triangles or from four adjacent triangles, like so:

Begin by looking for the smaller parallelograms. If you look for parallelograms leaning in the same direction as the one we drew, you'll find 3. But there are two other possible orientations for the smaller parallelogram; it could be flipped horizontally, or it could be rotated 90 degrees so that one triangle sits atop the other in the form of a diamond; both of these orientations also have 3 parallelograms, for a total of 9 smaller parallelograms.

Now look for larger parallelograms. Perhaps the easiest way to count these is to look along the sides of the larger composite triangle. You should be able to spot 2 of the larger parallelograms along each side, one originating at each vertex, for a total of 6 larger parallelograms.

Thus, there are a total of $9 + 6 = 15$ parallelograms in all.

12. H
Category: Plane Geometry
Difficulty: Medium
Getting to the Answer: The square has a perimeter of 16 inches, so each side of the square is 4 inches; the area of the square is, therefore, 16 square inches. If the side of the square is 4 inches, then the diameter of the circle is also 4 inches. The radius of the circle is then 2 inches, making the area of the circle 4π square inches. The area of the shaded region is then $16 - 4\pi$ square inches.

13. C
Category: Number Properties
Difficulty: Medium
Getting to the Answer: The safest strategy is simply to list out the possibilities. It's also helpful to realize that multiples of both 4 and 6 are multiples of 12 (the least common multiple between the two), so skip over all multiples of 12:

4, 8, ~~12~~, 16, 20, ~~24~~, 28, 32, ~~36~~, 40, 44, ~~48~~

So there are 8 in all.

14. H
Category: Variable Manipulation
Difficulty: Medium
Getting to the Answer: Don't be intimidated by the expression $f(x)$. In this case, you should just plug in the number that appears in the parentheses for the x in the expression the question has given you. So, if $f(x) = (8 - 3x)(x^2 - 2x - 15)$, $f(3) = [8 - 3(3)][(3)^2 - 2(3) - 15]$.

Once you get to this point, just remember PEMDAS.

$[8 - 3(3)][(3)^2 - 2(3) - 15] = (8 - 9)(9 - 6 - 15) = (-1)$
$(-12) = 12$, (H).

15. C
Category: Proportions and Probability

Difficulty: Medium

Getting to the Answer: A class contains five juniors and five seniors. If one member of the class is assigned at random to present a paper on a certain subject, and another member of the class is randomly assigned to assist him, then:
The probability that the first student picked will be a

$$\text{junior} = \frac{\text{\# of juniors}}{\text{Total \# of students}} = \frac{5}{10} = \frac{1}{2}.$$

Given that the first student picked was a junior, the probability that the second student picked will be a

$$\text{junior} = \frac{\text{\# of juniors remaining}}{\text{Total \# of students remaining}}.$$

So the probability that both students will be

$$\text{juniors} = \frac{1}{2} \times \frac{4}{9} = \frac{2}{9}.$$

16. G
Category: Plane Geometry

Difficulty: Medium

Getting to the Answer: Because the formula to find the area of a triangle is $\frac{1}{2}$(base) (height), you can plug in the base and area to find the height. You know that the area of this triangle is 45 units and that the base is $3 + 12 = 15$. Let x be the length of altitude $\overline{YS}$. Plug these into the area formula to get

$45 = \frac{15x}{2}$. Solve for x to get $x = 6$.

17. B
Category: Coordinate Geometry

Difficulty: Medium

Getting to the Answer: The y-coordinate is the point at which the x value is zero, so plug $x = 0$ into the equation:

$$6y - 3(0) = 18$$

$$6y = 18$$

$$y = 3$$

18. H
Category: Variable Manipulation

Difficulty: High

Getting to the Answer: This question involves common quadratics, so the key is to write these quadratic expressions in their other forms. For instance, $x^2 - y^2 = 12$, so $(x + y)(x - y) = 12$. Because $x - y = 4$, $(x + y)(4) = 12$, so $x + y = 3$. Finally, $x^2 + 2xy + y^2 = (x + y)^2 = (3)^2 = 9$.

19. B
Category: Plane Geometry

Difficulty: High

Getting to the Answer: This shape must be divided into three simple shapes. By drawing two perpendicular line segments down from the endpoints of the side that is 10 units long, you are left with a 3 × 10 rectangle, a triangle with a base of 4 and a height of 3, and a triangle with a base of 7 and a hypotenuse of $7\sqrt{2}$. The rectangle has an area of 3 × 10 = 30 square units. The smaller triangle has an area of $\frac{4 \times 3}{2} = 6$ square units. The larger triangle is a 45°-45°-90° triangle, so the height must be 7. Therefore, it has an area of $\frac{7 \times 7}{2} = 24.5$ square units. The entire shape has an area of 6 + 30 + 24.5 = 60.5 square units.

20. H

Category: Operations

Difficulty: High

Getting to the Answer: Although Backsolving is certainly possible with this problem, it's probably quicker to solve with arithmetic. The board is 12 feet long, which means it is $12 \times 12 = 144$ inches. The carpenter cuts off $3 \times 17 = 51$ inches. That leaves $144 - 51 = 93$ inches.

21. E

Category: Variable Manipulation

Difficulty: Low

Getting to the Answer: To answer this question, begin by setting the right side of the equation equal to zero:

$$x^2 - 4x - 6 = 6$$

$$x^2 - 4x - 12 = 0$$

Now use reverse-FOIL to factor the left side of the equation:

$$(x - 6)(x + 2) = 0$$

Thus, either $x - 6 = 0$ or $x + 2 = 0$, so $x = 6$ or -2.

22. H

Category: Variable Manipulation

Difficulty: Medium

Getting to the Answer: Here's another question that tests your understanding of FOIL, but you have to be careful. The question states that -3 is a possible solution for the equation $x^2 + kx - 15 = 0$, so in its factored form, one set of parentheses with a factor inside must be $(x + 3)$. Because the last term in the equation in its expanded form is -15, that means that the entire factored equation must read $(x + 3)(x - 5) = 0$, which in its expanded form is $x^2 - 2x - 15 = 0$. Thus, $k = -2$.

23. D

Category: Plane Geometry

Difficulty: Medium

Getting to the Answer: To solve this problem, you need to understand the triangle inequality theorem, which states: The sum of the lengths of any two sides of a triangle is always greater than the length of the third side. Therefore, the other sides of this triangle must add up to more than 7. You know from the problem that every side must be an integer. That means that the sides must add up to at least 8 inches (4 inches and 4 inches, or 7 inches and 1 inch, for example). The smallest possible perimeter is $7 + 8 = 15$.

24. F

Category: Trigonometry

Difficulty: Medium

Getting to the Answer: It's time to use SOHCAH-TOA, and drawing a triangle might help as well. If the sine of θ (opposite side over hypotenuse) is $\frac{\sqrt{11}}{2\sqrt{3}}$, then one of the legs of the right triangle is $\sqrt{11}$, and the hypotenuse is $2\sqrt{3}$. Now apply the Pythagorean theorem to come up with the other (adjacent) leg: $\left(\sqrt{11}\right)^2 + \left(n\right)^2 = \left(2\sqrt{3}\right)^2$, so $11 + n^2 = 12$, which means that $n^2 = 1$, and $n = 1$. Thus, cosine (adjacent side over hypotenuse) θ is $\frac{1}{2\sqrt{3}}$.

25. D

Category: Operations

Difficulty: Medium

Getting to the Answer: Take a quick look at the answer choices before simplifying an expression like this one. Notice that only one of these choices contains a radical sign in its denominator. So when you simplify the expression, try to eliminate that radical sign. Your calculations should look something like this:

$$\frac{\sqrt{3+x}}{\sqrt{3-x}} \times \frac{\sqrt{3-x}}{\sqrt{3-x}} = \frac{\sqrt{(3+x)(3-x)}}{\sqrt{(3-x)^2}} =$$

$$\frac{\sqrt{9-3x+3x-x^2}}{3-x} = \frac{\sqrt{9-x^2}}{3-x}$$

So (D) is correct.

26. G

Category: Proportions and Probability

Difficulty: Low

Getting to the Answer: If the ratio of the parts is 2:5, then the ratio total is $2 + 5 = 7$. Thus, the actual total number of cookies must be a multiple of 7. The only choice that's a multiple of 7 is (G), 35.

27. C

Category: Number Properties

Difficulty: Medium

Getting to the Answer: This question is a great opportunity to use your calculator. Notice that all your choices are decimals. In order to solve, convert $\frac{3}{16}$ into a decimal and add that to 0.175: $\frac{3}{16} = 0.1875$, so the sum equals $0.1875 + 0.175 = 0.3625$. Thus, (C) is correct.

28. H

Category: Plane Geometry

Difficulty: Low

Getting to the Answer: Remember that if you are given a perimeter for a rectangle, the rectangle with the greatest area for that perimeter will be a square. So you are looking for the area of a square with a perimeter of 20. The perimeter of a square equals $4s$, where s is the length of one side of the square. If $4s = 20$, then $s = 5$. The area of the square equals $s^2 = 5^2 = 25$, (H).

29. B

Category: Operations

Difficulty: High

Getting to the Answer: Be careful on this one. You can't start plugging numbers into your calculator without paying attention to the order of operations. This one is best solved on your own.

$$\frac{\dfrac{3}{2}+\dfrac{7}{4}}{\dfrac{15}{8}-\dfrac{3}{4}-\dfrac{4+3}{-4+3}} =$$

$$\frac{\dfrac{3}{2}+\dfrac{7}{4}}{\dfrac{9}{8}-\dfrac{7}{-1}} = \frac{\dfrac{13}{4}}{\dfrac{65}{8}} = \frac{13}{4} \times \frac{8}{65} = \frac{2}{5}$$

30. K

Category: Variable Manipulation

Difficulty: Medium

Getting to the Answer: You could solve this algebraically for x as follows:

$$x - 15 = 7 - 5(x - 4)$$

$$x - 15 = 7 - 5x + 20$$

$$x - 15 = -5x + 27$$

$$6x = 42$$

$$x = 7$$

Remember also that if you are ever stuck, you can Backsolve using the answer choices. Here, if you try them all out, only 7 works:

$$7 - 15 = 7 - 5(7 - 4)$$

$$-8 = 7 - 5(3)$$

$$-8 = 7 - 15$$

$$-8 = -8$$

31. C

Category: Plane Geometry

Difficulty: Medium

Getting to the Answer: Break strange figures like this one up into shapes that are more familiar and easier to handle. In this case, the quadrilateral can be split into a square and a right triangle. The square is 9×9, so the area of that part of the figure is 81 square meters. The right triangle has a height of 9 and a base of 4, so the area of the triangle would be

$$\frac{1}{2}bh = \frac{1}{2}(4 \times 9) = \frac{1}{2}(36) = 18$$

square meters. Therefore, the total area of the figure is (81 + 18) square meters = 99 square meters, (C).

32. H

Category: Coordinate Geometry

Difficulty: Medium

Getting to the Answer: The easiest way to solve this question is to put it in the form $y = mx + b$, where m equals the slope. In other words, you want to isolate y:

$$6y - 3x = 18$$
$$6y = 3x + 18$$
$$y = \frac{3x + 18}{6}$$
$$y = \frac{1}{2}x + 3$$

So the slope equals $\frac{1}{2}$.

33. A

Category: Coordinate Geometry

Difficulty: Low

Getting to the Answer: To answer this question, you have to know that perpendicular lines on the standard (x, y) coordinate plane have slopes that are negative reciprocals of each other. In other words, the line described by the equation $y = -\frac{4}{5}x + 6$ has a slope of $-\frac{4}{5}$, so a line perpendicular to it

has a slope of $\frac{5}{4}$. This eliminates all choices but (A). However, if you want to double-check, you can plug the coordinates you're given (4, 3) into the equation found in (A).

$$3 = \frac{5}{4}(4) - 2$$
$$3 = 5 - 2$$
$$3 = 3$$

34. K

Category: Coordinate Geometry

Difficulty: Medium

Getting to the Answer: Because the problem gives you the y-intercept, it is easy to look at the answer choices and rule out F, H, and J. Put the equation from the question in slope-intercept form to find its slope:

$$3x - 5y = 4$$
$$-5y = -3x + 4$$
$$y = \frac{-3x + 4}{-5}$$
$$y = \frac{3}{5}x - \frac{4}{5}$$

Because line t is parallel, it has the same slope. This matches (K).

35. A

Category: Variable Manipulation

Difficulty: Low

Getting to the Answer: To solve for x in the equation $y = mx + b$, isolate x on one side of the equation. Begin by subtracting b from both sides. You will be left with $y - b = mx$. Then divide both sides by m, and you will be left with $x = \frac{y - b}{m}$, (A).

36. J

Category: Plane Geometry

Difficulty: Medium

Getting to the Answer: In this figure, there are many right triangles and many similar triangles. If you know to be on the lookout for 3-4-5 triangles, it should be easy to spot that triangle *ABC* has sides of 15-20-25, so $\overline{AC}$ is 25. Now turn your attention to triangle *ABD*. Because it's a right triangle that shares ∠*BAC* with triangle *ABC*, it too must be a 3-4-5 triangle. So if the hypotenuse is 20, the shorter leg ($\overline{BD}$) must have a length of 12, and the longer leg ($\overline{AD}$) must have a length of 16.

37. A

Category: Coordinate Geometry

Difficulty: High

Getting to the Answer: The shortest distance to line *m* will be a line perpendicular to *m*. So the distance will be the difference between the *y*-coordinates of point *C* and the nearest point on line *m*. Because every point on *m* has a *y*-coordinate of 5, and point *C* has a *y*-coordinate of 3, the difference is 2.

38. G

Category: Variable Manipulation

Difficulty: Medium

Getting to the Answer: While you could try factoring the numerator, you'll find that you can't easily cancel out the denominator by doing so. Perhaps the easiest approach here is to Pick Numbers. Pick a simple number such as $x = 2$. Thus,

$$\frac{x^2 - 11x + 24}{8 - x} = \frac{(2)^2 - 11(2) + 24}{6} =$$
$$\frac{4 - 22 + 24}{6} = \frac{6}{6} = 1.$$

So 1 is your target number. When you plug $x = 2$ into the choices, the only choice that gives you 1 is (G).

39. C

Category: Coordinate Geometry

Difficulty: Medium

Getting to the Answer:

The textbook method for this problem would be to use the distance formula, but that's time-consuming. Instead, it may help to draw a picture. Draw a right triangle on the coordinate plane as shown above. Note that the distance between the two points represents the hypotenuse of the triangle. The legs of the triangle have lengths of 3 and 4, so the distance between the two points must be 5, (C).

40. G

Category: Plane Geometry

Difficulty: Medium

Getting to the Answer: To find the area of the shaded region, you must subtract the area of the circle from the area of the rectangle. Because the sides of the rectangle are 2*x* and 5*x*, it has an area of $2x \times 5x = 10x^2$. By examining the diagram, you can see that the circle has a diameter of 2*x*, so it has a radius of *x*. Its area is, therefore, πx^2. Thus, the shaded region has an area of $10x^2 - \pi x^2$.

41. B

Category: Trigonometry

Difficulty: High

Getting to the Answer: Because you are not given a diagram for this problem, it's best to draw a quick sketch of a right triangle to help keep the sides separate in your mind. Mark one of the acute angles θ. Because $\cos θ = \dfrac{5\sqrt{2}}{8}$, mark the adjacent side $5\sqrt{2}$ and the hypotenuse as 8. (Remember SOHCAHTOA.) Use the Pythagorean theorem to find that the side opposite θ is $\sqrt{14}$. The problem asks you to find tan θ. Tangent = $\dfrac{\text{opposite}}{\text{adjacent}}$, so $\tan\theta = \dfrac{\sqrt{14}}{5\sqrt{2}}$, which can be simplified to $\dfrac{\sqrt{7}}{5}$.

42. H

Category: Proportions and Probability

Difficulty: Medium

Getting to the Answer: This question is one where your calculator can come in handy. Divide 7 by integer values for n, and look for values between 0.5 and 0.8. Begin by looking for the integer values of n where $\dfrac{7}{n}$ is greater than 0.5. If $n = 14$, then $\dfrac{7}{n} = 0.5$, so n must be less than 14. Work through values of n until you get to the point where $\dfrac{7}{n} + 0.8$. When $n = 9$, $\dfrac{7}{n} = 0.778$, but when $n = 8$, $\dfrac{7}{n} = 0.875$. So the integer values that work in this case are $n = 9$, 10, 11, 12, and 13. Five integer values work, making (H) correct.

43. C

Difficulty: Medium

Category: Plane Geometry

Getting to the Answer: The points are as far apart as possible when separated by a diameter of X and a diameter of Y.

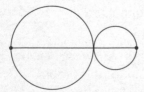

The circumference of a circle is π × (diameter), so the diameter of circle X is 12, and the diameter of circle Y is 8. The greatest possible distance between points then is 12 + 8 = 20.

44. K

Category: Variable Manipulation

Difficulty: Medium

Getting to the Answer: Begin by getting rid of the square root sign. If $y \geq 0$, then $\sqrt{y^2} = y$, so $\sqrt{(x^2 + 4)^2} = x^2 + 4$. Then $(x + 2)(x - 2) = x^2 - 4$, so you now have $(x^2 + 4) - (x^2 - 4) = ?$ Get rid of the parentheses, and you have $x^2 + 4 - x^2 + 4 = x^2 - x^2 + 4 + 4 = 8$.

45. A

Category: Variable Manipulation

Difficulty: Medium

Getting to the Answer: Here, you need to substitute −3 for s and solve. That gives you the expression $(-3)^3 + 2(-3)^2 + 2(-3)$, which equals $-27 + 18 - 6$, or −15. If you missed this problem, you probably made a mistake with the signs of the numbers.

46. G

Category: Variable Manipulation

Difficulty: High

Getting to the Answer: Be careful on this one. Begin by simplifying the equation by FOILing one side:

$$2x + 6 = (x + 5)(x + 3)$$

$$2x + 6 = x^2 + 8x + 15$$

Then get the right side of the equation to equal zero: $x^2 + 6x + 9 = 0$.

The left side of this equation is the perfect square $(x + 3)^2$, so $(x + 3)^2 = 0$, which has only one solution, $x = -3$. Choice (G) is correct.

47. E

Category: Pythagorean Theorem

Difficulty: Low

Getting to the Answer: The textbook method for this would be to use the Pythagorean theorem to find the length of a side and then multiply that by 4, but there's an easier way: eyeball it! The perimeter is greater than $\overline{AC}$, so you can get rid of A and B.

It appears to be quite a bit greater than $\overline{AC}$, more than twice as great, so C and D are out as well. That only leaves (E).

If you wanted to solve this the conventional way, because the perimeter is the sum of the lengths of all the sides of the square, you need to find the length of the square's sides. Let the length of each of the square's sides be x. $\overline{AC}$ divides the square into two right triangles, so you can apply the Pythagorean theorem: $\overline{AB}^2 + \overline{BC}^2 = \overline{AC}^2$. Because $\overline{AB}$ and $\overline{BC}$ are sides of the square, they have the same length. You can write that as $x^2 + x^2 = \overline{AC}^2$. $\overline{AC} = 8$, so $2x^2 = 8^2$, $2x^2 = 64$, $x^2 = 32$, $x = \sqrt{32} = \sqrt{16 \times 2} = 4\sqrt{2}$.

So each side of the square is $4\sqrt{2}$, and the perimeter of the square is $4 \times 4\sqrt{2} = 16\sqrt{2}$.

48. G
Category: Plane Geometry

Difficulty: Medium

Getting to the Answer: To find the area of this complex shape, you could divide it into two simple shapes by drawing a line 30 inches up, parallel to the horizontal base. This leaves you with a 4×30 rectangle and a triangle with height of 6 and a base of 4. The rectangle has an area of $4 \times 30 = 120$ square inches, and the triangle has an area of $\dfrac{4 \times 6}{2} = 12$ square inches. That makes a total of $120 + 12 = 132$ square inches.

49. E
Category: Plane Geometry

Difficulty: Medium

Getting to the Answer: Triangles are the secret to solving this one. Drawing $\overline{OD}$ divides quadrilateral $OCDE$ into two triangles, OCD and ODE. Both triangles are isosceles because $\overline{OC}$, $\overline{OD}$, and $\overline{OE}$ are all radii of circle O. Angles ODC and OCD have equal measures, because they're opposite equal sides, so $\angle ODC$ measures 70°. Similarly, $\angle ODE$ measures 45°.

Together, angles ODC and ODE make up $\angle CDE$, so its measure is $70° + 45° = 115°$.

50. K
Category: Coordinate Geometry

Difficulty: High

Getting to the Answer: Remember that lines intersect at the point that is a solution to both equations. So equations with no common solution don't intersect—they have the same slope and are parallel. To solve this problem, search through the answer choices to find the pair of equations representing lines with the same slope. If you write the equations in (K) in slope-intercept form, you'll get

$$y = -\frac{1}{3}x + 2, \quad y = -\frac{1}{3}x + \frac{7}{9},$$

so the slope is clearly the same for both equations.

51. E
Category: Number Properties

Difficulty: Medium

Getting to the Answer: To solve a repeating decimal question, begin by determining the pattern of the decimal on your calculator: $\dfrac{1}{7} = 0.142857142857\ldots$ so you know that this fraction repeats every six decimal places. Because you are looking for the 46th decimal place, you need to determine where in the six-term pattern you would be at the 46th place. Divide 46 by 6 and look for the remainder. The remainder in this case is 4, so you are looking for the 4th term in the sequence, which is 8, (E).

52. K
Category: Variable Manipulation

Difficulty: Medium

Getting to the Answer: Remember that you treat an inequality exactly like an equality, except that you need to flip the sign when you multiply or divide by a negative number. In this problem, you start with the inequality $-2 - 4x \le -6x$. Add $4x$ to both sides to get $-2 \leq -2x$. Divide by -2 and flip the sign to get $1 \geq x$, which matches (K).

53. B

Category: Operations

Difficulty: High

Getting to the Answer: For this problem, it would probably be easiest to Pick Numbers. Because you will be taking the square root of the numbers, it's easiest to pick perfect squares, like 4 and 9:

$$\frac{\sqrt{4}}{4} + \frac{\sqrt{9}}{9} = \frac{2}{4} + \frac{3}{9} = \frac{1}{2} + \frac{1}{3} = \frac{5}{6}$$

When you plug 4 and 9 into the answer choices, only (B) gives you $\frac{5}{6}$.

54. G

Category: Plane Geometry

Difficulty: Medium

Getting to the Answer: When transversals intersect parallel lines, corresponding line segments on the transversals are proportional. In other words, $\frac{\overline{DE}}{\overline{CB}} = \frac{\overline{EF}}{\overline{BA}}$. Thus, $\frac{6}{8} = \frac{\overline{EF}}{4}$, so $EF = 3$.

55. D

Category: Coordinate Geometry

Difficulty: High

Getting to the Answer: Divide the square into two right triangles by drawing the diagonal from (2, 7) to (2, 1). Remember that the area of each triangle is half its base times its height. Treat the diagonal as the base of a triangle. Its length is the distance from (2, 7) to (2, 1). Because the x-coordinates are the same, that distance is simply the difference between the y-coordinates, $7 - 1$, or 6. The diagonal bisects the square, so the height of the triangle is half the distance from $(-1, 4)$ to (5, 4). You already know that a diagonal of this square is 6, so half the distance is 3. Therefore, the base and height of either triangle are 6 and 3, making the area of each triangle $\frac{6 \times 3}{2}$, or 9 square units. The square is made up of

two such triangles and so has twice the area, or 18 square units.

Alternatively, you could use the Distance Formula to find the length of one side and square that side to find the area.

56. K

Category: Trigonometry

Difficulty: Medium

Getting to the Answer: Compared to the graph of $y = \cos \theta$, the graph of $y = 2 \cos \theta$ would have twice the amplitude and the same period, (K). Here you are doubling y, which represents the vertical coordinates, but the θ coordinates stay the same. The amplitude of a trigonometric equation refers to how high or low the curve moves from the horizontal axis. The period refers to the distance required to complete a single wave along the horizontal axis.

57. C

Category: Variable Manipulation

Difficulty: Medium

Getting to the Answer: To solve this problem with algebra, you need to translate each phrase into mathematics. Translated, the problem is $3(x + 15) = 4x - 65$. Solve for x to get 110. Alternatively, you could Backsolve starting with the middle value:

$$3(110 + 15) = 4(110) - 65$$

$$3(125) = 440 - 65$$

$$375 = 375$$

Because the two sides are equal, (C) is correct.

58. H

Category: Proportions and Probability

Difficulty: Medium

Getting to the Answer: You're given the formula for the volume of a cylinder in the equation so you can find the volume of both cylinders described. Then this becomes a ratio problem in which you're comparing the volumes of both cylinders. Pick Numbers to make this question more concrete and plug them into this volume formula.

Let's say the smaller cylinder has a height of 1 and a radius of 1 (diameter of 2), for a volume of $\pi(1)^2 \times 1 = \pi$. The larger cylinder would then have a height of 3 and a radius of 2 (diameter of 4), for a volume of $\pi(2)^2 \times 3 = 12\pi$. Thus, it would take 12 fillings of the smaller cylinder to fill the larger cylinder.

59. D

Category: Plane Geometry

Difficulty: High

Getting to the Answer: Draw a picture of the triangle and carefully apply your knowledge of the ratio of the lengths of the sides of a 30°-60°-90° triangle ($x : x\sqrt{3} : 2x$). If the longer leg has a length of 12, the shorter leg has a length of

$$\frac{12}{\sqrt{3}} = \frac{12\sqrt{3}}{\sqrt{3} \times \sqrt{3}} = \frac{12\sqrt{3}}{3} = 4\sqrt{3}.$$

Then, the hypotenuse is twice this, or $8\sqrt{3}$. Finally, the perimeter is the sum of the three sides, or

$$4\sqrt{3} + 12 + 8\sqrt{3} = 12\sqrt{3} + 12.$$

60. J

Category: Proportions and Probability

Difficulty: Medium

Getting to the Answer: Remember the average formula on this one. The average formula states,

$$\text{Average} = \frac{\text{Sum of the terms}}{\text{Number of the terms}}.$$ So to find the total average, find the total sum and divide it by the total number of terms. If a team averages x points in n games, then it scored nx points in n games. In the final game of the season, it scored y points. So the total sum of points for the season is $nx + y$, and the total number of games is $n + 1$. So the team's average score for the entire season is $\frac{nx + y}{n + 1}$, (J).

READING TEST

PASSAGE I

1. C

Category: Detail

Difficulty: Medium

Getting to the Answer: The answer can be found in lines 31–36: "The real evils, indeed, of Emma's situation were the power of having rather too much her own way, and a disposition to think a little too well of herself; these were the disadvantages which threatened alloy to her many enjoyments."

2. G

Category: Detai

Difficulty: High

Getting to the Answer: Isabella's name is given in line 73.

3. B

Category: Detail

Difficulty: Medium

Getting to the Answer: The answer can be found in lines 20–21: "Between them it was more the intimacy of sisters."

4. F

Category: Vocab-in-Context

Difficulty: Low

Getting to the Answer: As it is used in the sentence, *disposition* means "tendency" or "inclination." It would not make sense for Emma to have G, control; H, placement; or J, transfer "to think a little too well of herself" (lines 33–34).

5. D

Category: Detail

Difficulty: High

Getting to the Answer: The answer can be found in lines 62–69: "She recalled her past kindness—the kindness, the affection of sixteen years—how she had taught her and…how she had devoted all her powers to attach and amuse her in health—and how she had nursed her through the various illnesses of childhood."

6. H

Category: Inference

Difficulty: Medium

Getting to the Answer: Miss Taylor will continue to be a part of Emma's life, but they will not be as close because Miss Taylor no longer lives with Emma and because Miss Taylor will be primarily concerned with her husband's, not Emma's, well-being.

7. C

Category: Inference

Difficulty: Medium

Getting to the Answer: Emma is self-centered, as evidenced by her description of her relationship with Miss Taylor. Among Miss Taylor's admirable qualities, Emma includes the fact that Miss Taylor was "interested in her, in every pleasure, every scheme of hers—one to whom she could speak every thought as it arose, and who had such an affection for her as could never find fault" (lines 80–84). Emma is also clearly headstrong. She is described as "having rather too much her own way" (lines 32–33).

8. G

Category: Generalization

Difficulty: Medium

Getting to the Answer: Emma's description of her friendship with Miss Taylor suggests that Emma most highly values devotion in her friends.

9. B

Category: Detail

Difficulty: Medium

Getting to the Answer: The description of Mr. Weston is in lines 53–56: "The marriage had every promise of happiness for her friend. Mr. Weston was

a man of unexceptionable character, easy fortune, suitable age, and pleasant manners." None of the other choices match this description.

10. H

Category: Inference

Difficulty: Low

Getting to the Answer: The answer to the question is in lines 28–31: "Emma doing just what she liked, highly esteeming Miss Taylor's judgment, but directed chiefly by her own."

PASSAGE II

11. B

Category: Generalization

Difficulty: Medium

Getting to the Answer: Passage A discusses the Wright brothers' process for designing a successful airplane; (B) is correct. Although the passage mentions how the Wright brothers were regarded, A, this information appears in the first paragraph only, and is not the main focus of the passage. The passage discusses the approaches used by other inventors, but the author does not criticize them, as represented in C. The practical application of science, D, is too broad to be correct.

12. H

Category: Inference

Difficulty: High

Getting to the Answer: According to paragraph 2, most inventors would design an airplane, build it, and test it, but not know specifically what caused a plane to succeed or fail, (H). Choice F is opposite because Smeaton's coefficient was commonly accepted during that time in history. There's no indication that they considered the methods and rejected them, G. Choice J is opposite; people who were trying to build an airplane likely believed it was possible.

13. B

Category: Inference

Difficulty: High

Getting to the Answer: The passage says that the Wright brothers invented the wind tunnel as an alternative to building and testing "whole machines." They tested only parts of their design in the tunnel, such as wing shape. You can infer that the wind tunnel made it possible for them to deal with their airplane design one piece at a time. The author never implies that the data from the kites, A, was inaccurate. To work on controlling the plane laterally, they used a five-foot biplane kite rather than the wind tunnel, which rules out C. Choice D is opposite; they disproved a commonly-accepted theory of lift (called Smeaton's coefficient).

14. F

Category: Function

Difficulty: High

Getting to the Answer: Passage B deals mainly with how the Wright brothers were treated publicly following their discovery. The "legal battle" is mentioned as another example of how the brothers didn't receive the money and respect they deserved for their important contribution, (F). The author does not imply that it is unwise to publicize knowledge, G. Choice H is opposite; the author feels that their discovery was quite important. Choice J isn't directly related to the court case.

15. C

Category: Inference

Difficulty: Medium

Getting to the Answer: In the last paragraph, the author states that "this was too little, too late," so the author would agree that the honor did not properly compensate for the poor treatment of the brothers, (C). It was not a victory for Orville, A, because both brothers had passed away by 1948. The Smithsonian's choice was not a result of a refusal to recognize the brothers' achievements, B, because it was a great honor. There is no evidence to suggest that the craft would have been displayed sooner if European countries had issued the brothers a patent, D.

16. J

Category: Detail

Difficulty: High

Getting to the Answer: This Detail question requires very careful reading. The previous sentence talks about how "those who made airplanes" thought little of the Wright brothers' accomplishments. The following sentence is a continuation of that thought, and so it is "those who made airplanes," (J), who are expressing this opinion. The discussion of "the French aviation community" begins a new thought, ruling out F. The Wright brothers, G, didn't have a poor view of themselves. The author, H, has a positive view of the Wright brothers.

17. B

Category: Inference

Difficulty: Medium

Getting to the Answer: The passage says "the prevailing opinion among those who made airplanes was that two rustic, uneducated fellows from Ohio could never have accomplished such an historic feat except by accident." From this, you can infer that those who made airplanes didn't think that the Wright brothers were exceptional; in their eyes, the brothers' discovery must have been sheer luck, not the result of scientific experimentation. Eliminate A because the passage never says that they thought the Wrights hadn't made a working airplane, only that they thought little of the accomplishment. Choice C is opposite; they had a negative opinion the Wrights' breakthrough. Choice D is a distortion; they felt the brothers were lucky, not dishonest.

18. H

Category: Vocab-in-Context

Difficulty: Low

Getting to the Answer: The authors state that the Wrights were able to "marry all of these carefully designed components into a complete craft" (lines 72–73) and "deliberately marry the disparate components of air travel that are required for successful flight" (line 90–93). So, the Wright brothers brought together all the separate pieces into a whole airplane. Predict that "marry" means "bring together,"

(H). The airplane did prove, F, that the components worked when together, but it doesn't make sense to say that the brothers were able to deliberately prove the components. The Wright brothers had already rigorously tested each component separately, so G is incorrect. Airplane components can't be satisfied, so J won't work.

19. B

Category: Detail

Difficulty: Medium

Getting to the Answer: At the beginning of paragraph 3, Passage A states, "The Wright brothers proved to be adept scientists. With their keen analytical insight and love of engineering and all things mechanical, they were able to escape that endless loop of misguided 'improvements.'" This matches perfectly with (B). Choice A describes the approach that other, unsuccessful inventors used. Passage A does not provide evidence that the invention of the wind tunnel was a greater accomplishment than the airplane, C. The court case cited in D is included in Passage B, not in Passage A.

20. H

Category: Detail

Difficulty: Low

Getting to the Answer: Wrong answer choices for this type of question are commonly those that are true for one passage but not the other. Both passages agree that the Wright brothers did something great that no one else was capable of at the time, which is reflected in (H). The brothers' method of inquiry, F, is discussed in Passage A only. Choices G and J are included in Passage B, but not in Passage A.

PASSAGE III

21. B

Category: Inference

Difficulty: Medium

Getting to the Answer: In lines 11–13, Julia Margaret Cameron is described as "the first woman to

have achieved eminence in photography." The other answer choices contradict information supplied in the passage.

22. F

Category: Detail

Difficulty: Low

Getting to the Answer: The answer to this question can be found in lines 82–83, "Contemporary taste much prefers her portraits...," and in lines 88–89, "today her fame rests upon her portraits...."

23. D

Category: Detail

Difficulty: High

Getting to the Answer: The dates used in the passage tell you that this is a chronological account; the author begins with Cameron's birth in 1815, tells of her marriage and then her move to England in 1848, points out that she received her first photographic equipment in 1863, describes one of her photographs from 1864, and then concludes the paragraph with her death in 1874.

24. F

Category: Vocab-in-Context

Difficulty: Medium

Getting to the Answer: The dictionary definition of *cumbersome* is "difficult to handle because of weight or bulk." Choice (F) most closely fits this definition, and it is the only answer choice that makes sense within the context of the sentence.

25. B

Category: Inference

Difficulty: Medium

Getting to the Answer: Lines 55–56 describe how Cameron "devoted herself wholly to this art," which matches (B). Choice A contradicts information from the passage, which suggests that Cameron led anything but a conventional life. Neither the money that Cameron earned as a photographer nor her religious beliefs are discussed in the passage, making C and D incorrect.

26. F

Category: Generalization

Difficulty: Medium

Getting to the Answer: Lines 60–63 say, "she produced a large body of work that stands up as one of the notable artistic achievements of the Victorian period." To say that she is "the greatest photographer who ever lived" goes beyond anything stated or implied in the passage. The third paragraph does not compare her importance as an artist during her lifetime to her importance today. The passage also does not state that she "revolutionized" any photographic methods.

27. C

Category: Detail

Difficulty: Medium

Getting to the Answer: The answer to this question can be found in lines 7–10: "photography, being a new medium outside the traditional academic framework, was wide open to women and offered them opportunities that the older fields did not…"

28. G

Category: Detail

Difficulty: Low

Getting to the Answer: These titles refer to allegorical pictures, as described in lines 78–81: "Victorian critics were particularly impressed by her allegorical pictures, many of them based on the poems of her friend and neighbor Tennyson…."

29. D

Category: Detail

Difficulty: Medium

Getting to the Answer: The answer to this question can be found in lines 82–84: "Contemporary taste much prefers her portraits and finds her narrative scenes sentimental and sometimes in bad taste."

30. F

Category: Inference

Difficulty: Low

Getting to the Answer: The author says that Cameron "achieved eminence" (line 12) in her field, that she "devoted herself wholly to this art" (lines 55–56), and that "no other woman photographer has ever enjoyed such success" (lines 74–75). Only (F) fits these descriptions.

PASSAGE IV

31. C

Category: Detail

Difficulty: Low

Getting to the Answer: For details about the eye, look at paragraph 3. Only the cornea and stenopaic pupil are relevant, eliminating A and D. But the cornea, B, is helpful underwater, not on land.

32. G

Category: Inference

Difficulty: Medium

Getting to the Answer: The eye is covered in paragraph 3. The seal's cornea improves vision in the water (note the comparison to human underwater vision), but it distorts light moving through the air. Another adaptation was then needed to *minimize* (line 53) distortion, but that doesn't mean distortion is completely eliminated, so the seal's vision in the air is distorted, (G).

33. D

Category: Detail

Difficulty: Low

Getting to the Answer: The vibrissae are discussed only in the last paragraph. They sense wave disturbances made by nearby moving fish, so (D) is correct. Choice B, by using the phrase "in the air," distorts information in the passage.

34. F

Category: Detail

Difficulty: Low

Getting to the Answer: This is stated in the second paragraph, where the seal's hearing is discussed.

35. D

Category: Detail

Difficulty: Medium

Getting to the Answer: This appears in the first paragraph, which introduces the influences on the seal's adaptations. They include that the seal "does most of its fishing at night," that "noise levels are high," and that these factors are compounded by the seal's "two habitats."

36. H

Category: Detail

Difficulty: Medium

Getting to the Answer: Locating each of these claims in the passage, you find that (H) is *suggested* (line 68) and the subject of speculation, rather than stated as fact. All of the other choices are given in support of claims.

37. A

Category: Inference

Difficulty: High

Getting to the Answer: You learn in the first paragraph that they live along the northern Atlantic and Pacific coasts. Because they live both on the land and in the water, the coastlines must be accessible. You can infer that the waters are cold rather than warm, eliminating D. Choices B and C are too broad.

38. J

Category: Detail

Difficulty: Medium

Getting to the Answer: This feature is mentioned at the end of paragraph 2. It shouldn't be confused with echolocation, which is discussed in paragraph 4 but not associated with any particular sensory organ.

39. B

Category: Function

Difficulty: Medium

Getting to the Answer: The entire passage is about how the seal's sensory organs have adapted to life on land and in the water, making (B) the best choice. Generally, you are told about differences, not similarities, between the sensory organs of humans and harbor seals, eliminating A. The relative success of human and seal adaptation to their environments isn't discussed, thus eliminating C and D.

40. G

Category: Detail

Difficulty: Medium

Getting to the Answer: In paragraph 3, we see that human corneas refract light badly in water, while the seal's corneas perform well.

SCIENCE TEST

PASSAGE I

1. B

Category: Figure Interpretation

Difficulty: Medium

Getting to the Answer: To answer this question, you have to examine the third column of the table, transmittance range. For a material to transmit light at a wavelength of 25 μm, its transmittance range—the range of wavelengths over which the material is transparent—must include 25 μm. Only potassium bromide (0.3–29 μm) and cesium iodide (0.3–70 μm) have transmittance ranges that include 25 μm, so (B) is correct.

2. F

Category: Figure Interpretation

Difficulty: Medium

Getting to the Answer: The material that contradicts this hypothesis is going to have poor chemical resistance but a transmittance range less than 10 μm. Lithium fluoride, (F), fits the bill: Its chemical resistance is poor, and its transmittance range is less than 6 μm wide. Choices G and J are wrong because both flint glass and quartz have excellent chemical resistance. Choice H is out because cesium iodide has a transmittance range nearly 70 μm wide.

3. D
Category: Scientific Reasoning
Difficulty: High
Getting to the Answer: The correct answer is a pair of materials in which the refractive index of the first material is greater than that of the second. In A, B, and C, the refractive index of the first material is less than that of the second. In (D), however, flint glass has a refractive index of 1.66 while calcium fluoride's refractive index is only 1.43. That makes (D) the correct answer.

4. J
Category: Scientific Reasoning
Difficulty: Medium
Getting to the Answer: The easiest way to answer this question is to use the first couple materials and test each hypothesis on them. Choices F and G are incorrect because the transmittance range of lithium fluoride is wider than its useful prism range. Comparing the data on lithium fluoride and calcium fluoride rules out H because transmittance range does NOT increase as useful prism range decreases. In fact, looking down the rest of the table, you see that transmittance range seems to decrease as useful prism range decreases. Choice (J) is the only one left, and the data on lithium fluoride and calcium fluoride as well as all the other materials confirm that the transmittance range is always wider than, and includes within it, the useful prism range.

5. B
Category: Figure Interpretation
Difficulty: Medium
Getting to the Answer: According to the footnote to the table, quartz infused with lead oxide is flint glass. Comparison of the properties of pure quartz

and flint glass shows that the transmittance range of flint glass is narrower than that of quartz but its refractive index is greater. This supports (B).

6. G
Category: Scientific Reasoning
Difficulty: Medium
Getting to the Answer: Begin this question by looking at the answer choices and finding the transmittance range and useful range for prisms for lithium fluoride, sodium chloride, quartz, and flint glass. A quick glance at the chart shows that the ranges for lithium flouride (for transmittance and prisms, respectively) are slightly below 6 and 2. Sodium chloride shows ranges of just under 17 and 8. Quartz has ranges of less than 3 and 2, while flint glass has ranges of less than 2 for both categories. Therefore, sodium chloride, (G), is the correct answer.

PASSAGE II

7. D
Category: Scientific Reasoning
Difficulty: High
Getting to the Answer: Begin by looking at the equation in the question. Given that osmotic pressure is already isolated on one side, using some basic rules of math will make this question go much faster. R is a constant and therefore does not factor into the answer choices. Because temperature and osmotic pressure increase together, you can eliminate roman numeral I as well as A. Statement II describes what happens to Π when M and T are inversely related. The statement says that as one goes up and the other goes down, Π remains constant. That is true: Because both M and T are on the same side of the equation, the only way to keep Π constant and still vary M and T is to have an inverse relationship between the latter two variables. Statement II is correct, so you can eliminate C. For statement III, you can look at the equation and recognize that because M, R, and T are all multiplied together,

Π must increase if even one of those increases. Because statement III is also true, (D) is correct.

8. H
Category: Scientific Reasoning
Difficulty: Medium
Getting to the Answer: Use the results of both experiments to answer this question. The answer choices all involve temperature, concentration, and solvent in different combinations. To determine whether osmotic pressure is dependent upon a variable, look for a pair of trials in which all conditions except for that variable are identical. In doing so, you see that temperature and concentration affect osmotic pressure, but solvent does not.

9. C
Category: Figure Interpretation
Difficulty: High
Getting to the Answer: Find methanol at 0.5 mol/L, which is in Table 2. The text above the table states that all the trials were conducted under the same temperature (298 K). Therefore, simply look across the row that you identified. The osmotic pressure is 12.23, (C).

10. G
Category: Scientific Reasoning
Difficulty: High
Getting to the Answer: To figure out whether or not the sucrose solution will diffuse across the membrane under the conditions described in the question, go back to the definition of osmotic pressure given in the introduction. Once the external pressure reaches the osmotic pressure, osmosis will not occur. In order for osmosis to occur, the external pressure must be less than the osmotic pressure of the solution. The solution in this question is a 0.1 mol/L aqueous sucrose solution at 298 K; those conditions correspond to an osmotic pressure of 2.45 atm. Because the external pressure is 1 atm, which is less than the osmotic pressure, osmosis will occur. From the definition of osmosis in the passage, it is clear that the solution will diffuse from the side of the membrane with a lower concentration of dissolved material, in this case pure water, to the side with a higher concentration, in this case sucrose solution. Choice (G) is correct.

11. C
Category: Figure Interpretation
Difficulty: Medium
Getting to the Answer: To determine what the scientists investigated in Experiment 1, look at what they varied and what they measured. In Experiment 1, the scientists varied the concentration and the temperature of sucrose solutions, and they measured the osmotic pressure. Therefore, they were investigating the effect of concentration and temperature on osmotic pressure, (C). Watch out for A: It states what was investigated in Experiment 2, not Experiment 1.

12. F
Category: Patterns
Difficulty: Low
Getting to the Answer: The results in Table 2 indicate that osmotic pressure doesn't depend on the solvent, as discussed in the explanation to question 6. So Statement I is a valid conclusion, and G can be eliminated. Statement II is false. The results in Table 1 indicate that osmotic pressure is dependent on concentration as well as temperature. So H can be ruled out. Now consider Statement III. It is not a valid conclusion because osmotic pressure is the pressure required to prevent osmosis, so osmosis occurs only if the external pressure is less than the osmotic pressure.

13. D
Category: Scientific Reasoning
Difficulty: Medium
Getting to the Answer: To answer questions that ask about the design of an experiment, look at what the scientists are trying to measure. You're told that osmotic pressure is the pressure required to prevent osmosis. In order to measure the osmotic pressure

of a solution, scientists need to be able to tell when osmosis begins. If you have two clear solutions with sucrose dissolved in one of them, how can you tell when there's any movement of solvent between the two of them? If the sucrose is dyed, the blue solution will become paler when osmosis starts, i.e., when solvent moves across the membrane to create an equilibrium. Therefore, (D) is correct.

PASSAGE III

14. F
Category: Figure Interpretation
Difficulty: Low
Getting to the Answer: The question refers to Experiment 3, so look at Table 3. You see that when the temperature is 85 during the day and 85 at night, the leaves have the smallest measurements. Choice (F) is correct.

15. A
Category: Scientific Reasoning
Difficulty: Low
Getting to the Answer: The question refers to Experiment 2 only, so the correct answer will involve sunlight. Table 2 shows that the average length of the leaves increased from 5.3 cm to 12.4 cm as the amount of sunlight increased from 0 to 3 hours per day. But as the amount of sunlight increased further, leaf size decreased. Therefore, D is incorrect. Neither humidity, B, nor water, C, is relevant to Experiment 2.

16. G
Category: Figure Interpretation
Difficulty: Low
Getting to the Answer: Table 1 gives leaf widths at 35% and 55% humidity at 1.8 cm and 2.0 cm, respectively. The leaf width at 40% humidity would most likely be between those two figures. Choice (G) is the only choice within that range.

17. B
Category: Scientific Reasoning
Difficulty: Medium
Getting to the Answer: All the answer choices involve humidity and sunlight, which were investigated in Experiments 1 and 2, respectively. In Table 1, leaf length and width were greatest at 75% humidity. In Table 2, they were greatest at three hours per day of sunlight. Combining those two conditions, as in (B), would probably produce the largest leaves.

18. F
Category: Scientific Reasoning
Difficulty: Medium
Getting to the Answer: This question relates to the method of the study. Each experiment begins with a statement that five groups of seedlings were used. Therefore, (F) is correct. The other choices list variables that were manipulated.

19. D
Category: Scientific Reasoning
Difficulty: High
Getting to the Answer: Choice (D) is an assumption that underlies the design of all three experiments. If the seedlings were not equally capable of further growth, then changes in leaf size and density could not be reliably attributed to researcher-controlled changes in humidity, sunlight, and temperature. Choice A is incorrect because all the seedlings were 2–3 cm tall. The seedlings' abilities to germinate, B, or to produce flowers, C, were not mentioned in the passage.

20. H
Category: Scientific Reasoning
Difficulty: Medium
Getting to the Answer: Each of the three experiments investigated a different factor related to leaf growth. To produce the most useful new data, researchers would probably vary a fourth condition. Soil mineral content would be an appropriate factor to examine. None of the other choices relate directly

to the purpose of the experiments as expressed in paragraph 1 of the passage.

PASSAGE IV

21. B

Category: Figure Interpretation

Difficulty: Medium

Getting to the Answer: According to the table, decreasing the cross-sectional area of a given wire always increases resistance, so (B) is correct. Choice C is incorrect because resistivity, displayed in the second column, is constant for each material and thus cannot be responsible for variations in resistance for any given material. Gauge varies inversely with cross-sectional area, so D is incorrect.

22. G

Category: Patterns

Difficulty: High

Getting to the Answer: Because resistance varies inversely with cross-sectional area A, as discussed in the previous explanation, the correct answer to this question must place A in the denominator. The only choice that does so is (G).

23. D

Category: Patterns

Difficulty: Medium

Getting to the Answer: Compare the choices two at a time. The wires in A and B are made of the same material and have the same cross-sectional area; only their length is different. Doubling the length doubles the resistance, so B would have a higher resistance than A. By similar reasoning, (D) would have a higher resistance than C. The only difference between B and (D) is the material. Even though the research team didn't test wire with a 0.33 mm^2 cross-sectional area, Table 1 shows that tungsten wire has higher levels of resistance than aluminum wire across all factors.

24. J

Category: Scientific Reasoning

Difficulty: Medium

Getting to the Answer: The larger circle represents 10-gauge wire; its diameter is 2.59 mm. The smaller circle has a diameter of only 1.29 mm, but it represents 16-gauge wire, so Statement I is true, and you can eliminate G and H without even checking Statements II or III. To check Statement III, the table shows that the resistance of an iron (Fe) wire is much higher than that of an aluminum (Al) wire with the same length and cross-sectional area. The first sentence of paragraph 1 defined the resistance of a conductor as "the extent to which it opposes the flow of electricity." Because iron has a higher resistance than aluminum, iron must not conduct electricity as well. Therefore, Statement III is true, and (J) is correct.

25. D

Category: Patterns

Difficulty: Medium

Getting to the Answer: The data indicate that the resistivity of a material doesn't change when wire length changes. Therefore, the graph of resistivity versus length for tungsten (or any other) wire is a horizontal line.

26. J

Category: Patterns

Difficulty: Medium

Getting to the Answer: Refer to Table 1 to see the effect that wire length has on resistance. Regardless of wire gauge, resistance increases for each material when length is increased. Choice (J) is correct.

PASSAGE V

27. A

Category: Scientific Reasoning

Difficulty: Medium

Getting to the Answer: To answer this question, you have to refer to the examples presented by the scientists to find a point of agreement. Both use the example of giraffes to show how scarcity of food and the need to reach higher and higher branches led to the evolution of long necks; thus, they both agree that environment affects evolution.

28. H

Category: Scientific Reasoning

Difficulty: Medium

Getting to the Answer: This Principle question requires that you figure out how new evidence affects the two hypotheses. To answer it, all you have to consider are the hypotheses of the two scientists. Scientist 2 believes that characteristics acquired by an individual over a lifetime are passed on to its offspring, a theory that would be supported by this finding.

29. D

Category: Scientific Reasoning

Difficulty: Low

Getting to the Answer: This question requires some reasoning. Scientist 2 states that all of the changes that occur in an individual's life can be passed on to offspring. Because he believes that any characteristic can undergo change, he must also believe that any characteristic can be inherited.

30. G

Category: Scientific Reasoning

Difficulty: Medium

Getting to the Answer: You don't need any information other than the hypothesis of Scientist 1 to answer this question. He believes that random mutations continually occur within a species as it propagates and that advantageous mutations, such as long necks on giraffes, help the species adapt to environmental changes and thus become more prevalent within the species. This is what (G) states.

31. B

Category: Scientific Reasoning

Difficulty: Low

Getting to the Answer: Here, you don't need any information other than the hypotheses of the two

scientists. The crux of their disagreement is over how evolution occurs—whether through random mutations or through the inheritance of acquired characteristics.

32. G

Category: Scientific Reasoning

Difficulty: High

Getting to the Answer: Recall that Scientist 2 states that evolution occurs through the inheritance of acquired characteristics. In order to account for humans possessing nerve endings now that were not present before the discovery of fire, Scientist 2 would have to believe that new nerve endings could be acquired during a single lifetime. Choice (G) directly contradicts this idea and would therefore refute the hypothesis.

33. A

Category: Scientific Reasoning

Difficulty: Medium

Getting to the Answer: Recall that Scientist 1 explains that evolution occurs as a result of random mutation, while Scientist 2 credits the inheritance of acquired characteristics. Choice B can then be eliminated, because it is related to the explanation of the wrong scientist. Choice C would actually refute Scientist 1's hypothesis, and D is irrelevant. Only (A) provides a valid explanation for the increase in average height based on the random mutations described by Scientist 1.

PASSAGE VII

34. G

Category: Figure Interpretation

Difficulty: Low

Getting to the Answer: According to Figure 1, Group B had the greatest number of cows infected with BSE. Group B was fed meat from scrapie-infected sheep, which matches (G).

35. D

Category: Figure Interpretation

Difficulty: Medium

Getting to the Answer: In Experiment 1, the researchers vary what is fed to the cows by giving them meat from scrapie-free sheep and from scrapie-infected sheep. The cows are later examined for signs of BSE. One common type of incorrect answer choice for Experiment questions are choices, such as B for this question, that include factors that are outside the parameters of the experiment.

36. F

Category: Figure Interpretation

Difficulty: Medium

Getting to the Answer: In Experiment 2, the researchers vary what is injected into cows' brains. Any answer choice that discusses ingestion as a focus of this experiment is incorrect. This eliminates G, H, and J. Often, incorrect answer choices for Experiment questions, such as G for this question, will include the appropriate information from the wrong experiment.

37. B

Category: Scientific Reasoning

Difficulty: Medium

Getting to the Answer: By examining the method used in a given experiment, one can determine the assumptions the researchers made in carrying out the experiment and the sources of error. Often, an error enters the experiment because of the assumptions researchers make. In Experiments 1 and 2, the researchers examined the brains of cows a year and a half after the cows were fed scrapie-infected sheep meat or were injected with scrapie-infected sheep brains. If a year and a half is not a sufficient amount of time for BSE to develop, some of the cows that were counted as not infected might have developed BSE if they had been given more time.

38. H

Category: Scientific Reasoning

Difficulty: Low

Getting to the Answer: To answer this question, you need to determine how to test whether BSE can be transmitted via scrapie-infected goats. To test this, one would compare the effects of feeding cows scrapie-free goat meat with the effects of feeding cows scrapie-infected goat meat and compare the effects of injecting cows with scrapie-free goat brains with the effects of injecting them with scrapie-infected goat brains.

39. A

Category: Scientific Reasoning

Difficulty: Medium

Getting to the Answer: Remember that control groups are used as standards of comparison. The control group used in Experiment 1 is the group that is fed scrapie-free sheep meat. If the same proportion of Group A developed BSE as that of Group B, then the researchers would not have any evidence to support the hypothesis that the ingestion of scrapie-infected sheep meat causes BSE.

40. G

Category: Scientific Reasoning

Difficulty: High

Getting to the Answer: Because the proportion of the group of cows that ate scrapie-infected sheep meat and developed BSE was greater than the proportion of the group that were injected with scrapie-infected sheep brains and developed BSE, one can conclude that a cow that eats scrapie-infected sheep meat is more likely to develop BSE than a cow that is injected with scrapie-infected sheep brains. Mere exposure to scrapie-infected sheep, as opposed to ingestion of it, is never studied in either experiment, so conclusion I can be eliminated.

WRITING TEST

MODEL ESSAY

Below is an example of what a high-scoring essay might look like. Notice that the author states her position clearly in the introductory paragraph and supports that position with evidence in the following paragraphs. This essay also uses transitions, some advanced vocabulary, and an effective "hook" to draw in the reader.

Children are often asked, "What do you want to be when you grow up?" Little do they know, whether or not they go to college has a huge impact on their career choices. The issue under discussion is whether or not schools should develop dual curricula to serve both those students who are college bound and those who intend to forego college, instead entering a career directly after high school graduation. The fundamental concern is how to best serve all students, which I believe should be through two curricula working together.

The first point of view supports having all students pursue the same curriculum, one primarily directed at college-bound students. It essentially states that an academic-only curriculum is valuable for all students, regardless of their future plans. It is true that the ability to think critically, have a wide range of content knowledge, and be adept at the skills and techniques required to live a full and productive life are important to all students. A well-rounded person is able to take advantage of many more opportunities than those with limited skills. Furthermore, should a career-bound student change his mind and decide to go to college, he will have the basic requirements for a successful college experience. However, if a student is determined to start his career directly after high school, the college curriculum could be a waste of his time, and he would be better served by taking courses that prepare him for his career. I am in partial agreement with option one, since a broad, basic education is important for all students. However, it is similarly important to prepare students for their future lives, which may begin immediately after high school.

The second option supports career-readiness education. As stated above, it is important to recognize that some students are set on a embarking on a career after high school rather than on going to college. High school is the place to prepare these students, since it can offer the courses that are most applicable to them. Furthermore, students in danger of dropping out of high school are generally those who are uninterested in or bored by the academic curriculum. Such students would be more engaged and successful if they were able to take classes that fit their goals and interests, and they would be more likely not only to stay in school but also to be well-prepared for their careers. This option purposes a dual curriculum, one for the college bound and one for career readiness, and thus provides the best education for both. On the assumption that non-college-bound students are also taking an adequate number of general education classes, and supplementing them with courses designed to provide them with the skills they need for their careers, these students will now have a solid academic foundation as well as career skills. College-bound students will still have the option to take more academic classes. Thus, I support this option because it provides the best solution for both groups.

Those who agree that students who are not planning on going to college should not be offered career-centered classes are denying the fact that not all students go to college, even if given incentives to do so.

This option does not take into consideration the numerous facts that can affect whether or not a student goes to college. Some students cannot afford college fees, even with scholarships; some have a low GPA that would prohibit their acceptance at college; and some do poorly on pre-college tests such as the ACT. Encouraging students to go to college is not enough to ensure that they will. Though it may be true that college teaches how to be productive in the workforce, it is also true that being a fully qualified mechanic or electrician after high school is extremely productive for those who choose these careers. This option is an elitist one that would disregard those for whom college is not a goal, and it is one with which I completely disagree.

It is vital to all students that high schools prepare them for their future, whatever that may be. Those who choose college are well-served by an intensive academic curriculum that gives them a solid foundation for college. On the other hand, for those who choose, or are forced by circumstances, to forego college in favor of immediate entry into the workforce, it is important that, along with a sufficient academic foundation, they also receive training in their intended careers. Thus the second perspective, that of providing both an academic and a career-oriented curriculum, serves the needs of both and is the most effective one for all students.

You can evaluate your essay and the model essay based on the following criteria, which is covered in the Scoring section of Inside the ACT Writing Test:

- Does the author discuss all three perspectives provided in the prompt?

- Is the author's own perspective clearly stated?

- Does the body of the essay assess and analyze each perspective?

- Is the relevance of each paragraph clear?

- Does the author start a new paragraph for each new idea?

- Is each sentence in a paragraph relevant to the point made in that paragraph?

- Are transitions clear?

- Is the essay easy to read? Is it engaging?

- Are sentences varied?

- Is vocabulary used effectively? Is college-level vocabulary used?

Practice Test Two

ACT Practice Test Two
ANSWER SHEET

ENGLISH TEST

1. Ⓐ Ⓑ Ⓒ Ⓓ	11. Ⓐ Ⓑ Ⓒ Ⓓ	21. Ⓐ Ⓑ Ⓒ Ⓓ	31. Ⓐ Ⓑ Ⓒ Ⓓ	41. Ⓐ Ⓑ Ⓒ Ⓓ	51. Ⓐ Ⓑ Ⓒ Ⓓ	61. Ⓐ Ⓑ Ⓒ Ⓓ	71. Ⓐ Ⓑ Ⓒ Ⓓ
2. Ⓕ Ⓖ Ⓗ Ⓙ	12. Ⓕ Ⓖ Ⓗ Ⓙ	22. Ⓕ Ⓖ Ⓗ Ⓙ	32. Ⓕ Ⓖ Ⓗ Ⓙ	42. Ⓕ Ⓖ Ⓗ Ⓙ	52. Ⓕ Ⓖ Ⓗ Ⓙ	62. Ⓕ Ⓖ Ⓗ Ⓙ	72. Ⓕ Ⓖ Ⓗ Ⓙ
3. Ⓐ Ⓑ Ⓒ Ⓓ	13. Ⓐ Ⓑ Ⓒ Ⓓ	23. Ⓐ Ⓑ Ⓒ Ⓓ	33. Ⓐ Ⓑ Ⓒ Ⓓ	43. Ⓐ Ⓑ Ⓒ Ⓓ	53. Ⓐ Ⓑ Ⓒ Ⓓ	63. Ⓐ Ⓑ Ⓒ Ⓓ	73. Ⓐ Ⓑ Ⓒ Ⓓ
4. Ⓕ Ⓖ Ⓗ Ⓙ	14. Ⓕ Ⓖ Ⓗ Ⓙ	24. Ⓕ Ⓖ Ⓗ Ⓙ	34. Ⓕ Ⓖ Ⓗ Ⓙ	44. Ⓕ Ⓖ Ⓗ Ⓙ	54. Ⓕ Ⓖ Ⓗ Ⓙ	64. Ⓕ Ⓖ Ⓗ Ⓙ	74. Ⓕ Ⓖ Ⓗ Ⓙ
5. Ⓐ Ⓑ Ⓒ Ⓓ	15. Ⓐ Ⓑ Ⓒ Ⓓ	25. Ⓐ Ⓑ Ⓒ Ⓓ	35. Ⓐ Ⓑ Ⓒ Ⓓ	45. Ⓐ Ⓑ Ⓒ Ⓓ	55. Ⓐ Ⓑ Ⓒ Ⓓ	65. Ⓐ Ⓑ Ⓒ Ⓓ	75. Ⓐ Ⓑ Ⓒ Ⓓ
6. Ⓕ Ⓖ Ⓗ Ⓙ	16. Ⓕ Ⓖ Ⓗ Ⓙ	26. Ⓕ Ⓖ Ⓗ Ⓙ	36. Ⓕ Ⓖ Ⓗ Ⓙ	46. Ⓕ Ⓖ Ⓗ Ⓙ	56. Ⓕ Ⓖ Ⓗ Ⓙ	66. Ⓕ Ⓖ Ⓗ Ⓙ	
7. Ⓐ Ⓑ Ⓒ Ⓓ	17. Ⓐ Ⓑ Ⓒ Ⓓ	27. Ⓐ Ⓑ Ⓒ Ⓓ	37. Ⓐ Ⓑ Ⓒ Ⓓ	47. Ⓐ Ⓑ Ⓒ Ⓓ	57. Ⓐ Ⓑ Ⓒ Ⓓ	67. Ⓐ Ⓑ Ⓒ Ⓓ	
8. Ⓕ Ⓖ Ⓗ Ⓙ	18. Ⓕ Ⓖ Ⓗ Ⓙ	28. Ⓕ Ⓖ Ⓗ Ⓙ	38. Ⓕ Ⓖ Ⓗ Ⓙ	48. Ⓕ Ⓖ Ⓗ Ⓙ	58. Ⓕ Ⓖ Ⓗ Ⓙ	68. Ⓕ Ⓖ Ⓗ Ⓙ	
9. Ⓐ Ⓑ Ⓒ Ⓓ	19. Ⓐ Ⓑ Ⓒ Ⓓ	29. Ⓐ Ⓑ Ⓒ Ⓓ	39. Ⓐ Ⓑ Ⓒ Ⓓ	49. Ⓐ Ⓑ Ⓒ Ⓓ	59. Ⓐ Ⓑ Ⓒ Ⓓ	69. Ⓐ Ⓑ Ⓒ Ⓓ	
10. Ⓕ Ⓖ Ⓗ Ⓙ	20. Ⓕ Ⓖ Ⓗ Ⓙ	30. Ⓕ Ⓖ Ⓗ Ⓙ	40. Ⓕ Ⓖ Ⓗ Ⓙ	50. Ⓕ Ⓖ Ⓗ Ⓙ	60. Ⓕ Ⓖ Ⓗ Ⓙ	70. Ⓕ Ⓖ Ⓗ Ⓙ	

MATHEMATICS TEST

1. Ⓐ Ⓑ Ⓒ Ⓓ Ⓔ	11. Ⓐ Ⓑ Ⓒ Ⓓ Ⓔ	21. Ⓐ Ⓑ Ⓒ Ⓓ Ⓔ	31. Ⓐ Ⓑ Ⓒ Ⓓ Ⓔ	41. Ⓐ Ⓑ Ⓒ Ⓓ Ⓔ	51. Ⓐ Ⓑ Ⓒ Ⓓ Ⓔ
2. Ⓐ Ⓑ Ⓒ Ⓓ Ⓔ	12. Ⓕ Ⓖ Ⓗ Ⓙ Ⓚ	22. Ⓕ Ⓖ Ⓗ Ⓙ Ⓚ	32. Ⓕ Ⓖ Ⓗ Ⓙ Ⓚ	42. Ⓕ Ⓖ Ⓗ Ⓙ Ⓚ	52. Ⓕ Ⓖ Ⓗ Ⓙ Ⓚ
3. Ⓐ Ⓑ Ⓒ Ⓓ Ⓔ	13. Ⓐ Ⓑ Ⓒ Ⓓ Ⓔ	23. Ⓐ Ⓑ Ⓒ Ⓓ Ⓔ	33. Ⓐ Ⓑ Ⓒ Ⓓ Ⓔ	43. Ⓐ Ⓑ Ⓒ Ⓓ Ⓔ	53. Ⓐ Ⓑ Ⓒ Ⓓ Ⓔ
4. Ⓕ Ⓖ Ⓗ Ⓙ Ⓚ	14. Ⓕ Ⓖ Ⓗ Ⓙ Ⓚ	24. Ⓕ Ⓖ Ⓗ Ⓙ Ⓚ	34. Ⓕ Ⓖ Ⓗ Ⓙ Ⓚ	44. Ⓕ Ⓖ Ⓗ Ⓙ Ⓚ	54. Ⓕ Ⓖ Ⓗ Ⓙ Ⓚ
5. Ⓐ Ⓑ Ⓒ Ⓓ Ⓔ	15. Ⓐ Ⓑ Ⓒ Ⓓ Ⓔ	25. Ⓐ Ⓑ Ⓒ Ⓓ Ⓔ	35. Ⓐ Ⓑ Ⓒ Ⓓ Ⓔ	45. Ⓐ Ⓑ Ⓒ Ⓓ Ⓔ	55. Ⓐ Ⓑ Ⓒ Ⓓ Ⓔ
6. Ⓕ Ⓖ Ⓗ Ⓙ Ⓚ	16. Ⓕ Ⓖ Ⓗ Ⓙ Ⓚ	26. Ⓕ Ⓖ Ⓗ Ⓙ Ⓚ	36. Ⓕ Ⓖ Ⓗ Ⓙ Ⓚ	46. Ⓕ Ⓖ Ⓗ Ⓙ Ⓚ	56. Ⓕ Ⓖ Ⓗ Ⓙ Ⓚ
7. Ⓐ Ⓑ Ⓒ Ⓓ Ⓔ	17. Ⓐ Ⓑ Ⓒ Ⓓ Ⓔ	27. Ⓐ Ⓑ Ⓒ Ⓓ Ⓔ	37. Ⓐ Ⓑ Ⓒ Ⓓ Ⓔ	47. Ⓐ Ⓑ Ⓒ Ⓓ Ⓔ	57. Ⓐ Ⓑ Ⓒ Ⓓ Ⓔ
8. Ⓕ Ⓖ Ⓗ Ⓙ Ⓚ	18. Ⓕ Ⓖ Ⓗ Ⓙ Ⓚ	28. Ⓕ Ⓖ Ⓗ Ⓙ Ⓚ	38. Ⓕ Ⓖ Ⓗ Ⓙ Ⓚ	48. Ⓕ Ⓖ Ⓗ Ⓙ Ⓚ	58. Ⓕ Ⓖ Ⓗ Ⓙ Ⓚ
9. Ⓐ Ⓑ Ⓒ Ⓓ Ⓔ	19. Ⓐ Ⓑ Ⓒ Ⓓ Ⓔ	29. Ⓐ Ⓑ Ⓒ Ⓓ Ⓔ	39. Ⓐ Ⓑ Ⓒ Ⓓ Ⓔ	49. Ⓐ Ⓑ Ⓒ Ⓓ Ⓔ	59. Ⓐ Ⓑ Ⓒ Ⓓ Ⓔ
10. Ⓕ Ⓖ Ⓗ Ⓙ Ⓚ	20. Ⓕ Ⓖ Ⓗ Ⓙ Ⓚ	30. Ⓕ Ⓖ Ⓗ Ⓙ Ⓚ	40. Ⓕ Ⓖ Ⓗ Ⓙ Ⓚ	50. Ⓕ Ⓖ Ⓗ Ⓙ Ⓚ	60. Ⓕ Ⓖ Ⓗ Ⓙ Ⓚ

READING TEST

1. Ⓐ Ⓑ Ⓒ Ⓓ	6. Ⓕ Ⓖ Ⓗ Ⓙ	11. Ⓐ Ⓑ Ⓒ Ⓓ	16. Ⓕ Ⓖ Ⓗ Ⓙ	21. Ⓐ Ⓑ Ⓒ Ⓓ	26. Ⓕ Ⓖ Ⓗ Ⓙ	31. Ⓐ Ⓑ Ⓒ Ⓓ	36. Ⓕ Ⓖ Ⓗ Ⓙ
2. Ⓕ Ⓖ Ⓗ Ⓙ	7. Ⓐ Ⓑ Ⓒ Ⓓ	12. Ⓕ Ⓖ Ⓗ Ⓙ	17. Ⓐ Ⓑ Ⓒ Ⓓ	22. Ⓕ Ⓖ Ⓗ Ⓙ	27. Ⓐ Ⓑ Ⓒ Ⓓ	32. Ⓕ Ⓖ Ⓗ Ⓙ	37. Ⓐ Ⓑ Ⓒ Ⓓ
3. Ⓐ Ⓑ Ⓒ Ⓓ	8. Ⓕ Ⓖ Ⓗ Ⓙ	13. Ⓐ Ⓑ Ⓒ Ⓓ	18. Ⓕ Ⓖ Ⓗ Ⓙ	23. Ⓐ Ⓑ Ⓒ Ⓓ	28. Ⓕ Ⓖ Ⓗ Ⓙ	33. Ⓐ Ⓑ Ⓒ Ⓓ	38. Ⓕ Ⓖ Ⓗ Ⓙ
4. Ⓕ Ⓖ Ⓗ Ⓙ	9. Ⓐ Ⓑ Ⓒ Ⓓ	14. Ⓕ Ⓖ Ⓗ Ⓙ	19. Ⓐ Ⓑ Ⓒ Ⓓ	24. Ⓕ Ⓖ Ⓗ Ⓙ	29. Ⓐ Ⓑ Ⓒ Ⓓ	34. Ⓕ Ⓖ Ⓗ Ⓙ	39. Ⓐ Ⓑ Ⓒ Ⓓ
5. Ⓐ Ⓑ Ⓒ Ⓓ	10. Ⓕ Ⓖ Ⓗ Ⓙ	15. Ⓐ Ⓑ Ⓒ Ⓓ	20. Ⓕ Ⓖ Ⓗ Ⓙ	25. Ⓐ Ⓑ Ⓒ Ⓓ	30. Ⓕ Ⓖ Ⓗ Ⓙ	35. Ⓐ Ⓑ Ⓒ Ⓓ	40. Ⓕ Ⓖ Ⓗ Ⓙ

SCIENCE TEST

1. Ⓐ Ⓑ Ⓒ Ⓓ	6. Ⓕ Ⓖ Ⓗ Ⓙ	11. Ⓐ Ⓑ Ⓒ Ⓓ	16. Ⓕ Ⓖ Ⓗ Ⓙ	21. Ⓐ Ⓑ Ⓒ Ⓓ	26. Ⓕ Ⓖ Ⓗ Ⓙ	31. Ⓐ Ⓑ Ⓒ Ⓓ	36. Ⓕ Ⓖ Ⓗ Ⓙ
2. Ⓕ Ⓖ Ⓗ Ⓙ	7. Ⓐ Ⓑ Ⓒ Ⓓ	12. Ⓕ Ⓖ Ⓗ Ⓙ	17. Ⓐ Ⓑ Ⓒ Ⓓ	22. Ⓕ Ⓖ Ⓗ Ⓙ	27. Ⓐ Ⓑ Ⓒ Ⓓ	32. Ⓕ Ⓖ Ⓗ Ⓙ	37. Ⓐ Ⓑ Ⓒ Ⓓ
3. Ⓐ Ⓑ Ⓒ Ⓓ	8. Ⓕ Ⓖ Ⓗ Ⓙ	13. Ⓐ Ⓑ Ⓒ Ⓓ	18. Ⓕ Ⓖ Ⓗ Ⓙ	23. Ⓐ Ⓑ Ⓒ Ⓓ	28. Ⓕ Ⓖ Ⓗ Ⓙ	33. Ⓐ Ⓑ Ⓒ Ⓓ	38. Ⓕ Ⓖ Ⓗ Ⓙ
4. Ⓕ Ⓖ Ⓗ Ⓙ	9. Ⓐ Ⓑ Ⓒ Ⓓ	14. Ⓕ Ⓖ Ⓗ Ⓙ	19. Ⓐ Ⓑ Ⓒ Ⓓ	24. Ⓕ Ⓖ Ⓗ Ⓙ	29. Ⓐ Ⓑ Ⓒ Ⓓ	34. Ⓕ Ⓖ Ⓗ Ⓙ	39. Ⓐ Ⓑ Ⓒ Ⓓ
5. Ⓐ Ⓑ Ⓒ Ⓓ	10. Ⓕ Ⓖ Ⓗ Ⓙ	15. Ⓐ Ⓑ Ⓒ Ⓓ	20. Ⓕ Ⓖ Ⓗ Ⓙ	25. Ⓐ Ⓑ Ⓒ Ⓓ	30. Ⓕ Ⓖ Ⓗ Ⓙ	35. Ⓐ Ⓑ Ⓒ Ⓓ	40. Ⓕ Ⓖ Ⓗ Ⓙ

ENGLISH TEST

45 Minutes—75 Questions

Directions: In the following five passages, certain words and phrases are underlined and numbered. In the right-hand column are alternatives for each underlined portion. Select the one that best conveys the idea, creates the most grammatically correct sentence, or is the most consistent with the style and tone of the passage. If you decide that the original version is best, select NO CHANGE. You may also find questions that ask about the entire passage or a section of the passage. These questions will correspond to small numbered boxes in the text. For these questions, decide which choice best accomplishes the purpose set out in the question stem. After you've selected the best choice, fill in the corresponding oval in your Answer Grid. For some questions, you'll need to read the context in order to answer correctly. Be sure to read until you have enough information to determine the correct answer choice.

PASSAGE I

DUKE ELLINGTON, A JAZZ GREAT

[1]

By the time Duke Ellington published his autobiography, *Music is My Mistress,* in <u>1973 he had</u> traveled
1
to dozens of countries and every continent. "I pay rent in New York City," he answered when asked of his residence.

1. **A.** NO CHANGE
   B. 1973. He had
   C. 1973, it had
   D. 1973, he had

[2]

In the 1920s, though, Ellington <u>pays</u> more than rent
2
in New York; he paid his dues on the bandstand. Having moved to Harlem from Washington, D.C., in 1923,

2. **F.** NO CHANGE
   G. paid
   H. has to pay
   J. pay

Ellington <u>established: his own</u> band and achieved criti-
3
cal recognition with a polished sound and appearance. The first New York review of the Ellingtonians in 1923 commented, "The boys look neat in dress suits and labor hard but not in vain at their music." As Ellington made

3. **A.** NO CHANGE
   B. established the following: his own
   C. established his own
   D. took the time and effort to establish his own

GO ON TO THE NEXT PAGE

a name for himself as a <u>leader arranger and pianist,</u>
                              4
his Harlem Renaissance compositions and recordings
highlighted two enduring characteristics of the man.
First, Ellington lived for jazz. Second, Harlem sustained
<u>it,</u> physically and spiritually.
5

[3]

　　　Ellington himself admitted he was not a very
<u>good pianist. As a teenager</u> in Washington. He missed
             6

more piano <u>lessons then he took</u> with his teacher, Mrs.
                   7
Clinkscales, and spent more time going to dances than
practicing the the piano.

<u>Mrs. Clinkscales was really the name of his piano</u>
                              8
<u>teacher!</u> In the clubs,
   8

<u>therefore,</u> Ellington and his friends eventually caught
    9
word of New York and the opportunities

<u>that awaited and were there for</u> young musicians.
              10
Ellington wrote, "Harlem, to our minds, did indeed have
the world's most glamorous atmosphere. We had to go
there."

4. **F.** NO CHANGE
　　G. leader arranger, and pianist,
　　H. leader, arranger, and pianist
　　J. leader, arranger, and pianist,

5. **A.** NO CHANGE
　　B. him,
　　C. them,
　　D. itself,

6. **F.** NO CHANGE
　　G. good pianist as a teenager
　　H. good pianist, a teenager
　　J. good pianist, as a teenager

7. **A.** NO CHANGE
　　B. lessons then he had taken
　　C. lessons; he took
　　D. lessons than he took

8. **F.** NO CHANGE
　　G. That was really the name of his piano teacher: Mrs. Clinkscales!
　　H. Mrs. Clinkscales was really the name of his piano teacher.
　　J. OMIT the underlined portion.

9. **A.** NO CHANGE
　　B. however
　　C. despite
　　D. then

10. **F.** NO CHANGE
　　G. awaiting and being there for
　　H. that awaited
　　J. that were there for

GO ON TO THE NEXT PAGE ⟶

He left Washington with drummer Sonny Greer. Before

they could even unpack in Harlem, though, they found

themselves penniless. Not until Ellington was lucky

enough to find fifteen dollars on the street could he

return to Washington and recollect himself.

[4]

Ellington eventually did return to Harlem, and he

achieved great success as the bandleader at the Cotton

Club from 1927 to 1932. Located in the heart of Harlem at

142nd Street and Lenox Avenue, he played at the Cotton

Club, which was frequented by top entertainers and rich

patrons. Harlem's nightlife, "cut out of a very luxurious,

royal-blue bolt of velvet," was an inspirational backdrop,

and Ellington composed, arranged, and recorded prolifi-

cally to the rave of excited critical acclaim. "Black and Tan

Fantasy," "Hot and Bothered," and "Rockin' in Rhythm"

were Ellington's early hits during this period.

13 They exhibited his unique ability to compose music

that animated both dancers in search of a good time and

improvising musicians in search of good music.

11. **A.** NO CHANGE
    B. With drummer Sonny Greer, it was Washington that he left.
    C. Leaving Washington, he, Ellington, left with drummer Sonny Greer.
    D. OMIT the underlined portion.

12. **F.** NO CHANGE
    G. he played at the Cotton Club, a club that was frequented
    H. the Cotton Club, which was frequented
    J. the Cotton Club was frequented

13. The purpose of including the names of Ellington's songs is to:
    A. provide some details about Ellington's early music.
    B. contradict an earlier point that Ellington did not create his own music.
    C. illustrate the complexity of Ellington's music.
    D. discuss the atmosphere at the Cotton Club.

Before long, the once fumbling pianist from Washington, D.C., became the undisputed leader of hot jazz in decadent Harlem. [14]

14. The purpose of paragraph 4, as it relates to the previous paragraphs, is primarily to:

    F. demonstrate how accomplished Ellington had become.

    G. suggest that Ellington did not like living in New York.

    H. remind us how difficult it is to be a musician.

    J. make us skeptical of Ellington's abilities.

Question 15 asks about the preceding passage as a whole.

---

15. The writer wishes to insert the following detail into the essay:

> The combination of fun and seriousness in his music led to critical acclaim and wide mass appeal.

The sentence would most logically be inserted into paragraph:

    A. 1, after the last sentence.

    B. 3, before the first sentence.

    C. 4, after the first sentence.

    D. 4, before the last sentence.

GO ON TO THE NEXT PAGE

PASSAGE II

COLORING AS SELF-DEFENSE IN ANIMALS

The following paragraphs may or may not be in the most logical order. Each paragraph is numbered in brackets, and question 29 will ask you to choose the appropriate order.

[1]

Some animals change <u>its</u> coloring with the seasons.
16
The ptarmigan sheds its brown plumage

<u>in winter, replacing</u> it with white feathers. The stoat,
17

a member of the<u>weasel family is known</u> as the *ermine*
18
in winter because its brown fur changes to white. The

chameleon is perhaps the most versatile of all animals

<u>having changed</u> their protective coloration. The
19
chameleon changes its color in just a few minutes to

whatever surface it happens to be sitting on.

[2]

While animals like the chameleon <u>use their</u>
20
<u>coloring</u> as a way of hiding from predators, the skunk
20
uses its distinctive white stripe as a way of standing out

from its surroundings. Far from placing it in

16. **F.** NO CHANGE

G. their

H. it's

J. there

17. **A.** NO CHANGE

B. in winter and replacing

C. in winter: replacing

D. in winter replacing

18. **F.** NO CHANGE

G. weasel family known

H. weasel family, which is known

J. weasel family, is known

19. **A.** NO CHANGE

B. who changes

C. that change

D. that changed

20. **F.** NO CHANGE

G. their use coloring

H. use coloring their

J. coloring their use

GO ON TO THE NEXT PAGE

<u>danger; the skunk's</u> visibility actually protects it.
21

By distinguishing itself from other <u>animals. The</u> skunk
22
warns its predators to avoid its infamous stink. Think
about it:

<u>the question is would your appetite be whetted by the</u>
23
<u>skunk's odor?</u>
23

[3]

Researchers <u>have been investigating</u> how animal
24
species have come to use coloring as a means of protecting themselves. One study has shown that certain
animals have glands that release special hormones, resulting in the change of skin or fur color. <u>Therefore,</u> not
25
all the animals that camouflage themselves have
these glands. The topic <u>remains and endures as</u> one of
26
the many mysteries of the natural world.

21. **A.** NO CHANGE
    B. danger, the skunk's
    C. danger; the skunks'
    D. danger, it is the skunk's

22. **F.** NO CHANGE
    G. animals, therefore, the
    H. animals because
    J. animals, the

23. **A.** NO CHANGE
    B. would your appetite be whetted by the skunk's odor?
    C. the question is as follows, would your appetite be whetted by the skunk's odor?
    D. the question is would your appetite be whetted by the odor of the skunk?

24. **F.** NO CHANGE
    G. investigated
    H. were investigating
    J. investigate

25. **A.** NO CHANGE
    B. Nevertheless,
    C. However,
    D. Finally,

26. **F.** NO CHANGE
    G. remaining and enduring as
    H. remains and endures
    J. remains

GO ON TO THE NEXT PAGE

[4]

Animals have a variety of ways of protecting themselves from enemies. Some animals adapt in shape and color to their environment. The tree frog, for example, blends perfectly into its surroundings. When it sits motionless, <u>a background of leaves completely hides the tree frog.</u>
                    27

27

<u>This camouflage enables the tree frog to hide from other</u>
                                    28
<u>animals that would be interested in eating the tree frog.</u>
                        28

27. **A.** NO CHANGE
    B. the tree frog is completely hidden in a background of leaves.
    C. completely hidden is the tree frog in a background of leaves.
    D. a background of leaves and the tree frog are completely hidden.

28. **F.** NO CHANGE
    G. This camouflage enables the tree frog to hide from predators.
    H. This camouflage enables the tree frog to hide from other animals interested in eating the tree frog.
    J. OMIT the underlined portion.

Questions 29–30 ask about the preceding passage as a whole.

---

29. What would be the most logical order of paragraphs for this essay?
    A. 3, 1, 4, 2
    B. 1, 2, 4, 3
    C. 4, 1, 2, 3
    D. 2, 1, 3, 4

30. Suppose the author had been asked to write an essay on how animals use their coloring to protect themselves in the wild. Would this essay meet the requirement?
    F. Yes, because the author covers several aspects of how animals use their coloring to protect themselves.
    G. Yes, because the author thoroughly investigates how one animal protects itself with its coloring.
    H. No, because the author does not consider animals that exist in the wild.
    J. No, because the author does not include information from research studies.

GO ON TO THE NEXT PAGE ▷

PASSAGE III

THE HISTORY OF CHOCOLATE

The word *chocolate* is used to describe a variety of <u>foods made</u> from the beans of the cacao tree. The first
31
people known to have made chocolate were the

<u>Aztecs, a people who used</u> cacao seeds to make a bit-
32
ter but tasty drink. However, it was not until Hernan

Cortez's exploration of Mexico in

<u>1519. That</u> Europeans first learned of chocolate.
33
Cortez came to the New World in search of gold,

but his interest was also fired by the Aztecs' strange

drink. When Cortez returned to Spain, his ship's cargo

<u>included and held</u> three chests of cacao beans. It was
34
from these beans that Europe experienced its first

taste

of what <u>seemed to be</u> a very unusual beverage. The
35
drink soon became popular among those people

wealthy enough to afford it.

31. **A.** NO CHANGE
    B. foods, which are made
    C. foods and made
    D. foods and are

32. **F.** NO CHANGE
    G. Aztecs, and they used
    H. Aztecs a people that use
    J. Aztecs, who used

33. **A.** NO CHANGE
    B. 1519 that
    C. 1519, that
    D. 1519:

34. **F.** NO CHANGE
    G. included, held
    H. included
    J. including and holding

35. **A.** NO CHANGE
    B. seems to be
    C. seemingly is
    D. seemed being

GO ON TO THE NEXT PAGE

<u>Over the next century cafes specializing</u> in chocolate
36
drinks began to appear throughout Europe. ⬚37⬚

36. **F.** NO CHANGE
    G. Over the next century cafes specialize
    H. Over the next century, cafes specializing
    J. Over the next century, there were cafes specializing

37. The author is considering the addition of another sentence here that briefly describes one of the first European cafes to serve a chocolate drink. This addition would:
    A. weaken the author's argument.
    B. provide some interesting details.
    C. contradict the topic of the paragraph.
    D. highlight the author's opinion of chocolate.

Of course, chocolate is very popular today. People all over the world enjoy <u>chocolate bars chocolate sprinkles and even chocolate soda.</u>
38

38. **F.** NO CHANGE
    G. chocolate, bars, chocolate, sprinkles, and even chocolate soda.
    H. chocolate bars chocolate sprinkles— even chocolate soda.
    J. chocolate bars, chocolate sprinkles, and even chocolate soda.

<u>In fact</u>, Asia has cultivated the delicacy of chocolate-
39
covered ants! People enjoy this food as a snack at the movies or sporting events. The chocolate ant phenomenon has yet to take over America,

<u>but enjoy their chocolate Americans do</u> nonetheless.
40

39. **A.** NO CHANGE
    B. Unfortunately
    C. In spite of this
    D. The truth is

40. **F.** NO CHANGE
    G. but Americans enjoy their chocolate
    H. but enjoy their chocolate is what Americans do
    J. but Americans do enjoy their chocolate

Many chocolate lovers around the world were ecstatic to hear that chocolate may actually be good for you. Researchers

GO ON TO THE NEXT PAGE ⟩

<u>say: chocolate contains</u> a chemical that could prevent
                    41
cancer and heart disease. New research measures the

amount of catechins, the chemical thought to be behind

the benefits, in different types of chocolate.

<u>The substance is also found in tea.</u> The studies show
                    42
that chocolate is very high in catechins. The research is

likely to be welcomed

<u>by those</u> with a sweet tooth, although dentists
  43

<u>may less be pleased.</u>
        44

41. **A.** NO CHANGE
    B. have said the following: chocolate contains
    C. say that chocolate contains
    D. say: chocolate contained

42. **F.** NO CHANGE
    G. Another place where the substance is found is tea.
    H. Also, tea contains the substance.
    J. OMIT the underlined portion.

43. **A.** NO CHANGE
    B. with them
    C. by us
    D. to those

44. **F.** NO CHANGE
    G. pleased less they will be.
    H. may be pleased less.
    J. may be less pleased.

Question 45 asks about the preceding passage as a whole.

45. Suppose the author had been given the assignment of writing about culinary trends in history. Would this essay satisfy the requirement?

    A. Yes, because the essay discusses many culinary trends in history.
    B. Yes, because the essay shows how chocolate has been used over time.
    C. No, because the essay focuses too much on chocolate in present times.
    D. No, because the essay only covers chocolate.

GO ON TO THE NEXT PAGE

PASSAGE IV

THE MILITARY UNIFORM OF THE FUTURE

[1]

Scientists, in programs <u>administers by</u> the United
₄₆
States Army, are experimenting to develop the military

uniform of the future. As imagined, it

<u>would be light as silk, bulletproof, and able to</u> rapidly
₄₇
change at the molecular level to adapt to biological or

chemical threats. In response to a detected anthrax

threat, for example, it would become an impermeable

shield. The pant leg of a

<u>soldier who's</u> leg had been broken
₄₈

<u>would have been</u> able to morph into a
₄₉

<u>splint, or, even form</u> an artificial muscle. Nanosensors
₅₀
would transmit vital signs back to a medical team or

monitor the breath for increased nitric oxide, a sign of

stress.

[2]

The especially promising Invisible Soldier program

aims to make the long-held dream of human invisibility

a reality by using

46. **F.** NO CHANGE
    G. administering by
    H. administered by
    J. administers with

47. **A.** NO CHANGE
    B. would: be light as silk, bulletproof, and able to
    C. would be light as silk bulletproof and able to
    D. light as silk, bulletproof, and was able to

48. **F.** NO CHANGE
    G. soldier whose
    H. soldier, who's
    J. soldier that's

49. **A.** NO CHANGE
    B. would be
    C. will have been
    D. is

50. **F.** NO CHANGE
    G. splint or even form
    H. splint, or even, form
    J. splint or, even, form

GO ON TO THE NEXT PAGE ▷

technology. To create a covering capable of
51

concealing a soldier and making him invisible from
52
most wavelengths of visible light. [53] [54]

51. **A.** NO CHANGE
    B. technology to create
    C. technology, which were creating
    D. technology; create

52. **F.** NO CHANGE
    G. making a soldier invisible and concealing him
    H. concealing a soldier making that soldier invisible
    J. concealing a soldier

53. The writer's description of the U.S. Army's Invisible Soldier program seems to indicate that the army's opinion of the program is:
    A. skeptical.
    B. curious.
    C. enthusiastic.
    D. detailed.

54. What is the purpose of this paragraph, as it relates to the rest of the essay?
    F. To highlight one of the successes of the scientists' programs
    G. To predict the future of U.S. military uniforms
    H. To outline what will follow in the essay
    J. To introduce a specific example of the uniform of the future

[3]

A solution proposed in the early stages near the
55
beginning of the program's development was to construct
55
a suit or cape from fabric linked to sensors that could

detect the coloring and pattern of the background. The

sensors would then send varying intensities of electrical

current to the appropriate areas of the fabric,

55. **A.** NO CHANGE
    B. beginning and the early stages of
    C. early stages of
    D. OMIT the underlined portion.

GO ON TO THE NEXT PAGE

<u>they</u> would be impregnated with chemicals sensitive to
56
electricity. The coveralls would change colors continu-

ally as the soldier moved.

[4]

The problem with this solution from a military

standpoint, <u>you know, is</u>
57

<u>power: the fact that the suit</u> would require a continuous
58
flow of electricity means that a soldier would have to

carry a large number of batteries, which would hardly

contribute to ease of movement and camouflage.

[5]

[1] To address this problem, Army researchers have

developed a new kind of color-changing pixel, known as

the intererometric modulator or i-mod. [2] The research-

ers hope that a flexible suit made of i-mod pixels could

completely blend into any background. [3] In addition to

matching a background, the pixels could also be set to show

other colors, for example, a camouflage mode that would

render a soldier effectively invisible in the forest and a flash

mode that would enhance a soldier's visibility in a rescue

situation. [4] Changing the distance between the mirrors

changes the color of the light that they reflect. [5] Each i-

mod pixel is made up of a pair of tiny mirrors. 59

56. F. NO CHANGE
G. that
H. it
J. which

57. A. NO CHANGE
B. is, like,
C. however, is
D. therefore, is

58. F. NO CHANGE
G. power; the fact that the suit
H. power the fact that the suit
J. power the fact that, the suit

59. Which of the following sequences would make paragraph 5 most logical?
A. 2, 4, 5, 3, 1
B. 2, 3, 1, 5, 4
C. 1, 4, 5, 2, 3
D. 1, 5, 4, 2, 3

GO ON TO THE NEXT PAGE

Question 60 asks about the preceding passage as a whole.

60. The writer wishes to insert the following material into the passage:

> When H.G. Wells wrote *The Invisible Man*, there was no interest in camouflaging soldiers; the British army was garbed in bright red uniforms. Since that time, governments have learned the value of making soldiers difficult to see, first by using camouflage fabrics, and today by envisioning something even more effective that would change color to match the terrain.

The new material would most logically be placed in paragraph:

F. 2.

G. 3.

H. 4.

J. 5.

PASSAGE V

CALIFORNIA: A STATE BUILT ON DREAMS

It lasted fewer than 10 years, but when it was over, the United States had been radically and forever changed. The population had exploded on the West Coast of the country, <u>fortunes had been made and those same fortunes were lost,</u> and a new state had entered the
61
union—a state that would become a state of mind for all

Americans: California.
62

The United States <u>acquiring</u> the territory that would
63
later become California during the Mexican War (1846–1848). One of the many settlers who traveled to

the new territory was <u>John Sutter who was a shopkeeper</u>
64
from Switzerland who had left behind his wife, his children, and his debts, in search of a new life.

61. **A.** NO CHANGE
   B. fortunes had been made and lost,
   C. fortunes, which had been made, were then lost,
   D. made and lost were fortunes,

62. **F.** NO CHANGE
   G. Americans, and that place was called California.
   H. Americans, California.
   J. Americans. California.

63. **A.** NO CHANGE
   B. has acquired
   C. is acquiring
   D. acquired

64. **F.** NO CHANGE
   G. John Sutter, a shopkeeper
   H. John Sutter; a shopkeeper
   J. John Sutter, who was a shopkeeper

GO ON TO THE NEXT PAGE ⇨

<u>Hired he did</u> a carpenter named James Marshall to build
   65
a sawmill for him on the American River in the foothills

of the Sierra Nevada mountains.

65. **A.** NO CHANGE
   B. He hired
   C. Hiring
   D. He did hire

On January 24, 1848, <u>while inspecting the mill's</u>
   66
<u>runoff into the river</u>, Marshall saw two shiny objects be-
   66
low the surface of the water. He took the nuggets to Sut-

ter, who was annoyed by the discovery; Sutter didn't

want <u>them</u> mill workers distracted by gold fever.
   67

66. **F.** NO CHANGE
   G. (he was inspecting the mill's runoff into the river)
   H. inspecting the mill's runoff into the river all the while
   J. OMIT the underlined portion.

67. **A.** NO CHANGE
   B. this
   C. his
   D. there

<u>Keeping the discovery</u> quiet for a while, but then he
   68
couldn't resist bragging about it. Word got out, and

workers began quitting their jobs and heading into the

hills to look for the source of the gold that had washed

down the river.

[69] Thousands of people poured into California in

search of fortune and glory.

68. **F.** NO CHANGE
   G. The discovery he was keeping
   H. He kept the discovery
   J. Keeps he the discovery

69. Which of the following would provide the best transition here, guiding the reader from the topic of the previous paragraph to the new topic of this paragraph?
   A. Sutter and Marshall did not make a profit.
   B. The gold rush had officially begun.
   C. Can you image how a small discovery led to such a large state?
   D. Most of the "gold" turned out to be a hoax.

GO ON TO THE NEXT PAGE ⟹

This is similar to recent stock market increases. Dur-
70
ing the two years after Marshall's discovery, more than

90,000 people made their way to California, looking for

gold. In fact, so many people moved West in just

singularly one of those years, 1849, that all the prospec-
71
tors, regardless of when they arrived, became known as

Forty-niners. By 1850, so many people had moved to

the California territory that the United States Congress

was forced to declare it a new state. In 1854, the popula-

tion had increased by another 300,000 people. In fact, 1
72
out of every 90 people then living in the United States

was living in California.

Even after all of the gold had been taken from the

ground, California remained a magical place in the

American imagination. The 31st state had become a

place that lives could change, fortunes could be made,
73
and dreams could come true. For many

people, and California is still such a place.
74

70. **F.** NO CHANGE
G. The rush for gold was similar to recent stock market increases.
H. This was similar to recent stock market increases.
J. OMIT the underlined portion.

71. **A.** NO CHANGE
B. one
C. one and only one
D. singular

72. **F.** NO CHANGE
G. In spite of this,
H. Believe it or not,
J. Therefore,

73. **A.** NO CHANGE
B. where
C. through which
D. in

74. **F.** NO CHANGE
G. Forty-niners, California
H. people and California
J. people, California

GO ON TO THE NEXT PAGE

Question 75 asks about the preceding passage as a whole.

75. Suppose the writer had been assigned to write a brief essay detailing the life of a Forty-niner during the California gold rush. Would this essay successfully fulfill the assignment?

    A. Yes, because the essay tells about the lives of John Sutter and James Marshall.

    B. No, because the essay covers a historical rather than biographical perspective of the gold rush.

    C. Yes, because one can imagine the life of a Forty-niner from the details provided in the essay.

    D. No, because the essay does not discuss Forty-niners.

MATHEMATICS TEST

60 Minutes—60 Questions

Directions: Solve each of the following problems, select the correct answer, and then fill in the corresponding space on your answer sheet.

Don't linger over problems that are too time-consuming. Do as many as you can, then come back to the others in the time you have remaining.

The use of a calculator is permitted on this test. Though you are allowed to use your calculator to solve any questions you choose, some of the questions may be most easily answered without the use of a calculator.

Note: Unless otherwise noted, all of the following should be assumed.

1. Illustrative figures are *not* necessarily drawn to scale.
2. All geometric figures lie in a plane.
3. The term *line* indicates a straight line.
4. The term *average* indicates arithmetic mean.

1. The regular price for a certain bicycle is $125.00. If that price is reduced by 20%, what is the new price?

   A. $100.00
   B. $105.00
   C. $112.50
   D. $120.00
   E. $122.50

2. If $x = -5$, then $2x^2 - 6x + 5 = ?$

   F. −15
   G. 15
   H. 25
   J. 85
   K. 135

3. How many distinct prime factors does the number 36 have?

   A. 2
   B. 3
   C. 4
   D. 5
   E. 6

4. In the following figure, what is the value of x ?

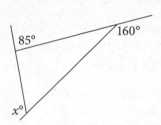

   F. 105°
   G. 115°
   H. 135°
   J. 245°
   K. 255°

5. What is the average of $\frac{1}{20}$ and $\frac{1}{30}$?

   A. $\frac{1}{25}$

   B. $\frac{1}{24}$

   C. $\frac{2}{25}$

   D. $\frac{1}{12}$

   E. $\frac{1}{6}$

GO ON TO THE NEXT PAGE

6. The toll for driving a segment of a certain freeway is $1.50 plus 25 cents for each mile traveled. Joy paid a $25 toll for driving a segment of the freeway. How many miles did she travel?

   F.   10
   G.   75
   H.   94
   J.   96
   K.   100

7. For all x, the product $3x^2 \times 5x^3 = ?$

   A. $8x^5$
   B. $8x^6$
   C. $15x^5$
   D. $15x^6$
   E. $15x^8$

8. How many units apart are the points $P(-1,-2)$ and $Q(2,2)$ in the standard (x,y) coordinate plane?

   F.   2
   G.   3
   H.   4
   J.   5
   K.   6

9. In a group of 25 students, 16 are female. What percentage of the group is female?

   A.   16%
   B.   40%
   C.   60%
   D.   64%
   E.   75%

10. For how many integer values of x will $\dfrac{7}{x}$ be greater than $\dfrac{1}{4}$ and less than $\dfrac{1}{3}$?

    F.   6
    G.   7
    H.   12
    J.   28
    K.   Infinitely many

11. Which of the following is a polynomial factor of $6x^2 - 13x + 6$?

    A. $2x + 3$
    B. $3x - 2$
    C. $3x + 2$
    D. $6x - 2$
    E. $6x + 2$

12. What is the value of a if $\dfrac{1}{a} + \dfrac{2}{a} + \dfrac{3}{a} + \dfrac{4}{a} = 5$?

    F. $\dfrac{1}{2}$
    G.   2
    H.   4
    J. $12\dfrac{1}{2}$
    K.   50

GO ON TO THE NEXT PAGE

13. In the following figure, $\overline{AD}$, $\overline{BE}$, and $\overline{CF}$ all intersect at point G. If the measure of $\angle AGB$ is 40° and the measure of $\angle CGE$ is 105°, what is the measure of $\angle AGF$?

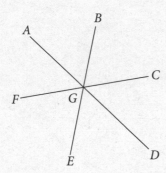

   A. 35°

   B. 45°

   C. 55°

   D. 65°

   E. 75°

14. Which of the following is the solution statement for the inequality $-3 < 4x - 5$?

   F. $x > -2$

   G. $x > \dfrac{1}{2}$

   H. $x < -2$

   J. $x < \dfrac{1}{2}$

   K. $x < 2$

15. In the following figure, $\overline{BD}$ bisects $\angle ABC$. The measure of $\angle ABC$ is 100°, and the measure of $\angle BAD$ is 60°. What is the measure of $\angle BDC$?

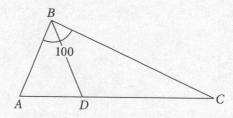

   A. 80°

   B. 90°

   C. 100°

   D. 110°

   E. 120°

16. If $x + 2y - 3 = xy$, where x and y are positive, then which of the following equations expresses y in terms of x?

   F. $y = \dfrac{3 - x}{2 - x}$

   G. $y = \dfrac{3 - x}{x - 2}$

   H. $y = \dfrac{x - 3}{2 - x}$

   J. $y = \dfrac{x - 2}{x - 3}$

   K. $y = \dfrac{6 - x}{x - 2}$

17. In a group of 50 students, 28 speak English and 37 speak Spanish. If everyone in the group speaks at least one of the two languages, how many speak both English and Spanish?

   A. 11

   B. 12

   C. 13

   D. 14

   E. 15

GO ON TO THE NEXT PAGE

18. A car travels 288 miles in 6 hours. At that rate, how many miles will it travel in 8 hours ?

    F. 216

    G. 360

    H. 368

    J. 376

    K. 384

19. When $\frac{4}{11}$ is written as a decimal, what is the 100th digit after the decimal point?

    A. 3

    B. 4

    C. 5

    D. 6

    E. 7

20. What is the solution for x in the following system of equations?

    $$3x + 4y = 31$$
    $$3x - 4y = -1$$

    F. 4

    G. 5

    H. 6

    J. 9

    K. 10

21. In the standard (x,y) coordinate plane, points P and Q have coordinates $(2,3)$ and $(12,-15)$, respectively. What are the coordinates of the midpoint of $\overline{PQ}$?

    A. $(6,-12)$

    B. $(6,-9)$

    C. $(6,-6)$

    D. $(7,-9)$

    E. $(7,-6)$

22. In the following figure, $\angle B$ is a right angle, and the measure of $\angle C$ is θ. What is the value of $\cos \theta$?

    F. $\frac{3}{4}$

    G. $\frac{3}{5}$

    H. $\frac{4}{5}$

    J. $\frac{5}{4}$

    K. $\frac{4}{3}$

23. In the following figure, the circle centered at P is tangent to the circle centered at Q. Point Q is on the circumference of circle P. If the circumference of circle P is 6 inches, what is the circumference, in inches, of circle Q ?

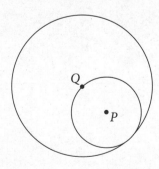

    A. 12

    B. 24

    C. 36

    D. 12π

    E. 36π

GO ON TO THE NEXT PAGE

24. If $f(x) = x^3 - x^2 - x$, what is the value of $f(-3)$?

    F. −39
    G. −33
    H. −21
    J. −15
    K.   0

25. If the lengths, in inches, of all three sides of a triangle are integers, and one side is 4 inches long, what is the least possible perimeter of the triangle, in inches?

    A.   6
    B.   8
    C.   9
    D. 12
    E. 16

26. What is the complete factorization of $2x + 3x^2 + x^3$?

    F. $x(x^2 + 2)$
    G. $x(x - 2)(x + 3)$
    H. $x(x - 1)(x + 2)$
    J. $x(x + 1)(x + 2)$
    K. $x(x + 2)(x + 3)$

27. If $xyz \neq 0$, which of the following is equivalent to $\dfrac{x^2 y^3 z^4}{\left(xyz^2\right)^2}$?

    A. $\dfrac{1}{y}$
    B. $\dfrac{1}{z}$
    C. y
    D. $\dfrac{x}{yz}$
    E. xyz

28. As a decimal, what is the sum of $\dfrac{2}{3}$ and $\dfrac{1}{12}$?

    F. 0.2
    G. 0.5
    H. 0.75
    J. 0.833
    K. 0.875

29. The formula for converting a Fahrenheit temperature reading to Celsius is $C = \dfrac{5}{9}(F - 32)$, where C is the reading in degrees Celsius and F is the reading in degrees Fahrenheit. Which of the following is the Fahrenheit equivalent to a reading of 95° Celsius?

    A.   35°F
    B.   53°F
    C.   63°F
    D. 203°F
    E. 207°F

30. A jar contains 4 green marbles, 5 red marbles, and 11 white marbles. If 1 marble is chosen at random, what is the probability that it will be green?

    F. $\dfrac{1}{3}$
    G. $\dfrac{1}{4}$
    H. $\dfrac{1}{5}$
    J. $\dfrac{1}{16}$
    K. $\dfrac{5}{15}$

GO ON TO THE NEXT PAGE

31. What is the average of the expressions $2x + 5$, $5x - 6$, and $-4x + 2$?

A. $x + \dfrac{1}{3}$

B. $x + 1$

C. $3x + \dfrac{1}{3}$

D. $3x + 3$

E. $3x + 3\dfrac{1}{3}$

32. The line that passes through the points $(1,1)$ and $(2,16)$ in the standard (x,y) coordinate plane is parallel to the line that passes through the points $(-10,-5)$ and $(a,25)$. What is the value of a ?

F. -8

G. 3

H. 5

J. 15

K. 20

33. In the following figure, $\overline{QS}$ and $\overline{PT}$ are parallel, and the lengths of $\overline{QR}$ and $\overline{PQ}$, in units, are as marked. If the perimeter of $\triangle QRS$ is 11 units, how many units long is the perimeter of $\triangle PRT$?

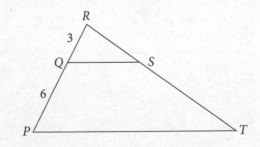

A. 22

B. 33

C. 66

D. 88

E. 99

34. The figure shown belongs in which of the following classifications?

I. Polygon
II. Quadrilateral
III. Rectangle
IV. Trapezoid

F. I only

G. II only

H. IV only

J. I, II, and III only

K. I, II, and IV only

35. If one solution to the equation $2x^2 + (a - 4)x - 2a = 0$ is $x = -3$, what is the value of a ?

A. 0

B. 2

C. 4

D. 6

E. 12

36. A menu offers 4 choices for the first course, 5 choices for the second course, and 3 choices for dessert. How many different meals, consisting of a first course, a second course, and a dessert, can one choose from this menu?

F. 12

G. 24

H. 30

J. 36

K. 60

GO ON TO THE NEXT PAGE

37. If an integer is divisible by 6 and by 9, then the integer must be evenly divisible by which of the following?

      I. 12

     II. 18

    III. 36

A. I only

B. II only

C. I and II only

D. I, II, and III

E. None

38. For all $x \neq 0$, $\dfrac{x^2 + x^2 + x^2}{x^2} = ?$

F. 3

G. $3x$

H. x^2

J. x^3

K. x^4

39. Joan has q quarters, d dimes, n nickels, and no other coins in her pocket. Which of the following represents the total number of coins in Joan's pocket?

A. $q + d + n$

B. $5q + 2d + n$

C. $0.25q + 0.10d + 0.05n$

D. $(25 + 10 + 5)(q + d + n)$

E. $25q + 10d + 5n$

40. Which of the following graphs represents the solutions for x of the inequality
$5x - 2(1 - x) \geq 4(x + 1)$?

F. ◄─┼─┼─⊕─┼─┼─┼─┼─┼─►
      −4 −3 −2 −1 0 1 2 3 4

G. ◄─┼─┼─●─┼─┼─┼─┼─┼─►
      −4 −3 −2 −1 0 1 2 3 4

H. ◄═══●─┼─┼─┼─┼─┼─►
      −4 −3 −2 −1 0 1 2 3 4

J. ◄═══════⊕─┼─┼─►
      −4 −3 −2 −1 0 1 2 3 4

K. ◄─┼─┼─┼─┼─┼─●─┼─┼─►
      −4 −3 −2 −1 0 1 2 3 4

41. In the standard (x,y) coordinate plane, line m is perpendicular to the line containing the points $(5,6)$ and $(6,10)$. What is the slope of line m ?

A. -4

B. $-\dfrac{1}{4}$

C. $\dfrac{1}{4}$

D. 4

E. 8

GO ON TO THE NEXT PAGE ▷

42. In the right triangle below, $\sin \theta = ?$

F. $\dfrac{5}{13}$

G. $\dfrac{5}{12}$

H. $\dfrac{12}{13}$

J. $\dfrac{13}{12}$

K. $\dfrac{13}{5}$

43. If $9^{2x-1} = 3^{3x+3}$, then $x = ?$

A. -4

B. $-\dfrac{7}{4}$

C. $-\dfrac{10}{7}$

D. 2

E. 5

44. From 1970 through 1980, the population of City Q increased by 20%. From 1980 through 1990, the population increased by 30%. What was the combined percent increase for the period 1970–1990 ?

F. 25%

G. 26%

H. 36%

J. 50%

K. 56%

45. Martin's average score after four tests is 89. What score on the fifth test would bring Martin's average up to exactly 90 ?

A. 90

B. 91

C. 92

D. 93

E. 94

46. Which of the following is an equation for the circle in the standard (x,y) coordinate plane that has its center at $(-1,-1)$ and passes through the point $(7,5)$?

F. $(x - 1)^2 + (y - 1)^2 = 10$

G. $(x + 1)^2 + (y + 1)^2 = 10$

H. $(x - 1)^2 + (y - 1)^2 = 12$

J. $(x - 1)^2 + (y - 1)^2 = 100$

K. $(x + 1)^2 + (y + 1)^2 = 100$

47. Which of the following is an equation for the graph in the following standard (x,y) coordinate plane?

A. $y = -2x + 1$

B. $y = x + 1$

C. $y = x + 2$

D. $y = 2x + 1$

E. $y = 2x + 2$

GO ON TO THE NEXT PAGE

48. What is $\frac{1}{4}$% of 16 ?

    F. 0.004

    G. 0.04

    H. 0.4

    J.   4

    K. 64

49. For all s, $(s + 4)(s - 4) + (2s + 2)(s - 2) = ?$

    A. $s^2 - 2s - 20$

    B. $3s^2 - 12$

    C. $3s^2 - 2s - 20$

    D. $3s^2 + 2s - 20$

    E. $5s^2 - 2s - 20$

50. Which of the following is an equation of the parabola graphed in the following (x, y) coordinate plane?

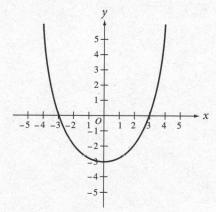

    F. $y = \dfrac{x^2}{3} - 3$

    G. $y = \dfrac{x^2 - 3}{3}$

    H. $y = \dfrac{x^2}{3} + 3$

    J. $y = \dfrac{x^2 + 3}{3}$

    K. $y = 3x^2 - 3$

51. In the following figure, $\sin a = \dfrac{4}{5}$. What is $\cos b$?

    A. $\dfrac{3}{4}$

    B. $\dfrac{3}{5}$

    C. $\dfrac{4}{5}$

    D. $\dfrac{5}{4}$

    E. $\dfrac{4}{3}$

52. For all $x \neq 0, \dfrac{x^2 + x^2 + x^2}{x} = ?$

    F. $3x$

    G. x^3

    H. x^5

    J. x^7

    K. $2x^2 + x$

53. One can determine a student's score S on a certain test by dividing the number of wrong answers (w) by 4 and subtracting the result from the number of right answers (r). This relation is expressed by which of the following formulas?

    A. $S = \dfrac{r - w}{4}$

    B. $S = r - \dfrac{w}{4}$

    C. $S = \dfrac{r}{4} - w$

    D. $S = 4r - w$

    E. $S = r - 4w$

GO ON TO THE NEXT PAGE ▷

54. What is the volume, in cubic inches, of the cylinder shown in the following figure?

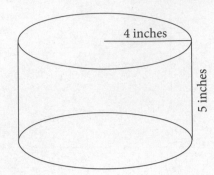

4 inches

5 inches

- **F.** 20π
- **G.** 40π
- **H.** 60π
- **J.** 80π
- **K.** 100π

55. In the following figure, $\overline{AB}$ is perpendicular to $\overline{BC}$. The lengths of $\overline{AB}$ and $\overline{BC}$, in inches, are given in terms of x. Which of the following represents the area of $\triangle ABC$, in square inches, for all $x > 1$?

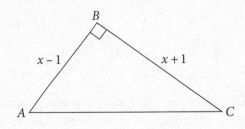

B

x − 1   x + 1

A   C

- **A.** x
- **B.** $2x$
- **C.** x^2
- **D.** $x^2 - 1$
- **E.** $\dfrac{x^2 - 1}{2}$

56. In 1990, the population of Town A was 9,400 and the population of Town B was 7,600. Starting then, each year the population of Town A decreased by 100, and the population of Town B increased by 100. In what year were the two populations equal?

- **F.** 1998
- **G.** 1999
- **H.** 2000
- **J.** 2008
- **K.** 2009

57. In a certain club, the average age of the male members is 35, and the average age of the female members is 25. If 20% of the members are male, what is the average age of all the club members?

- **A.** 26
- **B.** 27
- **C.** 28
- **D.** 29
- **E.** 30

GO ON TO THE NEXT PAGE

58. To determine the height h of a tree, Roger stands b feet from the base of the tree and measures the angle of elevation to be θ, as shown in the following figure. Which of the following relates h and b ?

F. $\sin\theta = \dfrac{h}{b}$

G. $\sin\theta = \dfrac{b}{h}$

H. $\sin\theta = \dfrac{b}{\sqrt{b^2 + h^2}}$

J. $\sin\theta = \dfrac{h}{\sqrt{b^2 + h^2}}$

K. $\sin\theta = \dfrac{\sqrt{b^2 + h^2}}{b}$

59. The formula for the lateral surface area S of a right circular cone is $S = \pi r\sqrt{r^2 + h^2}$, where r is the radius of the base and h is the altitude. What is the lateral surface area, in square feet, of a right circular cone with base radius 3 feet and altitude 4 feet?

A. $3\pi\sqrt{5}$

B. $3\pi\sqrt{7}$

C. 15π

D. 21π

E. $\dfrac{75\pi}{2}$

60. In the following figure, line t crosses parallel lines m and n. Which of the following statements must be true?

F. $a = b$

G. $a = d$

H. $b = e$

J. $c = g$

K. $d = g$

IF YOU FINISH BEFORE TIME IS CALLED, YOU MAY CHECK YOUR WORK ON THIS SECTION ONLY. DO NOT TURN TO ANY OTHER SECTION IN THE TEST. **STOP**

READING TEST

35 Minutes—40 Questions

Directions: There are four passages in this test. Each passage is followed by several questions. After reading a passage, choose the best answer to each question and fill in the corresponding oval on your Answer Grid. You may refer to the passages as often as necessary.

PASSAGE I

PROSE FICTION

This passage is adapted from Bleak House, *by Charles Dickens, which was first published in 1853. In this excerpt, Esther recounts some of her childhood experiences.*

I can remember, when I was a very little girl indeed, I used to say to my doll when we were alone together, "Now, Dolly, I am not
Line clever, you know very well, and you must be
(5) patient with me, like a dear!"

…My dear old doll! I was such a shy little thing that I seldom dared to open my lips, and never dared to open my heart, to anybody else. It almost makes me cry
(10) to think what a relief it used to be to me when I came home from school of a day to run upstairs to my room and say, "Oh, you dear faithful Dolly, I knew you would be expecting me!" and then to sit down on
(15) the floor, leaning on the elbow of her great chair, and tell her all I had noticed since we parted…

I was brought up, from my earliest remembrance—like some of the princesses
(20) in the fairy stories, only I was not charming—by my godmother. At least, I only knew her as such. She was a good, good woman! She went to church three times every Sunday, and to morning prayers on
(25) Wednesdays and Fridays, and to lectures whenever there were lectures, and never missed. She was handsome; and if she had ever smiled, would have been (I used to think) like an angel—but she never smiled.
(30) She was always grave and strict. She was so very good herself, I thought, that the

badness of other people made her frown all her life. It made me very sorry to consider how good she was and how unworthy of
(35) her I was, and I used ardently to hope that I might have a better heart; and I talked it over very often with the dear old doll, but I never loved my godmother as I ought to have loved her and as I felt I must have
(40) loved her if I had been a better girl.

I had never heard my mama spoken of. I had never been shown my mama's grave. I had never been told where it was.

Although there were seven girls at
(45) the neighboring school where I was a day boarder, and although they called me little Esther Summerson, I knew none of them at home. All of them were older than I, to be sure (I was the youngest there by a good
(50) deal), but there seemed to be some other separation between us besides that, and besides their being far more clever than I was and knowing much more than I did. One of them in the first week of my going to
(55) the school (I remember it very well) invited me home to a little party, to my great joy. But my godmother wrote a stiff letter declining for me, and I never went. I never went out at all.
(60) It was my birthday. There were holidays at school on other birthdays—none on mine. There were rejoicings at home on other birthdays, as I knew from what I heard the girls relate to one another—there were none
(65) on mine. My birthday was the most melancholy

GO ON TO THE NEXT PAGE →

day at home in the whole year…

Dinner was over, and my godmother and I were sitting at the table before the fire. The clock ticked, the fire clicked; not
(70) another sound had been heard in the room or in the house for I don't know how long. I happened to look timidly up from my stitching, across the table at my godmother, and I saw in her face, looking gloomily at me,
(75) "It would have been far better, little Esther, that you had had no birthday, that you had never been born!"

I broke out crying and sobbing, and I said, "Oh, dear godmother, tell me, pray do
(80) tell me, did Mama die on my birthday?"

"No," she returned. "Ask me no more, child!"

…I put up my trembling little hand to clasp hers or to beg her pardon with what
(85) earnestness I might, but withdrew it as she looked at me, and laid it on my fluttering heart. She…said slowly in a cold, low voice—I see her knitted brow and pointed finger—"The time will come—and soon
(90) enough—when you will understand this better and will feel it too.…I have forgiven her"—but her face did not relent—"the wrong she did to me, and I say no more of it, though it was greater than you will ever
(95) know…Forget your mother and leave all other people to forget her.…Now, go!"

….I went up to my room, and crept to bed, and laid my doll's cheek against mine wet with tears, and holding that solitary
(100) friend upon my bosom, cried myself to sleep. Imperfect as my understanding of my sorrow was, I knew that I had brought no joy at any time to anybody's heart and that I was to no one upon earth what Dolly was
(105) to me.

Dear, dear, to think how much time we passed alone together afterwards, and how often I repeated to the doll the story of my birthday and confided to her that I would
(110) try as hard as ever I could to repair the fault I had been born with.…I hope it is not self-indulgent to shed these tears as I think of it.

1. According to the passage, Esther only remembers:

   A. being brought up by her parents for a short time.
   B. being brought up by her mother for a short time.
   C. being brought up by her godmother for a short time.
   D. being brought up by her godmother.

2. It is most likely that Esther thought of her doll as:

   F. only an amusing plaything.
   G. her only friend and confidante.
   H. a princess in a fairy tale.
   J. a beautiful toy that was too fragile to touch.

3. As it is used in the passage, *stiff* (line 57) most closely means:

   A. difficult to bend.
   B. rigidly formal.
   C. unchanging.
   D. not moving easily or freely.

4. Which of the following most likely contributed to Esther's belief that she had been born with a fault (lines 110–111)?

   F. She is not very clever.
   G. Her birthday was never celebrated.
   H. She did not have any friends at school.
   J. Her mother died in childbirth.

GO ON TO THE NEXT PAGE

5. Esther's godmother's words, actions, and facial expression as described in paragraph 10 (lines 83–96) suggest that she:

   A. had a change of heart about celebrating Esther's birthday.

   B. did not know what had happened to Esther's mother.

   C. continued to resent Esther's mother.

   D. had truly forgiven Esther's mother.

6. According to the passage, Esther's childhood could be most accurately characterized as:

   F. an adventure.

   G. a time of loneliness and confusion.

   H. a period of dedication to education and self-improvement.

   J. a period of attempting to become more like her godmother.

7. From Esther's statement, "I was to no one upon earth what Dolly was to me" (lines 104–105), it is reasonable to infer that Esther:

   A. believed that her godmother loved her.

   B. believed that she would be able to become friends with the girls at school.

   C. believed that no one loved her.

   D. believed that her mother was alive.

8. In the passage, it is implied that all of the following contributed to separating Esther from the other girls at her school EXCEPT:

   F. the other girls were older than Esther.

   G. Esther's godmother did not allow Esther to socialize with the other girls outside of school.

   H. Esther believed that the other girls were much smarter.

   J. Esther was self-indulgent.

9. According to the passage, one reason that Esther thinks of her godmother as a "good, good woman" (lines 22–23) is:

   A. that when she smiles, she looks like an angel.

   B. that she forgave Esther's mother.

   C. that she frequently attends church services.

   D. that she gave Esther a doll.

10. In the passage, Esther describes herself as a child as:

   F. self-indulgent and not very clever.

   G. shy and not very clever.

   H. shy and faithful.

   J. self-indulgent and faithful.

PASSAGE II

SOCIAL SCIENCE

This passage is excerpted from "The Return of the Big Cats," by Mac Margolis, Newsweek, *December 11, 2000, © 2000 by Newsweek, Inc. All rights reserved. Reprinted by permission.*

Marcos Nunes is not likely to forget his first holiday in Brazil's Pantanal wilderness. One afternoon last October he was coaxing his *Line* horse through a lonely tuft of woods when *(5)* he suddenly found himself staring down a fully grown spotted jaguar. He held his breath while the painted cat and her cub paraded silkily through the grove, not 10 meters away.…"Thank you," he wrote later *(10)* in a hotel visitor's log, "for the wonderful fright!"

As Nunes and other ecotourists are discovering, these big, beautiful animals, once at the brink of extinction, are now *(15)* staging a comeback. Exactly how dramatic a comeback is difficult to say because jaguars—*Panthera onca*, the largest feline in the New World—are solitary, secretive,

GO ON TO THE NEXT PAGE

nocturnal predators. Each cat needs to
(20) prowl at least 35 square kilometers by itself. Brazil's Pantanal, vast wetlands that spill over a 140,000-square-kilometer swath of South America the size of Germany, gives them plenty of room to roam. Nevertheless,
(25) scientists who have been tagging jaguars with radio transmitters for two decades have in recent years been reporting a big increase in sightings. Hotels, campgrounds, and bed-and-breakfasts have sprung up to
(30) accommodate the half-million tourists a year (twice the number of five years ago) bent on sampling the Pantanal's wildlife, of which the great cats must be the most magnificent example.

(35) Most sightings come from local cattle herders—but their jaguar stories have a very different ring. One day last September, ranch hand Abel Monteiro was tending cattle near the Rio Vermelho, in the southern Pantanal,
(40) when, he says, a snarling jaguar leaped from the scrub and killed his two bloodhounds. Monteiro barely had time to grab his .38 revolver and kill the angry cat. Leonelson Ramos da Silva says last May he and a group
(45) of field hands had to throw flaming sticks all night to keep a prowling jaguar from invading their forest camp....The Brazilian interior, famous for its generous spirit and cowboy *bonhomie*, is now the scene of a
(50) political catfight between the scientists, environmentalists, and ecotourists who want to protect the jaguars and the embattled ranchers who want to protect themselves and their livelihood.

(55) The ranchers, to be sure, have enough headaches coping with the harsh, sodden landscape without jaguars attacking their herds and threatening their livelihoods. Hard data on cattle losses due to jaguars in
(60) the Pantanal are nonexistent, but there are stories. In 1995, Joo Julio Dittmar bought a 6,200-hectare strip of ideal breeding ground, only to lose 152 of his 600 calves to jaguars, he claims. Ranchers chafe at laws that forbid

(65) them to kill the jaguars. "This is a question of democracy," says Dittmar. "We ranchers ought to be allowed to control our own environment."

Man and jaguar have been sparring for
(70) territory ever since 18th-century settlers, traders, and herdsmen began to move into this sparsely populated *serto*, or back lands. By the 1960s, the Pantanal was a vast, soggy canvas, white with gleaming herds of Nelore
(75) cattle. Game hunters were bagging 15,000 jaguars a year in the nearby Amazon Basin (no figures exist on the Pantanal) as the worldwide trade in pelts reached $30 million a year. As the jaguars grew scarce, their
(80) chief food staple, the capybaras—a meter-long rodent, the world's largest—overran farmers' fields and spread trichomoniasis, a livestock disease that renders cows sterile.

Then in 1967, Brazil outlawed jaguar
(85) hunting, and a world ban on selling pelts followed in 1973. Weather patterns also shifted radically—due most likely to global warming—and drove annual floods to near-Biblical proportions. The waters are
(90) only now retreating from some inundated pasturelands. As the Pantanal herds shrank from 6 million to about 3.5 million head, the jaguars advanced. Along the way they developed a taste for the bovine intruders.

(95) The ranchers' fear of the big cats is partly cultural. The ancient Inca and Maya believed that jaguars possessed supernatural powers. In Brazil, the most treacherous enemy is said to be *o amigo da onca*, a
(100) friend to the jaguar....

Some people believe there may be a way for ranchers and jaguars to coexist. Sports hunters on "green safaris" might shoot jaguars with immobilizing drugs, allowing
(105) scientists to fit the cats with radio collars. Fees would help sustain jaguar research and compensate ranchers for livestock losses. (Many environmentalists, though, fear fraudulent claims.) Scientists are setting up
(110) workshops to teach ranchers how to protect

GO ON TO THE NEXT PAGE →

their herds with modern husbandry, pasture management, and such gadgets as blinking lights and electric fences.

(115) Like many rural folk, however, the wetland ranchers tend to bristle at bureaucrats and foreigners telling them what to do. When the scholars go home and the greens log off, the *pantaneiros* will still be there— left on their own to deal with the jaguars as

(120) they see fit.

11. As it is used in the passage, *canvas* (line 74) most closely means:

   A. a survey of public opinion.
   B. a background.
   C. a coarse cotton fabric.
   D. a painting.

12. According to the passage, one result of the decline of the jaguar population during the 1960s was:

   F. an increase in the population of human settlers.
   G. an increase in Brazil's ecotourist business.
   H. an increase in the price of a jaguar pelt.
   J. an increase in the population of jaguars' most common source of food, the capybaras.

13. According to the passage, it is difficult to determine the extent of the jaguar's comeback because:

   A. the area they inhabit is so large.
   B. the stories that the local ranchers tell about jaguars contradict the conclusions reached by scientists.
   C. jaguars are solitary, nocturnal animals that can have a territory of 35 square kilometers.
   D. scientists have only used radio transmitters to track the movements of the jaguar population.

14. The information about ecotourism in the first and second paragraphs of the passage (lines 1–34) suggests that:

   F. the jaguars are seen as a threat to the safety of tourists.
   G. the jaguars are important to the success of Brazil's growing ecotourism industry.
   H. the growth of the ecotourism industry is threatening the habitat of the jaguars.
   J. it is common for ecotourists to spot one or more jaguars.

15. According to the passage, which of the following is NOT a method for protecting cattle herds that scientists are teaching ranchers?

   A. "Green safaris"
   B. Pasture management
   C. The use of blinking lights and electric fences
   D. Modern husbandry

GO ON TO THE NEXT PAGE ⟶

16. It is most likely that the author of the passage included the jaguar stories of three ranchers (lines 35–47, 61–68) in order to:

   F. express more sympathy toward the ranchers than toward the environmentalists and scientists.

   G. illustrate the dangers and economic losses that the jaguars currently pose to ranchers.

   H. show the violent nature of the ranchers.

   J. provide a complete picture of the Pantanal landscape.

17. From information in the passage, it is most reasonable to infer that the cattle herds "shrank from 6 million to about 3.5 million head" (lines 91–92) because:

   A. the jaguars had killed so many cattle.

   B. environmentalists and scientists worked to convert pastureland into refuges for the jaguars.

   C. many cows had become sterile from trichomoniasis, and annual floods submerged much of the pastureland used by ranchers.

   D. the cattle could not tolerate the increase in the average temperature caused by global warming.

18. The main conclusion reached about the future of the relationship between the people and the jaguars in the Pantanal is that:

   F. the increase in ecotourism will ensure the continued growth in the jaguar population.

   G. the ranchers themselves will ultimately determine how they will cope with the jaguars.

   H. the jaguar population will continue to fluctuate with the number of tourists coming into the Pantanal.

   J. the scientists' new ranching methods will make it easy for the ranchers and jaguars to coexist.

19. According to the passage, which of the following groups want to protect the jaguar?

   I. Ecotourists
   II. Environmentalists
   III. Scientists

   A. I and II only

   B. I and III only

   C. II and III only

   D. I, II, and III

20. According to the passage, there are no accurate data available on:

   F. the number of cattle killed by jaguars.

   G. the number of ranchers attacked by jaguars.

   H. the growth rate of ecotourism in Brazil.

   J. the percentage of the Pantanal wetlands inhabited by jaguars.

GO ON TO THE NEXT PAGE

PASSAGE III

HUMANITIES

This passage is excerpted from Music Through the Ages Revised Edition, *© 1987 by Marion Bauer and Ethel R. Peyser, edited by Elizabeth E. Rogers, copyright © 1932 by Marion Bauer and Ethel R. Peyser, renewed copyright © 1960 by Ethel R. Peyser. Reprinted by permission of G. P. Putnam's Sons, a division of Penguin Group (USA), Inc.*

Greek instruments can be classified into two general categories—string and pipe, or lyre and aulos. Our knowledge of them comes *Line* from representations on monuments, vases,
(5) statues, and friezes and from the testimony of Greek authors. The lyre was the national instrument and included a wide variety of types. In its most antique form, the chelys, it is traced back to the age of fable and
(10) allegedly owed its invention to Hermes. Easy to carry, this small lyre became the favorite instrument of the home, amateurs, and women, a popular accompaniment for drinking songs and love songs as well as
(15) more noble kinds of poetry....Professional Homeric singers used a kithara, a larger, more powerful instrument, which probably came from Egypt. The kithara had a flat wooden sound box and an upper horizontal
(20) bar supported by two curving arms. Within this frame were stretched strings of equal length, at first but three or four in number. Fastened to the performer by means of a sling, the kithara was played with both
(25) hands. We are not sure in just what manner the instrument was used to accompany the epics. It may have been employed for a pitch-fixing prelude and for interludes, or it may have paralleled or decorated the vocal
(30) melody in more or less free fashion.

...Two types of tuning were used: the dynamic, or pitch method, naming the degrees "according to function"; and the thetic, or tablature, naming them "according
(35) to position" on the instrument.

As early as the eighth century B.C., lyres of five strings appeared. Terpander (fl. c. 675 B.C.), one of the first innovators, is said to have increased the number
(40) of strings to seven. He is also supposed to have completed the octave and created the Mixolydian scale. Aristoxenos claimed that the poetess Sappho, in the seventh century B.C., in addition to introducing a mode in
(45) which Dorian and Lydian characteristics were blended, initiated use of the plectrum or pick. At the time of Sophocles (495–406 B.C.), the lyre had eleven strings.

Another harplike instrument was the
(50) magadis, whose tone was described as trumpetlike. Of foreign importation, it had twenty strings, which, by means of frets, played octaves. As some of the strings were tuned in quarter tones, it was an instrument
(55) associated with the enharmonic mode. Smaller versions, the pectis and the barbitos, were also tuned in quarter tones. Greek men and boys had a style of singing in octaves that was called magadizing, after the octave-
(60) playing instruments.

The kithara was identified with Apollo and the Apollonian cult, representing the intellectual and idealistic side of Greek art. The aulos or reed pipe was the instrument of
(65) Dionysians, who represented the unbridled, sensual, and passionate aspect of Greek culture.

Although translated as "flute," the aulos is more like our oboe. Usually found
(70) in double form, the pipes set at an angle, the aulos was imputed to have a far more exciting effect than that produced by the subdued lyre. About 600 B.C., the aulos was chosen as the official instrument of
(75) the Delphian and Pythian festivals. It was also used in performances of the Dionysian dithyramb as well as a supplement of the chorus in classic Greek tragedy and comedy.

There was a complete family of auloi
(80) covering the same range as human voices. One authority names three species of simple pipes and five varieties of double pipes. (The double pipe was the professional

instrument.) An early specimen

(85) was supposed to have been tuned to the chromatic tetrachord D, C sharp, B flat, A— a fact that points to Oriental origin. Elegiac songs called aulodia were composed in this mode to be accompanied by an aulos.

(90) Although the first wooden pipes had only three or four finger holes, the number later increased so that the Dorian, Phrygian, and Lydian modes might be performed on a single pair. Pictures of auletes show them

(95) with a bandage or phorbeia over their faces; this might have been necessary to hold the two pipes in place, to modulate the tone or, perhaps, to aid in storing air in the cheeks for the purpose of sustained performance.

21. The passage suggests that the aulos was considered "the instrument of the Dionysians" (lines 64–65) because:

   A. it expressed the excitement and passion of that aspect of Greek culture.

   B. it was chosen as the official instrument of the Delphian and Pythian festivals.

   C. it represented the intellectual and idealistic side of Greek art.

   D. it was invented around the time that the Dionysian cult originated.

22. The statement that the chelys can be "traced back to the age of fable" (line 9) implies that the chelys:

   F. was invented by storytellers.

   G. was used to accompany the epics.

   H. probably existed in legend only.

   J. was a particularly ancient instrument.

23. The main purpose of the passage is to describe the:

   A. use of the lyre in different musical settings.

   B. connection between the ancient Greek arts of music and drama.

   C. references to music in ancient Greek literature.

   D. origin and development of various Greek instruments.

24. According to the passage, the kithara was:

   F. most likely of Greek origin.

   G. played with one hand.

   H. used by professional musicians.

   J. less powerful than a chelys.

25. Which of the following is NOT cited as a change that occurred to the lyre between the eighth and fifth centuries B.C.?

   A. Musicians began to use a plectrum.

   B. Lyres featured increasing numbers of strings.

   C. Musicians began to use different scales and modes.

   D. Lyres were used to accompany dramatic productions.

26. It can be inferred from the passage that the chromatic tetrachord D, C sharp, B flat, A (line 86) was:

   F. not appropriate for elegaic songs.

   G. only used by professional musicians.

   H. impossible on the first wooden pipes.

   J. present in ancient Oriental music.

GO ON TO THE NEXT PAGE ⟩

27. According to the passage, the most ancient form of the lyre was called a:

    A. magadis.
    B. kithara.
    C. chelys.
    D. barbitos.

28. According to the passage, one of Sappho's contributions to ancient Greek music was that she:

    F. completed the octave and created the Mixolydian scale.
    G. introduced a mode blending Dorian and Lydian characteristics.
    H. incorporated poetry into recitals of lyre music.
    J. helped increase the number of strings on the lyre.

29. According to the passage, which of the following is/are characteristic of the aulos?

    I. It was used in performances of the Dionysian dithyramb.
    II. It sounded more exciting than the lyre.
    III. It resembles the modern-day flute more than it does the oboe.

    A. I only
    B. I and II only
    C. II and III only
    D. I, II, and III

30. Which of the following does the passage suggest is true about our knowledge of ancient Greek instruments?

    F. Our knowledge is dependent on secondary sources.
    G. Little is known about how instruments were tuned.
    H. Very few pictures of ancient Greek instruments have survived.
    J. More is known about string instruments than about pipe instruments.

PASSAGE IV

NATURAL SCIENCE

The immune system can be divided into two major divisions: nonspecific and specific. The nonspecific immune system is composed of defenses that are used to fight off infection in general and are not targeted at specific pathogens. The specific immune system is able to attack very specific disease-causing organisms by means of protein-to-protein interaction and is responsible for our ability to become immune to future infections from pathogens we have fought off already.

PASSAGE A

Nonspecific defenses serve as the first line of defense for the body to fight off infection. The skin and mucous membranes form one part of these nonspecific defenses, which our body uses against
(5) foreign cells or viruses. Intact skin cannot normally be penetrated by bacteria or viruses, and oil and sweat secretions give the skin a pH that ranges from 3 to 5, which is acidic enough to discourage most microbes from growing there. In addition,
(10) saliva, tears, and mucous all contain the enzyme lysozyme, which can destroy bacterial cell walls (causing bacteria to rupture due to osmotic pressure) and some viral capsids. Mucous is able to trap foreign particles and microbes and transport them
(15) to the stomach through swallowing or to the outside by coughing or blowing the nose. Also, movement in the stomach due to peristalsis and in the airways due to cilia helps remove harmful agents. The gut

GO ON TO THE NEXT PAGE ⟶

flora, microorganisms that live in the stomach
(20) and intestines, secrete substances harmful to the
invader and compete with it for food. Inflamma-
tion is also a nonspecific defense as it attempts to
form a physical barrier, trapping the pathogen and
preventing it from spreading.

(25)   Certain white blood cells are another part of
the nonspecific defense systems. Macrophages are
large white blood cells that circulate, looking for
foreign material or cells to engulf, which
they do through phagocytosis. Macrophages circ-
(30) late through the blood and are able to transport
themselves through capillary walls and into tissues
that have been infected or wounded. Once in the
tissues, macrophages use their pseudopodia (like
amoebas) to pull in foreign particles and destroy
(35) them within lysosomes. Macrophages are called
antigen-presenting cells (APCs) because of their
ability to display on their own cell surface the
proteins that were on the surface of the cell or
viral particle they have just digested. Because
(40) macrophages and other APCs do not distinguish
between "self-proteins" destined for their cell
membrane and "non-self" proteins previously on
another organism's membrane, both types of proteins get shipped to the macrophage's cell surface.
(45) The advantage of this is that macrophages are able
to display to other more specific immune system
cells the antigens (foreign proteins) they have just
encountered. That, in turn, often results in a more
intensive immune response from these more speci-
(50) fic cells like B and T cells.

Neutrophils are white blood cells that are
actively phagocytic like macrophages, but are not
APCs. Our bodies normally produce approximately
1 million neutrophils per second, and they can be
(55) found anywhere in the body. They usually destroy
themselves as they fight off pathogens.

People who have decreased numbers of neutrophils circulating through their blood are extremely
susceptible to bacterial and fungal infections. Other
(60) white blood cells that secrete toxic substances without fine-tuned specificity include the eosinophils,
basophils, and mast cells.

PASSAGE B

The major specific defense of the immune
system includes specialized white blood cells
(65) known as lymphocytes which come in two varieties, B cells and T cells. Both are produced by stem
cells in the bone marrow, and although T cells
mature in the thymus, B cells do not. The thymus
is essential for "educating" T cells; those that recog-
(70) nize "self" antigens (proteins found on one's own
cell surfaces) are killed off to prevent the body from
attacking itself. This negative selection results in
the development of T cell tolerance, a necessity of
the specific immune system. Yet a positive selection
(75) process also exists whereby T cells that do not react
to a specific set of glycoproteins, called MHC (major histocompatibility complex) proteins, are killed
off because T cells need to be able to bond to both
self-MHC and foreign antigens simultaneously.

(80)   There are three types of T cells: helper (TH),
cytotoxic (TC), and suppressor (TS). While TH
cells are mediators between macrophages and B
cells, TC cells are essential in defending against
viruses because they can kill virally infected cells
(85) directly. Since virally infected cells display some
viral proteins on their surfaces, TC cells can bind
to those proteins and secrete enzymes that tear the
cell membrane, thereby killing the cell. TS cells are
involved in controlling the immune response so
(90) that it does not run amok; they do this by suppress-
ing the production of antibodies by B cells.

T cells cannot detect free antigens; they can
only respond to displayed antigens and MHC on
the surfaces of cells. When they do recognize a
(95) displayed antigen, it is always in combination with
a self-MHC protein displayed along with the antigen on the host cell surface. Interactions between
T cells and APCs are enhanced by certain proteins
that hold the T cell to the APC as it recognizes the
(100) antigen-MHC combination.

Every B cell has surface receptors that can
recognize a specific set of foreign antigens (proteins
found on the surfaces of foreign cells and viruses).
B cells can be "activated" in one of two ways: either
(105) they can come into contact with a foreign antigen
that can bind to the B cell surface receptors, or they
can engulf a pathogen, displaying its antigens on

GO ON TO THE NEXT PAGE

the B cell surface much as a macrophage would. Then they can get activated to divide by chemicals (110) released by a helper T cell that recognizes the foreign proteins sitting on the B cell surface.

B and T cells each have unique cell receptors. That means that almost every one of the several billion B and T cells in the body is capable of (115) responding to a slightly different foreign antigen. When a particular B or T cell gets activated, it begins to divide rapidly to produce identical clones.

In the case of B cells, these clones will all produce antibodies of the same structure, capable (120) of responding to the same invading antigens. B cell clones are known as plasma B cells and can produce thousands of antibody molecules per second as long as they live.

Questions 31–33 ask about Passage A.

---

31. According to first paragraph (lines 1–24), which of the following nonspecific defenses can kill bacteria?

    I. White blood cells that can engulf bacteria
    II. Skin secretions that have an acidic pH
    III. Mucous membranes that contain lysozyme

  A. I only
  B. III only
  C. II and III only
  D. I, II, and III

32. Which specific characteristic of macrophages often results in a more intensive immune response?

  F. The specific immune system detects the pathogens that the macrophage is engulfing.
  G. Macrophages are antigen-presenting cells.
  H. Macrophages will pass "non-self" proteins to the specific immune system division.
  J. Foreign particles are digested within macrophage lysosomes.

33. According to the passage, neutrophils:

  A. may cause people to be more susceptible to disease.
  B. are similar to macrophages because they engulf foreign material.
  C. display non-self proteins on their cell walls as do macrophages.
  D. will always destroy themselves in battling pathogens.

Questions 34–36 ask about Passage B.

---

34. As it is used in the passage, the word *mediators* (line 82) most nearly means:

  F. regulators.
  G. peacemakers.
  H. instigators.
  J. intermediaries.

35. According the passage, once a particular B cell gets activated, the cell:

  A. divides quickly to create plasma B cells.
  B. produces a foreign antigen.
  C. uses pseudopodia to destroy foreign particles.
  D. creates identical clones called neutrophils.

36. The passage describes a B cell as:

  F. a type of macrophage that can display antigens on its surface.
  G. using entirely different methods to capture foreign antigens than do macrophages.
  H. being able to self-replicate as soon as it displays foreign proteins on its cells surface.
  J. requiring other lymphocytes to act before it can replicate to produce antibodies.

GO ON TO THE NEXT PAGE →

Questions 37–40 ask about both passages.

37. The specific immune system differs from the nonspecific immune system in that it:

   A. is more complicated.
   B. uses white blood cells.
   C. is responsible for the body's ability to become immune.
   D. does not target specific pathogens.

38. Which of the following statements provides the most accurate comparison of the passages?

   F. Passage A provides a generic overview, while Passage B provides specific detail.
   G. Passage A includes nonspecific information about a concept, while Passage B provides specific information.
   H. Passage A provides information about one aspect of a system, while Passage B provides additional information about that system.
   J. Passage A provides an explanation of a process, while Passage B provides a different explanation of that same process.

39. It can be most reasonably inferred from both passages that:

   A. certain nonspecific defenses are required to occur before certain specific defenses can commence.
   B. nonspecific and specific defenses of the immune system operate independently.
   C. nonspecific defenses serve to communicate information to specific defenses.
   D. specific defenses are more important than nonspecific passages.

40. According to both passages, which defense mechanisms are cited as being able to kill pathogens by rupturing the cell membranes?

   I. Secretions such as mucous and saliva
   II. TC cells
   III. Disease-causing organisms

   F. I only
   G. I and II only
   H. III only
   J. I, II, and III

IF YOU FINISH BEFORE TIME IS CALLED, YOU MAY CHECK YOUR WORK ON THIS SECTION ONLY. DO NOT TURN TO ANY OTHER SECTION IN THE TEST. **STOP**

SCIENCE TEST

35 Minutes—40 Questions

Directions: There are several passages in this test. Each passage is followed by several questions. After reading a passage, choose the best answer to each question and fill in the corresponding oval on your Answer Grid. You may refer to the passages as often as necessary. You are NOT permitted to use a calculator on this test.

PASSAGE I

Acid-base indicators are used to determine changes in pH. The pH is a quantitative measure of the hydrogen ion concentration of a solution. For any solution, the pH ranges from 0 to 14. An acid-base indicator is a weak acid or base that is sensitive to the hydrogen ion concentration and changes color at a known pH. At any other pH, the acid-base indicator is clear.

Table 1

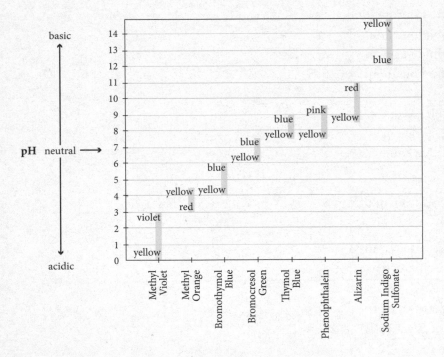

Figure 1

ph of Common Items	
14	Liquid drain cleaner
13	Bleach
12	Soapy water
11	Ammonia
10	Milk of magnesium
9	Toothpaste
8	Baking soda, seawater, eggs
7	Pure water
6	Milk
5	Black coffee
4	Tomato juice
3	Orange juice, soda
2	Lemon juice, vinegar
1	Gastric acid
0	Battery acid

GO ON TO THE NEXT PAGE

1. Which indicators undergo a color change in the region from pH 8 to pH 12?

   A. Bromocresol green, bromothymol blue, and thymol blue

   B. Thymol blue, phenolphthalein, and alizarin

   C. Phenolphthalein, alizarin, and sodium indigo sulfonate

   D. Phenolphthalein and bromothymol blue

2. Which of the following indicators undergoes a red-to-yellow or yellow-to-red color change?

   I.   Alizarin
   II. Thymol blue
   III. Methyl orange

   F. I only

   G. II only

   H. I and III only

   J. I, II, and III

3. A chemist is running an experiment in a solution that becomes basic upon completion. According to the diagram, the reaction is complete when:

   A. the addition of bromocresol green results in a blue color.

   B. any indicator turns violet.

   C. a white solid appears.

   D. the addition of bromothymol blue results in a blue color.

4. Which of the following hypotheses is consistent with the information in the passage and the diagram?

   F. Color changes for any given acid-base indicator occur in a solution with a pH less than 7.

   G. Color changes for any given acid-base indicator occur in a solution with a pH greater than 7.

   H. Color changes for acid-base indicators always occur within the same pH range.

   J. Color changes for acid-base indicators vary within the pH range.

5. Compared to bromothymol blue, phenolphthalein undergoes a color change at:

   A. a higher pH.

   B. a lower pH.

   C. the same pH.

   D. Cannot be determined from the data provided.

6. Based on Figure 1 and Table 1, which of the following indicators would be most useful in determining the pH of black coffee?

   F. Methyl Orange

   G. Bromothymol Blue

   H. Bromocresol Green

   J. Alizarin

GO ON TO THE NEXT PAGE

PASSAGE II

The Brazilian tree frog (*Hyla faber*) exchanges gases through both its skin and lungs. The exchange rate depends on the temperature of the frog's environment. A series of experiments was performed to investigate this dependence.

EXPERIMENT 1

Fifty frogs were placed in a controlled atmosphere that, with the exception of temperature, was designed to simulate their native habitat. The temperature was varied from 5°C to 25°C, and equilibrium was attained before each successive temperature change. The amount of oxygen absorbed by the frogs' lungs and skin per hour was measured, and the results for all the frogs were averaged. The results are shown in Table 1.

Table 1

Temperature (°C)	Moles O_2 absorbed/hr	
	Skin	Lungs
5	15.4	8.3
10	22.7	35.1
15	43.6	64.9
20	42.1	73.5
25	40.4	78.7

EXPERIMENT 2

The same frogs were placed under the same conditions as in Experiment 1. For this experiment, the amount of carbon dioxide eliminated through the skin and lungs was measured. The results are averaged and given in Table 2.

Table 2

Temperature (°C)	Moles CO_2 eliminated/hr	
	Skin	Lungs
5	18.9	2.1
10	43.8	12.7
15	79.2	21.3
20	91.6	21.9
25	96.5	21.4

7. Scientists want to determine if other atmospheric conditions affect gas exchange in frogs. Which of the following variables should they test?

    I. Skin color

    II. Humidity level

    III. Altitude

    IV. Wind speed

  A. I and II

  B. I, II, and III

  C. II and III

  D. II, III, and IV

8. The results of Experiment 1 suggest that the total amount of O_2 absorbed per hour is:

  F. affected by the temperature.

  G. independent of the temperature.

  H. an indication of how healthy a Brazilian tree frog is.

  J. always less than the total amount of CO_2 eliminated per hour.

9. According to Experiment 2, the total amount of CO_2 eliminated per hour at 17°C is closest to:

  A. 21 mol/hr.

  B. 85 mol/hr.

  C. 106 mol/hr.

  D. 115 mol/hr.

GO ON TO THE NEXT PAGE ▷

10. Ectotherms are animals whose bodily functions are affected by the temperature of their environment. Which of the following results supports the conclusion that *Hyla fabers* is an ectotherm?

    F. The oxygen absorbed at 25°C
    G. The carbon dioxide released by the lungs
    H. The oxygen absorbed over the entire temperature range
    J. The results do not support this conclusion.

11. According to the results of Experiment 2, which of the following plots best represents the amount of carbon dioxide eliminated through the skin and lungs as a function of temperature?

    A.

    B.

    C.

    D.

12. On the basis of the experimental results, one could conclude that as temperature increases:

    F. O_2 absorbed by the lungs increases, and CO_2 released by the skin decreases.
    G. O_2 absorbed by the lungs increases, and CO_2 released by the skin increases.
    H. O_2 absorbed by the lungs decreases, and CO_2 released by the lungs increases.
    J. O_2 absorbed by the lungs decreases, and CO_2 released by the lungs decreases.

13. According to the results of these experiments, as the temperature rises above 15°C, which of the following phenomena can be observed?

    A. The Brazilian tree frog's ability to absorb oxygen through the skin decreases, as does its ability to release carbon dioxide through the lungs.
    B. The Brazilian tree frog's ability to absorb oxygen through the skin decreases, while its ability to release carbon dioxide through the lungs remains about the same.
    C. The Brazilian tree frog's ability to absorb oxygen through the skin remains about the same, as does its ability to release carbon dioxide through the lungs.
    D. The Brazilian tree frog's ability to absorb oxygen through the skin increases, while its ability to release carbon dioxide through the lungs remains about the same.

GO ON TO THE NEXT PAGE

PASSAGE III

While the focus (point of origin) of most earthquakes lies less than 20 km below Earth's surface, certain unusual seismographic readings indicate that some activity originates at considerably greater depths. Below, two scientists discuss the possible causes of deep-focus earthquakes.

SCIENTIST 1

Surface earthquakes occur when rock in Earth's crust fractures to relieve stress. However, below 50 km, rock is under too much pressure to fracture normally. Deep-focus earthquakes are caused by the pressure of fluids trapped in Earth's tectonic plates. As a plate is forced down into the mantle by convection, increases in temperature and pressure cause changes in the crystalline structure of minerals such as serpentine. In adopting a denser configuration, the crystals dehydrate, releasing water. Other sources of fluid include water trapped in pockets of deep-sea trenches and carried down with the plates. Laboratory work has shown that fluids trapped in rock pores can cause rock to fail at lower shear stresses. In fact, at the Rocky Mountain Arsenal, the injection of fluid wastes into the ground accidentally induced a series of shallow-focus earthquakes.

SCIENTIST 2

Deep-focus earthquakes cannot result from normal fractures because rock becomes ductile at the temperatures and pressures that exist at depths greater than 50 km. Furthermore, mantle rock below 300 km is probably totally dehydrated because of the extreme pressure. Therefore, trapped fluids could not cause quakes below that depth. A better explanation is that deep-focus quakes result from the slippage that occurs when rock in a descending tectonic plate undergoes a phase change in its crystalline structure along a thin plane parallel to a stress. Just such a phase change and resultant slippage can be produced in the laboratory by compressing a slab of calcium magnesium silicate. The pattern of deep-quake activity supports this theory. In most seismic zones, the recorded incidence of deep-focus earthquakes corresponds to the depths at which phase changes are predicted to occur in mantle rock. For example, little or no phase change is thought to occur at 400 km, and indeed, earthquake activity at this level is negligible. Between 400 and 680 km, activity once again increases. Although seismologists initially believed that earthquakes could be generated at depths as low as 1,080 or 1,200 km, no foci have been confirmed below 700 km. No phase changes are predicted for mantle rock below 680 km.

14. If deep-focus earthquakes were found to be the result of rising liquid magma in the asthenosphere, this information would support which of the following?

    I. Scientist 1

    II. Scientist 2

    III. Neither scientist 1 nor scientist 2

F. I only

G. II only

H. III only

J. I and II

15. Scientists 1 and 2 agree on which point?

A. Deep-earthquake activity does not occur below 400 km.

B. Fluid allows tectonic plates to slip past one another.

C. Water can penetrate mantle rock.

D. Rock below 50 km will not fracture normally.

GO ON TO THE NEXT PAGE

16. Which of the following is evidence that would support Scientists 1's hypothesis?

 F. The discovery that water can be extracted from mantle-like rock at temperatures and pressures similar to those found below 300 km

 G. Seismographic indications that earthquakes occur 300 km below Earth's surface

 H. The discovery that phase changes occur in the mantle rock at depths of 1,080 km

 J. An earthquake underneath Los Angeles that was shown to have been caused by water trapped in sewer lines

17. Both scientists assume that:

 A. deep-focus earthquakes are more common than surface earthquakes.

 B. trapped fluids cause surface earthquakes.

 C. earth's crust is composed of mobile tectonic plates.

 D. deep-focus earthquakes cannot be felt on Earth's crust without special recording devices.

18. To best refute Scientist 2's hypothesis, Scientist 1 might:

 F. find evidence of other sources of underground water.

 G. record a deep-focus earthquake below 680 km.

 H. find a substance that does not undergo phase changes even at depths equivalent to 680 km.

 J. show that rock becomes ductile at depths of less than 50 km.

19. According to Scientist 1, the earthquake at Rocky Mountain Arsenal occurred because:

 A. serpentine or other minerals dehydrated and released water.

 B. fluid wastes injected into the ground compressed a thin slab of calcium magnesium silicate.

 C. fluid wastes injected into the ground flooded pockets of a deep-sea trench.

 D. fluid wastes injected into the ground lowered the shear stress failure point of the rock.

20. Scientist 2's hypothesis would be strengthened by evidence showing that:

 F. water evaporates at high temperatures and pressures.

 G. deep-focus earthquakes can occur at 680 km.

 H. stress has the same effect on mantle rock that it has on calcium magnesium silicate.

 J. water pockets exist at depths below 300 km.

21. According to Scientist 2, phase changes in the crystalline structure of a descending tectonic plate:

 A. occur only at Earth's surface.

 B. are not possible.

 C. cause certain minerals to release water, which exerts pressure within the plate.

 D. cause slippage that directly results in an earthquake.

GO ON TO THE NEXT PAGE

PASSAGE IV

Astronomers want to know the effects of atmospheric conditions on the impact of an asteroid-to-Earth collision. The most common hypothesis is that the presence of moisture in Earth's atmosphere significantly reduces the hazardous effects of such a collision. One researcher has decided to create a laboratory model of Earth. The researcher has the ability to control the amount of moisture surrounding the model. The researcher has also created models of asteroids of various sizes. The researcher will use a collision indicator (see table below) based on the Torino Scale to measure the results of two experiments.

Collision Indicator	
Torino Scale Collision Rating	Impact Effect
0 to 0.9	A collision capable of little destruction
1 to 3.9	A collision capable of localized destruction
4 to 6.9	A collision capable of regional destruction
7 to 10	A collision capable of global catastrophe

EXPERIMENT 1

The researcher simulated collisions on the Earth model of asteroid models representing mass equivalent to 1,000 kg to 1,000,000 kg. The controlled moisture level of the model Earth's atmosphere was 86%. The effects of the collisions were recorded and rated according to the collision indicator.

EXPERIMENT 2

The researcher simulated collisions on the Earth model of asteroid models representing the same masses as in Experiment 1. The controlled moisture level of the model Earth's atmosphere in this experiment was 12%. The effects of the collisions were recorded and rated according to the collision indicator. The results of both experiments are shown in the graph.

22. How was the experimental design of Experiment 1 different from that of Experiment 2?

    F. The impacts of more asteroids were measured.

    G. The impacts of larger asteroids were measured.

    H. There was more moisture in the atmosphere.

    J. There was a different collision indicator.

23. If the atmospheric moisture in Experiment 2 was increased to 50%, the collision rating for an asteroid with a mass of 400,000 kg would most likely be between:

    A. 2 and 3.

    B. 4.5 and 5.5.

    C. 6 and 7.

    D. 9 and 10.

GO ON TO THE NEXT PAGE

24. Based on the experimental results, one can generalize that an increase of moisture in the atmosphere would:

    F. decrease the impact of an asteroid-to-Earth collision, regardless of the size of the asteroid.

    G. decrease the impact of an asteroid-to-Earth collision involving an asteroid under 700,000 kg.

    H. increase the impact of an asteroid-to-Earth collision, regardless of the size of the asteroid.

    J. increase the impact of an asteroid-to-Earth collision involving an asteroid under 700,000 kg.

25. In a simulated asteroid-to-Earth collision, a 400,000 kg asteroid received a collision rating of 4. The amount of moisture in the atmosphere was most likely closest to:

    A. 0%.

    B. 12%.

    C. 86%.

    D. 100%.

26. According to the researcher's model, a 100,000 kg asteroid colliding in an atmosphere with a moisture level of 12% would be likely to have the same impact as an asteroid colliding in an atmosphere with a moisture level of 86% with a size closest to which of the following?

    F. 50,000 kg

    G. 120,000 kg

    H. 270,000 kg

    J. 490,000 kg

27. To be minimally capable of regional destruction, an asteroid entering an atmosphere with a moisture level of 86% would have to be roughly what percent larger than an asteroid capable of the same level of destruction entering an atmosphere with a moisture level of 12%?

    A. 20%

    B. 70%

    C. 150%

    D. 220%

28. If researchers were to find evidence of a 350,000 kg collision on Earth that resulted in a Torino Scale Collision Rating of 1.5, the moisture level would be:

    F. less than 12%.

    G. greater than 86%.

    H. exactly 12%.

    J. exactly 86%.

GO ON TO THE NEXT PAGE

PASSAGE V

The electrical conductivity of a material determines how it will react to various temperature conditions in a consumer product. Product researchers need to know how a material will react in order to determine its safety for consumer use. The electrical conductivity of two different samples of a platinum dithiolate compound was measured from 10 K to 275 K. The results and general conductivity versus temperature plots for conductors and semiconductors are shown here.

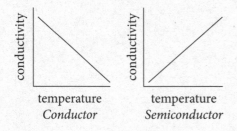

29. At what temperature do both samples demonstrate semiconductor-like behavior?

   A. 115 K

   B. 160 K

   C. 275 K

   D. They do not share a common temperature for semiconductor behavior.

30. For Sample HST-52, which of the following describes its behavior when the temperature is dropped from 200 K to 100 K?

   F. The sample remains a semiconductor.

   G. The sample remains a conductor.

   H. The sample undergoes a conductor to semiconductor transition.

   J. The sample undergoes a semiconductor to conductor transition.

31. In a material exhibiting conductor-like behavior, the conductivity:

   A. increases as the temperature increases.

   B. decreases as the temperature increases.

   C. decreases as the temperature decreases.

   D. remains the same at all temperatures.

GO ON TO THE NEXT PAGE

32. A newly developed material has a semiconductor to conductor transition at about 10 K as the temperature increases. Its conductivity versus temperature plot would resemble which of the following?

F.

G.

H.

J.

33. An industrial firm wishes to use HST-52 as a semiconductor in an assembly-line component. The experimental results indicate that:

   A. HST-52 is not a semiconductor; a new material will have to be chosen.

   B. HST-52 is suitable for the planned application.

   C. HST-52 is too brittle to be used in this manner.

   D. HST-52 will be usable only if the assembly line is maintained at less than 150 K.

34. The temperature at which a compound's conductivity-versus-temperature plot declines most quickly is known as its "optimal conductor" temperature. Which of the following could be the optimal conductor temperature for Sample HST-52?

   F. 20 K

   G. 80 K

   H. 160 K

   J. 180 K

GO ON TO THE NEXT PAGE

PASSAGE VI

Siamese cats have a genotype for dark fur, but the enzymes that produce the dark coloring function best at temperatures below the cat's normal body temperature. A Siamese cat usually has darker fur on its ears, nose, paws, and tail, because these parts have a lower temperature than the rest of its body. If a Siamese cat spends more than one hour a day for six consecutive days outdoors (an "outdoor" cat) during very cold weather, darker fur grows in other places on its body. If a Siamese cat does not spend this amount of time outdoors, it is an "indoor" cat. The amount of dark fur on its body remains constant throughout the year.

35. According to the graph, if the average temperature outdoors drops from 2°C to 0°C over the course of a month, what will most likely happen to the fur of an outdoor Siamese cat during the same time period? Over that time, the percentage of the cat's body covered in dark fur will:

A. increase.

B. decrease.

C. remain the same.

D. increase, then decrease.

36. A particular Siamese cat goes outdoors a total of three hours per week during the coldest part of the year. One could predict that the percentage of its body covered by dark fur would be closest to:

F. 0%.

G. 10%.

H. 40%.

J. 60%.

37. According to the graph, what is the most likely temperature outside if outdoor Siamese cats have 45% of their bodies covered in dark fur?

A. 0°C

B. 3°C

C. 6°C

D. 9°C

38. If a Siamese cat that lived indoors was lost and later found with dark fur over 30% of its body, which of the following could be inferred about the period during which it was missing:

    I. It was living in an area where temperatures fell below 5°C.

    II. It spent more time outdoors than indoors.

    III. It was missing for at least six days.

F. I and II only

G. I and III only

H. II and III only

J. I, II, and III

GO ON TO THE NEXT PAGE

39. If a Siamese cat has dark fur over 10% of its body, which of the following must be true about the cat?

   A. It lives indoors.

   B. It lives in an area where the temperature outdoors is usually 7°C or higher.

   C. It either lives indoors or it lives in an area where the temperature outdoors is usually 7°C or higher.

   D. None of the above

40. If a researcher wants to find out how fur color is affected by the amount of time a Siamese cat spends outside in cold weather, which experiment would be the most helpful?

   F. The indoor cats in the original experiment should be used as the control group, and their fur color should be compared to a group of Siamese cats spending six hours or more a day outside in cold weather for six consecutive days.

   G. A new group of Siamese cats should be formed and kept outside two or more hours a day at varying temperatures. Their fur color at different outdoor temperatures should be compared to that of the outdoor cats already charted.

   H. Siamese cats should be split into two groups, one group spending only one hour per day outside for six consecutive days in cold weather and the other group spending at least two hours a day outside for six consecutive days in the same weather.

   J. No new experiment is needed. The data already gathered show that the more time a Siamese cat spends outside in cold weather, the darker its fur will be.

WRITING TEST

40 Minutes—1 Question

Directions: This is a test of your writing skills. You will have forty (40) minutes to write an essay in English. Before you begin planning and writing your essay, read the writing prompt carefully to understand exactly what you are being asked to do. Your essay will be evaluated on the evidence it provides of your ability to do the following:

- Express judgments by evaluating the three perspectives given in the prompt, taking a position on an issue, and explaining the relationship among all four ideas
- Develop a position by using logical reasoning and by supporting your ideas
- Maintain a focus on the topic throughout the essay
- Organize ideas in a logical way
- Use language clearly and effectively according to the conventions of standard written English

You may use a separate piece of paper to plan your essay. *You must write your essay in pencil on the lined pages provided after the prompt.* Your writing on those lined pages will be scored. You may not need all the lined pages, but to ensure you have enough room to finish, do NOT skip lines. You may write corrections or additions neatly between the lines of your essay, but do NOT write in the margins of the lined pages. *Illegible essays cannot be scored, so you must write (or print) clearly.*

DO NOT OPEN THIS BOOKLET UNTIL TOLD TO DO SO.

GO ON TO THE NEXT PAGE

STUDENT ENGAGEMENT

Studies show that students not only retain more information but also enjoy learning more when they actively participate in the classroom. Teachers therefore strive to optimize engagement to foster a positive, effective instructional environment. In an effort to increase student interaction in the high school classroom, some educators argue that curriculum should take into account the interests and suggestions of students. Since teachers cannot allow students to choose every aspect of a lesson, is it worth the time and effort to actively seek relevant student feedback? As high schools aim to improve the quality of the education they offer to students, student opinion may prove to be valuable.

Read and carefully consider these perspectives. Each discusses the relevance of student feedback in lesson planning.

Perspective One	Perspective Two	Perspective Three
Many colleges require students to complete a course survey before they are eligible to receive their semester grades. Colleges use students' responses to evaluate course materials to ensure quality education. High schools would benefit from implementing a similar system of regular feedback on classroom lesson plans by students.	Students are not qualified to provide insight regarding lesson planning or curriculum design. Improving education quality is the responsibility of educators, and they are rightfully in charge of making effective changes.	Many school districts evaluate teachers using students' test scores and conducting in-classroom observations. Information gathered from student surveys could not only inform lesson design, but also provide another source of evaluation by which to measure teacher effectiveness.

ESSAY TASK

Write a unified, coherent essay in which you evaluate multiple perspectives on the relevance of student feedback in lesson planning. In your essay, be sure to:

- analyze and evaluate the perspectives given
- state and develop your own perspective on the issue
- explain the relationship between your perspective and those given

Your perspective may be in full agreement with any of the others, in partial agreement, or wholly different. Whatever the case, support your ideas with logical reasoning and detailed, persuasive examples.

GO ON TO THE NEXT PAGE ▷

PLANNING YOUR ESSAY

You may wish to consider the following as you think critically about the task:

Strengths and weaknesses of the three given perspectives

- What insights do they offer, and what do they fail to consider?
- Why might they be persuasive to others, or why might they fail to persuade?

Your own knowledge, experience, and values

- What is your perspective on this issue, and what are its strengths and weaknesses?
- How will you support your perspective in your essay?

_____

_____

_____

_____

_____

_____

_____

_____

_____

_____

_____

_____

_____

_____

_____

_____

_____

GO ON TO THE NEXT PAGE ⇨

GO ON TO THE NEXT PAGE

_____

_____

_____

_____

_____

_____

_____

_____

_____

_____

_____

_____

_____

_____

_____

_____

_____

_____

_____

_____

_____

IF YOU FINISH BEFORE TIME IS CALLED, YOU MAY CHECK YOUR WORK ON THIS SECTION ONLY. DO NOT TURN TO ANY OTHER SECTION IN THE TEST.   STOP

Practice Test Two
ANSWER KEY

ENGLISH TEST

1. D	11. A	21. B	31. A	41. C	51. B	61. B	71. B
2. G	12. J	22. J	32. J	42. J	52. J	62. F	72. F
3. C	13. A	23. B	33. B	43. A	53. C	63. D	73. B
4. J	14. F	24. F	34. H	44. J	54. J	64. G	74. J
5. B	15. D	25. C	35. A	45. D	55. C	65. B	75. B
6. G	16. G	26. J	36. H	46. H	56. J	66. F	
7. D	17. A	27. B	37. B	47. A	57. C	67. C	
8. J	18. J	28. G	38. J	48. G	58. F	68. H	
9. B	19. C	29. C	39. A	49. B	59. D	69. B	
10. H	20. F	30. F	40. G	50. G	60. F	70. J	

MATHEMATICS TEST

1. A	9. D	17. E	25. C	33. B	41. B	49. C	57. B
2. J	10. F	18. K	26. J	34. K	42. H	50. F	58. J
3. A	11. B	19. D	27. C	35. D	43. E	51. C	59. C
4. G	12. G	20. G	28. H	36. K	44. K	52. F	60. J
5. B	13. D	21. E	29. D	37. B	45. E	53. B	
6. H	14. G	22. H	30. H	38. F	46. K	54. J	
7. C	15. D	23. A	31. A	39. A	47. E	55. E	
8. J	16. F	24. G	32. F	40. K	48. G	56. G	

READING TEST

1. D	6. G	11. B	16. G	21. A	26. J	31. B	36. J
2. G	7. C	12. J	17. C	22. J	27. C	32. G	37. C
3. B	8. J	13. C	18. G	23. D	28. G	33. B	38. H
4. G	9. C	14. G	19. D	24. H	29. B	34. J	39. A
5. C	10. G	15. A	20. F	25. D	30. F	35. A	40. G

SCIENCE TEST

1. B	6. G	11. B	16. F	21. D	26. H	31. B	36. G
2. H	7. D	12. G	17. C	22. H	27. B	32. H	37. B
3. A	8. F	13. B	18. G	23. B	28. J	33. D	38. G
4. J	9. C	14. H	19. D	24. G	29. D	34. J	39. C
5. A	10. H	15. D	20. H	25. C	30. H	35. C	40. H

ANSWERS AND EXPLANATIONS

ENGLISH TEST

PASSAGE I

1. D
Category: Punctuation
Difficulty: Medium
Getting to the Answer: A comma is needed to set off the introductory phrase, so A cannot be correct. Choice B creates a sentence fragment, and the pronoun *it* in C does not match the subject of the sentence—Duke Ellington.

2. G
Category: Verb Tenses
Difficulty: Low
Getting to the Answer: The whole passage is in past tense, and there is no reason why this verb should not be in past tense as well. Also, the part of the sentence on the other side of the semicolon gives you a big clue by using *paid*.

3. C
Category: Punctuation
Difficulty: Medium
Getting to the Answer: The colon is used incorrectly in the original sentence, and B does not solve the problem. Choice D is unnecessarily wordy.

4. J
Category: Punctuation
Difficulty: High
Getting to the Answer: Commas are needed between items in a series, so eliminate F and G. A comma is also needed to set off the introductory phrase, so eliminate H.

5. B
Category: Word Choice
Difficulty: Medium
Getting to the Answer: In order to figure out the appropriate pronoun, identify the noun to which the pronoun refers. The only possible corresponding noun is *Ellington*; therefore, (B) is the correct answer.

6. G
Category: Sentence Sense
Difficulty: High
Getting to the Answer: "As a teenager in Washington" is not a complete sentence. Choice H does not make sense, and J is incorrect because the comma is unnecessary.

7. D
Category: Word Choice
Difficulty: Medium
Getting to the Answer: The word *then* should be *than*—(D) makes this correction.

8. J
Category: Wordiness
Difficulty: Low
Getting to the Answer: Even though the piano teacher's name is mentioned in the preceding sentence, more information about her name is unnecessary to make the sentence relevant to the passage.

9. B
Category: Connections
Difficulty: Medium
Getting to the Answer: There is a contrast between Ellington's not being a good pianist and his hearing about the opportunities for musicians in New York. The correct contrast is established by (B).

10. H
Category: Wordiness
Difficulty: Medium
Getting to the Answer: *Awaited* and *were there for* mean the same thing, so one part of the underlined portion should be deleted—that eliminates F and G. Choice J is also unnecessarily wordy.

11. A
Category: Sentence Sense
Difficulty: Medium
Getting to the Answer: The sentence is logical in the flow of the paragraph, so eliminate D. The paragraph discusses Ellington's move to Harlem, and the *they* in the next sentence indicates Ellington wasn't alone. Choice (A) is the simplest and most correct way to phrase the sentence.

12. J
Category: Word Choice
Difficulty: Medium
Getting to the Answer: The subject of the sentence is the Cotton Club, so choices with the pronoun *he*—F and G—should be eliminated. Choice H creates a sentence fragment.

13. A
Category: Writing Strategy
Difficulty: Low
Getting to the Answer: This list of songs follows a description of Ellington's early musical career, so (A) is correct. The songs do not contradict anything, so eliminate B. The names of the songs themselves do not illustrate complexity; therefore, C is incorrect. This part of the paragraph is no longer about the Cotton Club, so eliminate D.

14. F
Category: Writing Strategy
Difficulty: Medium
Getting to the Answer: The last paragraph of the essay lists the accomplishments of Ellington. Choice (F) is the only answer choice that makes sense.

15. D
Category: Organization
Difficulty: High
Getting to the Answer: Paragraph 4 is the only paragraph that covers elements of Ellington's music. The logical place for the insertion is before the last sentence of the essay where his musical ability is discussed.

PASSAGE II

16. G
Category: Word Choice
Difficulty: Medium
Getting to the Answer: The subject is *animals*, so a plural pronoun is needed. Choice F is a singular pronoun, H is a contraction, and J uses *there* instead of *their*.

17. A
Category: Punctuation
Difficulty: Medium
Getting to the Answer: The comma is needed to set off the second clause from the first, so eliminate B and D. Choice C incorrectly uses a colon.

18. J
Category: Punctuation
Difficulty: High
Getting to the Answer: The phrase "a member of the weasel family" is a nonessential clause and should be set off by commas. Eliminate G and H because they create sentence fragments.

19. C
Category: Verb Tenses
Difficulty: Medium
Getting to the Answer: "Having changed" is the incorrect verb tense. Ermines are nonhuman, so B is incorrect; choice (C) uses *that* correctly. The whole passage is in present tense, so eliminate D because it is in past tense.

20. F
Category: Sentence Sense
Difficulty: Low
Getting to the Answer: Choose the most logical order of the words. Choice (F) makes the most sense.

21. B
Category: Punctuation
Difficulty: Medium
Getting to the Answer: "Far from placing it in danger" is an introductory phrase and should be set off by a comma. Eliminate A and C. Choice D is unnecessarily wordy and doesn't make sense with the rest of the sentence.

22. J
Category: Wordiness
Difficulty: Medium
Getting to the Answer: "By distinguishing itself from other animals" is a sentence fragment. These words make sense as an introductory phrase and should therefore be set off by a comma. Choice (J) is the only choice that accomplishes this concisely.

23. B
Category: Wordiness
Difficulty: Low
Getting to the Answer: The unnecessary phrase "the question is" should be eliminated. Choice (B) is the simplest and most correct way to phrase the question.

24. F
Category: Verb Tenses
Difficulty: High
Getting to the Answer: The investigating has occurred in the past, and it is still occurring. The tense of the answer choice should be present perfect. Choices G and H only refer to the past, and J refers only to the present.

25. C
Category: Connections
Difficulty: Medium
Getting to the Answer: The previous sentence speaks of special glands, but this sentence says that some animals do not have these glands. This is a contrast, and *however* sets it up best.

26. J
Category: Wordiness
Difficulty: Low
Getting to the Answer: *Remains* and *endures as* are the same thing, so the correct choice will eliminate one of them. Choice (J) does just that.

27. B
Category: Word Choice
Difficulty: Low
Getting to the Answer: The pronoun *it* refers to the tree frog, not a background of leaves. Choice (B) fixes this modifier error by placing "the tree frog" after the modifying phrase.

28. G
Category: Wordiness
Difficulty: Medium
Getting to the Answer: The information pertains to the paragraph's topic, so eliminate J. Choice (G) is a simple and logical way of rephrasing all of the excess words.

29. C
Category: Organization
Difficulty: High
Getting to the Answer: Paragraph 4 begins with an introduction, and paragraph 3 ends with a conclusion. Choice (C) is the only choice that features this correct order.

30. F
Category: Writing Strategy
Difficulty: Medium
Getting to the Answer: The author covers a range of topics in the area and uses several animals as examples. All of the other answer choices are incorrect because they contradict things that the author does in the essay.

PASSAGE III

31. A
Category: Wordiness
Difficulty: Medium
Getting to the Answer: The other answer choices are unnecessarily wordy.

32. J
Category: Wordiness
Difficulty: Medium
Getting to the Answer: The other answer choices are unnecessarily wordy.

33. B
Category: Sentence Sense
Difficulty: High
Getting to the Answer: The sentences on both sides of the period are fragments. The best way to fix this mistake is to simply combine the sentences as (B) does.

34. H
Category: Wordiness
Difficulty: Low
Getting to the Answer: *Included* and *held* relay the same information. Choice (H) deletes one of the unnecessary words.

35. A
Category: Verb Tenses
Difficulty: Medium
Getting to the Answer: The drink was unusual to the people who had never experienced it before.

In other words, the verb form should be past tense. Eliminate B and C. Choice D does not make sense, so eliminate it.

36. H
Category: Sentence Sense
Difficulty: Medium
Getting to the Answer: "Over the next century" is an introductory phrase and should be set off by a comma. Choices (H) and J add the comma, but J also adds unnecessary words.

37. B
Category: Writing Strategy
Difficulty: Medium
Getting to the Answer: This description would add some "color" to the essay. It would not weaken or contradict anything, so eliminate A and C. It would not say anything about the author's opinion of chocolate either, so eliminate D.

38. J
Category: Punctuation
Difficulty: Low
Getting to the Answer: Commas are needed between items in a series. Choice G is incorrect because there are too many commas.

39. A
Category: Connections
Difficulty: Medium
Getting to the Answer: The sentence provides an example of the uses of chocolate worldwide. Choices B and C set up an unwarranted contrast. Choice D is not a good transition between the two sentences.

40. G
Category: Sentence Sense
Difficulty: Medium
Getting to the Answer: The word *do* is unnecessary in the sentence, especially with the presence of *nonetheless*. Choice (G) is the most concise statement of the information.

41. C
Category: Punctuation
Difficulty: Medium
Getting to the Answer: The colon is not used properly here, so eliminate A, B, and D.

42. J
Category: Wordiness
Difficulty: Low
Getting to the Answer: Tea has nothing to do with the topic, so the sentence should be eliminated.

43. A
Category: Word Choice
Difficulty: Low
Getting to the Answer: The research will be welcomed *by* people, not *to* or *with* them. Therefore, eliminate B and D. "Us with a sweet tooth" does not make sense, so (A) is the correct answer.

44. J
Category: Wordiness
Difficulty: Medium
Getting to the Answer: Choices F and G do not make any sense at all. Between H and (J), the latter is the best style.

45. D
Category: Writing Strategy
Difficulty: Medium
Getting to the Answer: This essay is about only chocolate, and it does not cover any other culinary trends in history. Therefore, it would not meet the requirement.

PASSAGE IV

46. H
Category: Word Choice
Difficulty: Medium
Getting to the Answer: Here, the verb is being used as part of a modifying phrase. Choice (H) is idiomatically correct.

47. A
Category: Punctuation
Difficulty: Medium
Getting to the Answer: Commas are needed in a series, so eliminate C. A colon is not appropriate; eliminate B. Choice D incorrectly switches to the past tense.

48. G
Category: Word Choice
Difficulty: Medium
Getting to the Answer: The form needed is the possessive of *who,* so (G) is correct.

49. B
Category: Verb Tenses
Difficulty: Medium
Getting to the Answer: This sentence is part of a list of proposed "uniform of the future" developments. The other sentences in that list use the verbs *would be*, *would become*, and *would transmit*; the correct form is (B).

50. G
Category: Punctuation
Difficulty: High
Getting to the Answer: No commas are needed in a list of only two items.

51. B
Category: Sentence Sense
Difficulty: Low
Getting to the Answer: Be wary of sentences that begin with *to*; they are often fragments like the one here. Choice (B) is the best and most concise way to combine the two parts of the sentence.

52. J
Category: Wordiness
Difficulty: Medium
Getting to the Answer: Two words in the underlined portion of the sentence have closely related meanings: *concealing* means "keeping from being

observed" or "hiding," and *invisible* means "hidden" or "impossible to see." Because these words convey the same idea, this is a redundancy that can be fixed by eliminating one of the two words. Therefore, eliminate F, G, and H and select (J) as the answer.

53. C
Category: Writing Strategy
Difficulty: Medium
Getting to the Answer: To determine the U.S. Army's opinion of the Invisible Soldier program, look at the words used to introduce and describe it: the army has dreamed of such a program and invested in it. So the army attitude is positive; eliminate the negative word *skeptical* in A and the neutral words *curious* and *detailed* in B and D, leaving *enthusiastic*, (C).

54. J
Category: Writing Strategy
Difficulty: High
Getting to the Answer: In context, this paragraph offers a specific example of the more general issues raised in paragraph 1.

55. C
Category: Wordiness
Difficulty: Medium
Getting to the Answer: Although the underlined segment is necessary, having *beginning* and *early stages* is redundant. Choice (C) is the most concise way to rephrase this.

56. J
Category: Sentence Sense
Difficulty: Medium
Getting to the Answer: As written, this is a run-on sentence, so eliminate F. To correct it, the new clause should be made subordinate by replacing the pronoun with a relative pronoun, so eliminate H. The correct form, because it follows a comma, is *which* rather than *that*, so eliminate G.

57. C
Category: Word Choice
Difficulty: Medium
Getting to the Answer: The passage has a formal, technical tone. It would, therefore, be inappropriate for the author to use the highly informal expressions "you know, is" or "is, like" eliminate A and B. The choice "however, is" is appropriate because this paragraph contrasts with the preceding one. Choice D would be appropriate if this paragraph drew a conclusion based on the prior paragraph, but it doesn't.

58. F
Category: Punctuation
Difficulty: High
Getting to the Answer: A colon is correct punctuation here because the material that follows it is an explanation of what precedes it.

59. D
Category: Organization
Difficulty: Medium
Getting to the Answer: Only sentence 2 and sentence 1 are choices for a first sentence. To put the sentences in logical order, first look for a good transition from paragraph 4, which discusses a problem. Sentence 1 explicitly refers to addressing the problem, so it's the better choice. Eliminate A and B. The second sentence should follow logically from sentence 1's description of the new color-changing pixel, and your choices are sentences 4 and 5. Sentence 4 in C refers to mirrors, which we haven't encountered before in the passage, rather than pixels, so eliminate this choice. That leaves us with (D), sentence 5, which refers to the pixels introduced in the first sentence.

60. F
Category: Organization
Difficulty: Medium
Getting to the Answer: To answer this question, you need an idea of the purpose of each

paragraph. Paragraph 1 introduces the "uniform of the future," paragraph 2 the Invisible Soldier program, paragraph 3 the program's early-stage solution, paragraph 4 a problem with that solution, and paragraph 5 a new advance that may solve that problem. The new sentences to be inserted do not discuss a problem with such a program. You can therefore eliminate G, H, and J. The material properly belongs in paragraph 2, (F), because it introduces camouflage generally.

PASSAGE V

61. B
Category: Sentence Sense
Difficulty: Low
Getting to the Answer: Choices A and C are too wordy, and D does not continue the verb tense established in the series.

62. F
Category: Punctuation
Difficulty: Medium
Getting to the Answer: The colon is used here to dramatically introduce California. The commas in G and H do not do this well, and the separate sentence in J does not work either.

63. D
Category: Verb Tenses
Difficulty: Low
Getting to the Answer: This paragraph is in the past tense, so the introductory sentence should be in the past tense as well.

64. G
Category: Punctuation
Difficulty: Medium
Getting to the Answer: This is a long nonessential clause that should be set off by a comma—eliminate F and H. Choice J is incorrect because it unnecessarily adds more words.

65. B
Category: Sentence Sense
Difficulty: Medium
Getting to the Answer: The word order is incorrect in A. Choice C creates a sentence fragment, and *did* in D is unnecessary.

66. F
Category: Wordiness
Difficulty: Medium
Getting to the Answer: The information is pertinent to the topic, and (F) is the clearest way to express it.

67. C
Category: Word Choice
Difficulty: Low
Getting to the Answer: The only choice that works here is (C), which uses the correct possessive form.

68. H
Category: Sentence Sense
Difficulty: Medium
Getting to the Answer: Choice F is a sentence fragment. Choices G and J are very awkward.

69. B
Category: Writing Strategy
Difficulty: Medium
Getting to the Answer: The last sentence of the previous paragraph talks about how workers began to quit their jobs to join the gold rush. The first sentence of this paragraph magnifies this point. Choice (B) is the only logical transition.

70. J
Category: Wordiness
Difficulty: Medium
Getting to the Answer: This information is not pertinent to the gold rush back in 1849.

71. B
Category: Wordiness
Difficulty: Low
Getting to the Answer: *Singularly* and *one* are redundant. Choice C is too wordy, and D is incorrect within the context of the sentence.

72. F
Category: Connections
Difficulty: Medium
Getting to the Answer: This sentence is a more specific detail that illustrates the preceding sentence. Choice (F) is the best transition between the two sentences.

73. B
Category: Word Choice
Difficulty: Medium
Getting to the Answer: Choice A makes it sound as though lives are changing the place rather than the other way around. Choice C does not make sense, and D is grammatically incorrect.

74. J
Category: Sentence Sense
Difficulty: Medium
Getting to the Answer: Choices F and H do not make sense because of the word *and*. Choice G is incorrect because the sentence is talking about people today, not the Forty-niners.

75. B
Category: Writing Strategy
Difficulty: High
Getting to the Answer: Though the Forty-niners are mentioned, the focus of the essay is on the history of the California gold rush. Therefore, the essay would not meet the requirements of the assignment.

MATHEMATICS TEST

1. A
Category: Proportions and Probability
Difficulty: Low
Getting to the Answer: To reduce a number by 20%, you could take 20% of the original number and subtract the result, or you could just take 80% of the original number:

$$\begin{aligned} \text{New price} &= 80\% \text{ of original price} \\ &= (0.80)(\$125) \\ &= \$100 \end{aligned}$$

2. J
Category: Variable Manipulation
Difficulty: Low
Getting to the Answer: Plug in $x = -5$ and see what you get:

$$\begin{aligned} 2x^2 - 6x + 5 &= 2(-5)^2 - 6(-5) + 5 \\ &= 2 \times 25 - (-30) + 5 \\ &= 50 + 30 + 5 \\ &= 85 \end{aligned}$$

3. A
Category: Number Properties
Difficulty: Medium
Getting to the Answer: The prime factorization of 36 is $2 \times 2 \times 3 \times 3$. That factorization includes two distinct prime factors, 2 and 3.

4. G
Category: Plane Geometry
Difficulty: Medium
Getting to the Answer: The exterior angles of a triangle (or any polygon, for that matter) add up to 360°:

$$\begin{aligned} x + 85 + 160 &= 360 \\ x &= 115 \end{aligned}$$

5. B

Category: Number Properties

Difficulty: High

Getting to the Answer: Don't jump to hasty conclusions—don't just average the denominators. Do it right—add the fractions and divide by 2:

Average of two numbers = $\dfrac{\text{Sum}}{2}$

$$\frac{\frac{1}{20} + \frac{1}{30}}{2} = \frac{\frac{3}{60} + \frac{2}{60}}{2} = \frac{\frac{5}{60}}{2} = \frac{\frac{1}{12}}{2} = \frac{1}{12} \times \frac{1}{2} = \frac{1}{24}$$

6. H

Category: Variable Manipulation

Difficulty: Medium

Getting to the Answer: Everyone pays $1.50, and the rest of the toll is based on the number of miles traveled. Subtract $1.50 from Joy's toll to see how much is based on distance traveled: $25.00 − $1.50 = $23.50. Then divide that amount by 25 cents per mile:

$$\frac{\$23.50}{\$0.25 \text{ per mile}} = 94 \text{ miles}$$

7. C

Category: Operations

Difficulty: Medium

Getting to the Answer: Multiply the coefficients and add the exponents:

$$3x^2 \times 5x^3 = 3 \times 5 \times x^2 + x^3 = 15x^5$$

8. J

Category: Coordinate Geometry

Difficulty: High

Getting to the Answer: You could use the distance formula, but it's easier here to think about a right triangle. One leg is the difference between the x's, which is 3, and the other leg is the difference between the y's, which is 4, so you're looking at a 3-4-5 triangle. The hypotenuse, which is the distance from P to Q, is 5.

9. D

Category: Proportions and Probability

Difficulty: Medium

Getting to the Answer: Percent times whole equals part:

$$(\text{Percent}) \times 25 = 16$$

$$\text{Percent} = \frac{16}{25} = 0.64 = 64\%$$

10. F

Category: Proportions and Probability

Difficulty: Medium

Getting to the Answer: For $\dfrac{7}{x}$ to be greater than $\dfrac{1}{4}$, the denominator x has to be less than 4 times the numerator, or 28. And for $\dfrac{7}{x}$ to be less than $\dfrac{1}{3}$, the denominator x has to be greater than 3 times the numerator, or 21. Thus, x could be any of the integers 22 through 27, of which there are 6.

11. B

Category: Variable Manipulation

Difficulty: Medium

Getting to the Answer: To factor $6x^2 − 13x + 6$, you need a pair of binomials whose "first" terms will give you a product of $6x^2$ and whose "last" terms will give you a product of 6. Because the middle term of the result is negative, the two last terms must both be negative. You know that one of the factors is among the answer choices, so you can use them in your trial-and-error effort to factor. You know you're looking for a factor with a minus sign in it, so the answer's either (B) or D.

Try (B) first: Its first term is $3x$, so the other factor's first term would have to be $2x$ (to get that $6x^2$ in the product). Choice (B)'s last term is −2, so the other factor's last term would have to be −3. Check to see whether $(3x − 2)(2x − 3)$ works:

$$\begin{aligned}(3x − 2)(2x − 3) &= (3x \times 2x) + [3x\,(−3)] \\ &\quad + [(−2)(2x)] + [(−2)(−3)] \\ &= 6x^2 − 9x − 4x + 6 \\ &= 6x^2 − 13x + 6\end{aligned}$$

It works. There's no need to check D.

12. G
Category: Variable Manipulation
Difficulty: Medium
Getting to the Answer: The four fractions on the left side of the equation are all ready to be added, because they already have a common denominator: a.

$$\frac{1}{a} + \frac{2}{a} + \frac{3}{a} + \frac{4}{a} = 5$$
$$\frac{1 + 2 + 3 + 4}{a} = 5$$
$$\frac{10}{a} = 5$$
$$10 = 5a$$
$$a = 2$$

13. D
Category: Plane Geometry
Difficulty: Medium
Getting to the Answer: $\angle CGE$ and $\angle BGF$ are vertical angles, so $\angle BGF$ measures 105°. If you subtract $\angle AGB$ from $\angle BGF$, you're left with $\angle AGF$, the angle you're looking for. So $\angle AGF$ measures 105° − 40°, or 65°.

14. G
Category: Variable Manipulation
Difficulty: Medium
Getting to the Answer: You solve an inequality much the way you solve an equation: Do the same things to both sides until you've isolated what you're solving for. (Just remember to flip the sign if you ever multiply or divide both sides by a negative number.) Here, you want to isolate x:

$$-3 < 4x - 5$$
$$2 < 4x$$
$$\frac{2}{4} < x$$
$$x > \frac{1}{2}$$

15. D
Category: Plane Geometry
Difficulty: Medium
Getting to the Answer: Because BD bisects $\angle ABC$, the measure of $\angle ABD$ is 50°. Now you know two of the three angles of $\triangle ABD$, so the third angle measures 180° − 60° − 50° = 70°.

$\angle BDC$, the angle you're looking for, is supplementary to the 70° angle, so $\angle BDC$ measures 180° − 70° = 110°.

16. F
Category: Variable Manipulation
Difficulty: High
Getting to the Answer: To express y in terms of x, isolate y:

$$x + 2y - 3 = xy$$
$$2y - xy = -x + 3$$
$$y(2 - x) = 3 - x$$
$$y = \frac{3 - x}{2 - x}$$

17. E
Category: Proportions and Probability
Difficulty: Medium
Getting to the Answer: If you add the number of English-speakers and the number of Spanish-speakers, you get 28 + 37 = 65. But there are only 50 students, so 65 − 50 = 15 of them are being counted twice—because those 15 speak both languages.

18. K
Category: Proportions and Probability
Difficulty: Medium
Getting to the Answer: Set up a proportion:

$$\frac{288 \text{ miles}}{6 \text{ hours}} = \frac{x \text{ miles}}{8 \text{ hours}}$$
$$6x = 288 \times 8$$
$$6x = 2{,}304$$
$$x = 384$$

19. D
Category: Number Properties
Difficulty: Medium
Getting to the Answer: To convert a fraction to a decimal, you divide the denominator into the numerator. Clearly, you don't have time to take the division out to 100 places after the decimal point. There must be a pattern you can take advantage of. Start dividing and continue just until you see what the pattern is:

$$11\overline{)4.000000\ldots} = 0.363636\ldots$$

The 1st, 3rd, 5th, etc. digits are 3; and the 2nd, 4th, etc. digits are 6. In other words, every odd-numbered digit is a 3 and every even-numbered digit is a 6. The 100th digit is an even-numbered digit, so it's a 6.

20. G
Category: Variable Manipulations
Difficulty: Low
Getting to the Answer: Because it's x you're looking for, eliminate y. Fortunately, the equations are all ready for you—just add them and the $+ 4y$ cancels with the $- 4y$:

$$3x + 4y = 31$$
$$3x - 4y = -1$$
$$6x = 30$$
$$x = 5$$

21. E
Category: Coordinate Geometry
Difficulty: Medium
Getting to the Answer: The coordinates of the midpoint are the averages of the coordinates of the endpoints. The average of the x's is $\frac{2 + 12}{2} = 7$, and the average of the y's is $\frac{3 + (-15)}{2} = -6$, so the coordinates of the midpoint are $(7, -6)$.

22. H
Category: Trigonometry
Difficulty: Medium
Getting to the Answer: Cosine is "adjacent over hypotenuse." Here, the leg adjacent to θ is 4 and the hypotenuse is 5, so $\cos \theta = \frac{4}{5}$.

23. A
Category: Plane Geometry
Difficulty: High
Getting to the Answer: The center of Q is on P's circumference, and the radius of circle Q is twice the radius of circle P. You could use the circumference of circle P to find the radius of circle P, then double that radius to get the radius of circle Q, and finally use that radius to calculate the circumference of circle Q. It's much easier and faster, however, if you realize that "double the radius means double the circumference." If the circumference of circle P is 6, then the circumference of circle Q is twice that, or 12.

24. G
Category: Variable Manipulation
Difficulty: Medium
Getting to the Answer: This looks like a functions question, but in fact it's just a "plug in the number and see what you get" question:

$$f(x) = x^3 - x^2 - x$$
$$f(-3) = (-3)^3 - (-3)^2 - (-3)$$
$$= -27 - 9 + 3$$
$$= -33$$

25. C
Category: Plane Geometry
Difficulty: Medium
Getting to the Answer: Use the Triangle Inequality Theorem here. If the two unknown side lengths are integers, and the sum of the two lengths has to be greater than 4, then the least amount the two unknown sides could add up to would be 5, which would make the perimeter $4 + 5 = 9$.

26. J

Category: Variable Manipulation
Difficulty: Medium
Getting to the Answer: First factor out an x from each term, then factor what's left:

$$2x + 3x^2 + x^3 = x(2 + 3x + x^2)$$
$$= x(x^2 + 3x + 2)$$
$$= x(x + 1)(x + 2)$$

27. C

Category: Operations
Difficulty: Low
Getting to the Answer: Get rid of the parentheses in the denominator, and then cancel factors the numerator and denominator have in common:

$$\frac{x^2 y^3 z^4}{\left(xyz^2\right)^2} = \frac{x^2 y^3 z^4}{x^2 y^2 z^4} = \frac{x^2}{x^2} \cdot \frac{y^3}{y^2} \cdot \frac{z^4}{z^4} = y$$

28. H

Category: Number Properties
Difficulty: Medium
Getting to the Answer: Normally you would have a choice: either convert the fractions to decimals first and then add, or add the fractions first and then convert the sum to a decimal. In this case, however, both fractions would convert to endlessly repeating decimals, which would be unwieldy when adding. In this case, it makes sense to add first, then convert:

$$\frac{2}{3} + \frac{1}{12} = \frac{8}{12} + \frac{1}{12} = \frac{9}{12} = \frac{3}{4} = 0.75$$

29. D

Category: Variable Manipulation
Difficulty: High
Getting to the Answer: This looks like a physics question, but in fact it's just a "plug in the number and see what you get" question. Be sure you plug 95 in for C (not F):

$$C = \frac{5}{9}(F - 32)$$
$$95 = \frac{5}{9}(F - 32)$$
$$\frac{9}{5} \times 95 = F - 32$$
$$F - 32 = 171$$
$$F = 171 + 32 = 203$$

30. H

Category: Proportions and Probability
Difficulty: Medium
Getting to the Answer: Probability equals the number of favorable outcomes divided by the total number of possible outcomes. In this problem, a favorable outcome is choosing a green marble—that's 4. The "total number of possible outcomes" is the total number of marbles, or 20:

$$\text{Probability} = \frac{\text{Favorable outcomes}}{\text{Total number of possible outcomes}}$$
$$= \frac{4}{20}$$
$$= \frac{1}{5}$$

31. A

Category: Number Properties
Difficulty: Medium
Getting to the Answer: To find the average of three numbers—even if they're algebraic expressions—add them and divide by 3:

$$\text{Average} = \frac{\text{Sum of terms}}{\text{Number of terms}}$$
$$= \frac{(2x + 5) + (5x - 6) + (-4x + 2)}{3}$$
$$= \frac{3x + 1}{3}$$
$$= x + \frac{1}{3}$$

32. F

Category: Coordinate Geometry
Difficulty: High
Getting to the Answer: Parallel lines have the same slope. Use the first pair of points to figure out the slope:

$$\text{Slope} = \frac{y_2 - y_1}{x_2 - x_1} = \frac{16 - 1}{2 - 1} = 15$$

Then use the slope to figure out the missing coordinate in the second pair of points:

$$\text{Slope} = \frac{y_2 - y_1}{x_2 - x_1}$$

$$15 = \frac{(25 - (-5))}{a - (-10)}$$

$$15 = \frac{30}{a + 10}$$

$$15a + 150 = 30$$

$$15a = -120$$

$$a = -8$$

33. B

Category: Plane Geometry

Difficulty: Medium

Getting to the Answer: When parallel lines make a big triangle and a little triangle as they do here, the triangles are similar (because they have the same angle measurements). Side $\overline{PR}$ is three times the length of $\overline{QR}$, so each side of the big triangle is three times the length of the corresponding side of the smaller triangle, and therefore the ratio of the perimeters is also 3:1. So the perimeter of ΔPRT is 3 times 11, or 33.

34. K

Category: Plane Geometry

Difficulty: Medium

Getting to the Answer: It is a polygon because it's composed of straight line segments. It is a quadrilateral because it has four sides. It is not a rectangle because opposite sides are not equal. It is a trapezoid because it has one pair of parallel sides.

35. D

Category: Variable Manipulation

Difficulty: Medium

Getting to the Answer: Plug in $x = -3$ and solve for a:

$$2x^2 + (a - 4)x - 2a = 0$$

$$2(-3)^2 + (a - 4)(-3) - 2a = 0$$

$$18 - 3a + 12 - 2a = 0$$

$$30 - 5a = 0$$

$$-5a = -30$$

$$a = 6$$

36. K

Category: Proportions and Probability

Difficulty: Medium

Getting to the Answer: The total number of combinations of a first course, second course, and dessert is equal to the product of the three numbers:

Total possibilities = 4 × 5 × 3 = 60

37. B

Category: Number Properties

Difficulty: High

Getting to the Answer: An integer that's divisible by 6 has at least one 2 and one 3 in its prime factorization. An integer that's divisible by 9 has at least two 3s in its prime factorization. Therefore, an integer that's divisible by both 6 and 9 has at least one 2 and two 3s in its prime factorization. That means it's divisible by 2, 3, 2 × 3 = 6, 3 × 3 = 9, and 2 × 3 × 3 = 18. It's not necessarily divisible by 12 or 36, each of which includes two 2s in its prime factorization. You could also do this one by Picking Numbers. Think of a common multiple of 6 and 9 and use it to eliminate some options. For example, 6 × 9 = 54 is an obvious common multiple—and it's not divisible by 12 or 36, but it is divisible by 18. The *least* common multiple of 6 and 9 is 18, which is also divisible by 18. In fact, every common multiple of 6 and 9 is also a multiple of 18.

38. F

Category: Variable Manipulation

Difficulty: Low

Getting to the Answer:

$$\frac{x^2 + x^2 + x^2}{x^2} = \frac{3x^2}{x^2} = 3$$

39. A

Category: Variable Manipulation

Difficulty: Medium

Getting to the Answer: Read carefully. This question's a lot easier than you might think. It's asking for the total number of coins, not the total value.

q quarters, *d* dimes, and *n* nickels add up to a total of *q* + *d* + *n* coins.

40. K
Category: Variable Manipulation
Difficulty: Medium
Getting to the Answer: You solve an inequality much the way you solve an equation: Do the same things to both sides until you've isolated what you're solving for. (Just remember to flip the sign if you ever multiply or divide both sides by a negative number.)

$$5x - 2(1 - x) \geq 4(x + 1)$$
$$5x - 2 + 2x \geq 4x + 4$$
$$5x + 2x - 4x \geq 4 + 2$$
$$3x \geq 6$$
$$x \geq 2$$

The "greater than or equal to" symbol is graphed as a solid circle.

41. B
Category: Coordinate Geometry
Difficulty: Low
Getting to the Answer: First find the slope of the line that contains the given points:

$$\text{Slope} = \frac{y_2 - y_1}{x_2 - x_1} = \frac{10 - 6}{6 - 5} = 4$$

Line *m* is perpendicular to the above line, so the slope of *m* is the negative reciprocal of 4, or $-\frac{1}{4}$.

42. H
Category: Trigonometry
Difficulty: Low
Getting to the Answer: Sine is "opposite over hypotenuse." Here, the leg opposite θ is 12 and the hypotenuse is 13, so:

$$\sin \theta = \frac{12}{13}$$

43. E
Category: Operations
Difficulty: Medium
Getting to the Answer: Express the left side of the equation so that both sides have the same base:

$$9^{2x - 1} = 3^{3x + 3}$$
$$(3^2)^{2x - 1} = 3^{3x + 3}$$
$$3^{4x - 2} = 3^{3x + 3}$$

Now that the bases are the same, just set the exponents equal:

$$4x - 2 = 3x + 3$$
$$4x - 3x = 3 + 2$$
$$x = 5$$

44. K
Category: Proportions and Probability
Difficulty: Medium
Getting to the Answer: Be careful with combined percent increase. You cannot just add the two percents, because they're generally percents of different wholes. In this instance, the 20% increase is based on the 1970 population, but the 30% increase is based on the larger 1980 population. If you just added 20% and 30% to get 50%, you fell into the testmaker's trap.

The best way to do a problem like this one is to pick a number for the original whole and just see what happens. As usual with percents, the best number to pick is 100. (That may be a small number for the population of a city, but verisimilitude is not important—all that matters is the math.)

If the 1970 population was 100, then a 20% increase would put the 1980 population at 120. Now, to figure the 30% increase, multiply 120 by 130%:

New # = (Original #) + (30% of Original #)
New # = 130% of Original #
$$x = 1.3(120)$$
$$= 156$$

The population went from 100 to 156, which is a 56% increase.

45. E
Category: Number Properties
Difficulty: Medium
Getting to the Answer: The best way to deal with changing averages is to go by way of the sums. Use the old average to figure out the total of the first four scores:

Sum of first 4 scores = 4 × 89 = 356

And use the new average to figure out the total he needs after the fifth score:

Sum of five scores = 5 × 90 = 450

To get his sum up from 356 to 450, Martin needs to score 450 − 356 = 94.

46. K
Category: Coordinate Geometry
Difficulty: High
Getting to the Answer: If you find the distance from the center to the given point on the circle, you'll have the radius. The difference between the x's is 8, and the difference between the y's is 6. If 8 and 6 are the lengths of the legs of a right triangle, then the hypotenuse is 10. The radius, then, is 10. Now you can plug the radius and the coordinates of the center point into the general form of the equation of a circle:

$$(x - h)^2 + (y - k)^2 = r^2$$
$$(x + 1)^2 + (y + 1)^2 = 10^2$$
$$(x + 1)^2 + (y + 1)^2 = 100$$

47. E
Category: Coordinate Geometry
Difficulty: Low
Getting to the Answer: In addition to picking coordinates from the line and plugging them into the answer choices, use the points where the line crosses the axes—(−1, 0) and (0, 2)—to find the slope:

$$\text{Slope} = \frac{y_2 - y_1}{x_2 - x_1} = \frac{2 - 0}{0 - (-1)} = 2$$

The y-intercept is 2. Now plug $m = 2$ and $b = 2$ into the slope-intercept equation form:

$$y = mx + b$$
$$y = 2x + 2$$

48. G
Category: Proportions and Probability
Difficulty: Medium
Getting to the Answer: Be careful. The question is not asking, "What is $\frac{1}{4}$ of 16?" It's asking, "What is $\frac{1}{4}$% of 16?" One-fourth of 1% is 0.25%, or 0.0025:

$$\frac{1}{4}\% \text{ of } 16 = 0.0025 \times 16 = 0.04$$

49. C
Category: Variable Manipulation
Difficulty: High
Getting to the Answer: Use FOIL to get rid of the parentheses, and then combine like terms:

$$(s + 4)(s - 4) + (2s + 2)(s - 2) = (s^2 - 16) + (2s^2 - 2s - 4)$$
$$= s^2 + 2s^2 - 2s - 16 - 4$$
$$= 3s^2 - 2s - 20$$

50. F
Category: Coordinate Geometry
Difficulty: Medium
Getting to the Answer: The easiest way to find the equation of a given parabola is to take a point or two from the graph and plug the coordinates into the answer choices, eliminating the choices that don't work. Start with a point with coordinates that are easy to work with. Here, you could start with (3, 0). Plug $x = 3$ and $y = 0$ into each answer choice, and you'll find that only (F) works.

51. C
Category: Trigonometry
Difficulty: Low
Getting to the Answer: Because $\sin a = \frac{4}{5}$, you could think of this as a 3-4-5 triangle:

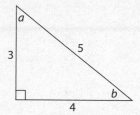

Cosine is "adjacent over hypotenuse." Here, the leg adjacent to b is 4, and the hypotenuse is 5, so $b = \frac{4}{5}$. (Notice that the sine of one acute angle in a right triangle is equal to the cosine of the other acute angle.)

52. F
Category: Variable Manipulation
Difficulty: Low
Getting to the Answer: Add the like terms in the numerator, and then divide by the denominator:

$$\frac{x^2 + x^2 + x^2}{x} = \frac{3x^2}{x} = 3x$$

If you weren't careful, you might have confused this with problem 38 and missed the change in the denominator.

53. B
Category: Variable Manipulation
Difficulty: Medium

Getting to the Answer: When you divide w by 4, you get $\frac{w}{4}$. When you subtract that result from r, you get $r - \frac{w}{4}$.

54. J
Category: Plane Geometry
Difficulty: Medium
Getting to the Answer: The formula for the volume of a cylinder is $V = \pi r^2 h$, where r is the radius of the circular base and h is the height. Here $r = 4$ and $h = 5$, so:

Volume $= \pi r^2 h$
$= \pi(4)^2(5)$
$= \pi(16)(5)$
$= 80\pi$

55. E
Category: Plane Geometry
Difficulty: Medium
Getting to the Answer: With a right triangle, you can use the two legs as the base and the height to figure out the area. Here, the leg lengths are expressed algebraically. Just plug the two expressions in for b and h in the triangle area formula:

$$\text{Area} = \frac{1}{2}(x - 1)(x + 1) = \frac{1}{2}(x^2 - 1) = \frac{x^2 - 1}{2}$$

56. G
Category: Proportions and Probability
Difficulty: Medium
Getting to the Answer: The difference between the populations in 1990 was $9,400 - 7,600 = 1,800$. Each year, as the larger population goes down by 100 and the smaller population goes up by 100, the difference decreases by 200. Thus, it will take $1,800 \div 200 = 9$ years to erase the difference.

57. B
Category: Number Properties
Difficulty: High
Getting to the Answer: The overall average is not simply the average of the two average ages. Because there are a lot more women than men, women carry more weight, and the overall average will be closer to 25 than 35. Pick particular numbers for the females and males, say 4 females and 1 male. The ages of the 4 females total 4 times 25, or 100, and the age of the 1 male totals 35. The average, then, is $(100 + 35)$ divided by 5, or 27.

58. J
Category: Trigonometry
Difficulty: High
Getting to the Answer: The height h of the tree is the leg opposite θ. The distance b from the base

of the tree is the leg adjacent to θ. "Opposite over adjacent" is tangent, but all the answer choices are in terms of the sine. Sine is "opposite over hypotenuse," so you're going to have to figure out the hypotenuse. Use the Pythagorean theorem:

$$(\text{hypotenuse})^2 = (\text{leg}_1)^2 + (\text{leg}_2)^2$$
$$(\text{hypotenuse})^2 = b^2 + h^2$$
$$\text{hypotenuse} = \sqrt{b^2 + h^2}$$

Now, to get the sine, put the opposite h over the hypotenuse $\sqrt{b^2 + h^2}$: $\sin\theta = \dfrac{h}{\sqrt{b^2 + h^2}}$

59. C
Category: Variable Manipulation
Difficulty: Medium
Getting to the Answer: This looks like a solid geometry question, but in fact it's just a "plug in the numbers" question:

$$S = \pi r\sqrt{r^2 + h^2} = \pi(3)\sqrt{3^2 + 4^2} = 3\pi\sqrt{9 + 16}$$
$$= 3\pi\sqrt{25} = 3\pi \times 5 = 15\pi$$

60. J
Category: Plane Geometry
Difficulty: Medium
Getting to the Answer: When a transversal crosses parallel lines, all the resulting acute angles are equal, and all the resulting obtuse angles are equal. (You can generally tell from looking which angles are equal.) In this problem's figure, $a = c = e = g$ and $b = d = f = h$. Only (J) is true: c and g are both obtuse. In all the other choices, you'll find an obtuse and an acute angle.

READING TEST

PASSAGE I

1. D
Category: Detail
Difficulty: Medium
Getting to the Answer: Lines 18–21 provide the answer: "I was brought up, from my earliest remembrance…by my godmother."

2. G
Category: Inference
Difficulty: Medium
Getting to the Answer: From the description of Dolly in the first two paragraphs, it is clear that Esther viewed her doll as her only friend. "I was such a shy little thing that I seldom dared to open my lips, and never dared to open my heart, to anybody else" (lines 6–9). This idea is repeated in lines 97–101: "I went up to my room, and crept to bed, and laid my doll's cheek against mine wet with tears, and holding that solitary friend upon my bosom, cried myself to sleep."

3. B
Category: Vocab-in-Context
Difficulty: Medium
Getting to the Answer: In this case, *stiff* is used to describe the tone of the letter that Esther's godmother wrote to decline the invitation to another student's birthday party. Choice (B), "rigidly formal," is the most appropriate definition in this context.

4. G
Category: Inference
Difficulty: High
Getting to the Answer: This is a Global question. Esther mentions that her birthday was never celebrated and the pivotal scene in the passage happens on her birthday. In lines 3–4, Esther tells her doll that she is not very clever, but that is not the focus of the passage. In lines 54–57, she mentions being invited to a friend's home for a party, so

H is not correct. In lines 79–82, you find out that Esther's mother did not die on her birthday, so J is not correct.

5. C
Category: Inference
Difficulty: Medium
Getting to the Answer: Although Esther's god-mother says that she has forgiven Esther's mother, her facial expression directly contradicts this. "I see her knitted brow and pointed finger...her face did not relent...." (lines 88–92).

6. G
Category: Detail
Difficulty: Low
Getting to the Answer: Esther is clearly lonely, as evidenced by her description of Dolly as her only friend and her explanation that there is a separation dividing her from the other girls at school. The birthday scene with her godmother also shows that Esther is quite confused about her own family past.

7. C
Category: Inference
Difficulty: Medium
Getting to the Answer: Her confrontation with her godmother gives Esther further reason to believe that no one loves her. The phrase before the cited line also points to (C) as the best answer: "I knew that I had brought no joy at any time to anybody's heart" (lines 102–103).

8. J
Category: Detail
Difficulty: Medium
Getting to the Answer: Choices F, G, and H are all mentioned in paragraph 5 (lines 44–59). At the end of the passage, Esther says, "I hope it is not self-indulgent to shed these tears as I think of it" (lines 111–112).

9. C
Category: Detail
Difficulty: Low
Getting to the Answer: Esther's evidence that her godmother is a "good, good woman" is explained in lines 22–27: "She went to church three times every Sunday, and to morning prayers on Wednesdays and Fridays, and to lectures whenever there were lectures, and never missed."

10. G
Category: Detail
Difficulty: High
Getting to the Answer: In the first paragraph, Esther says, "Now, Dolly, I am not clever..." (lines 3–4). In the second paragraph, Esther describes herself as "such a shy little thing" (lines 6–7).

PASSAGE II

11. B
Category: Vocab-in-Context
Difficulty: Low
Getting to the Answer: In the phrase "the Pantanal was a vast, soggy canvas, white with gleaming herds of Nelore cattle" (lines 73–75), *canvas* is used to mean "a background." None of the other choices makes sense.

12. J
Category: Detail
Difficulty: Medium
Getting to the Answer: The answer to this question can be found in lines 79–82: "As the jaguars grew scarce, their chief food staple, the capybaras—a meter-long rodent, the world's largest—overran farmers' fields..."

13. C
Category: Detail
Difficulty: Medium
Getting to the Answer: The answer to this question can be found in lines 15–20: "Exactly how dramatic

a comeback is difficult to say because jaguars—*Panthera onca*, the largest feline in the New World—are solitary, secretive, nocturnal predators. Each cat needs to prowl at least 35 square kilometers by itself."

14. G
Category: Inference
Difficulty: Medium
Getting to the Answer: The last sentence of the second paragraph provides the answer. "Hotels, campgrounds, and bed-and-breakfasts have sprung up to accommodate the half-million tourists a year…bent on sampling the Pantanal's wildlife, of which the great cats must be the most magnificent example" (lines 28–34). Tourists want to see the jaguars, and not having the jaguars might negatively affect the booming ecotourist business.

15. A
Category: Detail
Difficulty: Low
Getting to the Answer: The "green safari" example is mentioned as a way for "scientists to fit the cats with radio collars" (lines 103–105). The other three examples provided are listed in lines 109–113 as methods the scientists are teaching the ranchers.

16. G
Category: Generalization
Difficulty: Medium
Getting to the Answer: In lines 59–60, the author says, "Hard data on cattle losses due to jaguars in the Pantanal are nonexistent…." One reason for providing anecdotal information, then, is to tell the story of the hardships faced by the ranchers due to the jaguars. The author does not suggest that he empathizes with the ranchers more than the jaguars—in fact, he refers to the jaguars as "magnificent." The only examples that show rancher violence is Abel Monteiro shooting an attacking jaguar who had killed his two dogs (lines 37–43) and Ramos da Silva throwing burning sticks at a jaguar that was trying to invade his camp (43–47), both

acts of self-defense. The landscape of the Pantanal is not the focus of these two paragraphs, so J can be eliminated.

17. C
Category: Inference
Difficulty: Medium
Getting to the Answer: The passage explains that because of the decrease in the jaguar population, the capybara population increased. These rodents "spread trichomoniasis, a livestock disease that renders cows sterile" (lines 82–83). Lines 86–91 describe the effect of weather patterns and floods on the ranchers' land. "Weather patterns also shifted radically—due most likely to global warming—and drove annual floods to near-Biblical proportions. The waters are only now retreating from some inundated pasturelands."

18. G
Category: Detail
Difficulty: Medium
Getting to the Answer: The last sentence of the passage reads, "When the scholars go home and the greens log off, the *pantaneiros* will still be there—left on their own to deal with the jaguars as they see fit" (lines 117–120).

19. D
Category: Detail
Difficulty: Low
Getting to the Answer: Evidence is given throughout the passage that all three groups support protecting the jaguars. It is most concisely stated in lines 49–53: "a political catfight between the scientists, environmentalists, and ecotourists who want to protect the jaguars and the embattled ranchers.…"

20. F
Category: Detail
Difficulty: Medium
Getting to the Answer: The answer to this question can be found in lines 59–61: "Hard data on cattle

losses due to jaguars in the Pantanal are nonexistent, but there are stories."

PASSAGE III

21. A
Category: Inference
Difficulty: Medium
Getting to the Answer: This question asks you why the aulos was considered "the instrument of the Dionysians." In the fifth paragraph, you find out that the Dionysians "represented the unbridled, sensual and passionate aspect of Greek culture" (lines 65–67). The passage also says that the aulos had a "far more exciting effect" (lines 71–72) than the lyre. The suggestion here is clearly that the aulos must have been able to express the unbridled passion and excitement of the Dionysians, making (A) the best answer. Choice B is out because the fact that the aulos was chosen as the official instrument of the Delphian and Pythian festivals doesn't explain why it was the instrument of the Dionysians. Choice C contradicts the passage. The kithara, not the aulos, represented the intellectual, idealistic side of Greek art. Finally, the author never says when the Dionysian cult originated, so D is also out.

22. J
Category: Detail
Difficulty: Medium
Getting to the Answer: All the author means by saying that the chelys can be "traced back to the age of fable" is that it is an ancient instrument. The chelys was an actual, not an imaginary, instrument, so H is incorrect. G is out because the kithara was used to accompany the epics, not the chelys.

23. D
Category: Generalization
Difficulty: Low
Getting to the Answer: Choice (D) is the only answer choice that adequately covers the entire passage. Choice A focuses only on the lyre. The connection between Greek music and drama, B, is

mentioned only in passing, as are the references to music in ancient Greek literature, C. The passage is really all about the "origin and development of various Greek instruments," (D).

24. H
Category: Detail
Difficulty: Medium
Getting to the Answer: The first thing the author says about the kithara is that it was used by "professional Homeric singers" (lines 15–16). The kithara, according to the author, probably came from Egypt, so F is incorrect. Choice G and J contradict information in the paragraph to the effect that the kithara was more powerful than the chelys and was played with both hands.

25. D
Category: Detail
Difficulty: Medium
Getting to the Answer: Skim through the third paragraph to find the changes that occurred to the lyre between the eighth and fifth centuries B.C. Musicians began to use a plectrum in the seventh century B.C., A; lyres featured an increasing number of strings, B, during this period; and musicians also began to use different scales and modes, C. That leaves (D). Nothing in the paragraph indicates that lyres were used to accompany dramatic productions.

26. J
Category: Inference
Difficulty: Medium
Getting to the Answer: The final paragraph says that "an early specimen" of the aulos was tuned to the chromatic tetrachord, "a fact that points to Oriental origin" (line 87). From this, you can infer that the chromatic tetrachord must have been used in ancient Oriental music, (J). Choice F is contradicted by the author's assertion that elegiac songs were composed in the mode of the chromatic tetrachord. There is no evidence to support either G or H.

27. C
Category: Detail
Difficulty: Low
Getting to the Answer: In the fourth sentence of the first paragraph (lines 8–10), the author indicates that the chelys is the most antique form of the lyre.

28. G
Category: Detail
Difficulty: Medium
Getting to the Answer: Sappho did two things that you know about from lines 44–47. She introduced a mode "in which Dorian and Lydian characteristics were blended," and she "initiated the use of the plectrum."

29. B
Category: Detail
Difficulty: High
Getting to the Answer: All of the details you need to answer this question are in the sixth paragraph (lines 68–78). The first sentence states that the aulos is more like our oboe than our flute, so III is false. This means C and D can be eliminated. The second sentence of the paragraph confirms that the aulos sounded more exciting than the lyre (II). Because (B) is the only remaining answer choice that includes II, you know it has to be the best answer.

30. F
Category: Generalization
Difficulty: Medium
Getting to the Answer: Greek instruments are discussed as a whole at the very beginning of the passage. The author says that our knowledge of Greek instruments comes from "representations on monuments, vases, statues, and friezes and from the testimony of Greek authors" (lines 4–6). These are all "secondary sources" of information about the instruments, so (F) is the best answer. Choice G is incorrect because quite a bit is known about the tuning of the instruments, as represented in the second paragraph. Choice H is contradicted by the

same sentence that supports (F). Finally, there is no evidence to suggest that more is known about one type of instrument than the other, J.

PASSAGE IV

31. B
Category: Detail
Difficulty: High
Getting to the Answer: The first paragraph in Passage A states, "In addition, saliva, tears, and mucous all contain the enzyme lysozyme, which can destroy bacterial cell walls (causing bacteria to rupture due to osmotic pressure) and some viral capsids" (lines 9–13).

32. G
Category: Detail
Difficulty: High
Getting to the Answer: As described in the passage, "macrophages are able to display to other more specific immune system cells the antigens (foreign proteins) they have just encountered. That, in turn, often results in a more intensive immune response from these more specific cells like B and T cells" (lines 45–50).

33. B
Category: Generalization
Difficulty: Medium
Getting to the Answer: The second paragraph says that macrophages engulf materials through a process called phagocytosis, and the third paragraph states that neutrophils are phagocytic-like macrophages.

34. J
Category: Vocab-in-Context
Difficulty: Medium
Getting to the Answer: A TH cell is a "helper" cell. Additionally, clues in the passage indicate that macrophages/APCs and B cells cooperate: the third paragraph indicates that T cells interact with APCs,

and the fourth paragraph indicates that helper T cells cue B cells to activate. Predict that TH cells "help" or intervene in the situation.

35. A
Category: Detail
Difficulty: High
Getting to the Answer: Paragraphs 5 and 6 discuss the activation of B and T cells. The passage states, "When a particular B or T cell gets activated, it begins to divide rapidly to produce identical clones. In the case of B cells, these clones will all produce antibodies of the same structure, capable of responding to the same invading antigens. B cell clones are known as plasma B cells and can produce thousands of antibody molecules per second as long as they live" (lines 116–123).

36. J
Category: Detail
Difficulty: Medium
Getting to the Answer: The end of the fourth paragraph states that helper T cells (TH) must recognize the proteins and then release chemicals to tell the B cell to replicate, which, according to paragraph 6, will then produce antibodies.

37. C
Category: Generalization
Difficulty: High
Getting to the Answer: The introductory information states, "The specific immune system is able to attack very specific disease-causing organisms by means of protein-to-protein interaction and is responsible for our ability to become immune to future infections from pathogens we have fought off already."

38. H
Category: Detail
Difficulty: Medium
Getting to the Answer: Passage A provides information about the nonspecific functions of the system, while Passage B provides additional information about the system by addressing the specific functions.

39. A
Category: Inference
Difficulty: High
Getting to the Answer: Paragraph 4 in Passage B indicates that B cells can only be activated by TH cells that recognize pathogens the B cell has captured, but paragraph 3 indicates that T cells cannot recognize free antigens—they can only detect those displayed on cell surfaces. Additionally, paragraph 3 states that there are interactions between T cells and APCs, and paragraph 2 specifically states that TH cells will serve as mediators between the macrophages (certain APCs) and B cells. Passage A explains that macrophages are nonspecific functions that can display antigens on their cell walls for the specific system to see. It can thus be logically inferred that a macrophage in the nonspecific division must display information that a TH cell can see and pass to B cells before the B cells can be activated to then replicate and produce antibodies.

40. G
Category: Detail
Difficulty: Medium
Getting to the Answer: The first paragraph in Passage A states: "In addition, saliva, tears, and mucous all contain the enzyme lysozyme, which can destroy bacterial cell walls (causing bacteria to rupture due to osmotic pressure) and some viral capsids" (lines 9–13). The second paragraph of Passage B says, "Since virally infected cells display some viral proteins on their surfaces, TC cells can bind to those proteins and secrete enzymes that tear the cell membrane and kill the cell" (lines 85–88).

SCIENCE TEST

PASSAGE I

1. B
Category: Figure Interpretation
Difficulty: Medium
Getting to the Answer: Look at the *y*-axis of the graph between the region of pH 8 and pH 12, and then scan across at that level. The indicators that undergo color change in this pH range are thymol blue, phenolphthalein, and alizarin. These indicators correspond to (B).

2. H
Category: Figure Interpretation
Difficulty: Low
Getting to the Answer: Looking carefully at the graph, you can see that methyl orange changes from red to yellow between pH 3 and pH 5, and alizarin changes from yellow to red between pH 9 and pH 11. Thymol blue undergoes a yellow to blue color change, so it is not correct.

3. A
Category: Patterns
Difficulty: Medium
Getting to the Answer: In order to determine when the reaction is complete and the solution is basic, the chemist should select an indicator that turns color when the pH has risen into the region of basicity (above 7). When bromocresol green inches above the pH of 7, it turns blue, so (A) is correct.

4. J
Category: Scientific Reasoning
Difficulty: High
Getting to the Answer: This question requires you to form a broad conclusion about acid-base indicators. Choices F and G are incorrect because there are plenty of indicators that change colors above or below pH 7. Choice H is incorrect because different indicators change colors at different pH levels, and this fact also explains why (J) is correct.

5. A
Category: Figure Interpretation
Difficulty: Low
Getting to the Answer: Compare the two indicators on the graph, and you'll find that phenolphthalein undergoes a color change at a higher pH than bromothymol blue.

6. G
Category: Figure Interpretation
Difficulty: Low
Getting to the Answer: Locate black coffee in Table 1; it has a pH of 5. Then look in Figure 1 to determine which indicator responds to a pH of 5. Only Bromothymol Blue corresponds to this pH. Choice (G) is correct.

PASSAGE II

7. D
Category: Scientific Reasoning
Difficulty: Medium
Getting to the Answer: First, consider which of the listed options can be categorized as "atmospheric conditions." Because skin color is not an atmospheric condition, you can eliminate A and B. The other three options are atmospheric conditions. Choice (D) is correct.

8. F
Category: Figure Interpretation
Difficulty: Low
Getting to the Answer: The quickest way to answer the question is to eliminate the incorrect answer choices. A look at Table 1 rules out G because the total amount of oxygen absorbed is clearly affected by temperature. Choice H is incorrect because frog health is never an issue. The very mention of CO_2 makes J incorrect—Experiment 1 was only concerned with oxygen.

9. C
Category: Patterns
Difficulty: Medium
Getting to the Answer: There is no data for 17°C, so an estimate is necessary. The total (skin plus lungs) amount of carbon dioxide released per hour was about 100 mol/hr at 15°C and about 110 mol/hr at 20°C. The only choice that falls between these is (C).

10. H
Category: Scientific Reasoning
Difficulty: Medium
Getting to the Answer: To show that *Hyla faber* is an ectotherm, one must find evidence demonstrating that changes in temperature cause changes in gas exchange. Table 1 demonstrates that as temperature increases, *Hyla faber's* oxygen absorption increases, so (H) is correct. Choice F is not good evidence because data for only one temperature do not give an idea of how temperature changes affect gas exchange. Choice G is incorrect because the amount of carbon dioxide eliminated by the lungs is the same at 15°C, 20°C, and 25°C, making it look as though changes in temperature have little effect on gas exchange in the frog.

11. B
Category: Figure Interpretation
Difficulty: Low
Getting to the Answer: The amount of carbon dioxide eliminated by the skin increases over the range of temperatures; the increase levels off at the highest temperature. Carbon dioxide release by the lungs increases a bit over the lower temperatures and then levels off almost completely. The curve for skin release has to be much higher on the graph than the curve for lung release because the skin eliminated more carbon dioxide at each temperature than did the lungs. Choice (B) is the only graph that fits these patterns.

12. G
Category: Patterns
Difficulty: Medium
Getting to the Answer: When the answer choices all look similar, as in this problem, find the differences between them and rule out the ones that cannot be correct. You can eliminate H and J right away because the results show that as temperature increases, O_2 absorbed by the lungs increases. Choice F is not correct either—as temperature increases, CO_2 released by the skin increases, which is stated by (G).

13. B
Category: Figure Interpretation
Difficulty: Medium
Getting to the Answer: Here again, you want to be careful and refer to the answer choices as you review the tables to observe what happens as the temperature rises above 15°C. Each of the answer choices refers to the tree frog's ability to absorb oxygen through the skin, so start there. From Table 1, you can see that the skin's oxygen absorption rate goes down, so C and D are out. Now you need to refer to Table 2 to see what happens to the rate at which carbon dioxide is released from the lungs. It appears to remain about the same, so the correct answer is (B).

PASSAGE III

14. H
Category: Figure Interpretation
Difficulty: High
Getting to the Answer: This is a tricky question, so make sure you determine the opinions of both scientists. Scientist 1 states that deep-focus earthquakes are due to the release of water from crystalline structures, not magma. Because magma in the asthenosphere is not related to crystalline structures, it is unlikely to support Scientist 1's viewpoint. Scientist 2 states that deep-focus earthquakes are caused by slippage that occurs when rock in a descending plate undergoes a phase change. Liquid

magma in the asthenosphere fails to support Scientist 2's viewpoint. Because neither scientist is supported, (H) must be correct.

15. D
Category: Scientific Reasoning
Difficulty: Medium
Getting to the Answer: Scientist 1 states that "below 50 km, rock is under too much pressure to fracture normally." Scientist 2 gives the fact that "rock becomes ductile at the temperatures and pressures that exist at depths greater than 50 km" as the reason that "deep-focus earthquakes cannot result from normal fractures."

16. F
Category: Scientific Reasoning
Difficulty: High
Getting to the Answer: Scientist 1's theory is invalid unless water can be shown to exist in mantle rock at the level of deep-focus earthquakes. If researchers could subject mantle-like rock to those temperatures and pressures, and then extract water from it, (F), their experimental results would support the hypothesis of Scientist 1.

17. C
Category: Scientific Reasoning
Difficulty: Medium
Getting to the Answer: Both scientists believe that the Earth's crust (surface layer) is composed of mobile tectonic plates. In describing the plates as being "forced down into the mantle," Scientist 1 implies that they are normally in the crust, and Scientist 2 makes reference to "a descending tectonic plate." The introductory paragraph says that "most" earthquakes originate less than 20 km below Earth's surface, so A is incorrect. Neither scientist assumes that surface quakes are caused by trapped fluids, B; both state that such quakes are caused by normal fractures in Earth's crust. Neither scientist discusses how deep-focus earthquakes are detected, so D is not an assumption made by either scientist.

18. G
Category: Scientific Reasoning
Difficulty: Medium
Getting to the Answer: Scientist 2 believes that deep-focus quakes are the result of slippage caused by phase changes. Scientist 2 would, therefore, not expect deep quakes to occur below 680 km where, according to the last sentence of the passage, "no phase changes are predicted." Recording a quake with an origin below that depth would send Scientist 2 back to the drawing board, or at least in search of deeper phase changes.

19. D
Category: Scientific Reasoning
Difficulty: Low
Getting to the Answer: The final sentence of Scientist 1's paragraph mentions that when fluids were injected into the ground at the Rocky Mountain Arsenal, the unintended result was "a series of shallow-focus earthquakes." The opening words *in fact* signal that this final sentence is meant to illustrate the previous sentence, which refers to experiments in which trapped fluids caused rock to fail at lower than normal shear stresses. The implication is that the quakes at the arsenal occurred because the fluid wastes lowered the shear stress failure point of the rock, (D). Dehydration, A, is an important part of the hypothesis of Scientist 1 but is not specifically mentioned in the scientist's discussion of the Rocky Mountain Arsenal. The slab of calcium magnesium silicate, B, belongs in Scientist 2's paragraph. Choice C confuses the Rocky Mountain Arsenal incident with the deep-sea trenches that are mentioned in the previous two sentences.

20. H
Category: Scientific Reasoning
Difficulty: Medium
Getting to the Answer: Scientist 2 claims that the slippage involved in deep-focus quakes results from phase changes. To support this contention, she cites laboratory work that produced similar phase changes and slippage in a slab of calcium

magnesium silicate. But neither scientist says that mantle rock is composed of calcium magnesium silicate. If the slippery slab is to serve as evidence for Scientist 2's theory, it must at least be similar to mantle rock, so (H) is correct. Choice F might help refute Scientist 1's viewpoint, but it would not strengthen Scientist 2's theory. Choices G and J would tend to weaken Scientist 2's theory.

21. D
Category: Scientific Reasoning
Difficulty: Medium
Getting to the Answer: Phase changes are fundamental to the arguments of both scientists, and both agree that they occur deep beneath Earth's surface, so you can eliminate A and B. The release of water from minerals is part of the explanation of Scientist 1, so C is out as well. Only (D) agrees with the logic of Scientist 2.

PASSAGE IV

22. H
Category: Figure Interpretation
Difficulty: Medium
Getting to the Answer: The one variable that changes is the amount of moisture. Choice G cannot be correct because Experiment 2 says that the researcher used models representing equivalent mass as those in Experiment 1. There is no evidence for F or J.

23. B
Category: Scientific Reasoning
Difficulty: Medium
Getting to the Answer: The moisture in Experiment 1 is 86%, and the moisture in Experiment 2 is 12%. If the moisture were changed to 50%, the collision rating would fall between the lines of the two experiments on the graphs. At 400,000 kg, the collision rating would be between 4.5 and 5.5.

24. G
Category: Scientific Reasoning
Difficulty: High
Getting to the Answer: The collision ratings for Experiment 1, with a high percentage of moisture in the atmosphere, were mostly lower than those in Experiment 2. Therefore, an increase in moisture would decrease the impact of a collision. Eliminate H and J. However, for asteroids over 700,000 kg, the lines on the graph meet—the presence of moisture loses its effect. Choice (G) is correct.

25. C
Category: Figure Interpretation
Difficulty: Low
Getting to the Answer: Feel free to draw in your booklet on Test Day. To answer this question, draw a line from 4 on the x-axis straight up. Draw a line from 4 on the y-axis straight across. Those two lines meet on the line for Experiment 1. The moisture level for Experiment 1 was 86%, so (C) is correct.

26. H
Category: Figure Interpretation
Difficulty: Medium
Getting to the Answer: Again, it might help to draw on the graph to answer this question. Draw a vertical line up from 1 (100,000 kg) on the horizontal scale to see where it hits the curve representing Experiment 2. Then draw a horizontal line from this curve to the curve representing Experiment 1, and draw from that point down to the horizontal scale once again. You'll see that the size is closest to (H), 270,000 kg.

27. B
Category: Figure Interpretation
Difficulty: High
Getting to the Answer: To be minimally capable of regional destruction, an asteroid must have a collision rating of 4, so draw a horizontal line over from 4 on the vertical scale. If you do so, you'll see that size of an asteroid capable of such destruction goes from roughly 250,000 kg at a 12% moisture

level to about 400,000 kg at an 86% moisture level. Then 400,000 is roughly 70% larger than 250,000, so (B) is the correct answer.

28. J
Category: Patterns
Difficulty: Medium
Getting to the Answer: Use the graph to approximate where this collision would occur. A 1.5 on the Torino scale and a 350,000 kg asteroid would result in a point that is below and to the right of Experiment 1, so its moisture level would be above 86%. Choice (J) is the correct answer.

PASSAGE V

29. D
Category: Figure Interpretation
Difficulty: Medium
Getting to the Answer: Look at the graphs that clarify the relationship between conductivity and temperature for a conductor and a semiconductor. Semiconductors have a direct relationship: as temperature increases, so does conductivity. Look at the conductivity vs. temperature graph and find a temperature range in which both samples have positive slopes. Don't worry if you can't find a range—that means that both samples do not share a temperature range for semiconducting behavior, and therefore (D) is correct.

30. H
Category: Figure Interpretation
Difficulty: High
Getting to the Answer: Following HST-52 from right to left across the first figure (because the temperature is decreasing), conductivity increases and temperature decreases—just like the conductivity of a conductor—until 160 K, at which point HST-52's conductivity starts to decrease with decreasing temperature, like a semiconductor. With decreasing temperature, the sample undergoes a conductor to semiconductor transition, (H).

31. B
Category: Patterns
Difficulty: Low
Getting to the Answer: The plot for conductor-like behavior indicates that as the temperature increases, its conductivity decreases. Choices A and C describe the behavior of semiconductors, not conductors. Choice D is incorrect: If the conductivity of conductors were the same at all temperatures, the plot of conductivity versus temperature for conductors would be a horizontal line.

32. H
Category: Patterns
Difficulty: Medium
Getting to the Answer: A material that has a semiconductor to conductor transition at 10 K will show a brief increase and then, starting at 10 K, a steady decrease as the temperature increases. Choice (H) is the plot that shows this brief increase at low temperatures and then the decrease as the temperature rises.

33. D
Category: Scientific Reasoning
Difficulty: Medium
Getting to the Answer: The figure shows that HST-52 displays semiconductor behavior only up to about 150 K. Therefore, HST-52 will be usable as a semiconductor only at temperatures below about 150 K, (D). Choice A is incorrect because HST-52 is a semiconductor at certain temperatures, and B is incorrect because HST-52 is not a semiconductor at all temperatures. The brittleness of HST-52 is never discussed in the passage, so C should be eliminated from the outset.

34. J
Category: Patterns
Difficulty: High
Getting to the Answer: You are looking for the temperature at which the downward slope for Sample HST-52 is the steepest. This is somewhat difficult

to determine, but this much is clear: The slope does not begin to go down until the temperature rises above 160 K. Thus, the only answer that could make sense is (J), 180 K.

PASSAGE VII

35. C
Category: Figure Interpretation
Difficulty: Low
Getting to the Answer: The graph shows no difference in the percentage of body covered in dark fur for outdoor temperatures less than or equal to 2°C, making (C) correct. The phrase "According to the graph" should remind you to extract data directly from the graph. Based on the passage alone, you might incorrectly assume that because the temperature drops over that month the percentage of body covered in dark fur would increase, as in A. The graph shows, however, that this is only true for outdoor temperatures between 2°C and 7°C.

36. G
Category: Scientific Reasoning
Difficulty: High
Getting to the Answer: The key to this question is determining whether the cat in question is an outdoor or indoor cat. This cat goes outdoors a total of three hours per week, whereas an outdoor cat would spend at least six hours outdoors per week. Therefore, this cat is an indoor cat, and the percentage of dark fur on its body would remain just above 10%.

37. B
Category: Figure Interpretation
Difficulty: Medium
Getting to the Answer: You can draw a line from 45% dark fur across to the solid line representing outdoor cats. If you draw a line from that intersection straight down to the x-axis, you will hit 3°C.

38. G
Category: Patterns
Difficulty: High
Getting to the Answer: If the cat grew dark fur over 30% of its body, it must have been an outdoor cat as defined in the passage and, according to the graph, been exposed to temperature below 5°C (Statement I). To be an outdoor cat, a cat does not have to spend more time outdoors than indoors (Statement II), but it has to spend time outdoors for six consecutive days (Statement III).

39. C
Category: Patterns
Difficulty: Medium
Getting to the Answer: If a Siamese cat does not have dark fur over more than 10% of its body, then it must *either* be an indoor cat *or* live in an area where it is not regularly exposed to temperatures below 7°C.

40. H
Category: Scientific Reasoning
Difficulty: Medium
Getting to the Answer: Choice F is incorrect because the indoor cats will not help us, since they don't go outside. Choice G is not a good choice because the outdoor cats of the original experiment cannot be used as a control group: The time they spent outside was not monitored—you only know that they spent more than one hour outside a day. Choice J is incorrect because the data already gathered only show that outdoor cats turn darker in cold weather than indoor cats and do not provide any information about how varying the amount of time outdoors affects fur color. The correct answer is (H). A completely new experiment would have to be set up.

WRITING TEST

MODEL ESSAY

Below is an example of what a high-scoring essay might look like. Notice the author states her position clearly in the introductory paragraph and supports that position with evidence in the following paragraphs. This essay also uses transitions, some advanced vocabulary, and an effective "hook" to draw in the reader.

Teenagers have lots of opinions, many of which we share rather loudly. Taking into consideration the students' feelings about the courses they study in high school has both pros and cons. Some argue that schools should provide students a way to make their preferences known, others feel students are too young to make good decisions about what to study, and others argue that surveying students can help make the curriculum more relevant to them and provide another way to evaluate a teacher's effectiveness. I agree that students' interests should be surveyed as long as they are not, in and of themselves, the basis for creating a curriculum.

From the first perspective, it is argued that high schools should do what colleges do and survey students to see how they feel about their classroom lessons. Studies show that when high school students are engaged because they enjoy their studies and understand the relevance of what they are learning, they are more participatory in class and remember more of what they learn. However, one problem is that schools cannot let students create the lessons, since this would lead to chaos with so many students expressing different opinions. However, if it were made clear that not all suggestions would be used but that there would be some way to pare down the suggestions, implementing only those with most student support, it would be possible for the students' preferences to be included in a lesson. Schools could survey students, compile a list of five top suggestions, then have students vote on them. In this way at least some student suggestions, and hopefully the most popular ones, would be part of the curriculum and promote more interaction and learning in a classroom. Surely this is the goal of education, and therefore it should be encouraged.

On the other hand, there are those who think that only the teachers should be in charge of the curriculum because students are not qualified to make those changes. It's true that students don't have the education, knowledge, and maturity to design lessons, but the argument doesn't say that the curriculum would be totally in the hands of the students, but only that student preferences should be considered. Those who argue that students aren't capable of designing the curriculum have misunderstood the statement. Everybody can benefit from suggestions, including educators, so there is nothing wrong with finding out what students want and trying to incorporate at least some of it into the curriculum. Any good teacher does this already. For example, she tries to make her examples relevant to what the students are interested in, such as teaching math by using basketball or baseball examples. So the argument is already partially in force, and those who misread it by thinking that the entire curriculum would be made up by students are misinterpreting the argument and coming to a wrong conclusion.

Finally, some argue that allowing student surveys could make lessons more interesting and also be a way of evaluating a teacher's effectiveness. I personally think that this would be a better way to evaluate teachers

PRACTICE TEST TWO ANSWERS AND EXPLANATIONS

than using test scores, which don't always reflect real learning. But surveys are completely subjective, and it would be very difficult to tell which responses really reflect student satisfaction and which are just written because the student needs to write something. So this option is better than cold test scores, but I also see problems in it and so can't support it fully.

If a school administration makes it really clear that, just because students are being asked to make lesson plan suggestions doesn't mean that all suggestions will be used and that students are not in charge of making the curriculum, then the first perspective—allowing students to give their opinion about what they would like to study—is a good one. This one will make at least some lesson plans more interesting and relevant, and that will lead to better learning.

You can evaluate your essay and the model essay based on the following criteria, which is covered in the Scoring section of Inside the ACT Writing Test:

- Does the author discuss all three perspectives provided in the prompt?

- Is the author's own perspective clearly stated?

- Does the body of the essay assess and analyze each perspective?

- Is the relevance of each paragraph clear?

- Does the author start a new paragraph for each new idea?

- Is each sentence in a paragraph relevant to the point made in that paragraph?

- Are transitions clear?

- Is the essay easy to read? Is it engaging?

- Are sentences varied?

- Is vocabulary used effectively? Is college-level vocabulary used?

Practice Test Three

ACT Practice Test Three
ANSWER SHEET

ENGLISH TEST

1. Ⓐ Ⓑ Ⓒ Ⓓ   11. Ⓐ Ⓑ Ⓒ Ⓓ   21. Ⓐ Ⓑ Ⓒ Ⓓ   31. Ⓐ Ⓑ Ⓒ Ⓓ   41. Ⓐ Ⓑ Ⓒ Ⓓ   51. Ⓐ Ⓑ Ⓒ Ⓓ   61. Ⓐ Ⓑ Ⓒ Ⓓ   71. Ⓐ Ⓑ Ⓒ Ⓓ
2. Ⓕ Ⓖ Ⓗ Ⓙ   12. Ⓕ Ⓖ Ⓗ Ⓙ   22. Ⓕ Ⓖ Ⓗ Ⓙ   32. Ⓕ Ⓖ Ⓗ Ⓙ   42. Ⓕ Ⓖ Ⓗ Ⓙ   52. Ⓕ Ⓖ Ⓗ Ⓙ   62. Ⓕ Ⓖ Ⓗ Ⓙ   72. Ⓕ Ⓖ Ⓗ Ⓙ
3. Ⓐ Ⓑ Ⓒ Ⓓ   13. Ⓐ Ⓑ Ⓒ Ⓓ   23. Ⓐ Ⓑ Ⓒ Ⓓ   33. Ⓐ Ⓑ Ⓒ Ⓓ   43. Ⓐ Ⓑ Ⓒ Ⓓ   53. Ⓐ Ⓑ Ⓒ Ⓓ   63. Ⓐ Ⓑ Ⓒ Ⓓ   73. Ⓐ Ⓑ Ⓒ Ⓓ
4. Ⓕ Ⓖ Ⓗ Ⓙ   14. Ⓕ Ⓖ Ⓗ Ⓙ   24. Ⓕ Ⓖ Ⓗ Ⓙ   34. Ⓕ Ⓖ Ⓗ Ⓙ   44. Ⓕ Ⓖ Ⓗ Ⓙ   54. Ⓕ Ⓖ Ⓗ Ⓙ   64. Ⓕ Ⓖ Ⓗ Ⓙ   74. Ⓕ Ⓖ Ⓗ Ⓙ
5. Ⓐ Ⓑ Ⓒ Ⓓ   15. Ⓐ Ⓑ Ⓒ Ⓓ   25. Ⓐ Ⓑ Ⓒ Ⓓ   35. Ⓐ Ⓑ Ⓒ Ⓓ   45. Ⓐ Ⓑ Ⓒ Ⓓ   55. Ⓐ Ⓑ Ⓒ Ⓓ   65. Ⓐ Ⓑ Ⓒ Ⓓ   75. Ⓐ Ⓑ Ⓒ Ⓓ
6. Ⓕ Ⓖ Ⓗ Ⓙ   16. Ⓕ Ⓖ Ⓗ Ⓙ   26. Ⓕ Ⓖ Ⓗ Ⓙ   36. Ⓕ Ⓖ Ⓗ Ⓙ   46. Ⓕ Ⓖ Ⓗ Ⓙ   56. Ⓕ Ⓖ Ⓗ Ⓙ   66. Ⓕ Ⓖ Ⓗ Ⓙ
7. Ⓐ Ⓑ Ⓒ Ⓓ   17. Ⓐ Ⓑ Ⓒ Ⓓ   27. Ⓐ Ⓑ Ⓒ Ⓓ   37. Ⓐ Ⓑ Ⓒ Ⓓ   47. Ⓐ Ⓑ Ⓒ Ⓓ   57. Ⓐ Ⓑ Ⓒ Ⓓ   67. Ⓐ Ⓑ Ⓒ Ⓓ
8. Ⓕ Ⓖ Ⓗ Ⓙ   18. Ⓕ Ⓖ Ⓗ Ⓙ   28. Ⓕ Ⓖ Ⓗ Ⓙ   38. Ⓕ Ⓖ Ⓗ Ⓙ   48. Ⓕ Ⓖ Ⓗ Ⓙ   58. Ⓕ Ⓖ Ⓗ Ⓙ   68. Ⓕ Ⓖ Ⓗ Ⓙ
9. Ⓐ Ⓑ Ⓒ Ⓓ   19. Ⓐ Ⓑ Ⓒ Ⓓ   29. Ⓐ Ⓑ Ⓒ Ⓓ   39. Ⓐ Ⓑ Ⓒ Ⓓ   49. Ⓐ Ⓑ Ⓒ Ⓓ   59. Ⓐ Ⓑ Ⓒ Ⓓ   69. Ⓐ Ⓑ Ⓒ Ⓓ
10. Ⓕ Ⓖ Ⓗ Ⓙ   20. Ⓕ Ⓖ Ⓗ Ⓙ   30. Ⓕ Ⓖ Ⓗ Ⓙ   40. Ⓕ Ⓖ Ⓗ Ⓙ   50. Ⓕ Ⓖ Ⓗ Ⓙ   60. Ⓕ Ⓖ Ⓗ Ⓙ   70. Ⓕ Ⓖ Ⓗ Ⓙ

MATHEMATICS TEST

1. Ⓐ Ⓑ Ⓒ Ⓓ Ⓔ   11. Ⓐ Ⓑ Ⓒ Ⓓ Ⓔ   21. Ⓐ Ⓑ Ⓒ Ⓓ Ⓔ   31. Ⓐ Ⓑ Ⓒ Ⓓ Ⓔ   41. Ⓐ Ⓑ Ⓒ Ⓓ Ⓔ   51. Ⓐ Ⓑ Ⓒ Ⓓ Ⓔ
2. Ⓕ Ⓖ Ⓗ Ⓙ Ⓚ   12. Ⓕ Ⓖ Ⓗ Ⓙ Ⓚ   22. Ⓕ Ⓖ Ⓗ Ⓙ Ⓚ   32. Ⓕ Ⓖ Ⓗ Ⓙ Ⓚ   42. Ⓕ Ⓖ Ⓗ Ⓙ Ⓚ   52. Ⓕ Ⓖ Ⓗ Ⓙ Ⓚ
3. Ⓐ Ⓑ Ⓒ Ⓓ Ⓔ   13. Ⓐ Ⓑ Ⓒ Ⓓ Ⓔ   23. Ⓐ Ⓑ Ⓒ Ⓓ Ⓔ   33. Ⓐ Ⓑ Ⓒ Ⓓ Ⓔ   43. Ⓐ Ⓑ Ⓒ Ⓓ Ⓔ   53. Ⓐ Ⓑ Ⓒ Ⓓ Ⓔ
4. Ⓕ Ⓖ Ⓗ Ⓙ Ⓚ   14. Ⓕ Ⓖ Ⓗ Ⓙ Ⓚ   24. Ⓕ Ⓖ Ⓗ Ⓙ Ⓚ   34. Ⓕ Ⓖ Ⓗ Ⓙ Ⓚ   44. Ⓕ Ⓖ Ⓗ Ⓙ Ⓚ   54. Ⓕ Ⓖ Ⓗ Ⓙ Ⓚ
5. Ⓐ Ⓑ Ⓒ Ⓓ Ⓔ   15. Ⓐ Ⓑ Ⓒ Ⓓ Ⓔ   25. Ⓐ Ⓑ Ⓒ Ⓓ Ⓔ   35. Ⓐ Ⓑ Ⓒ Ⓓ Ⓔ   45. Ⓐ Ⓑ Ⓒ Ⓓ Ⓔ   55. Ⓐ Ⓑ Ⓒ Ⓓ Ⓔ
6. Ⓕ Ⓖ Ⓗ Ⓙ Ⓚ   16. Ⓕ Ⓖ Ⓗ Ⓙ Ⓚ   26. Ⓕ Ⓖ Ⓗ Ⓙ Ⓚ   36. Ⓕ Ⓖ Ⓗ Ⓙ Ⓚ   46. Ⓕ Ⓖ Ⓗ Ⓙ Ⓚ   56. Ⓕ Ⓖ Ⓗ Ⓙ Ⓚ
7. Ⓐ Ⓑ Ⓒ Ⓓ Ⓔ   17. Ⓐ Ⓑ Ⓒ Ⓓ Ⓔ   27. Ⓐ Ⓑ Ⓒ Ⓓ Ⓔ   37. Ⓐ Ⓑ Ⓒ Ⓓ Ⓔ   47. Ⓐ Ⓑ Ⓒ Ⓓ Ⓔ   57. Ⓐ Ⓑ Ⓒ Ⓓ Ⓔ
8. Ⓕ Ⓖ Ⓗ Ⓙ Ⓚ   18. Ⓕ Ⓖ Ⓗ Ⓙ Ⓚ   28. Ⓕ Ⓖ Ⓗ Ⓙ Ⓚ   38. Ⓕ Ⓖ Ⓗ Ⓙ Ⓚ   48. Ⓕ Ⓖ Ⓗ Ⓙ Ⓚ   58. Ⓕ Ⓖ Ⓗ Ⓙ Ⓚ
9. Ⓐ Ⓑ Ⓒ Ⓓ Ⓔ   19. Ⓐ Ⓑ Ⓒ Ⓓ Ⓔ   29. Ⓐ Ⓑ Ⓒ Ⓓ Ⓔ   39. Ⓐ Ⓑ Ⓒ Ⓓ Ⓔ   49. Ⓐ Ⓑ Ⓒ Ⓓ Ⓔ   59. Ⓐ Ⓑ Ⓒ Ⓓ Ⓔ
10. Ⓕ Ⓖ Ⓗ Ⓙ Ⓚ   20. Ⓕ Ⓖ Ⓗ Ⓙ Ⓚ   30. Ⓕ Ⓖ Ⓗ Ⓙ Ⓚ   40. Ⓕ Ⓖ Ⓗ Ⓙ Ⓚ   50. Ⓕ Ⓖ Ⓗ Ⓙ Ⓚ   60. Ⓕ Ⓖ Ⓗ Ⓙ Ⓚ

READING TEST

1. Ⓐ Ⓑ Ⓒ Ⓓ   6. Ⓕ Ⓖ Ⓗ Ⓙ   11. Ⓐ Ⓑ Ⓒ Ⓓ   16. Ⓕ Ⓖ Ⓗ Ⓙ   21. Ⓐ Ⓑ Ⓒ Ⓓ   26. Ⓕ Ⓖ Ⓗ Ⓙ   31. Ⓐ Ⓑ Ⓒ Ⓓ   36. Ⓕ Ⓖ Ⓗ Ⓙ
2. Ⓕ Ⓖ Ⓗ Ⓙ   7. Ⓐ Ⓑ Ⓒ Ⓓ   12. Ⓕ Ⓖ Ⓗ Ⓙ   17. Ⓐ Ⓑ Ⓒ Ⓓ   22. Ⓕ Ⓖ Ⓗ Ⓙ   27. Ⓐ Ⓑ Ⓒ Ⓓ   32. Ⓕ Ⓖ Ⓗ Ⓙ   37. Ⓐ Ⓑ Ⓒ Ⓓ
3. Ⓐ Ⓑ Ⓒ Ⓓ   8. Ⓕ Ⓖ Ⓗ Ⓙ   13. Ⓐ Ⓑ Ⓒ Ⓓ   18. Ⓕ Ⓖ Ⓗ Ⓙ   23. Ⓐ Ⓑ Ⓒ Ⓓ   28. Ⓕ Ⓖ Ⓗ Ⓙ   33. Ⓐ Ⓑ Ⓒ Ⓓ   38. Ⓕ Ⓖ Ⓗ Ⓙ
4. Ⓕ Ⓖ Ⓗ Ⓙ   9. Ⓐ Ⓑ Ⓒ Ⓓ   14. Ⓕ Ⓖ Ⓗ Ⓙ   19. Ⓐ Ⓑ Ⓒ Ⓓ   24. Ⓕ Ⓖ Ⓗ Ⓙ   29. Ⓐ Ⓑ Ⓒ Ⓓ   34. Ⓕ Ⓖ Ⓗ Ⓙ   39. Ⓐ Ⓑ Ⓒ Ⓓ
5. Ⓐ Ⓑ Ⓒ Ⓓ   10. Ⓕ Ⓖ Ⓗ Ⓙ   15. Ⓐ Ⓑ Ⓒ Ⓓ   20. Ⓕ Ⓖ Ⓗ Ⓙ   25. Ⓐ Ⓑ Ⓒ Ⓓ   30. Ⓕ Ⓖ Ⓗ Ⓙ   35. Ⓐ Ⓑ Ⓒ Ⓓ   40. Ⓕ Ⓖ Ⓗ Ⓙ

SCIENCE TEST

1. Ⓐ Ⓑ Ⓒ Ⓓ   6. Ⓕ Ⓖ Ⓗ Ⓙ   11. Ⓐ Ⓑ Ⓒ Ⓓ   16. Ⓕ Ⓖ Ⓗ Ⓙ   21. Ⓐ Ⓑ Ⓒ Ⓓ   26. Ⓕ Ⓖ Ⓗ Ⓙ   31. Ⓐ Ⓑ Ⓒ Ⓓ   36. Ⓕ Ⓖ Ⓗ Ⓙ
2. Ⓕ Ⓖ Ⓗ Ⓙ   7. Ⓐ Ⓑ Ⓒ Ⓓ   12. Ⓕ Ⓖ Ⓗ Ⓙ   17. Ⓐ Ⓑ Ⓒ Ⓓ   22. Ⓕ Ⓖ Ⓗ Ⓙ   27. Ⓐ Ⓑ Ⓒ Ⓓ   32. Ⓕ Ⓖ Ⓗ Ⓙ   37. Ⓐ Ⓑ Ⓒ Ⓓ
3. Ⓐ Ⓑ Ⓒ Ⓓ   8. Ⓕ Ⓖ Ⓗ Ⓙ   13. Ⓐ Ⓑ Ⓒ Ⓓ   18. Ⓕ Ⓖ Ⓗ Ⓙ   23. Ⓐ Ⓑ Ⓒ Ⓓ   28. Ⓕ Ⓖ Ⓗ Ⓙ   33. Ⓐ Ⓑ Ⓒ Ⓓ   38. Ⓕ Ⓖ Ⓗ Ⓙ
4. Ⓕ Ⓖ Ⓗ Ⓙ   9. Ⓐ Ⓑ Ⓒ Ⓓ   14. Ⓕ Ⓖ Ⓗ Ⓙ   19. Ⓐ Ⓑ Ⓒ Ⓓ   24. Ⓕ Ⓖ Ⓗ Ⓙ   29. Ⓐ Ⓑ Ⓒ Ⓓ   34. Ⓕ Ⓖ Ⓗ Ⓙ   39. Ⓐ Ⓑ Ⓒ Ⓓ
5. Ⓐ Ⓑ Ⓒ Ⓓ   10. Ⓕ Ⓖ Ⓗ Ⓙ   15. Ⓐ Ⓑ Ⓒ Ⓓ   20. Ⓕ Ⓖ Ⓗ Ⓙ   25. Ⓐ Ⓑ Ⓒ Ⓓ   30. Ⓕ Ⓖ Ⓗ Ⓙ   35. Ⓐ Ⓑ Ⓒ Ⓓ   40. Ⓕ Ⓖ Ⓗ Ⓙ

ENGLISH TEST

45 Minutes—75 Questions

Directions: In the following five passages, certain words and phrases are underlined and numbered. In the right-hand column are alternatives for each underlined portion. Select the one that best conveys the idea, creates the most grammatically correct sentence, or is the most consistent with the style and tone of the passage. If you decide that the original version is best, select NO CHANGE. You may also find questions that ask about the entire passage or a section of the passage. These questions will correspond to small numbered boxes in the text. For these questions, decide which choice best accomplishes the purpose set out in the question stem. After you've selected the best choice, fill in the corresponding oval in your Answer Grid. For some questions, you'll need to read the context in order to answer correctly. Be sure to read until you have enough information to determine the correct answer choice.

PASSAGE I

A SWIMMING CHANGE

[1]

Until three years ago, I had never considered myself to be athletically talented. I have never been able to hit, catch, throw, or kick a ball with any degree of confidence or accuracy. For years, physical <u>education being</u> [1] often the worst part of the school day for me. Units on tennis, touch football, volleyball, and basketball were torturous. I not only dreaded fumbling a pass,

1. A. NO CHANGE
   B. education, was
   C. education was
   D. education,

<u>so</u> I also feared being hit in the face by a ball. However, [2] at the beginning of my freshman year of high school, my attitude toward sports changed.

2. F. NO CHANGE
   G. and
   H. but
   J. though

GO ON TO THE NEXT PAGE →

[2]

Somehow, my good friend Gretchen convinced me

to join <u>our schools</u> swim team.
          3

<u>Knowing that I enjoyed swimming, over the course of</u>
                              4
<u>two summers, it was with Gretchen that I practically</u>
                              4
<u>had lived at the pool.</u> My mother had
          4

<u>insisted</u> that I take swimming lessons every summer
    5
since I was seven, so I was entirely comfortable in the

water. I was also eager to start my high school experience

with a new challenge and a new way to think of myself.

[3]

Of course, I had no idea what I was getting into

when Gretchen and I showed up for the first day of

practice. The team was made up of twenty young

<u>women, most of these swimmers</u> had been participat-
                              6
ing in the community swim team for years. I couldn't do

a flip turn at the end of the lane without getting water

up my nose. In contrast, most of the other swimmers,

3. **A.** NO CHANGE
    B. our schools'
    C. our school's
    D. ours school

4. **F.** NO CHANGE
    G. Because we had spent two summers
        practically living at the pool, it was
        Gretchen who knew that swimming was
        enjoyed by me.
    H. Having practically lived at the pool over
        two summers, the two of us, Gretchen
        knew it was swimming that I enjoyed.
    J. Gretchen knew I enjoyed swimming, as
        we had spent two summers practically
        living at the pool.

5. Of the four choices, which is the only one
    that does NOT indicate that the narrator's
    mother decided that the narrator must take
    swimming lessons?
    A. NO CHANGE
    B. suggested
    C. required
    D. demanded

6. **F.** NO CHANGE
    G. women, the majority of them
    H. women most of them
    J. women, most of whom

GO ON TO THE NEXT PAGE ⟹

who <u>had been swimming competitively, since elementa-</u>
              7
<u>ry school,</u> were able to gracefully somersault and begin
  7
the next lap. By the end of the first hour of practice, I

was exhausted and waterlogged.

[4]

However, I had no intention of <u>giving up, which</u>
                                            8
<u>would mean quitting.</u> I came back the next day and the
  8

next day for practice. Things <u>begun</u> to get serious in
                                 9
the second week, when we started the regular schedule

of four early morning and five afternoon practices. Our

coach,

<u>whom</u> had led the team to several state championships,
  10
demanded dedication from everyone on the team. The

hard work

<u>eventually paid off. By</u> the end of the first month, I had
         11
discovered that I was good at the butterfly,

7. **A.** NO CHANGE
    B. had been swimming competitively since
       elementary school,
    C. had been swimming, competitively since
       elementary school,
    D. had been swimming competitively since
       elementary school

8. **F.** NO CHANGE
    G. giving up and resigning myself to
       failure.
    H. giving up and quitting what I had set
       out to do.
    J. giving up.

9. **A.** NO CHANGE
    B. had been begun
    C. had began
    D. began

10. **F.** NO CHANGE
    G. for whom
    H. who
    J. which

11. **A.** NO CHANGE
    B. eventually paid off, so, as a result
    C. paid off eventually, however, by
    D. paid off, eventually, by

GO ON TO THE NEXT PAGE

a relatively new stroke that was first introduced in the
                                                        12
1930s. I rarely won individual races, but I became a
  12
solid member of our

team's medley relay.
        13

                         [5]

   After that intimidating first season, I continued

swimming. I even will have earned a varsity letter last
                       14
year. Now I'm hoping to earn a spot in the state compe-

tition my senior year. 15

12. Assuming each of the following creates a true statement, which provides the information most relevant to the narrator's experience on the swim team?

F. NO CHANGE

G. a difficult stroke that interested few other members of our team.

H. which is faster than the backstroke but somewhat slower than the crawl.

J. which is still sometimes called the dolphin because it incorporates a two-stroke dolphin kick.

13. A. NO CHANGE

B. team's medley relay (it consists of four swimmers).

C. team's medley relay, which the person swimming backstroke always begins.

D. team.

14. F. NO CHANGE

G. would have earned

H. earned

J. earn

15. If inserted here, which of the following would be the most appropriate sentence to conclude the essay?

A. My coach continues to schedule demanding practices, but I have come to enjoy the early morning swims.

B. For someone who thought she didn't have any athletic talent, I have come a long way.

C. Gretchen is also still on the team, but she does not swim the medley relay.

D. I've always enjoyed swimming, so I'm not all that surprised by my success as an athlete.

GO ON TO THE NEXT PAGE →

PASSAGE II

EXPLORING DUBUQUE'S AQUARIUM

[1]

One lazy day last summer, my parents decided that my younger sister and I needed a break from our vacation from academics. They took us to the National Mississippi River Museum and Aquarium in Dubuque, Iowa. I was prepared to be bored by this family educational trip. However, from the moment I walked through the museum's doors, I was <u>captivated; by</u> all that there was
16
to learn about life in the Mississippi.

[2]

[1] A large tank stocked with fish and turtles <u>was there</u> to greet us as we walked into the main hall. [2]
17
There were also animals I had never before glimpsed, such as a fish called the long-nosed gar. [3] I was amazed by this fish in particular. [4] Its long, tubular shape and distinctive rod-shaped <u>nose that</u> made it
18
appear like something that lived in the dark depths of the ocean. [5] This first of five freshwater aquariums offered a close-up view of <u>familiar animals that I had seen</u>
19
<u>before,</u> such as ducks. [20]
19

16. **F.** NO CHANGE
    G. captivated, by
    H. captivated by,
    J. captivated by

17. **A.** NO CHANGE
    B. is there
    C. are there
    D. were there

18. **F.** NO CHANGE
    G. nose, which
    H. nose, and this
    J. nose

19. **A.** NO CHANGE
    B. animals that were familiar sights to me,
    C. familiar animals to which I was no stranger,
    D. familiar animals,

20. To make paragraph 2 coherent and logical, the best placement of sentence 5 is:
    F. where it is now.
    G. before sentence 1.
    H. after sentence 1.
    J. after sentence 2.

GO ON TO THE NEXT PAGE

[3]

In the next aquarium, I <u>see</u> a catfish bigger than I
                                 21
had ever imagined this species could be. According to

the posted information, this specimen weighed more

than 100 pounds. With its long whiskers and slow, lazy

movements, this catfish looked like the grandfather of

all the other fish in the tank.

[4]

<u>I couldn't decide which I liked better, the catfish</u>
                             22
<u>or the long-nosed gar.</u> The next floor-to-ceiling tank,
       22
which represented the ecosystem of the Mississippi

bayou, held an animal I had never seen: an alligator. At

first, I had a hard time spotting the creature—it blended

in almost completely with a half-submerged log. [23]

Suddenly, though, it

21. **A.** NO CHANGE
    B. had been seeing
    C. saw
    D. spot

22. Which sentence most effectively connects this paragraph to the preceding paragraph?

    F. NO CHANGE
    G. Although the catfish was impressive, it was not the biggest animal on display in the museum.
    H. After seeing the catfish, I was interested in exhibits that were a bit more hands-on.
    J. Until my visit to the museum, I had never really considered what the Mississippi River was like south of my home.

23. At this point, the writer is considering removing the following phrase:

    it blended in almost completely with a half-submerged log.

    The primary effect of removing this phrase would be:

    A. a smoother transition between sentences.
    B. a greater contrast between images.
    C. a loss of descriptive information.
    D. an increased level of suspense.

GO ON TO THE NEXT PAGE

slides into the water and aims itself right at the glass
24
separating me from its ferocious claws and skin-tearing

teeth. I had a slightly moment of panic before I remem-
25
bered that, try as it might, this alligator would never

successfully hunt tourists like me. As

much of the onlookers squealed in delight as the alligator
26
moved through the tank, I noticed his companion. Far off

in a corner slept an enormous snapping turtle. I could im-

agine no better roommate for the alligator than this hook-

beaked turtle with rough ridges running along its shell.

[5]

Despite my initial expectations, I happily spent

the entire day soaking up information about creatures

that live in the Mississippi River. In one section of the

museum, I held a crayfish. [27] Later, I had the opportu-

nity to touch the cool, sleek skin of a stingray, which can

be found where the Mississippi empties into the Gulf of

Mexico.

24. **F.** NO CHANGE
    G. slides into the water to aim
    H. slid into the water and aiming
    J. slid into the water and aimed

25. **A.** NO CHANGE
    B. momentarily slight
    C. moment of slight
    D. momentarily of slight

26. **F.** NO CHANGE
    G. a large amount
    H. the many
    J. many

27. The writer would like to insert a sentence describing the appearance of the crayfish at this point. Which sentence would best accomplish the writer's goal?

    A. Also known as crawdads, crayfish are close relatives of the lobsters that live in freshwater.

    B. At an average length of three inches, the crayfish looks like a miniature lobster, complete with small but effective front pincers.

    C. Although they are found throughout the United States, crayfish populations are densest in Kentucky and Mississippi.

    D. At first, I was a bit nervous to touch the small creature, but then I relaxed and enjoyed the opportunity to look at it so closely.

GO ON TO THE NEXT PAGE ⟶

[6]

After seeing <u>all, I could inside the museum,</u> I wan-
                                    28
dered outside, only to find even more exhibits.

28. **F.** NO CHANGE
    G. all I could inside the museum,
    H. all, I could inside the museum
    J. all I could inside the museum

<u>Having just enough time, it was that I was able</u> to see
                              29
the otters and watch a riverboat launching, but it was
closing time before I was able to see the most impressive
thing the museum had to offer. A football-field-sized
steamboat from the 1930s is open to

<u>tourists. And operates</u> as a "boat-and-breakfast" that
              30
hosts overnight guests. I'm hoping that my family will
plan another educational trip to Dubuque soon so I can
experience life on a steamboat.

29. **A.** NO CHANGE
    B. It was that I had just enough time, so I
        was able
    C. Having just enough time, it was possible
    D. I had just enough time

30. **F.** NO CHANGE
    G. tourists and that operates
    H. tourists, it operates
    J. tourists and operates

PASSAGE III

THE MYSTERY DINER

The paragraphs in this essay may or may not follow the most logical order. Each paragraph
is numbered, and question 45 will ask you to determine the best placement of paragraph 6.

[1]

Although secret identities and elaborate disguises
are typically associated with the world of spies and vil-
lains, <u>it has</u> other uses. For six years, Ruth
      31

31. **A.** NO CHANGE
    B. it does have
    C. they do have
    D. and they have

GO ON TO THE NEXT PAGE

Reichl the restaurant critic for the *New York Times,* used
                    32
aliases and costumes as a regular part of her job.

[2]

Dining is big business in New York City, from the neighborhood noodle shops and diners to the upscale steak houses and four-star French restaurants.

33 Many of the more than one million people who read

the *Times* each day look to it for advice on where to eat.
                    34
A positive review from the *Times*

could have brought a restaurant unimagined suc-
      35
cess and month-long waiting lists for reservations. A

negative review, on the other hand, can undermine a

32. **F.** NO CHANGE
    G. Reichl, the restaurant critic, for the *New York Times,*
    H. Reichl, the restaurant critic for the *New York Times,*
    J. Reichl the restaurant critic for the *New York Times*

33. Should the following sentence be inserted into the passage at this point?

    The legendary French restaurant Le Bernardin received a four-star rating from the *Times* shortly after opening in 1986, an honor it has maintained ever since.

    A. Yes, because the added sentence emphasizes how important a positive review from the *Times* can be.
    B. Yes, because the specific information helps the reader develop a clearer picture of the type of restaurant reviewed by the *Times.*
    C. No, because it is unclear whether Reichl was responsible for reviewing this specific restaurant.
    D. No, because the specific information about one restaurant leads the reader away from the main topic of the essay.

34. **F.** NO CHANGE
    G. look with
    H. look by
    J. looking to

35. **A.** NO CHANGE
    B. can bring
    C. will have brought
    D. will be bringing

GO ON TO THE NEXT PAGE

restaurant's popularity and seriously cut into its profits.

Obviously, <u>restaurant owners and workers</u> have a lot at
                           36
stake when the restaurant critic for the *Times* walks in

the door. Waiters and chefs often pull out all of the stops

to impress the writer <u>that the</u> meal can make or break a
                         37
restaurant.

[3]

Reichl was acutely aware that <u>she received special</u>
                                            38
<u>treatment</u> once restaurant staff recognized her. She
  38
would be graciously greeted and led to the best table

in the restaurant, offered dishes prepared specially by

the head chef, and given multiple courses of amazing

desserts. In other words, the dining experience of the

restaurant critic was nothing like that of the <u>commonly</u>
                                                       39
<u>ordinary</u> person walking in from the street.
  39

[4]

To remedy this, <u>Reichl decided a solution would be</u>
                                  40
<u>to become,</u> for short periods of time, someone else.
  40

36. **F.** NO CHANGE
     G. restaurant owners and workers;
     H. restaurant, owners and workers
     J. restaurant owners, and workers

37. **A.** NO CHANGE
     B. who's
     C. whose
     D. which

38. **F.** NO CHANGE
     G. special treatment was received by her
     H. she was the recipient of special
              treatment
     J. she was in the position of receiving
              special treatment

39. **A.** NO CHANGE
     B. common, representative, and average
     C. typical
     D. extravagant

40. **F.** NO CHANGE
     G. she created a solution to the problem by
              becoming,
     H. Reichl decided to become,
     J. Reichl found a way to fix the problem,
              which involved becoming,

GO ON TO THE NEXT PAGE ⇨

<u>Transforming herself into different personas, Reichl used</u>
                                                        41
<u>wigs, special makeup, and carefully selected clothing,</u>
                                                        41
such as an attractive blonde named Chloe, a redhead

named Brenda, and an older woman named Betty. 42

41. A. NO CHANGE

B. With wigs, special makeup, and carefully selected clothing, Reichl transformed herself into different personas,

C. Transformed with wigs, special makeup, and carefully selected clothing, Reichl's different personas,

D. Reichl used wigs, special makeup, and carefully selected clothing, that transformed herself into different personas,

42. Which of the following true statements would make the most effective and logical conclusion for paragraph 4?

F. Reichl found that she could quickly disguise herself as Betty, but it took more time to become Chloe.

G. Her true identity hidden, Reichl would then dine at a restaurant she was currently evaluating.

H. After six years at the *Times,* Reichl moved on to become the editor of *Gourmet* magazine.

J. The former restaurant critic for the *Times* did not always agree with Reichl's methods or her selection of restaurants to review.

[5]

Sometimes, Reichl developed a different view about

the quality when she was not treated like a very impor-

tant person <u>of a restaurant</u>. Indeed, the difference be-
              43
tween the treatment she received as herself and as one

43. For the sake of logic and coherence, the underlined portion should be placed:

A. where it is now.

B. after the word *developed.*

C. after the word *view.*

D. after the word *quality.*

GO ON TO THE NEXT PAGE ⟩

of her characters was occasionally so great that Reichl would revise her initial impression of a restaurant and write a more negative review. [44]

[6]

By becoming an average customer, Reichl encouraged even the most expensive and popular restaurants to improve how they treated all of their customers. After all, waiters could never be certain when they were serving the powerful restaurant critic for the *New York Times*.

44. Would deleting the word *occasionally* from the previous sentence change the meaning of the sentence?

F. Yes, because without this word, the reader would not understand that Reichl had different experiences when she dined in disguise.

G. Yes, because without this word, the reader would think that Reichl always changed her impression of restaurants when she was not recognized and received different treatment as a result.

H. No, because this word repeats an idea that is already presented in the sentence.

J. No, because this word is used only to show emphasis, and it does not contribute to the meaning of the sentence.

Question 45 asks about the preceding passage as a whole.

45. To make the passage flow logically and smoothly, the best place for paragraph 6 is:

A. where it is now.
B. after paragraph 1.
C. after paragraph 3.
D. after paragraph 4.

GO ON TO THE NEXT PAGE →

PASSAGE IV

THE BENEFITS OF A SQUARE-FOOT GARDEN

[1]

[1] I used to start every spring with great hopes for my backyard vegetable garden. [2] After the last freeze in late March or early April, I devoted an entire weekend to preparing the soil in the garden. [3] I thinned out the rows that had too many plants and spent hours tugging out each weed that threatened to rob my little plants of the nutrients they needed to thrive. [4] Once spring truly arrived, I marked out my rows and scattered the packets of seeds that I <u>hoped, would</u> develop into prize-
46
winning vegetables. [5] In the first few weeks of the season, I was almost always in the garden. 47

[2]

Despite my best intentions, my garden never lived up to the vision I had for it. After I had devoted several weekends to watering and weeding, the garden always started to become more of a <u>burden</u> less of a hobby. By
48
July, the garden was usually in disarray, and I didn't have the energy or time to save it.

46. **F.** NO CHANGE
    G. hoped, would,
    H. hoped would,
    J. hoped would

47. To make paragraph 1 more logical and coherent, sentence 3 should be placed:
    A. where it is now.
    B. before sentence 1.
    C. after sentence 1.
    D. after sentence 4.

48. **F.** NO CHANGE
    G. burden:
    H. burden and
    J. burden, but,

GO ON TO THE NEXT PAGE ⇒

<u>July and August are always the hottest parts of the year.</u>
                                49

49. **A.** NO CHANGE
       B. The hottest months are July and August.
       C. (July, along with August, provides the hottest temperatures of the year.)
       D. OMIT the underlined portion.

[3]

This past year, <u>however,</u> my garden was finally the
                      50
success I had imagined it could be. Instead of planning

the traditional garden of closely planted

50. Of the following choices, which would be the LEAST acceptable substitution for the underlined word?
       F. on the other hand
       G. indeed
       H. though
       J. in contrast

<u>rows that is modeled after large-scale farming,</u> I tried a
                          51
new technique. My new approach is called square-foot

gardening.

51. **A.** NO CHANGE
       B. rows, which is modeled after large-scale farming,
       C. rows, which is based on the techniques for large-scale farming,
       D. rows,

[4]

<u>A square-foot garden is designed for efficiency.</u>
                      52

52. Which sentence most effectively links the topic of paragraph 3 to the topic of paragraph 4?
       F. NO CHANGE
       G. The technique of square-foot gardening was pioneered by Mel Bartholomew.
       H. One of the benefits of a square-foot garden is that it is less expensive to maintain than a traditional garden.
       J. My neighbor, who always has a beautiful garden, introduced me to the concept of square-foot gardening, and I have been grateful ever since.

GO ON TO THE NEXT PAGE ⟹

In a <u>traditionally</u> garden, you scatter a packet of seeds
          53
down a row. When the plants emerge,

<u>they spend</u> hours thinning each row by pulling out at
       54
least half of what was planted. In a square-foot garden,

you plant each seed individually, so there is never a need

for thinning <u>in the garden</u>. You create the garden plan
             55
1 square foot at a time, until you have a block of 16

squares. Sturdy pieces of lumber

<u>which could make</u> effective borders for each square.
      56
Walking paths that are at least 2 feet wide separate each

16-square-foot garden. The design is clean and simple,

and it eliminates the problem of getting to the rows in

the middle of a large garden. In fact,

<u>you can do</u> all the weeding, watering, and harvesting
      57
from the walking paths.

[5]

In addition to being easier to weed and water, a

square-foot garden takes up much less space than a

regular garden. I was able to grow <u>an increased number</u>
                                        58
<u>of more</u> vegetables in two square-foot gardens,
   58
which took up a total of 32 square feet, than I ever had

grown in my traditional garden, which took up

84 square feet. Preparing the soil for the smaller

---

53. A. NO CHANGE
B. conventionally
C. traditional
D. tradition

54. F. NO CHANGE
G. he spends
H. people spend
J. you spend

55. A. NO CHANGE
B. out the garden
C. in that garden
D. OMIT the underlined portion.

56. F. NO CHANGE
G. that make
H. make
J. OMIT the underlined portion.

57. A. NO CHANGE
B. you could have done
C. one can do
D. one is able to do

58. F. NO CHANGE
G. a larger quantity of more
H. an increased, bigger quantity
J. more

GO ON TO THE NEXT PAGE ⇨

space only required a few hours instead of a whole weekend. There was so much less weeding to do that the task never felt overwhelming. One season of using the square garden techniques <u>were all</u> it took for me
                                                      59
to convert to a completely new outlook on backyard gardening.

59. **A.** NO CHANGE
    B. were just what
    C. was all
    D. could be

Question 60 asks about the preceding passage as a whole.

---

60. If the writer had intended to write an essay detailing how to plan, prepare, and care for a square-foot garden, would this essay meet the writer's goal?

    F. No, because the writer relies on generalities rather than specifics when describing her square garden.

    G. No, because the writer focuses on comparing two different types of gardens instead of explaining how to begin and care for one type of garden.

    H. Yes, because the writer states specific measurements for her square garden.

    J. Yes, because the writer maintains that square gardens are superior to traditional gardens.

GO ON TO THE NEXT PAGE

PASSAGE V

THE IMPORTANCE OF MAINTAINING YOUR CAR

[1]

Most new car owners glance briefly at the owner's manual before depositing it in the glove compartment of their recently purchased automobile. Owners may dig out their manuals when something goes <u>wrong, such as a flat tire or a flashing engine light</u> but few take the time
61
to learn the basics about maintaining their new purchase. This is truly unfortunate, as a few simple and

61. A. NO CHANGE
   B. wrong; such as a flat tire or a flashing engine light
   C. wrong, such as a flat tire, or a flashing engine light
   D. wrong, such as a flat tire or a flashing engine light,

routine steps <u>improves the long-term performance of an automobile and decreases</u> the possibility of a traffic
62
accident.

62. F. NO CHANGE
   G. improve the long-term performance of an automobile and decreases
   H. improve the long-term performance of an automobile and decrease
   J. improves the long-term performance of an automobile and decrease

[2]

One of the easiest and most overlooked maintenance steps is caring for a car's wiper blades. Most people don't <u>notice a problem</u> until the blades fail to
63
clear the windshield during a rainstorm or heavy snowfall. When a driver's

63. A. NO CHANGE
   B. notice a problem that causes trouble
   C. recognize that their wiper blades are the source of a problem
   D. realize that their blades are failing and will become a problem

<u>vision being</u> obscured, an accident is more likely to happen. Replacing the
64

64. F. NO CHANGE
   G. vision, has been
   H. vision is
   J. vision,

GO ON TO THE NEXT PAGE ⇒

set blades at a time each year greatly reduces this risk.
65
In addition, frequently refilling the windshield washer

fluid reservoir guarantees that there will always be

enough fluid to wash away grime that accumulates on

the windshield.

[3]

Much of car maintenance focuses on preventing

problems before they occur. For example, checking the

levels of coolant, oil, brake fluid, and transmission fluid

can avert serious malfunctions. In general, these fluids
                                      66
should be checked monthly and refilled whenever the

need is indicated.

[4]

Cars are becoming more sophisticated every year,
                            67
but car owners without any expertise in mechanics can
                            67
still perform much of the basic upkeep of their vehicle.
                            67
You should change the oil in most cars every 3,000 to

7,000 miles. This task requires a willingness to get a bit

dirty, so you don't have to be a mechanic to change a
         68
car's oil. Before you get started, read the oil change

65. The underlined word would be most logically placed:

   A. where it is now.

   B. before the word *time.*

   C. before the word *year.*

   D. before the word *risk.*

66. **F.** NO CHANGE

   G. For generally,

   H. With usual

   J. By typically,

67. Which sentence is the most effective way to begin paragraph 4?

   A. NO CHANGE

   B. Changing the oil and oil filter regularly is another key to keeping your car's engine performing at its best.

   C. An entire industry now focuses on providing regular car maintenance, such as changing the oil and rotating the tires.

   D. Even if you haven't read your car owner's manual, you probably know that your car needs a tune-up every so often.

68. **F.** NO CHANGE

   G. but

   H. for

   J. because

GO ON TO THE NEXT PAGE ⟹

section, in your owner's manual and collect all of the
69

tools you will need. You won't need many tools, but you
70
will definitely need a car jack. Never get under a car that
70
is supported only by car

jacks: you do not want to risk being crushed by a car.
71
After you've secured the car, changing the oil is as

straightforward as sliding under the car with a drain

pan to catch the oil and a wrench to loosen the oil drain

plug. Then follow the instructions for changing the oil

filter, and fill the oil pan to the recommended level with

fresh oil. 72

[5]

These simple steps to maintaining the health of a

car can be done by just about anyone. However, success-

fully changing a car's oil does not turn a car owner into a

repair expert. More complicated tasks, such as adjusting

a carburetor or installing new brake pads, should be

69. **A.** NO CHANGE
    B. section, in your owner's manual,
    C. section in your owner's manual;
    D. section in your owner's manual,

70. In paragraph 4, the writer wants to provide an explanation of how to change the oil in an automobile. Which of the following would most logically fit the writer's intention for this paragraph?

    F. NO CHANGE
    G. need to get under the car to open the oil drain, so use car jacks to raise the car and sturdy car jack stands to support it.
    H. may find it helpful to watch someone else change the oil before you try to perform the job on your own.
    J. only need to follow a few basic steps in order to successfully change your car's oil.

71. **A.** NO CHANGE
    B. jacks, you
    C. jacks you
    D. jacks you,

72. Paragraph 4 of the essay uses the second person (*you, your*). Revising this paragraph to remove the second-person pronouns would have the primary effect of:

    F. disrupting the logical flow of the essay.
    G. making paragraph 4 more consistent with the voice used in the rest of the essay.
    H. underscoring the direct advice given to the reader.
    J. lightening the essay's formal tone.

GO ON TO THE NEXT PAGE ▷

<u>performed by a qualified</u> auto mechanic.
73

73. **A.** NO CHANGE
     B. professionally completed by a qualified
     C. performed by a certifiably qualified
     D. undertaken by qualifying

Questions 74–75 ask about the preceding passage as a whole.

---

74. After reading back through the essay, the writer decided that the following sentence contains important information:

> The owner's manual provides instructions on how to test the levels of these different fluids used to lubricate and cool the engine.

Logically, this sentence should be placed:

F. after the last sentence of paragraph 2.
G. before the first sentence of paragraph 3.
H. after the last sentence of paragraph 3.
J. after the last sentence of paragraph 4.

75. If the writer had intended to write an essay persuading readers to familiarize themselves with the basic safety features and maintenance needs of their cars, would this essay meet the writer's goal?

A. Yes, because the essay repeatedly encourages readers to refer to the owner's manual for their car.

B. Yes, because the essay lists many basic maintenance steps that owners can independently accomplish.

C. No, because the essay encourages readers to go beyond learning about the features of their car and actually perform some of the basic upkeep.

D. No, because the essay does not discuss a car's safety features in any detail.

MATHEMATICS TEST

60 Minutes—60 Questions

Directions: Solve each of the following problems, select the correct answer, and then fill in the corresponding space on your answer sheet.

Don't linger over problems that are too time-consuming. Do as many as you can, then come back to the others in the time you have remaining.

The use of a calculator is permitted on this test. Though you are allowed to use your calculator to solve any questions you choose, some of the questions may be most easily answered without the use of a calculator.

Note: Unless otherwise noted, all of the following should be assumed.

1. Illustrative figures are *not* necessarily drawn to scale.
2. All geometric figures lie in a plane.
3. The term *line* indicates a straight line.
4. The term *average* indicates arithmetic mean.

1. Tanya used $3\frac{3}{8}$ yards of fabric to make her dress, and she used $1\frac{1}{3}$ yards of fabric to make her jacket. What was the total amount, in yards, that Tanya used for the complete outfit of dress and jacket?

    A. $4\frac{1}{8}$

    B. $4\frac{1}{6}$

    C. $4\frac{4}{11}$

    D. $4\frac{1}{2}$

    E. $4\frac{17}{24}$

2. $5x^3y^5 \times 6y^2 \times 2xy$ is equivalent to:

    F. $13x^3y^7$.

    G. $13x^4y^8$.

    H. $60x^3y^7$.

    J. $60x^3y^{10}$.

    K. $60x^4y^8$.

3. Brandon puts 6% of his $36,000 yearly salary into savings, in 12 equal monthly installments. Jacqui deposits $200 every month into savings. At the end of one full year, what is the difference, in dollars, between the amount of money that Jacqui saved and the amount of money that Brandon saved?

    A. 20
    B. 24
    C. 240
    D. 1,960
    E. 2,800

4. Mikhail has received bowling scores of 190, 200, 145, and 180 so far in the state bowling tournament. What score must he receive on the fifth game to earn an average score of 180 for his five games?

    F. 179
    G. 180
    H. 185
    J. 200
    K. Mikhail cannot earn an average of 180.

GO ON TO THE NEXT PAGE

5. For steel to be considered stainless steel, it must have a minimum of 10.5% chromium in the metal alloy. If there are 262.5 pounds of chromium available, what is the maximum amount of stainless steel, in pounds, that can be manufactured?

A.   27.56

B.   252

C.   262.5

D.   2,500

E.   25,000

6. A homeowner wants to put a wallpaper border on the top edge of all the walls of his kitchen. The kitchen measures 6.5 meters by 4 meters. What is the required length, in meters, of the border?

F.   8

G.   10.5

H.   13

J.   21

K.   26

7. Which expression below is equivalent to $w(x - (y + z))$?

A. $wx - wy - wz$

B. $wx - wy + wz$

C. $wx - y + z$

D. $wx - y - z$

E. $wxy + wxz$

8. If $6n - 4 = 3n + 24$, $n = ?$

F.   28

G. $\dfrac{28}{3}$

H. $\dfrac{28}{9}$

J. $\dfrac{20}{9}$

K. $\dfrac{3}{28}$

9. What two numbers should be placed in the blanks below so that the difference between successive entries is the same?
26, ___, ___, 53

A. 36, 43

B. 35, 44

C. 34, 45

D. 33, 46

E. 30, 49

10. What is the real number value of $m^3 + \sqrt{12m}$ when $5m^2 = 45$?

F.   5

G.   27

H.   33

J.   38.09

K. 739.39

11. The radius of a sphere is $3\dfrac{3}{5}$ meters. What is the volume of the sphere, to the nearest cubic meter? Use the formula $V = \dfrac{4}{3}\pi r^3$

A.   42

B.   45

C.   157

D.   195

E. 3,429

GO ON TO THE NEXT PAGE

12. There are 10 peanuts, 6 cashews, and 8 almonds in a bag of mixed nuts. If a nut is chosen at random from the bag, what is the probability that the nut is NOT a peanut?

F. $\dfrac{5}{12}$

G. $\dfrac{7}{12}$

H. $\dfrac{5}{7}$

J. 10

K. 14

13. The number of people who shop at an electronics store during a given week is shown in the matrix below.

Adolescents	Adults	Senior Citizens
75	100	30

The ratio of people from each age group who will purchase a product to the number of people in that age group who shop at the store is shown in the following matrix:

Adolescents	0.20
Adults	0.35
Senior Citizens	0.10

Based on the matrices, how many people will make purchases?

A. 15

B. 41

C. 53

D. 133

E. 205

Use the following table to answer questions 14 and 15.

The table below shows the genres of radio music, broken down by the medium (AM, FM, or satellite) on which they are aired. In addition, the table shows the number of hours in which there is a live disc jockey.

Genre	Medium	# of Hours When There Is a Live Disc Jockey
Classical	AM	6
	FM	3
	Satellite	12
Country	AM	24
	FM	7
	Satellite	16
News	AM	24
	FM	24
	Satellite	24
Pop	AM	14
	Satellite	15
Rock	AM	12
	Satellite	24

14. What is the average number of hours, rounded to the nearest hour, that the country genre has a live disc jockey?

F. 3

G. 7

H. 14

J. 16

K. 24

GO ON TO THE NEXT PAGE

15. The time of day in which there is a live disc jockey does not matter, as long as there is a live disc jockey for the number of hours listed in the table. Assume that a disc jockey can switch from any genre and medium to another with the flip of a switch. Based on the table, what is the minimum number of disc jockeys needed to cover all genres and mediums, if each works an eight-hour shift?

    A.   5
    B.   13
    C.   25
    D.   26
    E.   205

16. In the following table, every row, column, and diagonal must have equivalent sums. Which term or value belongs in the lower left cell for this to be true?

m	$-4m$	$3m$
$2m$	0	$-2m$
	$4m$	$-m$

    F. $-4m$
    G. $-3m$
    H. -3
    J.   0
    K. m

17. The following standard coordinate plane is shown, with the four quadrants labeled. Point R, denoted by $R(x,y)$ is graphed on this plane, such that $x \neq 0$ and $y \neq 0$.

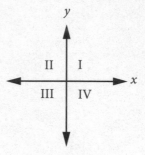

    If the product xy is a positive number, then point R is located in:

    A.   quadrant I only.
    B.   quadrant II only.
    C.   quadrant III only.
    D.   quadrant I or IV only.
    E.   quadrant I or III only.

18. The cafeteria offers 7 different sandwiches, 3 different soups, and 4 different drink choices on the luncheon menu. How many distinct meals are available if a meal consists of 1 sandwich, 1 soup, and 1 drink?

    F.   7
    G.   14
    H.   21
    J.   84
    K.   Cannot be determined from the given information.

19. At the university, there are 5 females for every 3 males. If there are 6,000 male students, how many students are female?

    A.   10,000
    B.   12,000
    C.   16,000
    D.   18,000
    E.   30,000

GO ON TO THE NEXT PAGE

20. What is the length, in inches, of the diagonal of a rectangle whose dimensions are 16 inches by 30 inches?

    F.   25

    G.   23

    H.   34

    J.   578

    K.   1,156

21. Which of the following expressions is NOT equivalent to $5n + 1$, if $n > 0$?

    A. $\dfrac{1}{5n + 1}$

    B. $5(n + 2) - 9$

    C. $\dfrac{1}{\dfrac{1}{5n + 1}}$

    D. $\dfrac{5n^2 + n}{n}$

    E. $\dfrac{25n^2 - 1}{5n - 1}$

22. Which of the following equations is equivalent to $3x + 2y = 16$?

    F. $y = -\dfrac{3}{2}x + 16$

    G. $y = -\dfrac{2}{3}x + 8$

    H. $y = \dfrac{3}{2}x + 8$

    J. $y = -\dfrac{3}{2}x + 8$

    K. $y = -\dfrac{2}{3}x + 8$

23. A solution to the equation $x^2 - 20x + 75 = 0$ is:

    A. -15.

    B. -5.

    C. 0.

    D. 3.

    E. 5.

24. Given the following right triangle, $\triangle LMN$, what is the value of $\cos N$?

    F. $\dfrac{5}{13}$

    G. $\dfrac{5}{12}$

    H. $\dfrac{12}{13}$

    J. $\dfrac{13}{12}$

    K. $\dfrac{13}{5}$

GO ON TO THE NEXT PAGE ⟩

25. In the following circle, chord AB passes through the center of circle O. If radius OC is perpendicular to chord AB and has a length of 7 centimeters, what is the length of chord BC, to the nearest tenth of a centimeter?

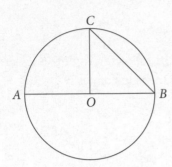

   A. 5.3

   B. 7.0

   C. 9.9

   D. 12.1

   E. 14.0

26. To convert a temperature in degrees Celsius to degrees Fahrenheit, the formula is $F = \frac{9}{5}C + 32$, where C is the temperature in degrees Celsius. What temperature, to the nearest degree Celsius, equals a temperature of 86 degrees Fahrenheit?

   F. 30

   G. 54

   H. 80

   J. 86

   K. 187

27. An Olympic-sized pool is 50 meters long, 25 meters wide, and holds 14,375 cubic meters of water. If the pool is the same depth in all parts, about how many meters deep is the water in the pool?

   A. Less than 9

   B. Between 9 and 10

   C. Between 10 and 11

   D. Between 11 and 12

   E. More than 12

28. In the following right triangle, $\triangle DEF$, the measure of segment DE is 42 inches, and the tangent of angle D is $\frac{5}{8}$. What is the length of segment EF, to the nearest tenth of an inch?

   F. 26.3

   G. 42.625

   H. 49.6

   J. 67.2

   K. 210.0

GO ON TO THE NEXT PAGE

29. The following bar graph shows the number of people at the spring prom, according to their grade level at the high school. According to the graph, what fraction of the people at the prom were sophomores?

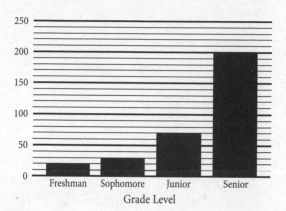

Number of Prom Attendees, by Grade Level

   A. $\dfrac{1}{16}$

   B. $\dfrac{3}{32}$

   C. $\dfrac{3}{29}$

   D. $\dfrac{3}{20}$

   E. $\dfrac{3}{10}$

30. In the following segment, point X is the midpoint of segment WZ. If the measure of WY is 26 cm and the measure of WZ is 44 cm, what is the length, in centimeters, of segment XY?

   F. 4

   G. 13

   H. 18

   J. 22

   K. 70

31. What is the x-coordinate of the intersection point, in the (x,y) coordinate system, of the lines $2x + 3y = 8$ and $5x + y = 7$?

   A. −1

   B. $\dfrac{15}{7}$

   C. 1

   D. 2

   E. 3

32. For all pairs of real numbers a and b, where $a = 2b - 8$, $b = ?$

   F. $a + 4$

   G. $2a - 8$

   H. $2a + 8$

   J. $\dfrac{a - 8}{2}$

   K. $\dfrac{a + 8}{2}$

33. What is the area, in square millimeters, of parallelogram $RSUT$ shown?

   A. 30

   B. 39

   C. 54

   D. 168

   E. 182

GO ON TO THE NEXT PAGE

34. If $x = -(y + 3)$, then $(x + y)^3 = ?$

    F.   –27

    G.   –9

    H.   9

    J.   27

    K.   Cannot be determined from the given information.

35. The following is a partial map of Centerville, showing 80 square miles: a total of 8 miles of Main Street and a total of 10 miles of Front Street. There is a fire station at the corner of Main and Front Streets, shown as point *F*. The town wants to build a new fire station exactly halfway between the hospital, at *H*, and the school, at *S*. What would be the driving directions to get from the current fire station to the new fire station, by way of Main and Elm streets? All streets and avenues shown intersect at right angles.

    A.   2.5 miles east, 4 miles north

    B.   2.5 miles west, 4 miles north

    C.   2.5 miles east, 6 miles south

    D.   5.5 miles west, 4 miles south

    E.   5.5 miles west, 6 miles south

36. There are two consecutive odd integers. The difference between four times the larger and twice the smaller is 36. If x represents the smaller integer, which of the following equations can be used to determine the smaller integer?

    F. $4x - 2x = 36$

    G. $4(x + 1) - 2x = 36$

    H. $4(x + 2) - 2x = 36$

    J. $(x + 3) - 2x = 36$

    K. $36 - 4x = 2x$

37. A 15-foot supporting wire is attached to a telephone pole 12 feet from the ground. The wire is then anchored to the ground. The telephone pole stands perpendicular to the ground. How far, in feet, is the anchor of the supporting wire from the base of the telephone pole?

    A.   3

    B.   6

    C.   9

    D.   12

    E.   15

38. In the following figure, the sides of the square are tangent to the inner circle. If the area of the circle is 100π square units, what is the unit length of a side of the square?

    F.   400

    G.   100

    H.   20

    J.   10

    K. π

GO ON TO THE NEXT PAGE

39. Rectangles *ABCD* and *EFGH* shown are similar. Using the given information, what is the length of side *EH*, to the nearest tenth of an inch?

A. 0.8

B. 1.3

C. 5.3

D. 7.0

E. 8.0

40. In parallelogram *VWXY* shown, points *U*, *V*, *Y*, and *Z* form a straight line. Given the angle measures as shown in the figure, what is the measure of angle ∠*WYX* ?

F. 25°

G. 30°

H. 50°

J. 100°

K. 150°

41. In the following figure, all interior angles are 90°, and all dimension lengths are given in centimeters. What is the perimeter of this figure, in centimeters?

A. 40

B. 61

C. 82

D. 122

E. Cannot be determined from the given information.

42. In the mayoral election, $\frac{3}{4}$ of the eligible voters at one site cast a vote. Three-fifths of the votes at this site were for candidate Martinez. If there are 3,500 eligible voters at this site, how many of them voted for Martinez?

F. 417

G. 1,575

H. 2,100

J. 2,625

K. 4,725

43. Given that *a* and *b* are positive integers, and the greatest common factor of a^4b^2 and a^3b is 54, what is a possible value for *b* ?

A. 2

B. 3

C. 6

D. 9

E. 27

GO ON TO THE NEXT PAGE ▷

44. If 40% of x is 70, then what is 160% of x?

    F. 28

    G. 45

    H. 112

    J. 175

    K. 280

45. Point M (2,3) and point N (6,5) are points on the coordinate plane. What is the length of the segment MN?

    A. $\sqrt{2}$ units

    B. $2\sqrt{3}$ units

    C. $2\sqrt{5}$ units

    D. 6 units

    E. 20 units

46. The ratio of the sides of two squares is 5:7. What is the ratio of the perimeters of these squares?

    F. 1:2

    G. 1:12

    H. 1:35

    J. 5:7

    K. 25:49

47. What is the equation of a circle in the coordinate plane with center (−2,3) and a radius of 9 units?

    A. $(x - 2)^2 + (y + 3)^2 = 9$

    B. $(x + 2)^2 + (y - 3)^2 = 9$

    C. $(x - 2)^2 + (y + 3)^2 = 81$

    D. $(x + 2)^2 + (y - 3)^2 = 3$

    E. $(x + 2)^2 + (y - 3)^2 = 81$

48. In the complex number system, $i^2 = -1$.

Given that $\dfrac{3}{5 - i}$ is a complex number, what is the result of $\dfrac{3}{5 - i} \times \dfrac{5 + i}{5 + i}$?

    F. $\dfrac{3}{5 + i}$

    G. $\dfrac{15 + 3i}{24}$

    H. $\dfrac{15 + 3i}{26}$

    J. $\dfrac{15 + i}{26}$

    K. $\dfrac{15 + i}{24}$

49. The following figures show regular polygons and the sum of the degrees of the angles in each polygon. Based on these figures, what is the number of degrees in an n-sided regular polygon?

    180°   360°   540°   720°

    A. $60n$

    B. $180n$

    C. $180(n - 2)$

    D. $20n^2$

    E. Cannot be determined from the information given.

GO ON TO THE NEXT PAGE

50. Fifty high school students were polled to see if they owned a cell phone and an MP3 player. A total of 35 of the students own a cell phone, and a total of 18 of the students own an MP3 player. What is the minimum number of students who own both a cell phone and an MP3 player?

F.   0

G.   3

H.   17

J.   32

K.   53

51. What is the solution set of all real numbers n such that $-4n + 3 > -4n + 1$?

A. All real numbers

B. All positive numbers

C. All negative numbers

D. All numbers such that $n > -\dfrac{1}{2}$

E. All numbers such that $n < -\dfrac{1}{2}$

52. If 3 people all shake hands with each other, there are a total of 3 handshakes. If 4 people all shake hands with each other, there are a total of 6 handshakes. How many total handshakes will there be if 5 people all shake hands with each other?

F.   7

G.   9

H.   10

J.   11

K.   12

53. The following chart shows the percentages of a county's budget expenses by category. The remainder of the budget will be placed in the category Miscellaneous. If these data are to be put into a circle graph, what will be the degree measure of the Miscellaneous wedge, rounded to the nearest degree?

Budget Category	Percentage of Budget
Salaries	23
Road Repair	5
Employee Benefits	22
Building Mainte-nance/Utilities	18

A.   32

B.   58

C.   68

D. 115

E. 245

54. If $\tan \theta = -\dfrac{4}{3}$, and $\dfrac{\pi}{2} < \theta < \pi$, then $\sin \theta = ?$

F. $-\dfrac{4}{5}$

G. $-\dfrac{3}{4}$

H. $-\dfrac{3}{5}$

J. $\dfrac{3}{5}$

K. $\dfrac{4}{5}$

GO ON TO THE NEXT PAGE

55. Which of the following systems of inequalities is represented by the shaded region on the coordinate plane below?

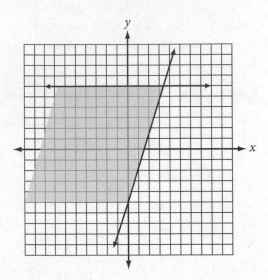

    A. $y < 6$ and $y > 3x - 5$

    B. $x < 6$ and $y > 3x - 5$

    C. $y < 6$ and $y < 3x - 5$

    D. $x < 6$ and $y < -3x - 5$

    E. $y < 6$ and $y > \dfrac{1}{3}x - 5$

56. If $f(x) = 2(x + 7)$, then $f(x + c) = ?$

    F. $2x + 2c + 7$

    G. $2x + c + 7$

    H. $2x + c + 14$

    J. $2x + 2c + 14$

    K. $2(x + 7) + c$

57. Which graph represents the solution set for the equation $y = \dfrac{2x^2 - 8}{x - 2}$?

    A.

    B.

    C.

    D.

    E.

GO ON TO THE NEXT PAGE

58. What are the coordinates of Q', the reflection of the point $Q(r,s)$ over the y-axis?

F. $(-r,s)$

G. $(-r,-s)$

H. $(s,-r)$

J. $(r,-s)$

K. $(-s,r)$

59. If $g = 4q + 3$ and $h = 2q - 8$, what is g in terms of h?

A. $g = \dfrac{h + 8}{2}$

B. $g = \dfrac{4h + 11}{2}$

C. $2h + 19$

D. $2h + 11$

E. $h = \dfrac{g - 3}{4}$

60. Find the $\cos(75°)$ knowing that $\cos(75°) = \cos(30° + 45°)$. Use the formula $\cos(\alpha + \beta) = \cos(\alpha)\cos(\beta) - \sin(\alpha)\sin(\beta)$ and the following table of values:

θ	$\sin\theta$	$\cos\theta$	$\tan\theta$
30°	$\dfrac{1}{2}$	$\dfrac{\sqrt{3}}{2}$	$\dfrac{\sqrt{3}}{3}$
45°	$\dfrac{\sqrt{2}}{2}$	$\dfrac{\sqrt{2}}{2}$	1
60°	$\dfrac{\sqrt{3}}{2}$	$\dfrac{1}{2}$	$\sqrt{3}$

F. $\dfrac{\sqrt{3} - \sqrt{2}}{4}$

G. $\dfrac{\sqrt{3} - \sqrt{2}}{2}$

H. $\dfrac{\sqrt{6} - \sqrt{2}}{4}$

J. $\dfrac{\sqrt{6} - \sqrt{2}}{2}$

K. $\dfrac{3 - \sqrt{2}}{4}$

READING TEST

35 Minutes—40 Questions

Directions: There are four passages in this test. Each passage is followed by several questions. After reading a passage, choose the best answer to each question and fill in the corresponding oval on your Answer Grid. You may refer to the passages as often as necessary.

PASSAGE I

PROSE FICTION

This excerpt from a short story describes a conversation between a woman and her husband, who is a twin.

Emily couldn't help but grin broadly after answering the phone. She frequently called us "two peas in a pod," but I'd always felt
Line like any time we were mentioned outside
(5) of my presence, he was "Bruce" and I was "Bruce's twin brother." Because of this, I wasn't surprised to hear my wife giggling uncontrollably and see her twirling the phone cord around her finger while talking
(10) to him. Despite the fact she was speaking to someone genetically identical to me, I couldn't help but wonder if she had ever responded so enthusiastically to one of my stories.
(15) "Okay, I'll tell him. Talk to you soon." After Emily hung up, I watched her take a deep, almost wistful breath before walking over to me.

"Bruce seems well," I said, trying to
(20) sound casual. "He told me about the new job and everything. What did you guys talk about?"

"Not much." Emily replied. She walked behind my chair and patted my shoulder
(25) before sitting on the couch and opening her magazine. It didn't appear as if she were really reading. She seemed to stop and start, pausing and reflecting about something unrelated to the smiling celebrities featured
(30) in the article.

"It's funny to think that he knows some of these people," she said, pointing at her magazine.

I looked at the gleaming teeth and
(35) chiseled features of the actors, and then looked over at a picture of Bruce and me resting on the mantel. Looking closely at the photo always made my stomach turn; as with every picture of us, there was an
(40) unmistakable vitality in Bruce's face that wasn't present in mine. It were as if I were wearing a "Bruce" costume; I was trying to mimic one of his trademark smiles, but I always seemed to produce a different failed
(45) attempt.

"You all right?" Emily asked, noticing my expression.

I grabbed the picture from the mantel and brought it to her. She looked at it and
(50) looked up at me quizzically.

"Can you tell which one is me?" I asked.

She looked back at the picture and pushed her lip out as she looked from one face to the next. After about five seconds she
(55) pointed to my face, then turned and looked at me confidently.

"How could you tell?" I asked.

"Well, it wasn't very hard," she responded. "You are my husband, and I love
(60) the way you smile. Bruce looks exactly the same in every picture, it looks practiced, but for you it always seems like you're thinking about something, even concentrating, to make sure you smile right."
(65) "Really?" I was surprised by how much thought she had put into this.

She took the picture and put it back on the mantel. I could still see the perfection in

GO ON TO THE NEXT PAGE ⇒

Bruce's smile and hesitation in mine, but at
(70) least Emily found a way to compliment my
insecurities.

Emily went back to perusing her
magazine.

"At least you ended up with a Fairholm,"
(75) I said, "even if it wasn't the famous one."

"Oh, was I supposed to pursue the
famous one?" she shot back.

She closed her magazine and put it
down on the coffee table. There wasn't an
(80) argument coming, but I saw her disappointment.
The problem was not that she actually
would have married my brother before me;
it was the simple fact that I couldn't help but
believe that to be the case. I saw myself as
(85) second to him and always had. With embarrassing
relatives, people will always point
out that one can't choose his or her family,
but when you're a twin, it's not the association
that you fear—it's the comparison.

(90) "Do you want to be where he is?" she
inquired, with an empty tone.

"This is exactly where I want to be,"
I replied. "I just never know how to explain
to people that I'm an insurance adjuster,
(95) not a Hollywood agent. They always want
to know how it happened when we had the
same upbringing and education. They look
at me as if I did something wrong."

"Do you ever call him?" she asked.
(100) "I figure he's busy, and he calls enough,"
I said.

She cradled her chin in her hand and
looked at me in mild disbelief. "You realize
that by not calling and turning down his
(105) invitations to visit, you make him feel
rejected, right?"

"Come on, Emily. He's surrounded
by famous people—he doesn't need my
approval."

(110) "Maybe not," she sighed, "but his favorite
stories to tell me aren't about Hollywood—
they're about you two growing up."

"Well, he was popular then, too," I said,
shrugging.

(115) "He doesn't look at it that way," she
responded. "He would give up a lot to have
your approval, Dave. He wants to be your
brother, not a competitor."

"It's okay, Emily. I'll call him soon, but I
(120) think that he'll be okay either way."

1. Dave would probably agree with which of the
   following statements regarding his relationship with Bruce?

   A. They would be better off not talking at
      all.
   B. Their phone conversations are vital to
      their relationship.
   C. Their bond as twins is stronger due to
      Emily's effort.
   D. Their competition makes it harder for
      them to get along.

2. Emily is best described as:

   F. aloof and ineffectual.
   G. needling and meddlesome.
   H. caring and diplomatic.
   J. pained and inconsolable.

3. Which of the following statements does
   NOT describe a feeling Dave has toward his
   brother?

   A. He is jealous of the reaction his brother
      gets from Emily during their phone
      conversation.
   B. He believes he would be better suited
      for his brother's type of work.
   C. He is resentful of his brother's superior
      social skills.
   D. He is skeptical of his brother's desire for
      his approval.

GO ON TO THE NEXT PAGE

4. The primary focus of the first paragraph is:

   F. Emily's attempt to make her husband jealous.

   G. Emily's desire for the brothers to resolve their differences.

   H. Dave's hope to distance himself from his twin brother.

   J. Dave's feelings of inferiority to his twin brother.

5. Lines 99–120 ("Do you ever...either way") suggest that Dave does not contact Bruce because Dave:

   A. believes that Bruce has great need for him but does not want to admit to Emily that she is right.

   B. feels guilty about being distant toward Bruce and worries that he will have to explain himself.

   C. wants to prove to Emily that he is not impressed by Bruce's high-profile job.

   D. still harbors resentment over Bruce getting preferential treatment during their childhood.

6. According to the passage, when Dave looks at the photograph, he sees:

   F. his brother being cruel to him.

   G. two indistinguishable faces.

   H. a comparison unfavorable to him.

   J. his wife paying more attention to Bruce.

7. Which of the following best summarizes Dave's feelings when he asks Emily to pick him out in the picture?

   A. Dave is confident that Emily will prefer his image to Bruce's.

   B. Dave is insecure; he feels the picture compares him unfavorably to Bruce.

   C. Dave is worried, because he thinks Emily will want to talk more about Bruce after seeing a picture of him.

   D. Dave is angry because he did not want to talk about the picture in the first place.

8. It can be logically deduced from the passage that Dave and Bruce:

   F. tell Emily different-sounding stories about their shared childhood.

   G. are frequently at odds regarding their different professions.

   H. have often fought over Emily's attention.

   J. were much closer shortly before Bruce moved.

9. It can be inferred from the passage that both Emily and Dave conclude that when pictures are taken of the brothers:

   A. Bruce looks much better than Dave.

   B. Dave appears angry at Bruce.

   C. pictures of Bruce are more consistent than those of Dave.

   D. Dave's expression makes a greater impression on the viewer than Bruce's.

GO ON TO THE NEXT PAGE ⟶

10. According to the passage, the reason Emily tells Dave about the content of Bruce's stories is that Emily:

F. wants to convince Dave that Bruce does not see himself as better than Dave.

G. wishes to hear Dave's version of the stories.

H. sees doing so as a way to make Dave more impressed with his brother.

J. thinks that doing so will make Dave sympathetic to Bruce's loneliness.

PASSAGE II

SOCIAL SCIENCE

This passage discusses the relationship between the media and public opinion.

Large-scale media would likely be traced back to ancient tribes sharing information about the edibility of berries or the
Line aggressiveness of animals. Despite constant
(5) evolution, the information most sought after is that regarding personal safety, personal opportunity, and the triumphs and misdeeds of others—the larger the persona and more laudatory or despicable the act,
(10) the better. When a story is of continued national interest, however, the focus shifts even further from facts and more to theater. To step back and compose an objective plot of goings-on is a distant possibility, but
(15) establishing the hero or villain of the day is paramount. Ultimately, the public's desire to have cold, dry, and correct facts is virtually nonexistent.

Current newscasts exacerbate this by
(20) delivering an assault on the senses with meaningless graphics and theatrical music; meanwhile, the monotone newscaster reads, verbatim from a teleprompter, often using phrases identical to those on other
(25) networks. Additionally, the viewer has

probably already read the same story on the Internet earlier. When television was limited to three networks, rather than ubiquitous news-only channels, the newscaster
(30) was a national figure, and audience members would eagerly await information that was new to them and would expect a relatively thorough explanation of any complicated events. For example, to this day many
(35) people, in explaining the Watergate scandal to those too young to know of it, use Walter Cronkite's delineation as the basis for their understanding.

The objective, trustworthy anchorperson
(40) has also given way to vociferous demagogues promising truth but delivering oversimplified, bias-driven sound bites. The idea of allowing individuals to draw their own conclusions is notably absent; in fact, many
(45) personalities mock those with opinions differing from those presented. The availability of neutral online sources mitigates this slightly, but not to any large degree. While the actual article may be impartial,
(50) electronic periodicals will still sensationalize headlines in order to attract casual readers, and those very headlines sway many readers to certain opinions before the article is even read. For example, if a headline mentions
(55) an "enraged public," the reader is far more likely to both read and take umbrage at the information than he or she would if the article mentioned a subject that "irked locals."

(60) In truth, though, the public is as desirous for dry and objective facts as finicky children are for brussels sprouts. The personalities willing to shrug off accountability in favor of wild accusations and bombastic
(65) slogans captivate a large demographic, while one would be generous by saying that objective fact-based programs occupy even a niche market. This not only damages the general accuracy of so-called
(70) "news" but also further polarizes the public. People now have the option to receive their

GO ON TO THE NEXT PAGE

news from hosts with a variety of political leanings, and one almost invariably chooses to watch the personality with opinions
(75) closest to one's own. This is more harmful than convenient because it allows viewers to simply parrot information they are given, eliminating any thought or scrutiny. It is this intellectual laziness that aids in
(80) distancing the general public from factual information: as a growing number become resigned to accept whatever their favorite host tells them, the more freedom networks have to pass sensationalist entertainment
(85) off as news. It boils down to the unfortunate truth that most are far more likely to accept inaccurate information as fact than to question the legitimacy of something that seems to fit with opinions a particular
(90) audience member holds.

   Those who make the news also obfuscate objective facts. A legion of employees is dedicated solely to the purpose of making the decisions of political figures sound
(95) flawless. Oftentimes, important decisions are made, yet throughout a lengthy press conference, not a single factual implication is discussed. The meeting becomes nothing more than an opportunity for political
(100) employees to test their infallible-sounding slogans, while the media dissects the semantics rather than the facts. Semantics, however, are all the media is presented with.

   Despite all these methods of prevarication,
(105) people still are better informed than they were in the past. Public knowledge of events often occurs minutes after the fact, rather than days or weeks. The populace has a strong desire for news in general,
(110) and amid all the unscrupulous presentation methods, facts do exist. However, the profitability of news has put a premium on presentation, not trustworthiness. Complicating matters further is the populace's impatience;
(115) the standard consumer would rather be presented with a minute and potentially inaccurate statement—one that may or may

not be retracted the following day—than suffer through a lengthy treatise comprised
(120) of all the known facts and nuances of a particular issue. The desire to know still exists, however; it just happens to be overshadowed by the public's desire for personal consensus and the media's desire to reel in
(125) the public.

11. One of the primary points the author attempts to make regarding the current news media is that:

   A. the media passes off made-up stories as facts.

   B. the news anchors are not as opinionated as they were in decades past.

   C. the media focuses more on presentation than substance.

   D. the media goes directly against what news audiences truly desire to see.

12. The author makes what claim about impartial news stories?

   F. They no longer exist.

   G. They can be sensationalized in ways other than their content.

   H. They often have headlines that correctly reflect the emotional level of the story.

   J. They all have headlines that attempt to make the reader feel involved in the story.

13. The author brings up Walter Cronkite's coverage of Watergate in order to assert that:

   A. Walter Cronkite was a particularly adept newsperson.

   B. a previous standard for news rightly included clarification of complex issues.

   C. current newscasters are far more forgettable than those before them.

   D. the expanding number of television channels has made individual newscasters less famous.

GO ON TO THE NEXT PAGE ⟶

14. By stating that "personal consensus" is of great importance to the public (lines 123–124), the author is probably suggesting that members of the public:

    F. do not want information that contradicts their own beliefs.

    G. work hard to find the source closest to truth, despite the difficulties present.

    H. wish to resolve any moral conflicts they may have with practices in news reporting.

    J. have difficulty finding news sources reflecting their personal views.

15. According to the passage, what type of news stories are sensationalized the most?

    A. Those with a fairly clear chain of events

    B. Those that stay in the public's consciousness for long periods of time

    C. Those that clearly support one political view

    D. Those with the most scandalous information

16. As it is used in line 14, the word *distant* most nearly means:

    F. separated.

    G. different.

    H. reserved.

    J. unlikely.

17. Based on the passage, which of the following headlines would the author be most likely to criticize?

    A. Earthquake Rocks Small Community, Arouses Questions Regarding Preparedness

    B. New Tax Protested by Idaho Farmers

    C. Parents Across Country Outraged at Offensive Song

    D. Governor Describes Proposed Legislation as "Monstrous"

18. The author asserts that individuals will often accept potentially inaccurate information because they:

    F. believe that most newscasters are honest.

    G. have no way to research correct facts.

    H. are forced to translate the guarded words of political employees.

    J. have political beliefs similar to those of specific media personalities.

19. In the fourth paragraph, the phrase "even a niche market" (line 68) expresses the author's feeling that:

    A. media companies are influenced greatly by public demand.

    B. cable television networks are unwilling to present objective facts.

    C. factual news media should look into better marketing practices.

    D. factual news would be profitable with greater exposure.

20. The author argues that in searching for a news source, audience members are most likely to choose the source that:

    F. features the most entertaining newscaster.

    G. validates the audience member's opinion.

    H. presents the shortest and simplest explanation for events.

    J. focuses on big stories rather than local ones.

GO ON TO THE NEXT PAGE ⟩

PASSAGE III

HUMANITIES

James Joyce was among the most influential writers of the early twentieth century and one of the leaders of a literary movement that became known as modernism. The following two passages are excerpted from essays written about Joyce during his lifetime.

PASSAGE A

Although the writer James Joyce has spent the majority of his adult life outside of Ireland, he has always thought
Line of himself as, and will be remembered
(5) as, a quintessentially Irish writer. His attachment to the nation, and especially his boyhood home of Dublin, is apparent in his works, which are invariably set in Ireland and often focus on the social
(10) and political issues of the Irish. One of his earliest works, a collection of short stories, is even entitled *Dubliners*, and his novel *Ulysses*, which is generally considered his greatest work, depicts 1904
(15) Dublin in almost staggering detail. Joyce was often quoted as saying that, were Dublin to be destroyed in some tremendous calamity, it could be re-created brick by brick from the depictions in
(20) *Ulysses*; in reading the novel, one finds it difficult to dispute the claim.

In addition to its focus on Dublin, *Ulysses* is somewhat narrowly focused in other ways as well. Its action takes place
(25) on a single day, and for the most part it is centered on a single protagonist. Its events are not the grand, sweeping historical landmarks found in other novels, such as Tolstoy's *War and Peace*, but
(30) rather the mundane events of everyday life; Joyce considered eating, running errands, and even making trips to the lavatory worthy of inclusion in his masterpiece. And yet, despite its tight focus,
(35) the novel is already considered one of

the most globally appealing of all time, a powerful representation of the complete human condition. Almost paradoxically, it is the level of detail in Joyce's micro-
(40) cosm of a single man on a single day in a single city that allows him to make statements and observations that apply to humanity as a whole. Perhaps human existence is not best contemplated on the
(45) great battlefields of history, which are experienced by only a few human beings for small portions of their lives. It might instead be better expressed in the minor struggles and idle musings of an ordi-
(50) nary Irishman who, by the very virtue of his ordinariness, is able to transcend the impediments of time and place in order to appeal to the entirety of the human dilemma.

PASSAGE B

(55) As one contemplates the state of literature in our modern era, it is hard to resist a longing for the great writers of eras gone by. At times, one must take great pains merely to remember that
(60) there were once authors such as Dante, Shakespeare, or Dickens: authors who were able to relate stories of great travels and struggles even as they compelled us to mull over the great philosophical
(65) questions of all time. They did not waste their time or ours with trivial affairs; their stories were unique and memorable, and they bore repeated readings and re-readings from generation to genera-
(70) tion. These writers never took perverse glee in conveying thoughts and actions that were better off forgotten. They took great care to depict accurately the best and worst aspects of human nature;
(75) they were well aware of the impact their works would have on culture and strove

GO ON TO THE NEXT PAGE ⟶

to ensure that they would enhance, rather than degrade, the public's intellect; they did not resort to tricks or devices in
(80) order to garner readership for their writings; and in all these regards, they are firmly distinguished from writers of the present day, the most notorious of which is the Irish novelist James Joyce.

(85)   The goal of art is to enlighten the consciousness of those who partake of it, to lift their minds and souls out of the trenches of ordinary activities and humanity's base instincts. It would seem
(90) that modern writers like Joyce have no interest in such enlightenment, instead preferring to revel in every detail of activities that should never have been committed to paper in the first place. In
(95) basing his novel *Ulysses* on Homer's *The Odyssey*, Joyce has sullied the very form of the epic genre. Whereas *The Odyssey* was a great tale of a noble hero's struggle against a seemingly insurmountable
(100) series of trials in order to restore order and honor to his household, Joyce's book is nearly the direct opposite. The protagonist is no hero, his actions are listless and forgettable, and his obsession with
(105) obscene and undignified behavior is virtually nauseating. It is a pity that Homer's epic hero has now been so distorted by his mere association with Joyce's antihero. And even more shame-
(110) ful is the waste of talent, for, subject matter aside, Joyce is no slouch as a wordsmith. Sadly, it is the literary world's loss that he was not born in a more dignified era where his talents could have been
(115) utilized in a more appropriate manner.

Questions 21–23 ask about Passage A.

21. Which of the following, if true, would most significantly weaken the main argument of Passage A?

A. Historical events are often depicted inaccurately in fictional writing.

B. Similar philosophical ideas often arise in cultures that have never had contact with each other.

C. People from some cultures find the thoughts and motivations of people in other cultures impossible to comprehend.

D. Thorough knowledge of the place where one grew up can lead to a stronger understanding of human nature.

22. Which of the following best conveys the meaning of "transcend...place" (lines 51–52)?

F. Make a specific statement about a particular group of people.

G. Write in such a way that precise information is obscured.

H. Ignore setting in order to focus solely on character.

J. Go beyond surface circumstance to reveal universal truth.

23. In lines 38–43 ("Almost paradoxically . . . as a whole"), the author of Passage A suggests that Joyce's widespread appeal is due to his:

A. knowledge of geography.

B. penchant for exciting prose.

C. attention to ordinary details.

D. use of exotic locales.

GO ON TO THE NEXT PAGE

Questions 24–26 ask about Passage B.

24. According to Passage B's first paragraph, the author is critical of James Joyce's writing on the grounds that Joyce:

   F. is not as dignified as the great authors of the past.

   G. lacks proper knowledge of his subject matter.

   H. copies too closely from the authors who preceded him.

   J. uses language that is unnecessarily elegant.

25. In the final sentence of Passage B (lines 112–115), the author suggests that Joyce:

   A. would sell many books whether his writing was obscene or not.

   B. never committed quite enough time to revising and improving his novels.

   C. would have been more successful if his prose style were stronger.

   D. might have produced greater literature in a more refined environment.

26. As used in line 89, the word *base* most nearly means:

   F. unrefined.

   G. foundational.

   H. nauseating.

   J. sophisticated.

Questions 27–30 ask about both passages.

27. It can be inferred that the author of Passage A would respond to Passage B's assertion that the goal of art is to enlighten by:

   A. providing evidence that Joyce's writing is more enlightened than older works.

   B. emphasizing the importance of appealing to readers throughout the world.

   C. agreeing that Joyce's attention to detail diminishes the value of his writing.

   D. refusing to acknowledge the significance of great philosophical questions.

28. Which of the following best captures the difference between the two authors' views of Joyce's writing?

   F. The author of Passage A despises its lack of importance, while the author of Passage B disparages its inaccuracy.

   G. The author of Passage A claims that it is insignificant, while the author of Passage B contends that it is obscene.

   H. The author of Passage A admires its universal appeal, while the author of Passage B deplores its lack of decorum.

   J. The author of Passage A laments its irrelevance, while the author of Passage B appreciates its craftsmanship.

29. Which of the following word pairs best reflects the perspective of each author on the word "detail" as used in Passage A (line 15) and Passage B (line 92)?

	Passage A	Passage B
A.	entertainment	dismay
B.	admiration	revulsion
C.	enthusiasm	shame
D.	support	glee

30. It can be inferred that the author of Passage B would most likely respond to Passage A's description of Joyce as "quintessentially Irish writer" (line 5) by:

   F. disagreeing that Joyce was of Irish descent.

   G. disagreeing that Joyce was an exemplary writer.

   H. agreeing that Joyce was a champion linguist.

   J. agreeing that Joyce was an unrelenting mystic.

GO ON TO THE NEXT PAGE

PASSAGE IV

NATURAL SCIENCE

This passage discusses the degree to which rattlesnakes pose a threat to humans.

In both recorded and oral history, rattle-snakes are categorized as malevolent beings. Their lance-shaped heads and angular brow-lines
Line make them look the perfect villain, and their
(5) venom cements this classification. Publicized reports of bite victims seem to prove their nefarious nature.

Unlike mammalian predators such as bears, rattlesnakes do not have the reputation
(10) of an animal deserving human respect. One imagines the rattlesnake hiding in our backyards, waiting to strike.

In recent long-term studies, however, the social behavior of rattlesnakes has been
(15) found to be quite different than many would expect. Herpetologists, scientists who study snakes, had long suspected a more complex and thoughtful existence for the reptiles, and now have hard information to back up
(20) their theories. When examined, the sinister opportunist lurking in the shadows better resembles a mild-mannered domestic. Unlike the nonvenomous king snake, rattlesnakes are entirely noncannibalistic, and
(25) tend to spend their entire lives with a single mate. The mating ritual in which two males will extend almost half of their bodies off the ground to wrestle is not lethal, and, once bested, a rattlesnake peacefully retreats to
(30) find a new den of eligible mates. Female rattlesnakes give birth to live young, and rattlesnakes often share their dens, even hibernating with tortoises without incident.

Sadly, it seems that only those with an
(35) existing fascination with snakes are aware of this socially functional rattlesnake. Another discovery that made little stir in the public consciousness is an experiment in which herpetologists tracked snakes with radio
(40) transmitters and saw their behavior when humans entered their habitat. While a few snakes did hold their ground and rattle, most saw or sensed a disturbance (snakes cannot hear) and immediately headed in
(45) the opposite direction. Many of the snakes that were handled by herpetologists did not coil or strike. This is not to say that a snake will not bite a human if disturbed, but the tendency is to retreat first and give warning
(50) second, before striking becomes a possibility.

Describing a more docile nature does not imply that rattlesnakes would make good pets for children, but considering the aggressiveness often displayed by a South
(55) American pit viper, the fer-de-lance, one familiar with both would have far less trepidation about passing by a rattlesnake. For one thing, rattlesnakes do coil and rattle, giving humans an opportunity to move
(60) away, while fer-de-lances will often strike at passersby without warning. Furthermore, when it comes down to statistics, American hospitals report an average of 7,000 snakebite patients a year; generally
(65) more than half are actually from nonvenomous snakes thought by victims to be venomous. On average, fewer than six people die of snake envenomation annually, and the vast majority of the serious bites are due
(70) to either handling the snake or stepping on it; most people bitten by snakes they were not engaging end up with very mild bites. Compare this with an average of over one million hospital visits for dog bites and
(75) twenty annual deaths at the jaws of man's best friend. With such minuscule statistics regarding snakebites, it is curious why they are still viewed as unfathomably dangerous, when bees, lightning—and yes, dogs—are
(80) responsible for far more human fatalities. The fer-de-lance, however, is responsible for thousands of deaths annually in Central and South America.

GO ON TO THE NEXT PAGE →

If one is looking for proof that rattlesnakes
(85) do not intend to harm humans, one
should consider perhaps the most stunning
evidence regarding bite behavior. Over
half of the bites rattlesnakes administer to
humans are "dry," meaning the rattlesnake
(90) purposely does not release venom. While I
will not posit that this is due to rattlesnakes
possessing an awareness of the well-being of
their non-food-source bite victim, there is
a great deal of thought present. The snake
(95) acknowledges that venom is needed for
immobilizing and digesting prey (venom
is actually saliva), producing venom takes
time, and the human is not a food source.
Therefore, if the snake is not surprised or
(100) fearing death, the damage of a rattlesnake
bite will likely be far less severe than if the
snake used all its venom. This has been
known for some time, but, in many cases, it
is probably better for humans to believe that
(105) the snakes are more liberal with venom than
they are, simply because a frightened and
cornered rattlesnake is very dangerous.

Unfortunately, some people take the
traditional view of the rattlesnake and use
(110) it as an excuse to harm the animals. People
in various areas use the fearsome reputation
of rattlesnakes, along with the more docile
reality, for profit. Rattlesnake roundups are
held, where people collect snakes
(115) beforehand and join in a festival celebrating their
conquest. The events are billed as both
entertainment and as making surrounding
residential areas safer for children; however,
the vast majority of snakes are collected
(120) from uninhabited areas, and people are
frequently bitten at the festivals while
handling the snakes for the audience. Eventually,
the snakes are killed to make clothing
or trophies, and these events are estimated
(125) to be responsible for 100,000 rattlesnake
deaths annually, in comparison to fewer
than 6 human deaths from rattlesnakes.

Behavior like this provides a better
reason for crotalid mythology. With

(130) statistics categorically showing a low level of
danger from rattlesnakes to humans, and an
extremely high level vice versa, it would be
a wonder to see what human-related folklore
rattlesnakes would come up with if they
(135) were able to speak or write.

31. In relation to the entire passage, the phrase
"the sinister opportunist lurking in the shadows better resembles a mild-mannered domestic" (lines 20–22) most likely implies that:

   A. adult rattlesnakes are considerably less
   aggressive than juveniles.

   B. recent studies regarding rattlesnakes
   found few incidents of aggressive
   behavior.

   C. rattlesnakes are more similar to
   mammals than once thought.

   D. rattlesnakes are entirely predictable in
   behavior.

32. The passage implies that the rattlesnake's fearsome reputation can be beneficial because:

   F. it influences people to avoid or move
   away from rattlesnakes.

   G. it protects the lives of rattlesnakes.

   H. it inspires medical advancement in
   treating snakebites, despite a low
   mortality rate.

   J. adventurous people may seek rattlesnakes as pets.

33. What evidence does the passage give regarding the social ability of rattlesnakes?

   A. Rattlesnakes are aware of the uses of
   their venom.

   B. Wrestling between males establishes a
   social hierarchy.

   C. Rattlesnakes can share their habitat
   with other species.

   D. Rattlesnakes rarely eat other snakes.

GO ON TO THE NEXT PAGE

34. The statement "it would be a wonder to see what human-related folklore rattlesnakes would come up with if they were able to speak or write" (lines 132–135) means that:

    F. humans and rattlesnakes both present great risks to each other's safety.

    G. humans and rattlesnakes behave in many similar ways.

    H. humans are a much greater threat to rattlesnakes than rattlesnakes are to humans.

    J. humans have traditionally assigned human emotions to rattlesnakes in folklore.

35. According to the passage, what is the correlation between human behavior and serious rattlesnake bites?

    A. There is no statistical relationship.

    B. Humans who move with quick motions attract strikes.

    C. Humans who actively seek interaction with snakes are less likely to receive a "dry" bite.

    D. Rattlesnakes deliver a variable amount of venom based on how threatening humans act.

36. What is suggested by lines 51–53 when the author states that the new evidence "does not imply that rattlesnakes would make good pets for children"?

    F. Only professional herpetologists should keep rattlesnakes.

    G. Dogs can also be dangerous pets.

    H. Nonaggressive behavior does not make a venomous animal harmless.

    J. Rattlesnakes in the wild are more docile than those in captivity.

37. The passage states that the relative likelihood of a human being killed by a rattlesnake bite is:

    A. greater than that of a dog bite.

    B. less than that of a bee sting.

    C. equal to that of a lightning strike.

    D. comparable to that of the South American fer-de-lance.

38. Which of the following correctly categorizes a rattlesnake's strategy in venom usage?

    F. The larger the prey or predator, the more venom is used.

    G. Even when threatened, a rattlesnake reserves venom to use on prey.

    H. Rattlesnakes are aware that they will wound larger animals.

    J. Rattlesnakes would rather use venom solely for prey.

39. The author states that rattlesnake roundups use contradictory logic because:

    A. children are rarely bitten by rattlesnakes.

    B. the rattlesnakes that bite people at roundups would have been far less likely to bite someone in their natural habitat.

    C. organizers use erroneous statistics to make the rattlesnakes seem more dangerous and the events more impressive.

    D. many who go to the events are unaware of how many snakes are killed.

GO ON TO THE NEXT PAGE ▷

40. As used in line 129, the term *crotalid* is most likely:

    F. an unfavorable characterization of humans.

    G. a scientific word meaning "rattlesnakes."

    H. a word describing a herpetologist who specializes in rattlesnakes.

    J. a general word for a group unfairly accused of wrongdoing.

IF YOU FINISH BEFORE TIME IS CALLED, YOU MAY CHECK YOUR WORK ON THIS SECTION ONLY. DO NOT TURN TO ANY OTHER SECTION IN THE TEST. **STOP**

SCIENCE TEST

35 Minutes—40 Questions

Directions: There are several passages in this test. Each passage is followed by several questions. After reading a passage, choose the best answer to each question and fill in the corresponding oval on your Answer Grid. You may refer to the passages as often as necessary. You are NOT permitted to use a calculator on this test.

PASSAGE I

Glaciers are large masses of ice that move slowly over Earth's surface due to the force of gravity and changes in elevation. Glacial *calving* occurs when one edge of a glacier borders a body of water. A calving glacier's *terminus* (the lower edge) periodically produces icebergs as they break away from the glacier and fall into the water.

STUDY 1

A computer was used to create a model of a typical calving glacier. It was hypothesized that a primary factor determining the calving rate is the glacier's velocity at its terminus. Figure 1 shows the calving rate, in meters per year, and length of the computer-generated glacier over a period of 2,000 years.

Figure 1

GO ON TO THE NEXT PAGE

STUDY 2

Four calving glaciers (A–D) were studied over a period of 10 years. The average velocity at the terminus of each glacier was recorded for years 1–5 and again for years 6–10. The calving rate of each glacier was estimated for the same time periods. The results are recorded in Table 1.

Table 1

Glacier	Years 1–5		Years 6–10	
	Average velocity (m/yr)	Calving rate (m/yr)	Average velocity (m/yr)	Calving rate (m/yr)
A	72	72	63	64
B	51	52	45	47
C	98	106	256	312
D	160	189	53	54

STUDY 3

Meteorologists reported unusually high average temperatures in the regions of Glacier C and Glacier D during the same 10-year period examined in Study 2. It was hypothesized that the high temperatures were responsible for the relatively rapid variations in velocity and calving rates evident for Glacier C and Glacier D in Table 1.

1. If the glacier model used in Study 1 is typical of all calving glaciers, the scientists would draw which of the following conclusions about the relationship between glacier length and calving rate?

    A. As calving rate decreases, glacier length always increases.

    B. As glacier length decreases, calving rate always decreases.

    C. A sharp increase in calving rate results in a sharp decrease in glacier length.

    D. A sharp increase in calving rate results in a sharp increase in glacier length.

2. The meteorologists in Study 3 hypothesized that the faster the calving rate, the faster the sea level at a calving glacier's terminus would rise. If this hypothesis is correct, which of the following glaciers resulted in the fastest rise in sea level during years 6–10?

    F. Glacier A

    G. Glacier B

    H. Glacier C

    J. Glacier D

3. Based on the results of Study 2, a calving glacier traveling at a velocity of 80 m/yr would most likely have a calving rate:

    A. between 72 m/yr and 106 m/yr.

    B. between 106 m/yr and 189 m/yr.

    C. between 189 m/yr and 312 m/yr.

    D. over 312 m/yr.

4. Which of the following statements best describes the behavior of the glaciers observed during Study 2?

    F. All of the glaciers observed traveled faster during the first five years than during the last five years.

    G. All of the glaciers observed traveled faster during the last five years than during the first five years.

    H. The calving rate is always less than the average velocity for all of the glaciers observed.

    J. The calving rate is always greater than or equal to the average velocity for all of the glaciers observed.

GO ON TO THE NEXT PAGE

5. Which of the following graphs best represents the relationship between the calving rate and the average velocity of the glaciers observed in Study 2 for years 6–10?

A.

B.

C.

D.

6. If the hypothesis made by the meteorologists in Study 3 is correct, the glacier modeled in Study 1 most likely experienced unusually high temperatures at approximately what time during the simulated 2,000-year study?

F. 500 years

G. 1,000 years

H. 1,500 years

J. 2,000 years

7. Based on Figure 1, what is the glacial length and calving rate, respectively, at 1,500 years?

A. 15 km and 125 m/yr

B. 23 km and 125 m/yr

C. 23 km and 350 m/yr

D. 125 km and 350 m/yr

GO ON TO THE NEXT PAGE ▷

PASSAGE II

Allergic rhinitis refers to a person's nasal reaction to small airborne particles called *allergens*. Table 1 shows the specific allergen, its type, and the approximate number of reported cases of allergic symptoms for a population of 1,000 people living in northern Kentucky during a single year.

Table 1

	Allergen type	Pollen			Mold		
Month	Specific allergen	Trees	Grass	Weeds	Alternaria	Cladosporium	Aspergillus
January					❀	❀	❀
February					❀	❀	❀
March		❀❀			❀	❀	❀
April		❀❀❀❀			❀	❀	❀
May		❀❀❀	❀❀❀		❀	❀	❀
June			❀❀❀❀❀		❀	❀	❀
July		❀❀		❀	❀❀	❀	❀
August				❀❀❀	❀❀❀❀	❀❀❀	❀❀❀❀
September				❀❀	❀❀❀	❀❀❀❀❀	❀❀❀❀
October				❀❀	❀❀❀❀	❀❀	❀❀
November					❀❀	❀	❀
December					❀	❀	❀

Note: Each ❀ equals 100 reported cases of allergic rhinitis.

Weekly tree pollen and total mold spore concentrations were measured in grains per cubic meter (gr/m^3) for samples of air taken in southern Iowa for eight weeks. The pollen and mold spore counts are shown in Figures 1 and 2, respectively.

Figure 1

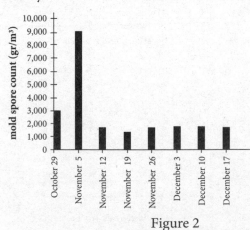

Figure 2

GO ON TO THE NEXT PAGE ⟶

8. If the 1,000 patients studied were given special air filters that greatly reduce allergic rhinitis symptoms, which of the following months would have the greatest decrease in the number of allergic rhinitis cases?

   F. March
   G. June
   H. September
   J. December

9. Based on Figure 1, the tree pollen count on March 2 was closest to:

   A.   75 gr/m³.
   B.   150 gr/m³.
   C. 1,500 gr/m³.
   D. 1,900 gr/m³.

10. According to Figure 2, the mold spore count in the weeks after November 5:

    F. increased.
    G. decreased.
    H. varied between 1,000 gr/m³ and 2,000 gr/m³.
    J. remained above 2,000 gr/m³.

11. Based on the data in Figure 1, the tree pollen count increased the most between which two dates?

    A. February 9 to February 16
    B. February 23 to March 2
    C. March 2 to March 9
    D. October 29 to November 5

12. According to Figure 1, which of the following conclusions about the tree pollen count is most valid?

    F. The tree pollen count was highest on March 9.
    G. The tree pollen count was highest on March 16.
    H. The tree pollen count was lowest on February 23.
    J. The tree pollen count was lowest on March 16.

13. Based on Table 1, most of the cases of allergic rhinitis in May in northern Kentucky were caused by which of the following allergens?

    A. Tree and grass pollen
    B. Grass and weed pollen
    C. Alternaria
    D. Aspergillus

GO ON TO THE NEXT PAGE

PASSAGE III

Simple harmonic motion (SHM) is motion that is *periodic*, or repetitive, and can be described by a frequency of oscillation. Students performed three experiments to study SHM.

EXPERIMENT 1

The students assembled the pendulum shown in Diagram 1. The mass at the end of the arm was raised to a small height, h, and released. The frequency of oscillation was measured in oscillations per second, or Hertz (Hz), and the process was repeated for several different arm lengths. The results are shown in Figure 1.

Diagram 1

Figure 1

EXPERIMENT 2

A spring was suspended vertically from a hook, and a mass was connected to the bottom of the spring, as shown in Diagram 2. The mass was pulled downward a short distance and released, and the frequency of the resulting oscillation was measured. The procedure was repeated with four different springs and four different masses, and the results are shown in Figure 2.

Diagram 2

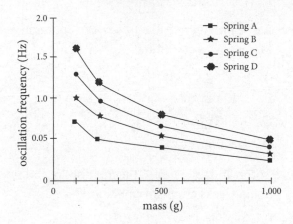

Figure 2

EXPERIMENT 3

Using the apparatus from Experiment 2, the mass-spring system was allowed to come to rest, and the *equilibrium length* of the spring was measured. The same four masses and four springs were used, and the results are shown in Figure 3.

Figure 3

GO ON TO THE NEXT PAGE ⟶

14. In Experiment 3, for which of the following masses would Spring B, Spring C, and Spring D have closest to the same equilibrium lengths?

    F. 100 g

    G. 270 g

    H. 500 g

    J. 1,000 g

15. A student has hypothesized that as the length of the arm of a pendulum increases, the oscillation frequency of the pendulum during SHM will decrease. Do the results of Experiment 1 support her hypothesis?

    A. Yes; the oscillation frequency of the pendulum observed in Experiment 1 decreased as the arm length increased.

    B. Yes; although the longest pendulum arm resulted in the highest oscillation frequency, the frequency decreased with increasing arm length for the other three lengths tested.

    C. No; the oscillation frequency of the pendulum observed in Experiment 1 increased as the arm length increased.

    D. No; although the longest pendulum arm resulted in the lowest oscillation frequency, the frequency increased with increasing arm length for the other three lengths tested.

16. Based on the results of Experiment 2, if an engineer needs a spring that oscillates most slowly after being stretched and released, which of the following springs should be chosen?

    F. Spring A

    G. Spring B

    H. Spring C

    J. Spring D

17. Based on the results of Experiment 3, if a 700 g mass were suspended from Spring A, at what equilibrium length would the system come to rest?

    A. Less than 20 cm

    B. Between 20 cm and 30 cm

    C. Between 30 cm and 50 cm

    D. Greater than 50 cm

18. The students tested a fifth spring, Spring E, in the same manner as in Experiment 2. With a 100 g mass suspended from Spring E, the oscillation frequency was 1.4 Hz. Based on the results of Experiment 2, which of the following correctly lists the five springs by their oscillation frequency with a 100 g mass suspended from *fastest* to *slowest*?

    F. Spring E, Spring B, Spring C, Spring A, Spring D

    G. Spring D, Spring A, Spring C, Spring B, Spring E

    H. Spring A, Spring B, Spring C, Spring E, Spring D

    J. Spring D, Spring E, Spring C, Spring B, Spring A

GO ON TO THE NEXT PAGE

19. Experiment 1 was repeated using a larger pendulum mass. Which of the following figures best expresses the comparison between the results found using the larger pendulum mass and using the original mass?

A.

B.

C.

D.

20. According to Figure 1, at what arm length will the oscillation frequency equal 0.35 Hz?

F.   13 cm

G.   16 cm

H.   19 cm

J.   21 cm

GO ON TO THE NEXT PAGE

PASSAGE IV

A person requires a certain percentage of oxygen in the blood for proper respiratory function. The amount of oxygen in the air varies enough with altitude that people normally accustomed to breathing near sea level may experience respiratory problems at significantly higher altitudes. Table 1 shows the average percentage of oxygen saturation in the blood, as well as the blood concentrations of three enzymes, GST, ECH, and CR, for three populations of high altitude (ha) dwellers and three populations of sea level (sl) dwellers. Enzyme concentrations are given in arbitrary units (a.u.). Figure 1 shows average oxygen partial pressure and average temperature at various altitudes.

Table 1

Population	Altitude range (m)	Oxygen saturation (%)	Enzyme concentration (a.u.)		
			GST	ECH	CR
ha 1	3,500–4,000	98.1	121.0	89.2	48.8
ha 2	3,300–3,700	99.0	108.3	93.5	45.6
ha 3	3,900–4,200	97.9	111.6	91.9	52.3
sl 1	0–300	98.5	86.7	57.1	44.9
sl 2	0–150	99.2	79.8	65.8	53.1
sl 3	0–200	98.7	82.5	61.4	47.0

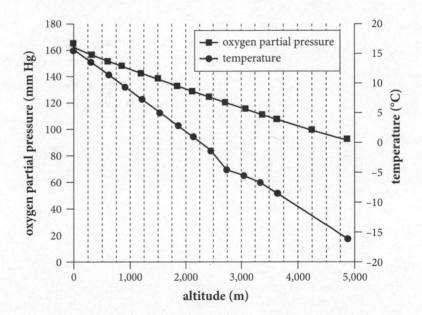

Figure 1

GO ON TO THE NEXT PAGE

21. Based on the data in Table 1, one would conclude that the blood of high altitude dwellers contains a higher concentration of:

    A. CR than ECH.

    B. CR than GST.

    C. ECH than GST.

    D. GST than CR.

22. Based on the information given, one would expect that, compared to the high-altitude dwellers, the sea-level dwellers:

    F. have blood with a lower percentage oxygen saturation.

    G. have blood with a lower GST concentration.

    H. can tolerate lower oxygen partial pressures.

    J. can tolerate lower temperatures.

23. According to Figure 1, an atmospheric sample found at an oxygen partial pressure of 110 mm Hg was most likely found at a temperature of about:

    A.   8.1°C.

    B.   0°C.

    C.   −5.4°C.

    D.   −12.5°C.

24. ECH is an enzyme that improves the efficiency of cellular energy production. Assume that people with higher ECH concentrations in the blood can function normally at higher altitudes without any respiratory difficulties. Based on Table 1, people from which population can function normally at the highest altitude?

    F. sl 1

    G. sl 2

    H. ha 2

    J. ha 3

25. Assume that a person's blood oxygen saturation percentage is determined only by the oxygen partial pressure at the location at which the person lives and the efficiency of the person's respiratory system at incorporating oxygen into the blood. Which of the following pieces of information supports the hypothesis that people from population ha 2 can incorporate oxygen into their blood more efficiently than can people from population sl 1?

    A. Population ha 2 lives where the oxygen partial pressure is lower than that of where population sl 1 lives, yet population ha 2 has a higher blood oxygen saturation percentage than does population ha 1.

    B. Population ha 2 lives where the oxygen partial pressure is higher than that of where population sl 1 lives, yet population ha 2 has a lower blood oxygen saturation percentage than does population ha 1.

    C. Population ha 2 has a higher CR concentration than does population sl 1.

    D. Population ha 2 has an unusually high GST concentration.

GO ON TO THE NEXT PAGE

26. If a population of dwellers living at 1,500–1,800 m was studied, which of the following assumptions about the enzyme levels is most likely true?

   F. The levels of GST, ECH, and CR would be the same as the high-altitude populations.

   G. The levels of GST, ECH, and CR would be the same as the sea-level populations.

   H. The level of GST would be lower than the level of the sea-level population, and the levels of ECH and CR would be lower than the the level of the high-altitude populations.

   J. The levels of GST and ECH would be higher than the level of the sea-level population, and the level of CR would be the same as both populations.

PASSAGE V

Two students explain why lakes freeze from the surface downward. They also discuss the phenomenon of the melting of ice under the blades of an ice skater's skates.

STUDENT 1

Water freezes first at the surface of lakes because the freezing point of water decreases with increasing pressure. Under the surface, *hydrostatic pressure* causes the freezing point of water to be slightly lower than it is at the surface. Thus, as the air temperature drops, it reaches the freezing point of water at the surface before reaching that of the water beneath it. Only as the temperature becomes even colder will the layer of ice at the surface become thicker.

Pressure is defined as *force* divided by the *surface area* over which the force is exerted. An ice skater exerts the entire force of his or her body weight over the tiny surface area of two very thin blades. This

results in a very large pressure, which quickly melts a small amount of ice directly under the blades.

STUDENT 2

Water freezes first at the surface of lakes because the density of ice is less than that of liquid water. Unlike most liquids, the volume of a given mass of water expands upon freezing, and the density therefore decreases. As a result, the *buoyant force* of water acting upward is greater than the force of gravity exerted downward by any mass of ice, and all ice particles float to the surface upon freezing.

Ice melts under an ice skater's skates because of friction. The energy used to overcome the force of friction is converted to heat, which melts the ice under the skates. The greater the weight of the skater, the greater the force of friction, and the faster the ice melts.

27. According to Student 1, which of the following quantities is *greater* for water molecules beneath a lake's surface than for water molecules at the surface?

   A. Temperature

   B. Density

   C. Buoyant force

   D. Hydrostatic pressure

GO ON TO THE NEXT PAGE

28. When two ice skaters, wearing identical skates, skated across a frozen lake at the same speed, the ice under the blades of Skater B was found to melt faster than the ice under the blades of Skater A. What conclusion would each student draw about which skater is heavier?

    F. Both Student 1 and Student 2 would conclude that Skater A is heavier.

    G. Both Student 1 and Student 2 would conclude that Skater B is heavier.

    H. Student 1 would conclude that Skater A is heavier; Student 2 would conclude that Skater B is heavier.

    J. Student 1 would conclude that Skater B is heavier; Student 2 would conclude that Skater A is heavier.

29. Which student(s), if either, would predict that ice will melt under the blades of an ice skater who is NOT moving?

    A. Student 1 only

    B. Student 2 only

    C. Both Student 1 and Student 2

    D. Neither Student 1 nor Student 2

30. A beaker of ethanol is found to freeze from the bottom upward, instead of from the surface downward. Student 2 would most likely argue that the density of frozen ethanol is:

    F. greater than the density of water.

    G. less than the density of ice.

    H. greater than the density of liquid ethanol.

    J. less than the density of liquid ethanol.

31. A toy boat was placed on the surface of a small pool of water, and the boat was gradually filled with sand. After a certain amount of sand had been added, the boat began to sink. Based on Student 2's explanation, the boat began to sink because:

    A. hydrostatic pressure became greater than the buoyant force of the water on the boat.

    B. atmospheric pressure became greater than the buoyant force of the water on the boat.

    C. the force of gravity of the boat on the water became greater than the buoyant force of the water on the boat.

    D. the force of gravity of the boat on the water became less than the buoyant force of the water on the boat.

32. According to Student 2, if friction between the ice and the blades of an ice skater's skates is reduced, which of the following quantities simultaneously decreases at the point where the blades and the ice are in contact?

    F. Pressure exerted by the blades on the ice

    G. Heat produced

    H. Force of gravity of the blades on the ice

    J. Freezing point of water

33. Based on Student 2's explanation, the reason a hot air balloon is able to rise above the ground is that the balloon and the air inside it are:

    A. less dense than the air outside the balloon.

    B. more dense than the air outside the balloon.

    C. at a higher pressure than the air outside the balloon.

    D. less buoyant than the air outside the balloon.

GO ON TO THE NEXT PAGE ⇨

PASSAGE VI

In many communities, chemicals containing fluoride ions (F^-) are added to the drinking water supply to help prevent tooth decay. Use of F^- is controversial because studies have linked F^- with bone disease. Students performed two experiments to measure F^- levels.

EXPERIMENT I

Five solutions, each containing a different amount of Na_2SiF_6 (sodium silicofluoride) in H_2O were prepared. Five identical *electrodynamic cells* were filled with equal volumes of each of the five solutions, and a sixth identical cell was filled with a *blank* solution (one containing no added Na_2SiF_6). The cells were activated to measure the electrical *conductivity* for each. The conductivities were then corrected by subtracting the conductivity of the blank solution from each value (see Table 1 and Figure 1).

Table 1

Concentration of F^- (mg/L*)	Measured conductivity (μS/cm**)	Corrected conductivity (μS/cm**)
0.0	15.96	0.00
0.1	16.13	0.17
0.5	16.80	0.084
1.0	17.63	1.67
2.0	19.30	3.34
4.0	22.64	6.68

*mg/L is milligrams per liter. **μS/cm is microsiemens per centimer.

Figure 1

GO ON TO THE NEXT PAGE

EXPERIMENT 2

A water sample was taken directly from the drinking water supply of one community. An electrodynamic cell identical to those used in Experiment 1 was filled with water from this sample, and the cell was activated. The procedure was repeated for water samples from several communities, and the conductivities were measured (Table 2).

Table 2

Community	Measured conductivity ($\mu S/cm$)	Concentration of F^- (mg/L)
Newtown	22.31	3.8
Springfield	16.46	0.3
Lakewood	18.63	1.6
Reading	19.47	2.1

34. Students subtracted the measured conductivity of the blank solution from the sample solutions in order to:

    F. determine the amount of conductivity solely due to F- ions.

    G. calibrate the electrodynamic cells.

    H. correct for non-ionic impurities.

    J. test the solubility of F-.

35. Based on the results of Experiment 1, if the concentration of F^- in a solution is doubled, then the corrected conductivity of the solution will approximately:

    A. remain the same.

    B. halve.

    C. double.

    D. quadruple.

36. A sample was also taken from the drinking water supply of the community of Bluewater in Experiment 2, and its conductivity was measured to be 20.69 $\mu S/cm$. Which of the following correctly lists the drinking water supplies of Newtown, Lakewood, and Bluewater in increasing order of F^- concentration?

    F. Lakewood, Newtown, Bluewater

    G. Bluewater, Newtown, Lakewood

    H. Newtown, Bluewater, Lakewood

    J. Lakewood, Bluewater, Newtown

37. Based on the results of Experiment 1, if a solution with a concentration of 3.0 mg/L F^- had been tested, the corrected conductivity would have been closest to which of the following values?

    A. 1.3 $\mu S/cm$

    B. 3.3 $\mu S/cm$

    C. 5.0 $\mu S/cm$

    D. 6.5 $\mu S/cm$

38. If Experiments 1 and 2 were repeated to measure the concentration of chloride ions (Cl^-) in drinking water, then which of the following changes in procedure would be necessary?

    F. The solutions in Experiment 1 should be prepared by adding different concentrations of NaCl (or another chemical containing Cl^-) to H_2O.

    G. The conductivity of the blank solution should be added to the measured conductivities.

    H. The electrodynamic cells should be set to measure resistivity instead of conductivity.

    J. Both NaCl and Na_2SiF_6 should be added to all of the samples.

GO ON TO THE NEXT PAGE

39. Based on the results of Experiments 1 and 2, if the measured conductivities for the samples tested in Experiment 2 were compared with their corrected conductivities, the measured conductivities would be:

   A. lower for all of the samples tested.

   B. higher for all of the samples tested.

   C. lower for some of the samples tested, higher for others.

   D. the same for all of the samples tested.

40. The presence of other negative ions, such as Cl^-, results in an increase in the electrical conductivity of a solution. If all of the samples tested in Experiment 2 contained trace concentrations of Cl^-, how would the measurements have been affected? Compared to the actual F^- concentrations, the F^- concentrations apparently measured would be:

   F. higher.

   G. lower.

   H. the same.

   J. higher for some of the samples, lower for others.

WRITING TEST

40 Minutes—1 Question

Directions: This is a test of your writing skills. You will have forty (40) minutes to write an essay in English. Before you begin planning and writing your essay, read the writing prompt carefully to understand exactly what you are being asked to do. Your essay will be evaluated on the evidence it provides of your ability to do the following:

- Express judgments by evaluating the three perspectives given in the prompt, taking a position on an issue, and explaining the relationship among all four ideas
- Develop a position by using logical reasoning and by supporting your ideas
- Maintain a focus on the topic throughout the essay
- Organize ideas in a logical way
- Use language clearly and effectively according to the conventions of standard written English

You may use a separate piece of paper to plan your essay. *You must write your essay in pencil on the lined pages provided after the prompt.* Your writing on those lined pages will be scored. You may not need all the lined pages, but to ensure you have enough room to finish, do NOT skip lines. You may write corrections or additions neatly between the lines of your essay, but do NOT write in the margins of the lined pages. *Illegible essays cannot be scored, so you must write (or print) clearly.*

DO NOT OPEN THIS BOOKLET UNTIL TOLD TO DO SO.

GO ON TO THE NEXT PAGE

EXPERIENTIAL EDUCATION

Experiential education is a philosophy that holds that students learn best through direct experience. Hands-on learning is said to promote deeper understanding because students are able to apply concepts and theories to physical situations. Rather than memorizing facts, students who are given the opportunity to create physical evidence of logical reasoning are better equipped to apply the same reasoning to new situations. Since all teachers aim to impart critical thinking in their classrooms, should they be expected to provide more hands-on learning opportunities? As educators aim to continuously improve the quality of the education they offer to students, consideration should be given to better incorporating hands-on learning.

Read and carefully consider these perspectives. Each suggests a particular approach regarding experiential education.

Perspective One	Perspective Two	Perspective Three
Some argue that to accept a theory without experiencing it is to learn nothing at all. Teachers need to provide opportunities for experiential involvement if they expect students to truly comprehend each lesson plan objective.	Experiential education is an integral part of readying students to pursue careers in the science, technology, engineering, and math fields, but not all disciplines. If students are expected to perform skill-based tasks in these fields after they graduate, they should be provided a strong foundation on which to build their careers. However, teachers should not be expected to supply experiential learning where it is not appropriate.	Schools cannot be expected to offer hands-on learning for students. Not only is it costly, but also it may not be effective for all learners. Students will be better served if schools invest money in other educational models and opportunities.

ESSAY TASK

Write a unified, coherent essay in which you evaluate multiple perspectives on experiential education. In your essay, be sure to:

- analyze and evaluate the perspectives given
- state and develop your own perspective on the issue
- explain the relationship between your perspective and those given

Your perspective may be in full agreement with any of the others, in partial agreement, or wholly different. Whatever the case, support your ideas with logical reasoning and detailed, persuasive examples.

GO ON TO THE NEXT PAGE ⟹

PLANNING YOUR ESSAY

You may wish to consider the following as you think critically about the task:

Strengths and weaknesses of the three given perspectives
- What insights do they offer, and what do they fail to consider?
- Why might they be persuasive to others, or why might they fail to persuade?

Your own knowledge, experience, and values
- What is your perspective on this issue, and what are its strengths and weaknesses?
- How will you support your perspective in your essay?

_____

_____

_____

_____

_____

_____

_____

_____

_____

_____

_____

_____

_____

_____

_____

_____

_____

GO ON TO THE NEXT PAGE ⟶

_____

_____

_____

_____

_____

_____

_____

_____

_____

_____

_____

_____

_____

_____

_____

_____

_____

_____

_____

_____

_____

_____

_____

_____

Practice Test Three
ANSWER KEY

ENGLISH TEST

1. C	11. A	21. C	31. C	41. B	51. D	61. D	71. A
2. H	12. G	22. G	32. H	42. G	52. F	62. H	72. G
3. C	13. A	23. C	33. D	43. D	53. C	63. A	73. A
4. J	14. H	24. J	34. F	44. G	54. J	64. H	74. H
5. B	15. B	25. C	35. B	45. A	55. D	65. B	75. D
6. J	16. J	26. J	36. F	46. J	56. H	66. F	
7. B	17. A	27. B	37. C	47. D	57. A	67. B	
8. J	18. J	28. G	38. F	48. H	58. J	68. G	
9. D	19. D	29. D	39. C	49. D	59. C	69. D	
10. H	20. H	30. J	40. H	50. G	60. G	70. G	

MATHEMATICS TEST

1. E	9. B	17. E	25. C	33. D	41. D	49. C	57. B
2. K	10. H	18. J	26. F	34. F	42. G	50. G	58. F
3. C	11. D	19. A	27. D	35. E	43. A	51. A	59. C
4. H	12. G	20. H	28. F	36. H	44. K	52. H	60. H
5. D	13. C	21. A	29. B	37. C	45. C	53. D	
6. J	14. J	22. J	30. F	38. H	46. J	54. K	
7. A	15. D	23. E	31. C	39. C	47. E	55. A	
8. G	16. G	24. H	32. K	40. J	48. H	56. J	

READING TEST

1. D	6. H	11. C	16. J	21. C	26. F	31. B	36. H
2. H	7. B	12. G	17. C	22. J	27. B	32. F	37. B
3. B	8. F	13. B	18. J	23. C	28. H	33. C	38. J
4. J	9. C	14. F	19. A	24. F	29. B	34. H	39. B
5. D	10. F	15. B	20. G	25. D	30. G	35. C	40. G

SCIENCE TEST

1. C	6. H	11. B	16. F	21. D	26. J	31. C	36. J
2. H	7. B	12. F	17. C	22. G	27. D	32. G	37. C
3. A	8. H	13. A	18. J	23. C	28. G	33. A	38. F
4. J	9. C	14. G	19. C	24. H	29. A	34. F	39. B
5. B	10. H	15. A	20. H	25. A	30. H	35. C	40. F

ANSWERS AND EXPLANATIONS

ENGLISH TEST

PASSAGE I

1. C
Category: Word Choice
Difficulty: Medium
Getting to the Answer: Choice (C) forms a complete sentence by using the simple past tense *was*. Choice A creates a sentence fragment; an *-ing* verb needs a helping verb, such as *was* or *is*, to be the main verb in a sentence. Choice B incorrectly uses a comma to separate the subject from the main verb. Choice D omits the verb entirely, creating a sentence fragment.

2. H
Category: Word Choice
Difficulty: Medium
Getting to the Answer: The phrase *not only* in the beginning of the sentence is your clue to the correct answer. Logically, the phrase *not only* is always followed by *but also*. The other choices neither complete the idiom correctly nor convey the necessary contrast between the ideas in the two clauses.

3. C
Category: Punctuation
Difficulty: High
Getting to the Answer: Add an apostrophe and an *s* to a singular noun to show possession. The narrator and Gretchen attend one school, so (C) is correct. Choice A omits the apostrophe needed to show that the *swim team* belongs to the *school*. Choice B incorrectly treats *school* as a plural, placing the apostrophe after the *s*. Choice D incorrectly uses *ours* and does not make *school* possessive.

4. J
Category: Wordiness
Difficulty: Medium
Getting to the Answer: The testmakers value simple and direct prose, so change passive constructions such as "it was with Gretchen that I" when you're given the opportunity. As is often the case on the English test of the ACT, the shortest choice—(J)—is correct. In addition to being verbose, F contains a sentence structure error: It is not clear who knows that the writer enjoyed swimming. Choices G and H are both also verbose.

5. B
Category: Writing Strategy
Difficulty: Low
Getting to the Answer: Slow down and carefully read a Nonstandard-Format question like this one. You just may see a question such as this that tests vocabulary. Choice (B) indicates that the narrator's mother recommended swimming lessons but did not decide that the narrator *must* take them. Choices A, C, and D all indicate that the mother's mind was made up.

6. J
Category: Sentence Sense
Difficulty: Medium
Getting to the Answer: If a sentence seems to have too many ideas, then it is probably a run-on. By itself, a comma cannot separate two clauses that could be independent sentences, as in F. Choice G replaces *swimmers* with a pronoun but does not correct the run-on. Similarly, H removes the comma but does not address the problem of two complete thoughts that are incorrectly joined. Choice (J) solves the problem by using *whom*, which turns the second half of the sentence into a dependent clause that describes the *women*.

7. B
Category: Punctuation
Difficulty: High
Getting to the Answer: This sentence contains a parenthetical phrase. If you omitted "who had been swimming competitively since elementary school," you would still have a complete sentence. Like all parenthetical phrases, this needs to be set off from the rest of the sentence. A comma is used at the beginning of the phrase, so a comma must also be used at the end of the phrase. This makes D incorrect. Choices A and C insert unnecessary commas within the parenthetical phrase.

8. J
Category: Wordiness
Difficulty: Low
Getting to the Answer: When in doubt, take it out. *Giving up,* by definition, means "quitting" or "failing." Choices F, G, and H create redundancies.

9. D
Category: Verb Tenses
Difficulty: Medium
Getting to the Answer: Trust your ear. *Begin* is an irregular verb; the simple past tense *began* can be used by itself, but the past participle *begun* cannot. Instead, *begun* always appears with *has,* *have,* or *had,* as in "I *have begun* to prepare for the ACT." Choice (D) correctly uses the simple past tense *began.* Choice B creates another verb usage error by inserting *been.* Choice C incorrectly uses *began* with *had.*

10. H
Category: Word Choice
Difficulty: High
Getting to the Answer: Don't panic if you see a question that tests the use of *who* and *whom.* The pronoun *who* serves as a subject, just like the pronouns *he* and *she* replace subjects. The pronoun *whom* serves as an object, just like the pronouns *him* and *her* replace objects. Here, *coach* is the subject

of the sentence, so *who,* (H), is correct. Never refer to a person as *which,* J.

11. A
Category: Wordiness
Difficulty: Medium
Getting to the Answer: Don't force a change where one isn't needed. The correct answer for some of the underlined portions will be NO CHANGE. The sentence "The hard work eventually paid off," is correct and concise as it is written. Choice B is verbose, and C and D create run-on sentences.

12. G
Category: Writing Strategy
Difficulty: Medium
Getting to the Answer: Start by asking yourself, "Does this information belong here?" The question asks for a sentence that is relevant to the narrator's experience on the swim team. Only (G) is connected to the narrator and the swim team; the sentence explains that the narrator was one of the only swimmers on the team to be interested in the butterfly. The history of the stroke, F; the relative speed of the stroke, H; and an alternative name for the stroke, J, are not as related to the narrator's personal experience.

13. A
Category: Writing Strategy
Difficulty: Medium
Getting to the Answer: The shortest answer is often, but not always, correct. Don't omit portions that add relevant information to the sentence. The sentence is about the narrator's swimming, so her participation in the medley relay is relevant. Choices B and C add descriptions of the medley relay that are not relevant to the topic.

14. H
Category: Verb Tenses
Difficulty: Medium
Getting to the Answer: The four choices offer different tenses of the same verb. The clue *last year* indicates that the narrator earned the varsity letter in the past. Choice (H), the simple past tense, is correct. Neither the future tense, F, nor the present tense, J, makes sense with the clue *last year*. Choice G would only make sense if something had prevented the narrator from earning the varsity letter.

15. B
Category: Writing Strategy
Difficulty: Low
Getting to the Answer: Keep the main point of the passage in mind. Before beginning high school, the narrator had never thought of herself as an athlete. Then she joined the swim team and became successful at the sport. Choice (B) is most relevant to the central ideas of the passage. Choices A and C focus too narrowly on details in the passage, while D contradicts the main point of the passage.

PASSAGE II

16. J
Category: Punctuation
Difficulty: Medium
Getting to the Answer: Don't assume that a comma or semicolon is needed just because a sentence is long. Read the sentence aloud to yourself, and you should be able to hear that a comma is not needed in the underlined portion. A semicolon, as in F, would only be correct if the second half of the sentence expressed a complete thought. Choices G and H both use an unnecessary comma.

17. A
Category: Word Choice
Difficulty: Low
Getting to the Answer: When a verb is underlined, check to see whether it agrees with its noun. Watch out for descriptive phrases that separate a verb from

its noun. Here, the verb *was* agrees with the singular noun *tank*. NO CHANGE is needed. Choice B uses the present tense, but the surrounding sentences use the past tense. Choices C and D incorrectly use a verb in the plural form.

18. J
Category: Sentence Sense
Difficulty: Medium
Getting to the Answer: When the word *that* or *which* is underlined, watch out for an incomplete sentence. As it is written, this is a sentence fragment; a complete verb is missing. Removing *that*, as in (J), turns *made* into the main verb of a complete and correct sentence. Choice G does not address the sentence fragment error, and H also fails to provide a clear and appropriate sentence.

19. D
Category: Wordiness
Difficulty: Medium
Getting to the Answer: If you are *familiar* with a type of animal, then you have almost certainly *seen it before*. Choice (D) creates a concise sentence that does not lose any of the original meaning. The other choices are redundant. Choice B repeats *sights* when *view* has already been used, and C uses the unnecessarily repetitive phrase "to which I was no stranger."

20. H
Category: Organization
Difficulty: High
Getting to the Answer: Scan the paragraph for connecting words and phrases that you can use as clues to determine the most logical order of sentences. In sentence 5, the word *first* suggests that the sentence should be placed close to the beginning of the paragraph. Sentence 2 says, "There were *also* animals I had never before glimpsed," which indicates that a preceding sentence discusses animals the writer had glimpsed. Sentence 5, which describes the writer's view of familiar animals, most logically belongs immediately after sentence 1.

21. C
Category: Verb Tenses
Difficulty: Low
Getting to the Answer: If an underlined verb agrees with its noun, then determine whether the verb's tense makes sense in the context of the passage. The surrounding verbs are in the past tense, so this sentence should use the simple past tense *saw*, (C). Choices A and D use the present tense, and B illogically uses the past progressive "had been seeing."

22. G
Category: Connections
Difficulty: High
Getting to the Answer: An effective first sentence for a paragraph will introduce the topic of the paragraph and connect that topic to ideas that have come before. Paragraph 3 focuses on the catfish, while paragraph 4 describes the large alligator and snapping turtle in the bayou tank. Choice (G) would provide an effective connection between these paragraphs, referring to the catfish and introducing the idea that there were even bigger animals on display. Neither F nor H leads into the topic of paragraph 4. Choice J doesn't provide a transition from the discussion of the catfish in paragraph 3.

23. C
Category: Writing Strategy
Difficulty: Medium
Getting to the Answer: The phrase in question provides a visual image; deleting the phrase would mean losing a description, (C). The removal of the phrase would not affect the transition between sentences, A. Contrary to B, the contrast between images would be decreased. The level of suspense may be somewhat decreased by the loss of the description, but it would not be increased, D.

24. J
Category: Verb Tenses
Difficulty: Medium
Getting to the Answer: The verbs *slides* and *aims* agree with the singular subject *it*, but they are in the wrong tense. The rest of the paragraph describes actions that took place in the past. For the sentence to make sense in context, these verbs should also be in the past tense, (J). Choices F and G use present-tense verbs. Choice H creates a logically incomplete sentence.

25. C
Category: Sentence Sense
Difficulty: Medium
Getting to the Answer: If something sounds awkward or unusual, there is probably an error. Most words that end in *-ly* are adverbs; they are used to modify verbs, adjectives, or other adverbs. Adverbs cannot be used to describe nouns, such as *moment*, A. Choice (C) correctly uses the adjective *slight* to modify *panic*. The sentences formed by B and D don't make sense.

26. J
Category: Idioms
Difficulty: Low
Getting to the Answer: The phrase "much of the onlookers" probably sounds strange to you. That's because *much* is used with noncountable things or concepts (as in "there isn't much time") or quantities (as in "there isn't much pizza left"). You could count the number of *onlookers*, so *many*, (J), is correct. Choices G and H also create idiomatic errors.

27. B
Category: Writing Strategy
Difficulty: Medium
Getting to the Answer: The question tells you that the writer's goal is to describe the appearance of the crayfish, so eliminate any sentences that do not have details about how crayfish look, C. Choice A suggests that crayfish look like lobsters, and D describes the crayfish as small. Neither of

these sentences offers the descriptive detail that is given in (B).

28. G
Category: Punctuation
Difficulty: Medium
Getting to the Answer: Trust your ear. You naturally pause when a comma or semicolon is needed in a sentence. A pause between *all* and *I* just doesn't sound right; that's because the full introductory phrase "After seeing all I could inside the museum" should not be interrupted. A comma should not separate a verb (*seeing*) from its object (*museum*). This eliminates F and H. A comma is needed between an introductory phrase and the complete thought that follows, making (G) correct and J incorrect.

29. D
Category: Wordiness
Difficulty: Medium
Getting to the Answer: Say it simply. The shortest answer here is correct: it turns the passive construction "it was that" in A and B into the active "I had." Choice C is unnecessarily wordy.

30. J
Category: Sentence Sense
Difficulty: High
Getting to the Answer: A sentence must have a subject and verb and express a complete thought. The sentence that begins "And operates" does not have a subject. Removing the period, (J), creates a grammatically correct sentence. Choice G is awkwardly worded. Choice H creates a run-on sentence; a coordinating conjunction such as *and* needs to be used along with a comma to link two complete thoughts.

PASSAGE III

31. C
Category: Pronouns
Difficulty: Medium
Getting to the Answer: When a pronoun is underlined, check to see that it agrees in number with the noun it replaces or refers to. In this sentence, the underlined pronoun refers back to the plural "secret identities and elaborate disguises." Choice (C) uses the correct plural pronoun *they*. Choices A and B create pronoun agreement errors by using the singular pronoun *it*. Choice D creates a sentence fragment.

32. H
Category: Punctuation
Difficulty: Medium
Getting to the Answer: Many English questions will focus on the correct use of commas. Commas should be used to separate an appositive or descriptive phrase from the main part of the sentence. The phrase "the restaurant critic for the *New York Times*" describes the noun *Ruth Reichl*, so the phrase should be set off with commas, (H). Choices F and J fail to use both necessary commas. On the other hand, G incorrectly inserts a third comma.

33. D
Category: Writing Strategy
Difficulty: High
Getting to the Answer: Only add sentences that are directly connected to the topic of a paragraph. Paragraph 2 discusses the importance of a *Times* review to restaurants in New York City. The suggested sentence provides a specific detail about one restaurant without explaining how the review from the *Times* affected business. Choice (D) best explains why the sentence should not be added.

34. F
Category: Idioms
Difficulty: Medium
Getting to the Answer: Trust your ear. You look *to* someone or something for advice. No change is needed. Choice G suggests that the paper is looking along *with* its readers, while H suggests that the readers are looking near the newspaper. Choice J uses an *-ing* verb without a helping verb, creating a sentence fragment.

35. B
Category: Verb Tenses
Difficulty: Low
Getting to the Answer: Verbs must make sense in the context of the passage. The next sentence says that a negative review "can undermine" a restaurant. Because the two sentences discuss possible results of a review, the underlined verb in this sentence should be in the same tense—"can bring," (B). Choice A illogically uses the conditional in the past tense, while C and D do not use the conditional at all.

36. F
Category: Punctuation
Difficulty: Medium
Getting to the Answer: The subject of the sentence is "restaurant owners and workers," and the verb is *have*. There isn't a descriptive phrase or clause separating the subject and verb, so no comma is needed. A semicolon should be used to connect two complete thoughts, G. Choice H incorrectly treats *restaurant* as the first item in a list; instead, *restaurant* identifies the type of *owners* and *workers*.

37. C
Category: Pronouns
Difficulty: Medium
Getting to the Answer: To whom does the meal belong? It belongs to the *writer,* so the possessive pronoun *whose* is correct. *Who's* is always a contraction for *who is* or *who has,* B. Choices A and D introduce sentence structure errors.

38. F
Category: Wordiness
Difficulty: Medium
Getting to the Answer: The shortest answer is often correct. The sentence is concise and direct as it is written. Each of the other choices adds unnecessary words to the underlined portion.

39. C
Category: Wordiness
Difficulty: Low
Getting to the Answer: On the ACT, there's no need to say the same thing twice. *Common, ordinary, representative,* and *average* all have very similar meanings; A and B use redundant language. Choice (C) makes the sentence concise by using only *typical.* Choice D uses a word that does not make sense in the context of the sentence.

40. H
Category: Wordiness
Difficulty: Medium
Getting to the Answer: If you have *decided* to do something to solve a problem, you have found a *solution*—there's no need to use both words. Choice (H) eliminates the redundancy and verbosity errors of the other choices.

41. B
Category: Sentence Sense
Difficulty: High
Getting to the Answer: As a rule, modifying words, phrases, and clauses should be as close as possible to the things or actions they describe. For instance, the list beginning "such as an attractive blonde named Chloe" describes the *different personas.* Therefore, *different personas* should come right before the list. This eliminates A. Choice (B) correctly uses an introductory phrase and makes *Reichl* the subject of the sentence. Choice C is a sentence fragment; a complete verb is missing. Choice D inserts an unnecessary comma between *clothing* and *that,* and the pronoun *herself* is incorrect in context.

42. G
Category: Writing Strategy
Difficulty: Medium
Getting to the Answer: The most logical and effective sentence will be connected to the main topic of the paragraph and make a transition to the following sentence. Paragraph 4 describes how Reichl turned herself into different characters, and paragraph 5 describes the result of reviewing a restaurant while in disguise. The best link between these ideas is (G). Choice F is a narrow detail that does not connect the two paragraphs, while H and J move completely away from the topic of Reichl's disguises.

43. D
Category: Organization
Difficulty: High
Getting to the Answer: Sometimes it helps to rephrase a question in your own words. For example, this question could be rewritten as "What does the phrase *of a restaurant* describe?" Reichl focuses on the quality of a restaurant, so the best placement is (D). The phrase does not describe *developed*, *view*, or *person*.

44. G
Category: Sentence Sense
Difficulty: High
Getting to the Answer: The word *occasionally* means "sometimes"; its placement in this sentence indicates that Reichl was sometimes treated very differently when she was in disguise, and sometimes she wasn't. Removing the word *occasionally* would indicate that Reichl always or typically had a different experience as one of her personas, (G).

45. A
Category: Organization
Difficulty: Medium
Getting to the Answer: Paragraph 6 describes the effect of Reichl's use of disguises when she reviewed restaurants. Logically, this information should follow the explanation of why and how Ruth dined as different people, the topics of paragraphs 3 and 4. Paragraph 6 should remain where it is.

PASSAGE IV

46. J
Category: Punctuation
Difficulty: Medium
Getting to the Answer: Trust your ear. A comma indicates a short pause, which you won't hear when you read this part of the sentence aloud. No comma is needed, (J). A comma can be used to separate a descriptive phrase from the rest of the sentence, F and H, but neither "would develop into prize-winning vegetables" nor "develop into prize-winning vegetables" is a descriptive phrase. Choice G incorrectly treats the underlined portion of the sentence as part of a list.

47. D
Category: Organization
Difficulty: High
Getting to the Answer: The paragraph describes events in chronological order, from the last freeze of the year to the time that spring "truly arrived." Sentence 3 describes thinning out the plants and pulling weeds so the new plants would grow; it would only make sense to do this *after* the seeds have been planted and have started to grow. Sentence 4 is about planting seeds, so sentence 3 must come after sentence 4, (D).

48. H
Category: Connections
Difficulty: Medium
Getting to the Answer: When you read this sentence aloud, you should be able to hear a short pause between *burden* and *less*. This pause indicates that the conjunction *and* is needed to separate the two descriptions, (H). Choice G is incorrect because a colon is used to introduce a brief definition, explanation, or list. Choice J uses the inappropriate conjunction *but*, which doesn't make sense in context.

49. D
Category: Wordiness
Difficulty: Medium
Getting to the Answer: When "OMIT the underlined portion" is an option, consider whether the underlined portion is relevant to the topic of the sentence or paragraph. Paragraph 2 is about the writer's failure to maintain her garden, not about the weather in July and August. Choice (D) is correct.

50. G
Category: Connections
Difficulty: Low
Getting to the Answer: Always read the questions carefully! This one asks for the choice that would NOT work in the sentence. In other words, three of the answer choices would make sense in the sentence. The first sentence of paragraph 3 contrasts with paragraph 2, so the contrasting transitions in F, H, and J are all possible substitutions for the underlined word. *Indeed,* (G), is a word used to show emphasis, not contrast.

51. D
Category: Wordiness
Difficulty: Medium
Getting to the Answer: The shortest answer is often correct. Choices A, B, and C all refer to large-scale farming, which is only loosely related to the topic of gardening. Choice (D) keeps the sentence focused on the topic of paragraph 3.

52. F
Category: Connections
Difficulty: High
Getting to the Answer: Before you answer this question, read enough of paragraph 4 to identify its main idea. Paragraph 3 introduces the topic of square-foot gardening, and paragraph 4 describes several of its advantages. The best link between these ideas is the original sentence, (F). Paragraph 4 doesn't mention the history of square-foot gardening or the writer's neighbor, so G and J don't make sense. Choice H is a detail about square-foot

gardening, but it does not function as a topic sentence for the paragraph.

53. C
Category: Sentence Sense
Difficulty: Low
Getting to the Answer: If an underlined word ends in *-ly,* you can be pretty sure that it is an adverb. Remember that adverbs can be used to describe verbs, adjectives, and other adverbs but not nouns. The word *garden* is a noun, so A and B are incorrect. The adjective *traditional,* (C), is correct. The phrase *tradition garden,* D, does not make sense.

54. J
Category: Word Choice
Difficulty: Medium
Getting to the Answer: Who spends hours thinning each row? From this sentence, it's unclear: you have no idea who *they* are. Other sentences in paragraph 4 use the pronoun *you,* so it makes sense to use *you* here.

55. D
Category: Wordiness
Difficulty: Medium
Getting to the Answer: "OMIT the underlined portion" is an option, so check to see whether the information is irrelevant to the topic or repetitive. This sentence begins with the phrase "In a square-foot garden," so it is unnecessary to repeat "in the garden." Choice (D) is correct.

56. H
Category: Sentence Sense
Difficulty: Low
Getting to the Answer: "OMIT the underlined portion" isn't always the correct answer. As it is written, the sentence does not express a complete thought. To correct the error, remove *which could* so that *make* becomes the main verb of the sentence. Choices G and J create sentence fragments.

57. A

Category: Word Choice

Difficulty: Medium

Getting to the Answer: Don't look too hard for an error—many English test questions will require NO CHANGE. The present tense and the pronoun *you* are used throughout paragraph 4, so this sentence is correct as it is written.

58. J

Category: Wordiness

Difficulty: Low

Getting to the Answer: Remember that the ACT values economy. If you can express an underlined portion in fewer words without changing or losing the original meaning, then the shortest answer is probably correct. The only choice that does not use redundant language is (J).

59. C

Category: Word Choice

Difficulty: Medium

Getting to the Answer: The verb in this sentence is separated from its singular subject "one season" by the phrase "of using the square garden techniques." Choice (C) corrects the subject-verb agreement error of the original sentence. Incorrect choices use the plural form of the verb, A and B, or the future tense, D, which does not make sense in the context of the sentence.

60. G

Category: Writing Strategy

Difficulty: High

Getting to the Answer: This question asks about the passage as a whole, so take a moment to think about the main idea of the passage. Paragraphs 1 and 2 describe the writer's failed attempts at a traditional garden, while paragraphs 3, 4, and 5 focus on the writer's success with a square-foot garden. The essay is not instructive; instead, it compares two types of gardens, (G).

PASSAGE V

61. D

Category: Punctuation

Difficulty: Medium

Getting to the Answer: When a coordinating conjunction such as *but* or *and* combines two independent clauses (complete thoughts), a comma must come before it. In this sentence, a comma should be inserted after *light,* (D). Choice C incorrectly places a comma in a compound phrase and fails to add one before the coordinating conjunction. Choice B incorrectly uses a semicolon between an independent and a dependent clause. You'll likely see at least one semicolon question on the ACT, so remember that a semicolon is used to separate two complete thoughts or to separate items in a series or list when one or more of those items already contains commas.

62. H

Category: Word Choice

Difficulty: Medium

Getting to the Answer: The answer choices present different forms of the verbs *improves* and *decreases*, so you know the issue is subject-verb agreement. The two underlined verbs need to agree with the plural subject *steps*; only (H) puts both *improve* and *decrease* in the correct form.

63. A

Category: Wordiness

Difficulty: Low

Getting to the Answer: The simplest way to say something is often the most correct option. The original sentence is the most concise and correct version. Choice B is redundant, using both *problem* and *trouble*. Choices C and D are both unnecessarily wordy in comparison to (A), which expresses the same meaning.

64. H
Category: Sentence Sense
Difficulty: Medium
Getting to the Answer: An *-ing* verb needs a helping verb to function as the main verb in a clause or sentence. Changing *being* to *is*, as in (H), corrects the sentence structure error. Choice G inserts an incorrect comma between *vision* and *has been*, while J creates a new sentence structure error by omitting the verb *being*.

65. B
Category: Sentence Sense
Difficulty: Medium
Getting to the Answer: Something that is *set* is established or predetermined. For the sentence to make sense, *set* should describe *time*; the wiper blades should be replaced at an *established* time each year. Choice (B) is correct. It does not make sense for the *blades*, A, the *year*, C, or the *risk*, D, to be *set*, or established.

66. F
Category: Word Choice
Difficulty: Low
Getting to the Answer: Trust your ear. With some idiom questions, you have to rely on your ear to hear what sounds correct. *In general* is an introductory phrase used to mean "usually" or "typically." Choice (F) provides the correct idiom for this context. The other choices contain idioms that are not typical of spoken English and do not fit this context.

67. B
Category: Writing Strategy
Difficulty: Medium
Getting to the Answer: To pick the best first sentence for paragraph 4, you must be able to identify the main idea of the paragraph. If you scan a few sentences of paragraph 4 before you answer the question, you'll see that the topic of the paragraph is changing a car's oil and oil filter. Only (B) introduces this topic. Choice A is too general, while C and D

refer to car maintenance procedures that are not discussed in paragraph 4.

68. G
Category: Connections
Difficulty: Medium
Getting to the Answer: The connecting word *so* is underlined, so consider the relationship between the two parts of the sentence. There is a slight contrast—the first part of the sentence explains what you *do* need, while the second part identifies what you *don't* need. The contrasting conjunction *but,* (G), makes the most sense in context. The other choices indicate a cause-and-effect relationship that is not present in the sentence.

69. D
Category: Punctuation
Difficulty: Medium
Getting to the Answer: Information that is key to the main idea of a sentence should not be set off by commas. Here, it's important to know that the section is "in your owner's manual," so commas are incorrect. Choice (D) is correct. Choice C incorrectly uses a semicolon; a complete thought is not expressed by "and collect all of the tools you need."

70. G
Category: Writing Strategy
Difficulty: High
Getting to the Answer: Carefully read the question so that you understand the writer's purpose. If the writer wants to explain how to change oil, then the sentence should explain at least one specific step in the process. Choice (G) provides the most detailed information about how to go about changing oil.

71. A
Category: Punctuation
Difficulty: Medium
Getting to the Answer: Use a semicolon to introduce or emphasize what follows. The warning "you do not want to risk being crushed by a car," is

certainly worthy of emphasis, so the sentence is correct as it is written. The other choices create run-ons, as the sentence expresses two complete thoughts; additionally, D incorrectly separates a subject noun from its verb with a comma.

72. G
Category: Writing Strategy
Difficulty: High
Getting to the Answer: Paragraph 4 uses the informal *you* and *your*, while the rest of the essay uses the more formal third person. Therefore, eliminating the second-person pronouns from paragraph 4 would make the paragraph match the tone and voice of the rest of the essay, (G). Choices H and J are opposite answers: eliminating *you* and *your* would make the advice less direct and would make the essay more formal.

73. A
Category: Wordiness
Difficulty: Low
Getting to the Answer: Watch out for redundant language! A "qualified mechanic" will do a *professional* job, just as a "qualified mechanic" is likely *certified*; B and C use repetitive language. Choice D introduces a sentence structure error. The best version of the underlined portion is (A).

74. H
Category: Writing Strategy
Difficulty: Medium
Getting to the Answer: Knowing the general topic of each paragraph will help you quickly answer a question like this one. The sentence refers to "these different fluids," so look for a part of the passage that discusses fluids. The second and third sentences of paragraph 3 refer to different fluids (*coolant, oil, brake fluid*, and *transmission fluid*), so the most logical placement for the sentence is at the end of paragraph 3, (H). Paragraph 2 and paragraph 4 each only refer to one fluid, so F and J are incorrect.

75. D
Category: Writing Strategy
Difficulty: Medium
Getting to the Answer: Use your Reading Comp skills to answer this question. Does the main idea of the passage fit with this purpose? Not really, as the passage focuses solely on basic maintenance that car owners can do themselves. The passage doesn't discuss the need to learn about a car's safety features. Choice (D) is correct.

MATHEMATICS TEST

1. E
Category: Operations
Difficulty: Medium
Getting to the Answer: To determine the total amount of fabric used, add the mixed numbers. To add mixed numbers, add the whole number parts, and then add the fractions. The whole number parts add to 4. To add the fractions, find the least common denominator of 8 and 3, which is 24. Convert each fraction to an equivalent fraction with a denominator of 24: $\frac{3 \times 3}{8 \times 3} = \frac{9}{24}$ and $\frac{1 \times 8}{3 \times 8} = \frac{8}{24}$.

Now, add the numerators, and keep the denominator: $\frac{9}{24} + \frac{8}{24} + \frac{17}{24}$. The total fabric used is $4\frac{17}{24}$. If you chose B, you found a common denominator, but you forgot to multiply the numerators by the same factor that you had multiplied the denominators by. A common error when adding fractions would result in C. This fraction was obtained by the incorrect procedure of adding the numerators, and then adding the denominators.

2. K
Category: Operations
Difficulty: Medium
Getting to the Answer: To simplify this expression, first multiply the numerical coefficients to get $5 \times 6 \times 2 = 60$. To multiply the variable

terms, keep the base of the variable and add the exponents. Remember that x denotes x^1. Multiply the x variable terms: $x^3 \times x = x^{3+1} = x^4$. Multiply the y variable terms: $y^5 \times y^2 \times y = y^{5+2+1} = y^8$. The resultant expression is $60x^4y^8$.

If your answer was J, you fell into the common trap of multiplying the exponents instead of using the correct method of adding the exponents. If your answer was either F or G, you added the numerical coefficients instead of multiplying. If your answer was H, you did not include the exponents of 1 for the single terms of x and y.

3. C

Category: Proportions and Probability
Difficulty: Medium
Getting to the Answer: First, find the amount each person saves yearly. Brandon saves 6% of his $36,000 salary, or $0.06 \times 36,000 = \$2,160$ each year. Jacqui saves $200 every month, or $12 \times 200 = \$2,400$ each year. The difference, in dollars, of their savings is therefore $2,400 - 2,160 = \$240$.

Choice A reflects the *monthly* difference in their savings. If you chose D, you incorrectly found the difference between Brandon's yearly savings and Jacqui's *monthly* savings. Choice E indicates Brandon's monthly *salary* minus Jacqui's monthly savings.

4. H

Category: Proportions and Probability
Difficulty: Medium
Getting to the Answer: An average is found by taking the total sum of the terms and dividing it by the total number of terms. Therefore, the sum = (average) $\times$ (number of terms). For Mikhail to have an average for the five games of 180, the sum = $180 \times 5 = 900$. The first four scores total $190 + 200 + 145 + 180 = 715$. Therefore, his score for the fifth game must be $900 - 715 = 185$.

Choice F is just the average of the first four scores. Choice G is the average of the first four scores added and averaged with 180.

5. D

Category: Proportions and Probability
Difficulty: Low
Getting to the Answer: The amount of chromium is a part of the whole alloy. Use the formula Part = Percent $\times$ Whole. There are 262.5 pounds of chromium available, which must reflect at least 10.5% of the whole. Let w represent the whole amount of alloy that can be manufactured, and write the algebraic equation: $262.5 = 10.5\%w$ or $262.5 = 0.105w$. Divide both sides of the equation by 0.105: $w = \frac{262.5}{0.105}$ pounds of steel.

Choice A represents 10.5% of 262.5. If you chose B, you simply subtracted 10.5 from 262.5, without regard to the percent or the whole amount. Choice C is simply the amount of chromium. If you chose E, you set up the problem correctly but incorrectly converted 10.5% to the decimal 0.0105.

6. J

Category: Plane Geometry
Difficulty: Low
Getting to the Answer: A wallpaper border is a strip that surrounds the perimeter of the kitchen. The perimeter of a rectangle = 2(length + width). The kitchen has a length of 6.5 meters and a width of 4 meters, so the amount of border needed is $2(6.5 + 4) = 2(10.5) = 21$ meters.

Choice G represents a common mistake made when calculating perimeter. This answer would result from just adding the two dimensions and not multiplying by 2. Choice K is the area, not the perimeter, of the kitchen.

7. A

Category: Operations
Difficulty: Medium
Getting to the Answer: To find an equivalent for the given expression, use the distributive property. First, evaluate the inner parentheses according to the order of operations, or PEMDAS. Distribute the negative sign to $(y + z)$ to get $w(x - y - z)$. Next,

distribute the variable *w* to all terms in parentheses to get *wx* – *wy* – *wz*.

Choice B fails to distribute the negative sign to the *z* term. Choices C and D only distribute the *w* to the first term. Choice E incorrectly distributes *wx* to the (*y* + *z*) term.

8. G
Category: Variable Manipulation
Difficulty: Medium
Getting to the Answer: This is an equation with a variable on both sides. To solve, work to get the *n* terms isolated on one side of the equation and the numerical terms on the other side. Subtract 3*n* from both sides to get 6*n* – 3*n* – 4 = 3*n* – 3*n* + 24. Combine like terms: 3*n* – 4 = 24. Now, add 4 to both sides: 3*n* – 4 + 4 = 24 + 4, or 3*n* = 28. Finally, divide both sides by 3: $n = \frac{28}{3}$. Choice F reflects a common trap: forgetting to divide by 3. If you chose H or J, you incorrectly added 6*n* and 3*n* and possibly subtracted 4 from 24 instead of adding 4. Dividing incorrectly at the last step would have led you to K.

9. B
Category: Patterns, Logic, and Data
Difficulty: Medium
Getting to the Answer: In this arithmetic sequence, you can think of the terms as 26, 26 + *s*, 26 + *s* + *s*, and 26 + *s* + *s* + *s*. In this example, *s* represents the difference between successive terms. The final term is 53, so set up an algebraic equation: 26 + *s* + *s* + *s* = 53. Solve this equation for *s*, by first combining like terms: 26 + 3*s* = 53. Subtract 26 from both sides to get 26 – 26 + 3*s* = 53 – 26, or 3*s* = 27. Divide both sides by 3 to find that *s*, the difference between terms, is 9. Therefore, the terms are 26, 26 + 9, 26 + 9 + 9, and 53 or 26, 35, 44, and 53.

Choice D results from taking 53 – 26, dividing by 4, adding this value to each term, and rounding. In all of the incorrect answer choices, there is a common difference between second-first and then fourth-third, but it is different from the difference between the third and the second terms.

10. H
Category: Variable Manipulation
Difficulty: High
Getting to the Answer: First, solve the equation $5m^2 = 45$ for *m*. Once a value is obtained for *m*, substitute this into the expression to evaluate and find the answer. To solve the equation, divide both sides of the equation by 5 to get $m^2 = 9$. Take the square root of each side to get *m* = 3, or *m* = –3.

Now, evaluate the expression. Because the expression contains the radical $\sqrt{12m}$, and the expression must be a real number, reject the value of *m* = –3. (When a radicand, the expression under the radical sign, is negative, the number does not have a value in the set of real numbers.) Substitute 3 for *m* in the expression:

$$(3)^3 + \sqrt{12(3)} = 27 + \sqrt{36} = 27 + 6 = 33$$

If you chose G, you just found the value of m^3. You might have selected J if you interpreted the 12*m* under the radical sign as the number 12^3 instead of 12 × 3. If you chose K, you probably failed to take the square root of 9 when solving the equation and used the value of 9 for *m*.

11. D
Category: Plane Geometry
Difficulty: Medium
Getting to the Answer: First, convert the mixed number radius to a decimal: $3\frac{3}{5} = 3.6$. Substitute 3.6 into the formula to get $V = \frac{4}{3} \times \pi \times (3.6)^3$. Use the π key on your calculator. If your calculator has fractional capability and follows the correct order of operations, type the entry in as listed above. Otherwise, first find 3.6 to the third power. Multiply the result by 4, then divide by 3. Finally, multiply by π. In either case, the result is approximately 195.43, or 195 to the nearest cubic meter.

If you chose A or B, you multiplied the radius by 3, instead of taking the radius to the third power. For C and A, you incorrectly converted $3\frac{3}{5}$ to 3.35, a common trap. If you arrived at E, you first multiplied $\frac{4}{3} \times \pi \times (3.6)$ and then raised this value to the third power.

12. G
Category: Proportions and Probability
Difficulty: Low
Getting to the Answer: Probability is a ratio that compares the number of favorable, or desired, outcomes to the total number of outcomes. Probability is always a number between 0 and 1. In this question, the favorable outcome is the number of nuts that are NOT peanuts, or $6 + 8 = 14$. The total number of outcomes is $10 + 6 + 8 = 24$. The probability that the nut is NOT a peanut is $\frac{14}{24} = \frac{7}{12}$, in lowest terms.

Choice F is the probability that the nut IS a peanut. Choice H is the ratio that compares peanuts to other nuts.

13. C
Category: Patterns, Logic, and Data
Difficulty: High
Getting to the Answer: The matrices outline the corresponding number of people who shop at the store to the ratio, written as a decimal, of the number of people who will make purchases, *with reference to their age group*. A ratio written as a decimal is essentially a percentage. So following the correspondence yields $75 \times 0.20 = 15$ adolescent purchases, $100 \times 0.35 = 35$ adult purchases, and $30 \times 0.10 = 3$ senior-citizen purchases. This is a total of $15 + 35 + 3 = 53$ people making purchases.

Choice A represents the adolescent purchases. If you chose B, you took the total number of people in the store, 205, and multiplied by the ratio for adolescents, 0.20. Choice D adds the total number of people, 205; multiplies by the sum of the ratios, 0.65; and then rounds. Choice E is the total number of people who shop at the store, not the total number of purchases.

14. J
Category: Patterns, Logic, and Data
Difficulty: Medium
Getting to the Answer: To find an average, calculate the sum of the data and then divide by the total number of data items. According to the table, the number of hours that the country genre has a live disc jockey is 24, 7, and 16. Find the sum: $24 + 7 + 16 = 47$. Divide: $47 \div 3 = 15.67$, which is 16 to the nearest hour.

Choice F is the number of *entries*, not hours, for the country genre.
Choice G is the average number of hours for the classical genre.
Choice K is the average number of hours for the news genre.

15. D
Category: Patterns, Logic, and Data
Difficulty: High
Getting to the Answer: When you add up all of the hours, you get 205. Divide 205 by 8 hours, which is the number of hours in each shift: $205 \div 8 = 25.625$. Round up to 26 because the question asks for the minimum number of disk jockeys needed to cover all genres and mediums if each works an eight-hour shift.

A common trap would be C because the answer would round down to 25 disc jockeys, but this would fall short of the requirement to cover all of the hours.

Choice E reflects the total number of hours needed. Choice A is the number of 24-hour segments that require a live disc jockey.

16. G
Category: Patterns, Logic, and Data
Difficulty: Medium
Getting to the Answer: To find the missing value, add the monomials in the first row: $m + -4m + 3m = 0$. This first row sums to zero. To be sure, check the rightmost column: $3m + -2m + -m = 0$. Every row, column, and diagonal must sum to 0. The first

column must therefore be $m + 2m + \square = 0$, or $3m + \square = 0$. Isolate the missing term on one side of the equation by subtracting $3m$ from both sides: $\square = -3m$.

If your choice was H, you ignored the m variable in the term. If your choice was F, J, or K, you may have just looked at the first column and the last row and found a value that would work with those, without considering the other rows, columns, and diagonals.

17. E
Category: Number Properties
Difficulty: Medium
Getting to the Answer: The algebraic expression xy means to multiply the point's x-value by its y-value. If the product is positive, then the x and y factors are either both positive or both negative, according to the rules for multiplying signed numbers. Positive x-coordinates are to the right of the origin. Positive y-coordinates are above the origin. In quadrant I, both coordinates are positive, and in quadrant III, both coordinates are negative. In quadrant II, the x-coordinate is negative (to the left of the origin), and the y-coordinate is positive (above the origin). In quadrant IV, the x-coordinate is positive (to the right of the origin), and the y-coordinate is negative (below the origin).

18. J
Category: Patterns, Logic, and Data
Difficulty: Medium
Getting to the Answer: The number of distinct lunches is determined by the fundamental counting principle. The counting principle directs you to multiply the different choices together to find the total number of combinations: $7 \times 3 \times 4 = 84$. If you consider just the sandwiches and soups alone, each sandwich can be paired with one of three soups, so there would be $7 \times 3 = 21$ different alternatives. These 21 alternatives would then become $21 \times 4 = 84$ different meals, because each of these 21 meals could be combined with four different drink choices.

A common trap answer is G, where the numbers are added together, instead of multiplied. Choice F is the number of sandwiches available, not the number of distinct meals. Choice H reflects the number of distinct choices of just sandwich and soup.

19. A
Category: Proportions and Probability
Difficulty: Low
Getting to the Answer: The question describes a comparison of the number of female to male students. This is a ratio—the ratio of female to male students is 5 to 3, or $\frac{5}{3}$. Let n represent the number of female students. Set up the proportion $\frac{5}{3} = \frac{n}{6,000}$ and cross multiply to get $3n = 5 \times 6,000$, or $3n = 30,000$. Divide both sides by 3 to get $n = 10,000$ females.

If you chose B, you may have used rounding and incorrectly considered the ratio to be twice as many females as males. Choice C represents the total number of students at the university. If you chose D or E, you may have stopped after multiplying 6,000 by 3 or by 5, respectively.

20. H
Category: Plane Geometry
Difficulty: Medium
Getting to the Answer: Draw a diagram of a rectangle:

Because a rectangle has four right angles, you can treat the diagonal, QS, as the hypotenuse of a right triangle with legs of 16 and 30 inches. Use the Pythagorean theorem to solve for the length of the hypotenuse. If c represents the length of the hypotenuse and a and b represent the length of the legs, then $a^2 + b^2 = c^2$. Substitute into the formula:

$$c^2 = 16^2 + 30^2$$
$$c^2 = 256 + 900$$
$$c^2 = 1{,}156$$

Take the square root of both sides of the equation to find that $c = 34$ inches.

If you chose F, you used 30 inches for c (the hypotenuse) in the formula, and then solved for one of the legs. Choice G adds the two dimensions and divides by 2. If you chose J, you incorrectly divided by 2 instead of taking the square root; for K, you added the squares but did not take the square root of the sum.

21. A
Category: Variable Manipulation
Difficulty: Medium
Getting to the Answer: Choice (A) is not equivalent to $5n + 1$—it is the reciprocal. If you chose B, you may have incorrectly simplified by not multiplying 5×2. The expression simplifies as $5n + 10 - 9$, or $5n + 1$. Choice C is also equivalent to $5n + 1$—when you divide fractions, you multiply by the reciprocal of the denominator, and

$$\frac{1}{1} \div \frac{1}{5n+1} = \frac{1}{1} \times \frac{5n+1}{1} = 5n + 1.$$

If you chose either D or E, you may have thought that they could not be equivalent because they have a squared variable. But when D is factored and simplified, you can see it is equivalent: $\dfrac{n(5n+1)}{n} = 5n + 1$.

The same is true for E: $\dfrac{(5n+1)(5n-1)}{5n-1} = 5n + 1$.

22. J
Category: Variable Manipulation
Difficulty: Medium
Getting to the Answer: Each of the answer choices is in the form $y = \dots$, so solve for y in terms of x. Isolate y on one side of the equation. First, subtract $3x$ from both sides: $3x - 3x + 2y = -3x + 16$. Combine

like terms to get $2y = -3x + 16$. Now, divide all terms on both sides by 2: $y = -\dfrac{3}{2}x + 8$.

In F, the numeric term 16 is not divided by 2. Choices G and K have the reciprocal of the coefficient of x. In H, $3x$ was added to both sides of the equation instead of subtracted, to get the incorrect term of $+\dfrac{3}{2}x$.

23. E
Category: Variable Manipulation
Difficulty: High
Getting to the Answer: To solve a quadratic equation, first factor the trinomial in the form $ax^2 + bx + c$. Because the c term is positive and the b term is negative, the factors will be $(x - \#)(x - \#)$. Look for factors of 75 that when added together will equal 20, the b coefficient. Some factor possibilities for 75 are 1 and 75, 3 and 25, and 5 and 15. Only the factors 5 and 15 will add to 20. The equation, after factoring, becomes $(x - 5)(x - 15) = 0$. The solutions are the values of x that result in either of the factors equaling 0: $x = 5$ or $x = 15$.

The common traps are A or B where you might have quickly looked at the factors and thought the answers were either -5 or -15. If you chose D, you may have thought the only factors of 75 were 3 and 25 and therefore chosen 3 as a solution. If you chose C, you may have ignored the term of 75 and found a solution of 0.

24. H
Category: Trigonometry
Difficulty: Medium
Getting to the Answer: The cosine (cos) ratio is the ratio of the side adjacent to angle N to the hypotenuse of the right triangle. The $\cos N = \dfrac{12}{13}$.

Choice F is the sine (sin) ratio of angle N. Choice G is the tangent (tan) ratio of angle N. Choice J is the secant (sec), or the reciprocal of the cos, to angle N. Choice K is the cosecant (csc), or the reciprocal of the sin, to angle N.

25. C
Category: Plane Geometry
Difficulty: Medium
Getting to the Answer: Because chord *AB* passes through the center, it is a diameter of the circle, and segment *OB* is a radius, equal to 7 cm. Because *OC* is perpendicular to *AB*, a right angle is formed. To find the length of chord *CB*, note that it is the hypotenuse of right triangle $\triangle COB$, with legs that each measure 7 cm. Because the legs have the same measure, this is a special right triangle, the 45°-45°-90° right triangle, and the sides are in the ratio of $n : n : n\sqrt{2}$. Chord *BC* is therefore $7\sqrt{2} \oplus 9.899$, or 9.9 to the nearest tenth of a centimeter. Alternately, you could have used the Pythagorean theorem, $a^2 + b^2 = c^2$, where $a = b = 7$:

$$7^2 + 7^2 = c^2$$
$$49 + 49 = c^2$$
$$c = \sqrt{98} \approx 9.9 \text{ cm}$$

If your answer was A, you used the Pythagorean theorem but evaluated 7^2 as 7×2, instead of 7×7. This is a common trap. Choice B is the length of the legs, not the hypotenuse. Choice D is $7\sqrt{3}$. Choice E is the length of the diameter of the circle.

26. F
Category: Variable Manipulation
Difficulty: Medium
Getting to the Answer: Substitute the value of 86 into the formula for *F*, the degrees in Fahrenheit, to get $86 = \frac{9}{5}C + 32$. Subtract 32 from both sides:

$$86 - 32 = \frac{9}{5}C + 32 - 32$$
$$54 = \frac{9}{5}C$$

Now, multiply both sides by the reciprocal of $\frac{9}{5}$ to isolate *C*:

$$\frac{5}{9} \times 54 = \frac{5}{9} \times \frac{9}{5} \times C$$
$$30 = C$$

If you chose G, you forgot to multiply by the reciprocal to get rid of the fraction on the right side of the equation. Choice H incorrectly multiplies 86 by $\frac{5}{9}$ first, then adds 32. Choice J is the degrees in Fahrenheit. Choice K would be the degrees in Fahrenheit of 86 degrees Celsius.

27. D
Category: Plane Geometry
Difficulty: Medium
Getting to the Answer: A swimming pool that is the same depth in all parts is a rectangular solid. The amount of water in the pool is the volume of the water. Use the formula $V = lwh$, and substitute in the volume, length, and width given in the problem. $14,375 = 50 \times 25 \times h$, or $14,375 = 1,250h$. Divide both sides of the equation by 1,250, to get $11.5 = h$. The depth is between 11 and 12 meters.

28. F
Category: Trigonometry
Difficulty: Medium
Getting to the Answer: The tangent is the ratio of the side opposite to the given angle over the side adjacent to the given angle. Segment *EF* is the side opposite to angle *D*, so call this side *m*. Segment *DE*, the adjacent side to angle *D*, equals 42 inches. Set up the equation:

$$\frac{5}{8} = \frac{m}{42}$$
$$(42)(5) = 8m$$
$$210 = 8m$$
$$m = 26.3$$

If you chose G, you added 42 and $\frac{5}{8}$. Choice H reflects the length of side *DF*, the hypotenuse of the right triangle. Choice J incorrectly uses 42 as the opposite side and side *EF* as the adjacent side.

29. B

Category: Proportions and Probability

Difficulty: Medium

Getting to the Answer: The fraction of the people who were sophomores would be the ratio of the number of sophomores to the total number of people at the prom. There were 30 sophomores and a total of 20 + 30 + 70 + 200 = 320 people at the prom. The fraction is $\frac{30}{320} = \frac{3}{32}$.

Choice A is the fraction of the attendees who were freshmen. Choice C is the ratio of sophomores to those who are NOT sophomores. Choice D is the ratio of sophomores to seniors. Choice E is a common trap—it compares the number of sophomores to 100, instead of to the total number of students in attendance.

30. F

Category: Number Properties

Difficulty: Low

Getting to the Answer: This problem requires you to understand that the sum of the parts of a segment is equal to the whole segment. It is given that X is the midpoint of segment WZ. Because the length of $WZ = 44$ cm, the length of WX is one-half of this, or 22 cm. From the relative positions of the points in the segment, $WX + XY = WY$, or alternately, $WY - WX = XY$. It is given that $WY = 26$ and calculated that WX is 22. Therefore, $XY = 26 - 22$, or 4 centimeters.

If you chose K, you just added the two numbers given in the problem. Choice J is the length of one-half of segment WZ, or the length of WX. If your answer was H, you subtracted the two numbers given in the problem. Choice G is one-half of segment WY.

31. C

Category: Variable Manipulation

Difficulty: Medium

Getting to the Answer: Find the point of intersection of two lines by solving the system of equations.

Use the elimination method by lining up the equations by like terms:

$$5x + y = 7$$
$$2x + 3y = 8$$

The problem asks for the x-coordinate, so multiply one of the equations so that when they are combined, the y-values are eliminated. If you multiply all terms in the top equation by -3, when you combine them, the y-values will be eliminated:

$$-3(5x + y = 7) \quad -15x - 3y = -21$$
$$2x + 3y = 8 \qquad 2x + 3y = 8$$

Combine like terms in the resulting equations: $(-15x + 2x) + (-3y + 3y) = -21 + 8$, or $-13x = -13$. Now, divide both sides of this simpler equation by -13 to get $x = 1$.

If you chose A, you probably divided the negative numbers incorrectly to get -1. Choice B may have resulted from only multiplying the y by -3 and not multiplying the terms of $5x$ and 7, and getting the result of $7x = 15$, or $x = \frac{15}{7}$. Choice D is the y-coordinate of the intersection of the two lines.

32. K

Category: Variable Manipulation

Difficulty: Medium

Getting to the Answer: To solve the equation for b, isolate b on one side of the equation. First, add 8 to both sides of the equation: $a + 8 = 2b - 8 + 8$, or $a + 8 = 2b$. Now, divide both sides by 2 to get $b = \frac{a + 8}{2}$.

If your answer was F, you forgot to divide a by 2. In G, you exchanged the variable a for the variable b, instead of solving for b. Choice H is similar to G, but the subtraction was changed to addition. In J, you may have subtracted 8 from both sides instead of adding 8.

33. D

Category: Plane Geometry

Difficulty: Low

Getting to the Answer: The area of a parallelogram is $A = bh$, where height h is the length of the perpendicular segment to one of the sides of the parallelogram. In the figure, segment RT, of length $9 + 5$, or 14 mm, is the base and the dotted segment, of length 12 mm, is the height. The area is $14 \times 12 = 168$ mm².

Choice A is the area of the little triangle at the top, not the parallelogram. If you chose B, you added the given numbers, without recognizing that the problem is asking for area. Choice C is the perimeter of the parallelogram. Choice E reflects a common error, where you multiplied the sides together instead of multiplying the base times the height.

34. F

Category: Variable Manipulation

Difficulty: Medium

Getting to the Answer: The problem asks you to evaluate $(x + y)^3$, so manipulate the given equation to isolate $x + y$ on one side of the equation. Once you have this value, cube it to find the answer to the problem. For the given equation $x = -(y + 3)$, first distribute the negative sign on the right-hand side to get $x = -y - 3$. Now add y to both sides of the equation: $x + y = -y + y - 3$. Combine like terms to arrive at $x + y = -3$. Now substitute -3 for $(x + y)$ in the expression to get $(-3)^3 = -3 \times -3 \times -3 = -27$.

Choice G is a common trap: evaluating $(-3)^3$ as $-3 \times 3 = -9$. Choices H and J result from not applying integer multiplication rules for negative numbers.

35. E

Category: Plane Geometry

Difficulty: High

Getting to the Answer: Because all streets and avenues shown intersect at right angles, the map is a rectangle in which opposite sides have the same measures. To find the location halfway between H and S, first think of the corner of Oak and 10th as the origin, or (0, 0). Just as in coordinate geometry, the first ordered pair represents the east-west direction, and the second ordered pair represents the north-south direction. The distance from the origin at Oak Street to the school is 5 miles east. The distance from the origin at 10th Avenue to the hospital is 8 miles north. The new station will be halfway between these coordinates, or $\frac{5}{2} = 2.5$ miles east of the origin and $\frac{8}{2} = 4$ miles north of the origin.

To drive from F to the new fire station, you would have to drive $8 - 2.5 = 5.5$ miles west on Main Street, then $10 - 4 = 6$ miles south on Elm Street (the first 2 miles south to get to 2nd Avenue, and then 4 more miles south to be halfway between the hospital and the school). Choice A is the directions to the new fire station starting from the origin at Oak and 10th. Choice B is the directions to the new fire station starting from the school. Choice C is the directions from the corner of Main and Oak to the new station. If you answered D, you forgot to add in the 2 miles on Elm Street to get from Main to 2nd Avenue.

36. H

Category: Variable Manipulation

Difficulty: Medium

Getting to the Answer: Consecutive integers are integers that differ by 1, such as 3, 4, 5. Consecutive odd integers are odd integers that differ by 2, such as 7, 9, 11, 13. Because the answer choices use the variable x, let x represent the smaller of the consecutive odd integers, so $(x + 2)$ would be the larger of the integers. Four times the larger is represented by $4(x + 2)$ and twice the smaller by $2x$. The key word *difference* means to subtract the smaller from the larger, and the key word *is* means "equal." The equation is $4(x + 2) - 2x = 36$.

Choice F represents four times a number minus twice the same number. Choice G is incorrect because it represents two consecutive integers rather than two consecutive *odd* integers. Choice J is an equation for two integers that differ by 3, which means that the numbers are too far apart on the number line to be consecutive odd integers. Choice K is an equation for the difference between 36 and four times the smaller integer.

37. C
Category: Plane Geometry
Difficulty: Low
Getting to the Answer: The question states that the telephone pole is perpendicular to the ground and a wire is attached to the pole. This will result in a right triangle. It helps to draw a quick figure to represent the situation. The thicker side of the triangle represents the telephone pole, and the hypotenuse is the wire:

To find out how far the anchor of the supporting wire is from the base of the telephone pole, solve for the length of the missing leg. Use the Pythagorean theorem, which is $a^2 + b^2 = hypotenuse^2$. Let b represent the missing leg, and substitute in the given values to get $12^2 + b^2 = 15^2$, or $144 + b^2 = 225$. Subtract 144 from both sides: $b^2 = 81$. To solve for b, take the square root of both sides: $\sqrt{b^2} = \sqrt{81}$, so $b = 9$ or -9. A length cannot be negative, so the length is 9 ft.

Choice A subtracts $15 - 12$ to get 3. If you chose B, you may have thought that 15^2 meant 15×2 and calculated $30 - 24 = 6$. Choice D is the length up the pole, and E is the length of the wire.

38. H
Category: Plane Geometry
Difficulty: Medium
Getting to the Answer: The area of a circle is $A = \pi r^2$, where r is the radius of the circle. Use the equation $100\pi = \pi r^2$ and solve for r by dividing both sides by π: $100 = r^2$. If you take the square root of both sides, then $r = 10$ or -10. Reject the -10 value, because a radius length cannot be negative. The radius of the circle is 10, so the diameter of the circle, which is the same as the length of a side of the square, is $2 \times 10 = 20$ units.

Choice F is the area of the square. Choice G is r^2. Choosing J is a common error that mistakes the radius of the circle for the side of the square.

39. C
Category: Proportions and Probability
Difficulty: Medium
Getting to the Answer: When figures are similar, the side lengths are in proportion. Let x represent the missing side length, and set up the proportion of shorter side to longer side: $\dfrac{3}{8} = \dfrac{2}{x}$.
Cross multiply to get $3x = 16$. Divide both sides by 3 to get $x = 16 \div 3 \approx 5.3$, to the nearest tenth of an inch.

If you chose A or B, you set up the proportion incorrectly—make sure to match up the long sides and the short sides on the same side of the fraction. Choice D is the most common error made with similar figures, resulting if you assumed that because $3 - 1 = 2$, the missing side was $8 - 1 = 7$. Similar figures have sides that are in proportion, which is not an additive relationship.

40. J
Category: Plane Geometry
Difficulty: Medium
Getting to the Answer: The figure shown is a parallelogram. Extend the top side out to make a parallel line to line *UZ*. Line *WY* is a transversal to the parallel

lines, forming alternate interior angles, ∠XWY and ∠WYV, which have the same measures of 50°. Line WV is another transversal line to the parallel lines, forming alternate interior angles ∠UVW and ∠VWX. Because they have the same measure, ∠VWX = 150°. In addition, ∠VWX and ∠VYX have the same measure—they are opposite angles in a parallelogram. Now ∠VYX − ∠WYV = ∠WYX, or 150 − 50 = 100°.

If your answer was H, you incorrectly thought that ∠WYX had the same measure as ∠XWY. Choice K is the measure of ∠VYX, not ∠WYX.

41. D
Category: Plane Geometry
Difficulty: Medium
Getting to the Answer: The key to solving this problem is to simplify the drawing, knowing that you are looking for the perimeter. This figure, for perimeter purposes, can be thought of as a rectangle—just lower all the bottom pieces and move all left pieces to the right and you have a rectangle, with side lengths of 40 centimeters, and top/bottom lengths of 12 + 5 + 4 = 21 centimeters:

The perimeter is two times the length plus two times the width, or 2(40) + 2(21) = 80 + 42 = 122 centimeters.

Choice A is the measure of the length. Choice B is just the measure of two sides of the figure (just the numbers that are shown).

42. G
Category: Proportions and Probability
Difficulty: High
Getting to the Answer: Convert the fractions into decimal equivalents and remember that the key word *of* means to multiply. Because $\frac{3}{4}$ of the 3,500 eligible voters cast a vote, this is 0.75 × 3,500 = 2,625 votes that were cast at the site. Three-fifths of these votes were for Martinez, or 0.6 × 2,625 = 1,575 votes for Martinez.

If you answered F, you followed the correct procedure, but incorrectly converted the fractions. Choice H is $\frac{3}{5}$ of all the eligible voters. Choice J is $\frac{3}{4}$ of the eligible voters. Choice K is the sum of H and J.

43. A
Category: Number Properties
Difficulty: Medium
Getting to the Answer: To find the greatest common factor, find all factor pieces that the two expressions have in common. In this case, the factors in common are a, a, a, and b, or a^3b. It is given that the greatest common factor is 54, so think of a cubic number that is a factor of 54. The first cubic numbers are 1^3 (1), 2^3 (8), and 3^3 (27). Twenty-seven is a factor of 54: 27 × 2 = 54, so a possible value for b is 2.

Choice B is the value of the variable a. Choice C, 6, is a factor of 54, but that leaves the value of 9 for a, and 9 is not a perfect cube. The same reasoning would eliminate D. Choice E is the value of a^3.

44. K
Category: Proportions and Probability
Difficulty: Medium
Getting to the Answer: To tackle this problem, break it up into its parts. First, find the value of x, given that 40% of x is 70. The key word *of* means to multiply. Write this as the equation $0.40x = 70$;

divide both sides by 0.40 to get $x = 175$. Now find 160% of x, or $1.60 \times 175 = 280$.

Choice F is 40% of 70. Choice G is 160% of 28, the incorrect value from F. Choice H is 160% of 70. A common trap is J, which is the value of the variable x.

45. C
Category: Coordinate Geometry
Difficulty: Medium
Getting to the Answer: To find the length of segment MN, use the distance formula: $d = \sqrt{(x_2 - x_1)^2 + (y_2 - y_1)^2}$. Substitute in the point values:

$$d = \sqrt{(6 - 2)^2 + (5 - 3)^2}$$
$$d = \sqrt{4^2 + 2^2}$$
$$d = \sqrt{20} = \sqrt{4} \times \sqrt{5} = 2\sqrt{5}$$

If you chose A, you may have used the distance formula incorrectly, using $(y_1 - x_1)$ and $(y_2 - x_2)$ instead of finding the difference between the x- and y-coordinates. Choice B multiplies by 2 instead of raising to the second power in the formula. Choice D is just the sum of the differences between the x- and y-coordinates. If your answer was E, you forgot to take the square root of 20, as indicated by the distance formula.

46. J
Category: Plane Geometry
Difficulty: Low
Getting to the Answer: If the sides are in the ratio of 5:7, the perimeter will be in this exact same ratio. When finding a perimeter, you add up the sides. Perimeter is measured in single units, just as is the side length. Therefore, the ratio will not change. If you are unsure about this fact, assign values and actually calculate the perimeters. Consider the smaller square to have sides $5s$ in length and the larger square to have sides $7s$ in length. The smaller square has a perimeter of $4 \times 5s = 20s$, and the larger $4 \times 7s = 28s$. The ratio $20s:28s$ is equivalent to 5:7, after dividing both terms of the ratio by $4s$.

If you chose F, you may have thought you needed to subtract $7 - 5 = 2$, to get the (incorrect) ratio 1:2. Likewise, G adds $7 + 5 = 12$. Choice H multiplies $7 \times 5 = 35$. Choice K confuses area and perimeter—the ratio of the *areas* is 25:49.

47. E
Category: Plane Geometry
Difficulty: Medium
Getting to the Answer: The equation of a circle, when you know the coordinates of the center (h,k) and the radius (r), is given by $(x - h)^2 + (y - k)^2 = r^2$. Substitute in the given values to get $(x - (-2))^2 + (y - 3)^2 = 9^2$. This simplifies to $(x + 2)^2 + (y - 3)^2 = 81$.

There are two common traps when finding the equation of a circle. One trap is to forget to square the radius, as in B. The other common trap is adding h and k to x and y, instead of subtracting, as in C. Choice A is both of these traps together. Choice D incorrectly takes the square root of the radius, instead of squaring the radius.

48. H
Category: Variable Manipulation
Difficulty: High
Getting to the Answer: In the complex number system, i^2 is defined to be equal to -1, as you are told in the question stem. Use the distributive property to multiply the fraction:

$$\frac{3}{5 - i} \times \frac{5 + i}{5 + i} = \frac{(3 \times 5) + 3i}{5^2 + 5i - 5i - i^2}$$
$$= \frac{15 + 3i}{25 - (-1)} = \frac{15 + 3i}{26}$$

If your answer was F, you may have cancelled incorrectly to simplify. Choice G reflects a common error when multiplying complex numbers: $25 - i^2$ was incorrectly interpreted as $25 - 1 = 24$. In J, the 3 in the numerator was not distributed to the i term. Choice K is the result of two errors—the common error described in G and the error in J.

49. C
Category: Plane Geometry
Difficulty: Low
Getting to the Answer: One way to solve this problem is to make a table. Each time the number of sides goes up by 1, the sum of the angles goes up by 180°. Make a third column in the table to discover a relationship.

Number of Sides	Sum of the Angles	
3	180°	180° × 1
4	360°	180° × 2
5	540°	180° × 3
6	720°	180° × 4

Notice that to find the sum of the angles, you can multiply 180 times 2 less than the number of sides of the polygon. This is (C).

If you chose A, you may have just considered the triangle and assumed that the relationship was $60n$. If your answer was B, you may have noticed that the number of degrees rose by 180°, but this did not consider the sides of the polygons. Choice D is a relationship that works for the three-sided and six-sided polygons, but not the other two.

50. G
Category: Patterns, Logic, and Data
Difficulty: Medium
Getting to the Answer: The key to solving this problem is to first assume that there are no students who have both a cell phone and an MP3 player. If this were the case, then there would be $35 + 18 = 53$ students polled. The problem states that 50 students were polled, so therefore at least 3 students have both electronic devices. This is the minimum number of students who own both.

If you chose F, you may have ignored the fact that 50 students were polled. Choice H is the difference between the number of cell phone owners and MP3 owners. Choice J is a possible number of students who own *only* a cell phone. Choice K is the sum of 35 and 18.

51. A
Category: Variable Manipulation
Difficulty: Medium
Getting to the Answer: To solve this inequality, attempt to get the variable on one side of the inequality by adding $4n$ to both sides: $-4n + 4n + 3 > -4n + 4n + 1$. Combine like terms to get $3 > 1$. This inequality is always true for the set of real numbers.

If you chose answer B or C, you may have thought that the term $-4n$ would limit the set of solutions. If your answer was D or E, you may have mistakenly added $-4n$ to both sides and added 3 to both sides to get $-8n > 4$, and then solved for n.

52. H
Category: Patterns, Logic, and Data
Difficulty: High
Getting to the Answer: Make this question easier to visualize by naming the five people:

A B C D E

Now you only need to identify the number of different combinations.

AB, AC, AD, AE

BC, BD, BE

CD, CE

DE

There are 10 distinct combinations, meaning 10 total handshakes.

If you chose F, you may have seen that 4 people have 2 more handshakes than other people and assumed this was the pattern for more people. If you chose G, you may have thought that the pattern in handshakes was multiples of 3. The key is to have a clear way to visualize the information given.

53. D

Category: Proportions and Probability

Difficulty: Medium

Getting to the Answer: First, determine the percentage in the category Miscellaneous. The total percentage must sum to 100%, so the percentage for Miscellaneous is 100 − 23 − 5 − 22 −18 = 32%. To find the number of degrees in a circle graph that corresponds with 32%, set up the ratio, where x represents the number of degrees for the Miscellaneous category. Recall that there are 360° in a circle: $\frac{32}{100} = \frac{x}{360}$. Cross multiply to get 32 × 360 = 100x, or 11,520 = 100x. Divide both sides by 100 to get x = 115°, rounded to the nearest degree.

Choice A is a common trap that represents the percentage, not the number of degrees in a circle graph. If your answer was B, you thought that there were 180° in a circle. Choice C is the percentage of categories that are *not* Miscellaneous, and E is the number of degrees that are *not* Miscellaneous.

54. K

Category: Trigonometry

Difficulty: High

Getting to the Answer: The information $\frac{\pi}{2} < \theta < \pi$ tells you that the angle is in quadrant II of the coordinate plane. In quadrant II, the sin values are positive. So the answer must be positive. Eliminate F, G, and H. You are given the value of tan θ, which is the ratio of the opposite side to the adjacent side of a right triangle. Sketch this triangle, using leg lengths of 4 and 3:

This is a special right triangle, the 3-4-5 Pythagorean triple, so the hypotenuse is 5 units in length. The sin of an angle is the ratio of the length of the opposite side to the length of the hypotenuse, or $\frac{4}{5}$.

If you chose F, you may have ignored the fact that the angle is in quadrant II and thought that the sin value would be negative. Choice G is the cotangent of the angle. Choices H and J are cosine values for the angle for quadrants II and I, respectively.

55. A

Category: Coordinate Geometry

Difficulty: Medium

Getting to the Answer: Look at the graphed boundary lines for the inequalities. Find the equation for these boundary lines and then determine whether the shading represents less than or greater than these boundary lines. The horizontal line has a slope of 0 and a y-intercept (where the line crosses the y-axis) of 6, so the equation of this boundary line is $y = 6$. It is shaded below this line, so the inequality is $y < 6$. The slanted line has a slope with a change in y-values of 3 and a change in x-values of 1, so the slope is $\frac{3}{1} = 3$. The y-intercept is −5. The line is increasing, so the slope is positive. The shading is greater than, or above, this boundary line, so the inequality is $y > 3x − 5$. If you chose B, you fell into a common trap of interpreting the horizontal boundary line equation to be $x < 6$. Choice C is another common error, representing the idea that the shading represents less than, or below, the slanted line. Choice D interprets the slope as −3. Negative slopes decrease, or slant downward, when going from left to right. Choice E represents a slope of $\frac{1}{3}$, not the correct slope of 3. A slope of $\frac{1}{3}$ would mean for every change of 1 in the y-values, the x-values would change by 3.

56. J
Category: Variable Manipulation
Difficulty: High
Getting to the Answer: The question asks you to evaluate the function f(x), replacing x with ($x + c$). Replace any instance of x in the function definition with $x + c$. This means that $2(x + 7)$ will be $2(x + c + 7)$. Use the distributive property and multiply each term in parentheses by 2 to get $2x + 2c + 2 \times 7$, or $2x + 2c + 14$.

In F, the 2 was not distributed to the constant term 7. Choice G only multiplies the 2 by the first term in the parentheses. In H and K, the c term was just added onto the end of the function definition, instead of replacing the x with ($x + c$).

57. B
Category: Coordinate Geometry
Difficulty: Medium
Getting to the Answer: First, simplify the equation by simplifying the fraction on the right-hand side. Factor the numerator and then cancel the ($x - 2$) factor from the numerator and denominator:

$$\frac{2x^2 - 8}{x - 2} = \frac{2(x^2 - 4)}{x - 2} = \frac{2(x + 2)(x - 2)}{x - 2} = 2(x + 2)$$

The simplified equation is $y = 2(x + 2)$, or $y = 2x + 4$. This equation is now in slope-intercept form, where the y-intercept is 4 and the slope is $\frac{2}{1}$. Choice (B) is the correct graph because the line has a slope of 2 and crosses the y-axis at 4.

If you ignored the denominator in the given equation, then you incorrectly chose A, the graph of the quadratic $y = 2x^2 - 8$.

Choice C is the graph of the equation $y = \frac{1}{2}x + 4$. If this was your choice, you may have misinterpreted the slope of a line. Choice D is the graph of a quadratic function, not the correct linear function. You cannot assume a function is a quadratic just because you see a variable that is squared; you must first try

to simplify the equation. Choice E is the graph of the linear function $y = -2x + 4$.

58. F
Category: Coordinate Geometry
Difficulty: Medium
Getting to the Answer: This problem tests your knowledge of line reflections in the coordinate plane.

When you reflect a point or a figure over the y-axis, the x-coordinate of each point is the opposite sign, and the y-coordinate stays the same. The reflection of the point Q (r,s) after a reflection over the y-axis is therefore Q' ($-r,s$).

Choice G would be the result of a reflection over the y-axis, followed by a reflection over the x-axis. Choice H is incorrect—the x- and y-coordinates were switched. Choice J is a common trap that represents a reflection over the x-axis.

59. C
Category: Variable Manipulation
Difficulty: High
Getting to the Answer: The problem is asking what is the value of g in terms of h. The two given equations do not show a direct relationship between g and h, so you must solve for q in the second equation to get q in terms of h, and then substitute this value for q in the first equation. To solve for q in the second equation, isolate q by first adding 8 to both sides of the equation: $h + 8 = 2q - 8 + 8$, or $h + 8 = 2q$. Divide both sides by 2 to get $\frac{h + 8}{2} = q$.

Use this value of q in the first equation: $g = 4q + 3$ becomes $g = \frac{4(h + 8)}{2} + 3$.

Factor out a 2 from the numerator and the denominator of the first term to get $g = 2(h + 8) + 3$. Multiply the terms in parentheses by 2, so $g = 2h + 16 + 3$, or $g = 2h + 19$.

Choice A is the value of *q* in terms of *h* from the second equation. In B, the constant term 3 in the first equation was incorrectly added to the numerator of the transformed first equation, and the 4 was not distributed to both terms of *h* and 8. In D, the 2 was factored out correctly, but the remaining 2 was not distributed to the constant term of 8. Choice E is the value of *q*, not *h*, in terms of *g* from the first equation.

60. H
Category: Trigonometry
Difficulty: High
Getting to the Answer: In this problem, you are asked to use the formula $\cos(\alpha + \beta) = \cos(\alpha)\cos(\beta) - \sin(\alpha)\sin(\beta)$ and the table of values to find the value of $\cos(75°) = \cos(30° + 45°)$. Substitute 30° for α and 45° for β to get: $\cos(30°)\cos(45°) - \sin(30°)\sin(45°)$. Now use the table to replace each sin or cos with the corresponding values in the table: $\frac{\sqrt{3}}{2} \times \frac{\sqrt{2}}{2} - \frac{1}{2} \times \frac{\sqrt{2}}{2}$. Using order of operations, multiply and then subtract the numerators and keep the denominator: $\frac{\sqrt{6}}{4} - \frac{\sqrt{2}}{4} = \frac{\sqrt{6} - \sqrt{2}}{4}$. Alternately, you could use your calculator to find the value of the $\cos(75°) \approx 0.2588$, and then test each answer choice to find the answer closest to this value. Choice (H) will be the only value to equal the $\cos(75°)$.

If you chose F or K, you probably used the wrong values in the table. In G, you used the wrong values in the table and also forgot to multiply the denominators, resulting in a denominator of 2 instead of 4. Choice J is a common trap—you correctly used the table but did not multiply the denominators to get a denominator of 4.

READING TEST

PASSAGE I

1. D
Category: Inference
Difficulty: Medium
Getting to the Answer: The question is asking about Dave's opinion specifically. Throughout the passage, Dave describes the problems with comparison between twins, and many of his comments to Emily are also focused on comparing himself to his twin. Choice (D) is correct because it mentions this competition and implies that it makes their relationship more difficult. Choice A is extreme, B implies that their relationship is stronger than it is, and C is not supported by the text because Emily doesn't seem to be able to convince Dave to make more of an effort.

2. H
Category: Detail
Difficulty: Low
Getting to the Answer: Emily has a good relationship with both brothers; she has an enjoyable conversation with Bruce and works to make Dave feel better. Also, she wants the brothers to be closer than they are. Because it reflects these details, (H) is the correct answer. Choice F is the opposite; Emily is very attentive, and G and J are both extreme and negative distortions of Emily's desire to help relations between the brothers.

3. B
Category: Detail
Difficulty: Medium
Getting to the Answer: This question is asking you to identify which answer choice is NOT represented in the passage, so the first step is to eliminate choices that ARE contained in the passage. In the first paragraph, Dave is envious of the reaction his wife has when talking to Bruce, eliminating A. The paragraph about Dave's reaction to the picture

captures his negative feelings regarding the difference in their popularity, eliminating C. The final conversation shows Dave as doubtful of Bruce's need for his approval, eliminating D. This leaves (B), which is not found in the passage and is therefore the correct answer.

4. J
Category: Function
Difficulty: Medium
Getting to the Answer: The first paragraph starts with a description of Emily on the phone, but the focus quickly shifts to Dave's reaction. It then moves to Dave making some points about his brother's popularity and questioning whether his own wife has ever reacted so favorably to him. Choice (J) summarizes this well. Choices F and H are not found in the passage, and G occurs much later.

5. D
Category: Inference
Difficulty: High
Getting to the Answer: Emily attempts to make Dave believe that he is important to Bruce, but Dave still feels he is in Bruce's shadow. It is unclear whether or not Dave entirely believes Emily, but when she brings up Bruce's desire to talk about the brothers' childhood, Dave's response suggests that he does not want to talk about it because it again reminds him of how Bruce has always been the more popular of the two. This makes (D) the correct answer. Choice A is out of scope; the passage does not suggest that Dave does anything to spite Emily. Choice B is incorrect because Dave does not feel guilty; he sees Bruce's success as proof that it doesn't matter whether he calls Bruce or not. Choice C is out of scope; Dave's reasons for not calling Bruce have to do with his feelings toward his brother, not any feelings related to Emily.

6. H
Category: Detail
Difficulty: Medium
Getting to the Answer: In lines 39–45, Dave explicitly talks about how Bruce's image has positive aspects (vitality) that his image lacks. This is a perfect match for (H), which restates this generally. Choices F and J are not found in the passage, and G is contradicted by the fact that both Dave and Emily can tell the difference between the twins.

7. B
Category: Inference
Difficulty: Medium
Getting to the Answer: Dave is uncomfortable at this point, because Emily is clearly thinking about Bruce. The previous paragraph describes the picture as a source of insecurity for Dave, suggesting that he is nervous and seeking reassurance that Emily is with him for reasons other than his connection to Bruce. Only (B) describes these feelings. Choice A is the opposite of what Dave is feeling, and neither C nor D can be deduced from the information in the passage.

8. F
Category: Inference
Difficulty: Medium
Getting to the Answer: With an open-ended question like this, the answer choices must be individually tested. Choice (F) can be logically deduced, especially from the last exchange: Emily mentions that Bruce tells her stories about their childhood, and when Dave makes a comment about Bruce's popularity, Emily responds that "[Bruce] doesn't look at it that way" (line 115). This suggests that there is a difference between each brother's childhood stories. Choice G is too extreme and better describes the reaction other people have to the different professions of Bruce and Dave. Choice H is also too extreme: Dave feels competitive with Bruce, but that does not imply that they have fought. Choice J is not

supported by the text; their childhood is the only time when it is stated that they spent time together.

9. C

Category: Detail

Difficulty: High

Getting to the Answer: Dave and Emily have different opinions regarding the picture. Dave is displeased with his image, while Emily professes to like his smile. However, Dave describes Bruce's smile as "trademark" (line 43), and Emily says that Bruce looks "exactly the same" (lines 60–61) in every picture. This makes (C) correct. Choices A and D depict opinions that are strictly Dave's and Emily's, respectively, and B is not supported by the passage at all.

10. F

Category: Inference

Difficulty: Medium

Getting to the Answer: Emily follows her comment about Bruce's stories by dismissing Dave's comment about Bruce's popularity, saying that Bruce "doesn't look at it that way" (line 115). Her response is in reaction to Dave's frequent comments suggesting that Bruce has been more successful socially and Dave's implication that Bruce feels superior to Dave. This matches (F), which correctly restates this idea. Choice G is not supported by the passage; H is opposite because Emily wants Dave to focus less on his brother's successes; and J is extreme, because Bruce wants more attention from his brother but is not necessarily lonely.

PASSAGE II

11. C

Category: Generalization

Difficulty: Medium

Getting to the Answer: The author is critical of the media throughout the passage and focuses mostly on ways in which the current media is not concerned enough with factual accuracy. Choice (C) matches this nicely. Choice A is too extreme; the author talks about distorting facts, not making them

up. Choice B contradicts paragraph 3, which characterizes some news personalities as "demagogues" with biased views. Choice D contradicts paragraph 4; the public's desire for this type of news is one of the reasons for its existence.

12. G

Category: Inference

Difficulty: High

Getting to the Answer: In paragraph 3, the author mentions how impartial stories can sway the opinions of readers through headlines rather than content. Choices H and J both mention headlines, but H makes the opposite point, and J is far too specific, using the example as a basis for a point that the author does not explicitly make. Choice F is contradicted by the passage. Choice (G) is general, but correct: the headline is another method used to sensationalize the story, as illustrated by the example of the "enraged public" (line 55) versus the "irked locals" (lines 58–59).

13. B

Category: Function

Difficulty: Medium

Getting to the Answer: The sentence preceding the Walter Cronkite example states that audience members expected to have complicated events explained to them; the Cronkite example follows this logic. Choice (B) matches this perfectly. Choice A may be inferred, but it is not the point the author is making—the author's concern is the treatment of the news, not specific news personalities. This reasoning also eliminates C. Choice D is never mentioned in or suggested by the passage.

14. F

Category: Inference

Difficulty: Medium

Getting to the Answer: In order to research this statement, it is a good idea to look back at paragraph 4 because it discusses the public. "Personal consensus" applies to the author's point about people looking for news reported by someone with a political opinion similar to their own. Choice (F) matches this. Choices G and J are both contradicted by information given in paragraph 4. Choice H is not supported by the passage and contradicts the author's main point.

15. B
Category: Detail
Difficulty: High
Getting to the Answer: In paragraph 1, the author states that in stories of "continued national interest" (lines 10–11), the focus shifts from facts to "theater" (line 12). Choice (B) is the best match. Choices A, C, and D are not explicitly mentioned as more or less likely to be sensationalized.

16. J
Category: Vocab-in-Context
Difficulty: Medium
Getting to the Answer: The sentence describes objective reporting as a "distant possibility." Questions like this are easier if you pick a word that means the same thing in context. In this case, you can predict *improbable* or something similar. This matches (J) perfectly. Choices F, G, and H do not address the likelihood of objective reporting.

17. C
Category: Writer's View
Difficulty: Medium
Getting to the Answer: The author is most likely to criticize a headline that sensationalizes or makes a value judgment, and the end of paragraph 3 gives an example. Choices A, B, and D are all basically factual and specific. Choice (C) is correct because it refers to a very broad group, like the example in paragraph 3 does, makes a value judgment by calling the song offensive, and uses emotional language.

18. J
Category: Detail
Difficulty: Low
Getting to the Answer: The fourth paragraph focuses on the flaws of the public and states that individuals who agree with certain politically biased hosts are unlikely to question the validity of the "facts" presented. This matches (J) perfectly. Choices F and G are not explicitly stated by the author. Choice H describes accuracy problems for the media, not the public.

19. A
Category: Detail
Difficulty: Medium
Getting to the Answer: The author makes the point that fact-based news only captures a small minority of the news audience. Also, the beginning of paragraph 4 states that the public is not interested in dry facts. Choice (A) can be inferred because the media companies are providing the type of programs that the public seems to want. Choice B is extreme—in fact, it could be inferred that if the greater public was interested in objective facts, the media (including cable) would provide programs of that sort. Choices C and D cannot be deduced from the passage; the author seems to believe that factual news will not draw a large audience no matter what.

20. G
Category: Inference
Difficulty: Low
Getting to the Answer: Because this question deals with the audience, paragraph 4 is a good place to look. The author states that audience members look for hosts who share their political opinions. Choice (G) is a general restatement of this idea, so it is correct. Choice F is not stated in the passage. Choice H distorts a detail from the last paragraph; audience members prefer short to lengthy, but there is no statement about audience members gravitating toward the shortest or simplest stories.

Choice J misuses the detail about headlines from paragraph 3.

PASSAGE III

21. C
Category: Generalization
Difficulty: Medium
Getting to the Answer: You should have already noted the main ideas of the passages, so all you need to do here is think about what statements could hinder the main idea of Passage A. The main idea of Passage A is that Joyce, despite, or even because of, the specific local detail in his work, has managed to create works of universal truth and appeal. Predict that the correct choice will somehow suggest a lack of ability to generate such widespread appeal. Choice A is a misused detail; though this author briefly mentions historical events in novels, the idea is not at all central to his point. Choice B is opposite; this might actually help the author's point, as it speaks to universal human ideals. Choice D is opposite; as is the case with B, this statement might actually help the author's point.

22. J
Category: Inference
Difficulty: Medium
Getting to the Answer: Use a paraphrase as your prediction, but keep in mind that the answer choices may be written in more general language. Here, the quoted phrase talks about escaping the boundaries of time and place to concentrate on greater truths that are independent of these factors. Expect to find a similar paraphrase among the answer choices. Choice F is opposite; the author is talking about revealing universal truths, not "specific" details. Choice G is out of scope; this author never claims that Joyce wrote in such a way as to "obscure information." Choice H is a distortion; although "ignoring setting" gets close to the right idea, focusing on "character" is not under discussion at this point.

23. C
Category: Inference
Difficulty: High
Getting to the Answer: When a question is phrased in this way, paraphrase the author's main point in the quoted lines to make a prediction. Remember that the answer choices may be phrased in more general language. Here, the author claims that Joyce's level of detail actually helps his work achieve greater appeal. Use such a paraphrase as the basis for your prediction. Choice A is a misused detail; though Dublin's "geography" is discussed earlier, it is not the main focus of discussion at this point in the passage. Choice B is opposite; the author of Passage A mostly describes Joyce's subject matter as mundane. Choice D is a distortion; though Dublin could perhaps be an "exotic locale" to some, this is not the point the author is making here.

24. F
Category: Detail
Difficulty: Medium
Getting to the Answer: One of the main criticisms in the first paragraph of Passage B is that Joyce's subject matter is more base and common than that of earlier authors. Use this idea as the foundation for your prediction. Choice G is out of scope; the author of Passage B never questions Joyce's factual knowledge. Choice H is opposite; if anything, Passage B argues that Joyce is too unlike his predecessors. Choice J is out of scope; the author of Passage B never makes claims about the elegance of Joyce's prose.

25. D
Category: Inference
Difficulty: Medium
Getting to the Answer: This is a fairly straightforward question; to make your prediction, just summarize the author's main point in the given sentence. In the final sentence, the author makes the claim that Joyce possessed the skill to have become a great writer, had he lived in an era more conducive to dignified writing. Use this as your

prediction. Choice A is out of scope; such a claim is never made in the passage and particularly not in the final sentence. Choice B is out of scope; this passage never mentions Joyce's need to "revise" his novels. Choice C is opposite; actually, the author suggests that Joyce's prose style was sufficiently strong and that all he needed was more refined subject matter.

26. F
Category: Vocab-in-Context
Difficulty: Medium
Getting to the Answer: Don't be fooled by familiar words; the challenge of questions like this is in the particular context, not the vocabulary itself. Here, the author uses "base" to describe crude details Joyce often includes, so you should predict something such as *indecent,* which matches (F), unrefined. Choice G is a distortion because it refers to the primary definition of the word. Choice H is a misused detail, referring to the phrase "virtually nauseating" later in the paragraph. Choice J is opposite; the author of Passage B is critical of Joyce's tendency to discuss unrefined activities.

27. B
Category: Inference
Difficulty: High
Getting to the Answer: Passage B criticizes Joyce for failing to provide enlightenment for readers, but Passage A has a favorable opinion of Joyce. The author of Passage A discusses how Joyce's works are globally appealing, which matches (B). Choice A is out of scope because Passage A does not discuss the level of enlightenment provided by older works. Choice C is opposite; the author of Passage A believes that Joyce's inclusion of details enhances his writing. Choice D is out of scope because Passage A does not address philosophical questions.

28. H
Category: Inference
Difficulty: Medium
Getting to the Answer: Although the question stem asks you to compare the passages, all you really have to do is summarize each author's opinion separately. Passage A is generally favorable towards Joyce, commending him for evoking many universal truths, while Passage B is mostly unfavorable, viewing him as undignified. Use this as the basis for your prediction. Choice F is opposite; the author of Passage A actually considers Joyce a great author, and "inaccuracy" is not really a criticism that Passage B employs. Choice G is opposite; similarly, this is incorrect because the author of Passage A promotes Joyce's "significance" as a writer. Choice J is a distortion; while Author B does mention Joyce's skill, Author A never laments any aspect of the writing nor deems it "irrelevant."

29. B
Category: Detail
Difficulty: Low
Getting to the Answer: Keep in mind the authors' general attitudes towards Joyce as you assess their tones at these particular points in the passages. In Passage A, the author is complementing the great degree of detail Joyce uses in describing Dublin, whereas the author of Passage B is expressing disgust at having to read the details of what he considers vulgar or insignificant acts. Use these tones as the basis for your predictions. Choice (B) is correct; this matches the perspectives of the authors. Choice A is a distortion; although both choices here get the general charge right, neither word is quite appropriate to the specific tone of each author. Choice C is a distortion; again, this choice gets the general positive/negative aspects of tone right, but the specifics aren't a good match with each author's attitude. Choice D is opposite; "glee" is contrary to the second author's tone.

30. G

Category: Inference

Difficulty: High

Getting to the Answer: The correct choice is likely to involve Passage B's main claim about Joyce's undignified writing. Choice (G) is correct; Passage B argues that Joyce's writing was not exemplary. Choice F is opposite; both authors agree that Joyce was of Irish descent. Choice H is out of scope; the author of Passage B is rarely complementary to Joyce, making this an unlikely choice. Choice J is out of scope; a "mystic" is someone concerned with religion or the occult, a choice inappropriate for either passage's discussion.

PASSAGE IV

31. B

Category: Inference

Difficulty: Medium

Getting to the Answer: The passage is most concerned with discrediting the myth that rattlesnakes are aggressive and very dangerous, and the selection refers to exactly that: the "sinister opportunist" is the myth, while the "mild-mannered domestic" is closer to fact. Choice (B) can be deduced from this. Choice A is incorrect, as juvenile snakes are not even mentioned. Choice C misuses the detail about rattlesnakes giving live birth, which is not treated as a recent discovery. Choice D is too extreme; the author describes rattlesnakes as fairly docile but not entirely predictable.

32. F

Category: Inference

Difficulty: Low

Getting to the Answer: At the end of paragraph 6, the author states that the reputation is good because a frightened and cornered rattlesnake is dangerous. Choice (F) fits this because if people did not avoid or move away from rattlesnakes, there would be more dangerous interaction between humans and snakes. Choices G and J are contradicted by the passage; in rattlesnake roundups, their reputation costs the snakes their lives, and the

author, who is aware of their docile nature, would certainly never believe a rattlesnake should be a pet. Choice H misuses the detail about snakebite deaths.

33. C

Category: Detail

Difficulty: Medium

Getting to the Answer: The passage gives quite a few examples of the social behavior of rattlesnakes, so be prepared to find a restated fact among the answer choices. Choice (C) fits this nicely, because the second paragraph states that rattlesnakes have been known to hibernate with tortoises. Choice A is not a social behavior. Choice B goes beyond the text; the wrestling is used to claim a mate, but the losing snake will leave, rather than take a place within a hierarchy. Choice D also misuses a detail; rattlesnakes are described as "entirely noncannibalistic" (line 24), meaning they never eat other snakes.

34. H

Category: Inference

Difficulty: Medium

Getting to the Answer: The mythology referred to is that of the heartless, aggressive rattlesnake. This relates to rattlesnake roundups (line 113) to which the author clearly objects, so it would follow that the author sees this particular human behavior as heartless and aggressive. Choice (H) matches this perfectly, and the statistical comparison in paragraph 7 supports this. Choice F contradicts the author's belief that rattlesnakes are not as dangerous as commonly thought. Choices G and J do not relate to the point the author is making.

35. C

Category: Detail

Difficulty: Medium

Getting to the Answer: The sixth paragraph states that serious bites can usually be traced to people who either handle or step on snakes, in contrast to those who were not engaging the snakes. Choice (C) fits this nicely, specifically focusing on those handling snakes as an example of individuals purposefully seeking interaction. Choice A is incorrect because a relationship is mentioned. Choice B is not mentioned in the text. Choice D is a distortion because rattlesnakes deliver venom based on how threatened they feel, not necessarily based on how threatening humans act.

36. H
Category: Inference
Difficulty: High
Getting to the Answer: The selection's sentence starts with describing the docile behavior of rattlesnakes, as a follow-up to scientific findings in the previous paragraph. The implication is that snakes, while not as dangerous as often thought, can still be dangerous. Choice (H) matches this perfectly. Choice F is outside the scope of the passage; there is no mention of herpetologists keeping snakes. Choice G misuses a later detail; the author is not comparing the rattlesnake as a pet to dogs. Choice J states a comparison that is never made.

37. B
Category: Detail
Difficulty: Medium
Getting to the Answer: In paragraph 5, the author lists various statistics and states that dogs, bees, and lightning are all responsible for more annual deaths than rattlesnakes and that the fer-de-lance is responsible for substantially more. Choice (B) is the only answer that fits; every other choice is contradicted by the facts given.

38. J
Category: Detail
Difficulty: Medium
Getting to the Answer: In paragraph 6, the author explains that the rattlesnake knows that it needs its venom for food and goes on to state that the only situation in which a rattlesnake would release all of its venom is when it feels threatened. Choice (J) fits with this; the rattlesnake wishes to conserve its venom, specifically for prey. Choice F is incorrect because humans are large in comparison and

receive mostly "dry" bites. Choice G contradicts the statement about rattlesnakes potentially using all their venom if threatened. Choice H contradicts the statement that rattlesnakes are not aware of the well-being of nonfood sources.

39. B
Category: Inference
Difficulty: High
Getting to the Answer: The author examines two pieces of contradictory logic. The first is that the organizers use the reputation of the rattlesnake to promote interest but rely on the more docile nature of the snakes to manage the event. The second is the fact that most of the snakes are taken from areas without people and put into contact with people, thus creating a more dangerous situation. Choice (B) matches the second piece of information. Choice A is not stated as fact in the text. Choice C brings up erroneous statistics, but organizers use the rattlesnake's erroneous reputation. Choice D is not mentioned in the passage.

40. G
Category: Vocab-in-Context
Difficulty: Medium
Getting to the Answer: The answer lies in the last sentence, which speculates on the status of humans in rattlesnake folklore "if [rattlesnakes] were able to speak or write." This makes it clear that *crotalid* must have something to do with actual rattlesnakes. Choice (G) is the only choice that fits because the sentence is mocking the way that humans have characterized rattlesnakes within human mythology. Choices F, H, and J all are incorrect because they mention groups that are not specifically rattlesnakes.

SCIENCE TEST

PASSAGE I

1. C
Category: Patterns
Difficulty: High
Getting to the Answer: Be careful of extreme language, such as the use of *always* in A and B. While the general trend is that decreasing glacier length corresponds to decreasing calving rate, the opposite is true at the sharp peak in calving rate at around 1,500 years, which (C) correctly describes.

2. H
Category: Figure Interpretation
Difficulty: Low
Getting to the Answer: This question asks you to find the glacier with the largest calving rate for years 6–10 in Table 1. Make sure you are looking in the right place, which in this case is the far right column of Table 1.

3. A
Category: Patterns
Difficulty: Medium
Getting to the Answer: This question requires a little deeper understanding of the data presented in Table 1. For all four glaciers during both time periods, the calving rate is slightly greater than or equal to the average velocity. To predict the calving rate of a glacier with a velocity of 80 m/yr, you must look for glaciers traveling at similar velocities. The closest values come from glaciers A and C during years 1–5, which had velocities of 72 m/yr and 98 m/yr, respectively. The corresponding calving rates for these two glaciers are 72 m/yr and 106 m/yr. The correct answer should fall within this range, as described by (A).

4. J
Category: Figure Interpretation
Difficulty: Medium
Getting to the Answer: With open-ended questions like this one, a simple process of elimination is usually most efficient. Comparison of each choice with the data in Table 1 reveals that only (J) accurately reflects the "behavior of the glaciers."

5. B
Category: Figure Interpretation
Difficulty: Medium
Getting to the Answer: Don't be too concerned with the strange scale of the horizontal axis of each choice. The values on the axis correspond exactly to the calving rates for years 6–10 given in Table 1. Simply find the graph that correctly plots the four points given by the data in the last two columns of Table 1.

6. H
Category: Scientific Reasoning
Difficulty: Low
Getting to the Answer: The meteorologists in Study 3 hypothesized that high temperatures cause rapid variations in velocity and calving rate. Figure 1 shows a rapid change in calving rate at around 1,500 years. If the hypothesis is true, then the glacier modeled in Study 1 experienced a rapid change in temperature approximately 1,500 years ago, and (H) is correct.

7. B
Category: Figure Interpretation
Difficulty: Low
Getting to the Answer: The question is asking you to identify two data points—the glacier length and calving rate—in Figure 1. To get to the answer, find 1,500 years on the *x*-axis and draw a vertical line. Find where the vertical line intersects with glacier length curve and trace back to the *y*-axis on the left hand side to find that the glacier length is 23. You can eliminate A and D. Find the point where

the calving rate line intersects with the vertical line that was drawn, and trace over to the *y*-axis on the right hand side to find that the calving rate is approximately 125. Therefore, (B) is correct.

PASSAGE II

8. H
Category: Scientific Reasoning
Difficulty: Low
Getting to the Answer: The question states that the air filters greatly reduce rhinitis symptoms and asks which month would have the greatest decrease in the number of allergic rhinitis cases. To get to the answer, look at Table 1 and count the total number of cases associated with the four months in the answer choices. September has the greatest number of cases. Therefore, (H) is correct.

9. C
Category: Figure Interpretation
Difficulty: Low
Getting to the Answer: Sometimes, you will be asked to simply read information directly from a graph. If you are careful to refer to the right part of the right graph, you will find correct answers to these kinds of questions very quickly. The bar for March 2 on Figure 1 rises to approximately 1,500 gr/m³, (C).

10. H
Category: Patterns
Difficulty: Medium
Getting to the Answer: You are asked to describe a trend in the data in Figure 1 beyond the high value given for November 5. After this value, the data maintain no discernible trend, but they do stay within a relatively small range of values, as is correctly described in (H).

11. B
Category: Figure Interpretation
Difficulty: Low
Getting to the Answer: Be careful to answer the correct question. "Increased the most" doesn't necessarily mean the count increased to its largest value, which is the trap set in C. Choice D is also a trap, set for those who refer to the wrong figure.

12. F
Category: Figure Interpretation
Difficulty: Medium
Getting to the Answer: This question asks about the tree pollen count shown in Figure 1. Process of elimination reveals that only (F) correctly reflects the data shown in the figure.

13. A
Category: Figure Interpretation
Difficulty: Low
Getting to the Answer: You are finally asked to refer to the rather complicated Table 1. Find the row for the month of May, and look for the corresponding column(s) containing the most reported cases of allergic rhinitis. In this case, that means the most ❀ symbols. Tree and grass pollen account for six of the nine total ❀ symbols in the May row and indeed constitute most of the cases.

PASSAGE III

14. G
Category: Figure Interpretation
Difficulty: Medium
Getting to the Answer: Notice that in Figure 3, the lines plotted for Springs B, C, and D intersect at approximately the same mass. The exact mass value is not completely clear from the figure, but it is definitely larger than F and smaller than H, which leaves (G) as the only possibility.

15. A
Category: Figure Interpretation
Difficulty: Medium
Getting to the Answer: According to Figure 1, oscillation frequency does indeed decrease with increasing arm length, so you can eliminate C and D. The second part of B is simply false, which leaves only (A).

16. F
Category: Scientific Reasoning
Difficulty: Medium
Getting to the Answer: This question requires a couple of steps of logic. First, you must realize what *slowly* means in terms of oscillation frequency. Recall from the passage that oscillation frequency is measured in "oscillations per second." The faster the spring oscillates, the more oscillations it will complete per second. Therefore, you are looking for the spring with the lowest value for oscillation frequency, which is Spring A.

17. C
Category: Figure Interpretation
Difficulty: Medium
Getting to the Answer: Refer to the line plotted for Spring A in Figure 3. On that line, a mass of 700 g corresponds to an equilibrium length of just less than 40 cm. Only (C) includes this estimate.

18. J
Category: Patterns
Difficulty: High
Getting to the Answer: According to Figure 2, an oscillation frequency of 1.4 Hz at a mass of 100 g would be represented by a data point that would fall in between the frequency values for Spring C and Spring D at that mass. Only H and (J) place Spring E correctly between Springs C and D, and (J) correctly lists the springs in order of *decreasing* oscillation frequency.

19. C
Category: Scientific Reasoning
Difficulty: High
Getting to the Answer: The effects of mass are not mentioned in Experiment 1. Only the pendulum arm length affects the oscillation frequency, so the plots for the original mass and the larger mass should be identical, as in (C).

20. H
Category: Figure Interpretation
Difficulty: Low
Getting to the Answer: Figure 1 shows the relationship between arm length and oscillation frequency. To find the corresponding arm length, draw a line from 0.35 on the y-axis to the curve. At the point of intersection, draw a line down to the x-axis. The line will be closer to 20 than 15, which is why the correct answer is 19 cm, (H).

PASSAGE IV

21. D
Category: Figure Interpretation
Difficulty: Low
Getting to the Answer: Make sure you refer to the correct part of Table 1 for the enzyme concentration values of populations ha 1, ha 2, and ha 3. The table shows that for all three high-altitude populations, GST levels are highest, CR levels are lowest, and ECH levels are intermediate. Only (D) does not violate this relationship.

22. G
Category: Figure Interpretation
Difficulty: Low
Getting to the Answer: The process of elimination works best here. Choice F is not universally true; the oxygen saturation percentages are pretty similar for high-altitude and sea-level dwellers. Neither Table 1 nor Figure 1 shows a comparison between high- or low-altitude populations and temperature or partial

oxygen pressure, so H and J cannot be correct. Only (G) is directly supported by the values in the table.

23. C
Category: Figure Interpretation
Difficulty: Medium
Getting to the Answer: The answer to this question comes directly from Figure 1, but you must be careful to not confuse the two data sets. You can draw a horizontal line from 110 mm Hg on the left vertical axis until it intersects with the oxygen partial pressure data (squares). That intersection happens at about 3,200 m. To find the temperature at this altitude, draw a horizontal line from the temperature plot (circles) at 3,200 m to the right axis. It intersects at between –5°C and –10°C, meaning the correct answer must be (C). Accidentally reversing the two data sets likely results in selecting trap answer A.

24. H
Category: Figure Interpretation
Difficulty: Medium
Getting to the Answer: You are asked to find the highest ECH concentration for any of the six populations, which occurs for population ha 2.

25. A
Category: Scientific Reasoning
Difficulty: High
Getting to the Answer: Only (A) and C agree with the information in Table 1. You can eliminate C, though, because nothing in the passage or data suggests that CR concentration has anything to do with efficiency at incorporating oxygen into the blood.

26. J
Category: Scientific Reasoning
Difficulty: High
Getting to the Answer: The question is asking you to identify the relationship between altitude and enzyme levels, and then predict the levels for an intermediate population. The population at 1,500-1,800 m (intermediate) is located between sea level and high altitude. When comparing GST between the sea-level and high-level populations, GST is higher for the high-altitude populations. It's safe to assume that the intermediate population would have a GST level higher than the sea level and lower than the high-altitude populations. Therefore, F, G, and H can be eliminated. Double-check EST and CR values to confirm that (J) is correct.

PASSAGE V

27. D
Category: Scientific Reasoning
Difficulty: Medium
Getting to the Answer: Recall that Student 1 credits pressure for the freezing phenomenon. Choices B and C reflect elements of the viewpoint of Student 2 and can therefore be eliminated. If A were true, the temperature and pressure effects would work against each other, so only (D) makes sense.

28. G
Category: Scientific Reasoning
Difficulty: Low
Getting to the Answer: According to Student 1, pressure causes the ice to melt, and pressure increases with increasing weight. Student 2 states that friction causes the ice to melt and that the force of friction increases with increasing weight. Therefore, the students would agree that ice would melt faster under the heavier skater, as in (G).

29. A
Category: Scientific Reasoning
Difficulty: Medium
Getting to the Answer: In the explanation of Student 2, ice melts when heat is generated as the skater overcomes the force of friction by *moving* across the ice. If the skater is not moving, then no heat should be generated. Student 1, though, explains that ice melts due to pressure, which is

present whether or not the skater is moving, making (A) correct.

30. H
Category: Scientific Reasoning
Difficulty: Medium
Getting to the Answer: Student 2 explains that less dense materials float above more dense materials. Because the frozen ethanol remains below the liquid ethanol, (H) must be true.

31. C
Category: Scientific Reasoning
Difficulty: Low
Getting to the Answer: You can eliminate A and B due to the mention of pressure in both, which is a concept only Student 1 contemplates. Student 2 describes floating as the case in which the buoyant force exceeds the force of gravity, so the sinking boat is evidence of the opposite situation, as described in (C).

32. G
Category: Scientific Reasoning
Difficulty: Medium
Getting to the Answer: Eliminate F because only Student 1 considers pressure, and eliminate J because the only possible support for this explanation also comes from Student 1. Eliminate H because the force of gravity will only change as the mass of the skater changes. Student 2 states that heat is produced by overcoming friction, so less friction would mean less heat, as in (G).

33. A
Category: Scientific Reasoning
Difficulty: Medium
Getting to the Answer: Recall that the viewpoint of Student 2 focuses on a difference in *density*, and eliminate C. Choices B and D both actually mean the same thing, but the term *buoyant* is included in D to entice the unwary test taker. In either case, the balloon would remain on the ground. The less

dense balloon described in (A) would indeed rise above the ground.

34. F
Category: Scientific Reasoning
Difficulty: Medium
Getting to the Answer: To get to the answer, focus on the relationship between measured and corrected conductivity in Table 1. The measured data demonstrates that there is conductivity in the sample solutions even when F^- is not present. Subtracting the intrinsic conductivity allows the scientist to better see how much conductivity is due to just F^-. Choice H is out of scope, because the passage does not mention the presence of impurities, and non-ionic molecules do not conduct electricity. Choice J is also incorrect because the question states that Na_2SiF_6 is already in solution. The data is normalized after it has been collected, so it would not be used to calibrate the electrodynamic cells.

35. C
Category: Patterns
Difficulty: Low
Getting to the Answer: Either Table 1 or Figure 1 can provide the answer here. Table 1 contains numerical examples of cases where the F^- concentration is indeed doubled (from 0.5 mg/L to 1 mg/L, for example) and gives the corresponding change in conductivity. Taking care to look in the *corrected* conductivity column, you can see that 2 times the concentration results in 2 times the corrected conductivity. Likewise, Figure 1 makes it clear that relationship between the two quantities is linear, which means that any multiplication of the concentration results in the same multiplication of the conductivity.

36. J
Category: Figure Interpretation
Difficulty: Medium
Getting to the Answer: Compare the new conductivity value to those given in Table 2, specifically those for Newtown and Lakewood, and recall

the direct relationship between conductivity and F⁻ concentration. Noticing that Bluewater's conductivity value lies between the values for Newtown and Lakewood allows you to eliminate F and G. Taking care to list the towns in order of *increasing* F⁻ leads you to (J).

37. C
Category: Patterns
Difficulty: Medium
Getting to the Answer: Refer to Table 1 to see where a value of 3.0 mg/L would fit in. This new concentration is between the 2.0 mg/L and 4.0 mg/L values given in the table, so the corrected conductivity should lie between 3.34 µS/cm and 6.68 µS/cm. Choices B and D are too close to the extremes of this range, but (C) is exactly in the middle as it should be. Alternatively, you could read the corrected conductivity for a concentration of 3.0 mg/L directly from Figure 1.

38. F
Category: Scientific Reasoning
Difficulty: Medium
Getting to the Answer: Questions that ask you to change the procedure of an experiment usually require you to review the original experiment before answering. In this case, the description of Experiment 1 tells you that F⁻ is added in the form of dissolved Na_2SiF_6. To study Cl⁻ concentrations, the students must use a chemical that contains Cl⁻ when preparing the solutions, as in (F).

39. B
Category: Scientific Reasoning
Difficulty: Low
Getting to the Answer: Experimental data are not required to answer this question. The last sentence of the description of Experiment 1 explains that the corrected conductivity is calculated by *subtracting* the measured conductivity of the blank solution. This always results in the corrected conductivity being less than the measured conductivity, as in (B).

40. F
Category: Scientific Reasoning
Difficulty: Medium
Getting to the Answer: You are told that Cl⁻ results in an increase in conductivity, and the data show that F⁻ results in an increase in conductivity. Therefore, in a solution containing both F⁻ and Cl⁻, it would be impossible to distinguish the contributions to conductivity from each ion given only conductivity measurements. Conductivity would be increased by the presence of Cl⁻, and the apparent values for F⁻ concentration would be falsely high, as in (F). If you miss this point, you could at least eliminate J because the question asks only about the case where *all* of the samples have Cl⁻ concentrations. The effect of the Cl⁻ should not be different for different solutions.

WRITING TEST

MODEL ESSAY

Below is an example of what a high-scoring essay might look like. Notice that the author states her position clearly in the introductory paragraph and supports that position with evidence in the following paragraphs. The essay also uses transitions, some advanced vocabulary, and an effective "hook" to draw in the reader.

Teachers often tell us that learning is fun, and the best way to convince us that learning is enjoyable is to give us activities that keep us engaged (and awake). The issue here is whether teachers should provide more hands-on learning experiences because doing so would help all students learn and remember better. On the other hand, others say that it's possible to learn without doing and that schools should use their money for other educational purposes rather than trying to make everything hands-on learning. I believe that the best learning comes from hands-on work.

I know from experience that I learn better when I can actually *do* something myself. When students do projects such as growing plants, they really learn about the science because they are part of making that science work. This is analogous to learning how to ride a bike. A child can read about it, watch videos on it and even watch someone actually ride a bike, but he doesn't learn how to do it until he gets on a bike and pedals away. Thus, it is important that the teacher provide opportunities for students to do as much hands-on learning as possible. However, those who think that students don't learn anything unless they actually *do* it are wrong. There are ideas that can't be experimented with. How can students re-create the Big Bang or evolution? But just because they can't actually do this doesn't mean students don't learn. There is a lot that can be learned from reading and learning from experts. However, if there is a choice between learning by doing and not having that opportunity, learning by doing is the better way to teach and learn.

On the other hand, other people think that experiential education is important only for students who will work in a career that requires that they do things themselves, such as engineering and technology. It is important that students who will enter careers that are skill based have the opportunity to practice this in school. School is supposed to teach what is needed for students later in life, and knowing how to do experiments or re-create what others have done should be part of this. But the people who argue for this say it is important only for students who will need it in their future careers. This means that some students, particularly those who don't know what career they want, will not get the benefit of hands-on experiences. That splits students into two groups: those who learn by doing and those who don't. All students learn well by doing, so it would not be fair to offer it only to some students. How can teachers know what is appropriate for students in their future careers if even the students don't yet know? This solution is not a good one because it assumes things that can't be supported.

Finally, it is shortsighted to argue that rather than create opportunities for hands-on learning, schools should spend their money on other things because learning by doing is expensive and may not be good for all students. There's always the problem that not all students learn in the same way so there's no one kind of learning that is best for everyone. But that doesn't mean teachers shouldn't provide hands-on opportunities. Actually, this is a good way to reach all students because it involves working with your hands, maybe some reading and talking too, and critical thinking, so it uses lots of ways of learning. It is foolish to have the opportunity to do something important and not do it just because some people may not benefit from it or it will cost money. Teachers should give students the opportunity to learn in a hands-on way as much as possible.

In the real world, when we need to learn something new, like how to cook or use a computer program, if it's possible to learn by doing while having someone help and direct us, that is the best way to learn and the way that schools should teach. Studies, and my own experience, show that everyone can benefit from hands-on education; that is the way we learn and remember best.

You can evaluate your essay and the model essay based on the following criteria, which is covered in the Scoring section of Inside the ACT Writing Test:

- Does the author discuss all three perspectives provided in the prompt?

- Is the author's own perspective clearly stated?

- Does the body of the essay assess and analyze each perspective?

- Is the relevance of each paragraph clear?

- Does the author start a new paragraph for each new idea?

- Is each sentence in a paragraph relevant to the point made in that paragraph?

- Are transitions clear?

- Is the essay easy to read? Is it engaging?

- Are sentences varied?

- Is vocabulary used effectively? Is college-level vocabulary used?

Compute Your Score

1. **Figure out your score in each subject test.** Refer to the answer keys to figure out the number right in each test. Enter the results in the chart:

		TEST 1	TEST 2	TEST 3
RAW SCORES	English:			
	Math:			
	Reading:			
	Science:			

2. **Find your Practice Test scores.** Find your raw score on each subject test in the following table. The score on the far left column indicates your estimated scaled score if this were an actual ACT.

SCALED SCORE	RAW SCORES			
	English	**Mathematics**	**Reading**	**Science**
36	75	60	40	40
35	74	60	40	40
34	73	59	39	39
33	72	58	39	39
32	71	57	38	38
31	70	55–56	37	37
30	69	53–54	36	36
29	68	50–52	35	35
28	67	48–49	34	34
27	65–66	45–47	33	33
26	63–64	43–44	32	32
25	61–62	40–42	31	30–31
24	58–60	38–39	30	28–29
23	56–57	35–37	29	26–27
22	53–55	33–34	28	24–25
21	49–52	31–32	27	21–23
20	46–48	28–30	25–26	19–20
19	44–45	26–27	23–24	17–18
18	41–43	23–25	21–22	16
17	39–40	20–22	19–20	15
16	36–38	17–19	17–18	14
15	34–35	15–16	15–16	13
14	30–33	13–14	13–14	12
13	28–29	11–12	12–13	11
12	25–27	9–10	10–11	10
11	23–24	8	9	9
10	20–22	7	8	8
9	17–19	6	7	7
8	14–16	5	6	6
7	12–13	4	5	5
6	9–11	3	4	4
5	7–8	2	3	3
4	4–6	1	2	2
3	3	1	1	1
2	2	0	0	0
1	1	0	0	0

		TEST 1	TEST 2	TEST 3
SCALED SCORES	English:			
	Math:			
	Reading:			
	Science:			

3. **Find your estimated Composite score.** To calculate your estimated Composite score, simply add together your scaled scores on each subject test and divide by four.

COMPOSITE SCORE

TEST 1	TEST 2	TEST 3